A Tutorial Guide to The Student Edition of

Lotus. 1-2-3®

RELEASE 2.3

Limited Warranty

Addison-Wesley warrants that the enclosed Student Edition ("the program") will substantially conform to the published specifications and to the documentation during the period of 90 days from the date of original purchase, provided that it is used on the computer hardware and with the operating system for which it was designed. Addison-Wesley also warrants that the magnetic media on which the program is distributed and the documentation are free from defects in materials and workmanship during the period of 90 days from the date of original purchase. Addison-Wesley will replace defective media or documentation or correct substantial program errors at no charge provided you return the item with dated proof of purchase to Addison-Wesley within 90 days of the date of original purchase. If Addison-Wesley is unable to replace defective media or documentation or correct substantial program errors, your license fee will be refunded. These are your sole remedies for any breach of warranty.

Except as specifically provided above, Addison-Wesley makes no warranty or representation, either express or implied, with respect to this program, documentation or media, including their quality, performance, merchantability or fitness for a particular purpose. Lotus makes no warranty or representation, either express or implied, with respect to this program, documentation or media, including their quality, performance, merchantability or fitness for a particular purpose.

Because programs are inherently complex and may not be completely free of errors, you are advised to verify your work. In no event will Publisher or Lotus be liable for direct, indirect, cover, special, incidental or consequential damages arising out of the use of or inability to use the program, documentation or media, even if advised of the possibility of such damages. In no case shall the liability of Publisher exceed the amount of the license fee and in no case shall Lotus have any liability.

The warranty and remedies set forth above are exclusive and in lieu of all others, oral or written, express or implied. No Publisher dealer, distributor, agent or employee is authorized to make any modification or addition to this warranty.

Some states do not allow the exclusion or limitation of implied warranties or limitation of liability for incidental or consequential damages, so these limitations may not apply to you.

U.S. Government Restricted Rights

The enclosed software and documentation are provided with RESTRICTED AND LIMITED RIGHTS. Use duplication, or disclosure by the Government is subject to restrictions as set forth in FAR § 52.227-14 (June 1987) Alternate III(g)(3) (June 1987), FAR § 52.227-19 (June 1987), or DFARS § 52.227-7013 (c)(1)(ii) (June 1988) as applicable. Contractor/Manufacturer is Addison-Wesley Publishing Company, Inc., Educational Software Division, Jacob Way, Reading, MA 01867.

General

Addison-Wesley and Lotus retain all rights not expressly granted. Nothing in this License Agreement constitutes a waiver of Addison-Wesley's or Lotus' rights under the U.S. Copyright laws or any other federal or state law.

To obtain performance of this warranty, return the item with dated proof of purchase within 90 days of the purchase date to: Addison-Wesley Publishing Company, Inc., Educational Software Division, Jacob Way, Reading, MA 01867.

A Tutorial Guide to The Student Edition of

Lotus.123.

RELEASE 2.3

TIMOTHY J. O'LEARY
Arizona State University

LINDA I. O'LEARY

Addison-Wesley Publishing Company, Inc.

The Benjamin/Cummings Publishing Company, Inc.

Reading, Massachusetts • Redwood City, California • New York
Don Mills, Ontario • Wokingham, England • Amsterdam • Bonn
Sydney • Singapore • Tokyo • Madrid • San Juan • Milan • Paris

A Tutorial Guide to The Student Edition of Lotus 1-2-3, Release 2.3 is published by Addison-Wesley Publishing Company, Inc. and The Benjamin/Cummings Publishing Company, Inc.

Sponsoring Editor: *Elizabeth Burr*

Project Manager: *Rachel Bunin*

Development Editor: *Lois Refkin*

Software Production Supervisor: *Karen Wernholm*

Production Coordinator: *Myrna D'Addario*

Text Design: *Jean Hammond*

Cover Design: *Gex, Inc.*

Compositor: *Gex, Inc.*

Manufacturing Supervisor: *Trish Gordon*

Dedicated to our parents

Charles D. O'Leary
Jean Larson O'Leary
Irene A. Perley Coats

and in memory of

Albert Lawrence Perley

Preface

The *Student Edition of Lotus 1-2-3, Release 2.3* is a significant revision of the existing *Student Edition*, which teaches basic 1-2-3 concepts using a clear, simple, and easy-to-follow keystroke based approach. The revision features completely new cases for each lab, new Release 2.3 commands, an additional chapter on advanced macros, and completely revised and expanded exercise sets.

This text is written for students who have little or no experience with computers or with Lotus 1-2-3. The cases at the beginning of each lab are general interest cases, and are designed to appeal to students from a variety of disciplines.

Key Features and Organization

Getting Started Section

The text begins with a Getting Started section. This provides students with the basic information they need to install, start, run, and end Lotus 1-2-3. It is written in an easy-to-follow step-by-step format, and assumes no prior computer experience on the part of the students. This section also contains information about the rest of the text, including the typographical conventions used in the 1-2-3 labs, assumptions about hardware usage, and an overview to introduce students to the features and power of 1-2-3.

1-2-3 Labs

After the Getting Started section, there are ten 1-2-3 labs, each designed to teach students the basics of Lotus 1-2-3. Each lab takes about 45 minutes to complete, although this may vary somewhat from lab to lab, student to student, and instructor to instructor. The lab pedagogy includes the following:

Case-Based Approach   Students learn 1-2-3 commands as they develop the spreadsheet that is described in the case study that begins each lab. The subject of these case studies can range from analyzing living expenses to financial planning for a gourmet food chain. They are designed to appeal to students from a variety of majors.

Step-by-Step Labs   Each lab leads students step-by-step through the keystrokes required to develop the spreadsheet presented in the case study. The presentation is clear, direct, easy-to-follow, and concise, with an emphasis on 1-2-3 skills and commands.

Extensive Exercises   The exercise sets throughout the text include a variety of off-line and on-line exercises and case problems. For off-line practice and review, the text provides both multiple choice and matching exercises, while for on-line practice, each exercise set includes several case problems. Some of the case problems are structured, providing students with step-by-step instructions for working through the problem solution. The remaining cases are open-ended and require students to synthesize the Lotus 1-2-3 skills they have learned.

1-2-3 Command Reference   The text concludes with a comprehensive Lotus 1-2-3, Release 2.3 Command Reference. This contains descriptions of the 1-2-3 commands, menus, and functions and includes all of the Release 2.3 capabilities. Capabilities not included in the student software are marked with an asterisk (*).

What's New in This Edition?

The Student Edition of Lotus 1-2-3, Release 2.3 has been thoroughly revised in response to user feedback. Key revisions include the following:

- New case studies

- Revised and expanded problem sets

- Coverage of additional Release 2.3 features — principally the dialog boxes, use of the mouse, new types of graphs, and additional range functions

- More extensive coverage of @ functions, including @IF

- A new lab that covers advanced macros

- New conceptual material on graphing that explains when different types of graphs should be used and why

- Reorganization of graphing material so that it now immediately precedes the database labs, and follows all of the basic worksheet material

- A new overview section

How to Use This Book

If students are installing their own software:

Students who have purchased this text with the Lotus 1-2-3, Release 2.3 Educational Software Series software and are installing it themselves should read through each chapter of the Getting Started section, and carefully follow the installation instructions included there.

If students are using preinstalled software:

Students who are using this text with software that has been installed for them already can skip Chapter 2 of the Getting Started section. However, they should read all the other Getting Started chapters carefully.

Flexibility of labs:

The labs have been designed in a modular fashion, to allow instructors the greatest flexibility in course development. After students have mastered the basic spreadsheet commands in Labs 1 and 2, they may proceed directly to the graphics, database, macro, or advanced spreadsheet labs. The numerous alternative paths that are available are detailed in the Instructor's Manual.

Students completing all ten labs will be able to organize and analyze information in a spreadsheet effectively and efficiently. In addition, they will be able to create and use macros and 1-2-3 databases.

About the Software

This text is available with or without the Addison-Wesley Lotus 1-2-3, Release 2.3 Educational Software Series software.

What's New in the Professional Lotus 1-2-3, Release 2.3 Software

Following are some of the new features in Lotus 1-2-3, Release 2.3. A complete listing of new Release 2.3 features may be found in Appendix B.

- New graph types and options for greater control over the appearance of graphs

- New printing features including background printing and the ability to save printer information in an encoded file

- The ability to edit the current file directory

- The ability to specify a range before selecting a command
- Use of (DEL) to delete contents of current cell
- Improved prompts to more closely reflect selected commands
- Interactive dialog boxes replace settings sheets
- Mouse support
- New add-in features including the ability to identify and check formulas in the worksheet (Auditor), an interactive online tutorial for learning 1-2-3 (1-2-3 Go!), the ability to view the contents of files on disk (Viewer), and enhanced spreadsheet publishing for 1-2-3 worksheets (Wysiwyg).

Limitations to the Lotus 1-2-3 Educational Software Series Software

This is a full capacity, fully compatible version of the professional Release 2.3 software. It is fully functional except that the following features have been omitted:

Access menu

Translate Utility

Add-ins: Wysiwyg*, Viewer, Auditor, 1-2-3 Go!

In addition, a header, "Addison-Wesley: 1-2-3 for Education," and the student's name automatically print at the top of all printed worksheets.

* The Wysiwyg software packaged with a tutorial guide is available separately from Addison-Wesley. Contact your local sales representative for more information.

Supplements

Addison-Wesley has developed an extensive supplements package to provide lecture and testing support to adopters of *The Student Edition of Lotus 1-2-3, Release 2.3*. A description of each ancillary follows.

Instructor's Manual by Kenneth L. Weimer, Kellogg Community College

This is designed as a teaching aid to provide answers and solutions to text problems, transparency masters for critical or difficult to demonstrate areas of the software, and helpful teaching suggestions for first time instructors and teaching assistants.

It includes the following:

- Product support information (includes technical support information and a list of Addison-Wesley Lotus 1-2-3 texts)

- Teaching hints and recommendations for each lab

- Answers and discussion of end-of-lab exercises and cases

- Additional cases for each lab designed to be used for group projects, lab assignments, and end of the semester assignments

- Transparency masters

Printed Test Bank by Parker Granger, Jacksonville State University

This will contain supplemental problems for each lab designed to be used in "off-line" testing.

It includes:

- 30 multiple choice and true/false questions for each lab

- 20 open-ended questions for each lab. At least 10 of the open-ended questions are based on a sample spreadsheet.

Computerized Test Bank — OmniTest II

The printed test items described above will also be available on Addison-Wesley's powerful computerized testing system, OmniTest II. OmniTest II allows users to easily create, store, and print out multiple versions of exams and worksheets, includes sophisticated graphics, and allows professors to edit questions and add their own.

Data Show

This is preprogrammed on-line lecture support that is designed to allow professors to demonstrate the key concepts in each lab using only the space bar.

Acetates

Thirty transparencies illustrate key 1-2-3 concepts from each lab. Includes material on creating worksheets, graphs, databases, and macros.

On-line Concurrent Testing for Key Lotus 1-2-3 Skills — The Addison-Wesley Judd Test

The Addison-Wesley Judd Test, developed by the Mentrix Corporation, runs concurrently with Lotus 1-2-3 software, allowing on-line testing of twenty key 1-2-3 skill areas. The Addison-Wesley Judd Test automatically evaluates keystrokes, and accepts any "legal" solution. It will score accuracy and test taking time, and provides both summary and detailed results of testing. The Addison-Wesley Judd Test is ideal as a screening device for a course that requires a certain level of 1-2-3 competency. In addition, students can purchase Addison-Wesley Judd Test "Remote Assessment Disks" that allow them to use the test at sites that are remote from the professor's full version, and to test any given skill area once. This is ideal for self study, semester quizzes, or an on-line final exam. Contact your Addison-Wesley representative for more information on availability of The Addison-Wesley Judd Test.

Acknowledgments

The development of the *Student Edition of Lotus 1-2-3, Release 2.3* has required a tremendous team effort from many individuals, and we would like to thank all those who have contributed to it. Through their combined efforts, we have built upon and improved the previous student editions of Lotus 1-2-3.

We are particularly grateful to a team of three people who worked very closely with us on this project. This team was lead by Jim Elam, a professor in the computer information systems department at Scottsdale Community College, who through his several years of writing and teaching experience offered clear insight and focus to the project. Thanks to Karl Konrad, who has worked with us on each of three previous editions, for his dedicated technical expertise. Also, thanks to Colleen Hayes for her energy, enthusiasm, and insightful suggestions.

We are grateful for the contributions of many people at Addison-Wesley. In particular, we thank Jim Behnke, Director of the Higher Education Publishing Group, for his interest and support for this project. Without his efforts, we could not have completed this revision. Also, thanks to Betsy Burr, Senior Editor, and Karen Wernholm, Production Supervisor, for contributing to the smooth production of this book.

For the day-to-day coordination of the development of this book, we would like to thank Rachel Bunin, Project Manager, for her good humor, persistence, and organizational skills. It has always been a pleasure working with her. Credit also needs to be given to Lois Refkin for her conscientious editing skills, and to Myrna D'Addario for production coordination. Without their combined efforts and pleasant natures, this project would not have been the success it is. Thanks also go to our field testers, Bryan Krauthamer and David Toebes.

Our thanks to the staff and programmers of Lotus Development Corporation, who provided us with their technical expertise and created the software for this package.

Timothy J. O'Leary
Linda I. O'Leary
November, 1991

Contents

Getting Started

Contents

Chapter 1

Before You Begin

This chapter describes the contents of *The Student Edition of Lotus 1-2-3, Release 2.3* package as well as information about product support. It also discusses the typographical conventions used in this manual. You should read this chapter before you install the Lotus 1-2-3, Release 2.3 Educational Software Series software.

Note If you have purchased a copy of this text without the 1-2-3 Educational Software Series software, you can skip the following section. You should, however, read the rest of this chapter.

Checking Your Package

The Student Edition of Lotus 1-2-3, Release 2.3 package should contain:

- The *User's Manual* (this book)
- Two 3½" program disks or four 5¼" program disks, and one 5¼" data files disk
- License Agreement (printed on the disk box)
- Warranty and Registration Card
- Keyboard templates (printed on the disk box)

The *User's Manual* and the keyboard templates are described in the following sections.

The User's Manual

The *User's Manual* contains the following three parts:

- Getting Started
- Lab Activities
- Reference Section

Getting Started

This part includes information on installing the Lotus 1-2-3, Release 2.3, Educational Software Series software, starting and quitting a 1-2-3 session, starting and quitting PrintGraph, and an overview, which is an interactive lab designed to familiarize you with the power and scope of the 1-2-3 program.

Lab Activities

The ten hands-on, interactive labs cover worksheets, graphics, databases, and macros. They teach you to use 1-2-3 by providing clear, concise, step-by-step keystroke instructions for creating spreadsheets that solve problems presented in case studies.

Reference Section

This section is a comprehensive discussion of 1-2-3 commands and procedures. It also includes three appendixes that describe compatible printer emulations, features new to Release 2.3, and instructions for creating a floppy disk version of Release 2.3.

The Keyboard Templates

A keyboard template is a guide that you place on the keyboard to remind you what each function key or special key combination does in 1-2-3, Release 2.3. There are two templates printed on the box that holds the software disks; you can cut out a template and tape it to the keyboard.

If the function keys on the keyboard are on the left of the typewriter key section, use the rectangular template. If the function keys lie across the top, use the horizontal template.

Product Support

Neither Addison-Wesley nor Lotus Development Corporation provides phone assistance to students using *The Student Edition of Lotus 1-2-3, Release 2.3*. Phone assistance is provided to *registered* instructors who adopt *The Student Edition of Lotus 1-2-3, Release 2.3*.

If you encounter difficulty using the Lotus 1-2-3, Release 2.3 software,

- Consult the Reference Section of this manual for information on the commands or procedures you are trying to perform.

• Use the 1-2-3 on-line Help screens to locate specific program or error message information.

If you need to ask your instructor for assistance, describe your question in detail. Write down what you were doing (that is, the steps or procedures you followed) when the problem occurred. Also write down the exact error message, if applicable.

Terminology and Typographical Conventions

You tell 1-2-3 what you want to do by selecting a series of commands from menus. To select commands, you either highlight the commands in the menu and then press the ⏎ key, or you type the first character of each command you want.

If you have installed a mouse you can select a command by clicking any character in the command. You will learn more about each of these techniques in Part 2, Lab Activities.

Table 1 describes the terminology used in this manual.

This Term	Means You Should
Highlight:	Use the arrow keys to highlight a menu option and the arrow keys or the mouse to highlight a block of cells.
Move to:	Move the cell pointer to a particular location in the worksheet. You can use the arrow keys, F5 (GOTO), or the mouse if you have one installed. For example, the instruction to move the cell pointer to cell D10 would be
	Move to: D10
Press:	Press the specified key or keys. "Press" is used primarily with the arrow keys, the function keys, and special keys such as ⏎ to perform a procedure. For example, the instruction to press ⏎ would be
	Press: ⏎
Select:	Choose the specified information that follows. In the labs you will learn several methods for selecting menu options, range names, and file names.
Type:	Strike or press a key. "Type" is used primarily with the standard typewriter keys to enter information into a worksheet. Letters, numbers, or symbols you type are printed in boldface. For example, the instructions to type the word "TOTAL" would be printed as follows:
	Type: **TOTAL**

Table 1

Mouse Conventions   Table 2 describes the mouse terminology used in this manual.

This Term	Means You Should
Click:	Press the left mouse button one time and then release it. Do not hold the mouse button down for longer than a fraction of a second. "Click" assumes that you have positioned the mouse pointer on the item you want to select.
Drag:	Press and hold down the mouse button as you move the mouse.
Point to:	Position the mouse pointer over a particular word or icon on the screen.

Table 2

Keyboard Conventions

Key symbols designate special keys on the keyboard such as the arrow keys ((←)), function keys ((F1) (HELP)), the escape key ((ESC)), or the enter key ((↵)).

Key Combinations

When two keys are separated by a hyphen (-), such as (CTRL)-(→), you press and hold down the first key, press the second key, and then release both keys. For example, you would press and hold down (CTRL), press (→), and then release both keys.

When two keys are separated by a space, such as (END) (HOME), press the first key and release it, then press the second key and release it. For example, press (END) and release it, then press (HOME) and release it.

Command Sequences

Typically you select a series of commands to perform an action in 1-2-3. In the labs, the first letter of each command option is printed in boldface, indicating that it should be typed. Any other parts of the command sequence to be typed are also in boldface. For example, the command to retrieve the file DATA would be shown as

/**F**ile **R**etrieve **DATA** (↵)

In this case, you would type **/FRDATA** and then press (↵).

1-2-3 Key Terms

Key terms appear in boldface type the first time they are defined. In the Lab Activities section, these terms are also listed in the Glossary at the end of each lab.

Icons

The following icon is used throughout this manual.

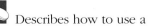 Describes how to use a mouse to perform a task.

| **Function Keys** | These are keys labeled $F1$, $F2$, $F3$, and so on; they are located either at the left side or along the top row of your keyboard. In the labs, you will learn how to use these keys to perform specific operations such as Edit, Help, or Run. For details on the use of function keys, refer to Chapter 1 in the Reference section of this manual. |

Assumptions

Following are assumptions this manual makes about moving around the keyboard, working with the mouse, and working with the data disk.

| **About Terminology** | Throughout this manual, the "move to" instruction assumes you'll use the arrow keys to move to the specified cell unless otherwise instructed. |

Note If you use $F5$ (GOTO) or the mouse to move, your screen will not match the screen shown in the manual.

| **About Using a Mouse** | The command sequences in the labs provide keyboard instructions, and assume that you are not using a mouse. The labs do provide mouse instructions for selected command sequences. These instructions are located in special mouse text, which is indicated by the mouse icon ⬛ . If you are using a mouse, you can substitute the mouse techniques described in those summaries for the keyboard instructions. |

- The mouse instructions assume that you use the left mouse button to select items unless the right button is specified.

- When a mouse instruction uses the term "click," it assumes that you have already moved the mouse pointer to the object you want to select. ("Click" means to press and release the left mouse button.)

| **About the Data Disk** | The labs assume that you insert a data disk in drive A before you start 1-2-3. This data disk should remain in place throughout the labs, because the default drive for saving and retrieving all worksheet files is drive A. You will learn how to set this default drive in Chapter 3, Starting and Quitting a 1-2-3 Session. |

Chapter 2

Installing Lotus 1-2-3, Release 2.3 Educational Software Series Software

Before you can use the 1-2-3, Release 2.3 Educational Software Series software, you must transfer the program files from the original disks to your hard disk. Because the files on the original disks are compressed, you must use the Install program to decompress them. You can't simply copy the files onto your hard disk.

This chapter describes the steps you should follow to transfer the files. It also explains how to choose the equipment 1-2-3 asks you to identify during the Install process.

Note If you have purchased this text without the 1-2-3 Educational Software Series software, or have already installed 1-2-3, you can skip to the section titled "Creating the Data Disk for the 5¼" Version" on page GS-28 for instructions on creating your data disk, or skip to Chapter 3.

What You Will Need

To complete the installation, you will need:

- The four original 1-2-3 program disks and the 1-2-3 Data Files disk if you are using the 5¼" version; the two original 1-2-3 program disks if you are using the 3½" version

- A hardware list describing the equipment in your system

- A DOS system disk (version 2.1 or higher), or DOS installed on your hard disk (see the system requirements on the back cover of your package)

- 2.5 MB of free hard disk space

- Six 5¼" blank disks with sleeves and labels if you are using the 5¼" version; three 3½" blank disks with labels if you are using the 3½" version

- Write-protect tabs (for the original 5¼" disks only)

The Installation Procedure

There are two sets of installation instructions:

- The quick installation instructions list only the basic installation steps. If you feel comfortable installing new applications, you can probably install the Lotus 1-2-3, Release 2.3 Educational Software Series software using just these general guidelines.

- The detailed installation instructions list step-by-step procedures that walk you through the installation process.

In either case, you should allow about fifteen minutes for the installation process, and try not to rush. If you need assistance, you can press (F1) (HELP) for help on the installation screen you're currently viewing.

Quick Installation Instructions

The following instructions assume you're installing 1-2-3 from your A drive onto your hard disk drive. If you are installing 1-2-3 from a drive other than A, substitute that drive name throughout.

1. Start the computer and format the blank disks.

2. Insert the original Program Disk 1 disk into the A drive, change to the A drive (A:\>), and type **INSTALL**.

   Note You must run the Install program from the drive that has your 1-2-3 disks in it.

3. Follow the instructions on the screen, inserting disks and making selections as prompted.

   Note If you need assistance with any part of this procedure, press the (F1) (HELP) key for on-line help, or refer to the detailed installation instructions section "Specifying Your Equipment" on page GS-20. If you still need assistance, exit Install, and follow the detailed installation instructions from the beginning.

4. After you have completed the installation procedure, copy the disks that came in your package onto blank formatted disks. Store these backup copies in a safe place, away from the computer system.

5. Reserve one formatted blank disk for use as your data files disk.

6. If you are using the 3½" version of the software, you must transfer the data files from the hard disk to your data disk after you have installed 1-2-3. See "Copying the Data Files to Your Data Disk" on page GS-26. You will use the data disk to store and retrieve data files as you work through the labs.

Detailed Installation Instructions

The following instructions provide step-by-step guidance for installing 1-2-3 on your hard disk drive. If you have any problems during this process, you can press (F1) (HELP) or ask your technical resource person for help.

Preparing a Hardware List

Before you begin the Install program, you need to know what type of equipment you have and how much memory you have available. Complete the hardware list shown in Table 3 so you will be prepared to answer the questions that appear on your screen during the installation. If you are unsure of how to complete this list, consult your computer dealer or technical resource person. Be sure to include the brand name and model or type for each piece of equipment.

Hardware List

Item	Manufacturer	Model/Type
Screen display card (monochrome, EGA, VGA, and so on)	_____	_____
Monitor type (for example, 80 x 25)	_____	_____
Text Printer #1	_____	_____
Text Printer #2 (if used)	_____	_____
Graphics Printer #1	_____	_____
Graphics Printer #2 (for example, plotter)	_____	_____

Table 3

If your computer does not have a graphics card and a monitor with graphics capability, you cannot view 1-2-3 graphs on your monitor.

Working with Floppy Disks

Your computer has at least one disk drive that uses either a 5¼" or 3½" removable disk (also called a **diskette** or **floppy disk**). These two types of disks are illustrated in Figure 1.

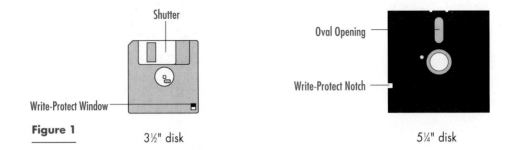

Figure 1

3½" disk   5¼" disk

You will use the disks that accompany this manual to install the 1-2-3 program. You will also format a separate data disk to store copies of the data files for the worksheets, databases, and graphs you create.

Whenever you work with disks, keep the following tips in mind.

- Keep disks away from heat, sunlight, smoke, and magnetic fields such as telephones, televisions, and transformers.

- Label each disk with the contents of the disk.

- Insert a floppy disk carefully into a drive; push the disk in the drive as far as it will go, but do not force the disk.

- Do not remove a disk while the drive access light is on.

- Do not touch the disk media with your fingers or other objects.

- Keep food and drinks away from disks.

About 3½" Disks

- Do not open the shutter (the sliding metal door at the top center of the disk). This exposes the surface of the disk to dust that could damage the data.

- Insert the metal shutter into the drive first. If the drive is horizontal, be sure the label is facing up; if the drive is vertical, consult your instructor or technical resource person if you are not sure how to insert the disk.

About 5¼" Disks

- Be careful when you write on a disk label. A sharp point or hard pressure may damage a disk. Use a felt-tip pen to write on a label that is already on a disk.

- When you're finished working with a 5¼" disk, always place it back in a disk sleeve.

- Insert the oval opening into the drive first. If the drive is horizontal, be sure the label is facing up; if the drive is vertical, consult your instructor or technical resource person if you are not sure how to insert the disk.

- Close the drive door after you insert a disk.

Starting the Computer

Before you can install 1-2-3, you must start the computer and load DOS (Disk Operating System), which lets the computer do basic tasks such as copying and formatting disks. When you start this section, your computer should be off.

Note If you make a typing error as you are going through the instructions in this chapter, use the BACKSPACE key to erase the letters and then type the entry correctly.

1. Turn on the computer. If the monitor has a separate switch, turn it on as well.

   It may take up to one minute for the **cursor** (small blinking underscore) to appear in the upper left corner of the screen. When the computer is ready, it either displays the date or asks you to enter it.

2. If you need to enter the date, use the form mm-dd-yy. For example, if the date is January 3, 1992,

   Type: **01-03-92**

   Press: ⏎

3. If you need to enter the time, use the twenty-four hour format HH:MM. For example, if the time is 1:45 p.m.,

   Type: **13:45**

   Press: ⏎

   If you enter the time or date incorrectly, DOS prompts you to try again. When you finish entering the date and time, the DOS prompt appears. This manual uses A:\> for the floppy-disk drive prompt and C:\> for the hard-disk drive prompt. Your prompt may look somewhat different.

Using the Install Program

The 1-2-3 Install program is straightforward and simple to follow. As you use it, messages appear on the screen that explain the information requested. If you need help at any point in the installation procedure, press the [F1] (HELP) key to see an on-line Help screen that gives further information.

Note The following instructions assume you're installing 1-2-3 from your A drive onto your C hard-disk drive. If you're using other drive names, be sure to substitute the correct drive designations in the following steps. If you are not sure, ask your instructor or technical resource person for assistance. You must run the Install program from the drive that has your 1-2-3 program disks in it.

The first time you use the Install program, you must use the original Install disk (Program Disk 1) to start the program.

Starting the Install Program

To start the Install program,

1. Insert Program Disk 1 in drive A.

2. At the DOS prompt,

   Type: **A:**

   Press: [⏎]

3. When the prompt changes to A:\>,

   Type: **INSTALL**

   Press: [⏎]

   Notice the drive light comes on after you press [⏎] indicating that Install is being loaded (that is, copied into the computer's memory). After a moment, a message confirms that Install is loading.

   After the Install program is loaded, it displays an introductory screen.

4. After you read the introductory screen,

   Press: [⏎]

   to display the Install initialization screen.

Following the Install Program

The Install screens provide instructions to guide you through the program. If the screen does not give you all the information you need, press (F1) (HELP) to see additional information.

The first time you use the Install program, you must complete the following steps:

- Record your name and school name; this will **initialize** your copy of the software.

- Transfer the 1-2-3 program files to your hard disk.

- Specify your equipment so that 1-2-3 can work correctly.

The following sections describe each of these steps.

Recording Your Name and School Name The first time you use Install, it asks you to record your name and school name on the initialization screen.

Note Once Install records this information, you cannot change it. You will see it every time you start 1-2-3, and your name will appear on your printed worksheets exactly as it appears on this screen.

Let's step through the process now.

Figure 2 shows the Install initialization screen. It asks you to record your name in the upper highlighted box.

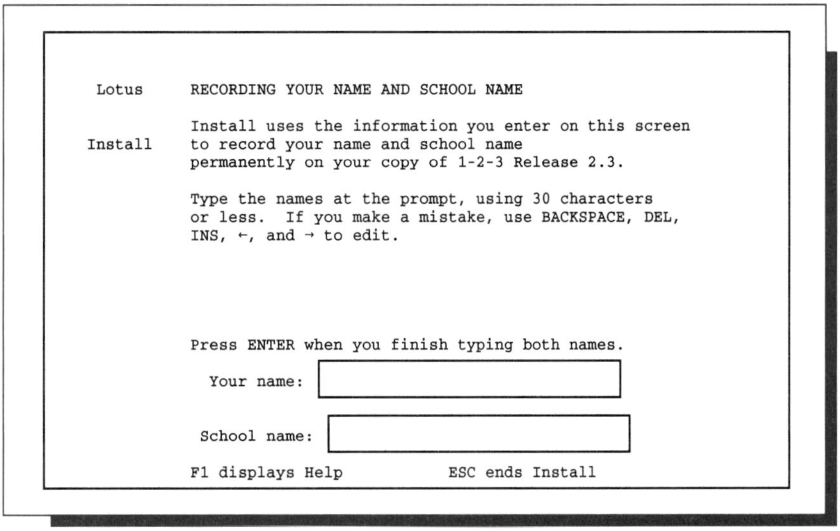

Figure 2

```
Lotus       RECORDING YOUR NAME AND SCHOOL NAME

            Install uses the information you enter on this screen
Install     to record your name and school name
            permanently on your copy of 1-2-3 Release 2.3.

            Type the names at the prompt, using 30 characters
            or less.  If you make a mistake, use BACKSPACE, DEL,
            INS, ←, and → to edit.




            Press ENTER when you finish typing both names.

              Your name: [                                ]


            School name: [                                ]

            F1 displays Help            ESC ends Install
```

You can type up to 30 characters. If you make a typing error, use the BACKSPACE key to erase letters, then retype the entry. To insert characters, use ← or → to move the cursor to the desired position, then type the new characters.

1. At the prompt,

   Type: (your first and last names)

2. Check your typing carefully. When you are satisfied that the entry is correct and appears as you would like it to appear on your worksheet printouts,

   Press: ↓

   The cursor moves to the lower highlighted box, where you enter your school name. Again, you can type up to 30 characters.

3. At the prompt,

   Type: (your school name)
   Press: ↵

   A confirmation dialog box, shown in Figure 3, asks if your entry is correct. This is your final chance to correct your name and/or your school name. If you select Y and press ↵ the information will be recorded as it is displayed on the screen, making you the licensee of record. Once you record this information, you cannot change it.

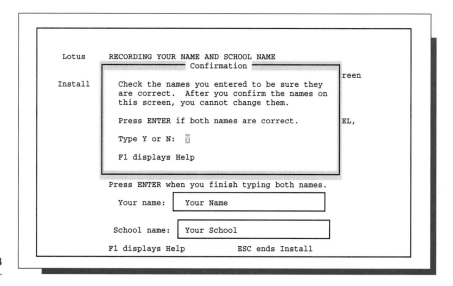

Figure 3

Note To leave Install without recording your name and school name, you must do so before you select Y and press ⏎ at the confirmation screen. If you want to leave Install at this time,

Press: (CTRL)-(BREAK)

(The (BREAK) key is normally located in the upper right corner of the keyboard. Look for the word Break on the *front*, not the top, of a key marked Scroll Lock or Pause.)

Any information you typed is deleted; the next time you run Install, you must start the program from the beginning.

4. If you have made an error and want to reenter your name or school name, at the prompt,

Type: N

Press: ⏎

Make any necessary corrections.

5. To accept the information,

Select: Yes

Press: ⏎

The Install program now displays the file transfer screen, and is ready to begin transferring the program files.

Transferring the Program Files

The file transfer screen indicates that Install is ready to transfer the 1-2-3 program files to your hard disk (Figure 4).

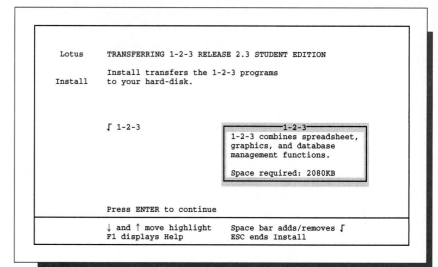

```
        Lotus       TRANSFERRING 1-2-3 RELEASE 2.3 STUDENT EDITION

                    Install transfers the 1-2-3 programs
        Install     to your hard-disk.



                    ∫ 1-2-3                     ┌─────────1-2-3─────────┐
                                                │ 1-2-3 combines spreadsheet, │
                                                │ graphics, and database │
                                                │ management functions. │
                                                │                        │
                                                │ Space required: 2080KB │
                                                └────────────────────────┘


                    Press ENTER to continue
                 ───────────────────────────────────────────────────────
                    ↓ and ↑ move highlight       Space bar adds/removes ∫
                    F1 displays Help             ESC ends Install
```

Figure 4

1. To begin,

   Press: ⏎

The next screen that appears asks you to specify the disk drive (C, D, or E) where Install will store the 1-2-3 program files.

Specifying the Hard-Disk Name

1. Unless you supply other instructions, Install assumes the drive is C. To accept this drive,

   Press: ⏎

   or, if you want to store the 1-2-3 files on another disk (for instance, D or E),

   Type: (letter of the drive to use)

   Press: ⏎

   Note If your hard disk drive has less that 2.5 MB of disk space free, you may need to remove some of the files from it before you can install 1-2-3. See your technical resource person for assistance.

Specifying the Program Directory Name The next Install screen asks you to specify the directory (that is, the name of a disk subdivision) where Install will store the 1-2-3 program files. Install recommends that you use the directory name \123R23.

1. To accept this name,

Press: ⏎

After you have specified a disk drive letter and a directory name, Install transfers the 1-2-3 program files to that directory.

As Install transfers each file, it displays the name of the file being transferred and flashes the message "Please Wait" near the bottom of the screen.

When Install has transferred all files from one disk, it asks you to insert another disk and press ⏎.

After all files are transferred, Install reports that the file transfer was successful, and begins the next part of the Install program, Specifying Your Equipment.

2. To continue,

Press: ⏎

Install displays the Main Menu screen (Figure 5).

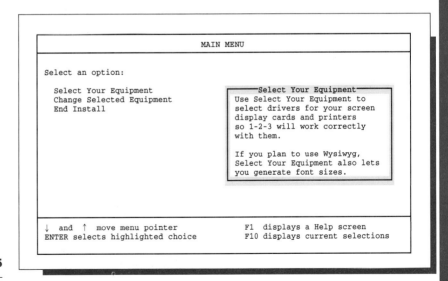

Figure 5

Using the Install Main Menu

The Install Main Menu has three choices:

Select Your Equipment	Provides step-by-step instructions for selecting equipment used with your computer system. You select drivers that allow 1-2-3 to display graphs and print your 1-2-3 worksheets and graphs.
	Use Select Your Equipment the first time you install 1-2-3 or whenever you need to create a new driver set.
Change Selected Equipment	Lets you change or add a screen display, text printer, or graphics printer driver in the current driver set.
	Use Change Selected Equipment to update an existing driver set when you get a new monitor or a new printer, or use it to change the equipment selections if your system is not working correctly.
End Install	Returns you to the DOS prompt.

The Install program includes Help screens that further explain menu choices. After you read the box at the right of the screen, if you want more information, press (F1) (HELP) to display the related Help screen. When you've read the screen, press (ESC) to return to the menu.

Specifying Your Equipment

Before you start 1-2-3 the first time, you must tell Install what equipment you plan to use with 1-2-3.

If you choose the first option, Select Your Equipment, 1-2-3 will ask you to specify the following:

- Screen display
- Text printer(s)
- Graphics printer(s)

Each time you choose a piece of equipment to use with 1-2-3, you are selecting a special program known as a **driver**. That driver tells 1-2-3 how to work with the equipment you specify.

As you make these selections, refer to the Hardware List you completed earlier in this chapter (Table 3 on page GS-11). It should make it easier for you to choose from the lists displayed on the screen.

Note If you do not want to select your equipment right now,

Press: ↓ twice

to select End Install, then

Press: ↵

to leave the Install program.

1. Make sure the option Select Your Equipment is highlighted, and

    Press: ↵

The next screen that appears describes video detection.

2. After reading this screen,

    Press: ↵

    to continue.

Specifying a Screen Display   The Install program helps you select a screen display by automatically highlighting the type of screen display detected in your computer. This is the screen display type you should choose.

Note If you want to explore the other choices, you can use ↓ to scroll down the list. As you do, notice that the text changes in the information window on the right.

1. To select a screen display, make sure it is highlighted and,

Press: ⏎

Next you are asked to select a display option that is compatible with the type of monitor you have. This option determines how many columns and rows are displayed, and establishes the background color. Again, the highlighted option is the one recommended by the Install program.

Note If you are not sure what to select, check with your technical resource person.

2. To select a display option, make sure it is highlighted, and

Press: ⏎

Note You can only display graphics if you have:

- A graphics monitor (monochrome or color)
- A graphics card (such as a Hercules card for a monochrome monitor or an enhanced graphics adapter)

If you are not sure whether your computer can display graphics, check your hardware chart or ask your technical resource person. This will not affect your ability to run the 1-2-3 program. You simply will not be able to see the graphs you create on your screen.

Specifying Text Printers   Next you are asked to select a text printer or printers. The Install program uses the term **text printer** to describe the printer you use to print numbers and letters, as well as the special characters that 1-2-3 produces.

Install asks, "Do you have a text printer?"

1. If you have a printer connected to your computer system that you will use for your work in 1-2-3, or, if you currently do not have a printer but know which one you will eventually be using,

Select: Yes

If you do not have a printer or if you do not want to print in 1-2-3,

Select: No

Install will proceed to the graphics printer selection screen.

2. If you selected Yes, now select the name of the printer manufacturer that you included in the Hardware List on page GS-11. Use the arrow keys to scroll through the options. As each option is highlighted, additional information appears in the box on the right of the screen.

Note If you do not know which option to choose, consult your printer manual or your technical resource person. Appendix A provides a list of suggested compatible printers for 1-2-3.

After you have highlighted the appropriate printer manufacturer,

Press: ⏎

Next you are asked to select the model or model series for your text printer.

3. Again, refer to the Hardware List on page GS-11, highlight the appropriate option and,

Press: ⏎

Now you are asked if you have another text printer connected to the system.

4. If you do,

Select: Yes

5. Identify the printer manufacturer and printer series or model for the second text printer.

6. After you have identified all the text printers and Install asks if you have another text printer connected to the system,

Select: No

Specifying Graphics Printers   Finally, you are asked to select a graphics printer or printers. The Install program uses the term **graphics printer** for the printer you use to print graphs. Even if you plan to use the same printer for graphs that you use for text, you must still select it again from the graphics printer menu.

Install asks, "Do you have a graphics printer?"

1. If your printer is capable of printing graphs,

Select: Yes

Note If you do not have a printer capable of printing graphs,

Select: No

Install will proceed to the next screen, Naming Your Driver Set.

If you selected Yes, now select a graphics printer: select the name of the graphics printer manufacturer, then select the specific printer series or model.

2. Repeat the procedure you used to select your text printer manufacturer and model to select your graphics printer manufacturer and model.

Then you are asked if you have another graphics printer.

3. If you do,

Select: Yes

4. Identify the name of the printer manufacturer and the printer series or model.

5. After you have identified all the printers and Install asks if you have another graphics printer,

Select: No

Note If your printer does not have graphics capability, you cannot print 1-2-3 graphs, even though they are displayed on the screen.

Naming and Saving Driver Sets

After you have finished selecting the equipment, Install stores your choices in a file with a .SET extension. This file is called a **driver set**.

In order to name the driver set, the Install program asks, "Do you want to name your driver set?"

1. To use 1-2-3's default name,

Select: No

1-2-3 automatically saves the driver information in a file called 123.SET. Each time you start 1-2-3 or any of its companion programs, 1-2-3 looks for this driver set.

You can also give the driver set a name other than 123.SET. You should do this only if you want to create more than one driver set, as described in the following section. Otherwise, skip to the section "Exiting from the Install Program" on page GS-25.

Creating More Than One Driver Set

If you want to use 1-2-3 with more than one type of computer (for instance, a personal computer at school and a portable computer at home), you need to create a different driver set for each computer system. Each driver set you create must have a different name.

1. To give your driver set a name other than 123.SET, when the Install program asks you if you want to name your driver set,

    Select: Yes

The program then prompts you to enter the driver set name. You can use descriptive names, such as HOME.SET and SCHOOL.SET, to distinguish different drivers. The name you give your driver set can contain up to eight characters, but may not contain any of these characters: ( ) ; , . / ? : + = < > \ '

Do not type the extension .SET after the name of the driver set; the extension is added automatically by the Install program. See the Reference section for instructions on starting 1-2-3 with a driver set other than 123.SET.

Once you have created and named the first driver set, you can create additional driver sets by returning to the Install main menu. Use Selecting Your Equipment again and make the selections for the second driver set.

Note To change only one or two selections to make the second driver set (perhaps you added a graphics printer), use the Change Selected Equipment option on the Install main menu. This allows you to make minor changes to the current driver set without having to repeat all the equipment selections.

You must give each driver set a different name so that the previous sets remain unchanged on the disk.

Exiting from the Install Program

After Install has finished copying and saving the driver set you created, it displays a screen saying that you have finished the installation procedure. At this point, you can do one of the following:

- Press ⏎ to leave the Install program. Install displays an exit screen, where you can choose to end the program or to return to the Install main menu.

- Press F9 to return to the Install main menu.

- Press (F10) to display a list of the drivers in the set you created or to create another driver set.

1. Return to the Install main menu and

   Select: End Install

   You are returned to the DOS prompt, in the directory where the 1-2-3 files are installed.

Copying the Data Files to Your Data Disk

As you work through the 1-2-3 labs, you will use sample data files from the data disk in drive A. You will also configure 1-2-3 so that it stores your worksheet files and graphs on this disk. (The procedure for doing this is described in Chapter 3.)

In order to create the data disk you will use with the 1-2-3 labs, you need to format a blank disk.

Formatting Disks

You use DOS, or disk operating system, commands to format disks.

Note If you are experienced with formatting disks, skip ahead to "Creating the Data Disk."

1. To format a disk for use as the data disk, make sure you are at the DOS (C:\>) prompt and

   Type: **FORMAT A:**

   CAUTION You *must* include the drive name (A:) in the command or else you can accidentally erase all the files from your hard disk.

   Press: (↵)

   Your screen prompts you to "Insert new diskette for drive A: and strike any key when ready."

2. Insert a blank disk in drive A.

   Note Use a blank disk, *not* a program disk from your package.

3. To start formatting,

Press: ⏎

The message "Formatting..." appears on the screen. The drive indicator light next to the drive door goes on, and the drive makes a whirring noise. Formatting can take as long as one minute. When the process is finished, the light goes out, and the message "Format complete" appears. DOS displays information about available space on the disk and asks "Format another (Y/N?)"

4. If you want to continue formatting blank disks,

Type: **Y**

With some versions of DOS, you also have to press ⏎. After you have formatted all the disks you need, when the prompt appears,

Type: **N**

5. As you remove each formatted disk, place a blank label on it to show that it is formatted.

Creating the Data Disk for the 3½" Disk Version*

To create the data disk, you will use the DOS COPY command to copy the sample data files to a formatted, blank 3½" floppy disk. This disk will be your data disk. It will hold the files you need to work through the labs.

Remember, a floppy disk must be formatted before you can use it. Follow the procedure outlined in the previous section to format a floppy disk.

Now you are ready to copy the sample data files to the data disk.

*Note If you purchased this package without the 1-2-3 software, see the following section, "Creating the Data Disk for the 5¼" Disk Version," for instructions on creating the data disk.

1. Label a formatted floppy disk "1-2-3 Data Disk 1." This will become your data disk.

2. Insert the blank formatted disk into drive A.

3. Make sure you are in the \123R23 directory.

4. Then, at the DOS prompt,

Type: **COPY *.WK1 A:**

Press: ⏎

The asterisk (*) is a **wildcard** character that stands for any combination of letters. This command tells DOS to copy every file ending with the file extension .WK1. .WK1 is the file extension 1-2-3 attaches to the name of the data files.

When all .WK1 files have been copied, DOS reports the total number of files copied, then displays the DOS prompt. The data disk now contains the sample data files you will use as you work through the labs.

Creating the Data Disk for the 5¼" Disk Version

If your copy of *The Student Edition of Lotus 1-2-3, Release 2.3* contains 5¼" disks, or if you purchased this package without the Lotus 1-2-3, Release 2.3 software, the 1-2-3 files that you need to work through the labs are on a separate disk labeled Data Files Disk.

To create a data disk that you can use to work through the labs, you should copy the contents of the Data Files Disk onto a blank formatted disk. Follow the procedure outlined in the previous section to format a floppy disk. Then follow the instructions in one of the following two sections to copy the data files to your data disk.

Copying the Data Files on a System with Two Floppy Drives

1. Label a formatted floppy disk "1-2-3 Data Disk 1." This will become your data disk.

2. Insert the disk labeled Data Files Disk into drive A.

3. Insert the blank formatted disk into drive B.

4. Make sure you are at the DOS prompt for the A drive (A:\>) and,

Type: **COPY *.* B:**

Press: ⏎

The asterisk (*) is a wildcard character that stands for any combination of letters. This command tells DOS to copy every file on the disk in drive A onto the disk in drive B.

When all the files have been copied, DOS reports the total number of files copied, then displays the DOS prompt. The data disk now contains the sample files you will use in the labs.

Copying the Data Files on a System with One Floppy Drive

1. Label a formatted floppy disk "1-2-3 Data Disk 1." This will become your data disk.

2. Insert the disk labeled Data Files Disk into drive A.

3. Make sure you are at the DOS prompt for the A drive (A:\>), and

Type: **DISKCOPY A: A:**

Press: ⏎

This command tells DOS to copy every file from a source diskette in drive A to a target diskette in drive A.

DOS will prompt you to insert the source diskette, or disk you are copying from, into drive A. Since you have already inserted the Data Files Disk into drive A,

4. Press: ⏎

After a short time, DOS will prompt you to insert the target disk, or disk you are copying to, into drive A.

5. Insert the blank formatted disk into drive A.

6. Press: ⏎

Depending on the amount of information on the source disk, DOS may repeat this process several times.

After DOS has finished copying all of the files from the Data Files Disk onto your data disk, it will display the prompt

Copy another diskette (Y/N)?

7. Type: **N**

DOS will return you to the A drive DOS prompt. Your data disk now contains the files you will use in the labs.

Making Backup Copies of the 1-2-3 Disks

You may want to make backup copies of the original 1-2-3 program disks after you have completed installation in case your 1-2-3 files become damaged as you run the 1-2-3 program. To do this, follow the instructions for copying disks in the section "Creating the Data Disk for the 5¼" version" that starts on page GS-28.

Repeat this procedure until all the 1-2-3 disks are copied. Be sure to label each disk.

Write-Protecting the Backup Disks

Remember that disks are vulnerable to human error. You can avoid some accidents by **write-protecting** a disk when you are not planning to save files on it. This ensures that you do not accidentally alter or erase any information on the disk. Write-protecting backup disks is a wise precaution. You can run programs and retrieve information from a write-protected disk.

However, you cannot save files to a write-protected disk. Thus you probably won't want to write-protect your data disk.

The procedure for write-protecting a disk depends on what kind of disk you are using:

- For a 5¼" disk, use a write-protect tab to cover the notch on the side of the disk. Place half of the tab on the notch, then fold the tab over so it sticks to the other side. In this way the notch is completely covered by the write-protect tab. Do not use white or clear household tape. Use only write-protect tabs manufactured specifically for disks.

- For a 3½" disk, there is a small write-protect window in the lower right corner of the disk. When the window is open, the disk is protected. If necessary, slide the small plastic tab over to uncover the window. Remember, if you can see through the window in the right corner of the disk, the disk is protected. If you cannot see through the window, the disk is *not* protected.

Modifying Your 1-2-3 Installation

After you have finished the installation procedure, you may decide to change some of your original selections. To do this, you start the Install program from the hard disk. Otherwise, you may skip to Chapter 3, "Starting and Quitting a 1-2-3 Session."

1. Make sure you are at the C:\> prompt.

2. To change to the 1-2-3 directory, at the C:\> prompt,

Type: **CD\123R23**

Press: ⏎

3. To run the Install program,

Type: **INSTALL**

Press: ⏎

4. Read the opening screen when it is displayed, then,

Press: ⏎

When you start Install from the hard disk, the main menu lists the options available to you:

Select Your Equipment	Creates a new driver set.
Change Selected Equipment	Changes the selected equipment.
End Install	Quits Install.

Note If you want to review the use of the Install menus, read "Using the Install Main Menu" earlier in this chapter.

5. Select: Change Selected Equipment

Changing Equipment Options

The Change Selected Equipment option lets you do many things you cannot do elsewhere in the Install program. The options available from this menu are listed below.

Return to Main Menu	Returns to the Install Main Menu.
Make Another Driver Set Current	Allows you to enter the name of another driver set so you can modify it with the Change Selected Equipment or Modify the Current Driver Set commands.
	If you do not use this option, the Install program assumes you want to make changes in 123.SET.
Modify the Current Driver Set	Makes changes in the current driver set.
	The Modify Current Driver Set screen lets you select from the Graph Display menu, then from the Text Display menu. Some text-display and graphics driver combinations are not available through the screen display option in other Install menus.
Save the Current Driver Set	Saves changes in the driver set.
	You can save the driver set with the same name or a new name.
Switch Mouse Buttons	1-2-3 uses the left mouse button by default for selecting items. Left-handed people might want to use this option to switch to use the right mouse button to select items.
Add New Drivers to the Library	Adds 1-2-3 driver programs that came with your equipment.
	These separate drivers should have a .DRV file extension. This option creates a library (SINGLE.LBR) consisting of all the separate drivers. You can then select the new drivers from the Install menus.
End Install	Returns you to the DOS prompt.

Revising the Current Driver Set

If you select Modify the Current Driver Set from the Change Selected Equipment menu, you can choose the equipment (or options) you want to change. A triangle (▶) appears next to your current selection for each driver.

If you make any changes to a driver set and you want to save those changes,

Select: Save the Current Driver Set

from the Change Selected Equipment menu.

The Install program asks you to supply a name for the revised driver set. If you do not plan to create more than one driver set,

Press: (↵)

Your driver set will be called 123.SET. If you use a name other than 123.SET, you will have to type that name whenever you start 1-2-3 or any of its companion programs. See the Reference section for instructions on starting 1-2-3 with a driver set other than 123.SET.

If you select the End Install option before you save your changes, the Install program prompts you to save them. If you want to save the changes,

Select: Yes

Chapter 3

Starting and Quitting a 1-2-3 Session

This chapter provides step-by-step instructions for starting and quitting 1-2-3. It also describes how to change the drive or directory where 1-2-3 stores the files you create, and how to use the 1-2-3 on-line help system.

Starting 1-2-3, Release 2.3

Before you can begin using 1-2-3, it must be installed on your hard disk drive. If it is not already installed on your hard drive, refer to Chapter 2 for instructions.

These instructions assume that DOS and the directory \123R23 are on the hard disk on drive C. If your hard disk is called by some other letter (for example, D) substitute that letter in the following instructions. If you specified a different directory name for 1-2-3, substitute that name in the instructions. For further assistance, contact your technical resource person.

If the computer is on and you see the DOS prompt, skip to step 2. If your computer is off, start with step 1.

1. Make sure the floppy disk drive is empty and turn on the computer. In a few moments you should see the DOS prompt, C:\>, on your screen.

    Note If you need help starting your computer, refer to "Starting the Computer" in Chapter 2.

2. To change to the directory that contains the 1-2-3, Release 2.3 program files,

Type: **CD\123R23**

Press: ⏎

If you used a different name for the 1-2-3 directory, substitute that name.

3. To start 1-2-3, insert your data disk into the A drive and,

Type: **123**

Press: ⏎

Note You can also have 1-2-3 retrieve a worksheet file, select a certain driver set, or specify other settings when it starts. For more information, refer to Chapter 2 in the Reference section.

First, 1-2-3 displays its logo screen, including the information you entered during installation. Next, a blank 1-2-3 worksheet should appear on the screen.

Note If the screen displays the message "Bad command or file name,"

- Make sure that you are in the directory that contains the 1-2-3 files. If the name of the directory does not appear beside the C:\> prompt, type **CD** and press ⏎. DOS displays the complete prompt, including the directory. If you are in the wrong directory, start again from step 2.

- Check that you typed 123 correctly. If you did not, repeat step 3.

If your screen goes blank, the logo screen freezes, or an invalid driver set message appears, you must modify your driver set using the instructions previously discussed in the "Modifying Your 1-2-3 Installation" section in Chapter 2.

Changing the Default Drive or Directory

When you start 1-2-3 for the first time, the program automatically retrieves files from and saves files to the drive or directory from which you started the program. This is called the **default directory**. If you start 1-2-3 directly from a hard disk drive directory, such as C:\123R23, 1-2-3 automatically designates that directory as the default directory.

In order to work with the data files on the data disk, make drive A the default drive. Although you can specify a different drive and directory as you work with files in 1-2-3, changing the default drive and directory once is easier than specifying a drive and directory every time you retrieve or save a file.

1. A blank worksheet should be displayed on your screen. To access the 1-2-3 main menu,

   Press: / (slash)

2. To select the command sequence to change the default drive (Worksheet Global Default Directory),

   Press: **W**

   Press: **G**

   Press: **D**

   Press: **D**

3. The Default Settings dialog box is on the screen. The default drive and directory path are shown at the top of the box. Outside the box, on the second line of the screen, 1-2-3 also displays the drive and directory from which you started 1-2-3, which is probably C:\123R23. To change the default directory,

   Press: (ESC)

   This will clear the original default directory. The line at the top of the screen now prompts you to enter the new default directory.

4. Make sure the data disk is in the A drive. If the disk is not locked in place, 1-2-3 will not be able to accept the command in step 5.

5. Type the name of the drive and directory where you want 1-2-3 to store files. The labs in this book assume you are storing files on the data disk in drive A.

Type: **A:**

Press: ⏎

Note If your hard-disk drive is C and you created a subdirectory named DATA in the \123R23 directory, change the 123R23 default directory to DATA.

Type: **C:\123R23\DATA**

Press: ⏎

If necessary, substitute the name of your 1-2-3 directory in the command. Be sure you correctly specify both the drive and directory path.

6. To save the directory destination, select Update. To do this,

Press: **U**

7. To close the Default Settings dialog box, leave the 1-2-3 worksheet menu and select Quit.

Press: **Q**

Getting On-Line Help

1-2-3, Release 2.3 includes an on-line Help system. You can start this system by pressing (F1) (HELP) whenever you are using 1-2-3.

The 1-2-3 Help system is context-sensitive, which means that the Help topic you see when you press (F1) (HELP) is directly related to the task you are performing. For example, if you select **\Worksheet Insert** from the 1-2-3 menu and press (F1) (HELP), you see a Help screen that describes the Insert command (Figure 6).

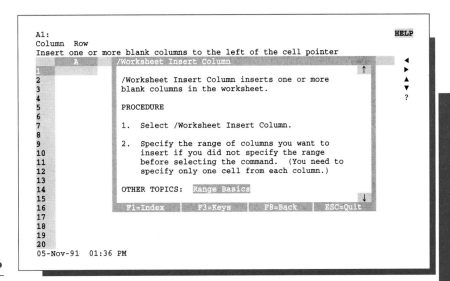

Figure 6

If the Help screen contains more information than a single screen can display, you use the ↓ key to see the additional information. You can also move the pointer to any of the highlighted words (words that appear in a brighter intensity or a different color) and press ↵ to learn more about that topic.

You can access the Help index by pressing F1 (HELP) again. Figure 7 shows the Main Help Index.

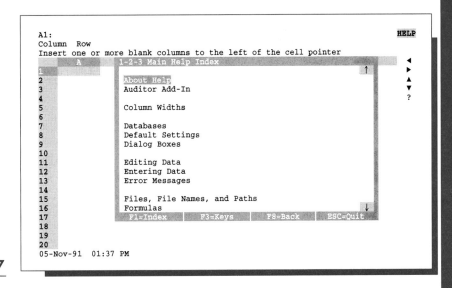

Figure 7

The Help index provides an alphabetical list of topics. You scroll down the alphabetical list and select any topic you want to learn about. If you want information about a 1-2-3 procedure, you select the entry called "How do I…" For example, if you select "How do I…", then select Add Columns or Rows, you see the Help screen in Figure 8.

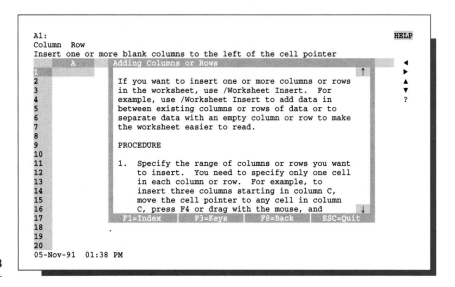

Figure 8

Help also includes a glossary of 1-2-3 terms. To access the glossary, you scroll down the list and select Glossary of Terms from A to L or Glossary of Terms from M to Z (depending on the term you want to look up). When you press ⏎, you see an alphabetical list of terms; when you select a term, its definition is displayed.

Note Reminders at the bottom of the Help screen describe the keys used in Help. As indicated, the (F8) key returns you to the previous Help screen, (F3) describes the various ways to use keys in Help, and you leave Help by pressing (ESC).

For additional instructions on using the on-line Help system, see the Reference section. As you work through the labs, you are encouraged to use Help as often as you like.

Ending a 1-2-3 Session

Follow the instructions in this section to quit a 1-2-3 session.

1. To access the 1-2-3 main menu,

   Press: / (slash)

2. To select Quit,

   Press: **Q**

3. To leave 1-2-3, select Yes.

   Press: **Y**

   1-2-3 returns you to the DOS prompt.

Chapter 4

Starting and Quitting PrintGraph

You can use the 1-2-3 Print command to print text and numbers, but you must use a separate program, PrintGraph, to print or plot graphs you have created and saved during a 1-2-3 session. This chapter introduces PrintGraph.

PrintGraph lets you select colors (if you have a color graphics printer or plotter), fonts (type styles), density (number of dots per character), and the position of the graph on the paper.

The sections that follow assume that your hard disk is drive C and that 1-2-3 is installed in a directory named \123R23. If you are using different drive or directory names, substitute the names you selected in the following procedures.

Starting PrintGraph

1. Make sure your computer is turned on and the DOS prompt is displayed.

2. To access the 1-2-3 directory,

   Type: **CD\123R23**

   Press: ⏎

3. To start the PrintGraph program,

   Type: **PGRAPH**

   Press: ⏎

PrintGraph uses the driver sets you created when you used the Install program. To use a driver set with a name other than 123.SET, type **PGRAPH** followed by a space and the name of the driver set, then press ⏎. It is not necessary to type the extension .SET. For example, to start PrintGraph with a driver set called HOME.SET, type **PGRAPH HOME**. If you do not type the name of the driver set, PrintGraph uses 123.SET.

Note If the screen displays the message "Bad command or file name,"

- Check that you typed **PGRAPH** correctly. If you did not, repeat step 3.

- Make sure that you are in the directory that contains the 1-2-3 files. If the name of the directory does not appear beside the C:\> prompt, type **CD** and press ⏎. DOS displays the complete prompt, including the directory. If you are in the wrong directory, start again from step 2.

If your screen goes blank, the logo screen freezes, or an invalid driver set message appears, you must modify your driver set using the instructions previously discussed in the "Modifying Your 1-2-3 Installation" section in Chapter 2.

Using PrintGraph

When PrintGraph starts, the logo screen appears briefly, followed by the menu screen, shown in Figure 9.

```
Copyright 1986, 1991 Lotus Development Corp.  All Rights Reserved.      MENU

Select graphs to print or preview
Image-Select  Settings  Go  Align  Page  Exit

       GRAPHS     IMAGE SETTINGS                      HARDWARE SETTINGS
       TO PRINT   Size              Range colors      Graphs directory
                    Top       .395  X                   C:\123R23
                    Left      .750  A                 Fonts directory
                    Width    6.500  B                   C:\123R23
                    Height   4.691  C                 Interface
                    Rotation  .000  D                   Parallel 1
                                    E                 Printer
                  Font              F
                  1  BLOCK1                            Paper size
                  2  BLOCK1                              Width     8.500
                                                        Length   11.000

                                                      ACTION SETTINGS
                                                      Pause  No   Eject  No
```

Figure 9

You perform all PrintGraph operations — selecting graphs to print or preview; changing image, hardware, and action settings; printing; aligning and advancing the paper; and exiting — from this menu screen.

The PrintGraph menu works like the 1-2-3 menu at the top of a worksheet screen. To select a command, you use the arrow keys to move the highlighted rectangle across the menu bar (above the double line near the top of the screen). As you do, notice that the line of text just above the menu line changes. This upper line explains the function of each command.

Once you become familiar with the PrintGraph menu, you can select commands as you do in the 1-2-3 worksheet menu, by typing the first letter of the command you want.

In the next section, you will learn how to customize the hardware settings.

Customizing the PrintGraph Hardware Setup

The first time you start PrintGraph, you need to change two hardware settings: the type of graphics printer and the default directory.

During installation, you chose one or more printers to use for printing graphs. When you start PrintGraph, you must "remind" the program of your choice. If you chose more than one graphics printer, you must tell PrintGraph which one to use.

When you start PrintGraph for the first time, the program automatically retrieves files from and saves files to the default drive and directory. The labs in this book assume that you have set the default drive to A, so you also need to change the default drive and directory for PrintGraph.

Setting the Printer Type

The following sections describe the procedures for setting the printer type and changing the default drive or directory. Once you make these changes, they remain in effect until you change them again.

1. To select Settings Hardware Printer from the main PrintGraph menu,

   Press: **S**

   Press: **H**

   Press: **P**

2. 1-2-3 displays a list of the printers you selected during installation. To specify the printer you want to use, press ⬆ or ⬇ to move the highlight bar to the appropriate printer and press the SPACEBAR to mark a selection. (The SPACEBAR also deselects a selected item, if you want to change printers.) A number sign (#) marks the selected printer or plotter. When you have marked the printer you want to use,

   Press: ⏎

3. To save the printer name and font directory settings,

Press: Q

Press: S

The main PrintGraph menu reappears. To change the default drive or directory, follow the procedure in the next section.

Changing the Default Drive or Directory for Graphs

1-2-3 stores graphs as "picture" files with a .PIC extension. You create these graph files in a 1-2-3 worksheet and print them using the PrintGraph program. 1-2-3 stores the .PIC files in the same location as the worksheet data files; if the data files are stored on a floppy disk in drive A, the graphs are stored there as well.

You can designate a default drive or directory from which you retrieve the stored .PIC files. Because the graph files are stored on a data disk in drive A, follow the directions below for changing the default drive and directory in PrintGraph.

1. To select Settings Hardware Graphs-Directory from the main PrintGraph menu,

Press: S

Press: H

Press: G

PrintGraph displays the default directory, C:\123R23.

2. To change the default directory to the A drive, make sure your data disk is in the A drive and,

Type: A:

Press: ⏎

Note If you wanted to retrieve your graph files from a hard-disk sub-directory, enter the directory's path. For example, if your .PIC files are filed in a subdirectory of your 123 directory named GRAPHS (on your hard disk),

Type: C:\123R23\GRAPHS

Press: ⏎

3. To save the new default directory,

Press: **Q**

Press: **S**

The main PrintGraph menu reappears.

Quitting a PrintGraph Session

Follow the instructions in this section to leave the PrintGraph program and return to DOS.

1. To select Exit,

Press: **E**

2. To confirm that you want to exit,

Press: **Y**

The DOS prompt appears on the screen.

Chapter 5

An Overview to 1-2-3

Case Study

T om Adams, a student at Northern University, is preparing a report on the future population growth for the state. While researching the report, he collected the population estimates of four cities for the years 1992 through 1995.

Tom recently acquired *The Student Edition of Lotus 1-2-3 Release 2.3* and has been using it to record and analyze the data. We will use the file Tom created to track population growth to explore 1-2-3's worksheet, graphics, and database capabilities.

Turn the computer on and load 1-2-3. If you need assistance, refer to Chapter 3, Starting and Quitting 1-2-3. Your screen should look similar to Figure 10.

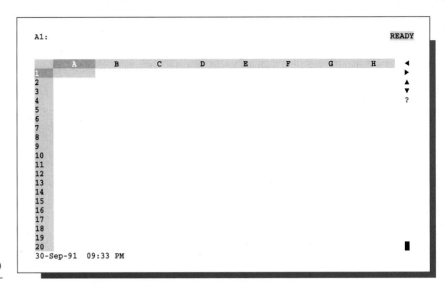

Figure 10

This is a blank 1-2-3 **worksheet**. A worksheet is an electronic representation of a spreadsheet used to enter and analyze data. The worksheet
consists of cells that are created by the intersection of a numbered row
and a lettered column. The highlight bar inside the worksheet is the **cell
pointer**. The cell pointer displays your cell location in the worksheet. It
is currently in cell A1 (column A, row 1).

The parts of a worksheet will be described in detail in Lab 1.

Moving Around the Worksheet

The keyboard allows you to communicate with 1-2-3. For example, you
use the pointer-movement keys to move the cell pointer around the
worksheet. The keyboard is described in detail in Lab 1. Watch the
movement of the cell pointer as you do the following:

Press: ⬇ three times

Press: ➔ two times

Your screen should now look similar to Figure 11.

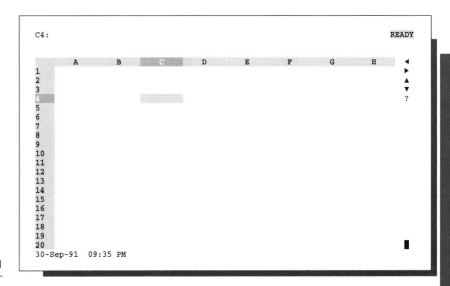

```
C4:                                                          READY

          A        B        C        D        E        F        G        H    ◄
 1                                                                            ►
 2                                                                            ▲
 3                                                                            ▼
 4                                                                            ?
 5
 6
 7
 8
 9
10
11
12
13
14
15
16
17
18
19
20
30-Sep-91  09:35 PM                                                       ■
```

Figure 11

The cell pointer is now in cell C4. Next, use the pointer-movement keys to move the cell pointer to cell D15, then to cell E12.

Many other keys also control the cell pointer. You will learn about them in Lab 1.

Tom has created a worksheet file that contains the data for the cities he is tracking. To see this worksheet file,

Press: /

Notice the two lines of new information displayed in the second and third lines of the screen. This is the 1-2-3 **main menu**. Pressing / accesses this menu. You use the main menu to enter all commands to 1-2-3.

Tom has entered his population data into a file named CITIES. To retrieve this file, issue the command **F**ile **R**etrieve **CITIES** by doing the following:

Press: **F**

Press: **R**

Type: **CITIES**

Press: ⏎

Your screen should now look similar to Figure 12.

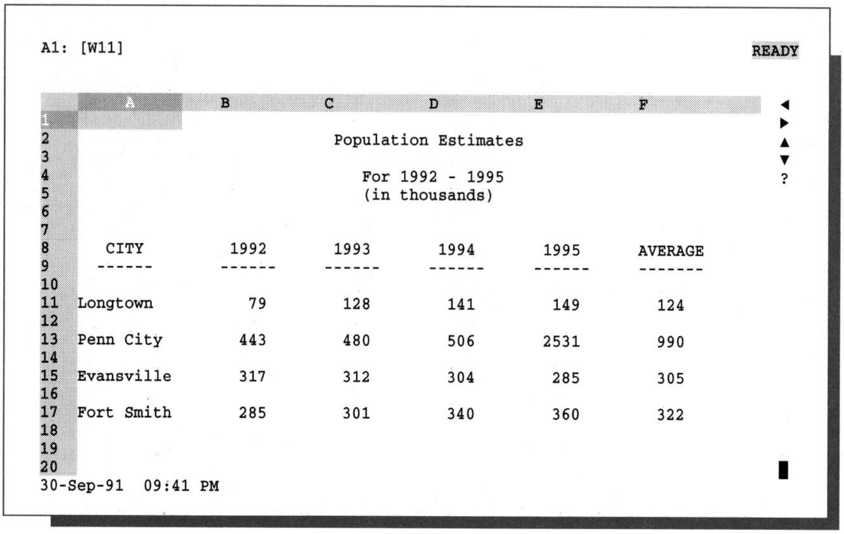

```
A1: [W11]                                                              READY

            A          B         C         D         E         F        ◄
  1                                                                      ►
  2                        Population Estimates                          ▲
  3                                                                      ▼
  4                          For 1992 - 1995                             ?
  5                           (in thousands)
  6
  7
  8       CITY        1992      1993      1994      1995     AVERAGE
  9       ------      ------    ------    ------    ------   -------
 10
 11  Longtown          79       128       141       149       124
 12
 13  Penn City        443       480       506      2531       990
 14
 15  Evansville       317       312       304       285       305
 16
 17  Fort Smith       285       301       340       360       322
 18
 19
 20                                                                      ■
     30-Sep-91   09:41 PM
```

Figure 12

Tom created this worksheet to track the yearly population for four cities — Longtown, Penn City, Evansville, and Fort Smith. The average population of each city has been calculated using a 1-2-3 @function. In Labs 1 and 2, you will learn how to enter data, formulas, and @functions into a worksheet.

Tom notices that he made an error when he entered the data in cell E13. The population for Penn City in 1995 should be 531, not 2531. To correct this error, use the ⟶ and ⟱ pointer-movement keys to

Move to: E13

Type: **531**

To enter the new value, you will press ⏎. Watch your screen carefully, and notice how the AVERAGE column automatically changes to reflect the new value.

Press: ⏎

Your screen should now look similar to Figure 13.

```
E13: [W11] 531                                                      READY

          A          B          C          D          E          F      ◄
 1                                                                       ►
 2                         Population Estimates                          ▲
 3                                                                       ▼
 4                           For 1992 - 1995                             ?
 5                            (in thousands)
 6
 7
 8      CITY         1992       1993       1994       1995    AVERAGE
 9      ------       ------     ------     ------     ------   -------
10
11   Longtown          79        128        141        149        124
12
13   Penn City        443        480        506        531        490
14
15   Evansville       317        312        304        285        305
16
17   Fort Smith       285        301        340        360        322
18
19
20
     30-Sep-91   09:43 PM                                            ■
```

Figure 13

The formula in cell F13 has been recalculated to reflect the new value in cell E13. This recalculation feature allows 1-2-3 to perform what-if analysis. What-if analysis and many worksheet commands are presented in Labs 1, 2, 3, and 4.

Exploring Graphics

Looking at the data in the worksheet, you can see that the population changes each year. To visualize these changes more clearly, 1-2-3 provides graphing capabilities.

Note In this section, you will be viewing graphs. If your computer system does not support graphics, skip to the next section, "Exploring Databases."

Tom has created both a line graph and a bar graph of the data. To view the line graph, we will issue the command /Graph Name Use, followed by the name of the graph. To do this,

Press: /

Press: G

Press: N

Press: U

If you have a color monitor, to enter the name of the graph,

Type: **LINE-C**

Press: ⏎

If you have a monochrome monitor, to enter the name of the graph,

Type: **LINE**

Press: ⏎

Your screen should look similar to Figure 14.

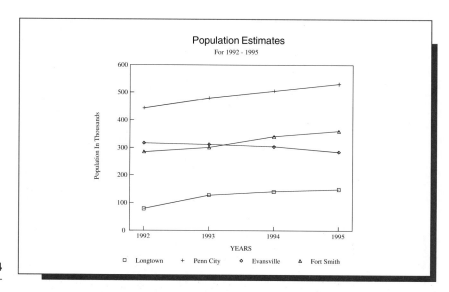

Figure 14

The line graph clearly shows the trends in population for the four cities over the four-year period.

To clear the graph from the screen,

Press: SPACEBAR

To see the same data represented as a bar graph,

Press: **N**

Press: **U**

If you have a color monitor, to enter the name of the graph,

Type: **BAR-C**

Press: ⏎

If you have a monochrome monitor, to enter the name of the graph,

Type: **BAR**

Press: ⏎

Your screen should look similar to Figure 15.

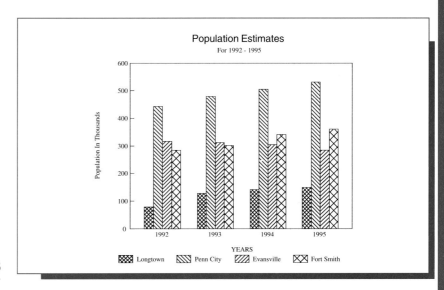

Figure 15

As you can see, the use of graphs to display the data in a worksheet helps you visualize trends and patterns of change. To clear the graph from the screen,

Press: SPACEBAR

To leave (quit) the Graph menu,

Press: **Q**

Creating and printing graphs are presented in Labs 5 and 6.

Exploring Databases

After speaking with his professor, Tom decided to expand his worksheet to include a database of additional cities.

The 1-2-3 worksheet is much larger than the area you can view on your display screen at one time. The area of the worksheet that you can see on your screen at one time is called a **window**. To see the area of the worksheet where Tom entered the data for his database,

Press: (PGDN)

Your screen should look similar to Figure 16.

```
E33: [W11] 127                                                    READY

        A        B         C         D          E        F        ◄
21                                                                 ►
22                                                                 ▲
23                    Database of Cities Populations               ▼
24                          (in thousands)                         ?
25
26 CITY          1992      1993      1994       1995    AVERAGE
27 Longtown        79       128       141        149       124
28 Penn City      443       480       506        531       490
29 Evansville     317       312       304        285       305
30 Fort Smith     285       301       340        360       322
31 Allen Park      82        90        99        108        95
32 Norton          82        90        99        109        95
33 Racine          96       105       116        127       111
34 Niagara        218       240       264        291       253
35 Little Fall    309       340       374        412       359
36 Lake Hayes     105       116       128        140       122
37 Minet            5         6         6          7         6
38 Mission         98       108       119        130       114
39 Covina          85        93       102        113        98    ■
40 Brook Park      96       105       116        128       111
30-Sep-91  10:08 PM
```

Figure 16

The area of the worksheet that contains the database of additional cities is now visible in the window. A **database** simply contains information that is organized in a specific way. Tom's database contains the population for each city by year.

The information in a database can be sorted or arranged alphabetically or numerically by 1-2-3. Tom would like to see the cities listed in alphabetical order. To sort the file, we will use the command **/D**ata **S**ort **G**o. To do this,

Press: /

Press: D

Press: S

Press: G

Your screen should look similar to Figure 17.

```
E33: [W11] 285                                                          READY

             A        B        C        D        E         F         ◄
21                                                                    ►
22                                                                    ▲
23                     Database of Cities Populations                 ▼
24                          (in thousands)                            ?
25
26  CITY           1992     1993     1994     1995    AVERAGE
27  Allen Park       82       90       99      108        95
28  Apple Grove      96      105      115      126       111
29  Brook Park       96      105      116      128       111
30  Camptown         30       33       37       40        35
31  Caroltown        20       22       25       27        24
32  Covina           85       93      102      113        98
33  Evansville      317      312      304      285       305
34  Fairview         81       89       95      105        93
35  Fort Smith      285      301      340      360       322
36  Galion           70       78       85       94        82
37  Hanson          219      241      265      291       254
38  Hometown         70       77       85       94        82
39  Hutch           220      242      267      293       256        ■
40  Inver Grove     207      227      250      275       240
30-Sep-91  10:09 PM
```

Figure 17

The database is now listed in alphabetical order, making it easier for Tom to find the cities.

The database can also be searched to locate specific information, much as you would search through a filing cabinet to locate a specific record or group of records. Tom would like to produce a separate list of all the cities in the database that have an average population over 250,000. He already has an area of the worksheet designated to hold this data. To see this area,

Press: (PGDN) twice

Your screen should look similar to Figure 18.

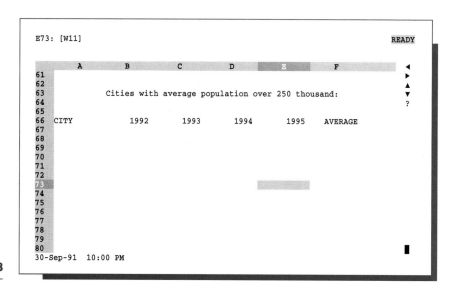

Figure 18

The necessary commands to select the cities with populations over 250,000 have already been selected. To produce the list of cities, you will use the QUERY function key, (F7) ,

Press: (F7) (QUERY)

Your screen should look similar to Figure 19.

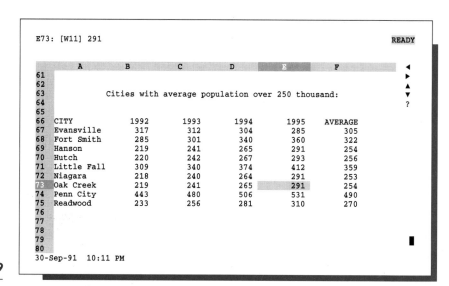

Figure 19

The nine cities with average populations over 250,000 are displayed. Creating and using a database is described in detail in Labs 7 and 8.

Leaving 1-2-3

The command to leave 1-2-3 is **/Q**uit **Y**es. To issue this command,

Press: /

Press: Q

Press: Y

1-2-3 reminds you that you have made changes to your worksheet and have not saved these changes on your data disk. At this point, you do not want to save your changes and you want to exit from 1-2-3.

Press: Y

Introducing Macros

Another more advanced topic covered in the labs is macros. A macro is a set of commands and instructions that are stored in a worksheet. The commands are executed whenever you run (invoke) the macro. The final two labs, 9 and 10, describe how to use and create macros.

Now turn to Lab 1, and get started using 1-2-3.

Lab Activities

Contents

Lab 1

Creating a Worksheet

In Lab 1, you will learn how to:

Objectives

- **Design a worksheet**
- **Move around the worksheet**
- **Use the mouse with 1-2-3 if you have one installed**
- **Enter labels and values**
- **Edit entries**
- **Use the 1-2-3 menus**
- **Retrieve a file**
- **Enter formulas**
- **Save a worksheet**
- **Print a worksheet**
- **Erase a worksheet**

Colleen Hayes is a new employee at a mountain ski resort who needs to find an apartment. Colleen recently purchased the 1-2-3 program, and wants to use it to help her analyze expenses at different apartment complexes in the area and select the most economical one.

Colleen found three apartment complexes near the ski area. She will consider renting either an efficiency or a one-bedroom apartment at each complex. Colleen will look at the various expenses associated with the apartments before deciding on the one she will rent.

The total monthly expense for an apartment will include rent, electricity, basic phone, renter's insurance, and the cost of driving to work each day. The rent, phone, and renter's insurance will be the same amount every month. Colleen has estimated the cost of electricity based on the size of the apartment. The car expenses are based on the number of miles she must drive to work.

Designing Worksheets

In Lab 1, you will create Colleen's worksheet, which is shown in Figure 1.1.

```
                    NEW APARTMENT ANALYSIS FOR COLLEEN HAYES

                        TANGLEWOOD        ORANGE GROVE       WIND COVE

                      EFF    BDRM 1     EFF    BDRM 1     EFF    BDRM 1
                      -------------------------------------------------------

          EXPENSES

          Rent         399      450      350      425      405      475
          Electricity   30       45       45       65       25       30
          Telephone     12       12       12       12       12       12
          Renter's Ins. 10       10       10       10       10       10
          Car Exp. to Work 50    50       75       75       25       25

          TOTAL MONTHLY COST 501 567      492      587      477      552

          Miles to  Work   10    10       15       15        5        5
```

Figure 1.1

Before creating a worksheet, you must develop a plan. There are four steps in this planning process.

1. **Specify purpose.** As your first step, you must decide exactly what you want the worksheet to do for you. Colleen wants her worksheet to analyze apartment expenses.

2. **Create paper model.** Once you know what you want the worksheet to do for you, you must use a pencil and paper to make a sketch of the worksheet. Your design should include titles, headings, and sample data.

3. **Build and test.** Once your design is complete, you are ready to use 1-2-3 to create and then test the worksheet for errors.

4. **Document.** Well-designed worksheets typically are documented within the worksheet. However, sometimes large or complex worksheets are documented on a separate paper document. Either way, documentation is important to ensure that whoever uses the worksheet will be able to clearly understand its objectives and procedures.

As the complexity of the problem increases, the importance of following the design process increases. Even for simple worksheets like Colleen's, the design process is important.

Colleen's purpose is to analyze apartment expenses. Her paper model is shown in Figure 1.2.

	New Apartment Analysis for Colleen Hayes					
	TANGLEWOOD		ORANGE GROVE		WIND COVE	
	EFF	BDRM 1	EFF	BDRM 1	EFF	BRDM 1
Expenses						
Rent	399	450	350	425	405	475
Electricity	38	45	45	65	25	30
Phone	12	12	12	12	12	12
Renter's Ins.	18	18	18	18	18	18
Car Exp. to Work						
Total Monthly Cost						
Miles to Work	10	10	15	15	5	5

Figure 1.2

We will follow Colleen as she plans, builds, tests, and documents her worksheet.

Exploring 1-2-3's Worksheet

After you load 1-2-3, your screen should look similar to Figure 1.3. (If you need help loading, see Chapter 3 in "Getting Started.") If you plan to use a mouse, be sure the mouse is installed before you start 1-2-3.

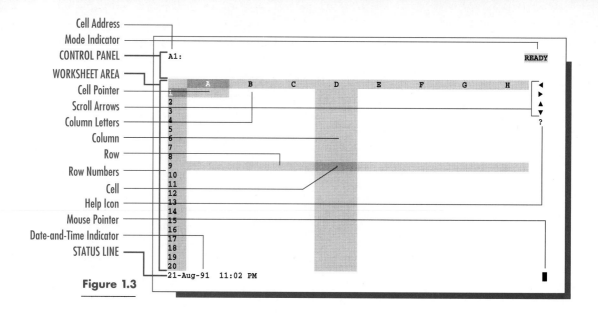

Cell Address
Mode Indicator
CONTROL PANEL
WORKSHEET AREA
Cell Pointer
Scroll Arrows
Column Letters
Column
Row
Row Numbers
Cell
Help Icon
Mouse Pointer
Date-and-Time Indicator
STATUS LINE

Figure 1.3

Figure 1.3 shows a blank 1-2-3 display screen. It is divided into three areas: the worksheet area, the control panel, and the status line.

The **worksheet area** is located in the center of the display screen and occupies the largest amount of space on the screen. The **worksheet** consists of a rectangular grid of **rows** and **columns.** The border of **row numbers** down the left side of the worksheet area identifies each row in the worksheet. The border of **column letters** across the top of the worksheet area identifies each column in the worksheet.

The part of the worksheet you see on your screen is called a **window,** which displays only a portion of the entire worksheet area. The entire worksheet has a total of 256 columns, labeled A through IV, and 8,192 rows, numbered 1 through 8192.

The basic unit of a worksheet is a **cell,** which is formed by the intersection of a column and a row. For example, cell A1 is the intersection of column A and row 1.

The highlight bar shown in cell A1 is the **cell pointer.** It identifies the cell you are using. The cell containing the cell pointer is the **current cell.** Notice that the column letter and the row number corresponding to the current cell are highlighted in the worksheet borders. In Figure 1.3, the current cell is A1, and the corresponding A and 1 in the worksheet borders are highlighted.

The **control panel** is located above the worksheet area. It consists of three lines that display information, command choices, and prompts. The first line currently displays two pieces of information. On the left side of the first line, the **cell address** of the current cell is displayed. The cell address always consists of the column letter followed by the row number of the current cell. Because the cell pointer is now located in cell A1, the cell address displays A1:.

The highlighted box on the right side of the first line is the **mode indicator.** It indicates the current **mode,** or state, of the 1-2-3 program. Here, the current mode is READY. There are 14 different modes of operation, and as you use the program, the mode indicator will change to display the current mode. Modes will be discussed as they appear throughout the labs.

The bottom line of the display screen contains the **status line.** This line displays the date and time as well as status indicators. Currently, it displays the **date-and-time indicator** on the left side. This indicator displays the date and time as maintained by DOS. **Status indicators** tell you that a certain key or program condition is in effect. Status indicators will be displayed as they are activated and will be discussed as they appear throughout the labs.

Sometimes your worksheet will be replaced with a dialog box containing an **error message**. These messages tell you about a program error that has been detected. Both dialog boxes and error messages will be discussed in further detail throughout the labs.

Mouse Features

If you have installed a mouse, an icon panel is displayed on the right side of the worksheet. The four icons (symbols) that appear as directional arrows are called **scroll arrows**. They can be activated by the mouse to move around the worksheet. The ? (question mark) is the Help icon and is used to access 1-2-3's Help facility.

The following are instructions for using a mouse.

You may also see a vertical rectangle displayed on your screen. It is the **mouse pointer**. In Figure 1.3, the mouse pointer is located in the lower right corner of the screen, but it could be located anywhere on your screen. You will learn about using the mouse in this lab in the sections "Moving Around the Worksheet," "Getting Help," and "Selecting a Command."

The icon panel and the mouse pointer are displayed only if you have installed a mouse. If you have not installed a mouse, you will not see the icon panel or the mouse pointer on your screen even though they are displayed in the figures in these labs.

Examining the Keyboard

The keyboard allows you to communicate with 1-2-3. Figure 1.4 shows two typical keyboards.

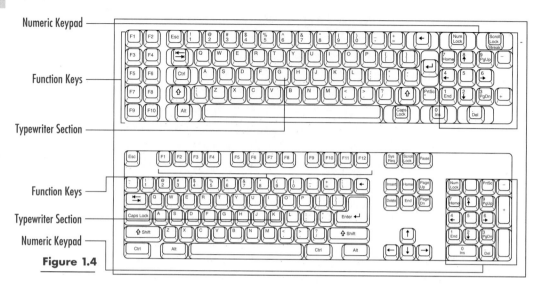

Numeric Keypad

Function Keys

Typewriter Section

Function Keys

Typewriter Section

Numeric Keypad

Figure 1.4

The keyboard has three general areas: the typewriter section, the function keys, and the numeric keypad.

The typewriter section is arranged like a standard typewriter keyboard. Letter and number keys are in their usual places, and holding the (SHIFT) key down and typing a letter key produces a capital letter.

In addition to the standard operations, the typewriter section has keys for special operations. Table 1.1 lists these special keys and their operations in 1-2-3.

Key	Description
(ESC)	Cancels a command
(CTRL)	Causes keys to take on new meanings
(ALT)	Causes keys to take on new meanings
(INS)	Switches between inserting and typing over existing characters
(DEL)	Deletes a character
(TAB)	Moves the cell pointer one screen to the right
(SHIFT)-(TAB)	Moves the cell pointer one screen to the left
(↵)	Allows the user to enter data or command sequences
(NUM LOCK)	Switches the cursor movement keys to number keys, or vice versa

Table 1.1

Key	Description
(CAPS LOCK)	Switches the letters to uppercase or lowercase
BACKSPACE	Moves the cursor back one space and deletes the character
(SCROLL LOCK)	Switches the cell pointer to a stationary position during scrolling
(CTRL)-(BREAK)	Cancels current procedure

**Table 1.1
Continued**

The function keys execute special 1-2-3 commands. They are labeled (F1) through (F10) (or (F12) on some keyboards). The role of the function keys will be discussed as they appear in the labs.

The numeric keypad, which is to the right of the typewriter section, can be used for moving around a worksheet and for entering numeric data. To use the keypad to enter numbers, you must first press the (NUM LOCK) key. If (NUM LOCK) is not on (for some keyboards, a light indicates (NUM LOCK) is on), pressing these keys moves the cell pointer around the worksheet.

Typically, you use the numeric keypad to move the cell pointer around the worksheet, and you use the number keys in the typewriter section to enter numeric data.

Some keyboards have a separate keypad for the four directional arrow keys. Use of these keys moves the cell pointer in the direction of the arrow on the key.

Moving Around the Worksheet

You can move around the worksheet using either the keyboard or the mouse. Even if you have a mouse installed, follow the instructions in "Using the Keyboard" before you complete the section "Using the Mouse."

Using the Keyboard

The arrow keys in the numeric keypad are used to move the cell pointer around the worksheet in the direction of the arrow. Note the changes in the control panel and the movement of the cell pointer as you

Press: (↓) three times

Press: (→) two times

Your screen should look similar to Figure 1.5.

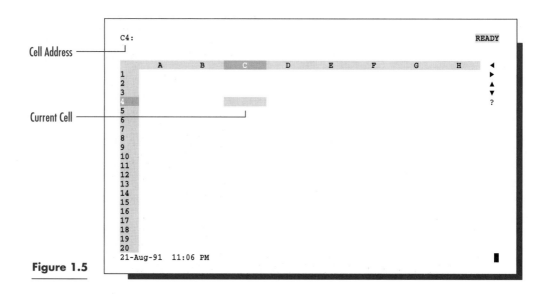

Cell Address ——

Current Cell ——

Figure 1.5

The cell pointer should now be in cell C4, making this cell the current cell. The cell address in the control panel reflects the new location of the cell pointer. The column letter C and the row number 4, along the borders of the worksheet, are highlighted.

Practice moving around the worksheet by using the four arrow keys, (↓), (↑), (→), and (←), to move the cell pointer to cells D9, F18, and B12.

The (HOME) key will return you to the top left corner of the worksheet. This position in the worksheet is also called the **home position.**

Press: (HOME)

The cell pointer should now be back in cell A1.

The worksheet has more columns than those you can see on your screen at one time. To view the next full window of the worksheet, you would hold down the (CTRL) key and press either (→) to move right one full screen or (←) to move left one full screen.

To move right one full screen:

Press: (CTRL)-(→)

Note When two keys are separated by a hyphen (-), you must hold down the first key while pressing the second key. Do *not* press the hyphen key.

Your screen should show columns I through P, as shown in Figure 1.6.

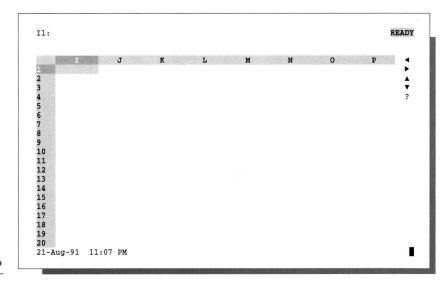

I1:   READY

	I	J	K	L	M	N	O	P
1								
2								
3								
4								
5								
6								
7								
8								
9								
10								
11								
12								
13								
14								
15								
16								
17								
18								
19								
20								

21-Aug-91   11:07 PM

Figure 1.6

To return to the previous window,

Press: CTRL-←

The screen should again show columns A through H.

By holding down the CTRL key while pressing either → or ←, you can quickly move horizontally through the worksheet. This is called **scrolling.**

Pressing the PGDN key allows you to move down one full screen (20 rows) at a time.

Press: PGDN

Your screen should now look similar to Figure 1.7.

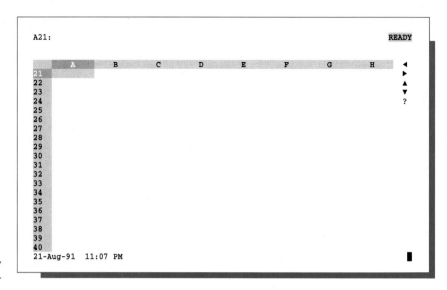

A21:   READY

```
        A        B        C        D        E        F        G        H      ◄
  21                                                                           ►
  22                                                                           ▲
  23                                                                           ▼
  24                                                                           ?
  25
  26
  27
  28
  29
  30
  31
  32
  33
  34
  35
  36
  37
  38
  39
  40
  21-Aug-91   11:07 PM                                                         ■
```

Figure 1.7

You have moved down one full screen, and rows 21 through 40 are now
displayed in the window. Similarly, pressing the (PGUP) key allows you to
move up one full screen.

Press: (PGUP)

Your screen has moved up one full window on the worksheet, returning
you to the screen that displays rows 1 through 20. By holding down the
(PGUP) or (PGDN) key, you can quickly scroll vertically through the
worksheet.

To move to the last row of the worksheet,

Press: (END)

Notice that the status indicator END is displayed in the status line. This
tells you the (END) key is being used.

Press: (↓)

The cell pointer moved to cell A8192. Your screen should look similar to
Figure 1.8.

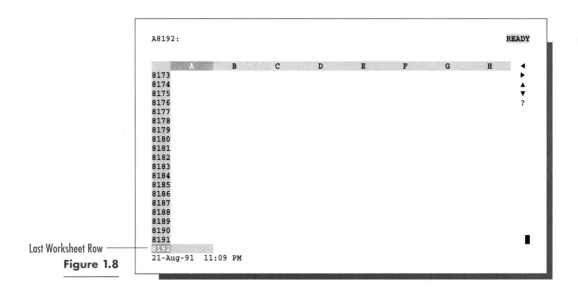

Last Worksheet Row

Figure 1.8

Columns are sequenced first from A to Z, then from AA to AZ, and then from BA to IV. To move to the last column of the worksheet,

Press: (END)

Press: (→)

The cell pointer moved to cell IV8192. Your screen should look similar to Figure 1.9.

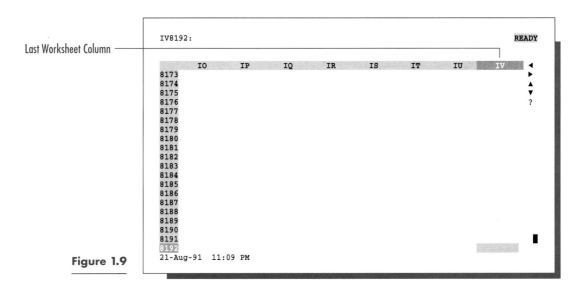

Last Worksheet Column

Figure 1.9

Cell IV8192 is at the bottom right corner of the worksheet.

Sometimes a faster method of moving around the worksheet is to use the GOTO function key, ⬚F5⬚. For example, to go to cell H128, first

Press: ⬚F5⬚ (GOTO)

Look at the second line of the control panel. The message, or **prompt,** "Enter address to go to:" is displayed. The current location of the cell pointer follows the prompt. A prompt is how 1-2-3 communicates with you, and now it is prompting you to enter the new cell address to move to. 1-2-3 automatically entered the current location of the cell pointer in response to the prompt. Since this is not the address you want to move to, you need to enter the correct cell address. You can enter the cell address in lowercase or uppercase characters.

Type: **H128**

To tell 1-2-3 that your response to the prompt is complete,

Press: ⬚⏎⬚

Your screen should look similar to Figure 1.10.

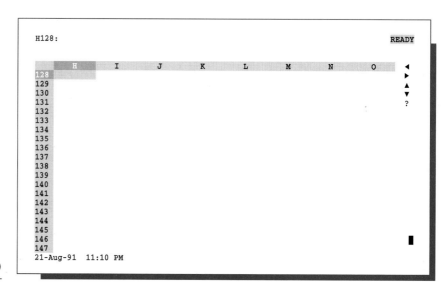

Figure 1.10

Cell H128 is placed in the upper left corner of the window, and the cell pointer is positioned in that cell.

To return quickly to cell A1,

Press: `HOME`

Now move the cell pointer to cell A45 using the `↓` key. The row numbers on the screen now go from 26 to 45. You have moved the window down the worksheet by individual rows rather than by a full screen.

Practice each of the following key sequences, and watch how your screen changes.

`↑`	`HOME`	`PGUP`
`↓`	`CTRL`-`→`	`END` `↓`
`←`	`CTRL`-`←`	`END` `→`
`→`	`PGDN`	`F5` *cell address*

When you are ready to go on,

Press: `HOME`

Using the Mouse

The following are instructions for using a mouse.

If you have installed a mouse, you will want to read this section to find out how to use your mouse to move around the worksheet. If you did not install a mouse or you do not plan to use a mouse, you can proceed to the next section titled "Entering Labels."

Before continuing, be sure that your mouse is installed. You will know the mouse is installed if you see the four scroll arrows and ? (Help icon) on the right side of your screen.

The mouse controls the **mouse pointer**, which may be visible on your screen and appears as a tall rectangular box. You move the mouse pointer on the screen by moving the mouse over the desk top in the same direction you want the mouse pointer to move. On the top of the mouse are two or three buttons that you will use to make selections.

When you are using 1-2-3, you can use three mouse actions: Point, Click, and Drag. These actions enable you to initiate work in the program, to select commands, or to enter information. The actions are defined as follows:

Point: Move the mouse until the mouse pointer rests on what you want to point to on the screen. (This action precedes clicking and dragging.)

Click: Press and release the mouse button quickly without moving the mouse. (This action is used in combination with pointing.)

Drag: Press and hold down the mouse button while moving the mouse pointer to a new location on the screen.

For additional information about the mouse, refer to Part 1, "Getting Started."

Practice moving the mouse in all directions (up, down, left, and right), and note the movement of the mouse pointer on the screen. Be sure your mouse is in contact with the desk top on which it is resting.

Pick up the mouse and move it to a different location on your desk top. Notice that the mouse pointer did not move on the screen. This is because the mouse pointer movement is controlled by the rubber-coated ball on the bottom of the mouse. This ball must move within its socket for the pointer to move on the screen. The ball's movement is translated into signals that tell the computer how to move the on-screen pointer.

To move from cell to cell within the worksheet, point to the cell you want to move to, and click the left button.

You will use the left button to select items since this is the default button set by 1-2-3 during the install process.

Note For all future mouse directions, we will refer to the Point to and Click actions more simply as Click. For example, the preceding direction would, in future, be stated as

Click: the cell you want to move to

Now,

Click: D10

Click: G16

Click: B4

Click: A1

You may find that using the mouse to move the cell pointer in an empty worksheet is difficult because you cannot tell the exact location of the mouse pointer. When the worksheet contains data, it is much easier to position the mouse pointer accurately.

To use the mouse to move the cell pointer one row or column at a time, click the scroll arrow corresponding to the direction you want to move. The scroll arrows are located on the upper right side of the worksheet area in the icon panel. If you are having difficulty identifying the scroll arrows on your screen, you may want to refer to Figure 1.3, which shows the icon panel containing the scroll arrows.

To move down three rows,

> **Click:**   the down scroll arrow three times

Cell A4 should be highlighted.

To scroll continuously,

> **Click:**   a scroll arrow until the row and column you want to see are displayed on the screen

Practice continuous scrolling:

> **Click:**   the down scroll arrow until row 45 comes into view on the screen

Now, to scroll continuously to the right,

> **Click:**   the right scroll arrow until columns I through P can be seen on the screen

Practice moving the cell pointer around the worksheet using the mouse techniques described in this section.

The mouse can be used with most of the exercises in this book. Specific instructions on how to use the mouse will be provided when new topics involving the mouse are introduced.

When you are ready to go on,

> **Press:**   HOME

Entering Labels

Next, you will learn how to enter information into a worksheet and how to correct, or **edit,** entries.

Entries into the worksheet are either labels or values. **Labels** are text entries, such as words and symbols that describe other worksheet entries. They cannot be used for arithmetic calculations. **Values** are numbers and formula entries.

The first character you enter in a cell determines how 1-2-3 will define the cell contents. Cell entries that begin with a number from 0 through 9 or any of the **numeric symbols** +, −, ., (, @, #, and $ are values. Cell entries that begin with an alpha character (A through Z), ', ", ^, or any other character are defined as labels.

For example, if you entered the number 14 into a cell, it would be a value and could be used to calculate other values. However, if you preceded the number 14 with an apostrophe ('14), 1-2-3 would interpret it as a label and could not use it to calculate other arithmetic values.

To show how the first character of a cell entry is interpreted, the mode indicator displays either LABEL or VALUE. When the cell entry is complete, the mode indicator returns to READY.

You will begin creating Colleen Hayes's worksheet by entering the labels for the type of apartment in row 5. The first label is for an efficiency apartment.

Move to: C5

Check the cell address in the control panel to be sure that the cell pointer is in cell C5.

Type: **efficiency**

Your screen should now look similar to Figure 1.11.

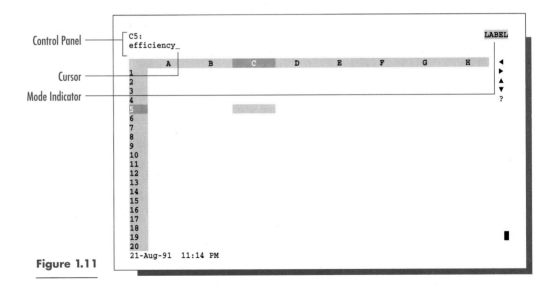

Figure 1.11

If you make a typing error, use the BACKSPACE key to erase the letters back to your mistake, and then type the entry correctly.

The mode indicator changed from READY to LABEL. The second line of the control panel displays the label **efficiency** followed by a blinking underscore, or **cursor.** The cursor shows you where each character will appear as you type. Notice, however, that the label has not yet been entered into cell C5 of the worksheet.

To enter the label into cell C5,

Press: ⏎

Your screen should now look similar to Figure 1.12.

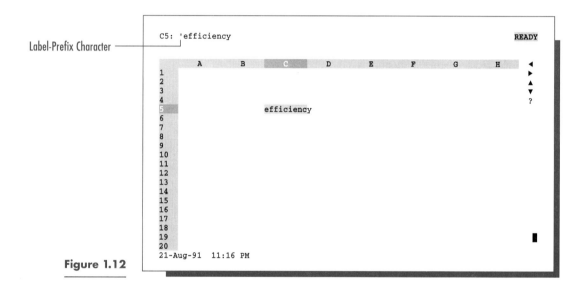

Label-Prefix Character

Figure 1.12

The label, **efficiency,** should be displayed in cell C5. (If you entered the label in the wrong cell location, move the cell pointer to the cell containing the label and press ⃝DEL. The cell entry will be erased. Deleting entries will be discussed in more detail in Lab 2. You should then move to cell C5 and enter the label **efficiency.**)

Notice that, following the cell address in the control panel, the contents of the current cell are displayed as **'efficiency.** The apostrophe (') before the label is a **label-prefix character.** This character is automatically entered before all label entries (in the control panel but not in the current cell). It controls the placement or alignment of the label within the cell space. The apostrophe aligns a label at the left side of the cell space. You will see shortly how label alignment can be changed.

Also notice that the **y** in **efficiency** appears to be outside cell C5 and displayed in cell D5. This occurred because the word *efficiency* is longer than the nine spaces in cell C5. A label that is longer than the cell width is called a **long label.** As long as the cells to the right of C5 are empty, the long label can be fully displayed. If cell D5 contained data, the long label would be cut off. Adjusting columns to accommodate long labels will be discussed in Lab 2.

To simplify our worksheet, we want to change **efficiency** to **eff.** This can be accomplished in either READY mode or EDIT mode.

To use READY mode, simply type over the existing entry. With the cell pointer in cell C5,

Type: **eff**

Press: ⏎

When you press ⏎, **eff** is entered in the worksheet, and **efficiency** is replaced. Another way to enter information in the worksheet without using ⏎ is to move the cell pointer to another cell. For example, with the cell pointer still in cell C5,

Type: **Eff**

Press: →

The label is entered in cell C5, and the cell pointer is moved to cell D5.

The second method of changing entries uses EDIT mode, which is accessed by using the EDIT function key, (F2). To change **Eff** to **EFF** using EDIT mode,

Move to: C5

Press: (F2) (EDIT)

Your screen should look similar to Figure 1.13.

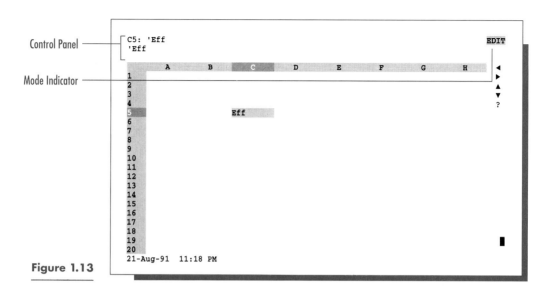

Control Panel ——

Mode Indicator ——

```
C5:  'Eff                                          EDIT
'Eff
            A       B       C       D       E       F       G       H     ◄
1                                                                        ►
2                                                                        ▲
3                                                                        ▼
4                                                                        ?
5                       Eff
6
7
8
9
10
11
12
13
14
15
16
17
18
19                                                                       ▮
20
21-Aug-91   11:18 PM
```

Figure 1.13

The second line of the control panel now displays **'Eff,** and the mode indicator has changed from READY to EDIT. In EDIT mode, you can use the keys in Table 1.2 for specific tasks.

Key	Action
←	Moves the cursor one space left in the entry
→	Moves the cursor one space right in the entry
HOME	Moves the cursor to the first character in the entry
END	Moves the cursor to the space after the last character
CTRL-→ or TAB	Moves the cursor five spaces to the right
CTRL-← or SHIFT-TAB	Moves the cursor five spaces to the left
BACKSPACE	Deletes characters to the left of the cursor
INS	Overwrites text
DEL	Deletes characters at the cursor
ESC	Erases all characters in the entry

Table 1.2

To delete the **ff** from **Eff** in the second line of the control panel,

Press: ← two times

Press: DEL two times

To complete the edit,

Type: **FF**

Press: ⏎

Your screen should look similar to Figure 1.14.

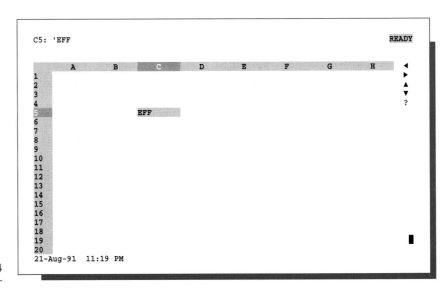

C5: 'EFF   READY

	A	B	C	D	E	F	G	H
1								
2								
3								
4								
5			EFF					

21-Aug-91   11:19 PM

Figure 1.14

You have returned to READY mode, and **EFF** is now entered into cell C5.

As you can see, editing would be particularly useful for changing long or complicated entries.

Next, you will practice using READY and EDIT modes to enter the column label for a one bedroom apartment in cell D5.

Move to: D5

Type: **bedroom-1**

Press: ⏎

To change **bedroom-1** to **Bdrm 1** in READY mode,

Type: **Bdrm 1**

Press: ⏎

To change **Bdrm 1** to **BDRM 1** using EDIT mode,

Press:	(F2) (EDIT)
Press:	BACKSPACE five times
Type:	**DRM 1**
Press:	(↵)

Your screen should look similar to Figure 1.15.

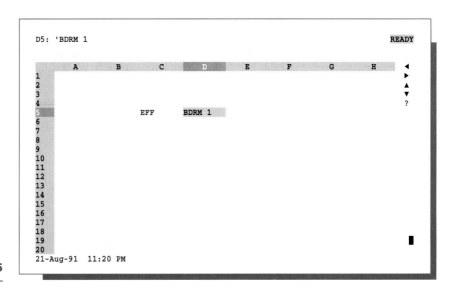

Figure 1.15

Notice that both **EFF** and **BDRM 1** are displayed to the left side of their cell space. This is because the default label-prefix character (') was automatically entered by 1-2-3. Labels can be displayed in their cell space as left-aligned, centered, or right-aligned. You can specify the alignment of a label within the cell space by entering the following label-prefix characters before the label:

Label-prefix character	Effect
' (apostrophe)	left-aligned
^ (caret)	centered
" (quote)	right-aligned

If no label-prefix character is specified, 1-2-3 automatically enters an apostrophe, and the label is left-aligned.

To change **EFF** to right alignment,

> **Move to:** C5
>
> **Type:** "EFF
>
> **Press:** ⏎

Your screen should now look similar to Figure 1.16.

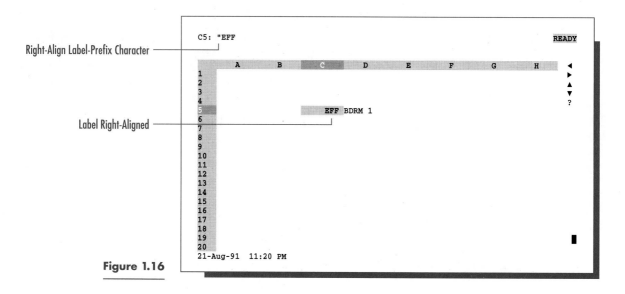

Right-Align Label-Prefix Character ⟶

Label Right-Aligned ⟶

Figure 1.16

EFF is displayed right-aligned in the cell space. Notice that there is a blank space to the right of the label. 1-2-3 reserves this space for special characters, such as a close parenthesis or a percent sign, used in numeric entries.

Now, change **BDRM 1** to right alignment in either EDIT or READY mode.

You are ready to enter the labels for the other two apartment complexes. Because we want the labels entered as all capital letters,

> **Press:** (CAPS LOCK)

The status indicator, CAPS, appears in the status line to tell you the (CAPS LOCK) key is on. The (CAPS LOCK) key affects only the letter keys, not the number or punctuation keys. Do not use the (SHIFT) key with letters when (CAPS LOCK) is on. However, you will need to use the (SHIFT) key to create the " (quotation mark) character.

Now enter and right-align the labels **EFF**, **BDRM 1**, **EFF**, and **BDRM 1** in cells E5 through H5. Use ⟶ to enter the first three labels, and use ⏎ to enter the last label in cell H5. Your screen should look similar to Figure 1.17.

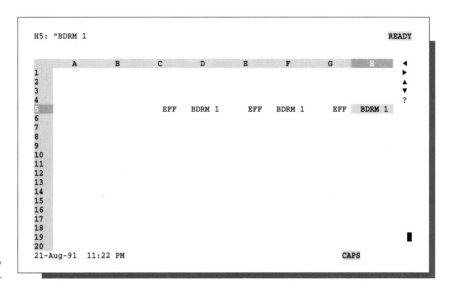

Figure 1.17

To turn off CAPS LOCK,

Press: CAPS LOCK

Next, you want to underline the first **EFF** column title. To do this, you will enter nine hyphen characters in the cell below the first **EFF**.

Move to: C6

Type: '---------

Press: ⏎

The apostrophe preceding the entry defines the entry as a label. Without it, the first character in the entry (-) would have been interpreted as a value (a negative sign), and an error would have resulted.

Cell C6 should be completely filled with a series of hyphens.

An easier way to fill a cell with repeated characters is to begin the entry with another label-prefix character, the backslash (\). This label-prefix character tells 1-2-3 to fill the cell with the character(s) following the backslash.

Move to: D6

Type: \-

Press: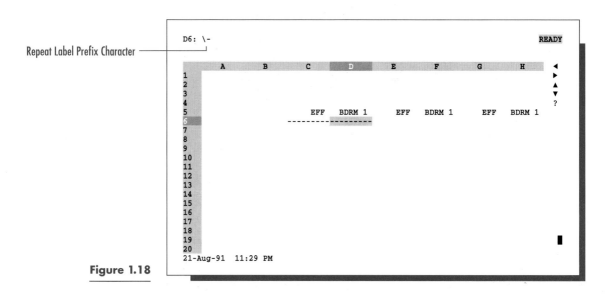

Your screen should look similar to Figure 1.18.

Repeat Label Prefix Character

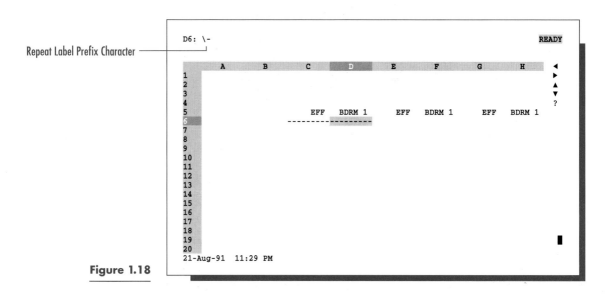

Figure 1.18

You can use the backslash character to fill a cell with any repeated character. For example, if you want all asterisks in a cell, you would type *.

Now, underline the other column titles.

To enter a title for the worksheet,

Move to: C1

Type: **New Apartment Analysis For Colleen Hayes**

Press: ⏎

Although the title is a long label, it is fully displayed in the worksheet since the cells to the right of C1 are empty.

You can now enter the names of the apartment complexes that Colleen wants to compare. Enter **TANGLEWOOD** in cell C3, **ORANGE GROVE** in cell E3, and **WIND COVE** in cell G3.

Notice that the complex names are not centered over the column labels. To center a title over multiple columns, you will need to enter extra blank spaces before the title.

Move to: C3

The title in C3 is 10 characters long and needs to be centered over the headings in column C and column D. From the E in EFF to the 1 in BDRM 1 is 12 spaces. TANGLEWOOD is 10 spaces long. To center TANGLEWOOD over EFF and BDRM 1, you want to leave a blank space on either side of TANGLEWOOD, which is the same as 1 space + 10 spaces + 1 space = 12 spaces.

When you center TANGLEWOOD, you must also take into account that the headings in column C and column D are right-aligned. EFF starts 6 spaces to the right. You will need to move a total of 7 spaces to the right for TANGLEWOOD to be centered over the headings.

Press:	(F2) (EDIT)
Press:	(HOME)
Press:	(→) one time so that the cursor is under the T in TANGLEWOOD
Press:	SPACEBAR (six times) so that the cursor has moved a total of seven spaces
Press:	(↵)

The title is now centered over the column names EFF and BDRM 1. Now center the titles ORANGE GROVE and WIND COVE using EDIT mode.

The row labels for Colleen's worksheet are entered in the same manner as the column labels. This has already been done for you and saved in the file LABELS.WK1 on your data disk. You will retrieve this file in the section "Selecting a Command."

We now explore the structure of the 1-2-3 menus.

Examining the 1-2-3 Menus

You access the 1-2-3 menus by pressing the slash key, /, located on the bottom right of the typewriter section of your keyboard.

Press:	/

To display the 1-2-3 menu by using the mouse, move the mouse pointer into the control panel, and the menu will automatically be displayed.

Your screen should look similar to Figure 1.19.

Menu Pointer
Command Menu (Main Menu)
Worksheet Menu Options
(Submenu)

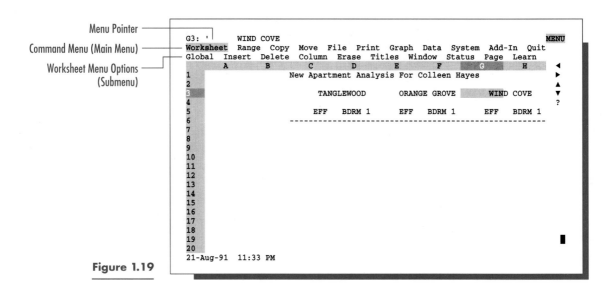

Figure 1.19

Look at the control panel. The first line has changed to indicate MENU in the mode indicator. The second line now shows the main 1-2-3 **menu**, or list, of 11 different **commands**, beginning with **W**orksheet and ending with **Q**uit.

The highlight bar that is currently on **W**orksheet is the **menu pointer**. The third line shows the submenu of commands associated with the highlighted main menu command, in this case, **W**orksheet.

Getting Help

1-2-3 provides a Help facility for all commands that can be accessed using the keyboard or the mouse. Even if you are using a mouse, complete the following section, "Using the Keyboard."

Using the Keyboard

To obtain help (information) on a particular command, begin the command, and then press the HELP function key, (F1). For example, we wish to obtain help on the **F**ile command. To move the menu pointer to **F**ile and obtain help,

Press: (→) four times

Press: (F1) (HELP)

Your screen should look similar to Figure 1.20.

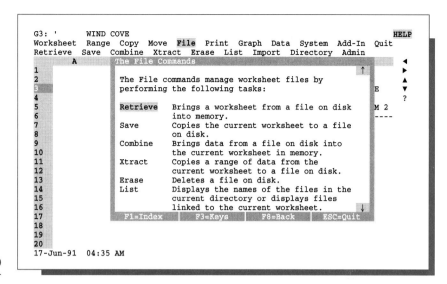

```
G3: '        WIND COVE                                            HELP
Worksheet  Range  Copy  Move  File  Print  Graph  Data  System  Add-In  Quit
Retrieve  Save  Combine  Xtract  Erase  List  Import  Directory  Admin
        A          The File Commands                                    ◄
1                                                             ↑          ►
2                  The File commands manage worksheet files by          ▲
3                  performing the following tasks:               E       ▼
4                                                                        ?
5                  Retrieve  Brings a worksheet from a file on disk   M 2
6                            into memory.                            ----
7                  Save      Copies the current worksheet to a file
8                            on disk.
9                  Combine   Brings data from a file on disk into
10                           the current worksheet in memory.
11                 Xtract    Copies a range of data from the
12                           current worksheet to a file on disk.
13                 Erase     Deletes a file on disk.
14                 List      Displays the names of the files in the
15                           current directory or displays files
16                           linked to the current worksheet.    ↓
17                  F1=Index      F3=Keys      F8=Back      ESC=Quit
18
19
20
17-Jun-91  04:35 AM
```

Figure 1.20

The mode indicator now displays HELP, and the screen provides information on the **F**ile commands.

You can get more information now about any of the topics that are highlighted on the screen. (If you have a color monitor, highlighting is displayed as a different color.) Simply use the arrow keys to move the menu pointer until it highlights the topic of your choice, and then press ⏎.

For example, in Figure 1.20, the menu pointer is highlighting the **R**etrieve command. For information on this command,

Press: ⏎

Your screen should look similar to Figure 1.21.

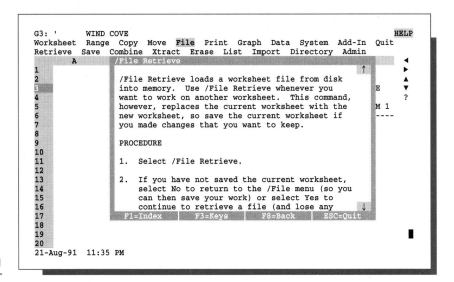

```
G3: '      WIND COVE                                              HELP
Worksheet  Range  Copy  Move  File  Print  Graph  Data  System  Add-In  Quit
Retrieve  Save  Combine  Xtract  Erase  List  Import  Directory  Admin
           A          /File Retrieve                                      ◄
  1                                                              ↑         ►
  2                   /File Retrieve loads a worksheet file from disk     ▲
  3                   into memory.  Use /File Retrieve whenever you    E  ▼
  4                   want to work on another worksheet.  This command,
  5                   however, replaces the current worksheet with the M 1
  6                   new worksheet, so save the current worksheet if  ----
  7                   you made changes that you want to keep.
  8
  9                   PROCEDURE
 10
 11                   1.  Select /File Retrieve.
 12
 13                   2.  If you have not saved the current worksheet,
 14                       select No to return to the /File menu (so you
 15                       can then save your work) or select Yes to
 16                       continue to retrieve a file (and lose any   ↓
 17                    F1=Index      F3=Keys      F8=Back      ESC=Quit
 18
 19                                                                   ■
 20
21-Aug-91  11:35 PM
```

Figure 1.21

The screen now shows information on the **/F**ile **R**etrieve command. Read the information about **R**etrieve on this Help screen. It tells you that **/F**ile **R**etrieve accesses other worksheets you have created and replaces the current worksheet. If you want to save the current worksheet, you would have to use the **/F**ile **S**ave command before accessing a new worksheet with the **/F**ile **R**etrieve command. If you want to save the worksheet, use the **/F**ile **S**ave command before you retrieve another file.

Notice that all the information about **/F**ile **R**etrieve is not displayed on this screen. To read more about **/F**ile **R**etrieve, press ⬇ until you have read all the information about **R**etrieve.

When you reach the end of the information on **R**etrieve, Help gives you a list of other topics related to **/F**ile **R**etrieve. You could select one of these topics and receive additional help.

To turn off the Help facility and return to your original position in the worksheet,

Press: (ESC)

To review, you access the main menu by pressing /, select the main menu topic, ask for help by pressing (F1) (HELP), and then select the desired Help topic for more detailed information. By using the Help system, you can obtain an explanation of each command. This is a good way to find out about 1-2-3. You can access the Help menu at any time by pressing (F1) (HELP).

Using the Mouse

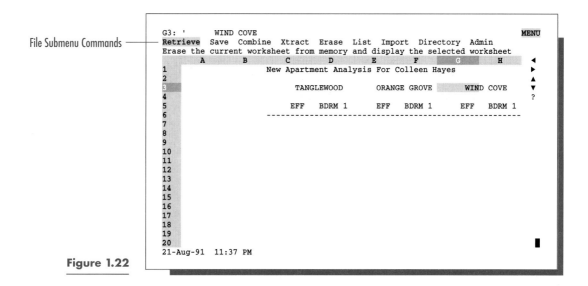

The following are instructions for using a mouse.

If you do not have a mouse installed, skip to the next section, "Selecting a Command."

You can also use the mouse to access the 1-2-3 menus and 1-2-3 Help. Move the mouse pointer to the second line of the control panel.

To select the **F**ile command,

Click: any character in the word File

You can click **F**ile whether or not it is highlighted by the menu pointer so long as the mouse pointer is on it. Your screen should look similar to Figure 1.22.

File Submenu Commands ————

```
G3: '      WIND COVE                                              MENU
Retrieve  Save  Combine  Xtract  Erase  List  Import  Directory  Admin
Erase the current worksheet from memory and display the selected worksheet
          A        B        C        D        E        F        G        H        ◄
1                      New Apartment Analysis For Colleen Hayes                    ►
2                                                                                  ▲
3                      TANGLEWOOD          ORANGE GROVE          WIND COVE          ▼
4                                                                                  ?
5                      EFF   BDRM 1        EFF   BDRM 1        EFF   BDRM 1
6                      -----------------------------------------------------
7
8
9
10
11
12
13
14
15
16
17
18
19
20                                                                                 ■
21-Aug-91  11:37 PM
```

Figure 1.22

The **F**ile submenu commands, which were on the third line of the control panel, are now on the second line. The third line now presents a brief description of the highlighted **R**etrieve command.

To obtain more information on the **R**etrieve command,

Click: ? (Help icon)

Your screen should now look similar to Figure 1.23.

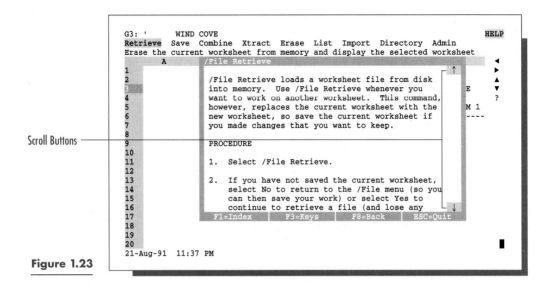

Scroll Buttons

Figure 1.23

```
G3: '      WIND COVE                                                HELP
Retrieve  Save  Combine  Xtract  Erase  List  Import  Directory  Admin
Erase the current worksheet from memory and display the selected worksheet
          A        /File Retrieve                              ◄
1                                                          ↑    ►
2                 /File Retrieve loads a worksheet file from disk  ▲
3                 into memory.  Use /File Retrieve whenever you   E ▼
4                 want to work on another worksheet.  This command,  ?
5                 however, replaces the current worksheet with the  M 1
6                 new worksheet, so save the current worksheet if   ----
7                 you made changes that you want to keep.
8
9                 PROCEDURE
10
11                1.  Select /File Retrieve.
12
13                2.  If you have not saved the current worksheet,
14                    select No to return to the /File menu (so you
15                    can then save your work) or select Yes to
16                    continue to retrieve a file (and lose any   ↓
17                 F1=Index       F3=Keys       F8=Back      ESC=Quit
18
19
20
21-Aug-91  11:37 PM                                              ■
```

Notice that all the information about **/F**ile **R**etrieve is not displayed on the screen. To read more about **/F**ile **R**etrieve,

Click: the down arrow scroll button in the lower right corner of the Help screen

This scrolls the information on the screen so that you can read the next line. Continue to use the down arrow scroll button until you have read all the information about **R**etrieve. You can click the scroll button to move one line at a time or press the scroll button for continuous scrolling.

To turn off Help, you could click the ESC button at the bottom of the Help screen, or you could click the right mouse button. Clicking the right mouse button is like pressing (ESC) on the keyboard; either action will back you out of a menu. Using the second method,

Click: the right mouse button

Your screen should again look like Figure 1.22.

To return to the main menu, you could press (ESC) or you could click the right mouse button. Using the second method,

Click: the right mouse button

Selecting a Command

Once again, you can use a mouse or the keyboard to select commands.

You can select a command in one of four different ways:

1. Type the first letter (in uppercase or lowercase) of the command.

2. Use the ⊖ and ⊝ keys to move the menu pointer to highlight the command, and then press ⏎. (This is called menu pointing.)

3. Use a combination of methods 1 and 2.

4. Use the mouse to click a command. This is discussed in detail in the section "Using the Mouse."

In the next section, "Using the Keyboard," you will retrieve a file using the keyboard.

Using the Keyboard

The third line of the control panel lists the various submenu commands associated with the highlighted command.

You want to retrieve a file. Since the **F**ile command is already highlighted, you can either press ⏎ or type **F** to select this command.

Select: File

Your screen should now look similar to Figure 1.24.

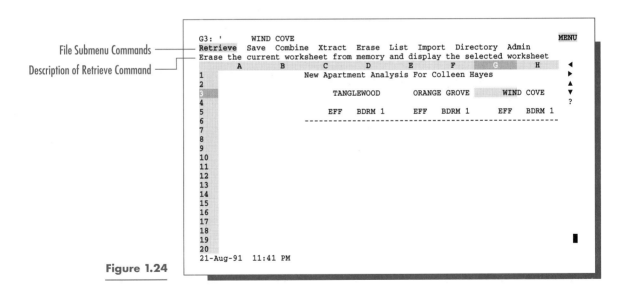

File Submenu Commands

Description of Retrieve Command

Figure 1.24

The **F**ile submenu commands, which were on the third line of the control panel, are now on the second line. The third line now presents a brief description of the highlighted **R**etrieve command. You now want to retrieve a file, so

Select: **R**etrieve

Since you have a worksheet on your screen, 1-2-3 beeps to remind you to save the worksheet if you wish to. Notice that the menu has only two choices, **N**o and **Y**es, and that the third line displays the message "WORKSHEET CHANGES NOT SAVED! Retrieve file anyway?" Selecting **N**o would enable you to issue the **/F**ile **S**ave command to save the worksheet. You do not need to save this worksheet, however, so

Select: **Y**es

Your screen should now look similar to Figure 1.25.

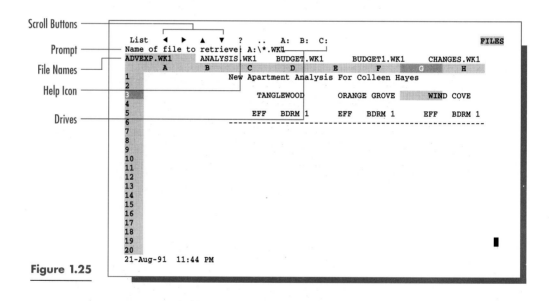

Figure 1.25

If you have a mouse installed, the first line of the control panel displays the scroll buttons, ? (Help icon), and letters indicating the drives.

Whether or not you have a mouse installed, the mode indicator displays FILES. The second line of the control panel prompts you to specify the name of the file you want to retrieve. Following the prompt, the drive (A:) that 1-2-3 is using is displayed. (If you are saving your data files on a hard disk, your prompt will probably display C:.) The third line lists worksheet files on your data disk.

You can select the name of the file to be retrieved by typing the file name or by using the menu pointer. Besides using the (→) and (←) keys, you can move the menu pointer even more quickly through the list of files, or see a full screen list, by using the keys shown in Table 1.3.

Key	Description
(END)	Takes you to the last file
(HOME)	Takes you to the first file
(↑)	Takes you to the previous list of files
(↓)	Takes you to the next list of files
(F3) (NAME)	Displays a full screen of file names

Table 1.3

These keys are especially helpful when you have a disk that contains many files.

Move the menu pointer by using the arrow keys to highlight the file named LABELS.WK1. You will not see this file right away in the third row since the worksheet files are alphabetically arranged. Use both the (→) and the (↓) keys until LABELS.WK1 is highlighted. Then, to select this file,

Press: (↵)

Your screen should now look similar to Figure 1.26.

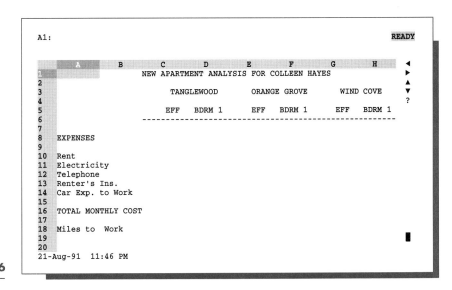

Figure 1.26

The worksheet that contains the column and row labels is now displayed on your screen, and the mode indicator displays READY.

To review, the command sequence used to retrieve the file LABELS.WK1 was:

/**F**ile **R**etrieve **Yes** **LABELS.WK1** ⏎

You can issue a command by typing the first letter of each command, by using the menu pointer, or by a combination of the two methods. The most efficient way (fewest keystrokes) is to type the first letter of the command.

Using the Mouse

In the next section, "Using the Mouse," you will retrieve the file LABELS.WK1 again. If you do not have a mouse installed, skip this section and go to the nex section, "Entering Values." Activate the menu by using the mouse to move the control panel.

The following are instructions for using a mouse.

Click: File Retrieve

Note If the message "WORKSHEET CHANGES NOT SAVED! Retrieve the file anyway?" appears, select the YES option.

Your screen should now look similar to Figure 1.27.

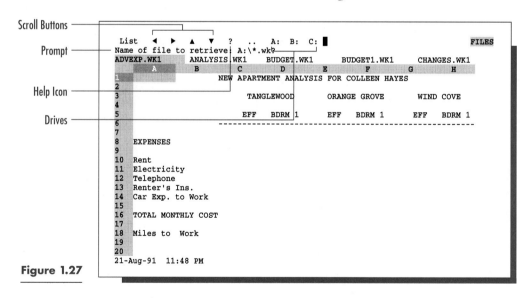

Figure 1.27

The first line of the control panel displays the scroll buttons, ? (Help icon), and letters indicating the drives. The second line of the control panel prompts you to specify the name of the file you want to retrieve. Following the prompt, the drive (A:) that 1-2-3 is using is displayed. (If you are saving your data files on a hard disk, your prompt will probably display C:.) The third line lists worksheet files on your data disk. The mode indicator displays FILES.

As you did when you selected **F**ile and **R**etrieve, you can select the name of the file to be retrieved by moving to any character in the file name and clicking. If the name of the file you want to retrieve is not displayed, click the appropriate scroll arrow in the first line of the control panel. If the file you want to retrieve is not on the drive shown in the prompt message in the second line, click the letter corresponding to the drive you want in the list of drives displayed in the first line. To retrieve the file LABELS.WK1, scroll until you see its name and then

Click: LABELS.WK1

Your screen should now look similar to Figure 1.26. The worksheet that contains the column and row labels is now displayed on your screen, and the mode indicator displays READY.

Throughout these labs, you can use the keyboard, the mouse, or a combination of both to select commands or get help.

Entering Values

We are now ready to enter some values into the worksheet. Values are numbers or the results of formulas. All values begin with a number from 0 through 9 or one of the following numeric symbols: +, -, ., (, @, #, or $.

You will begin by entering the values for the rent Colleen would have to pay for the different apartments.

Move to: C10

Type: **399**

Press: ⏎

Continue by entering the following values in D10 through G10.

Move to: D10

Type: **450**

Move to: E10

Type: **350**

Move to: F10

Type: **425**

Move to: G10

Type: **405**

Observe the mode indicator as it changes from READY to VALUE.

Your screen should now look similar to Figure 1.28.

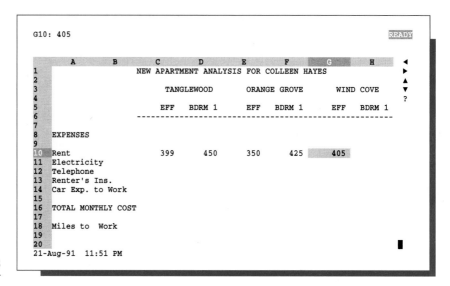

```
G10: 405                                                              READY

         A        B       C       D       E       F       G       H    ◄
  1              NEW APARTMENT ANALYSIS FOR COLLEEN HAYES               ►
  2                                                                     ▲
  3                   TANGLEWOOD       ORANGE GROVE      WIND COVE      ▼
  4                                                                     ?
  5                EFF   BDRM 1     EFF   BDRM 1     EFF   BDRM 1
  6              ---------------------------------------------------------
  7
  8   EXPENSES
  9
 10   Rent              399     450     350     425     405
 11   Electricity
 12   Telephone
 13   Renter's Ins.
 14   Car Exp. to Work
 15
 16   TOTAL MONTHLY COST
 17
 18   Miles to  Work
 19
 20
 21-Aug-91  11:51 PM                                               ▮
```

Figure 1.28

The values are all right-aligned in their cells. Unlike labels, which can be left-aligned ('), right-aligned ("), or centered (^), values can only be right-aligned.

If you insert an ', ", or ^ before a value, the entry is defined as a label, and it will have a numeric value of zero if used in arithmetic operations. For example, to enter the rent for the last apartment as "475,

Move to: H10

Type: "475

The mode indicator displays LABEL because the first character in the entry is a nonnumeric character.

Press: ⏎

The number appears correct in cell H10; however, because the number is a label, calculations using the data in this cell will be incorrect, as you will soon see.

The rest of the values for the apartment analysis have been entered for you and saved in a file named ANALYSIS.WK1. To retrieve the file and not save LABELS.WK1,

Select: /**F**ile **R**etrieve **Y**es

Use the arrow keys to move the menu pointer to the file name ANALYSIS.WK1.

Then, to select this file

Press: ⏎

Your screen should look similar to Figure 1.29.

```
A1:                                                                    READY

          A        B       C       D       E       F       G       H    ◄
    1                    NEW APARTMENT ANALYSIS FOR COLLEEN HAYES        ►
    2                                                                    ▲
    3                      TANGLEWOOD      ORANGE GROVE     WIND COVE    ▼
    4                                                                    ?
    5                     EFF   BDRM 1    EFF   BDRM 1    EFF   BDRM 1
    6                    ------------------------------------------------
    7
    8    EXPENSES
    9
   10    Rent            399     450     350     425     405     475
   11    Electricity      30      45      45      65      25      30
   12    Telephone        12      12      12      12      12      12
   13    Renter's Ins.    10      10      10      10      10      10
   14    Car Exp. to Work 50      50      75      75      25      25
   15
   16    TOTAL MONTHLY COST 501   567     492     587     477
   17
   18    Miles to  Work   10      10      15      15       5       5
   19
   20                                                                ■
         21-Aug-91  11:54 PM
```

Figure 1.29

Notice that the worksheet values have been entered for you and all the columns have been totaled except for column H.

Entering a Formula

You are now ready to enter a formula to calculate the total for column H. A **formula** is an entry that performs a calculation and displays the results of the calculation in the cell containing the formula. You can use either numeric values or cell addresses in a formula. If you use cell addresses, 1-2-3 performs the calculation using the values contained in the cells referenced in the formula.

For example, move to cell C14 and look at the control panel. The formula +C18*0.25*20 is displayed. To calculate car expenses, this formula multiplies the value in cell C18 times 25 cents per mile and then multiplies the result by 20 working days a month. The result is displayed in cell C14.

There are three types of formulas: numeric, text, and logical. The most common type, numeric, calculates numeric values using the following **arithmetic operators:**

+ for addition

– for subtraction

/ for division

* for multiplication

^ for exponentiation

A numeric formula can begin with a number or with one of the numeric symbols that defines an entry as a value. When the first entry in a formula is a cell address (which begins with a letter), begin the formula with a plus (+) symbol. This is necessary to define the cell entry as a value. The letter of the cell address can be typed in either uppercase or lowercase. A numeric formula cannot contain any spaces.

Note In many of the worksheets, you will be asked to enter the date. If you enter August 15, 1992, for example, as 8/15/92, 1-2-3 will assume that you are entering a formula using division. Similarly, if you enter that date as 8-15-92, 1-2-3 will assume you are entering a formula using subtraction. To enter the date so that it is not a formula, either use the label format in which you spell out the month (Aug. 15, 1992) or put an ' before the first number ('8-15-92) to indicate that the entry is a label, not a value.

You are now ready to add the entries in cells H10, H11, H12, H13, and H14 and have the sum displayed in cell H16.

Move to: H16

Type: **+H10+H11+H12+H13+H14**

Press: ⏎

Your screen should now look similar to Figure 1.30.

Formula

```
H16: +H10+H11+H12+H13+H14                                    READY

        A        B       C       D       E       F       G       H      ◄
 1                 NEW APARTMENT ANALYSIS FOR COLLEEN HAYES            ►
 2                                                                      ▲
 3                   TANGLEWOOD       ORANGE GROVE     WIND COVE        ▼
 4                                                                      ?
 5                   EFF   BDRM 1     EFF   BDRM 1     EFF   BDRM 1
 6                   --------------------------------------------------
 7
 8    EXPENSES
 9
10    Rent          399     450     350     425     405     475
11    Electricity    30      45      45      65      25      30
12    Telephone      12      12      12      12      12      12
13    Renter's Ins.  10      10      10      10      10      10
14    Car Exp. to Work 50    50      75      75      25      25
15
16    TOTAL MONTHLY COST 501 567     492     587     477      77
17
18    Miles to  Work  10     10      15      15       5       5
19
20                                                                     ∎
      21-Aug-91  11:57 PM
```

Figure 1.30

The formula appears in the control panel, and the numeric result appears in the worksheet cell.

But the total value displayed in cell H16 is incorrect; it should be 552. The error occurs because the entry in cell H10 is a label and so has a value of zero.

To correct the error,

Move to: H10

Press: (F2) (EDIT)

Press: (HOME)

Press: (DEL)

Press: (↵)

Your screen should look similar to Figure 1.31.

```
H10: 475                                                              READY

        A       B        C       D       E       F       G       H       ◄
1                      NEW APARTMENT ANALYSIS FOR COLLEEN HAYES          ►
2                                                                        ▲
3                       TANGLEWOOD      ORANGE GROVE     WIND COVE        ▼
4                                                                        ?
5                       EFF   BDRM 1    EFF   BDRM 1    EFF   BDRM 1
6
7                      -------------------------------------------------
8    EXPENSES
9
10   Rent              399     450     350     425     405     475
11   Electricity        30      45      45      65      25      30
12   Telephone          12      12      12      12      12      12
13   Renter's Ins.      10      10      10      10      10      10
14   Car Exp. to Work   50      50      75      75      25      25
15
16   TOTAL MONTHLY COST 501     567     492     587     477     552
17
18   Miles to  Work     10      10      15      15       5       5
19
20
     21-Aug-91  11:57 PM                                          ▮
```

Figure 1.31

Now that the entry in cell H10 is a value, it can be used in calculations. The formula in cell H16 has been recalculated using the new data in cell H10. The **automatic recalculation** of formulas as data is changed is one of the most powerful features of electronic worksheets.

Saving the Worksheet

Before you save the worksheet, your instructor may want to have you enter your name in cell A1.

If you exit the 1-2-3 program without saving the current worksheet, the changes you made to it would be lost. To save the current version of the worksheet,

Select: /**F**ile **S**ave

The prompt "Enter name of file to save:" appears in the control panel. The current drive and the name of the file you retrieved, ANALYSIS.WK1, are displayed following the prompt. You can save the current worksheet as it appears on the screen using this file name, or you can save it using a new file name. In case you want to use the original file ANALYSIS.WK1 again to repeat the exercises, you should give your completed worksheet a new name like FINALANS.WK1. A 1-2-3 file name should be no longer than eight characters and can include any combination of letters, numbers, underscores, and hyphens. It cannot include any blank spaces. To enter the new file name, in either uppercase or lowercase characters,

Type: **FINALANS**

Press: ↵

The current version of the worksheet has been saved on your disk as FINALANS.WK1. Lotus 1-2-3 automatically adds the file extension .WK1 to all worksheet files created using the program unless you enter a file name extension of your own when saving the file. The files LABELS.WK1 and ANALYSIS.WK1 are still on your data disk, unchanged.

To verify that the current worksheet has been saved on the disk, erase the screen and the current worksheet from memory by issuing the following command sequence:

/Worksheet **E**rase

In response to the prompt confirming that you want to erase the worksheet,

Select: **Y**es

This prompt is another safety precaution to prevent the accidental loss of a worksheet file that might not have been saved.

Your screen should now display a blank worksheet. Retrieve the file FINALANS by issuing the following command sequence:

/File **R**etrieve **FINALANS** ↵

Your screen should again look similar to Figure 1.31. The worksheet is displayed as you saved it. Even the cell pointer is in the same cell as it was at the time the file was saved.

Whenever a file is retrieved, the current worksheet is automatically erased from the screen and memory and is replaced by the retrieved worksheet file. Therefore, it is not necessary to use the **/W**orksheet **E**rase command before you retrieve a file.

Printing a Worksheet

You will now print the worksheet using the 1-2-3 **P**rint command. For this lab, you will obtain a simple printout. Many of 1-2-3's print options will be discussed in later labs.

If your printer is off, turn it on. Check to see that it is on line. If your printer uses continuous form paper, adjust the printer paper so that the perforated line is just above the printer's scale. Begin the **P**rint command as follows:

Select: /**P**rint

The four print options are displayed in the control panel. Since you want to send the output directly to the printer,

Select: **P**rinter

You will now see a dialog box for Print Settings. You will learn how to use dialog boxes and ranges in Lab 2. A **range** is a cell or a rectangular group of adjoining cells in the worksheet. For now, the only option that you must select is the range. The default settings for the other options in the dialog box are satisfactory for this lab.

You will specify the range using the menu. Notice that the menu option **R**ange is highlighted in the control panel. To select the **R**ange command,

Press: (↵)

The dialog box is cleared from the screen so you can see the worksheet while specifiying the range. You are now prompted for the range address. The **range address** specifies the portion of the worksheet you want to print by using that portion's upper left cell and lower right cell, separated by one or two periods. Since you want to print the entire worksheet, and its upper left cell is A1 and its lower right cell is H18,

Type: **A1..H18**

Press: (↵)

The dialog box is displayed again, reflecting the range you specified.

Finally, to tell the program that the paper is aligned with the top of the printer's scale and to begin printing,

Select: **A**lign

Select: **G**o

Your printer may take a few moments before it begins to print the worksheet. Do not select **G**o again because it will result in multiple printouts of the worksheet.

When the printing is finished, issue the following command to advance the printed page:

Select: **P**age

Your printer output should look similar to Figure 1.32.

```
                        NEW APARTMENT ANALYSIS FOR COLLEEN HAYES

                          TANGLEWOOD       ORANGE GROVE      WIND COVE

                        EFF    BDRM 1     EFF    BDRM 1     EFF    BDRM 1
                        - - - - - - - - - - - - - - - - - - - - - - - - - -

             EXPENSES

             Rent       399     450       350     425       405     475
             Electricity  30      45        45      65        25      30
             Telephone   12      12        12      12        12      12
             Renter's Ins. 10     10        10      10        10      10
             Car Exp. to Work 50  50        75      75        25      25

             TOTAL MONTHLY COST 501 567    492     587       477     552

             Miles to  Work 10    10        15      15         5       5
```

Figure 1.32

The header "The Student Edition of Lotus 1-2-3" and your name are automatically printed at the top of your worksheet.

Return to READY mode by issuing the following command:

Select: **Q**uit

Colleen's worksheet is complete. Based on her analysis of the worksheet, Colleen has decided to rent an efficiency apartment at Wind Cove Apartments.

Leaving 1-2-3

Always be sure, before you retrieve a file, erase a worksheet, or end a 1-2-3 session, that you save the current worksheet if you want to use it again. If you do not save it, you will lose it.

If you want to leave 1-2-3 at this time, issue the following command:

Select: **/Q**uit **Y**es

Glossary

Arithmetic operator: The symbols used in a formula that control the type of calculation to be performed: +, −, /, *, ^.

Automatic recalculation: The recalculation of all formulas in a worksheet when data in cells referenced by the formula change.

Cell: The basic unit of a worksheet formed by the intersection of a row and a column.

Cell address: The column letter and row number of the current cell displayed in the first line of the control panel.

Cell pointer: The highlight bar that identifies the current cell location in the worksheet.

Column: A vertical line of cells down the worksheet.

Column letter: The border of letters across the top of the worksheet area that labels the columns in the worksheet.

Command: An instruction you give 1-2-3 by selecting from the menu that appears when you press /.

Control panel: The top three lines of the screen, which display information about the current cell, command choices, and prompts.

Current cell: The cell that the cell pointer is on.

Cursor: A blinking underscore that shows you where each character will appear as you type.

Date-and-time indicator: The date and time displayed in the status line.

Edit: To correct entries made in a worksheet.

Error message: A program message displayed in the dialog box when a program error is detected.

Formula: A mathematical expression that defines the relationship among two or more cells in a worksheet.

Home position: The upper left corner cell of the worksheet, usually cell A1.

Label: An entry beginning with an alphabetical character, ', ", ^, or any other character not considered a value.

Label-prefix character: Special characters entered before a label that control the display of the label: ', ", ^, or \.

Long label: A label that is longer than the cell width.

Menu: The series of choices that appears on the control panel after you access the main 1-2-3 menu.

Menu pointer: The highlight bar that identifies the current menu selection.

Mode: The current state of operation of the program.

Mode indicator: A highlighted word in the top right line of the control panel that indicates the current mode of operation of the worksheet.

Mouse pointer: The vertical rectangle that is displayed on the screen when a mouse has been installed. The mouse pointer mirrors the movement of the mouse.

Numeric symbol: The characters *, -, ., (, @, #, and $ that define an entry as a value.

Prompt: A program response displayed in the control panel that requires a user response.

Range: A cell or rectangular group of adjoining cells in the worksheet.

Range address: The section of the worksheet defined by any two diagonally opposite corners, separated by two periods.

Row: A horizontal line of cells across the worksheet.

Row number: The border of numbers down the left side of the worksheet area that labels the rows in the worksheet.

Scroll arrows: Directional arrows displayed on the screen and activated by the mouse to scroll in the direction of the arrow.

Scrolling: The process of moving several rows or columns or full screens horizontally or vertically through the worksheet.

Status indicator: A highlighted word displayed in the status line that describes a program or special key condition.

Status line: The bottom line of the screen, which displays the date-and-time indicator, status indicators, and error messages.

Value: A number (0 through 9) or the result of a formula.

Window: The part of the worksheet displayed on the screen.

Worksheet: The electronic representation of a financial spreadsheet created from a rectangular grid of rows and columns.

Worksheet area: The center of the screen, which contains the worksheet.

Practice Problems and Cases

Matching

1. (F2) ___4___ **a.** moves the cell pointer to upper left corner

2. (F5) ___1___ **b.** enters EDIT mode

3. (F1) ___3___ **c.** accesses Help facility

4. (HOME) ___7___ **d.** saves worksheet

5. (ESC) ___2___ **e.** moves to particular cell

6. /FR ___9___ **f.** erases worksheet from memory

7. /FS ___6___ **g.** retrieves worksheet from disk

8. /PP ___5___ **h.** cancels command

9. /WE ___10___ **i.** leaves 1-2-3 but does not save file

10. /QY ___8___ **j.** accesses Print menu

Cases

1. In the following worksheet, several items are identified by letters. In the space below the worksheet, enter the correct term for each item. The first one has been completed for you. (*Hint:* Use the Glossary for this lab.)

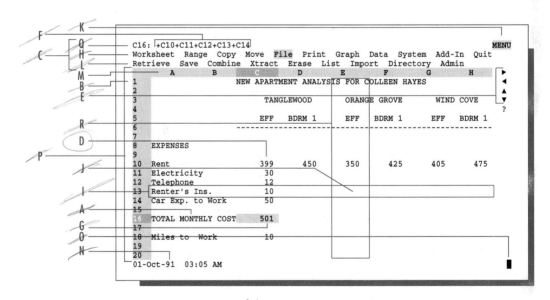

a. label   d. Value

b. RowNo.   e. Scroll Arrows Omit

c. Control Panel   f. formula

g. _Current Cell_   m. _Column Letter_

h. _Main Menu_   n. _Date Indicator_

i. _Row_   o. _Mouse Pointer / Unit_

j. _Cell_   p. _Work Sheet Area_

k. _Mode Indicator_   q. _Cell Address_

l. _Sub-Menu_   r. _Column_

2. Retrieve the file PROB1-2.WK1. This is a worksheet file similar to the case we started in this lab. However, it contains several errors. Follow these steps to locate and correct the errors.

   a. Change the column labels so that they are all capital letters and right-aligned. Change the row labels so that only the first letter of each word is capitalized and the labels are left-aligned.

   b. Look at the values in column D and in row 9. Correct those that have been entered incorrectly.

   c. Use the repeat label-prefix character to underline the column headings in row 5.

   d. Enter your name in cell A1 and the current date in cell A2. (You may need to use a label prefix to enter the date.)

   e. Save the corrected worksheet file as HWLAB1-2.

   f. Print the corrected worksheet.

3. Thomas Long is considering moving to a new townhouse. He is considering three different townhouses: Villa Way, Village North, and West Gate. Thomas has estimated the following monthly expenses for a two- and a three-bedroom unit at each townhouse:

| | Villa Way | | Village North | | West Gate | |
	BDRM 2	BDRM 3	BDRM 2	BDRM 3	BDRM 2	BDRM 3
Rent	495	545	510	550	540	605
Electricity	35	50	45	60	40	55
Telephone	50	50	75	75	35	35
Renter's Ins.	25	25	25	25	25	25
Car Expense						

   a. In cell C1, enter the worksheet title:

   NEW TOWNHOUSE ANALYSIS FOR THOMAS LONG

b. Enter the labels Villa Way, Village North, and West Gate in cells C3, E3, and G3.

c. Enter and center the labels BDRM 2 and BDRM 3 in cells C5 and D5. Repeat for cells E5 and F5 and for cells G5 and H5.

d. Use the repeat label-prefix character to underline the labels in rows 3 and 5.

e. Using (F2) (EDIT) and the SPACEBAR, center each townhouse name over the columns BDRM 2 and BDRM 3.

f. Enter the row labels Rent, Electricity, Telephone, Renter's Ins., and Car Expense in rows A10 through A14.

g. Enter the labels EXPENSES in cell A8, TOTAL MONTHLY COST in cell A16, and Miles to Work in cell A18.

h. Enter the appropriate numbers into cells C10 through H13.

i. Enter the formula +C18*0.25*20 into cell C14. (Do not enter any other formulas into row 14.)

j. In cell C16, enter the formula to calculate total cost for the two-bedroom unit at Villa Way. (Do not enter any other formulas into row 16.)

k. Enter your name in cell A1 and the current date in cell A2.

l. Save the worksheet using the file name HWLAB1-3.

m. Print the worksheet.

You will complete this worksheet in Practice Case 2 in Lab 2.

4. Alan Black earns $1,900 a month as an assistant store manager. He has the following fixed monthly expenses:

Rent	475
Food	225
Clothing	100
Telephone	35
Car Loan	275

He also has two periodic expenses. In February, he has a six-month car insurance payment due for $475. In March, his automobile license registration of $175 is due. Create a worksheet for Alan using the following steps:

a. Enter the labels JAN, FEB, MAR, APR, MAY, JUN, and TOTAL in cells B3 through H3. Enter them in all capital letters and right-aligned.

b. Use the repeat label-prefix character to underline the column headings.

c. Enter the row labels so that only the first letter of each word is capitalized and the labels are left-aligned. The labels should all be entered in column A as follows:

Row 5	Wages:
Row 7	Expenses:
Row 8	Rent
Row 9	Food
Row 10	Clothing
Row 11	Telephone
Row 12	Car Loan
Row 13	Insurance
Row 14	License
Row 16	Total Exp:
Row 18	Balance:

d. Enter the monthly wage in cells B5 through G5.

e. Enter the fixed monthly expenses for January only.

f. Enter the two periodic expenses.

g. Enter the formula to calculate the total for wages in cell H5.

h. Enter your name in cell A1 and the current date in cell A2.

i. Save the worksheet using the file name HWLAB1-4.

j. Print the worksheet.

You will complete this worksheet in Practice Case 3 in Lab 2.

5. Retrieve the file PROB1-5.WK1. Enter your name in cell A1 and the current date in cell A2. Notice that the worksheet contains several errors. Locate and correct the errors. Save the corrected worksheet file as HWLAB1-5, and then print the worksheet. You will complete this worksheet in Practice Case 6 in Lab 2.

6. Have you considered buying a new car recently? Following the four steps in the planning process for worksheets, create an analysis for four different cars. You might select one car to be your ideal, another to be the most practical, and the remaining two as compromises. In the purchase cost of the cars, you might include such items as air-conditioning, cruise control, or air bags. In some cars these may be standard, and in others they may be optional. In the operating cost of each car, you might include insurance, licensing, fuel, and maintenance. You may wish to use the apartment analysis created in Lab 1 as a rough guide.

   Be sure to complete the paper model first. After you create the 1-2-3 worksheet, enter your name in cell A1 and the date in cell A2. Then save your worksheet as HWLAB1-6 and print the worksheet.

7. Following the four steps in the planning process for worksheets, create a simple six-month budget for yourself using 1-2-3. Include any sources of income such as wages or monthly allowances. List and estimate each of your monthly costs such as food, clothing, and car expenses. You might even include some planned savings. Be realistic and experiment a bit with your income and expenses.

   Be sure to complete the paper model first. After you create the 1-2-3 worksheet, enter your name in cell A1 and the date in cell A2. Then save your worksheet as HWLAB1-7 and print the worksheet.

Lab 2

Enhancing a Worksheet

Objectives

In Lab 2, you will learn how to:

- Change column widths
- Use a dialog box
- Insert and delete rows and columns
- Point a range
- Copy formulas
- Copy cell entries
- Use absolute cell references
- Use @functions
- Enable and use the Undo feature
- Use what-if analysis
- Erase cell entries
- Save and replace files

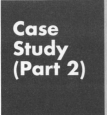

I n Lab 1, you created an apartment analysis for Colleen Hayes. You entered labels, values, and a simple formula into a worksheet that helped Colleen decide which apartment to rent. Now that Colleen has started her job, you will use the information from the apartment analysis to create a working budget in this lab.

Part of the budget is already done for you. To complete the worksheet, you will enter the values for Colleen's expenses as well as formulas to calculate her total expenses and balance. You will also redefine the column widths and insert and delete columns and rows to improve the appearance of the worksheet.

Changing Column Widths

After loading 1-2-3, retrieve the worksheet file BUDGET.WK1 by issuing the following command sequence:

/**F**ile **R**etrieve **BUDGET.WK1** ↵

Your screen should now look similar to Figure 2.1.

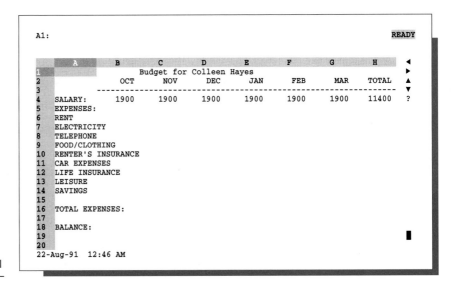

```
A1:                                                              READY

          A         B        C        D        E        F        G        H
 1                    Budget for Colleen Hayes
 2                   OCT      NOV      DEC      JAN      FEB      MAR    TOTAL
 3        --------------------------------------------------------------------
 4   SALARY:        1900     1900     1900     1900     1900     1900    11400
 5   EXPENSES:
 6   RENT
 7   ELECTRICITY
 8   TELEPHONE
 9   FOOD/CLOTHING
10   RENTER'S INSURANCE
11   CAR EXPENSES
12   LIFE INSURANCE
13   LEISURE
14   SAVINGS
15
16   TOTAL EXPENSES:
17
18   BALANCE:
19
20
     22-Aug-91  12:46 AM
```

Figure 2.1

This worksheet contains the column and row labels for Colleen's budget. It also contains her monthly take-home salary of $1,900 that she will receive from the ski resort. Since her job begins in October, she wants to set up a budget for the next six months.

Before you enter more data into the worksheet, you will improve its appearance by adjusting **column widths** and inserting rows and columns.

Some of the row labels in column A are longer than the initial or default column width setting of nine spaces and overflow into column B. For example, the label RENTER'S INSURANCE in cell A10 overlaps into cell B10.

Move to: A10

Although the label is 18 characters long, it is fully displayed in the worksheet because the cell to the right (B10) is empty. If cell B10 contained data, the long label in cell A10 would be truncated, or cut off. Since you will be entering data in column B, you should increase the width of column A so that the labels will not be truncated.

To change the width of a single column, with the cell pointer anywhere within the column you want to change, issue the following command sequence:

/Worksheet **C**olumn **S**et-Width

The prompt "Enter column width (1..240):" is displayed in the control panel. The column width can be set between 1 and 240 spaces. The current column width, 9, is displayed following the prompt. To increase the column width to 18, continue the command sequence as follows:

Type: **18**

Press: ⏎

Your screen should now look similar to Figure 2.2.

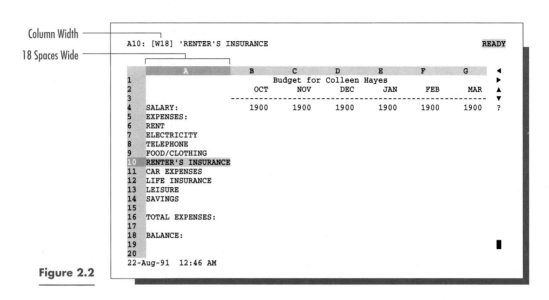

Column Width ————
18 Spaces Wide ————

```
A10: [W18] 'RENTER'S INSURANCE                                    READY

              A          B      C      D      E      F      G    ◄
 1                         Budget for Colleen Hayes                ►
 2                       OCT    NOV    DEC    JAN    FEB    MAR    ▲
 3                      ----------------------------------------  ▼
 4       SALARY:         1900   1900   1900   1900   1900   1900  ?
 5       EXPENSES:
 6       RENT
 7       ELECTRICITY
 8       TELEPHONE
 9       FOOD/CLOTHING
10       RENTER'S INSURANCE
11       CAR EXPENSES
12       LIFE INSURANCE
13       LEISURE
14       SAVINGS
15
16       TOTAL EXPENSES:
17
18       BALANCE:
19
20
22-Aug-91  12:46 AM
```

Figure 2.2

Column A has expanded to 18 spaces wide, and the label is fully displayed within the cell space. The new column width is displayed in the control panel in brackets following the cell address, [W18]. When the cell pointer is anywhere within a column whose column width has been changed using the /**W**orksheet **C**olumn command, the control panel will display the column width setting.

As a result of increasing the width of column A, the TOTAL column (H) was pushed to the right and is no longer visible in the window. To provide space in the window for the TOTAL column, we will decrease the width of all other columns in the worksheet to five spaces. Although this could be done by decreasing the width of each column individually, you can also change these column widths together. To do this, select the /**W**orksheet **G**lobal command using either the keyboard or the mouse. If you are using the keyboard, issue the following command sequence:

> /**W**orksheet **G**lobal

If you are accessing the /**W**orksheet **G**lobal command using the mouse, first access the main menu by pointing to the empty second line of the control panel. Once the main menu is displayed,

Click: Worksheet

Click: Global

to display the Global Settings dialog box.

Your screen should look similar to Figure 2.3.

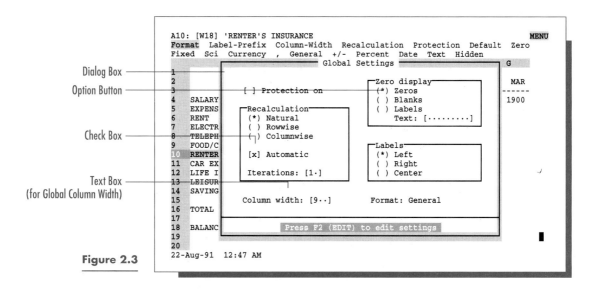

Dialog Box
Option Button

Check Box

Text Box
(for Global Column Width)

Figure 2.3

```
A10: [W18] 'RENTER'S INSURANCE                                    MENU
Format Label-Prefix Column-Width Recalculation Protection Default Zero
Fixed  Sci  Currency  ,  General  +/-  Percent  Date  Text  Hidden
                        Global Settings                           G
 1
 2                                           ┌Zero display┐        MAR
 3          [ ] Protection on                │(*) Zeros   │       ------
 4  SALARY                                    │( ) Blanks  │       1900
 5  EXPENS    ┌Recalculation┐                 │( ) Labels  │
 6  RENT      │(*) Natural  │                 │   Text: [.........] │
 7  ELECTR    │( ) Rowwise  │                 └───────────────────┘
 8  TELEPH    │( ) Columnwise                 
 9  FOOD/C    │                               ┌Labels┐
10  RENTER    │[x] Automatic                  │(*) Left  │
11  CAR EX    │                               │( ) Right │
12  LIFE I    │Iterations: [1.]               │( ) Center│      ↵
13  LEISUR    └───────────────────            └──────────┘
14  SAVING
15             Column width: [9..]         Format: General
16  TOTAL
17
18  BALANC          Press F2 (EDIT) to edit settings
19                                                            ▮
20
22-Aug-91  12:47 AM
```

Using a Dialog Box

The worksheet has been replaced by the Global Settings dialog box. Many commands in 1-2-3 will use a **dialog box**. This is one way 1-2-3 communicates with you either to show you current settings or to obtain information from you to complete a command. As you make choices from the menu, the dialog box will change to reflect those choices. You can also change options directly in the dialog box using the keyboard or the mouse.

Dialog boxes consist of option buttons, check boxes, text boxes, command buttons, and list boxes.

Option buttons allow you to select only one option from a group of options. Once you select an option, it is marked with an * (asterisk).

Check boxes allow you to select one or more options, or no options, from a group. A check box is marked when an x appears next to the option.

Text boxes consist of information in square brackets ([...]). You enter information into a text box by typing the appropriate text or number that the command requires.

Command buttons are used to confirm selections or display other dialog boxes. The most common command button is OK. It is used to confirm the current selections and complete the dialog box. When a command button is followed by ..., it will display another dialog box with more detailed choices.

List boxes allow you to select from a list of several choices, such as a list of names.

The Global Settings dialog box displays the current global settings for the worksheet. Global settings are settings that affect the entire worksheet. The option we want to change is the Column width option, which appears in the lower left corner of the dialog box. The Column width text box shows that the current setting for all columns in the worksheet is 9.

To use a dialog box, you must first activate the dialog box. Once again, you can do so using either the keyboard or the mouse. If you are using a mouse, read this section before completing the mouse instructions.

Using the Keyboard

Press:　　(F2) (EDIT)

Notice the menu disappears from the control panel, and one letter of each option in the dialog box is highlighted, including the "C" in Column width. To make the new global column width setting five spaces,

Press:　　**C**

The cursor appears in the Column width text box. To change the width,

Type:　　**5**

Press:　　(↵)

All column widths will now change to five spaces except column A, which was individually set. Changes made using the /**W**orksheet **C**olumn command always override global settings.

Notice the OK command button (lower right corner of the dialog box) is now highlighted. To confirm the changes made in the dialog box,

Press:　　(↵)

You will now see a revised dialog box confirming your choices. To exit the dialog box and return to the READY mode,

Press:　　(CTRL)-(BREAK)

Note Pressing (CTRL)-(BREAK) has the same effect as pressing (ESC) to exit a menu and return to the worksheet in READY mode.

Using the Mouse 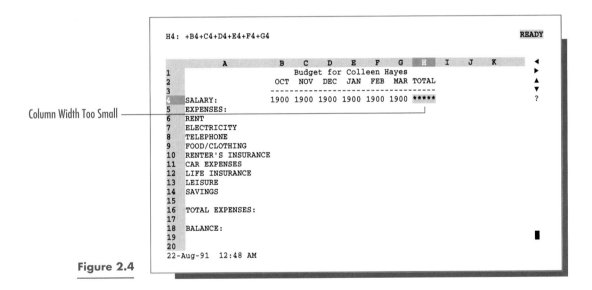 When the Global Settings dialog box appears on your screen, look for the Column width option in the lower left corner, followed by a text box.

To select Column width,

Click: anywhere on Column width or on the text box

The option should turn a different color or shade once you activate it. To indicate the desired column width,

Type: 5

Click: the OK command button

To exit from the menu,

Click: the right mouse button three times

Although the TOTAL column is now visible, a series of asterisks (*****) appears in cell H4.

Move to: H4

Your screen should now look similar to Figure 2.4.

```
H4: +B4+C4+D4+E4+F4+G4                                      READY

              A       B    C    D    E    F    G   H    I   J   K    ◄
   1                    Budget for Colleen Hayes                      ►
   2                  OCT  NOV  DEC  JAN  FEB  MAR TOTAL               ▲
   3                 ---------------------------------                ▼
   4    SALARY:        1900 1900 1900 1900 1900 1900 *****            ?
   5    EXPENSES:
   6    RENT
   7    ELECTRICITY
   8    TELEPHONE
   9    FOOD/CLOTHING
   10   RENTER'S INSURANCE
   11   CAR EXPENSES
   12   LIFE INSURANCE
   13   LEISURE
   14   SAVINGS
   15
   16   TOTAL EXPENSES:
   17
   18   BALANCE:                                                     ■
   19
   20
   22-Aug-91  12:48 AM
```

Column Width Too Small

Figure 2.4

The correct formula is displayed in the control panel. However, the value 11400 does not appear in the worksheet because the cell is not wide enough. Whenever the width of a cell containing a value is too small to fully display the entry, asterisks are displayed. The cell's width has to be at least one space larger than the value. (1-2-3 reserves one extra space for special numeric displays, such as a percent sign.)

Individual cells cannot be expanded in 1-2-3. To correct the problem, you could change the width of column H (individually) or change the width of all columns in the worksheet (globally) or change the width of column H and several adjacent columns. Since the values for the months look crowded, we will increase the column width for columns B through H. To change the width of several adjacent columns, issue the following command sequence:

/Worksheet **C**olumn **C**olumn-Range **S**et-Width

In response to the prompt in the control panel, you must specify the range of columns whose width you want to change. A range is a cell or rectangular group of adjoining cells in the worksheet. In Figure 2.5, the unshaded boxes show examples of valid and invalid ranges.

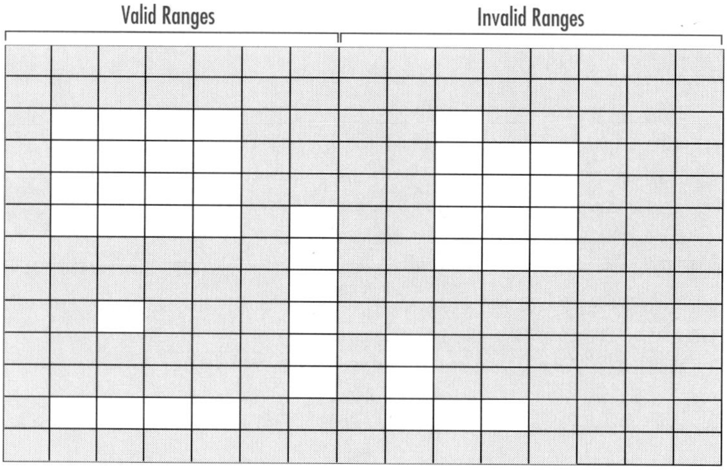

Figure 2.5

A range is entered using the beginning cell address and ending cell address separated by two periods. In response to the prompt, 1-2-3 displays the cell address of the current cell as the default response. To specify the range of columns, any row can be used. Since the cell pointer is already on row H4, we will enter the range as B4..H4.

Type: **B4..H4**

The default response is cleared, and the new range is displayed following the prompt. You can type one or two periods in the range, but 1-2-3 will always display a range with two periods.

Press: 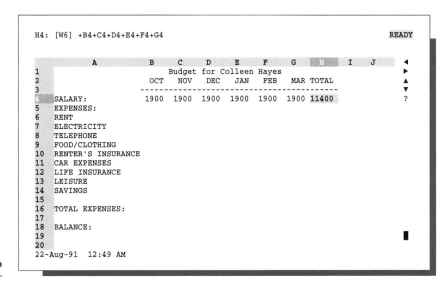 ↵

To enter the new width,

Type: 6

Press: ↵

Your screen should look similar to Figure 2.6.

```
H4: [W6] +B4+C4+D4+E4+F4+G4                                        READY

                    A        B     C     D     E     F     G     H    I    J    ◄
    1                        Budget for Colleen Hayes                           ►
    2                        OCT   NOV   DEC   JAN   FEB   MAR TOTAL             ▲
    3               --------------------------------------------                ▼
    4        SALARY:         1900  1900  1900  1900  1900  1900 11400           ?
    5        EXPENSES:
    6        RENT
    7        ELECTRICITY
    8        TELEPHONE
    9        FOOD/CLOTHING
   10        RENTER'S INSURANCE
   11        CAR EXPENSES
   12        LIFE INSURANCE
   13        LEISURE
   14        SAVINGS
   15
   16        TOTAL EXPENSES:
   17
   18        BALANCE:
   19                                                                           ■
   20
            22-Aug-91  12:49 AM
```

Figure 2.6

The width of columns B through H changed to six spaces each, and the value in cell H4 is fully displayed. The column width setting, [W6], is displayed in the control panel because the width of these columns was changed using the /**W**orksheet **C**olumn command.

Inserting and Deleting Columns

You can further improve the worksheet's appearance by inserting a blank column after column A. Move the cell pointer to any cell in column B, and issue the following command sequence:

/**W**orksheet **I**nsert **C**olumn ↵

Your screen should now look similar to Figure 2.7.

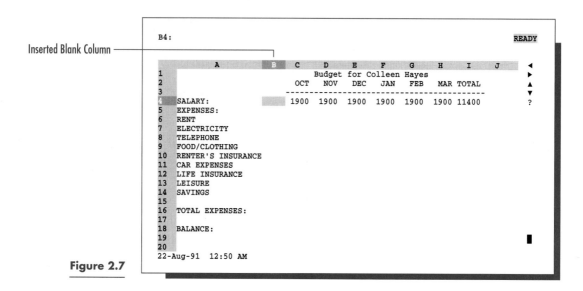

Inserted Blank Column ──

```
B4:                                                              READY

              A        B   C    D    E    F    G    H    I   J     ◄
  1                        Budget for Colleen Hayes               ►
  2                    OCT  NOV  DEC  JAN  FEB  MAR TOTAL          ▲
  3                    --------------------------------------     ▼
  4   SALARY:              1900 1900 1900 1900 1900 1900 11400     ?
  5   EXPENSES:
  6   RENT
  7   ELECTRICITY
  8   TELEPHONE
  9   FOOD/CLOTHING
 10   RENTER'S INSURANCE
 11   CAR EXPENSES
 12   LIFE INSURANCE
 13   LEISURE
 14   SAVINGS
 15
 16   TOTAL EXPENSES:
 17
 18   BALANCE:
 19                                                           ■
 20
 22-Aug-91  12:50 AM
```

Figure 2.7

A blank column has been inserted into the worksheet by moving all the cell entries to the right one column.

A second blank column between MAR and TOTAL would improve the worksheet's appearance even more. Move the cell pointer to column I, and issue the following command sequence:

/**W**orksheet **I**nsert **C**olumn ⏎

To delete a column, follow the same procedure, except select **D**elete instead of **I**nsert. Everything in the column will then be deleted.

Inserting and Deleting Rows

You can insert and delete rows in nearly the same manner that you inserted and deleted columns. The only difference in the command sequence is that you replace **C**olumn with **R**ow.

To insert a row between the worksheet's title and the months, move the cell pointer to any cell in row 2, and issue the following command sequence:

/**W**orksheet **I**nsert **R**ow ⏎

Your screen should now look similar to Figure 2.8.

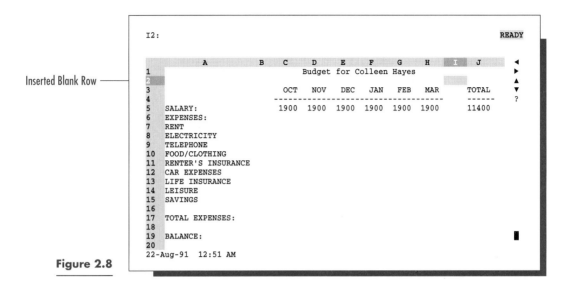

Inserted Blank Row

Figure 2.8

A blank row (row 2) has been inserted into the worksheet by moving all cell entries below row 2 down one row.

To insert another row between SALARY and EXPENSES, move the cell pointer to any cell in row 6, and issue the following command sequence:

/**W**orksheet **I**nsert **R**ow ⏎

To delete a row, use the same procedure, except select **D**elete instead of **I**nsert. When you are deleting rows and columns, be careful that you do not accidentally delete any rows or columns of important information.

Using the Copy Command

In Lab 1, you entered the values one cell at a time. The fastest way to enter identical data into several cells is to use the **C**opy command.

Colleen's rent expense will be $405 per month for her efficiency apartment at Wind Cove Apartments. You will enter this value into cell C8 for her October rent and then copy this value into cells D8 through H8 for her November through March rent expenses.

Move to: C8

Type: **405**

Press: ⏎

To copy the contents of cell C8 to cells D8, E8, F8, G8, and H8,

Select: **/C**opy

Your screen should now look similar to Figure 2.9.

Prompt

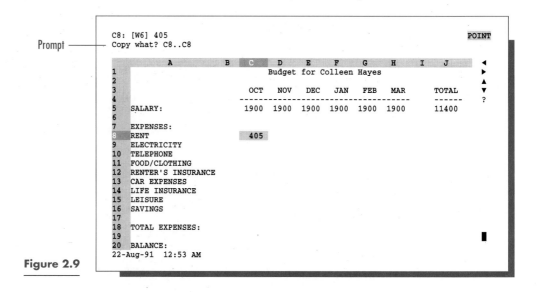

Figure 2.9

The second line of the control panel displays the prompt "Copy what?"

1-2-3 anticipated that the current position of the cell pointer (C8..C8) is the cell you want to copy from.

If you wanted to copy from another cell or range of cells, you would enter that cell location. In this case, however, you do want to copy from cell C8. To confirm this selection,

Press: ⏎

The second line of the control panel now displays the prompt "To where?" Again, 1-2-3 has anticipated your response. This time, however, it is not correct.

64   **Lab 2**   Enhancing a Worksheet

To specify the correct range, D8 through H8, continue the command sequence as follows:

Type: **D8..H8**

Press: ⟨↵⟩

Your screen should now look similar to Figure 2.10.

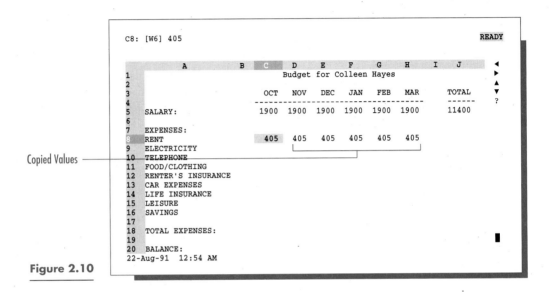

```
C8: [W6] 405                                                    READY

                    A       B   C   D    E    F    G    H    I   J    ◄
1                                   Budget for Colleen Hayes              ►
2                                                                        ▲
3                                   OCT  NOV  DEC  JAN  FEB  MAR    TOTAL ▼
4                                   ----------------------------    ----- ?
5            SALARY:                1900 1900 1900 1900 1900 1900   11400
6
7            EXPENSES:
8            RENT                   405  405  405  405  405  405
9            ELECTRICITY
10           TELEPHONE
11           FOOD/CLOTHING
12           RENTER'S INSURANCE
13           CAR EXPENSES
14           LIFE INSURANCE
15           LEISURE
16           SAVINGS
17
18           TOTAL EXPENSES:                                            ▮
19
20           BALANCE:
             22-Aug-91  12:54 AM
```

Copied Values

Figure 2.10

The value 405 has been copied to the specified range of cells.

Practice using the **C**opy command by moving to C9, entering the value 25 for electricity expense and copying the contents of cell C9 to cells D9 through H9.

You have used the **C**opy command to copy from a single cell to a range of cells. You can also copy from a range of cells by specifying the beginning and ending cells of the range following the "Copy what?" prompt.

Pointing a Range

Another method of defining the data range to be copied is to use the cell pointer to highlight the cell or range of cells. Whenever 1-2-3 displays POINT in the mode indicator, you can use this method to specify a range. To see how this works,

Move to: C10

Type: **12**

Press: ⏎

Using the Keyboard This value needs to be copied to cells D10 through H10, which can be done using either the keyboard or the mouse. If you are using a mouse, read this section before following the mouse instructions. Using the keyboard, begin the **C**opy command as usual:

Select: /**C**opy

The prompt will read "Copy what? C10..C10." To accept cell C10 as the cell to be copied,

Press: ⏎

You are now ready to specify the range to copy to.

Notice that the mode indicator now displays POINT. Instead of typing in the cell range to copy to, you will use the cell pointer to highlight the range. To move the cell pointer to the cell beginning the range,

Move to: D10

To **anchor**, or specify, this cell as the beginning of the range,

Type: **.** (period)

This cell is now the **anchor cell**. Next, to move the cell pointer to the last cell of the range (H10),

Press: → four times

Your screen should now look similar to Figure 2.11.

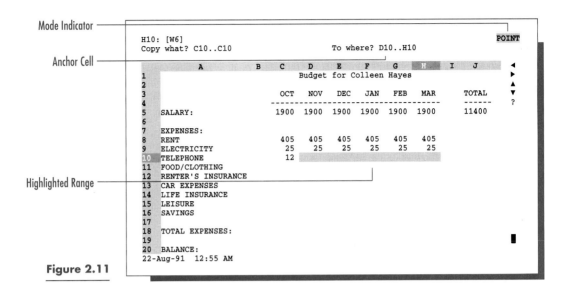

Mode Indicator ———

Anchor Cell ———

Highlighted Range ———

Figure 2.11

```
H10: [W6]                                                            POINT
Copy what? C10..C10                       To where? D10..H10
               A      B    C    D    E    F    G    H    I    J   ◄
1                      Budget for Colleen Hayes                    ►
2                                                                  ▲
3                     OCT  NOV  DEC  JAN  FEB  MAR   TOTAL         ▼
4                    -------------------------------  ------       ?
5   SALARY:          1900 1900 1900 1900 1900 1900   11400
6
7   EXPENSES:
8   RENT             405  405  405  405  405  405
9   ELECTRICITY      25   25   25   25   25   25
10  TELEPHONE        12
11  FOOD/CLOTHING
12  RENTER'S INSURANCE
13  CAR EXPENSES
14  LIFE INSURANCE
15  LEISURE
16  SAVINGS
17
18  TOTAL EXPENSES:                                          ▮
19
20  BALANCE:
22-Aug-91  12:55 AM
```

The range D10 to H10 is highlighted on the screen. The highlighted range is also displayed as D10..H10 following the "To where?" prompt in the control panel.

The final step is to tell 1-2-3 that this is the end of the range:

Press: ⏎

Using the Mouse

The mouse can also be used in POINT mode to copy cells. For example, to copy the October telephone expenses using the mouse, activate the main menu by pointing to the control panel, and then

Click: Copy

1-2-3 should display the prompt "Copy what?" To indicate that C10 is the cell to be copied,

Click: cell C10 on the worksheet

You must then click a second time on C10 to confirm it as the cell to copy and to display the prompt "To where?" To indicate D10..H10 as the "To where" range, point to cell D10 and drag (hold the left mouse button down) the mouse pointer to H10, the last cell of the range. 1-2-3 will enter the period automatically for you.

Click the left mouse button again to confirm the "Copy where?" range and complete the command.

Your screen should now look similar to Figure 2.12.

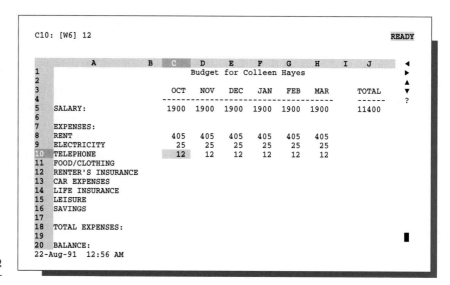

```
C10: [W6] 12                                                    READY

            A        B   C     D     E     F     G     H     I     J   ◄
     1                       Budget for Colleen Hayes                  ►
     2                                                                 ▲
     3                      OCT   NOV   DEC   JAN   FEB   MAR   TOTAL   ▼
     4                    --------------------------------------------  ?
     5    SALARY:          1900  1900  1900  1900  1900  1900   11400
     6
     7    EXPENSES:
     8    RENT              405   405   405   405   405   405
     9    ELECTRICITY        25    25    25    25    25    25
    10    TELEPHONE          12    12    12    12    12    12
    11    FOOD/CLOTHING
    12    RENTER'S INSURANCE
    13    CAR EXPENSES
    14    LIFE INSURANCE
    15    LEISURE
    16    SAVINGS
    17
    18    TOTAL EXPENSES:
    19                                                               ■
    20    BALANCE:
    22-Aug-91  12:56 AM
```

Figure 2.12

The telephone expense is now copied across the range you defined.

POINT mode is available in many command options and can be particularly helpful in a large worksheet.

Now use the **C**opy command to fill in food/clothing expenses (row 11) at 400 a month and renter's insurance (row 12) at 10 a month.

Colleen figured car expenses to be $25 a month when she did her apartment analysis, but she forgot to include car insurance. Use the **C**opy command to fill in car expenses (row 13) at $90 a month; this figure includes $25 a month for gas and $65 a month for car insurance.

Complete row 14 by entering 277 for life insurance expense in the month of January only (cell F14). Your screen should now look similar to Figure 2.13.

```
F14: [W6] 277                                                         READY

                 A      B   C    D    E    F    G    H    I    J    ◄
 1                          Budget for Colleen Hayes                ►
 2                                                                  ▲
 3                          OCT  NOV  DEC  JAN  FEB  MAR   TOTAL     ▼
 4                          ---------------------------   ------    ?
 5       SALARY:            1900 1900 1900 1900 1900 1900  11400
 6
 7       EXPENSES:
 8       RENT               405  405  405  405  405  405
 9       ELECTRICITY         25   25   25   25   25   25
10       TELEPHONE           12   12   12   12   12   12
11       FOOD/CLOTHING      400  400  400  400  400  400
12       RENTER'S INSURANCE  10   10   10   10   10   10
13       CAR EXPENSES        90   90   90   90   90   90
14       LIFE INSURANCE                     277
15       LEISURE
16       SAVINGS
17
18       TOTAL EXPENSES:
19
20       BALANCE:
         22-Aug-91  12:59 AM
```

Figure 2.13

Copying a Formula

To complete the worksheet, you need to enter the formulas to calculate Colleen's leisure expense, savings, total expenses, and balance. Colleen feels she can budget 10 percent of her salary for leisure and 20 percent for savings.

The formula to calculate October's leisure expense will take the value in cell C5 (salary) and multiply it by .10. The arithmetic operator that indicates multiplication is an asterisk (*).

To enter this formula,

Move to: C15

Type: +C5*.10

Press: ⏎

Notice that 1-2-3 displays the formula in the control panel as +C5*0.1. Although you entered the formula using the multiplier .10, 1-2-3 always displays a decimal with a leading zero followed by the decimal value.

Copy the formula in cell C15 to cells D15 through H15. The calculated value, 190, appears in each cell.

Your screen should now look similar to Figure 2.14.

```
C15: [W6] +C5*0.1                                                  READY

              A        B    C    D    E    F    G    H    I    J    ◄
         1                     Budget for Colleen Hayes                ►
         2                                                             ▲
         3                   OCT  NOV  DEC  JAN  FEB  MAR    TOTAL     ▼
         4                   ------------------------------- ------    ?
         5    SALARY:        1900 1900 1900 1900 1900 1900   11400
         6
         7    EXPENSES:
         8    RENT           405  405  405  405  405  405
         9    ELECTRICITY    25   25   25   25   25   25
        10    TELEPHONE      12   12   12   12   12   12
        11    FOOD/CLOTHING  400  400  400  400  400  400
        12    RENTER'S INSURANCE 10   10   10   10   10   10
        13    CAR EXPENSES   90   90   90   90   90   90
        14    LIFE INSURANCE                 277
        15    LEISURE        190  190  190  190  190  190
        16    SAVINGS
        17
        18    TOTAL EXPENSES:
        19                                                           ■
        20    BALANCE:
        22-Aug-91  01:00 AM
```

Figure 2.14

Move to: D15

The formula in this cell is +D5*0.1. The formula reflects the new column location of the formula in the worksheet. The formula in cell C15 references the value in cell C5, and the formula in cell D15 references the value in cell D5. This way, the formula appropriately calculates the value based on the salary earned for that month.

When the formula in cell C15 was copied, the cell addresses in the copied formulas were automatically adjusted relative to their new location in the worksheet. This occurs because the formula in cell C15 contains a **relative cell reference**. Whenever a cell address is entered in a formula using just the column letter and row number, the cell address will change to reflect its new location in the worksheet when the formula is copied. 1-2-3 interprets the formula in cell C15 as "multiply the contents of the cell ten rows above times 0.1." When the formula is copied to cell D15, 1-2-3 still interprets the formula as "multiply the contents of the cell ten rows above times 0.1." To do this, 1-2-3 adjusts the relative cell reference so that the formula becomes +D5*0.1.

To see how the other formulas adjusted relative to their new location in the worksheet, move the cell pointer to each formula in the range (E15 through H15), and read the formulas in the control panel.

Since Colleen wants to put 20 percent of her salary into savings, the formula to calculate October's savings will multiply October's salary by .20. To enter the formula,

Move to: C16

Type: **+C5*.20**

Press: ⊣

Copy the formula across to H16.

Using @Functions

Next, you need to enter the formula to calculate the total expenses for each month in cell C18 and then copy it across the row through cell H18. The formula to compute the total could be entered as +C8+C9+C10+C11+C12+C13+C14+C15+C16. However, using 1-2-3's @functions is easier.

@Functions are built-in formulas that perform certain types of calculations automatically. To learn more about @functions, you can use either the keyboard or the mouse to access the Help facility. If you are using the keyboard,

Press: F1 (HELP)

If you are using the mouse,

Click: ?

Then, click either the down arrow scroll button located on the icon panel or the down arrow located in the bottom right corner of the Help screen until @Function Basics appears. Then,

Click: @Function Basics

The 1-2-3 Main Help Index is displayed. (If the Main Help Index is not on your screen, refer to Chapter 5 in "Getting Started.") The index displays an alphabetized list of topics. To obtain information about a topic using the keyboard, highlight the topic and press ⊣. As you move through the list, the screen will scroll. To get help about @functions, use the down arrow key to

Move to: @Function Basics

Press: ⊣

Your screen should now look similar to Figure 2.15.

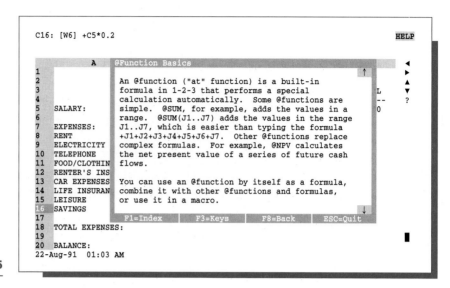

```
C16: [W6] +C5*0.2                                                    HELP

            A   @Function Basics
  1             ┌─────────────────────────────────────────────────┐  ◄
  2             │An @function ("at" function) is a built-in     ↑ │  ►
  3             │formula in 1-2-3 that performs a special          │ L  ▲
  4             │calculation automatically.  Some @functions are   │ -- ▼
  5   SALARY:   │simple.  @SUM, for example, adds the values in a   │ 0  ?
  6             │range.  @SUM(J1..J7) adds the values in the range  │
  7   EXPENSES: │J1..J7, which is easier than typing the formula    │
  8   RENT      │+J1+J2+J3+J4+J5+J6+J7.  Other @functions replace   │
  9   ELECTRICITY│complex formulas.  For example, @NPV calculates   │
 10   TELEPHONE │the net present value of a series of future cash   │
 11   FOOD/CLOTHIN│flows.                                          │
 12   RENTER'S INS│                                                │
 13   CAR EXPENSES│You can use an @function by itself as a formula,│
 14   LIFE INSURAN│combine it with other @functions and formulas,  │
 15   LEISURE   │or use it in a macro.                           ↓ │
 16   SAVINGS   └─────────────────────────────────────────────────┘
 17             │ F1=Index    │  F3=Keys   │  F8=Back   │  ESC=Quit │
 18   TOTAL EXPENSES:
 19                                                                     ■
 20   BALANCE:
22-Aug-91  01:03 AM
```

Figure 2.15

Carefully read the information about @Function Basics on this screen. Remember that there is additional information beyond the screen, and you will need to scroll down by pressing ⬇ to read it.

The structure, or **syntax**, of an @function is as follows:

@function name(argument1,argument2,. . .,argument*n*)

The @function name tells 1-2-3 which type of calculation to perform. The arguments are the data that 1-2-3 uses in the calculation of the @function. When you enter @functions, be sure to follow these basic rules of syntax:

- Do not leave spaces between the @function name and the arguments.

- Separate multiple arguments in an @function by a comma or a semicolon, not a space.

- Enclose the arguments in parentheses.

- Use either uppercase or lowercase letters to type an @function name.

To return to the worksheet using the mouse,

Click: the right mouse button

When you have finished reading about @functions, to return to the worksheet using the keyboard,

Press: (ESC)

You will use the **@SUM** function to calculate the total monthly expenses. This function uses a list of values for the arguments. A list can be a cell, a range, a formula, or any combination of these separated by commas. In this case, the list is the range C8..C16. To enter this @function,

Move to: C18

Type: **@SUM(C8..C16)**

Press: ⏎

Note If the @function contains an error, 1-2-3 will beep and change to EDIT mode when you try to enter the @function. Locate and correct the error, and then reenter the @function.

Your screen should now look similar to Figure 2.16.

```
C18: [W6] @SUM(C8..C16)                                          READY

              A        B   C    D    E    F    G    H    I    J    ◄
1                          Budget for Colleen Hayes                 ►
2                                                                   ▲
3                         OCT  NOV  DEC  JAN  FEB  MAR     TOTAL    ▼
4                         ------------------------------   ------   ?
5   SALARY:              1900 1900 1900 1900 1900 1900    11400
6
7   EXPENSES:
8   RENT                  405  405  405  405  405  405
9   ELECTRICITY            25   25   25   25   25   25
10  TELEPHONE              12   12   12   12   12   12
11  FOOD/CLOTHING         400  400  400  400  400  400
12  RENTER'S INSURANCE     10   10   10   10   10   10
13  CAR EXPENSES           90   90   90   90   90   90
14  LIFE INSURANCE                            277
15  LEISURE               190  190  190  190  190  190
16  SAVINGS               380  380  380  380  380  380
17
18  TOTAL EXPENSES:      1512
19
20  BALANCE:
22-Aug-91  01:04 AM
```

Figure 2.16

The calculated value, 1512, is displayed in cell C18.

As you can see, using an @function to calculate this sum was a lot easier than typing in the formula.

Copy the @function in cell C18 to cells D18 through H18. The range specified in the @function is adjusted appropriately because of relative cell referencing.

Next, you need to enter the formula to compute Colleen's monthly balance (row 20). The monthly balance is the monthly salary minus monthly total expenses. You can also use the cell pointer to specify cell addresses in a formula or an @function. This action can be accomplished using either the keyboard or the mouse.

To use the cell pointer using the keyboard,

Move to: C20

Type: +

Move to: C5

Notice that the mode indicator now displays POINT.

Type: − (minus)

Move to: C18

Press: ⏎

The complete formula is displayed in the control panel, and the calculated value, 388, is displayed in cell C20.

Now copy this formula across row 20 through March.

Your screen should now look similar to Figure 2.17.

```
C20: [W6] +C5-C18                                              READY

              A          B   C      D      E      F      G      H    I    J     ◄
1                                Budget for Colleen Hayes                       ►
2                                                                               ▲
3                                OCT    NOV    DEC    JAN    FEB    MAR   TOTAL  ▼
4                                ----------------------------------     ------  ?
5    SALARY:                     1900   1900   1900   1900   1900   1900  11400
6
7    EXPENSES:
8    RENT                         405    405    405    405    405    405
9    ELECTRICITY                   25     25     25     25     25     25
10   TELEPHONE                     12     12     12     12     12     12
11   FOOD/CLOTHING                400    400    400    400    400    400
12   RENTER'S INSURANCE            10     10     10     10     10     10
13   CAR EXPENSES                  90     90     90     90     90     90
14   LIFE INSURANCE                                    277
15   LEISURE                      190    190    190    190    190    190
16   SAVINGS                      380    380    380    380    380    380
17
18   TOTAL EXPENSES:             1512   1512   1512   1789   1512   1512
19                                                                          ■
20   BALANCE:                     388    388    388    111    388    388
     22-Aug-91  01:07 AM
```

Figure 2.17

To complete the worksheet, the formula to calculate the TOTAL in column J needs to be entered. This has already been done for you and saved in the file NUMBERS.WK1. To erase your current worksheet from the screen and the computer's memory and to retrieve the file NUMBERS.WK1, issue the following command sequence:

/File **R**etrieve **Y**es **NUMBERS.WK1** ⏎

Your screen should now look similar to Figure 2.18.

```
A1: [W18]                                                              READY

              A          B    C     D     E     F     G     H   I    J     ◀
1                            Budget for Colleen Hayes                      ▶
2                                                                          ▲
3                             OCT   NOV   DEC   JAN   FEB   MAR     TOTAL   ▼
4                            ------------------------------------   ------  ?
5        SALARY:             1900  1900  1900  1900  1900  1900     11400
6
7        EXPENSES:
8        RENT                 405   405   405   405   405   405      2430
9        ELECTRICITY           25    25    25    25    25    25       150
10       TELEPHONE             12    12    12    12    12    12        72
11       FOOD/CLOTHING        400   400   400   400   400   400      2400
12       RENTER'S INSURANCE    10    10    10    10    10    10        60
13       CAR EXPENSES          90    90    90    90    90    90       540
14       LIFE INSURANCE                         277                   277
15       LEISURE              190   190   190   190   190   190      1140
16       SAVINGS              380   380   380   380   380   380      2280
17
18       TOTAL EXPENSES:     1512  1512  1512  1789  1512  1512      9349
19                                                                           ▮
20       BALANCE:             388   388   388   111   388   388      2051
         22-Aug-91  01:11 AM
```

Figure 2.18

Using an Absolute Cell Reference

Colleen now wants to know what proportion of her total salary for six months (J5) is allocated to expenses each month. To begin, place a new descriptive label in cell A19.

Move to: A19

Type: **PROPORTION**

Press: ⏎

To enter the formula to make this calculation,

Move to: C19

Type: **+C18/J5** ⏎

Press: ⏎

More than 13 percent of her total salary is allocated to October expenses. Copy this formula to cells D19 through H19.

Although the value in cell C19 appears to have been calculated properly, all the other cells in that row display the message ERR. This is because the formula in cell C19 was entered using a relative cell reference.

Move to: D19

Your screen should now look similar to Figure 2.19.

```
D19: [W6] +D18/K5                                              READY

              A        B    C    D    E    F    G    H   I   J
                             Budget for Colleen Hayes
 1
 2
 3                             OCT  NOV  DEC  JAN  FEB  MAR    TOTAL
 4                            -----------------------------   ------
 5    SALARY:                 1900 1900 1900 1900 1900 1900   11400
 6
 7    EXPENSES:
 8    RENT                     405  405  405  405  405  405    2430
 9    ELECTRICITY               25   25   25   25   25   25     150
10    TELEPHONE                 12   12   12   12   12   12      72
11    FOOD/CLOTHING            400  400  400  400  400  400    2400
12    RENTER'S INSURANCE        10   10   10   10   10   10      60
13    CAR EXPENSES              90   90   90   90   90   90     540
14    LIFE INSURANCE                          277              277
15    LEISURE                  190  190  190  190  190  190    1140
16    SAVINGS                  380  380  380  380  380  380    2280
17
18    TOTAL EXPENSES:         1512 1512 1512 1789 1512 1512    9349
19    PROPORTION             0.132  ERR  ERR  ERR  ERR  ERR
20    BALANCE:                 388  388  388  111  388  388    2051
      22-Aug-91  01:13 AM
```

Figure 2.19

The formula in cell D19 now references cell K5, which is a blank cell. Since cell K5 contains nothing, 1-2-3 assumes that its value is zero. The formula in cell D19 requires division by zero, which is impossible. Therefore, ERR is displayed in the worksheet. Look at the other formulas in this row, and you will see the same problem.

The formula in cell C19 should have been entered in such a way that the reference to cell J5 would not be changed when the formula was copied. To do this, you need to use an absolute cell reference in the formula.

An **absolute cell reference** prevents the relative adjustment of a cell address in a formula when it is copied. To maintain the reference to a specific cell address when you are copying formulas, enter a dollar sign ($) before both the column letter and the row number of the cell address in the formula.

It is also possible to enter a formula using a **mixed cell reference**. This is done by entering a dollar sign ($) before either the column letter or the row number of the cell address, but not before both. The result is that either the row or the column will not be adjusted during the copy. For example, the address A$5 would be copied by changing the column letters, but the row number would always be 5.

You can enter the dollar sign directly by typing it or by using (F4), the ABS (absolute) key. To edit the formula in cell C19 to have absolute cell referencing and to demonstrate the use of the ABS key,

Move to: C19

Press: (F2)(EDIT)

We need to change the reference to cell J5 in the formula to an absolute reference. The edit cursor should be positioned on or immediately to the right of the cell address before using the ABS key. This tells 1-2-3 which cell address to alter. Since the edit cursor is in the correct location,

Press: (F4)(ABS)

The cell address to the left of the edit cursor now contains a dollar sign before the column letter and the row number, making it absolute. Each time you press (F4) (ABS), the cell address will change from absolute to mixed to relative. To see this change, watch the control panel as you

Press: (F4)(ABS) slowly four times

The cell address cycles through all possible combinations of the different reference types. It should now be absolute. To complete the edit,

Press: (↵)

Copy this formula across row 19 through March.

Your screen should now look similar to Figure 2.20.

Absolute Cell Address ——

```
C19: [W6] +C18/$J$5                                                  READY

            A          B    C     D     E     F     G     H     I     J     ◄
 1                          Budget for Colleen Hayes                        ►
 2                                                                          ▲
 3                          OCT   NOV   DEC   JAN   FEB   MAR       TOTAL    ▼
 4                          --------------------------------       ------   ?
 5  SALARY:                 1900  1900  1900  1900  1900  1900      11400
 6
 7  EXPENSES:
 8  RENT                     405   405   405   405   405   405       2430
 9  ELECTRICITY               25    25    25    25    25    25        150
10  TELEPHONE                 12    12    12    12    12    12         72
11  FOOD/CLOTHING            400   400   400   400   400   400       2400
12  RENTER'S INSURANCE        10    10    10    10    10    10         60
13  CAR EXPENSES              90    90    90    90    90    90        540
14  LIFE INSURANCE                             277                    277
15  LEISURE                  190   190   190   190   190   190       1140
16  SAVINGS                  380   380   380   380   380   380       2280
17
18  TOTAL EXPENSES:         1512  1512  1512  1789  1512  1512       9349
19  PROPORTION             0.132 0.132 0.132 0.156 0.132 0.132
20  BALANCE:                 388   388   388   111   388   388       2051
    22-Aug-91  01:14 AM
```

Figure 2.20

Move across row 19 to confirm that each formula references cell J5. Using an absolute cell reference easily solved the problem.

Enabling Undo

Since she will be changing and erasing some data, Colleen would like to make 1-2-3's Undo feature available. Undo is an optional feature that allows you to cancel the most recent operation that changed the worksheet. If you wish to use Undo, you must first enable (activate) it. Once Undo is enabled, it can be used to restore the worksheet after a change is made. (You cannot undo changes made before Undo is enabled.) Undo may require memory that is currently being used for a worksheet. Therefore, before you enable Undo, you will save this worksheet, replacing the original, and then clear it from memory. We will discuss saving and replacing files in detail later in this lab. Issue the following command sequences:

/File Save **NUMBERS.WK1** ⏎ **R**eplace

/**W**orksheet **E**rase **Y**es

To turn on the Undo feature, you will use the menu to access the Default Settings dialog box. You can turn on Undo using either the keyboard or the mouse. Using the keyboard, issue the following command sequence:

/**W**orksheet **G**lobal **D**efault

After erasing the worksheet from memory, display the menu. Then,

Click: Worksheet Global Default

The Default Settings dialog box should appear.

Click: Undo on

to place an x in the check box. Click OK to confirm the settings. To exit the menu,

Click: Quit

The Default Settings dialog box appears. To activate the dialog box,

Press: (F2) (EDIT)

Notice the "n" in Undo is highlighted. To enable Undo,

Type: **n**

Press: (↵)

To select OK and leave the menu,

Press: (↵)

Select: **Q**uit

Notice the UNDO status indicator at the bottom of the screen.

Now that Undo is enabled, retrieve the file NUMBERS.WK1 by issuing the following command sequence:

/File Retrieve NUMBERS.WK1 (↵)

Erasing Entries

If you are using the mouse, display the menu. Then,

Click: Range Erase

To specify the range A19..H19,

Point to: cell A19

Drag to: cell H19

Click: the left mouse button

Colleen decides that the PROPORTION row of data does not really belong in her budget, so she wants to clear, or erase, the entire row.

Move to: A19

Using the keyboard, issue the following command sequence:

/Range **E**rase **A19..H19** (↵)

Your screen should now look similar to Figure 2.21.

```
A19: [W18]                                                      READY

            A        B    C    D    E    F    G    H    I    J    ◄
  1                           Budget for Colleen Hayes              ►
  2                                                                 ▲
  3                      OCT  NOV  DEC  JAN  FEB  MAR      TOTAL     ▼
  4                      ---------------------------      ------     ?
  5   SALARY:            1900 1900 1900 1900 1900 1900     11400
  6
  7   EXPENSES:
  8   RENT               405  405  405  405  405  405       2430
  9   ELECTRICITY         25   25   25   25   25   25        150
 10   TELEPHONE           12   12   12   12   12   12         72
 11   FOOD/CLOTHING      400  400  400  400  400  400       2400
 12   RENTER'S INSURANCE  10   10   10   10   10   10         60
 13   CAR EXPENSES        90   90   90   90   90   90        540
 14   LIFE INSURANCE                     277                 277
 15   LEISURE            190  190  190  190  190  190       1140
 16   SAVINGS            380  380  380  380  380  380       2280
 17
 18   TOTAL EXPENSES:   1512 1512 1512 1789 1512 1512       9349
 19
 20   BALANCE:           388  388  388  111  388  388       2051
      22-Aug-91  01:18 AM    UNDO
```

Figure 2.21

The entire row is now erased.

Note Using the **/R**ange **E**rase command is the fastest way to erase a range of cells. However, if you wish to erase only a single cell, simply highlight the cell and press (DEL). You do not need to try this now.

Using the Undo Feature

Colleen realizes that she erased the row of data too soon. She wanted to record the values for later use. To cancel the most recent operation that changed worksheet data or settings, Colleen can use the Undo ((ALT)-(F4)) feature. This feature restores the worksheet to the way it was the last time 1-2-3 was in READY mode.

Press: (ALT)-(F4) (UNDO)

The row of data that Colleen had erased is redisplayed. It appears exactly as it did before she used the **E**rase command.

After recording the information, Colleen now wants to erase the row again. Rather than using the **E**rase command, she can press Undo again, and 1-2-3 will redo the entry or command.

Press: (ALT)-(F4) (UNDO)

The status indicator at the bottom of the screen displays UNDO whenever 1-2-3 can activate the Undo feature. The row is again erased from the worksheet.

This feature is an important safeguard against mistakes that may take a lot of time to fix. However, be careful when you use this command since you may get some unexpected results. Each time you begin a command, start an entry, or use certain function keys that affect the worksheet data, 1-2-3 creates a temporary backup copy of the worksheet as it last appeared in READY mode. The backup copy is stored in memory. Since 1-2-3 does not wait until the command or entry is complete before backing up the worksheet, you must use the Undo feature immediately after executing the command or making the entry that you want to undo. A backup worksheet is not created if the key you press does not cause a change in the worksheet data.

Using the Worksheet

Colleen would now like to use her proposed budget to help her plan her financial needs for the future. Colleen plans to buy a new car in April. She estimates the down payment to be $3,000. At her current rate of savings, however, Colleen will have only $2,280 in April. She will have to increase her savings rate to reach her goal of $3,000 for her down payment and still have a reserve to cover unexpected expenses.

To see the effect on Colleen's budget, change her monthly savings (C16..H16) to 30 percent of her salary. To make this change, use the EDIT function key, (F2), and change the formula in cell C16 to +C5*0.3; then copy this formula to cells D16 through H16.

The process of changing selected factors in a worksheet is called **what-if analysis**. What if her savings changed to 30 percent of her salary a month?

After you change the data in row 16, your screen should look similar to Figure 2.22.

```
C16: [W6] +C5*0.3                                                    READY

              A            B   C    D    E    F    G    H   I   J    ◄
1                              Budget for Colleen Hayes                 ►
2                                                                       ▲
3                              OCT  NOV  DEC  JAN  FEB  MAR   TOTAL      ▼
4                              ------------------------------ ------     ?
5     SALARY:                  1900 1900 1900 1900 1900 1900  11400
6
7     EXPENSES:
8     RENT                     405  405  405  405  405  405   2430
9     ELECTRICITY               25   25   25   25   25   25    150
10    TELEPHONE                 12   12   12   12   12   12     72
11    FOOD/CLOTHING            400  400  400  400  400  400   2400
12    RENTER'S INSURANCE        10   10   10   10   10   10     60
13    CAR EXPENSES              90   90   90   90   90   90    540
14    LIFE INSURANCE                          277              277
15    LEISURE                  190  190  190  190  190  190   1140
16    SAVINGS                  570  570  570  570  570  570   3420
17
18    TOTAL EXPENSES:         1702 1702 1702 1979 1702 1702  10489
19                                                                      ■
20    BALANCE:                 198  198  198  -79  198  198    911
      22-Aug-91  01:21 AM     UNDO
```

Figure 2.22

The completed worksheet shows that Colleen has a cash flow problem in January, with a negative balance of $79. Colleen's life insurance payment is due that month. However, over the six-month period, Colleen has a positive balance of $911. Colleen is not too concerned about the deficit in January because she has her savings to borrow from.

When 1-2-3 recalculates a worksheet, only those formulas directly affected by a change in the data are recalculated. This is called **minimal recalculation**. Without this feature, in large worksheets the time it takes to recalculate all formulas each time a value is changed could take several minutes. The minimal recalculation feature decreases the recalculation time by recalculating only affected formulas.

Colleen now has a total balance of $911 and a total savings of $3,420. Colleen feels she can afford a more active social life, so she decides to increase her leisure allowance from 10 to 15 percent of her salary. To make this change, use the EDIT function key, (F2), and change the formula in cell C15 to +C5*0.15; then copy this formula to cells D15 through H15.

Your screen should look similar to Figure 2.23.

```
C15: [W6] +C5*0.15                                               READY

              A        B    C      D      E      F      G      H    I    J     ◄
1                             Budget for Colleen Hayes                         ►
2                                                                              ▲
3                            OCT    NOV    DEC    JAN    FEB    MAR             ▼
4                         ------------------------------------------  ------    ?
5      SALARY:             1900   1900   1900   1900   1900   1900     11400
6
7      EXPENSES:
8      RENT                 405    405    405    405    405    405      2430
9      ELECTRICITY           25     25     25     25     25     25       150
10     TELEPHONE             12     12     12     12     12     12        72
11     FOOD/CLOTHING        400    400    400    400    400    400      2400
12     RENTER'S INSURANCE    10     10     10     10     10     10        60
13     CAR EXPENSES          90     90     90     90     90     90       540
14     LIFE INSURANCE                            277                     277
15     LEISURE              285    285    285    285    285    285      1710
16     SAVINGS              570    570    570    570    570    570      3420
17
18     TOTAL EXPENSES:     1797   1797   1797   2074   1797   1797     11059
19                                                                            ■
20     BALANCE:             103    103    103   -174    103    103       341
       22-Aug-91  01:22 AM  UNDO
```

Figure 2.23

Even by increasing her leisure allowance, Colleen still has a positive balance of $341. She feels this balance is enough to cover any unexpected expense.

Next, you will save and print the worksheet.

Saving and Replacing a File

Before 1-2-3 will allow you to save any worksheet, it checks to see if another worksheet with the same name exists on the disk. If one does not exist, the worksheet is automatically saved. If one does exist, 1-2-3 prompts you to select either **C**ancel, **R**eplace, or **B**ackup.

To save the current worksheet by copying it over the partial worksheet BUDGET.WK1, issue the following command sequence:

/File Save **BUDGET.WK1** ⏎

The second line of the control panel prompts you to select **C**ancel, **R**eplace, or **B**ackup. If you select **C**ancel, the file will not be saved as BUDGET.WK1, and you could reissue the command using another file name. If you select **R**eplace, the current worksheet will be saved as BUDGET.WK1, and the previous worksheet will be lost. If you select **B**ackup, the current worksheet will be saved as BUDGET.WK1, and a backup copy of the existing file on disk would be saved as BUDGET.BAK.

Since you want to replace the old worksheet,

Select: **R**eplace

This feature protects against your accidentally saving one file over another with the same name.

Printing a File

You will now print the worksheet using the 1-2-3 Print Settings dialog box, as you did in Lab 1.

If your printer is off, turn it on. Check to see that it is on-line. If your printer uses continuous form paper, adjust the printer paper so that the perforated line is just above the printer's scale. Begin the **P**rint command as follows:

Select: /**P**rint **P**rinter

The Print Settings dialog box is displayed. The only option that you must select is the range. To specify the range as the entire worksheet,

Press: (F2) (EDIT)

Select: **R**ange

Type: **A1..J20**

Press: (↵)

The default settings for the other options in the dialog box are satisfactory for now. To confirm the settings,

Press: (↵)

Finally, to tell the program that the paper is aligned with the top of the printer's scale and to begin printing,

Select: **A**lign **G**o

Your printer may take a few moments before it begins to print the worksheet. Do not select **Go** again because it will result in multiple printouts of the worksheet.

When the printing is finished, your printer will advance your printout forward when you issue the following command:

Page

Your printer output should look similar to Figure 2.24.

```
Addison-Wesley: 1-2-3 for Education                          Linda O'Leary


                          Budget for Colleen Hayes

                   OCT   NOV   DEC   JAN   FEB   MAR     TOTAL
                   -----------------------------------     ------
         SALARY:   1900  1900  1900  1900  1900  1900    11400

         EXPENSES:
         RENT       405   405   405   405   405   405     2430
         ELECTRICITY  25    25    25    25    25    25      150
         TELEPHONE    12    12    12    12    12    12       72
         FOOD/CLOTHING 400  400   400   400   400   400     2400
         RENTER'S INSURANCE 10  10  10   10    10    10       60
         CAR EXPENSES  90    90    90    90    90    90      540
         LIFE INSURANCE                277                   277
         LEISURE     285   285   285   285   285   285     1710
         SAVINGS     570   570   570   570   570   570     3420

         TOTAL EXPENSES: 1797 1797 1797 2074 1797 1797    11059

         BALANCE:    103   103   103  -174   103   103      341
```

Figure 2.24

The header "The Student Edition of Lotus 1-2-3" and your name are automatically printed at the top of your worksheet.

Return to READY mode by issuing the following command:

Quit

Exit 1-2-3.

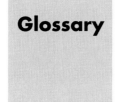

Glossary

Absolute cell reference: A cell address that always refers to the same cell even if it is copied to a new cell location.

Anchor: Defines the cell that begins a range of cells to be highlighted while in POINT mode.

Anchor cell: The beginning cell of a range.

Check boxes: Option from a group on a dialog box and marked by an x next to the option.

Column width: The number of spaces that a column contains.

Command buttons: Appear when the dialog box is active; they carry out the action of the command.

Default: A setting that 1-2-3 automatically uses unless another setting is specified.

Dialog box: Displays the current settings for the options associated with the command in use.

@function: A built-in formula that automatically performs certain types of calculations.

Global: A setting that affects the entire worksheet.

List boxes: Appear in a dialog box when you must select from menu choices, such as a list of range names.

Minimal recalculation: The recalculation of only those formulas affected by a change in data in the worksheet.

Mixed cell reference: A cell address that is part absolute and part relative.

Option buttons: Options on a dialog box marked by an * (asterisk).

Pointing: Using the cell pointer to specify a cell or a range of cells.

Range: A cell or a rectangular group of adjoining cells in the worksheet.

Relative cell reference: A cell address that refers to a cell's position rather than to the cell itself and adjusts relative to its new position when copied.

@SUM: An @function that calculates the total value of cells in a specified range of cells.

Syntax: The structure that must be followed when entering @functions.

Text boxes: Appear in a dialog box and accept any type of entry, including numbers, range names, or text, depending on what the command requires.

What-if analysis: A technique used to evaluate the effects of changing selected values or formulas in a worksheet.

Matching

1. F4	_10_	a. erases a range of cells
2. ALT-F4	_5_	b. rectangular block of adjacent cells
3. Dialog box	_6_	c. absolute cell reference
4. @functions	_9_	d. inserts a new column
5. Range	_3_	e. displays current settings
6. +F$10	_8_	f. copies a range of cells
7. +$C$12	_4_	g. built-in formula
8. /C	_2_	h. Undo feature key sequence
9. /WIC	_7_	i. mixed cell reference
10. /RE	_1_	j. switches a cell reference among absolute, mixed, and relative

Multiple Choice

Mike Kelly has created a worksheet to record and total scores. Refer to the figure below to answer the following questions.

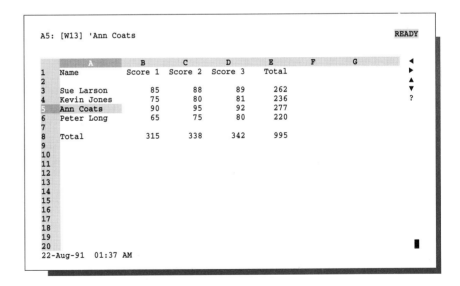

1. The current worksheet cell is:

   a. C6   c. B8

   b. A5   d. A1

2. The range of Peter Long's scores is:

    a. A4..D4   c. A6..E6

    b. B3..D3   d. B6..D6

3. The width of column A is:

    a. 11   c. 13

    b. 9   d. 14

4. The value in cell D8 is:

    a. 342   c. 338

    b. 80   d. 995

5. The command to insert a column between Name and Score 1 would be:

    a. /ICB   c. /WIB

    b. /WICB   d. /WIC

6. The command to globally change the widths of the columns would be:

    a. /WGC   c. /IGC

    b. /WCG   d. /WC

7. The formula to total the scores for Score 1 would be:

    a. +B3+C3+D3   c. +B3+B4+B5+B6

    b. +D3+D4+D5+D6   d. +B3+B4+D5+B6

8. If the formula in cell E3 is +B3+C3+D3 and it is copied down the column, the formula in cell E6 would be:

    a. +B3+B4+B5   c. +C3+D3+E3

    b. +B6+C6+D6   d. +E3+E4+E5

9. If you were using the @SUM function to add column A, the value in cell A10 would be:

    a. 0   c. 338

    b. 315   d. 65

10. If you copied the @SUM function from cell E4 to cell F4, the value in cell F4 would be:

    a. 236   c. 0

    b. 397   d. 81

Cases

1. Cory Owens has been trying to create a worksheet for his personal budget and has been having some problems. Retrieve the worksheet file PROB2-1.WK1.

   a. The entries in row 4 represent Cory's monthly wages. These figures should not be there. Use the **E**rase command to correct this error.

   b. Look at row 18. The month labels should be in row 1. Move the labels in row 18 to row 1. (*Hint:* Although you could retype all the labels in row 1 and then erase row 18, there is a much easier way using one of 1-2-3's commands.)

   c. You have probably noticed the asterisks in the worksheet. Globally change the column widths to seven spaces.

   d. Insert two blank rows as rows 1 and 2. Delete row 7, and insert a row at row 4.

   e. In cell B4, use the repeat label-prefix character to enter a series of underline (_) characters, and copy this entry from cell B4 to cell C4 through cell H4.

   f. Enter your name in cell A1 and the date in cell A2.

   g. Save your corrected version of the worksheet using the file name HWLAB2-1.

   h. Print the worksheet.

2. To complete this problem, you first must have built the worksheet as specified in Practice Case 3 of Lab 1. If you have already completed that problem, retrieve the file HWLAB1-3.WK1. Continue to create the New Townhouse Analysis for Thomas Long by following these steps:

   a. Enter the Miles to Work values in row 18 as 20 for Villa Way, 15 for Village North, and 8 for West Gate.

   b. Copy the formula in cell C14 to cells D14 through H14.

   c. Enter an @SUM formula to calculate the TOTAL MONTHLY COST. Copy this formula across row 16.

   d. Enter the current date in cell A2. Make sure your name appears in cell A1.

   e. Save your completed version of the worksheet using the file name HWLAB2-2.

   f. Print the worksheet.

3. To complete this problem, you first must have built the worksheet as specified in Practice Case 4 of Lab 1. If you have already completed that problem, retrieve the file HWLAB1-4.WK1. Continue to create the budget for Alan Black by following these steps:

a. Fill in the monthly expenses for February through June. (Remember, Insurance and License are periodic expenses.)

b. Alan would like to add an entry for Savings and to allocate 5 percent of his monthly wages toward this expense. Enter the label Savings in cell A15. Enter a formula to calculate savings in cell B15, and then copy it to cells C15 through G15.

c. Alan forgot to allow for expenses for leisure activities and other miscellaneous items. He feels $120 would be adequate. He would like to enter the label Misc Exp in the row below License. Insert a row in the appropriate space, enter the label Misc Exp, and enter the value 120 for JAN through JUN.

d. Enter a blank row below Savings.

e. Copy the TOTAL formula from cell H5 to cells H8 through H16.

f. Enter the formulas required to calculate the Total Exp and Balance. Copy these formulas across through the TOTAL column (H).

g. Alan realizes he has much more money left over each month (Balance) than he needs to cover unexpected expenses. He decides to increase his monthly savings. The monthly savings is currently calculated as 5 percent of monthly wages. Change the percent used to calculate savings for all months except JAN so that the balance for each month is as close as possible to, but no more than, $200. (Limit your adjustment to two decimal places.) What is the total savings now?

h. Increase the width of column A to 10. Decrease all other column widths to 8.

i. Enter the current date in cell A2.

j. Save your completed version of this worksheet using the file name HWLAB2-3.

k. Print the worksheet.

4. Retrieve the file PROB2-4.WK1. Enter your name in cell A1 and the current date in cell A2. Complete the worksheet by inventing a reasonable salary and expenses for Brian so that the ending balance is as close as possible to $2000. Save the corrected worksheet file as HWLAB2-4, and print the worksheet.

5. Following the four steps in the planning process for worksheets, create an analysis for four different vacations. Select four destinations using all practical modes of transportation. The cost of the vacations may include hotel accommodations, car rental, meals, and other expenses. Figure your spending money as a percent of the total cost.

After you complete the paper model, create and complete the 1-2-3 worksheet. Enter your name in cell A1 and the date in cell A2, save as HWLAB2-5, and print the worksheet.

6. To complete this problem, you first must have completed the worksheet as specified in Practice Case 5 in Lab 1. If you have already completed that problem, retrieve the file HWLAB1-5.WK1. Complete the worksheet so that the ending balance is as close as possible to $1500.

Enter the current date in cell A2, save the completed worksheet as HWLAB2-6, and print the worksheet.

Lab 3

Using Worksheets

In Lab 3, you will learn how to:

Objectives

- **Display the file name**
- **Locate and eliminate circular references**
- **Hide and unhide columns**
- **Link files**
- **Name a range of cells**
- **Use the @MIN, @MAX, and @AVG functions**
- **Format cells**
- **Back up a file**

Case Study

an Walker, manager of a chain of restaurants in the Southwest called Walker's Gourmet Sandwiches, is concerned about his company's finances and has decided to incorporate more long-range planning into company policies and strategies. Dan has recently learned about the worksheet capabilities of 1-2-3 and has decided to use the program to help him with his financial planning.

Displaying the File Name

Dan has just started to use 1-2-3 to create an income statement for Walker's Gourmet Sandwiches, and he is having some problems.

To see his worksheet, load 1-2-3, and retrieve the file JANUARY.WK1.

This income statement extends beyond row 20. To view the rest of the worksheet, use ⬇ to

Move to: A23

Your screen should look similar to Figure 3.1.

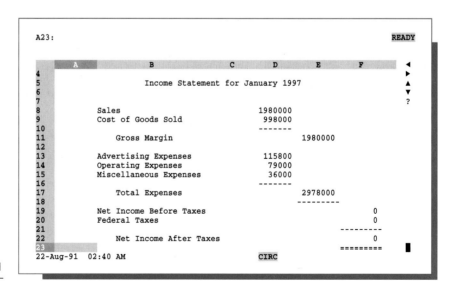

Figure 3.1

In this lab, you will be working with several different files. To help keep track of the file you are using, you can display the file name in the status line in place of the date-and-time indicator.

Using the Keyboard

You can accomplish this change using either the keyboard or the mouse. If you are using the mouse, see the section that follows. If you are using the keyboard, issue the following command sequence:

> /**W**orksheet **G**lobal

The date-and-time indicator is a default 1-2-3 worksheet setting. To change this setting,

> **Select:** **D**efault

The Default Settings dialog box is displayed. Notice that the currently selected option under Clock is Standard. This indicates a standard date-and-time display. To turn off the date-and-time display and turn on the file name display,

> **Select:** **O**ther **C**lock **F**ilename **Q**uit

Using the Mouse

To change the date-and-time indicator to the file name using the mouse, first display the main menu. Then,

> **Click:** Worksheet Global

The date-and-time indicator is a default 1-2-3 worksheet setting. To change this setting,

> **Click:** Default

To turn off the date-and-time display and turn on the file name display,

> **Click:** the Filename option button located near the upper right corner of the Default Settings dialog box

Once Filename is selected, to confirm your choice and leave the menu,

> **Click:** OK
> **Click:** Quit

Your screen should look similar to Figure 3.2.

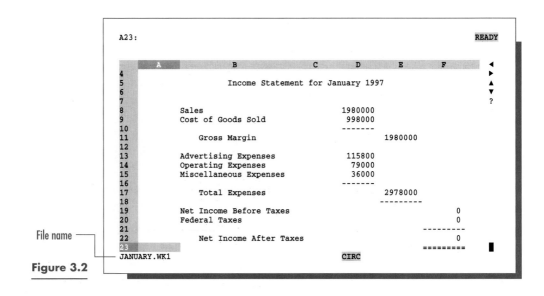

A23:   READY

	A	B	C	D	E	F

```
4
5                      Income Statement for January 1997
6
7
8          Sales                              1980000
9          Cost of Goods Sold                  998000
10                                            -------
11             Gross Margin                             1980000
12
13         Advertising Expenses                115800
14         Operating Expenses                   79000
15         Miscellaneous Expenses               36000
16                                            -------
17             Total Expenses                           2978000
18                                                     ---------
19         Net Income Before Taxes                                0
20         Federal Taxes                                          0
21                                                     ---------
22             Net Income After Taxes                             0
23                                                     =========
```

JANUARY.WK1   CIRC

File name —

Figure 3.2

The file name JANUARY.WK1 is displayed in the status line.

The worksheet has errors in the formulas used to calculate the Gross Margin and Total Expenses. The correct equations should be:

Gross Margin = Sales – Cost of Goods Sold (+D8 – D9)

Total Expenses = Advertising Expenses + Operating Expenses + Miscellaneous Expenses (+D13+D14+D15)

Correct the formulas in cells E11 and E17 to calculate Gross Margin and Total Expenses.

Locating a Circular Reference

There is also an error in the formula to calculate Net Income Before Taxes. To see this formula,

Move to: F19

Your screen should look similar to Figure 3.3.

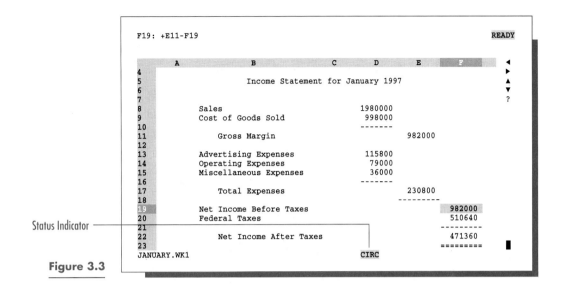

```
F19: +E11-F19                                                              READY

          A              B                C       D       E       F       ◄
    4                                                                     ►
    5                 Income Statement for January 1997                   ▲
    6                                                                     ▼
    7                                                                     ?
    8              Sales                         1980000
    9              Cost of Goods Sold             998000
   10                                            -------
   11                 Gross Margin                        982000
   12
   13              Advertising Expenses          115800
   14              Operating Expenses             79000
   15              Miscellaneous Expenses         36000
   16                                            -------
   17                 Total Expenses                      230800
   18                                                     ---------
   19              Net Income Before Taxes                        982000
   20              Federal Taxes                                  510640
   21                                                             ---------
   22                 Net Income After Taxes                      471360
   23                                                             =========  ■
JANUARY.WK1                                         CIRC
```

Status Indicator ──────

Figure 3.3

The formula in cell F19 is +E11 – F19. The formula should be:

Net Income Before Taxes = Gross Margin – Total Expenses
(+E11 – E17)

Because the incorrect formula in cell F19 references itself as part of the computation, a **circular reference** error occurs, and the status indicator CIRC is displayed. A circular reference occurs whenever a cell's formula refers to itself, either directly or indirectly.

For some special applications, you may want to have circular referencing. Such cases, however, are not very common. Generally, whenever CIRC appears, stop and locate the cell or cells causing the circular reference by using the /**W**orksheet **S**tatus command.

To see how this works, issue the following command sequence:

/**W**orksheet **S**tatus

Your screen should look similar to Figure 3.4.

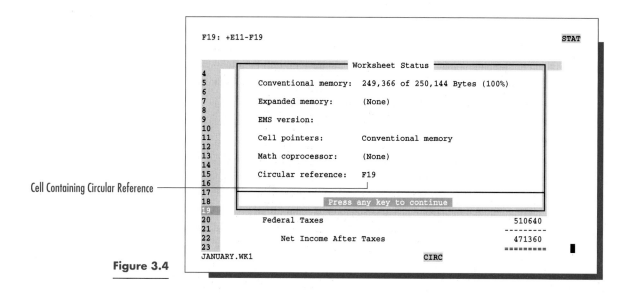

F19: +E11-F19   STAT

```
        ┌──────────────────── Worksheet Status ────────────────────┐
 4      │                                                           │
 5      │  Conventional memory:   249,366 of 250,144 Bytes (100%)   │
 6      │                                                           │
 7      │  Expanded memory:       (None)                            │
 8      │                                                           │
 9      │  EMS version:                                             │
10      │                                                           │
11      │  Cell pointers:         Conventional memory               │
12      │                                                           │
13      │  Math coprocessor:      (None)                            │
14      │                                                           │
15      │  Circular reference:    F19                               │
16      │                                                           │
17      ├───────────────────────────────────────────────────────────┤
18      │              Press any key to continue                    │
19      └───────────────────────────────────────────────────────────┘
20          Federal Taxes                                510640
21                                                      ---------
22            Net Income After Taxes                    471360
23                                                      =========
JANUARY.WK1                                    CIRC
```

Cell Containing Circular Reference ──────

Figure 3.4

The **Worksheet Status screen** displays information about available memory and the type of memory cell pointers are using, as well as whether there is a math coprocessor installed or any circular references in the worksheet. The Worksheet Status screen tells us that the location of the circular reference is in cell F19.

The cell location of only one circular reference can be displayed at a time. If you correct the CIRC cell reference in the worksheet and the message is still displayed in the status indicator, recall the Worksheet Status screen to locate the source of another circular reference.

To clear the screen of the Worksheet Status screen and return to the worksheet, press any key.

In this case, solving the problem is easy. The equation in cell F19 to calculate Net Income Before Taxes should be the difference between Gross Margin and Total Expenses. Now correct the formula in cell F19.

Your screen should look similar to Figure 3.5.

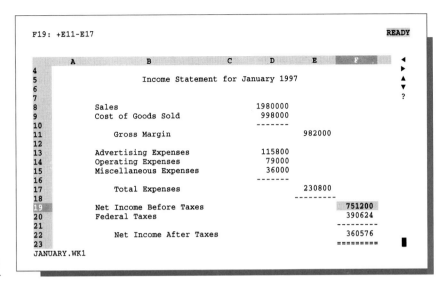

Figure 3.5

The CIRC message has disappeared.

Other circular references may be more complex. For example, as shown in Figure 3.6, a formula in cell B5 could refer to cell B15, which contains a formula referring to cell E15, which contains a formula referring to E5, which refers to cell B5.

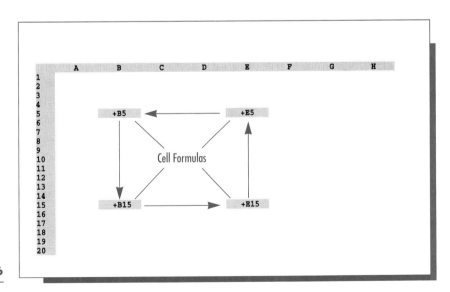

Figure 3.6

Even in complex cases, however, circular references are usually easy to locate and correct with the help of the Worksheet Status screen.

Save the corrected worksheet as JANEXP.

Hiding and Unhiding Columns

Another useful feature of 1-2-3 is its ability to hide a column of information. This is particularly helpful when you want to print a worksheet without displaying all the columns. You will see how this works by hiding column E.

Move to: E19

Issue the following command sequence:

/**W**orksheet **C**olumn **H**ide ⏎

This command sequence uses cell E19 to refer to column E. (You could have used any cell address in column E.)

Your screen should look similar to Figure 3.7.

Hidden Column E —————

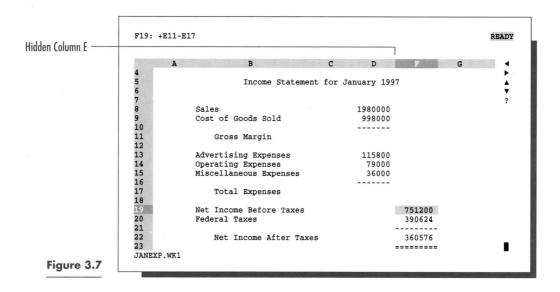

Figure 3.7

Column E is no longer visible in the worksheet; even the column letter has disappeared. When you hide several columns, only those areas of the worksheet that are not hidden will be printed.

To redisplay the hidden column, issue the following command sequence:

/**W**orksheet **C**olumn **D**isplay

Your screen should now look similar to Figure 3.8.

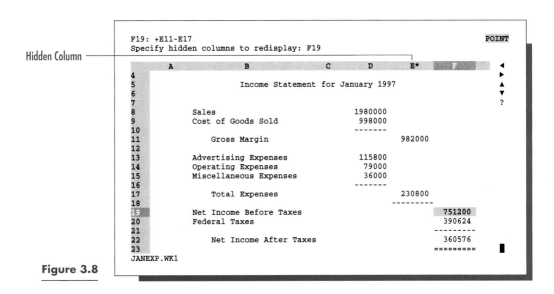

Hidden Column

Figure 3.8

```
F19: +E11-E17                                                    POINT
Specify hidden columns to redisplay: F19
              A              B              C         D       E*      F
4
5                        Income Statement for January 1997
6
7                                                                       ?
8                Sales                            1980000
9                Cost of Goods Sold                998000
10                                                 -------
11                   Gross Margin                            982000
12
13                Advertising Expenses             115800
14                Operating Expenses                79000
15                Miscellaneous Expenses            36000
16                                                 -------
17                   Total Expenses                          230800
18                                                          ---------
19               Net Income Before Taxes                              751200
20               Federal Taxes                                        390624
21                                                                  ---------
22                   Net Income After Taxes                           360576
23                                                                  =========
JANEXP.WK1
```

The hidden column is now displayed and marked with an asterisk (*) to identify it.

The control panel prompts you to specify which column to unhide. 1-2-3 has left the cell pointer in F19. To unhide column E, you can either specify column E or position the cell pointer in any cell in column E. Using the second approach, complete the command as follows:

Again, any cell address in column E would be acceptable.

Column E is again displayed on the screen.

File Linking

After looking at the values in the January statement, Dan asks the advertising director to check his January expense figures. Dan thinks the advertising expenses are too high.

The advertising director has created a worksheet of the department's expenses. To see the file containing the advertising expense report, retrieve the file ADVEXP.WK1.

Your screen should look similar to Figure 3.9.

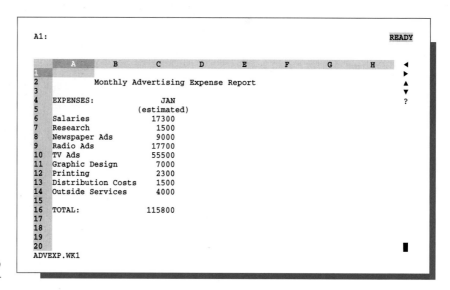

Figure 3.9

The advertising director initially estimated his January monthly expenses for the report. Now he has the actual figures for January and needs to change the worksheet to reflect the new values. First, to change the label in cell C5 to Actual and to make the word right-aligned,

Move to: C5

Type: **"Actual**

Press: ⏎

Next, enter the following new values in the worksheet:

Cell	Value
C7	1540
C8	8850
C9	18650
C10	48180
C11	6750
C12	4070
C13	2340
C14	4120

The TOTAL advertising expense (cell C16) is now 111800.

Save the revised worksheet as ADVEXP.WK1 using the **R**eplace option.

Dan decides that this may be a good time to see how the file linking feature of 1-2-3 works. This feature allows you to use values from cells in other worksheets in the current worksheet. The file that receives the value is the **target file,** and the file that supplies the data is the **source file.** To link files, Dan needs to know the name of the file and the cell in the worksheet containing the January advertising expense total. He is told that the file name is ADVEXP and the cell containing the January advertising expense is C16.

Retrieve the target file, JANEXP.WK1.

To create a link between two files, you enter a **linking formula** in the target file that refers to a cell in the source file. The JANEXP file will be the target file, and the ADVEXP file will be the source file. Dan wants the value in cell D13 of the target file to be the same as the value in cell C16 of the source file.

Move to: D13

The linking formula uses the following format:

+<<file reference>>cell reference

The file reference is the file name of the source file enclosed in double angle brackets. The cell reference is the cell address of the source file cell containing the value to be copied to the target file.

Type: +<<ADVEXP>>C16

Press: ⏎

Your screen should be similar to Figure 3.10.

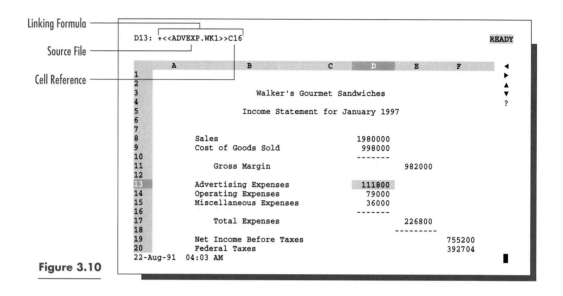

Linking Formula

Source File

Cell Reference

```
D13: +<<ADVEXP.WK1>>C16                                          READY

        A              B              C         D         E         F       ◄
  1                                                                          ►
  2                                                                          ▲
  3                         Walker's Gourmet Sandwiches                      ▼
  4                                                                          ?
  5                      Income Statement for January 1997
  6
  7
  8            Sales                            1980000
  9            Cost of Goods Sold               998000
 10                                             -------
 11               Gross Margin                            982000
 12
 13          Advertising Expenses             111800
 14          Operating Expenses                79000
 15          Miscellaneous Expenses            36000
 16                                            -------
 17               Total Expenses                         226800
 18                                                     ---------
 19          Net Income Before Taxes                               755200
 20          Federal Taxes                                         392704
22-Aug-91  04:03 AM                                                      ▮
```

Figure 3.10

The value in cell C16 of ADVEXP, 111800, is copied from the source file into the target file. The target file is recalculated using the new data.

Once a linking formula is entered in a worksheet, whenever the value in the cell referenced in the source file changes, the target file is automatically updated when it is retrieved. Another way to update the target file is to use the command /**F**ile **A**dmin **L**ink-Refresh. This command will immediately update the linked cells.

Dan likes how the file linking feature works. Some time in the future, when the corporate income statement is running smoothly, he plans to require that all departments create worksheets for their monthly expense reports, and then he will link them directly to the corporate income statement.

Save the revised worksheet using the **R**eplace option with the same file name, JANEXP.

Using @Functions: @SUM, @MIN, @MAX, @AVG

For the next six months, Dan Walker continues to create monthly income statements similar to the one shown in Figure 3.10.

At the end of six months, Dan wants to summarize the firm's performance. He prepares a combined income statement showing the monthly statements from January through June, along with totals for the first half of the year.

To see the worksheet Dan created for the combined income statement, retrieve the file SIXMONTH.WK1. The worksheet title tells you that the values represent thousands of dollars.

The worksheet extends below row 20. To see the rest of the worksheet, use ⬇ to

Move to: A24

Your screen should now look similar to Figure 3.11.

```
A24: [W18] '   % Sales Increase                                    READY

                A       B    C    D    E    F    G    H     I    J    K    ◄
5                       Jan  Feb  Mar  Apr  May  Jun  TOTAL MIN  MAX        ►
6                       ---- ---- ---- ---- ---- ---- ----- ---- ----      ▲
7       Sales           1998 1856 1901 1654 1733 1840                      ▼
8       Cost of Goods Sold 998 980  960  934 1010  945                     ?
9                       ---- ---- ---- ---- ---- ---- ----- ---- ----
10          Gross Margin 1000 876  941  720  723  895
11
12      Adv Expenses     112  100   85  110  124  102
13      Opr Expenses      79   88   74   88   95   99
14      Misc Expenses     36   42   31   34   22   36
15                       ---- ---- ---- ---- ---- ---- ----- ---- ----
16          Total Expenses 227 230  190  232  241  237
17          Average Expense
18
19      Net Before Tax   773  646  751  488  482  658
20      Federal Taxes    402  336  391  254  251  342
21                       ------------------------------------------------
22          Net After Tax 371 310  360  234  231  316
23                       ================================================
24          % Sales Increase                                            ■
SIXMONTH.WK1
```

Figure 3.11

The column labeled Jan is similar to the January income statement shown in Figure 3.10. The only difference is that the income figures are now displayed down a single column.

In addition to the income figures for January, this new worksheet shows the figures for February, March, April, May, and June. Dan also plans to calculate totals, as well as the minimums and maximums, for the six months. You will use 1-2-3's @functions to calculate these values.

You will begin by using the @SUM function to calculate the column TOTAL in the worksheet. Cell addresses and ranges can also be pointed in an @function. To see how to use pointing to specify the range B7 through G7 in this @function,

Move to: H7

Type: @SUM(

Move to: G7

Click: G7

Drag to: B7

The mode indicator displays POINT. You can specify a range beginning at either end of the range of cells using the keyboard or the mouse. If you are using the keyboard, you will anchor cell G7 as the beginning of the range when you

Type: . (period)

Then, using ⬅ to highlight the rest of the range,

Move to: B7

To complete the @function,

Type:)

Press: ⏎

Your screen should look similar to Figure 3.12.

```
H7: [W7] @SUM(G7..B7)                                          READY

              A          B    C    D    E    F    G    H    I    J    K   ◄
 5                       Jan  Feb  Mar  Apr  May  Jun  TOTAL MIN  MAX      ►
 6                       ---- ---- ---- ---- ---- ---- ----- ---- -----   ▲
 7   Sales              1998 1856 1901 1654 1733 1840 10982             ▼
 8   Cost of Goods Sold  998  980  960  934 1010  945                    ?
 9                       ---- ---- ---- ---- ---- ---- ----- ---- -----
10      Gross Margin     1000  876  941  720  723  895
11
12   Adv Expenses         112  100   85  110  124  102
13   Opr Expenses          79   88   74   88   95   99
14   Misc Expenses         36   42   31   34   22   36
15                       ---- ---- ---- ---- ---- ---- ----- ---- ----
16      Total Expenses    227  230  190  232  241  237
17      Average Expense
18
19   Net Before Tax       773  646  751  488  482  658
20   Federal Taxes        402  336  391  254  251  342
21                       ------------------------------------------------
22      Net After Tax     371  310  360  234  231  316
23                       ================================================
24   % Sales Increase
SIXMONTH.WK1
```

Figure 3.12

The total, 10982, is now displayed in cell H7.

Naming a Range

The same range, B7..G7, is needed in the @functions to calculate the minimum and maximum values to be displayed in columns I and J. Rather than reselect the same range, you can name the range. The named range is then used in the @function in place of the cell addresses of the range. You can use either the keyboard or the mouse to name a range.

Note If you are using a mouse, try performing the actions described here using the mouse instead of the keyboard. In this case, you can perform the same actions using your mouse.

To assign the name SALES to the range of cells B7..G7,

Move to: B7

Select: /**R**ange **N**ame

Five **R**ange **N**ame options are displayed in the control panel. They have the following effects:

Create   Assigns or modifies a range name

Delete   Removes a range name

Labels   Creates range names from a range of labels

Reset   Deletes all range names

Table   Creates a list of range names and their range addresses

A range name, which can have up to 15 characters, should be descriptive of the range contents. The following guidelines should be observed:

- Do not include spaces, semicolons, or numeric symbols in range names.

- Do not create a range name that looks like a cell address, such as B25.

- Do not begin a range name with a number or create a range name that consists entirely of numbers.

To assign the name SALES to cells B7 through G7, complete the command sequence as follows:

Create **SALES** ⏎ **B7..G7** ⏎

Another way to issue this command sequence would be to specify the range before bringing up the menu. This is called **preselecting** a range. In this example, you would move to G7, press (F4) (ABS) to anchor, highlight the range with (←), press (⏎), and then select /**R**ange **N**ame Create **SALES** (⏎). You can preselect a range any time a 1-2-3 command requires a range.

With the cell pointer in cell H7, look at the @function in the control panel. Your screen should look similar to Figure 3.13.

Named Range

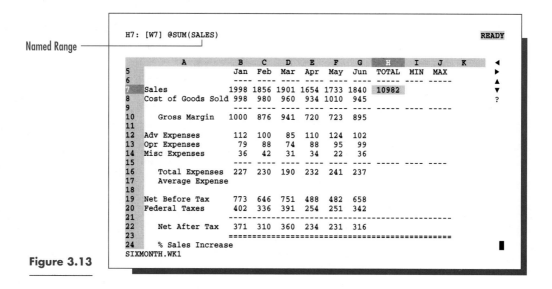

```
H7: [W7] @SUM(SALES)                                                    READY

            A        B    C    D    E    F    G    H    I    J    K     ◄
5                   Jan  Feb  Mar  Apr  May  Jun TOTAL  MIN  MAX        ►
6                   ---- ---- ---- ---- ---- ---- ----- ---- -----     ▲
7  Sales           1998 1856 1901 1654 1733 1840 10982                 ▼
8  Cost of Goods Sold 998  980  960  934 1010  945                     ?
9                   ---- ---- ---- ---- ---- ---- ----- ---- -----
10    Gross Margin 1000  876  941  720  723  895
11
12 Adv Expenses     112  100   85  110  124  102
13 Opr Expenses      79   88   74   88   95   99
14 Misc Expenses     36   42   31   34   22   36
15                  ---- ---- ---- ---- ---- ---- ----- ---- -----
16   Total Expenses 227  230  190  232  241  237
17   Average Expense
18
19 Net Before Tax   773  646  751  488  482  658
20 Federal Taxes    402  336  391  254  251  342
21                  -------------------------------------------------
22   Net After Tax  371  310  360  234  231  316
23                  =================================================
24   % Sales Increase                                                  ■
SIXMONTH.WK1
```

Figure 3.13

The @function in cell H7 uses the named range, SALES, in place of B7..G7. Naming ranges makes the range easier to enter and the worksheet easier to read and understand.

You will now use this named range with the @MIN function to find the smallest value in the defined range.

Move to: I7

Type: @MIN(SALES)

Press: ⏎

Your screen should look similar to Figure 3.14.

```
I7: @MIN(SALES)                                                    READY

          A             B    C    D    E    F    G    H    I    J    K    ◀
5                      Jan  Feb  Mar  Apr  May  Jun TOTAL  MIN  MAX       ▶
6                      ---- ---- ---- ---- ---- ---- ----- ---- -----     ▲
7  Sales             1998 1856 1901 1654 1733 1840 10982 1654            ▼
8  Cost of Goods Sold 998  980  960  934 1010  945                       ?
9                      ---- ---- ---- ---- ---- ---- ----- ---- -----
10     Gross Margin   1000  876  941  720  723  895
11
12 Adv Expenses        112  100   85  110  124  102
13 Opr Expenses         79   88   74   88   95   99
14 Misc Expenses        36   42   31   34   22   36
15                      ---- ---- ---- ---- ---- ---- ----- ---- ----
16     Total Expenses  227  230  190  232  241  237
17     Average Expense
18
19 Net Before Tax      773  646  751  488  482  658
20 Federal Taxes       402  336  391  254  251  342
21                     ----------------------------------------------
22     Net After Tax   371  310  360  234  231  316
23                     ==============================================
24     % Sales Increase                                               ▮
SIXMONTH.WK1
```

Figure 3.14

The entry in cell I7, 1654, is the smallest, or minimum, value in the SALES range. The @function is displayed in the control panel using the range name.

Next, to use the @MAX function in cell J7 to find the largest value in the defined range of cells,

Move to: J7

Type: **@MAX(SALES)**

Press: ⏎

The maximum value in the SALES range, 1998, has been entered into cell J7.

Now use the **C**opy command to copy the @functions in cells H7 through J7 to cells H8 through J8.

Move to cells H8, I8, and J8, and look at the @function in each cell. The correct range, B8..G8, is used in the @function, not the named range SALES. A named range, like an unnamed range, adjusts relative to its new location in the worksheet when it is copied. To make a named range absolute, you would enter a dollar sign before the range name (for example, $SALES).

Next, Dan Walker wants to calculate the average monthly expenses of his chain of Gourmet Sandwiches restaurants. The @AVG function will calculate the average of a range of cells.

Name the range for January's expenses by issuing the following command sequence:

/Range Name Create **JANEXP** ⏎ **B12..B14** ⏎

Then, to enter the @function,

Move to: B17

Type: **@AVG(JANEXP)**

Press: ⏎

Your screen should look similar to Figure 3.15.

```
B17: @AVG(JANEXP)                                                      READY

              A          B    C    D    E    F    G    H      I    J    K    ◄
5                       Jan  Feb  Mar  Apr  May  Jun  TOTAL  MIN  MAX        ►
6                       ---- ---- ---- ---- ---- ---- -----  ---- -----      ▲
7       Sales           1998 1856 1901 1654 1733 1840  10982 1654 1998      ▼
8       Cost of Goods Sold 998 980  960  934 1010  945   5827  934 1010
9                       ---- ---- ---- ---- ---- ---- -----  ---- -----      ?
10        Gross Margin  1000  876  941  720  723  895
11
12      Adv Expenses    112  100   85  110  124  102
13      Opr Expenses     79   88   74   88   95   99
14      Misc Expenses    36   42   31   34   22   36
15                      ---- ---- ---- ---- ---- ---- -----  ---- ----
16        Total Expenses 227  230  190  232  241  237
17        Average Expense 76
18
19      Net Before Tax  773  646  751  488  482  658
20      Federal Taxes   402  336  391  254  251  342
21                      -----------------------------------------------------
22        Net After Tax 371  310  360  234  231  316
23                      =====================================================
24        % Sales Increase                                                  ■
SIXMONTH.WK1
```

Figure 3.15

The average expense for the month of January appears in cell B17.

To complete the worksheet, the next step would be to name the other ranges and to copy the @functions for TOTAL, MIN, and MAX down their respective columns and the @function for the Average Expense across the row. This has already been done for you and saved in the file COMPLETE.WK1. Retrieve this file. (You do not need to save the current file.)

To see the rest of the worksheet, use ⬇ to

Move to: A24

Setting Cell Formats

Dan would like to determine the percentage increase (or decrease) in each month's sales over the previous month's sales. To enter the formula for this calculation,

Move to: C24

Type: **(C7 – B7)/B7**

Press: ⏎

Your screen should look similar to Figure 3.16.

```
C24: (C7-B7)/B7                                                    READY

                A       B      C     D     E     F     G     H     I     J      ◄
        5               Jan    Feb   Mar   Apr   May   Jun   TOTAL MIN   MAX    ►
        6               -----  ----- ----- ----- ----- ----- ----- ----- -----  ▲
        7  Sales        1998   1856  1901  1654  1733  1840  10982 1654  1998   ▼
        8  Cost of Goods Sold  998  980  960  934  1010  945  5827  934  1010   ?
        9               -----  ----- ----- ----- ----- ----- ----- ----- -----
       10     Gross Margin 1000  876  941  720  723  895  5155  720  1000
       11
       12  Adv Expenses  112    100   85    110   124   102   633   85    124
       13  Opr Expenses  79     88    74    88    95    99    523   74    99
       14  Misc Expenses 36     42    31    34    22    36    201   22    42
       15               -----  ----- ----- ----- ----- ----- ----- ----- ----
       16     Total Expenses 227  230  190  232  241  237  1357  190  241
       17     Average Expense 76  77   63   77   80   79   452   63    80
       18
       19  Net Before Tax 773   646   751   488   482   658   3798  482   773
       20  Federal Taxes  402   336   391   254   251   342   1975  251   402
       21               -------------------------------------------------------
       22     Net After Tax 371  310  360  234  231  316  1823  231  371
       23               =======================================================
       24     % Sales Increase       0                                          ■
      COMPLETE.WK1
```

Figure 3.16

The calculated value, 0 (actually −0 on screen), does not seem correct. If you manually evaluated the formula in cell C24, you would find that the value should be approximately −7 percent.

To find the problem, access the Global Settings screen by issuing the following command:

/**W**orksheet **G**lobal

Your screen should look similar to Figure 3.17.

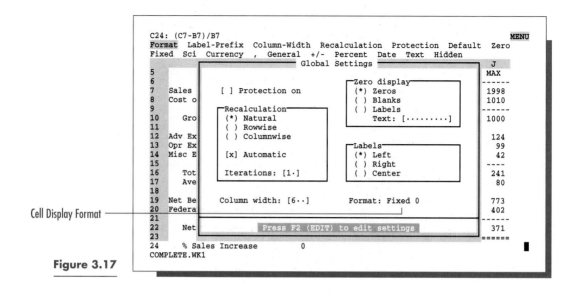

Cell Display Format

Figure 3.17

```
C24: (C7-B7)/B7                                                    MENU
Format  Label-Prefix  Column-Width  Recalculation  Protection  Default  Zero
Fixed  Sci  Currency  ,  General  +/-  Percent  Date  Text  Hidden
                          ═══ Global Settings ═══                    J
 5                                                                   MAX
 6                                                                   ------
 7   Sales       [ ] Protection on        ┌Zero display┐            1998
 8   Cost o                                (*) Zeros                 1010
 9               ┌Recalculation┐           ( ) Blanks                ------
10      Gro      (*) Natural               ( ) Labels                1000
11               ( ) Rowwise                   Text: [.........]
12   Adv Ex      ( ) Columnwise                                       124
13   Opr Ex                                └────────────┘              99
14   Misc E      [x] Automatic            ┌Labels┐                     42
15                                         (*) Left                  ----
16      Tot      Iterations: [1.]          ( ) Right                  241
17      Ave                                ( ) Center                  80
18
19   Net Be      Column width: [6..]        Format: Fixed 0           773
20   Federa                                └──────────────           402
21                                                                   ------
22      Net       Press F2 (EDIT) to edit settings                    371
23                                                                   ======
24      % Sales Increase            0                                    ▮
COMPLETE.WK1
```

The bottom right corner of the screen indicates that the current format is Fixed 0. This tells you that the worksheet has been formatted to display numbers without decimals (zero decimal places). Therefore, 0.07 appeared on the screen as merely 0. You can correct this by changing the format of 0.07 to 7%. To return to the worksheet,

Press: (CTRL)-(BREAK)

To change the cell display format to Percent, issue the following command sequence:

/Range **F**ormat

Your screen should look similar to Figure 3.18.

Format Options ────
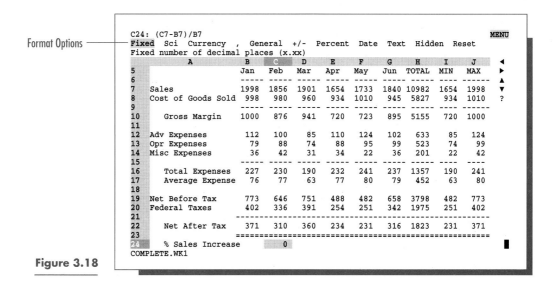

Figure 3.18

The **F**ormat command lists 11 options in the control panel. From these, you can specify how numeric values are to be displayed in the worksheet. Since you want to convert the value in cell C24 to a percentage,

Select: **P**ercent

The control panel prompts you to specify the number of decimal places you want displayed. The default setting for decimal places is 2, but you want 0. Continue the command sequence as follows:

0

The next prompt asks you to define the range of cells to be formatted. To accept the displayed range (C24..C24),

Press:

Your screen should look similar to Figure 3.19.

Cell Format

```
C24: (P0) (C7-B7)/B7                                                    READY

            A        B     C     D     E     F     G     H     I     J    ◄
    5                Jan   Feb   Mar   Apr   May   Jun  TOTAL   MIN   MAX  ►
    6               ----- ----- ----- ----- ----- ----- ----- ----- -----  ▲
    7  Sales        1998  1856  1901  1654  1733  1840 10982  1654  1998   ▼
    8  Cost of Goods Sold 998   980   960   934  1010   945  5827   934  1010  ?
    9               ----- ----- ----- ----- ----- ----- ----- ----- -----
   10      Gross Margin  1000   876   941   720   723   895  5155   720  1000
   11
   12  Adv Expenses   112   100    85   110   124   102   633    85   124
   13  Opr Expenses    79    88    74    88    95    99   523    74    99
   14  Misc Expenses   36    42    31    34    22    36   201    22    42
   15               ----- ----- ----- ----- ----- ----- ----- ----- ----
   16      Total Expenses  227   230   190   232   241   237  1357   190   241
   17      Average Expense  76    77    63    77    80    79   452    63    80
   18
   19  Net Before Tax  773   646   751   488   482   658  3798   482   773
   20  Federal Taxes   402   336   391   254   251   342  1975   251   402
   21               -------------------------------------------------------
   22      Net After Tax  371   310   360   234   231   316  1823   231   371
   23               =======================================================
   24      % Sales Increase    -7%                                         ▮
   COMPLETE.WK1
```

Figure 3.19

The **F**ormat **P**ercent command took the calculated value in cell C24 and multiplied it by 100. It also displays a percent sign (%) after the value. The result, −7%, shows that Dan's sales declined by 7 percent from the previous month.

The first line in the control panel now displays the cell format as (P0). The P tells you the cell format is Percent, and the zero shows the number of decimal places.

Copy the formula in cell C24 to cells D24 through G24.

The **C**opy command not only copied the formula, it also copied the cell format.

Next Dan wants to add dollar signs and commas to the worksheet. You just used the **R**ange **F**ormat command to format the values in a selected range of cells. Now you will use the /**W**orksheet **G**lobal **F**ormat command to format the values in all worksheet cells, except those previously formatted with the **R**ange **F**ormat command.

To format the worksheet globally to display values with dollar signs and zero decimal places, issue the following command sequence:

/**W**orksheet **G**lobal **F**ormat **C**urrency **0** ⏎

Your screen should look similar to Figure 3.20.

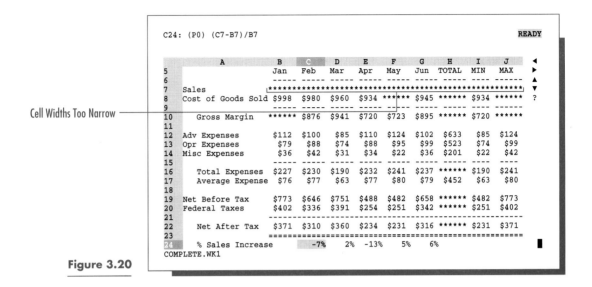

Cell Widths Too Narrow

Figure 3.20

All the values in the worksheet are now formatted to display dollar signs and commas except the values in cells C24 through G24, which were formatted with the **R**ange **F**ormat command.

As indicated by the asterisks, some cells are not large enough to display the cell contents including the dollar sign and commas.

To increase the column widths of columns B through J, issue the following command sequence:

/**W**orksheet **C**olumn **C**olumn-Range **S**et-Width **B24..J24** ⏎

The current width of these columns is six characters. Since you cannot be sure how wide the column widths need to be to display the values, you can increase the width space by space and see how the worksheet adjusts at the same time. Try doing this:

Press: →

The column width increased to seven characters, but that is still not enough to display all the values.

Press: →

All the values are displayed with the column width set at eight characters. To complete the command sequence,

Press: ⌨

Your screen should look similar to Figure 3.21.

```
C24: (P0) [W8] (C7-B7)/B7                                              READY

              A           B        C        D        E        F        G      ◄
5                        Jan      Feb      Mar      Apr      May      Jun     ►
6                      -------  -------  -------  -------  -------  -------    ▲
7     Sales           $1,998   $1,856   $1,901   $1,654   $1,733   $1,840    ▼
8     Cost of Goods Sold $998    $980     $960     $934   $1,010     $945    ?
9                      -------  -------  -------  -------  -------  -------
10       Gross Margin $1,000     $876     $941     $720     $723     $895
11
12    Adv Expenses      $112     $100      $85     $110     $124     $102
13    Opr Expenses       $79      $88      $74      $88      $95      $99
14    Misc Expenses      $36      $42      $31      $34      $22      $36
15                     -------  -------  -------  -------  -------  -------
16       Total Expenses $227     $230     $190     $232     $241     $237
17       Average Expense $76      $77      $63      $77      $80      $79
18
19    Net Before Tax    $773     $646     $751     $488     $482     $658
20    Federal Taxes     $402     $336     $391     $254     $251     $342
21                     --------------------------------------------------
22       Net After Tax  $371     $310     $360     $234     $231     $316
23                     ==================================================
24       % Sales Increase        -7%       2%     -13%       5%       6%    ■
COMPLETE.WK1
```

Figure 3.21

The asterisks have been replaced by the values in the cells. However, because you increased the column widths, the TOTAL, MIN, and MAX columns are no longer displayed in the window.

To see the TOTAL, MIN, and MAX columns, use → to

Move to: J24

Your screen should look similar to Figure 3.22.

Row Labels in Column A
Not Displayed

```
J24: [W8]                                                      READY

        B       C       D       E       F       G       H       I       J     ◄
5      Jan     Feb     Mar     Apr     May     Jun    TOTAL    MIN     MAX    ►
6     -------  -------  -------  -------  -------  -------  ------   ----   --------  ▲
7    $1,998  $1,856  $1,901  $1,654  $1,733  $1,840 $10,982  $1,654  $1,998  ▼
8      $998    $980    $960    $934  $1,010    $945  $5,827    $934  $1,010   ?
9     -------  -------  -------  -------  -------  -------  ------   ----   --------
10   $1,000    $876    $941    $720    $723    $895  $5,155    $720  $1,000
11
12     $112    $100     $85    $110    $124    $102    $633     $85    $124
13      $79     $88     $74     $88     $95     $99    $523     $74     $99
14      $36     $42     $31     $34     $22     $36    $201     $22     $42
15    -------  -------  -------  -------  -------  -------  ------   ----   ----
16     $227    $230    $190    $232    $241    $237  $1,357    $190    $241
17      $76     $77     $63     $77     $80     $79    $452     $63     $80
18
19     $773    $646    $751    $488    $482    $658  $3,798    $482    $773
20     $402    $336    $391    $254    $251    $342  $1,975    $251    $402
21    ---------------------------------------------------------------------------
22     $371    $310    $360    $234    $231    $316  $1,823    $231    $371
23    ===========================================================================
24  e          -7%      2%    -13%      5%      6%                            ■
COMPLETE.WK1
```

Figure 3.22

Although you can now see the TOTAL, MIN, and MAX columns, you cannot see the row labels in column A. This makes it difficult to understand the information displayed in the window. Lab 4 will help you correct this problem.

Creating a Backup File

Many times you may want to use the same file name when you save a file, but you also want to keep a copy of the last version of the file on the disk. You can do this by creating a backup file when you save the worksheet. Issue the following command sequence:

/**F**ile **S**ave ⏎ **B**ackup

The old version of the worksheet has been saved as COMPLETE.BAK and the current version as COMPLETE.WK1. To retrieve a backup file, you must enter the file name with the .BAK file extension. The backup file will not be displayed in the list of .WK1 files. Alternatively, you could rename the backup file and change the file extension to .WK1. Then you could retrieve it like any other worksheet file.

Finally, print Dan's six-month income statement, and exit 1-2-3.

@AVG: Calculates the average in a range of cells.

Circular reference: Occurs when a formula refers directly or indirectly to the cell that contains that formula. The status indicator displays CIRC whenever 1-2-3 detects a circular reference.

Linking formula: A formula entered in the target file that creates a link to a cell in the source file.

@MAX: Calculates the highest value in a range of cells.

@MIN: Calculates the lowest value in a range of cells.

Source file: The file that supplies the data when files are linked.

@SUM: Calculates the total value in a range of cells.

Target file: The file that retrieves the data when files are linked.

Worksheet Status screen: Displays the current worksheet settings.

Practice Problems and Cases

Matching

1. @MAX
2. @AVG
3. CIRC
4. $10.99
5. *****
6. +<<MRKEXP>>C10
7. /FSR
8. /WGFC0
9. /WS
10. /RNC

_____ 5 **a.** indicates insufficient cell width

_____ 7 **b.** saves and replaces a worksheet file

_____ 6 **c.** linking formula

_____ 3 **d.** status indicator for circular reference

_____ 8 **e.** globally formats a range as currency with no decimals

_____ 1 **f.** calculates the highest value in a range

_____ 9 **g.** displays a Worksheet Status screen

_____ 4 **h.** a number in currency format

_____ 2 **i.** calculates the average in a range

_____ 10 **j.** names a range

Multiple Choice

Jenna has been working on a quarterly income statement worksheet. The figure below shows Jenna's current worksheet screen. Use the screen to answer the following questions.

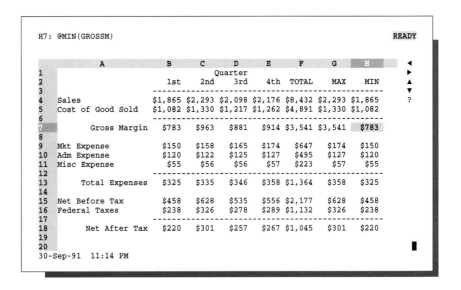

```
H7: @MIN(GROSSM)                                                    READY

              A          B      C      D      E      F      G      H      ◄
1                             Quarter                                     ►
2                        1st    2nd    3rd    4th  TOTAL    MAX    MIN     ▲
3                     ------------------------------------------------    ▼
4   Sales             $1,865 $2,293 $2,098 $2,176 $8,432 $2,293 $1,865    ?
5   Cost of Good Sold $1,082 $1,330 $1,217 $1,262 $4,891 $1,330 $1,082
6                     ------------------------------------------------
7         Gross Margin  $783   $963   $881         $914 $3,541 $3,541   $783
8
9   Mkt Expense         $150   $158   $165   $174   $647   $174   $150
10  Adm Expense         $120   $122   $125   $127   $495   $127   $120
11  Misc Expense         $55    $56    $56    $57   $223    $57    $55
12                     ------------------------------------------------
13       Total Expenses  $325   $335   $346   $358 $1,364   $358   $325
14
15  Net Before Tax       $458   $628   $535   $556 $2,177   $628   $458
16  Federal Taxes        $238   $326   $278   $289 $1,132   $326   $238
17                     ------------------------------------------------
18        Net After Tax  $220   $301   $257   $267 $1,045   $301   $220
19
20
30-Sep-91  11:14 PM
```

1. The current worksheet cell is:

   a. C6   c. H7

   b. A5   d. A1

2. The named range for Sales would be:

   a. A4..D4   c. A6..E6

   b. B4..E4   d. B6..D6

3. The file name is displayed on the ___status___ line.

   a. control panel   c. worksheet

   b. mode indicator   d. status

4. The entry in cell G12 has the value of:

   a. 0   c. 881

   b. 2177   d. 301

5. The command to globally change the format to currency with zero decimal places would be:

   a. /WGFC0   c. /WFC0

   b. /FGC0   d. /WWFC0

6. The command to hide column F is:

   a. /WGCH   c. /CH

   b. /WCH   d. /WH

7. The formula in cell G7 references cells:

   a. B4..F4   c. B7..E7

   b. C5..F5   d. B7..F7

8. If the formula in cell F4 is @SUM(SALES) and it is copied down to cell F9, the formula in cell F9 would be:

   a. @SUM(SALES)   c. @SUM(B9..E9)

   b. @SUM(GROSSM)   d. +B9+C9+D9+E9

9. If the function @MIN(C4..C16) were included in a cell in the worksheet, the value appearing in that cell would be:

   a. 0   c. 301

   b. 56   d. 335

10. The location of a circular reference is displayed on the _____.

   a. status line   c. worksheet area

   b. status screen   d. control panel

Cases

1. Lisa Oswald has been working on a six-month income statement for her Antique Doll Shop. She has been having some problems. Retrieve the file PROB3-1.WK1 to see the worksheet Lisa has created.

   a. Put your name in cell A1 and the current date in cell A2.

   b. Locate the source of the CIRC reference, and correct the formula or @function causing the reference. Does the CIRC message disappear? If not, again locate the source of the CIRC reference, and correct it until it disappears.

   c. Appropriately name the ranges for Sales and the individual expenses. Complete the TOTAL column by entering the @function to SUM the columns B through G.

d. Complete the MIN and MAX columns by entering the @functions to calculate the minimum and maximum values in columns B through G.

e. Hide columns B through G. Print the worksheet. Unhide columns B through G.

f. Enter the formula to calculate the percentage increase (or decrease) in each month's sales over the previous month's sales in cell C24. Format the cell to display percent with zero decimal places. Copy the formula from cell C24 to D24 through G24.

g. Globally change the worksheet to display currency with zero decimal places. Increase the column widths to display the values. What is the new column width?

h. Save the new version of the worksheet as HWLAB3-1.

i. Print the worksheet.

2. Lee Ramage has asked the marketing director to create a worksheet of his department's expenses for January.

a. Retrieve the file PROB3-2.WK1.

b. Complete the worksheet by entering the @SUM function to total the marketing expenses for January.

c. Note the location of the total, and save the file using the **R**eplace option.

d. Lee is now ready to include the total from the Marketing Director's worksheet in her Income Statement for January 1997. Retrieve the file PROB3-2A.WK1.

e. Enter the formula in cell E8 to calculate Gross Margin.

f. Enter a linking formula in cell D10 that refers to the cell that contains the total of the Marketing Director's worksheet.

g. Enter a formula in cell E14 to calculate total expenses.

h. Enter your name in cell A1 and the current date in cell A2.

i. Save the new worksheet as HWLAB3-2.

j. Print the worksheet.

3. Donna's Confectionery Delights is having a summer sale. The four salespeople at one of her stores decide it would be fun to see who could sell the most chocolate in August. The following table shows the amount of their sales by week.

Sales

Name	Week 1	Week 2	Week 3	Week 4	Total	Avg
Jill	398	250	343	145		
David	250	410	174	268		
Kari	243	344	290	399		
Thomas	189	375	313	250		

Use this data to create a worksheet. Enter your name in cell A1 and the current date in cell A2.

a. Appropriately name each person's sales range.

b. Use the @SUM function and the named ranges to calculate each person's total sales.

c. Use the @AVG function and the named ranges to calculate each person's average sales.

d. Donna decides she would like to know what total sales are for each week. Enter the label and function to calculate total sales for the four weeks.

e. Enter the @AVG function to find the average of total weekly sales.

f. Hide the columns containing the individual weekly sales numbers. Print the worksheet.

g. Unhide the columns, save the file as HWLAB3-3, and print the worksheet.

4. Retrieve the file PROB3-4.WK1. Enter your name in cell A1 and the current date in cell A2. The file contains some circular references that need correcting. Complete the worksheet by entering the appropriate formulas. Save the corrected worksheet file as HWLAB3-4, and then print the worksheet.

5. Create a six-month income statement for Joe's Drive-In Burgers. (*Note:* The format will be the same as the one used in the lab.) Use appropriate formulas, and format it to display dollar signs with zero decimal places.

Enter your name in cell A1 and the current date in cell A2, save the file as HWLAB3-5, and print the worksheet.

6. Retrieve the file PROB3-6.WK1. The file contains labels for a six-month income statement. Change the file to contain titles, underlines, values, and formulas. Include columns to find the MAX, MIN, and AVG of each named range. What is your percentage of sales increase? Enter your name in cell A1 and the current date in cell A2, save the file as HWLAB3-6, and print the worksheet.

Lab 4

Managing a Large Worksheet

Objectives

In Lab 4, you will learn how to:

- Freeze horizontal and vertical titles
- Create, scroll, and use windows
- Extract and combine worksheets
- Use what-if analysis
- Use the @NOW function
- Enter and justify text
- Print in compressed mode
- Restrict file access using passwords

Case Study (Part 2)

At the end of Lab 3, Dan Walker had completed an income statement for a six-month period. Once the income statement was formatted to display currency, however, it could no longer be contained in one window. In Lab 4, Dan has expanded the income statement to cover a one-year period. The increased size of the worksheet has made it more difficult to handle. You will follow Dan as he learns how to manage a large worksheet and use what-if analysis to help with his company's long-range financial planning.

Freezing Titles

Dan Walker has extended the six-month statement for Walker's Gourmet Sandwiches to a full year. To see this worksheet, load 1-2-3, and retrieve the file YEAR.WK1.

This worksheet contains income statement figures for 12 months. The worksheet extends beyond column F and below row 20. Although there are quicker ways to move around the worksheet for this lab, use the arrow keys as directed. You need to do this so that your display screen will appear the same as the figures in this lab.

To view the rest of the worksheet, use ⬇ and ➔ to:

Move to: P24

Your screen should look similar to Figure 4.1.

```
P24:                                                              READY

          I        J        K        L        M        N        O        P      ◄
5                                                                                ►
6        Aug      Sep      Oct      Nov      Dec     TOTAL      MIN      MAX     ▲
7      -------  -------  -------  -------  -------  -------  -------  -------     ▼
8      $1,872   $1,921   $1,741   $1,675   $1,891  $21,976   $1,654   $1,998    ?
9      $1,157   $1,194   $1,235   $1,232   $1,575  $13,395     $934   $1,575
10     -------  -------  -------  -------  -------  -------  -------  -------
11       $716     $727     $506     $443     $317   $8,581     $317   $1,000
12
13       $114     $116     $116     $171     $181   $1,422      $85     $181
14        $99      $79      $73     $100      $65   $1,032      $65     $100
15        $36      $47      $24      $35      $17     $403      $17      $47
16     -------  -------  -------  -------  -------  -------  -------  -------
17       $249     $242     $213     $306     $263   $2,857     $190     $306
18
19       $466     $486     $293     $137      $53   $5,724      $53     $773
20       $242     $253     $152      $71      $28   $2,977      $28     $402
21     -------  -------  -------  -------  -------  -------  -------  -------
22       $224     $233     $141      $66      $26   $2,748      $26     $371
23     =======  =======  =======  =======  =======  =======  =======  =======
24        -1%       3%      -9%      -4%      13%                              ▮
22-Aug-91  04:19 AM
```

Figure 4.1

This worksheet provides a convenient way for Walker's management team to summarize the company's annual financial performance and to analyze its monthly performance. However, the worksheet is difficult to read.

Look, for example, at the entry $716 in cell I11. It is difficult to remember what that figure represents. Is it income, an expense, a total, or a tax?

To see the row labels in column A, use ⬅ to

Move to: A24

You can now see that the figures in row 11 are for gross margin.

Whenever a worksheet extends beyond a single window and the row labels are no longer visible, understanding the worksheet is difficult. It would be much more convenient if you could keep the titles in column A in the window all the time. **Freezing titles** keeps row and column headings on the screen even when you scroll the windows.

To freeze a vertical column of titles, locate the cell pointer one column to the right of the column you want to freeze. To freeze column A,

Move to: B24

Then issue the following command sequence:

/**W**orksheet **T**itles **V**ertical

Nothing appears to have happened.

Press: ⬅

The program does not allow the cell pointer to move into column A, the frozen column.

Now watch the monthly figures scroll as you use ➡ to

Move to: P24

Your screen should look similar to Figure 4.2.

Frozen Vertical Titles

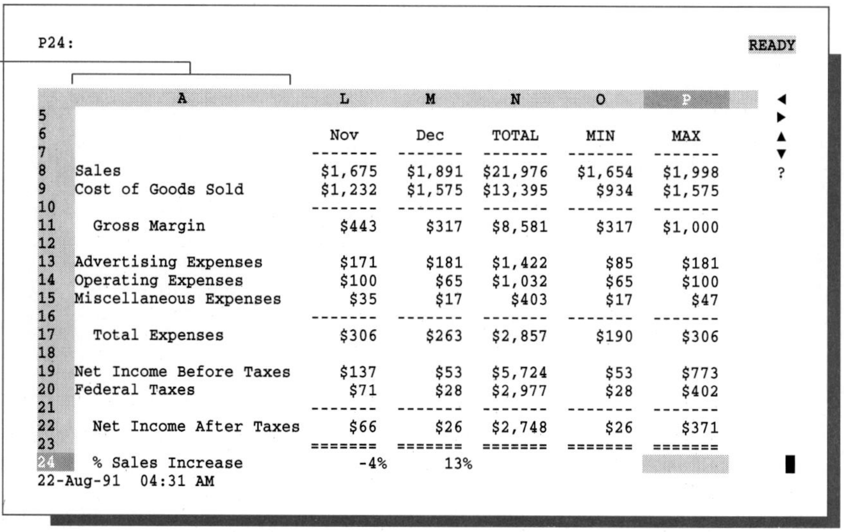

```
P24:                                                                    READY

                  A          L       M       N       O       P
 5
 6                          Nov     Dec    TOTAL    MIN     MAX
 7                        -------  ------- ------- ------- -------
 8    Sales               $1,675  $1,891 $21,976  $1,654  $1,998
 9    Cost of Goods Sold  $1,232  $1,575 $13,395    $934  $1,575
10                        -------  ------- ------- ------- -------
11      Gross Margin        $443    $317  $8,581    $317  $1,000
12
13    Advertising Expenses  $171    $181  $1,422     $85    $181
14    Operating Expenses    $100     $65  $1,032     $65    $100
15    Miscellaneous Expenses $35     $17    $403     $17     $47
16                        -------  ------- ------- ------- -------
17      Total Expenses      $306    $263  $2,857    $190    $306
18
19    Net Income Before Taxes $137   $53  $5,724     $53    $773
20    Federal Taxes          $71     $28  $2,977     $28    $402
21                        -------  ------- ------- ------- -------
22      Net Income After Taxes $66   $26  $2,748     $26    $371
23                        ======= ======= ======= ======= =======
24    % Sales Increase       -4%     13%
22-Aug-91  04:31 AM
```

Figure 4.2

Column A does not move. You have frozen column A so that the row labels always appear in the window. This makes the worksheet much easier to read and to use.

To unfreeze, or clear, the frozen titles, issue the following command sequence:

/**W**orksheet **T**itles **C**lear

Your screen should now look similar to Figure 4.3.

```
P24:                                                              READY

        K       L       M       N       O       P       Q    R   ◄
5                                                                ►
6      Oct     Nov     Dec    TOTAL    MIN     MAX              ▲
7    ------- ------- ------- ------- ------- -------            ▼
8    $1,741  $1,675  $1,891 $21,976  $1,654  $1,998            ?
9    $1,235  $1,232  $1,575 $13,395    $934  $1,575
10   ------- ------- ------- ------- ------- -------
11    $506    $443    $317   $8,581    $317  $1,000
12
13    $116    $171    $181   $1,422     $85    $181
14     $73    $100     $65   $1,032     $65    $100
15     $24     $35     $17     $403     $17     $47
16   ------- ------- ------- ------- ------- -------
17    $213    $306    $263   $2,857    $190    $306
18
19    $293    $137     $53   $5,724     $53    $773
20    $152     $71     $28   $2,977     $28    $402
21   ------- ------- ------- ------- ------- -------
22    $141     $66     $26   $2,748     $26    $371
23   ======= ======= ======= ======= ======= =======
24     -9%     -4%     13%                                      ■
22-Aug-91   04:32 AM
```

Figure 4.3

Column A no longer appears in the window.

To confirm that the titles are unfrozen, use ⬅ to

Move to: A24

The cell pointer can now be moved into column A.

Freezing and unfreezing titles horizontally across a row is just as easy as freezing and unfreezing them vertically down a column. To do so, position the cell pointer one row below the row to be frozen. Everything above that row will remain stationary on your screen.

To freeze the rows above row 8, use ⬆ to

Move to: A8

Then issue the following command sequence:

/**W**orksheet **T**itles **H**orizontal

To confirm that the titles are frozen,

Press: ⬆

Next, use ⊥ to

Move to: A28

Your screen should now look similar to Figure 4.4.

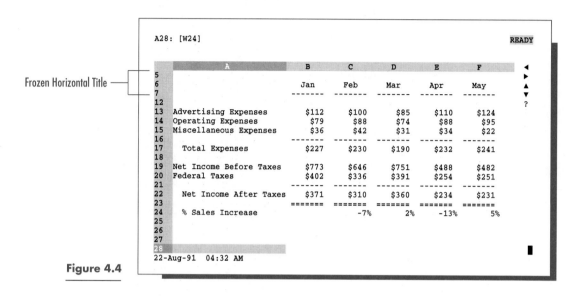

Frozen Horizontal Title

```
A28: [W24]                                                            READY

              A            B        C        D        E        F       ◄
 5                                                                     ►
 6                        Jan      Feb      Mar      Apr      May      ▲
 7                      -------  -------  -------  -------  -------     ▼
12                                                                     ?
13   Advertising Expenses  $112    $100     $85     $110     $124
14   Operating Expenses     $79     $88     $74      $88      $95
15   Miscellaneous Expenses $36     $42     $31      $34      $22
16                       -------  -------  -------  -------  -------
17      Total Expenses    $227    $230     $190     $232     $241
18
19   Net Income Before Taxes $773  $646    $751     $488     $482
20   Federal Taxes         $402    $336     $391     $254     $251
21                       -------  -------  -------  -------  -------
22      Net Income After Taxes $371 $310    $360     $234     $231
23                       =======  =======  =======  =======  =======
24      % Sales Increase           -7%      2%      -13%      5%
25
26
27
28

22-Aug-91  04:32 AM
```

Figure 4.4

As you scroll the worksheet, rows 5, 6, and 7 remain fixed on the screen.

There may be times when you will want to move the cell pointer to a cell that is within a frozen row or column, such as cell A5 in this worksheet. To do this, use F5, the GOTO feature.

Press: F5 (GOTO)

Type: **A5**

Press: ↵

Your screen should look similar to Figure 4.5.

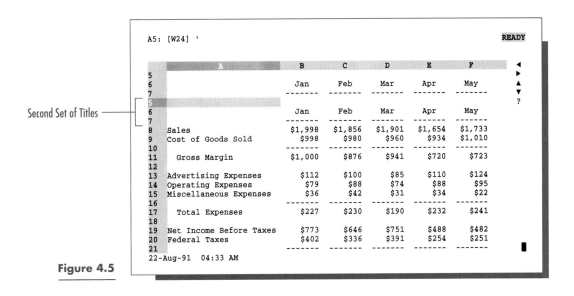

Second Set of Titles

```
A5: [W24] '                                                          READY

                              A           B       C       D       E       F      ◄
   5                                                                             ►
   6                                       Jan     Feb     Mar     Apr     May    ▲
   7                                      ------- ------- ------- ------- -------  ▼
   5                                                                             ?
   6                                       Jan     Feb     Mar     Apr     May
   7                                      ------- ------- ------- ------- -------
   8   Sales                             $1,998  $1,856  $1,901  $1,654  $1,733
   9   Cost of Goods Sold                  $998    $980    $960    $934  $1,010
  10                                      ------- ------- ------- ------- -------
  11     Gross Margin                    $1,000    $876    $941    $720    $723
  12
  13   Advertising Expenses               $112    $100     $85    $110    $124
  14   Operating Expenses                  $79     $88     $74     $88     $95
  15   Miscellaneous Expenses              $36     $42     $31     $34     $22
  16                                      ------- ------- ------- ------- -------
  17     Total Expenses                   $227    $230    $190    $232    $241
  18
  19   Net Income Before Taxes            $773    $646    $751    $488    $482
  20   Federal Taxes                      $402    $336    $391    $254    $251
  21                                      ------- ------- ------- ------- -------    ■
  22-Aug-91  04:33 AM
```

Figure 4.5

A second set of frozen horizontal titles is displayed immediately below the first set. The cell pointer is positioned in a previously frozen cell.

Press: (↑) four times

You can now move into and use any of the previously frozen rows. To clear the second set of frozen titles:

Press: (PGDN)

Press: (PGDN)

To verify that the original frozen horizontal titles are again in effect,

Press: (↑)

The cell pointer cannot be moved above row 8.

Note To clear a second set of frozen vertical titles, you would use the (CTRL)-(→) and (CTRL)-(←) sequence.

Clear the frozen titles by issuing the following command sequence:

/**W**orksheet **T**itles **C**lear

As you have probably already guessed, you can also freeze titles horizontally and vertically at the same time. To do this, you must position the cell pointer one column to the right of the column to be frozen and one row below the row to be frozen. In the case of Dan's worksheet, the appropriate cell is B8. Everything to the left and above that cell will be frozen.

Move to: B8

Freeze the titles to the left of and above the cell pointer by issuing the following command sequence:

/**W**orksheet **T**itles **B**oth

Press: ⬆

Press: ⬅

The rows above row 8 and the column to the left of column B are frozen. Now, watch your screen closely as you use ➡ and ⬇ to

Move to: P8

Move to: P28

Your screen should look similar to Figure 4.6.

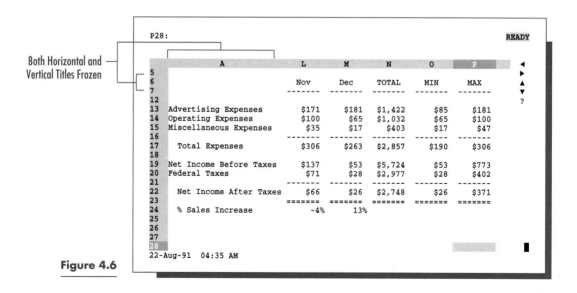

Both Horizontal and Vertical Titles Frozen

Figure 4.6

The vertical titles (column A) and the horizontal titles (above row 8) remain frozen on the screen as you scroll through the worksheet. To return to the upper left position of the worksheet,

Press: (HOME)

The HOME key returns the cell pointer to cell B8 rather than to cell A1 because all cells above and to the left of cell B8 are frozen.

Creating and Scrolling Windows

The frozen titles greatly improve the readability of the worksheet, but it is still awkward for Walker's management team to make certain types of comparisons.

Dan Walker wants to compare his monthly income figures to the annual totals. For example, he wants to compare the income figures for the month of April, located in column E, with the annual totals, located in column N. Because of the size of the worksheet, however, these two columns cannot be displayed at the same time in a single window.

Worksheets are viewed through windows. So far, you have used only one window at a time. You will now use the /**W**orksheet **W**indow command to create two windows on your screen at the same time.

To create a vertical window between columns M and N, move the cell pointer anywhere in column N. Using (→),

Move to: N8

Issue the following command sequence:

/**W**orksheet **W**indow **V**ertical

Your screen should look similar to Figure 4.7.

```
M8: 1891.4405075                                                    READY

              A          J        K        L        M         N    ◄
        5                                                   5       ►
        6                 Sep      Oct      Nov      Dec     6 TOTAL ▲
        7               -------  -------  -------  ------- 7        ▼
        8  Sales        $1,921   $1,741   $1,675   $1,891  8 $21,976 ?
        9  Cost of Goods Sold $1,194 $1,235 $1,232 $1,575 9 $13,395
       10               -------  -------  -------  ------- 10
       11    Gross Margin $727    $506     $443     $317  11 $8,581
       12                                                  12
       13  Advertising Expenses $116 $116   $171     $181 13 $1,422
       14  Operating Expenses  $79    $73    $100      $65 14 $1,032
       15  Miscellaneous Expenses $47 $24    $35      $17 15  $403
       16               -------  -------  -------  ------- 16
       17    Total Expenses $242   $213     $306     $263 17 $2,857
       18                                                  18
       19  Net Income Before Taxes $486 $293 $137     $53 19 $5,724
       20  Federal Taxes  $253    $152     $71      $28 20 $2,977
       21               -------  -------  -------  ------- 21 -------
       22    Net Income After Taxes $233 $141 $66     $26 22 $2,748
       23               =======  =======  =======  ======= 23 =======
       24    % Sales Increase  3%     -9%      -4%     13% 24
     22-Aug-91  04:36 AM
```

Row Numbers for
Second Window

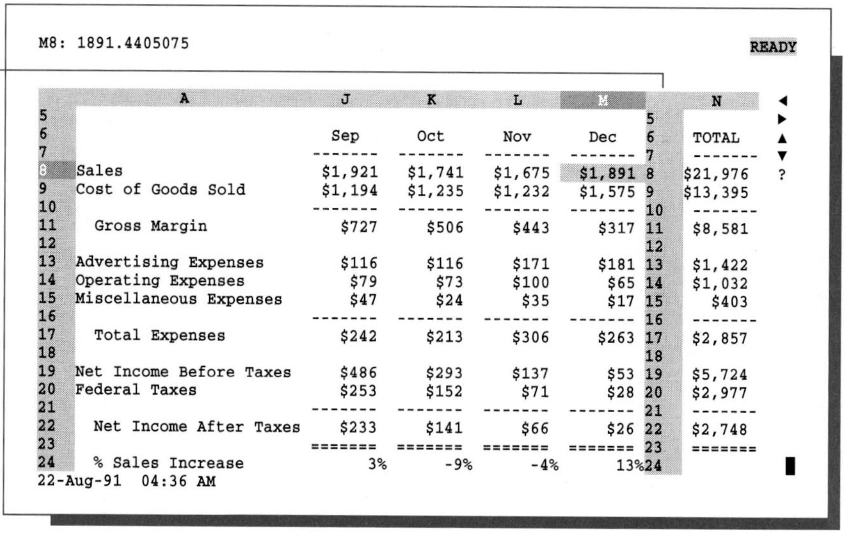

Figure 4.7

A new column of row numbers appears between columns M and N, separating the two windows. The cell pointer is currently in the left window. Now watch your screen closely as you use ⬅ to

Move to: B8

Your screen should look similar to Figure 4.8.

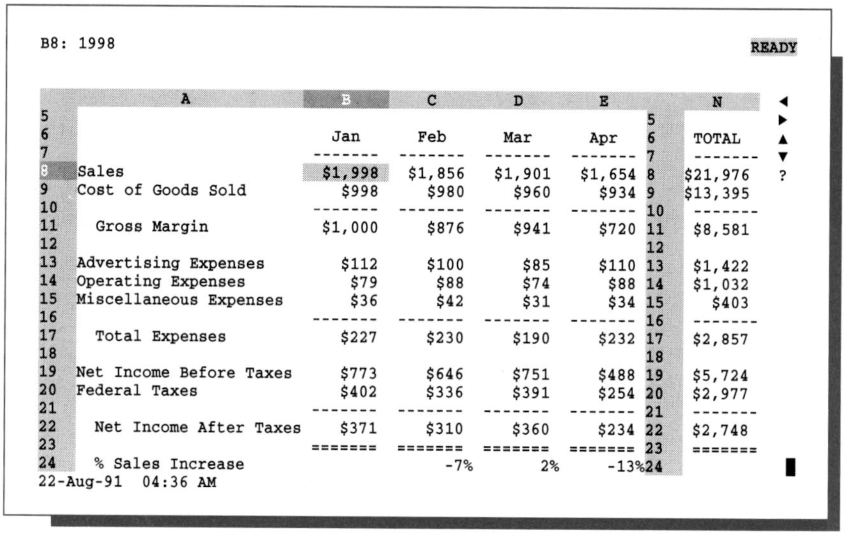

```
B8: 1998                                                           READY

              A          B        C        D        E         N    ◄
        5                                                   5       ►
        6                 Jan      Feb      Mar      Apr     6 TOTAL ▲
        7               -------  -------  -------  ------- 7        ▼
        8  Sales        $1,998   $1,856   $1,901   $1,654  8 $21,976 ?
        9  Cost of Goods Sold $998 $980    $960     $934  9 $13,395
       10               -------  -------  -------  ------- 10
       11    Gross Margin $1,000  $876     $941     $720  11 $8,581
       12                                                  12
       13  Advertising Expenses $112 $100   $85     $110 13 $1,422
       14  Operating Expenses  $79    $88    $74      $88 14 $1,032
       15  Miscellaneous Expenses $36 $42    $31      $34 15  $403
       16               -------  -------  -------  ------- 16
       17    Total Expenses $227   $230     $190     $232 17 $2,857
       18                                                  18
       19  Net Income Before Taxes $773 $646 $751    $488 19 $5,724
       20  Federal Taxes  $402    $336     $391     $254 20 $2,977
       21               -------  -------  -------  ------- 21 -------
       22    Net Income After Taxes $371 $310 $360   $234 22 $2,748
       23               =======  =======  =======  ======= 23 =======
       24    % Sales Increase          -7%      2%    -13% 24
     22-Aug-91  04:36 AM
```

Figure 4.8

The columns in the left window move as the cell pointer moves, but the columns in the right window remain stationary. Now Dan can easily compare the income figures for April in column E to the annual total in column N.

Now watch your screen again as you use ⬇ to

Move to: B28

The rows in both windows move together. This is called **synchronized scrolling**.

You can move the cell pointer from one window to the other using (F6), the WINDOW function key.

To move the cell pointer to the right window,

Press: (F6) (WINDOW)

(F6) (WINDOW) is simply a switch that makes the cell pointer jump from one window to the other. Try pressing it a few times.

If the cell pointer is not in the right window, put it there. Now watch your screen as you use ⬆ to

Move to: N8

Again, the windows scroll together, synchronized. The windows can also operate independently. This is called **unsynchronized scrolling.** To change to unsynchronized scrolling, issue the following command sequence:

/**W**orksheet **W**indow **U**nsync

No difference is immediately visible. However, watch your screen as you use ⬇ to

Move to: N28

Your screen should look similar to Figure 4.9.

```
N28: [W9]                                                              READY

             A              B        C        D        E        N      ◄
5                                                             5        ►
6                          Jan      Feb      Mar      Apr    6  TOTAL   ▲
7                        -------  -------  -------  ------- 7  ------- ▼
8    Sales               $1,998   $1,856   $1,901   $1,654 12          ?
9    Cost of Goods Sold    $998     $980     $960     $934 13  $1,422
10                       -------  -------  -------  ------- 14  $1,032
11     Gross Margin      $1,000     $876     $941     $720 15    $403
12                                                         16  -------
13   Advertising Expenses  $112     $100      $85     $110 17  $2,857
14   Operating Expenses     $79      $88      $74      $88 18
15   Miscellaneous Expenses $36      $42      $31      $34 19  $5,724
16                       -------  -------  -------  ------- 20  $2,977
17     Total Expenses      $227     $230     $190     $232 21  -------
18                                                         22  $2,748
19   Net Income Before Taxes $773    $646     $751     $488 23 =======
20   Federal Taxes         $402     $336     $391     $254 24
21                       -------  -------  -------  ------- 25
22     Net Income After Taxes $371   $310     $360     $234 26
23                       =======  =======  =======  ======= 27
24     % Sales Increase             -7%       2%     -13% 28          ■
22-Aug-91  04:38 AM
```

Figure 4.9

The left window remains stationary while the rows in the right window scroll.

Switch to the left window and scroll down to B28. The rows in both windows should now be lined up.

You can create a horizontal window as easily as you made a vertical window. The command sequence is identical, except that you select **H**orizontal rather than **V**ertical.

Before continuing, remove the window and clear the frozen titles by issuing the following command sequences:

/**W**orksheet **W**indow **C**lear

/**W**orksheet **T**itles **C**lear

Extracting and Combining Files

Dan Walker has reviewed his company's financial statements and is pleased with the company's performance. He is also pleased with the worksheet analysis, particularly with the basic design of the worksheet.

Dan decides to create a new worksheet to help him develop a five-year financial plan. This new worksheet will contain some of the current worksheet's information, such as the row titles and the values in the TOTAL column.

To set up the framework for this new file, you will use the **X**tract and the **C**ombine commands.

The **X**tract command takes a portion of the current worksheet and saves it as a new file. First, you will extract the labels in column A to the file FRAME.

Press: HOME

Move to: A6

Issue the following command sequence:

/**F**ile **X**tract

Your screen should look similar to Figure 4.10.

Xtract Options

```
A6: [W24]                                                        MENU
Formulas  Values
Save data including formulas
                   A              B        C        D        E        F       ◄
 1                        Walker's Gourmet Sandwiches                         ►
 2                                                                            ▲
 3                        Income Statement for the Year 1997                  ▼
 4                             (in thousands of dollars)                      ?
 5
 6                                Jan      Feb      Mar      Apr      May
 7                              -------  -------  -------  -------  -------
 8  Sales                       $1,998   $1,856   $1,901   $1,654   $1,733
 9  Cost of Goods Sold            $998     $980     $960     $934   $1,010
10                              -------  -------  -------  -------  -------
11    Gross Margin             $1,000     $876     $941     $720     $723
12
13  Advertising Expenses         $112     $100      $85     $110     $124
14  Operating Expenses            $79      $88      $74      $88      $95
15  Miscellaneous Expenses        $36      $42      $31      $34      $22
16                              -------  -------  -------  -------  -------
17    Total Expenses             $227     $230     $190     $232     $241
18
19  Net Income Before Taxes      $773     $646     $751     $488     $482
20  Federal Taxes                $402     $336     $391     $254     $251   ■
22-Aug-91  04:39 AM
```

Figure 4.10

The control panel prompts you to select either the **F**ormulas or **V**alues command. If the cells you are extracting contain formulas, you can extract either the values displayed in the worksheet or the formulas used to calculate the values; however, you cannot extract both.

In this case, all the entries in column A are labels; therefore, either response is acceptable. To continue the command sequence,

Press: ⏎

The next prompt is to assign a name to the extracted file. Continue the command sequence as follows:

FRAME ⟨↵⟩

To complete the command sequence, define the range to be extracted as

A6..A24 ⟨↵⟩

After a few moments, the defined range is copied into the new file.

Next, you will extract the values in the TOTAL column to another file. Using ⟨→⟩,

Move to: N6

To extract the label and values in cells N6 through N23 to the file TOTAL, issue the following command sequence:

/File **X**tract

In this command sequence, you need to select values rather than formulas. This is because the new worksheet will not contain the monthly income figures used by the formulas and @functions in column N. If the formulas were copied, they would reference blank cells, and the calculated value would be zero. Continue the command sequence as follows:

Values **TOTAL** ⟨↵⟩ **N6..N23** ⟨↵⟩

Next, you will combine the two files, FRAME and TOTAL, to create a new worksheet file. Begin by retrieving the file FRAME. You do not need to save the current file.

Your screen should look similar to Figure 4.11.

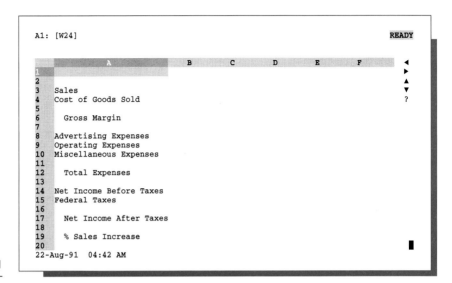

```
A1: [W24]                                                         READY

                        A              B      C      D      E      F       ◄
  1                                                                        ►
  2                                                                        ▲
  3    Sales                                                               ▼
  4    Cost of Goods Sold                                                  ?
  5
  6      Gross Margin
  7
  8    Advertising Expenses
  9    Operating Expenses
 10    Miscellaneous Expenses
 11
 12      Total Expenses
 13
 14    Net Income Before Taxes
 15    Federal Taxes
 16
 17      Net Income After Taxes
 18
 19      % Sales Increase
 20                                                                        ■
       22-Aug-91  04:42 AM
```

Figure 4.11

The file FRAME contains the labels in column A extracted from the file YEAR.

The **C**ombine command incorporates all or part of a file into the current worksheet. You will use the **C**ombine command to copy the file TOTAL into the file FRAME. Before you use this command, however, the cell pointer must be positioned in the upper left corner of the area in the worksheet where the file is to be inserted.

Move to: B1

Then issue the following command sequence:

/**F**ile **C**ombine **C**opy

The control panel prompts you to select either the **E**ntire-File or a **N**amed/Specified-Range to be copied.

You want the entire contents of the file TOTAL to be copied, so complete the command sequence as follows:

Entire-File **TOTAL** ⊖

Your screen should look similar to Figure 4.12.

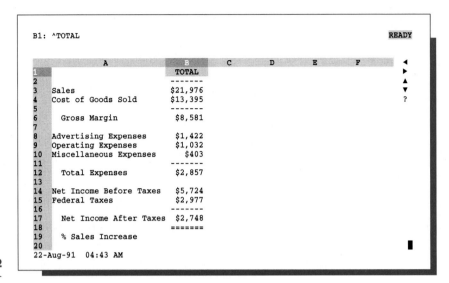

```
B1: ^TOTAL                                                       READY

                A                B        C      D      E      F      ◄
1                             TOTAL                                   ►
2                             -------                                 ▲
3    Sales                   $21,976                                  ▼
4    Cost of Goods Sold      $13,395                                  ?
5                             -------
6       Gross Margin          $8,581
7
8    Advertising Expenses     $1,422
9    Operating Expenses       $1,032
10   Miscellaneous Expenses     $403
11                            -------
12      Total Expenses        $2,857
13
14   Net Income Before Taxes  $5,724
15   Federal Taxes            $2,977
16                            -------
17      Net Income After Taxes $2,748
18                            =======
19      % Sales Increase
20
     22-Aug-91  04:43 AM                                         ■
```

Figure 4.12

The TOTAL column has been copied into the file FRAME. Dan Walker
wants to develop a five-year financial plan using this basic worksheet.
The data in the TOTAL column will become the data for the year 1997.
He asks his management team to prepare an income statement for the
following year (1998) and to project this statement another five years
(1999 through 2003).

After hours of discussion and analysis, the management team develops
a projected income statement. To see this statement, retrieve the file
PROJECT.WK1. You do not need to save the current file.

To see the rest of the worksheet, use $\rightarrow$ and $\downarrow$ to

Move to: G27

Your screen should now look similar to Figure 4.13.

```
G27: (P2) (G11-F11)/F11                                          READY

          B      C      D      E      F      G      H      I     ◀
8      Actual Budget  x==============Projections===============x  ▶
9       1997   1998   1999   2000   2001   2002   2003  TOTAL    ▲
10      ------ ------ ------ ------ ------ ------ ------ ------    ▼
11      21976  25400  29100  34000  39000  45700  52000 247176   ?
12      13395  15800  16000  18000  18940  20000  20900 123035
13      ------ ------ ------ ------ ------ ------ ------ ------
14       8581   9600  13100  16000  20060  25700  31100 124141
15
16       1422   2100   2800   3300   4300   5450   6250  25622
17       1032   1700   2000   2300   2600   3150   3950  16732
18        403    700   1200   1600   2000   2550   3450  11903
19      ------ ------ ------ ------ ------ ------ ------ ------
20       2857   4500   6000   7200   8900  11150  13650  54257
21
22       5724   5100   7100   8800  11160  14550  17450  69884
23       2976   2652   3692   4576   5803   7566   9074  36340
24      ------ ------ ------ ------ ------ ------ ------ ------
25       2748   2448   3408   4224   5357   6984   8376  33544
26      ======================================================
27             15.58% 14.57% 16.84% 14.71% 17.18% 13.79%         ▮
22-Aug-91  04:44 AM
```

Sales ——— (pointing to row 11)

Figure 4.13

Dan Walker evaluates this worksheet by first looking at the projected growth in sales (row 11).

Future sales are increasing from $25,400 in 1998 (cell C11) to $52,000 in 2003 (cell H11). Although dollar sales are increasing each year, the percentage of the increase varies from a high of 17.18 percent in 2002 (cell G27) to a low of 13.79 percent in 2003 (cell H27). Dan would prefer to see a steady rate of growth over these years.

Using What-If Analysis

Dan decides to revise this five-year plan based on a constant annual sales increase of 15 percent. He wants to know what effect this revision would have on his firm's growth; that is, what if sales increased at a constant rate of 15 percent a year? As previously discussed, **what-if analysis** is a technique that evaluates the effects of changing selected factors in a worksheet.

Begin by entering a formula to calculate the projected sales in 1998 (cell C11) as 15 percent more than the previous year's sales (cell B11). To do this,

Move to: C11

Type: **+B11*1.15**

Press: ⏎

For a better view of the worksheet, use ⬅ to

Move to: A11

The Gross Margin (C14), Net Income Before Taxes (C22), Federal Taxes (C23), and Net Income After Taxes (C25) for 1998 have all been instantaneously recalculated. The % Sales Increase (C27) now reflects the 15 percent increase as calculated by the formula.

Copy the formula to calculate projected sales from 1998 (C11) to 1999 (D11) through 2003 (H11). Then move the cell pointer to cell G11 for a better view of the worksheet.

Your screen should look similar to Figure 4.14.

```
G11: +F11*1.15                                                    READY

      B        C        D        E        F        G        H        I
8   Actual   Budget   x=============Projections=================x
9    1997     1998     1999     2000     2001     2002     2003    TOTAL
10  -------  -------  -------  -------  -------  -------  -------  -------
11   21976    25272    29063    33423    38436    44202    50832   243204
12   13395    15800    16000    18000    18940    20000    20900   123035
13  -------  -------  -------  -------  -------  -------  -------  -------
14    8581     9472    13063    15423    19496    24202    29932   120169
15
16    1422     2100     2800     3300     4300     5450     6250    25622
17    1032     1700     2000     2300     2600     3150     3950    16732
18     403      700     1200     1600     2000     2550     3450    11903
19  -------  -------  -------  -------  -------  -------  -------  -------
20    2857     4500     6000     7200     8900    11150    13650    54257
21
22    5724     4972     7063     8223    10596    13052    16282    65912
23    2976     2586     3673     4276     5510     6787     8467    34274
24  -------  -------  -------  -------  -------  -------  -------  -------
25    2748     2387     3390     3947     5086     6265     7815    31638
26  ================================================================
27            15.00%   15.00%   15.00%   15.00%   15.00%   15.00%
22-Aug-91   04:48 AM
```

Figure 4.14

The entire worksheet has been recalculated.

Dan discusses his plans for constant growth at 15 percent a year with his management team. The purchasing director notes that the cost of goods sold will, of course, change whenever sales change. He suggests that the annual cost of goods sold expense be calculated at 60 percent of sales.

The advertising director points out that if sales are to increase 15 percent a year, advertising expenses will have to increase 20 percent a year.

The financial director suggests that the worksheet be modified to compute annual profit margins, which are calculated as follows:

$$\text{Profit Margins} = \frac{\text{Net Income Before Taxes}}{\text{Gross Margin}} \times 100\%$$

He comments that it would be interesting to see how Walker's profit margin compares with the industry average of 56 percent.

The worksheet has been modified to reflect all these suggestions. To see the modified worksheet, retrieve the file REVISED.WK1. You do not need to save the current file.

To get a better view of the worksheet, use ⬇ to

Move to: A28

To freeze the titles above row 11 and in column A, use ⬆ and ➡ to

Move to: B11

Then issue the command sequence to freeze both titles.

Your screen should now look similar to Figure 4.15.

```
B11: 21976                                                      READY

              A          B        C        D        E        F      ◄
9                       1997     1998     1999     2000     2001     ►
10                    -------  -------  -------  -------  -------     ▲
11  Sales              21976    25272    29063    33423    38436     ▼
12  Cost of Goods Sold 13395    15163    17438    20054    23062     ?
13                    -------  -------  -------  -------  -------
14    Gross Margin      8581    10109    11625    13369    15374
15
16  Advertising Expenses 1422    1706     2048     2457     2949
17  Operating Expenses   1032    1800     2000     2200     2300
18  Miscellaneous Expenses 403   1000     1300     1600     1850
19                    -------  -------  -------  -------  -------
20    Total Expenses    2857     4506     5348     6257     7099
21
22  Net Income Before Taxes 5724  5603    6278     7112     8276
23  Federal Taxes       2976     2913     3264     3698     4303
24                    -------  -------  -------  -------  -------
25    Net Income After Taxes 2748  2689   3013     3414     3972
26                    =================================================
27    % Sales Increase           15.00%   15.00%   15.00%   15.00%
28    Profit Margins             55.42%   54.00%   53.20%   53.83%   ▮
22-Aug-91  05:07 AM
```

Figure 4.15

Confirm that the cost of goods sold entries have been changed to 60 percent of sales by examining the formulas in cells C12 through H12. Confirm that the advertising expenses have been increased 20 percent annually by examining the formulas in cells C16 through H16. Confirm that the correct equations have been used to calculate profit margins in cells C28 through H28.

Walker's profit margins, shown in row 28, are below the industry average of 56 percent. Dan decides that the financial plan should have profit margins that at least equal the industry average.

After talking with his management team, he concludes that the only way for Walker's to increase profit margins is to reduce expenses and that only operating expenses can realistically be cut. The goal is to achieve a profit margin of 56 percent by reducing operating expenses.

To see what happens when you reduce operating expenses for 1998 from $1800 to $1700,

Move to: C17

Type: **1700**

Press: ⏎

Your screen should look similar to Figure 4.16.

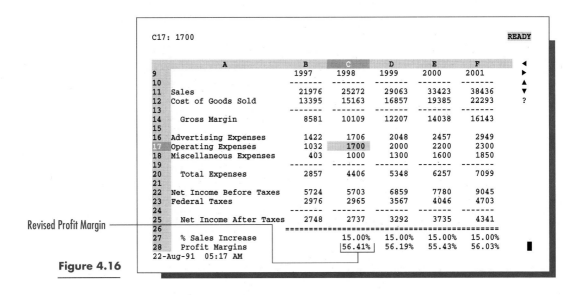

Revised Profit Margin

Figure 4.16

The profit margin increased from 55.42 percent to 56.41 percent, which is more than enough. You now know that the appropriate level is between $1800 and $1700.

Try increasing the operating expense for 1998 to $1750. The profit margin decreases from 56.41 percent to 55.92 percent, which is a bit too low.

Now try $1740.

How about $1745?

The profit margin is now 55.97 percent.

How about $1742?

Your screen should look similar to Figure 4.17.

```
C17: 1742                                                          READY

              A                B       C       D       E       F       ◄
9                             1997    1998    1999    2000    2001      ►
10                           ------- ------- ------- ------- -------    ▲
11  Sales                    21976   25272   29063   33423   38436     ▼
12  Cost of Goods Sold       13395   15163   17438   20054   23062     ?
13                           ------- ------- ------- ------- -------
14     Gross Margin           8581   10109   11625   13369   15374
15
16  Advertising Expenses      1422    1706    2048    2457    2949
17  Operating Expenses        1032    1742    2100    2200    2300
18  Miscellaneous Expenses     403    1000    1300    1600    1850
19                           ------- ------- ------- ------- -------
20     Total Expenses         2857    4448    5448    6257    7099
21
22  Net Income Before Taxes   5724    5661    6178    7112    8276
23  Federal Taxes             2976    2943    3212    3698    4303
24                           ------- ------- ------- ------- -------
25     Net Income After Taxes 2748    2717    2965    3414    3972
26                           =================================================
27     % Sales Increase              15.00%  15.00%  15.00%  15.00%
28     Profit Margins                56.00%  53.14%  53.20%  53.83%      ■
    22-Aug-91  05:21 AM
```

Revised Profit Margin

Figure 4.17

The profit margin is now 56 percent. The budget for 1998 will have operating expenses set at $1742.

Determine the operating expenses for the years 1999 to 2003 in the same way.

Year	Value
1999	1768
2000	1825
2001	1966
2002	2241
2003	2500

When you are done,

Press: (HOME)

Unfreeze the worksheet titles.

Preparing a Memo

Dan Walker wants to send a copy of this worksheet, along with a brief, explanatory message, to his father, the president of Walker's Gourmet Sandwiches.

Move to: B31

Type: **TO:**

Move to: C31

Type: **President, Dan Walker Sr.**

Move to: B32

Type: **FROM:**

Move to: C32

Type: **Manager, Dan Walker Jr.**

Move to: B33

Type: **DATE:**

Move to: C33

Entering the Date Using @NOW

You can enter the current date into a worksheet using the @NOW function. This @function calculates the date using the DOS system date by assigning a number to each of the 73,050 days from January 1, 1900, through December 31, 2099. They are called **date numbers**.

Type: **@NOW**

Press: (↵)

Your screen should look similar to Figure 4.18.

```
C33: @NOW                                                              READY

              A            B        C        D        E        F      ◄
 14    Gross Margin        8581     10109    11625    13369    15374   ►
 15                                                                    ▲
 16  Advertising Expenses  1422     1706     2048     2457     2949    ▼
 17  Operating Expenses    1032     1742     1768     1825     1966    ?
 18  Miscellaneous Expenses 403     1000     1300     1600     1850
 19                        -------  -------  -------  -------  -------
 20    Total Expenses      2857     4448     5116     5882     6765
 21
 22  Net Income Before Taxes 5724   5661     6510     7487     8610
 23  Federal Taxes         2976     2943     3385     3893     4477
 24                        -------  -------  -------  -------  -------
 25    Net Income After Taxes 2748  2717     3125     3594     4133
 26                        =================================================
 27    % Sales Increase             15.00%   15.00%   15.00%   15.00%
 28    Profit Margins               56.00%   56.00%   56.00%   56.00%
 29
 30
 31                        TO:     President, Dan Walker Sr.
 32                        FROM:   Manager, Dan Walker Jr.
 33                        DATE:     35817                            ▮
     22-Aug-91  05:28 AM
```

Date Serial Number

Figure 4.18

The value displayed in cell C33 is the date number for the system date on your computer system. (Of course, this value on your screen will likely be different from the number in Figure 4.18.)

To change the display of the date number to a date, use the **/R**ange **F**ormat **D**ate command, as follows:

/Range **F**ormat **D**ate

Five date format options are displayed in the control panel. Use the Help facility for information on the date formats. You want to display the date as month/day/year. The option that displays the date in this manner is **4** (Long Intn'l). Continue the command sequence as follows:

4

Your screen should look similar to Figure 4.19.

```
C33: (D4) @NOW                                                    READY

          A                   B        C        D        E        F      ◄
14    Gross Margin          8581    10109    11625    13369    15374     ►
15                                                                        ▲
16  Advertising Expenses    1422     1706     2048     2457     2949     ▼
17  Operating Expenses      1032     1742     1768     1825     1966     ?
18  Miscellaneous Expenses   403     1000     1300     1600     1850
19                         -------  -------  -------  -------  -------
20     Total Expenses       2857     4448     5116     5882     6765
21
22  Net Income Before Taxes 5724     5661     6510     7487     8610
23  Federal Taxes           2976     2943     3385     3893     4477
24                         -------  -------  -------  -------  -------
25    Net Income After Taxes 2748    2717     3125     3594     4133
26                         ===========================================
27    % Sales Increase              15.00%   15.00%   15.00%   15.00%
28    Profit Margins                56.00%   56.00%   56.00%   56.00%
29
30
31                       TO:      President, Dan Walker Sr.
32                       FROM:    Manager, Dan Walker Jr.
33                       DATE:    01/22/98                              ■
22-Aug-91  05:30 AM
```

Figure 4.19

Your current date should be displayed in cell C33. If you did not enter a date at the DOS date prompt, the DOS default date is displayed.

Justifying Text

You are now ready to enter the body of the memo.

> **Move to:** B35

Without pressing ⏎ until directed, enter the following message as one long label in cell B35.

> **Type:** **I have been working with our management group to develop a projected income statement for the next five years. I think you will be pleased with the results.**
>
> **Press:** ⏎

The sentences are entered as a long label in cell B35. To change this long label into a paragraph, 1-2-3 lets you rearrange, or **justify**, the long label to fit within a specified width. Issue the following command sequence:

> /**R**ange **J**ustify **B35..F35** ⏎

> **Move to:** B40

Your screen should look similar to Figure 4.20.

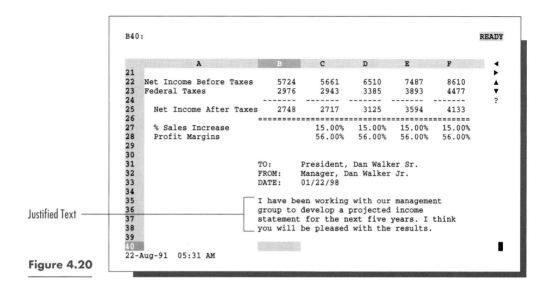

Figure 4.20

Justified Text

```
B40:                                                              READY

          A              B        C        D        E        F      ◄
21                                                                  ►
22  Net Income Before Taxes   5724     5661     6510     7487     8610    ▲
23  Federal Taxes             2976     2943     3385     3893     4477    ▼
24                           -------  -------  -------  -------  -------   ?
25    Net Income After Taxes  2748     2717     3125     3594     4133
26                           ========================================
27    % Sales Increase                15.00%   15.00%   15.00%   15.00%
28    Profit Margins                  56.00%   56.00%   56.00%   56.00%
29
30
31                      TO:        President, Dan Walker Sr.
32                      FROM:      Manager, Dan Walker Jr.
33                      DATE:      01/22/98
34
35                     ┌ I have been working with our management
36                     │ group to develop a projected income
37                     │ statement for the next five years. I think
38                     └ you will be pleased with the results.
39
40
22-Aug-91  05:31 AM
```

The long label in cell B35 has been broken into four long labels contained in cells B35 through B38. The long labels do not exceed the specified width and look like a paragraph.

Enter the following text in cell B40 as one long label without pressing ⏎ until directed.

Type: **To meet the industry standard of a 56 percent profit
margin, we decreased the operating expenses.
As you can see, we will need to watch the operating
expenses closely if we want to attain our goal.**

Press: ⏎

Justify the text in cell B40 in the same manner. For a better view of the memo,

Move to: B46

Your screen should now look similar to Figure 4.21.

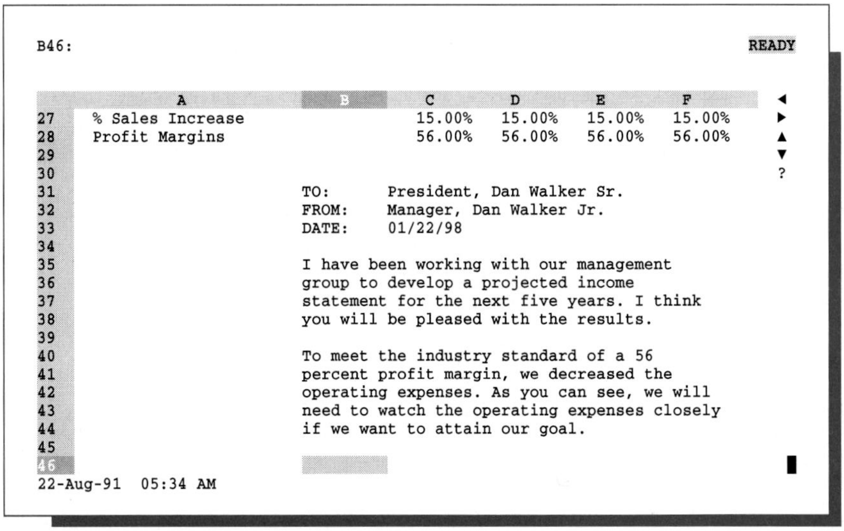

```
B46:                                                                    READY

              A              B        C        D        E        F      ◄
27   % Sales Increase                15.00%   15.00%   15.00%   15.00%   ►
28   Profit Margins                  56.00%   56.00%   56.00%   56.00%   ▲
29                                                                       ▼
30                                                                       ?
31                        TO:       President, Dan Walker Sr.
32                        FROM:     Manager, Dan Walker Jr.
33                        DATE:     01/22/98
34
35                        I have been working with our management
36                        group to develop a projected income
37                        statement for the next five years. I think
38                        you will be pleased with the results.
39
40                        To meet the industry standard of a 56
41                        percent profit margin, we decreased the
42                        operating expenses. As you can see, we will
43                        need to watch the operating expenses closely
44                        if we want to attain our goal.
45
46
     22-Aug-91  05:34 AM
```

Figure 4.21

The worksheet is ready to be printed.

Printing in Compressed Mode

To print the entire worksheet on a single page, Dan decides to use compressed printing. **Compressed printing** reduces the size of characters and the space between them, increasing the amount of text that can be printed across the width of a page.

Note The following procedure works for most printers, but it may not work for your particular printer. You may need to consult your printer manual before proceeding.

Issue the following command sequence:

/**P**rint **P**rinter

You will now see the Print Settings dialog box. Continue the command sequence:

Range **A1..I44** ⏎ **O**ptions

The print options are as follows:

Header Prints a line of text just below the top margin of every page

Footer Prints a line of text just above the bottom margin of every page

Margins Sets margins for the printed page

Borders Prints specified rows or columns on every page

Setup Specifies font size and style

Pg-Length Indicates the number of printed lines on the page

Other Selects other printing procedures

Quit Returns to the Print menu

To compress the print size,

Select: **S**etup

Now, turn on the compressed print option by entering

\015 ⏎

Note The setup string \015 creates compressed printing on many, but not all, printers. Consult your printer manual if you need alternative setup values.

The maximum margin size you can use with compressed print is 132 spaces. To increase the right margin to that number of spaces, continue the command sequence:

Margins **R**ight **132** ⏎

Check to see that the printer is on. If you are using continuous form paper, make sure that the top of the paper is aligned with the top of the printer's scale.

To print the worksheet,

Select: **Q**uit **A**lign **G**o

When the printer stops printing, advance the page and return to READY mode by completing the command sequence:

Page **Q**uit

The printed document should look similar to Figure 4.22. The header and your name are automatically printed at the top of the page.

```
Addison-Wesley: 1-2-3 for Education                              Linda O'Leary


                              Walker's Gourmet Sandwiches

                              Five Year Financial Plan
                              (in thousands of dollars)

                          Income Statement for the Year Ending:

                   Actual  Budget  x==============Projections=================x
                   1997    1998    1999    2000    2001    2002    2003   TOTAL
                   ------- ------- ------- ------- ------- ------- ------- -------
Sales              21976   25272   29063   33423   38436   44202   50832  243204
Cost of Goods Sold 13395   15163   17438   20054   23062   26521   30499  146132
                   ------- ------- ------- ------- ------- ------- ------- -------
   Gross Margin     8581   10109   11625   13369   15374   17681   20333   97072

Advertising Expenses   1422    1706    2048    2457    2949    3538    4246   18366
Operating Expenses     1032    1742    1768    1827    1966    2241    2500   13076
Miscellaneous Expenses  403    1000    1300    1600    1850    2000    2200   10353
                   ------- ------- ------- ------- ------- ------- ------- -------
   Total Expenses   2857    4448    5116    5884    6765    7779    8946   41795

Net Income Before Taxes 5724   5661    6510    7485    8610    9901   11387   55277
Federal Taxes          2976    2943    3385    3892    4477    5149    5921   28744
                   ------- ------- ------- ------- ------- ------- ------- -------
   Net Income After Taxes 2748  2717    3125    3593    4133    4753    5466   26533
                   ===============================================================
   % Sales Increase        15.00%  15.00%  15.00%  15.00%  15.00%  15.00%
   Profit Margins          56.00%  56.00%  55.99%  56.00%  56.00%  56.00%

                   TO      President, Dan Walker Sr.
                   FROM:   Manager, Dan Walker Jr.
                   DATE:   01/22/98

                   I have been working with our management
                   group to develop a projected income
                   statement for the next five years.  I think
                   you will be pleased with the results.

                   To meet the industry standard on a 56
                   percent profit margin, we decreased the
                   operating expenses.  As you can see, we will
                   need to watch the operating expenses closely
                   if we want to attain our goal.
```

Figure 4.22

Using Passwords to Restrict Access to Files

The data contained in this worksheet file are confidential. To restrict access to it, Dan decides to save the file with a password. To tell 1-2-3 that you want to save a file with a password, following the file name in the **S**ave command, press SPACEBAR and the letter **P**.

To save this worksheet as FUTURE with a password, issue the following command sequence:

/File Save **FUTURE P** ⏎

The prompt, "Enter password:" is displayed in the control panel. A password can be up to 15 characters long. However, it cannot contain any spaces. To enter the password RESTRICT,

Type: **RESTRICT**

Press: ⏎

The password is not displayed following the prompt. Instead, for each letter of the password you type, a blank is displayed (or, possibly, a solid block or underscore). This feature further ensures the privacy of the password as it is entered.

Your screen should look similar to Figure 4.23.

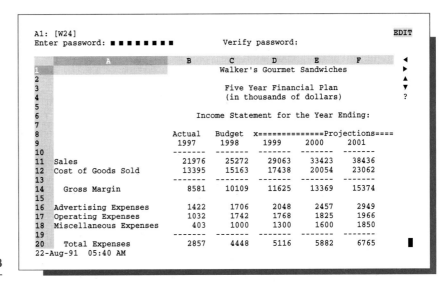

```
A1: [W24]                                                    EDIT
Enter password: ■ ■ ■ ■ ■ ■ ■ ■        Verify password:
                 A              B       C       D       E       F    ◄
 1                                      Walker's Gourmet Sandwiches       ►
 2                                                                        ▲
 3                                      Five Year Financial Plan          ▼
 4                                      (in thousands of dollars)         ?
 5
 6                                  Income Statement for the Year Ending:
 7
 8                              Actual  Budget  x==============Projections====
 9                              1997    1998    1999    2000    2001
10                              -------  -------  -------  -------  -------
11  Sales                       21976   25272   29063   33423   38436
12  Cost of Goods Sold          13395   15163   17438   20054   23062
13                              -------  -------  -------  -------  -------
14      Gross Margin            8581    10109   11625   13369   15374
15
16  Advertising Expenses        1422    1706    2048    2457    2949
17  Operating Expenses          1032    1742    1768    1825    1966
18  Miscellaneous Expenses      403     1000    1300    1600    1850
19                              -------  -------  -------  -------  -------
20      Total Expenses          2857    4448    5116    5882    6765    ■
22-Aug-91  05:40 AM
```

Figure 4.23

In response to the prompt to verify the password,

Type: **RESTRICT**

Press: ⏎

You have now saved this file under the file name FUTURE with the password RESTRICT.

Erase the worksheet from your screen and the computer's memory by issuing the following command sequence:

/**W**orksheet **E**rase **Y**es

To retrieve the password-restricted file, issue the following command sequence:

/File Retrieve FUTURE (↵)

Your screen should look similar to Figure 4.24.

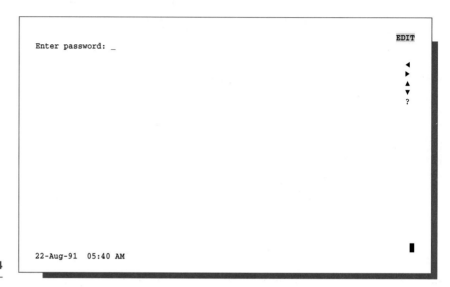

```
                                                            EDIT

    Enter password: _

                                                              ◄
                                                              ►
                                                              ▲
                                                              ▼
                                                              ?









                                                              ■
    22-Aug-91  05:40 AM
```

Figure 4.24

To respond to the prompt in the control panel, you must enter the password exactly as you entered it during the **S**ave command. Since password protection is case sensitive, you must enter the password so that it matches exactly, including uppercase and lowercase letters. To complete the command,

Type: **RESTRICT**

Press: (↵)

The file FUTURE is loaded into your computer's memory and displayed on your screen. If you enter the password incorrectly, the error message "Incorrect password" is displayed. Press (ESC) to clear the message, and then try again.

You can retrieve a password-protected file only if you enter the correct password. If you forget the password, there is no way of retrieving the file.

Exit from 1-2-3.

Glossary

Compressed printing: A print option that reduces the space between characters and the size of characters to create a smaller (compressed) type.

Date numbers: An integer from 1 to 73,050 assigned to each day from January 1, 1900, through December 31, 2099.

Freezing titles: Fixes row and column titles on the screen.

Justify: Converts a long label of text in a cell so that none of the lines is longer than a specified width.

Synchronized scrolling: The simultaneous scrolling of rows or columns in two windows.

Unsynchronized scrolling: The independent scrolling of rows or columns in two windows.

What-if analysis: A technique that evaluates the effects of changing selected factors in a worksheet.

Practice Problems and Cases

Matching

1. /RJ
2. /PPOM
3. @NOW
4. /WTC
5. /FS filename P
6. /WWU
7. /RFD
8. /FCCE
9. /FX
10. /WWV

_____ **a.** enters the current date

_____ **b.** saves a file with a password

_____ **c.** freezes window vertically

_____ **d.** unsynchronizes two windows

_____ **e.** sets date format

_____ **f.** changes print margins

_____ **g.** clears frozen titles

_____ **h.** writes a part of the worksheet to a file

_____ **i.** rearranges text

_____ **j.** copies an entire file

Multiple Choice

Justin Kopps has been working on the income statement worksheet shown in the figure below. Refer to the figure to answer the following questions.

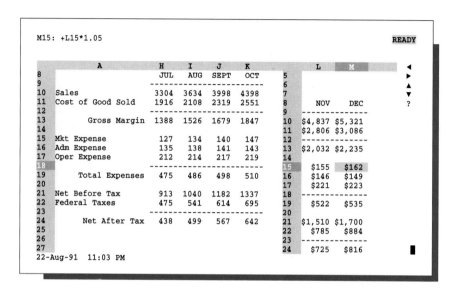

1. The current worksheet cell is:

   a. L16

   b. M15

   c. L8

   d. A1

2. To keep the names of the months at the top of the left window, you would freeze the titles above row:

   a. 7

   b. 8

   c. 9

   d. 10

3. The command to move the cell pointer to the other window would be:

   a. (F4)

   b. (F6)

   c. (F9)

   d. /WWC

4. If the cell pointer was located at cell B9 and the titles were frozen above row 9 and to the left of column B, which of the following arrow keys could you use?

   a. (←), (→)

   b. (←), (↑)

   c. (→), (↓)

   d. (→), (↑)

5. The command to globally change the format to currency with zero decimal places is:

    a. /WGFC0   c. /WFC0

    b. /FGC0   d. /WWFC0

6. The left and right windows are:

    a. dependent and synchronized   c. dependent and unsynchronized

    b. independent and synchronized   d. independent and unsynchronized

7. The formula in cell M15 is +L15*1.05. This increases the value of L15 by:

    a. 50%   c. .05%

    b. 5%   d. 105%

8. The window was created between columns:

    a. K and L   c. A and L

    b. L and M   d. K and M

9. The command to clear the window would be:

    a. /WTC   c. /WC

    b. /WGWC   d. /WWC

10. Column A is wider than the other columns. The command that was used to widen it was:

    a. /WGC   c. /WCR

    b. /WCS   d. /RCS

Cases

1. Lisa Oswald has expanded her worksheet from six months to a full year. You will use this worksheet to practice many of the 1-2-3 commands you learned for managing a large worksheet. Retrieve the worksheet PROB4-1.WK1.

    a. Put your name in cell A1 and the current date in cell A2.

    b. Move to cell C28, and create a vertical window at this location.

    c. Switch to the right window, and move to cell C6. Freeze the titles above row 7. While moving the cell pointer to column M, compare the sales figures for FEB through DEC to the figure for JAN. In which month were sales almost identical to JAN?

d. Move to cell I26. What happened in the left window?

e. Switch to the left window. Change the window scrolling to unsynchronized. Move to cell B9, and observe the movement in the screen.

f. Freeze the titles in the left window above row 7.

g. Switch to the right window. Line up the rows in the two windows.

h. Use the **G**lobal command to display currency with zero decimal places. What happens in the left window?

i. Print a copy of the worksheet.

j. Clear the window. Clear the titles. What happens to the format?

2. Lisa Oswald is planning a meeting with the department directors. The purpose of the meeting is to plan the budget for the first quarter of 1998. She wants to generate a report that will show the income statement figures for 1997. She feels this information should help the directors plan for the next quarter.

a. Retrieve the file PROB4-2.WK1. Use this file to extract the labels in column A and the first three months of income figures (columns B to D) to a new file, HWLAB4-2.WK1.

b. Retrieve the file HWLAB4-2.WK1, and add a new column to calculate the row totals. Label this column TOTAL. Make adjustments to improve the appearance of the new worksheet. (Insert or delete rows and columns, and adjust column widths if necessary.) Add the title: Lisa's Antique Doll Shop, First Quarter 1997 Income Statement.

c. Lisa would like to add a memo to the worksheet below the report. Enter the header of the memo starting in cell B26 as:

   TO: Department Directors

   FROM: (your name)

   DATE: (enter the current date using the @NOW function)

d. Enter the body of the memo in cell B30.

   I am distributing this first-quarter 1997 income statement for your information and reference. Please have your comments prepared for the meeting scheduled for next Monday.

e. Reformat the text of the memo so that it is displayed under the whole worksheet in cells B30 to D30.

f. Print the worksheet so that it fits on one page.

g. Save the worksheet as HWLAB4-2 using the **R**eplace option.

3. To complete this problem, you must have completed the worksheet in Practice Case 4 in Lab 3. If you have completed that problem, retrieve the file HWLAB3-4. Then complete the following steps.

a. Add six columns between JUN and TOTAL. Enter the appropriate labels to expand the worksheet to a one-year income statement. Sales and Cost of Goods Sold will increase by 10 percent for each new month.

b. Correct the formulas to reflect the new data ranges.

c. Insert two blank rows above the worksheet. Center a title above the worksheet that describes the worksheet.

d. Add a column to show the Average of each column.

e. Globally change the worksheet to display currency with two decimal places. Increase the column widths to display the values. What is the new column width?

f. Move your name and date from cells A3 and A4 to cells A1 and A2.

g. Save the worksheet as HWLAB4-3.

h. Print the worksheet.

4. To complete this problem, you must have completed the worksheet in Practice Case 5 in Lab 3. If you have completed that problem, retrieve the file HWLAB3-5.

Complete the worksheet by making it a one-year income statement. Correct the formulas and column widths, and enter the current date in cell A2. Save the worksheet as HWLAB4-4, and print the worksheet.

5. To complete this problem, you must have completed the worksheet in Practice Case 7 in Lab 1. If you have completed that problem, retrieve the file HWLAB1-7.

Expand your six-month income statement to a yearly statement. You might even add blank rows, underlines, and totals to make the worksheet easier to read. Enter and justify a memo below the worksheet. Change the date in cell A2 to the current date. Save the worksheet as HWLAB4-5, and print the worksheet.

6. To complete this problem, you must have completed the worksheet in Practice Case 6 in Lab 3.

Extract the labels from the file HWLAB3-6. Create a four-year projected budget with a 30 percent increase in sales and a 45 percent profit margin. Enter your name in cell A1 and the current date in cell A2. Save the worksheet as HWLAB4-6, and print the worksheet.

Lab 5

Creating and Printing a Line Graph

In Lab 5, you will learn how to:

- Create line graphs
- Specify the X axis
- Specify data to be graphed
- Create and edit titles
- Create and edit legends
- Use data labels
- Use grids
- Save current graph settings
- Save a graph for printing
- Print a graph

Dave Robson, a student at Southwestern State University, has an economics report due on the recent changes in income within the United States. The first part of his report will focus on changes in the work force, for different age groups, between 1980 and 1990. Dave has researched his report and found the data we will use in Labs 5 and 6.

Dave has entered this data into a worksheet file. Although the data is nicely displayed, he feels it would look better and be easier to understand in graph form. We will follow Dave in Labs 5 and 6 as he uses 1-2-3 to create and print graphs.

Note To be able to view the graphs in Labs 5 and 6, you will need a computer with graphics capabilities and to have properly installed 1-2-3 to display graphs. (See "Installing Lotus 1-2-3, Release 2.3" in Chapter 2 of "Getting Started.")

Load 1-2-3 in the usual manner.

Dave has entered the income data for households, men in the work force, women in the work force, and heads of households in a worksheet file named CHANGES.WK1. To see this worksheet, issue the following command sequence:

/File Retrieve CHANGES.WK1 (⏎)

Note Remember that you can use (F3) (NAME) as well as the arrow keys, (HOME), and (END) to find the file you wish to retrieve.

Your screen should look similar to Figure 5.1.

```
A1: [W20]                                                          READY

              A              B      C      D      E      F      G      ◄
                            Changes in Income                           ►
   2                        From 1980 to 1990                           ▲
   3                                                                    ▼
   4                        16-24  25-34  35-44  45-54  55-64   65+     ?
   5                        -------------------------------------------
   6    Household           -10.0    1.0    4.0    4.5   -2.0   14.0
   7    Men in Work Force   -15.0   19.0   47.0   16.0  -10.0   -8.0
   8    Women in Work Force -10.0   38.0   75.0   38.0  -38.0    2.0
   9    Head of Household   -30.2   15.5   51.0   13.5   -2.1   25.9
  10
  11
  12
  13
  14
  15
  16
  17
  18
  19
  20
  22-Aug-91   09:15 PM                                                  ■
```

Figure 5.1

Source: *The Wall Street Journal,* March 9, 1990, p. R12.

The worksheet shows percentage changes in income for four different population groups. The percentage changes are based on the comparison of 1980 data to 1990 data. For example, the value in cell B6 indicates that household income for people between the ages of 16 and 24 was 10 percent lower in 1990 than in 1980, and the value in cell D8 indicates that the income of women in the work force between the ages of 35 and 44 increased 75 percent from 1980 to 1990.

Different Graph Types

Graphs are visual representations that show the relationships between variables. These relationships may be evident from a worksheet like the one on your screen. Graphs, however, make trends and relationships easier to identify.

1-2-3 has seven graph types: bar, HLCO, line, mixed, pie, stacked bar, and XY.

Type of Graph	Description
1.	Bar graphs are frequently used to compare different ranges of values to one another. You can include up to six different bars in a **bar graph** with each bar appearing in a different pattern or color. Each bar represents a range of data displayed in the worksheet.

2. An **HLCO graph** is typically used for tracking stock market prices. The graph shows the high (H), low (L), closing (C), and opening (O) values of stocks. Each stock's values are indicated along a vertical line.

3. **Line graphs** are often used to show changes in data over time. A line graph can have up to six different lines. Each line represents a range of data; each value in the range is represented by a point on the line.

4. **Mixed graphs** display bars and lines in the same graph.

5. **Pie graphs** show the relationship of each value in a range to the range as a whole. Each slice of the pie represents a single value in the range. The largest value in the range displays as the largest slice of the pie.

6. **Stacked bar graphs** are often used to compare values and totals by stacking up to six different bars on top of one another.

7. **XY graphs** are used to show the relationship between two ranges of numeric data, such as age and income.

Parts of the Graph

Graphs consist of several important parts, which are illustrated in Figure 5.2.

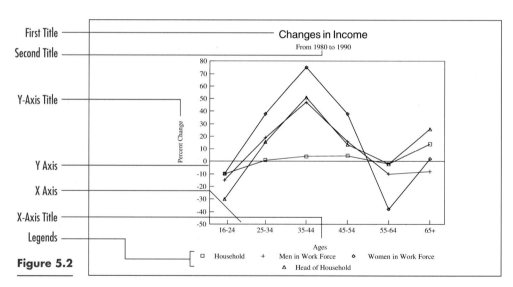

Figure 5.2

Line, bar, stacked bar, and XY graphs contain two reference lines, or axes:

X axis   a horizontal line at the bottom of the graph

Y axis   a vertical line at the left edge of the graph

A 1-2-3 graph can have four different **titles**:

first title   a short description of the entire graph

second title   an additional description of the first title

X-axis title   a short description of the X axis

Y-axis title   a short description of the Y axis

At the bottom of the graph, **legends** briefly describe or reference data in the graph.

In 1-2-3, you use the **G**raph command to create and modify graphs. Issue the following command:

/**G**raph

Your screen should look similar to Figure 5.3.

Graph Menu —

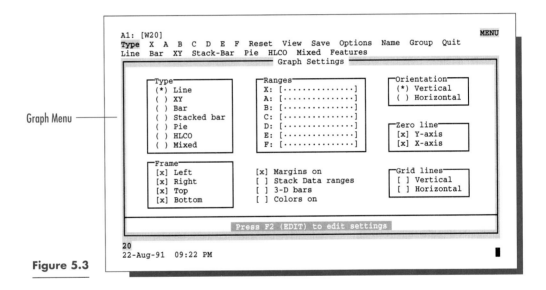

Figure 5.3

The Graph Settings dialog box is displayed on the screen. Like the Global Settings dialog box, this dialog box helps you keep track of the choices you will make. The Graph Settings dialog box shows you the current graph settings for the **G**raph commands displayed in the **Graph menu.** Since no graph settings have been specified yet, the dialog box contains only the default settings.

To briefly preview the **G**raph commands displayed in the second line of the control panel,

Press: [F1] (HELP)

Information on the /Graph Type command is displayed. Read this screen carefully, and then return to the control panel. Highlight the other Graph commands in turn, and press F1 (HELP) to read the Help information on each of them.

When you have finished reviewing Help for the Graph commands, you will be ready to create a line graph.

Dave is not sure which type of graph will work best for this data. He will begin by creating a line graph to visually display the percentages.

Creating Line Graphs

The first step is to select the type of graph you want to create. To do this using the Graph Settings dialog box,

Press: F2 (EDIT)

Select: Type

Your screen should now look similar to Figure 5.4.

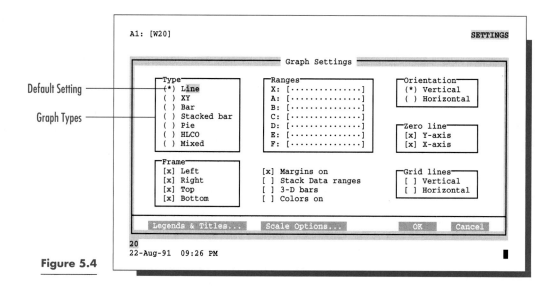

Figure 5.4

The dialog box lists the seven types of graphs. The asterisk (*) next to Line in the dialog box shows that the default graph type is a line graph. Since this is the type of graph we want to create, to accept the default,

Press: ↵

Defining X-Axis Labels

In a line graph, the X option in the **R**anges section of the dialog box can be used to label the horizontal, or X, axis. However, it is more convenient to view the worksheet when specifying graph ranges. In order to view the worksheet when specifying ranges for a graph, you will define the ranges by using the Graph menu. To leave the dialog box and return to the menu,

Press: ⏎

Select: **X**

The worksheet appears, and the control panel displays the "Enter x-axis range:" prompt. This lets you set the range of cells containing the data to be specified as the X-axis range.

The X-axis labels must be contained in a continuous range of cells in the worksheet. For Dave's line graph, the X axis will be the ages 16–24 through 65+, which are in the continuous range of cells B4 through G4.

You can use the mouse to specify any graph range by dragging the mouse. In this instance, define the range by dragging from B4 to G4.

To set the ages as the X-axis labels, you can use either the keyboard or the mouse. Using the keyboard, issue the command sequence as follows:

B4..G4 ⏎

The Graph Settings dialog box appears again, and the range of cells you specified for the X data range is displayed in the **R**anges section next to X:.

Defining Data Ranges

Now that you have specified the type of graph and the X-axis labels, the next step is to specify the worksheet ranges that contain the numbers to be graphed.

Up to six different numeric data ranges, represented by the letters A, B, C, D, E, and F displayed in the Graph menu, can be shown on a single graph.

For now, you are going to graph only one data range: the percentages for household income, which are located in cells B6 through G6. To specify the data range, you use the same procedure you used to specify the X axis. To specify cells B6 through G6 as the A data range, continue the command sequence as follows:

A B6..G6 ⏎

The A data range is displayed in the dialog box. Once the X and A data ranges are specified, you can view your graph. To view the graph,

Press: (F10) (GRAPH)

Using the GRAPH function key, (F10), allows you to view the graph as you create it. You can also view the graph by selecting **V**iew from the Graph menu.

Your screen should look similar to Figure 5.5.

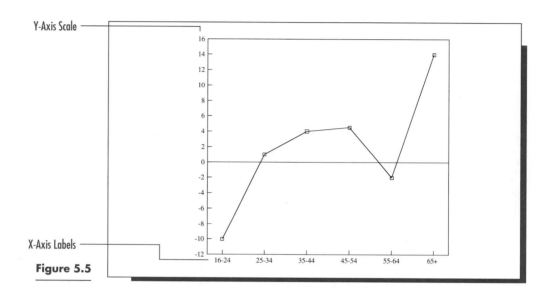

Y-Axis Scale

X-Axis Labels

Figure 5.5

The ages are displayed on the X axis, and the percentage data for household income is plotted in the graph as a series of square symbols connected by a line. 1-2-3 automatically set the scale of values on the Y axis. The Y-axis values were determined by the high and low values in the A range.

To clear the graph and return to the Graph Settings dialog box, you can press any key, for example,

Press: SPACEBAR

Adding Titles

You can greatly improve the appearance and clarity of the graph by adding some titles. The command to add titles is found under **L**egends & Titles, which is not yet visible on your screen. You can activate the dialog box using either the keyboard or the mouse. Using the keyboard to activate the dialog box and select **L**egends & Titles,

Press: (F2) (EDIT)

Select: **L**egends & Titles...

Click anywhere in the dialog box to activate it; then click on Legends & Titles.

Your screen should look similar to Figure 5.6.

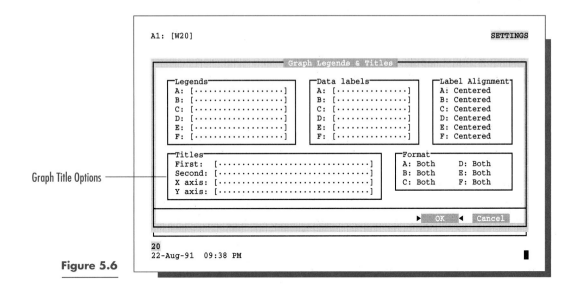

A1: [W20]   SETTINGS

┌─────────────────────── Graph Legends & Titles ───────────────────────┐

┌Legends─────────────┐ ┌Data labels─────────┐ ┌Label Alignment┐
A: [····················]   A: [················]   A: Centered
B: [····················]   B: [················]   B: Centered
C: [····················]   C: [················]   C: Centered
D: [····················]   D: [················]   D: Centered
E: [····················]   E: [················]   E: Centered
F: [····················]   F: [················]   F: Centered

┌Titles────────────────────────────────────┐ ┌Format────────────────┐
First: [····································]   A: Both   D: Both
Second: [····································]   B: Both   E: Both
X axis: [····································]   C: Both   F: Both
Y axis: [····································]

                                        ▶ OK ◀   Cancel

20
22-Aug-91 09:38 PM   ■

Figure 5.6

Graph Title Options

The Graph Legends & Titles dialog box is displayed. The four options
listed under **T**itles in the dialog box will allow you to enter titles for
the first (main title) and second (subtitle) lines at the top of the graph,
as well as titles for the X and Y axes. To enter the first line (main title)
select:

Titles **F**irst

You can respond to the prompt for the title in one of two ways. You can
type in the title, or you can reference a cell in the worksheet containing
the label you want to use as the title. In this case, you want to use the
title Changes in Income, displayed in cell C1 of the worksheet as the first
title line of the graph. To enter worksheet labels directly into graph titles
use the backslash (\) key followed by the cell address containing the
label.

To specify the label in cell C1 as the first title line, complete the command sequence as follows:

\C1 (↵)

To view the graph,

Press: (F10) (GRAPH)

Your screen should look similar to Figure 5.7.

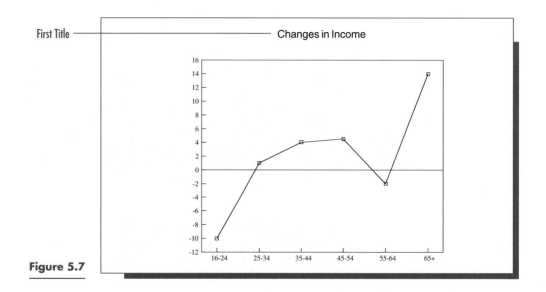

First Title ——————— Changes in Income

Figure 5.7

The backslash feature inserted the contents of cell C1 from the worksheet into the graph. 1-2-3 automatically centered the title over the graph.

To return to the Graph Legends & Titles dialog box,

SPACEBAR (or any other key)

Next, you want to add a second title, For Households, to the graph. Issue the following command sequence:

Titles **S**econd

Since this title is not a worksheet label that can be copied into the graph, you must enter it directly. Continue the command sequence as follows:

Type: **For Households**

Press: ⏎

To specify titles for the X axis and the Y axis, issue the following command sequences:

Titles **X** axis **Ages** ⏎

Titles **Y** axis **Percent Change** ⏎

To leave this dialog box and see the titles you have added to the graph,

Press: ⏎ F10 (GRAPH)

Your screen should look similar to Figure 5.8.

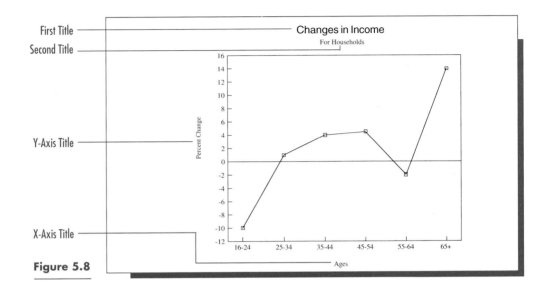

Figure 5.8

Both the first and second titles are centered over the graph. The X-axis title, Ages, and the Y-axis title, Percent Change, are also centered along their respective axes.

To return to the Graph Settings dialog box,

Press: SPACEBAR (or any other key)

Adding New Data Ranges

Dave wants to add the percentage data for the other populations to the graph. Again, you will use the Graph menu to reference the ranges directly from the worksheet.

First, you need to close the Graph Settings dialog box.

Press: ⏎

The Graph menu appears in the control panel. To specify the second data range,

Select: **B**

The Graph Settings dialog box is cleared from the screen, and the worksheet is displayed. Men in Work Force will be the second data variable. In response to the "Enter second data range:" prompt, you can continue by using the keyboard or dragging the mouse. Using the keyboard,

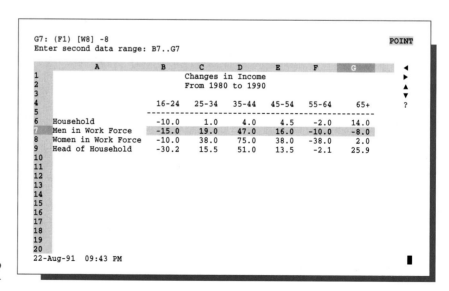

Type: **B7..G7**

Press: ⏎

Did you notice that POINT was displayed in the mode indicator? You can also use pointing to specify the range. This is especially helpful when the range extends beyond the window and you do not know which cell ends the range.

The Graph Settings dialog box is displayed again. The range of cells you specified for the B data range is displayed in the dialog box. It is easy to check the range of cells defined as the B data range. Simply reselect the B data range from the Graph menu, and 1-2-3 will highlight the range.

To see how this works,

Select: **B**

Your screen should look similar to Figure 5.9.

If you are using the mouse, you can continue to specify any graph range by dragging the mouse. In this instance, drag the mouse from B7 to G7.

```
G7: (F1) [W8] -8                                                    POINT
Enter second data range: B7..G7

                A          B       C       D       E       F       G        ◄
1                        Changes in Income                                   ►
2                        From 1980 to 1990                                   ▲
3                                                                            ▼
4                       16-24   25-34   35-44   45-54   55-64    65+         ?
5                       ----------------------------------------------
6    Household          -10.0     1.0     4.0     4.5    -2.0    14.0
7    Men in Work Force  -15.0    19.0    47.0    16.0   -10.0    -8.0
8    Women in Work Force -10.0    38.0    75.0    38.0   -38.0    2.0
9    Head of Household  -30.2    15.5    51.0    13.5    -2.1    25.9
10
11
12
13
14
15
16
17
18
19
20
22-Aug-91  09:43 PM                                                         ■
```

Figure 5.9

The range B7..G7 should now be highlighted. If it is not, enter the correct range before continuing.

To accept this range,

Press: ⏎

To view the graph,

Press: F10 (GRAPH)

Your screen should look similar to Figure 5.10.

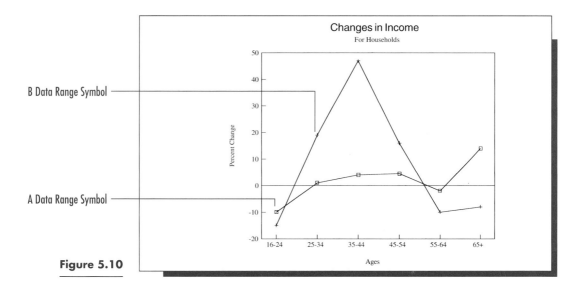

B Data Range Symbol

A Data Range Symbol

Figure 5.10

Dave still needs to enter the data ranges for Women in Work Force and Head of Household as the third and fourth data ranges (C and D). To return to the Graph menu and specify the ranges,

Press: SPACEBAR

Type: **C B8..G8**

Press: ⏎

Type: **D B9..G9**

Type: ⏎

To view this new graph,

Select: **V**iew

Your screen should now look similar to Figure 5.11.

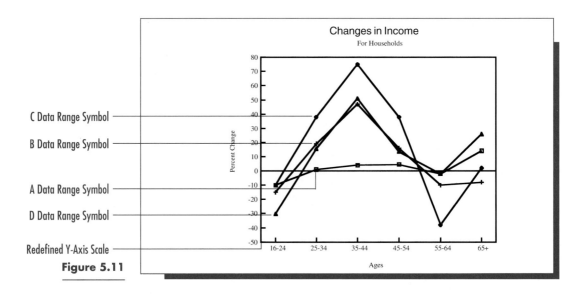

C Data Range Symbol ──────────

B Data Range Symbol ──────────

A Data Range Symbol ──────────

D Data Range Symbol ──────────

Redefined Y-Axis Scale ──────────

Figure 5.11

The data ranges for all four variables are now displayed in the graph. Notice that each data range is distinguished by a different symbol. Also notice that 1-2-3 automatically redefines the scale of the Y axis based on the highest and lowest values in the four data ranges.

To return to the Graph Settings dialog box,

Press: SPACEBAR

Press: (F2) (EDIT)

If you have a color monitor and want to view the graph in color, you should use the keyboard or the mouse to select the **C**olors on check box in the Graph Settings dialog box. Using the keyboard to view the graph in color,

Select: **C**olors on (↵) (F10) (GRAPH)

Each data range is displayed in a different color. If the graph is displayed on your screen, return to the Graph Settings dialog box.

Press: SPACEBAR

Editing Titles

The graph title is no longer appropriate since the graph now represents percentages for four different variables. Dave decides to change the title to Changes in Income From 1980 to 1990.

To change the second title line,

Select: Legends & Titles... Titles Second

Your screen should look similar to Figure 5.12.

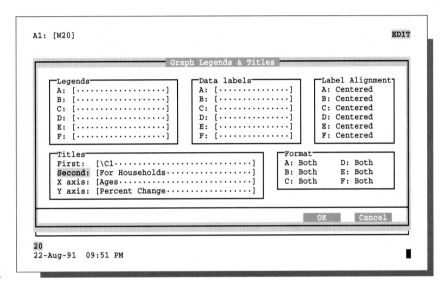

Figure 5.12

The current second title line is displayed following the prompt **S**econd:. To erase the title For Households,

Press: [ESC]

Cell C2 contains the label "From 1980 to 1990." To specify this label as the new second title in the graph, complete the command sequence as follows:

\C2 [↵]

View the graph again.

Press: [F10] (GRAPH)

Your screen should look similar to Figure 5.13.

New Second Title

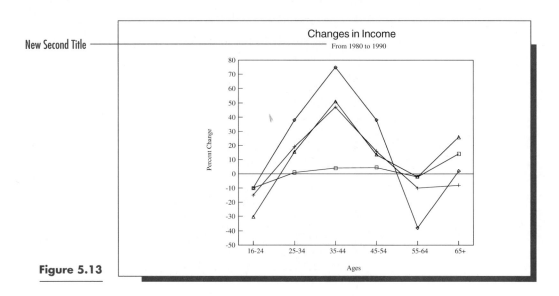

Figure 5.13

The new second title line is displayed centered over the graph.

Creating and Editing Legends

The four data ranges in the graph are distinguished from one another by a different symbol placed on each line. It is difficult, however, to know which line goes with which data range. Legends, which are descriptions of each line, will solve this problem. 1-2-3 will accept long legends (up to 19 characters), but it will wrap long legends to a second line. For readability, it is best to keep legends short.

To clear the graph from the screen and return to the Graph Legends & Titles dialog box,

Press: SPACEBAR

The command to add legends is found under **L**egends.

Select: **L**egends

Legends are specified using the same procedure as the graph titles: by typing the actual legend or by using the backslash key followed by the cell address of the worksheet entry to be used as the graph legend.

You can enter the label, Household, from cell A6, as the legend for the A data range by entering the cell reference. To see how this works,

Select: **A \A6**

Press: ⏎ (F10) (GRAPH)

The legends, Household, is displayed below the x axis title. Clear the graph. Individually entering legends allows you to change the legends from the labels you used on the worksheet. However, Dave wants to use the labels he entered on the worksheet. You can enter all the legends at one time by using the **R**ange command in the Graph Legend menu. To leave the Graph Legends & Titles dialog box,

Press: ⏎

To close the Graph Settings dialog box and display the Graph menu,

Press: ⏎

To specify a range of labels as the legends, continue the command sequence as follows:

Options **L**egend **R**ange

The **R**ange command allows you to specify a range of cells in the worksheet that contains entries that you want to be the legends for the graph data ranges. 1-2-3 uses the first entry in the range as the A data range legend, the second entry as the B data range legend, and so forth.

To specify the labels in cells A6 through A9 as the legends for the A through D data ranges, continue the command sequence as follows:

A6..A9 ⏎

The cell addresses are now entered in the Graph Legends & Titles dialog box as if you had entered them individually using the backslash feature. To see how the legends are displayed on the Graph Legends & Titles dialog box,

Select: (F2) (EDIT) **L**egends & Titles...

To view the graph and the legends,

Press: (F10) (GRAPH)

Your screen should look similar to Figure 5.14.

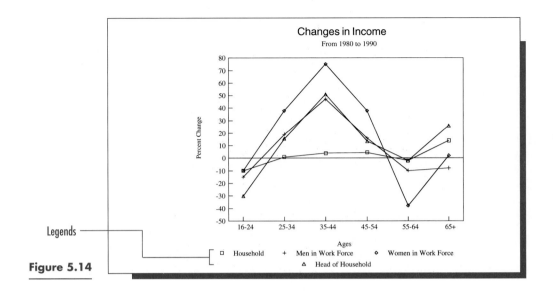

Legends

Figure 5.14

The four legends are displayed at the bottom of the graph.

Using Data Labels

For many graphs, it is important to display the exact value being plotted. To do this, **data labels** are used. Dave wants to see if adding data labels to the plotted points for Women in Work Force will improve his graph.

To do this, you will use the Graph menu rather than the dialog box.

Press:	SPACEBAR
Press:	⏎ twice
Select:	**D**ata-Labels

Your screen should look similar to Figure 5.15.

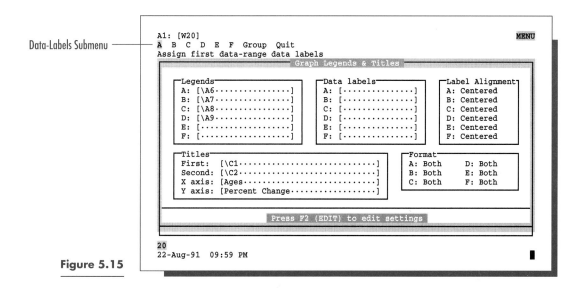

Data-Labels Submenu

```
A1: [W20]                                                      MENU
A  B  C  D  E  F  Group  Quit
Assign first data-range data labels
                    ╔═══════ Graph Legends & Titles ═══════╗
  ┌Legends──────────────────┐  ┌Data labels─────────────┐  ┌Label Alignment┐
  A: [\A6················]      A: [···············]        A: Centered
  B: [\A7················]      B: [···············]        B: Centered
  C: [\A8················]      C: [···············]        C: Centered
  D: [\A9················]      D: [···············]        D: Centered
  E: [··················]      E: [···············]        E: Centered
  F: [··················]      F: [···············]        F: Centered

  ┌Titles───────────────────────────────────┐  ┌Format──────────────┐
  First:  [\C1····························]      A: Both    D: Both
  Second: [\C2····························]      B: Both    E: Both
  X axis: [Ages·························]        C: Both    F: Both
  Y axis: [Percent Change··················]

                 ▓▓▓▓ Press F2 (EDIT) to edit settings ▓▓▓▓

20
22-Aug-91  09:59 PM                                              ■
```

Figure 5.15

The Graph Legends & Titles dialog box is displayed.

Data labels on the dialog box allow you to specify data labels for each individual range of data (A–F). Since Dave wants to see how the data labels would look only for the C data range (Women in Work Force),

Select: C

To specify the range containing the values to be displayed as the data labels, continue the command sequence,

B8..G8 (⏎)

Your screen should look similar to Figure 5.16.

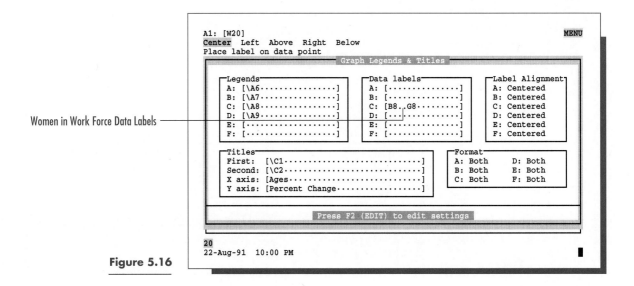

Women in Work Force Data Labels ———

```
A1: [W20]                                                        MENU
Center  Left  Above  Right  Below
Place label on data point
┌──────────────────── Graph Legends & Titles ────────────────────┐
│ ┌─Legends──────────────┐  ┌─Data labels──────────┐  ┌─Label Alignment─┐
│  A: [\A6················]   A: [················]   A: Centered
│  B: [\A7················]   B: [················]   B: Centered
│  C: [\A8················]   C: [B8·.G8··········]   C: Centered
│  D: [\A9················]   D: [···│··········]    D: Centered
│  E: [··················]    E: [················]   E: Centered
│  F: [··················]    F: [················]   F: Centered
│                                                    └─────────────────┘
│ ┌─Titles────────────────────────────────────────┐  ┌─Format──────────┐
│  First:  [\C1······························]       A: Both     D: Both
│  Second: [\C2······························]       B: Both     E: Both
│  X axis: [Ages·····························]       C: Both     F: Both
│  Y axis: [Percent Change··················]      └─────────────────┘
│                                                   
│             Press F2 (EDIT) to edit settings
└──────────────────────────────────────────────────────────────────┘

20
22-Aug-91  10:00 PM
```

Figure 5.16

Next, the control panel displays five options that control the placement of the data labels in the graph. They can be displayed centered, to the left, above, to the right, or below each data point.

To place the data labels to the left of the data points,

Select: **L**eft **Q**uit

To view the graph,

Press: (F10) (GRAPH)

Your screen should look similar to Figure 5.17.

Data Labels ——

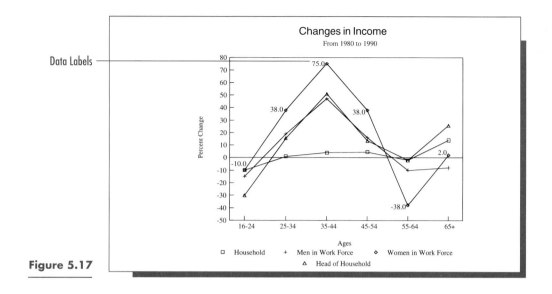

Figure 5.17

The data labels are displayed in the graph to the left of the data points for Women in Work Force.

Dave feels that data labels next to each data point for the four variables will clutter the graph too much. Instead of data labels, he decides to add grid lines to improve the readability of the graph.

Using Grids

The **G**rid lines option allows you to specify horizontal lines, vertical lines, or both to form a **grid** within the graph. A grid makes it easier to read the value of a data point or the height of a bar.

Return to the Graph Settings dialog box.

Press: SPACEBAR

Using the mouse to mark the check box for Horizontal (under Grid lines), click anywhere on Horizontal.

To display grids, mark the check box for **H**orizontal (under **G**rid lines), using either the keyboard or the mouse. Using the keyboard, issue the following command sequence:

F2 (EDIT) **G**rid lines **H**orizontal ⏎

To view the graph,

Press: F10 (GRAPH)

Your screen should look similar to Figure 5.18.

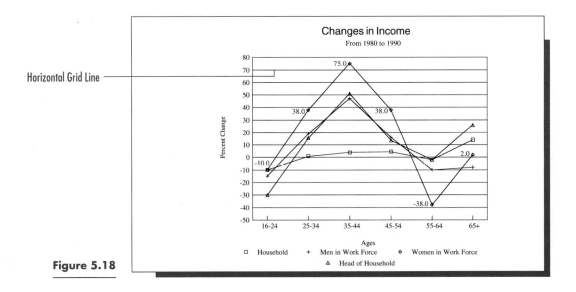

Horizontal Grid Line

Figure 5.18

Use grids and data labels sparingly because they can clutter a graph, making it more difficult to read.

Clearing Graph Settings

After looking at the graph, Dave decides to clear the data labels from the graph.

To return to the Graph Settings dialog box:

> **Press:** SPACEBAR

If you are using the mouse,

Click: Legends & Titles...

Click: C under Data labels

Click: the right mouse button

You can use either the keyboard or the mouse to clear the data labels for Women in Work Force range (C). Using the keyboard,

> **Select:** **L**egends & Titles... **D**ata labels **C**
> **Press:** ⌨ESC ⌨↵

The Graph Legends & Titles dialog box shows that the data label range is cleared.

To view the graph,

> **Press:** ⌨F10 (GRAPH)

Your screen should look similar to Figure 5.19.

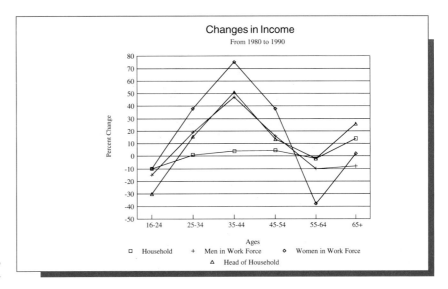

Figure 5.19

This looks better, but Dave feels the horizontal grid lines also detract from the graph. To return to the Graph Settings dialog box:

Press: SPACEBAR

Press: ⏎

Using the mouse to clear the horizontal grid from the graph,

Click: Horizontal (in Grid lines box)

To clear the horizontal grid from the graph, use either the keyboard or the mouse. Using the keyboard, issue the following command sequence:

Grid lines **H**orizontal ⏎

To view the graph,

Press: F10 (GRAPH)

The graph is now displayed without grid lines.

Saving Current Graph Settings

To save the current graph in the worksheet so that you can use it again, all you need to do is save the worksheet. The current graph settings will be saved as well. The next time you retrieve the file, you can view the graph again.

To clear the graph,

Press: SPACEBAR

To close the Graph Settings dialog box and return to READY mode,

Press: ⏎

Select: **Q**uit

Save this worksheet and the graph settings in a new file by issuing the following command sequence:

/File Save CHANGESG.WK1 ⏎

Now erase the worksheet from the screen and the computer's memory by issuing the following command sequence:

/Worksheet Erase Yes

It is always wise to save your worksheet before you use the **E**rase command; otherwise, you will lose your work.

On your screen, you should have a blank worksheet that has no current graph settings. To confirm this,

Press: (F10) (GRAPH)

The computer displays a blank screen, indicating that the current worksheet has no graph settings.

To return to the worksheet,

Press: SPACEBAR

Retrieve the file CHANGESG.WK1.

Now try viewing the graph.

Press: (F10) (GRAPH)

Your line graph is displayed on your screen just the way you left it.

Dave is not sure the line graph is right for his report, so in the next lab we will look at different types of graphs that Dave can use instead.

To return to the worksheet,

Press: SPACEBAR

Saving the current graph settings with the worksheet allows you to retrieve and view the graph when you retrieve the worksheet. However, saving the worksheet does not allow you to print the graph using PrintGraph.

Saving Graphs for Printing

To print your graph using the Lotus 1-2-3 PrintGraph program, you must first save the graph settings in a special file. This file is called a **graph file** and has a file extension of .PIC.

To save the current graph settings for printing, you use the **/G**raph **S**ave command. However, if you do not have a color printer and you are viewing your graph in color, you must reset the graph to black and white before you save the graph settings for printing. If you do not reset the graph to black and white, the graph will not print correctly. If you are displaying the graph in color and do not have a color printer, unmark the **C**olors on check box by issuing the following command sequence:

/Graph (F2) (EDIT) **C** (↵) (↵) **Q**uit

To save the graph for printing, issue the following command sequence:

/Graph **S**ave **LINE** (↵) **Q**uit

A description of the graph is saved on your data disk in a file called LINE.PIC. 1-2-3 automatically adds the .PIC extension to any graph you save for printing. A graph file name can have no more than eight characters and must follow the same naming conventions as other 1-2-3 files.

You are now ready to print the graph you saved. To print the graph, you will use 1-2-3's PrintGraph program. Before you start this program, you must exit 1-2-3. To return to the DOS prompt, issue the following command sequence:

/Quit **Y**es

Using PrintGraph

To complete this section, you must have properly installed and established your hardware setup for the PrintGraph program. (For details, see "Starting and Ending PrintGraph" in Chapter 4 of "Getting Started.")

Note If you are not at the DOS prompt, a menu probably appears on your screen that offers an option to return to DOS. Use this option now and at any other time we ask you to return to the DOS prompt.

To access PrintGraph,

Type: **PGRAPH**

In a few minutes, your screen should look similar to Figure 5.20.

PrintGraph Menu

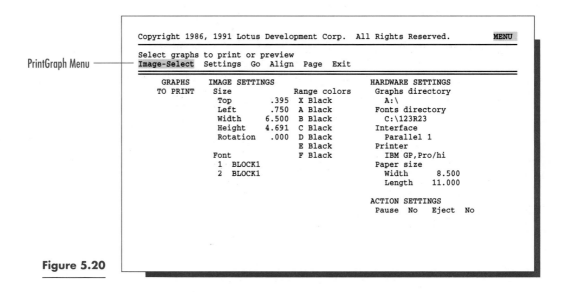

```
Copyright 1986, 1991 Lotus Development Corp.  All Rights Reserved.      MENU

Select graphs to print or preview
Image-Select  Settings  Go  Align  Page  Exit

    GRAPHS    IMAGE SETTINGS                      HARDWARE SETTINGS
   TO PRINT   Size                Range colors    Graphs directory
             Top          .395    X Black            A:\
             Left         .750    A Black         Fonts directory
             Width       6.500    B Black            C:\123R23
             Height      4.691    C Black         Interface
             Rotation     .000    D Black            Parallel 1
                                  E Black         Printer
             Font                 F Black            IBM GP,Pro/hi
             1  BLOCK1                            Paper size
             2  BLOCK1                               Width      8.500
                                                     Length    11.000

                                                  ACTION SETTINGS
                                                  Pause  No    Eject  No
```

Figure 5.20

Note Your hardware settings may differ from those in Figure 5.20 depending on your particular computer system.

The PrintGraph menu is automatically displayed in the second line of the control panel. You do not press / to display the menu. Move the menu pointer to each command, and read the short description on the line above the menu. You select commands from the menu just as you do in 1-2-3.

Printing a graph involves three simple steps: selecting the graph to be printed, preparing the printer, and printing.

First, to select the graph to be printed, issue the following command:

Image-Select

Your screen should look similar to Figure 5.21.

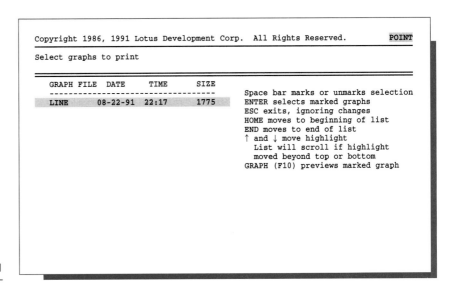

Figure 5.21

Although you cannot change any of the graph settings in the graph files, you can preview them by using the GRAPH function key, (F10).

Press: (F10) (GRAPH)

Your screen should look similar to Figure 5.22.

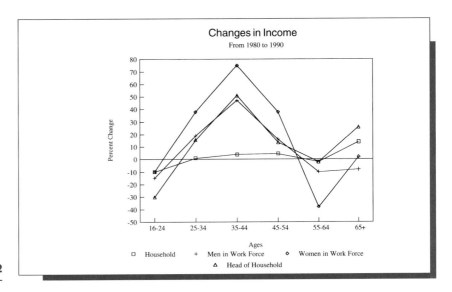

Figure 5.22

To return to the Image-Select screen,

Press: SPACEBAR

To select or mark the graph to be printed,

Press: SPACEBAR

A # sign appears next to the selected graph file. To complete your selection,

Press: ⏎

Your screen should look similar to Figure 5.23.

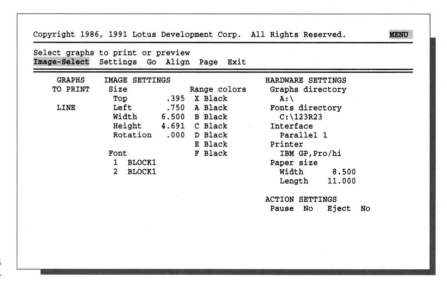

```
Copyright 1986, 1991 Lotus Development Corp.  All Rights Reserved.     MENU

Select graphs to print or preview
Image-Select  Settings  Go  Align  Page  Exit

      GRAPHS    IMAGE SETTINGS                       HARDWARE SETTINGS
      TO PRINT  Size               Range colors     Graphs directory
                Top          .395   X Black            A:\
      LINE      Left         .750   A Black          Fonts directory
                Width       6.500   B Black            C:\123R23
                Height      4.691   C Black          Interface
                Rotation     .000   D Black            Parallel 1
                                    E Black          Printer
                Font                F Black            IBM GP,Pro/hi
                1  BLOCK1                            Paper size
                2  BLOCK1                              Width      8.500
                                                       Length    11.000

                                                   ACTION SETTINGS
                                                   Pause  No   Eject  No
```

Figure 5.23

The selected graph file name is displayed on the PrintGraph settings sheet.

Next, prepare the printer by turning it on. If you are using continuous form paper, adjust the page so that the perforation is near the first print position. Make sure the printer is on line.

Finally, issue the following command sequence:

Align **G**o

Align tells the printer that the paper is now at the top of a page. In a few moments, your printer should begin to print the graph.

To advance the paper to the top of the next page and to leave the PrintGraph program, issue the following command:

Page **E**xit **Y**es

You should be returned to the DOS prompt.

Glossary

Bar graph: A graph that shows numeric data as a set of evenly spaced bars, each bar representing a value in the range being graphed.

Data labels: The labels attached to data points on a graph with the /Graph Options Data-Labels command.

Graph menu: The selection of menu items displayed when /Graph is selected.

Grid: The horizontal, vertical, or intersecting lines that can be specified in a graph with the /Graph Options Grid command.

HLCO graph: A graph used for tracking the high, low, closing, and opening values of stocks.

Legends: The patterns and symbols used in a graph and the text that defines them.

Line graph: A graph that represents numeric data as a set of points along a line.

Mixed graph: A graph that displays data using both bars and lines.

Pie chart: A graph that compares parts to the whole, with each value in a range being a slice of the pie.

Stacked bar graph: A graph that compares totals as well as individual values, with each part representing a value in one of the data ranges.

Title: A descriptive label placed at the top of a graph or along the X or Y axis.

X axis: The horizontal boundary of a graph.

XY graph: A graph that shows the relationship between two variables by plotting pairs of values.

Y axis: The vertical boundary of a graph.

Matching

1. F10

2. Type

3. Legend

4. Data-Labels

5. Grids

6. Reset

7. X

8. /GS

9. Image-Select

10. /G

_____ **a.** saves a graph for printing

_____ **b.** erases a data range

_____ **c.** displays value next to the corresponding point on a graph

_____ **d.** labels the horizontal axis

_____ **e.** displays graph on screen

_____ **f.** chooses graph to be printed

_____ **g.** accesses the Graph menu

_____ **h.** displays symbols and descriptive labels

_____ **i.** determines the kind of graph

_____ **j.** adds horizontal or vertical reference lines to the graph

Multiple Choice

In the following graph, several items are identified by letters. In the space below the worksheet, enter the correct term for each item. The first one has been completed for you. (*Hint:* Use the glossary for this lab.)

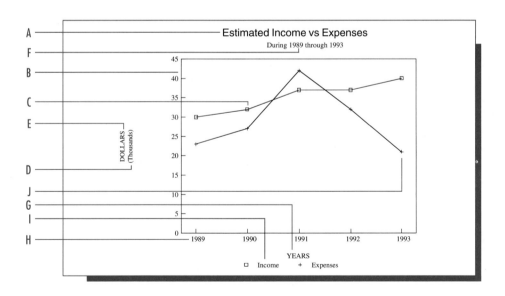

a. First title   f. _____

b. _____   g. _____

c. _____   h. _____

d. _____   i. _____

e. _____   j. _____

Cases

1. The following table presents the leasing cost per acre of private and federal lands:

| | **Years** | | | |
	1975	**1980**	**1985**	**1990**
Federal	2.00	2.40	1.85	1.90
Private	6.00	7.80	8.90	9.00

Source: General Accounting Office. Printed in *USA Today*, May 17, 1991, p. 6A.

Display this data as a line graph by completing the following steps:

a. Create a worksheet file of this data. Put your name in cell A1 and the date in cell A2.

b. Specify a line graph.

c. Set the X axis as the years.

d. Specify the data for the two categories as the data ranges.

e. Enter a first title line: Cost for Leasing Lands.

f. Enter a second title line that displays your name and the current date.

g. Enter an X-axis title line: Years.

h. Enter a Y-axis title line: Price per Acre.

i. Create a legend to identify the two data ranges.

j. Display the graph, and save the graph as LINE5-1.

k. Save this worksheet with the current graph settings as HWLAB5-1, and then print the worksheet.

l. Print the graph using PrintGraph.

2. The following data from the Census Bureau presents statistics on adults 25 to 34 years old living with parents.

	Years			
	1960	1970	1980	1990
Men	11	9	10.1	15
Women	7.5	6	7	8

Source: *The Arizona Republic,* June 16, 1991, p. A4.

To show this data in the form of a line graph, complete the following steps.

a. Create a worksheet file of this data. Put your name in cell A1 and the date in cell A2.

b. Specify a line graph.

c. Set the X axis as the years.

d. Specify the percentages of adults living with parents as the two data ranges.

e. Enter a first title line: Adults Living with Parents.

f. Enter a second title line that displays your name and the current date.

g. Enter an X-axis title: Years.

h. Enter a Y-axis title: Percent.

i. Create a legend to identify the two groups of data.

j. Add horizontal grid lines.

k. Display the graph, and save the graph as LINE5-2.

l. Save the worksheet with the current graph settings as HWLAB5-2, and then print the worksheet.

m. Print the graph using PrintGraph.

3. To complete this problem, you first must have built the worksheet as specified in Practice Case 3 in Lab 3. If you have completed that problem, retrieve the file HWLAB3-3.WK1. Complete the following steps:

a. Specify a line graph.

b. Set the X axis to display the weeks 1 through 4.

c. Specify the four employees' sales as data ranges A, B, C, and D.

d. Enter an appropriate first title line.

e. Enter a second title line that displays your name and the current date.

f. Enter an appropriate Y-axis title line.

g. Create appropriate legends to identify the four data ranges.

h. Display the graph. Save the graph as LINE5-3. Save the worksheet as HWLAB5-3, and then print the worksheet.

i. Print the graph using PrintGraph.

4. To complete this problem, you must have completed the worksheet in Practice Case 1 in Lab 3. If you have completed that problem, retrieve the file HWLAB3-1.WK1.

Create a line graph showing gross margin, total expenses, and net income before taxes. Add an appropriate first title and X- and Y-axis titles. Specify your name and the current date as the second title line. Enter appropriate legends. Save the graph as LINE5-4. Save the worksheet as HWLAB5-4. Print the worksheet and the graph.

5. Jay Tucker did a random survey of 200 people to find the average income based on the number of years they spent in college. Jay will use the data he collected for his report. Retrieve the file PROB5-5.WK1. This file contains the average income by age based on the number of years in college.

Create a line graph of the five data ranges. Add a first title line, legends, and X- and Y-axis labels. Enter your name and the current date as the second title line. Save the graph as LINE5-5. Save the worksheet as HWLAB5-5, and then print the graph.

6. Retrieve the file PROB5-6.WK1. This file contains data on the cost of driving in 1990 and 1991. Use this data to create a line graph that best represents the data. Enter your name and the current date as the second title line. Save the graph as LINE5-6. Print the graph, and then save the worksheet as HWLAB5-6.

Lab 6

Creating and Printing Graphs

In Lab 6, you will learn how to:

- Modify graph types
- Name graphs
- Create bar, stacked bar, mixed, pie, and exploded pie graphs
- Enhance a graph
- Use the /Data Fill command
- Recall previously named graphs

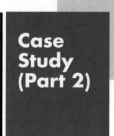

Case Study (Part 2)

Dave Robson's economics report is due in a few days. He was not happy with the line graph created in Lab 5, and he thinks a bar graph would be more appropriate. Dave has also found data for other sections of his report that he needs to put into graph form. We will follow Dave as he creates the graphs for his report.

Changing the Graph Type

Dave has modified his worksheet slightly from Lab 5 and has added some more data. To see the line graph, load the 1-2-3 program in the usual manner, and retrieve the file REPORT.WK1. View the graph by pressing (F10) (GRAPH).

Your screen should look similar to Figure 6.1.

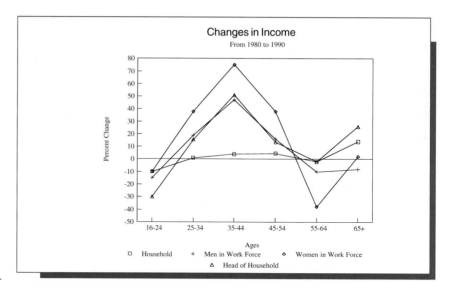

Figure 6.1

In Lab 5, you learned about line graphs. There are six other types of graphs: bar, stacked bar, XY, mixed, HLCO, and pie. Bar and stacked bar graphs use data ranges in the same way line graphs do. However, a bar graph shows numeric data as a set of evenly spaced bars, each of which represents a value in the range that you are graphing.

The data in Dave's worksheet shows the percentage change for four variables over six different age groups. Dave could use this line graph for his report, but a bar graph will show the differences in percentages more clearly.

If you are using a mouse, access the main menu and

Click: Graph

Click: Type

Click: Bar

To create a bar graph of this data, you need to access the Graph menu to change the type of graph. If you are using the keyboard, return to the worksheet by pressing any key, and then complete the following command sequence:

/**G**raph **T**ype **B**ar

The option button asterisk (*) is now next to **B**ar. To see how this has changed the graph,

Press: (F10) (GRAPH)

Dave feels the bar graph represents the data better than the line graph. He will use the bar graph in his report. To save the graph for printing, return to the Graph menu, and then issue the following command sequence:

Save **BAR** (↵)

Naming Graphs

Dave would like to create another graph using the worksheet data. To create more than one graph in a worksheet, each graph needs to be named. When you name a graph, the graph's specifications are stored with the graph's name. You can view and modify the graph simply by recalling the name of the graph. If the current graph settings are not named, they will be deleted as you specify new graph settings. If you want the **named graph** to display in color, you will have to turn on the color option before naming the graph.

A graph name can be up to 15 characters long and should be descriptive of the graph. The name cannot contain spaces, commas, semicolons, or the characters +, −, /, $, >, <, @, *, or #. It can be entered using either uppercase or lowercase characters; 1-2-3 will always display the graph name in uppercase. To save the current graph settings under the name BAR, issue the following command sequence:

Name **C**reate **BAR** (↵)

The bar graph settings are named and stored in the computer's memory for later recall. Named graphs are not saved to the disk with the worksheet file until the worksheet is saved.

Canceling Graph Settings

To demonstrate how to recall named graphs, you will reset, or clear, the current graph settings and then recall the named graph BAR. The Reset menu lets you cancel all the current graph settings (**G**raph), individual data ranges (**X** and **A–F**), all data ranges (**R**anges), or all graph options (**O**ptions).

To erase the current graph settings using the **R**eset command, issue the following command sequence:

Reset **G**raph ⌗F10⌗ (GRAPH)

1-2-3 beeps and displays a blank screen. This means that there are no current graph settings in memory. When using the **R**eset command, be very careful that you select the correct submenu command. Otherwise, you can inadvertently cancel many graph settings that are time consuming to respecify.

Now, to recall the named graph BAR, press SPACEBAR, and then issue the following command sequence:

Name **U**se **BAR** ⌗←⌗

The bar graph should be displayed on your screen.

Naming graphs is an important feature because it allows you to have more than one set of graph settings in a single worksheet.

It is perfectly acceptable to name the graph specifications and then use the same name to save the graph for printing. The graph settings will be stored in the worksheet with the name BAR, and the graph image will be saved on the disk as BAR.PIC for printing.

Understanding the difference between naming graphs, saving graphs, and saving files is important:

- **/G**raph **N**ame **C**reate names a graph so that it can be recalled later and displayed on your screen.

- **/G**raph **S**ave creates a new file on your data disk with a .PIC extension for printing with the PrintGraph program.

- **/F**ile **S**ave creates a worksheet file with a .WK1 extension. The worksheet file includes all values and labels, along with all named graph settings and current graph settings.

Clear the graph, and quit the Graph menu.

Dave has other data he needs to include in his report. For his section on "Changes in Leisure Activities," Dave has statistics on the number of subscribers to pay television stations. Dave has entered the data into this worksheet. To see the data,

Press: (PGDN)

Your screen should look similar to Figure 6.2.

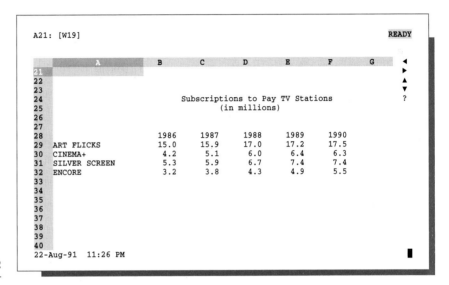

Figure 6.2

A21: [W19]   READY

	A	B	C	D	E	F	G
21							
22							
23							
24		Subscriptions to Pay TV Stations					
25		(in millions)					
26							
27							
28		1986	1987	1988	1989	1990	
29	ART FLICKS	15.0	15.9	17.0	17.2	17.5	
30	CINEMA+	4.2	5.1	6.0	6.4	6.3	
31	SILVER SCREEN	5.3	5.9	6.7	7.4	7.4	
32	ENCORE	3.2	3.8	4.3	4.9	5.5	
33							
34							
35							
36							
37							
38							
39							
40							

22-Aug-91   11:26 PM

Each of the pay stations available is listed in column A. The number of subscribers, in millions, is listed in columns B through F.

The data in Dave's worksheet compares the number of subscribers during the years 1986 through 1990 in the United States. Dave could create a line graph using this data, but a bar graph will show the differences more clearly.

To create a bar graph of this data, begin by resetting the current graph. Issue the following command sequence:

/**G**raph **R**eset **G**raph

Notice the Graph Settings dialog box displays the default settings. Define the new graph type as follows:

Select: **T**ype **B**ar

Using the Group Command

Next you will need to specify the data ranges. The X data range will display the five years 1986, 1987, 1988, 1989, and 1990 as the X-axis labels. The X data range is B28 through F28. The data ranges for the numeric data to be graphed are the numbers for the four different pay stations. The data is located in cells B29 through F32.

1-2-3 has a quick way to define the data range settings for a graph if the data in the worksheet are located in consecutive columns or rows. Since the X data range and the A through D data ranges are in the worksheet range B28 through F32, we can use the /Graph Group command to quickly define the graph data ranges.

Select: **G**roup

In response to the prompt "Enter group range:," continue the command sequence by highlighting the range as:

B28..F32

1-2-3 will automatically divide the group range into all the data ranges for the graph beginning with the X data range and continuing with the A through D ranges.

Press: ⏎

The next menu displays the choices **C**olumnwise or **R**owwise. This tells 1-2-3 whether to divide the ranges by columns or rows. Since we want each row of the graph to be a data range for the graph,

Select: **R**owwise

The X and A through D data ranges have been specified and are displayed in the Graph Settings dialog box.

To view the graph,

Select: **V**iew

Your screen should look similar to Figure 6.3.

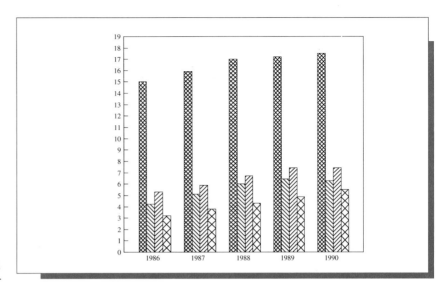

Figure 6.3

Remember that the **V**iew command works the same as (F10) (GRAPH). You can use **V**iew whenever the Graph menu is displayed. (F10) (GRAPH) will display the current graph whenever a graph is defined for a worksheet.

Using the **G**roup command to specify the data ranges can save a lot of time; however, the worksheet must be set up so that the X and A through F data ranges are in a continuous range.

Each yearly group of bars shows the number of subscribers for each pay station. For example, the first group of bars shows Dave the difference in the number of subscribers for each of the four stations.

The bars in the graph contain different **hatch patterns,** or designs, to identify the different variable percentages. If you have a color monitor and want to view the graph in color, press SPACEBAR to clear the graph. Color can be turned on using either the Graph menu or the Graph Settings dialog box. You used the dialog box in Lab 5 to turn the color on. Another way to turn the color on is to issue the following command sequence:

Options **C**olor **Q**uit

You can switch to and from color by using the **O**ptions **C**olor command and the **O**ptions **B**&W command. In color, each bar is filled with a solid color. In black and white, each bar contains a different hatch pattern. If you have changed the color, view the graph again.

Press SPACEBAR to clear the graph and return to the Graph menu.

Complete the graph by adding the following:

- Legends for the A through D data ranges (use **O**ptions **L**egend **R**ange)
- First title: Subscriptions to Pay TV Stations
- Second title: By [Your Name]
- X-axis title: Years
- Y-axis title: People (in millions)

When you have finished, view the graph. Your screen should be similar to Figure 6.4.

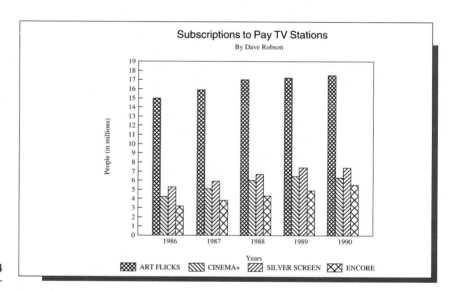

Figure 6.4

Clear the graph from your screen, quit the Graph menu, and return to the worksheet.

Creating a Stacked Bar Graph

By creating a stacked bar graph, Dave can show the total number of subscribers for each year. Dave can change the current bar graph to a stacked bar graph simply by changing the graph type.

A stacked bar graph compares totals as well as individual values. Each part of a stacked bar graph represents a value in one of the data ranges.

Change the graph type to stacked bar, and view it by issuing the following command sequence:

/Graph **T**ype **S**tack-Bar (F10) (GRAPH)

Your screen should look similar to Figure 6.5.

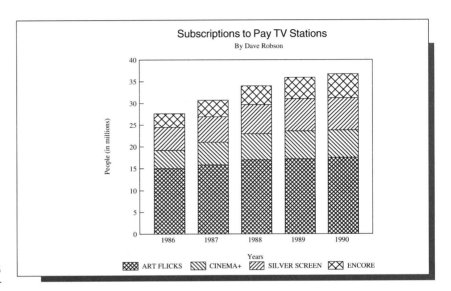

Figure 6.5

In this graph, the bars representing number of subscribers for each pay station are stacked on top of one another in a single bar. The parts of the bar are differentiated by various hatch patterns or colors. Each bar represents the total number of subscriptions for each year.

Return to the Graph menu.

Enhancing a Graph

Dave can make the graph look better by giving the bars a 3-D effect and adding grid lines. To see how this works, keyboard users should issue the following command sequence:

(F2) (EDIT) **3**-D bars (↵) (F10) (GRAPH)

If you are using a mouse,
Click: 3-D bars
and then press (F10) (GRAPH).

Your screen should look similar to Figure 6.6.

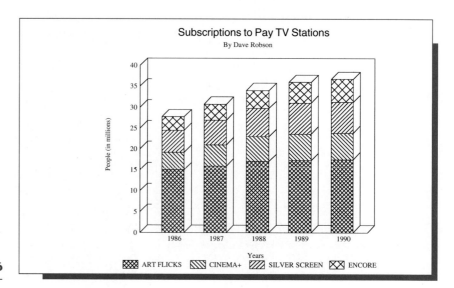

Figure 6.6

The stacked bar graph is now displayed as three-dimensional bars. By making the bars look three-dimensional, the graph is harder to read. Dave thinks that adding horizontal grid lines will make it clearer. To add grid lines, return to the Graph Settings dialog box. If you are using the keyboard, issue the following command sequence:

Grid lines **H**orizontal ⏎

View the graph.

If you are using the mouse, you can access grid lines by clicking Horizontal in the Grid lines box.

Your screen should look similar to Figure 6.7.

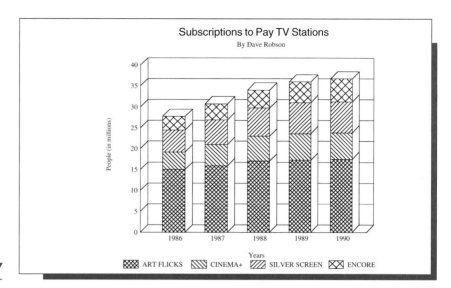

Figure 6.7

The grid lines make the graph easier to read. Another option available on the Graph Settings dialog box is orientation. The **O**rientation option displays the X axis on the left and places the Y axis along the top. The bars are then drawn from left to right instead of bottom to top. But since Dave likes the way the graph is drawn, we will not change the orientation of the graph.

The graph is now ready to be saved for printing. (If you were viewing the graph in color but you don't have a color printer, remember to turn off the color option before you save the graph as a .PIC file.)

To save the graph for printing as STACKED.PIC, clear the graph from the screen, and then press ⏎ to return to the Graph menu. Continue with the following command sequence:

Save **STACKED** ⏎

Name the graph settings by issuing the following command sequence:

Name **C**reate **STACKED** ⏎ **Q**uit

Creating a Pie Chart

Dave would like to see what percentage each pay station attracts of the total number of subscriptions to these stations in 1986. The best graph for this purpose is a pie chart.

A **pie chart** shows the relationship between a whole and its parts. In a pie chart, each value in a range is a slice of the pie, and the size of each slice corresponds to a percentage of the total.

Graph settings for pie charts are different from line or bar graphs. Before you can create a pie chart, you need to reset the current graph settings.

Issue the following command sequence:

> **/G**raph **R**eset **G**raph

Then specify a pie chart by issuing the following command sequence:

> **T**ype **P**ie

In pie charts, you use the X data range to label the slices of the pie and the A data range to specify the numeric data to be graphed. To display the worksheet screen so that you can easily refer to cells in the worksheet,

> **Press:** (F6) (WINDOW)

Whenever the Graph menu is displayed on the screen and you are in MENU mode, you can use (F6), the WINDOW function key, to clear the dialog box and display the worksheet. The worksheet will continue to be displayed until (F6) (WINDOW) is pressed again to redisplay the dialog box.

The labels for the slices are located in cells A29 through A32. The A data range is the number of subscribers for each pay station during the year 1986, located in cells B29 through B32. Since the data for this graph is located in a continuous range, you can use the **G**roup command to define the data ranges. To do this, issue the following command sequence:

> **G**roup **A29..B32** (↵)

To use the columns of data for the graph ranges,

> **Select:** **C**olumnwise

To redisplay the dialog box,

> **Press:** (F6) (WINDOW)

To view the pie chart,

> **Press:** (F10) (GRAPH)

Your screen should look similar to Figure 6.8.

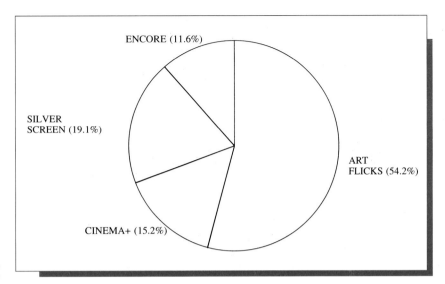

Figure 6.8

Each pay station, defined in the X range, labels a slice of the pie. The percentage for each station is a portion of the total number of subscribers in 1986. 1-2-3 automatically calculated the percentages. For example, 11.6 percent of all subscribers in 1986 subscribed to Encore.

Note If you have a color monitor and the graph on your screen is not in color, you may want to turn color on.

Shading the Pie Chart

To further differentiate the pie's slices, you can add shading (color or hatch patterns) to the pie chart. There are eight different hatch patterns. To assign a hatch pattern or color to each of the four slices of the pie, you will fill a worksheet column with the values 1 to 4. The **shading values** are specified as the B data range and can be any number from 1 to 8. Shading values can appear almost anywhere in the worksheet, so long as the cells can be defined in a single range.

Clear the graph, and then leave the Graph menu.

Select:　**Q**uit

You will enter the shading values in column G of the worksheet.

Move to:　G29

Rather than typing in each number, you can use the **D**ata **F**ill command to fill the column with a sequence of numbers. To do this,

Select: /**D**ata **F**ill

To specify the range of cells to fill, continue the command sequence as follows:

G29..G32 ⏎

To enter the number 1 as the **start value,** or the first value 1-2-3 enters in the range,

Type: 1

Press: ⏎

To accept the number 1 as the **step value,** or the increment between each of the values,

Press: ⏎

The **stop value** is the number 1-2-3 uses as the upper limit for the sequence. Since the range contains only four cells, it will reach the end of the range before the default stop value (8191). You could enter the number 4 or simply accept the default. To accept the default,

Press: ⏎

Your screen should look similar to Figure 6.9.

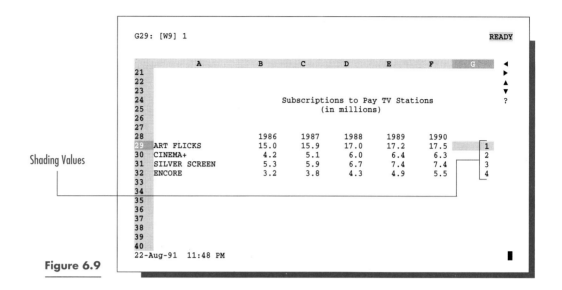

Shading Values

```
G29: [W9] 1                                                  READY

             A           B       C       D       E       F      G    ◄
21                                                                   ►
22                                                                   ▲
23                                                                   ▼
24                         Subscriptions to Pay TV Stations          ?
25                                (in millions)
26
27
28                       1986    1987    1988    1989    1990
29  ART FLICKS           15.0    15.9    17.0    17.2    17.5    1
30  CINEMA+               4.2     5.1     6.0     6.4     6.3    2
31  SILVER SCREEN         5.3     5.9     6.7     7.4     7.4    3
32  ENCORE                3.2     3.8     4.3     4.9     5.5    4
33
34
35
36
37
38
39
40
22-Aug-91  11:48 PM                                              ∎
```

Figure 6.9

The numbers 1 through 4 are entered in the specified range of cells. To define these values as the B data range, issue the following command sequence:

/Graph **B G29..G32** ⏎

View the graph.

Your screen should look similar to Figure 6.10.

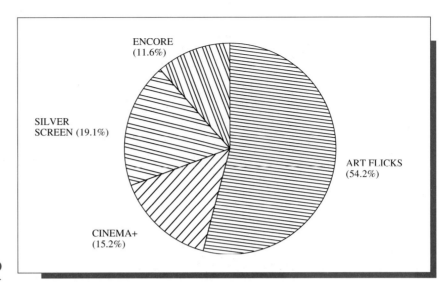

ENCORE
(11.6%)

SILVER
SCREEN (19.1%)

ART FLICKS
(54.2%)

CINEMA+
(15.2%)

Figure 6.10

The shading values specified in the B range determine the shading for each slice of the pie. If you changed the values in the worksheet, the shading would change correspondingly.

Creating an Exploded Pie Chart

A slice or several slices of the pie can be further emphasized by exploding the slice(s) from the pie. To do this, you add 100 to the value in the B data range of the slice(s) to be exploded.

To return to READY mode, clear the graph, then leave the Graph menu:

Select: **Q**uit

To explode the Encore slice from the pie,

Move to: G32

Type: **104**

Press: ⏎

The last digit (in this case, 4) determines the shading for the exploded slice.

View the graph.

Your screen should now look similar to Figure 6.11.

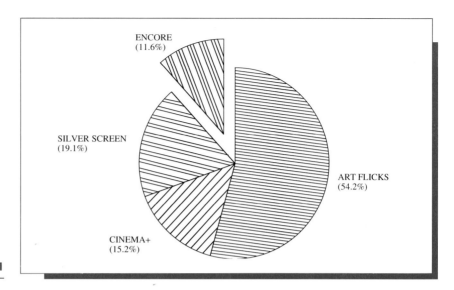

Figure 6.11

The slice of the pie chart representing Encore is exploded.

Complete the pie chart as follows:

- Set the first graph title: Subscriptions for 1986.
- Enter your name as the second graph title.
- View the graph.
- Name the graph PIE.
- Save the graph as PIE.

Using What-If Graphing

Dave would like to see what the effect of Art Flicks having 10 million fewer subscribers in 1986 would have on the total percentages. To do this, you will use what-if graphing, which shows how changes in the worksheet data affect the graphs using that data. To change the worksheet, return to READY mode.

Select: **Q**uit

To reflect this change in the number of Art Flicks' subscribers, you need to reduce the number of subscribers.

Move to: B29

Type: 5

Press: ⏎

Your screen should look similar to Figure 6.12.

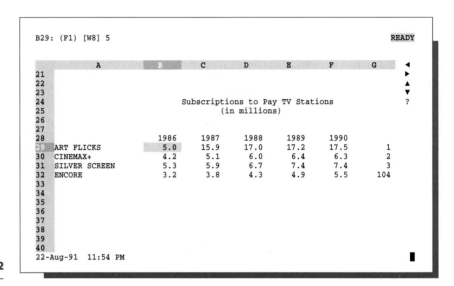

```
B29: (F1) [W8] 5                                                    READY

              A          B        C        D        E        F        G     ◄
    21                                                                      ►
    22                                                                      ▲
    23                                                                      ▼
    24                       Subscriptions to Pay TV Stations               ?
    25                              (in millions)
    26
    27
    28                     1986     1987     1988     1989     1990
    29 ART FLICKS          5.0      15.9     17.0     17.2     17.5      1
    30 CINEMAX+            4.2      5.1      6.0      6.4      6.3       2
    31 SILVER SCREEN       5.3      5.9      6.7      7.4      7.4       3
    32 ENCORE              3.2      3.8      4.3      4.9      5.5      104
    33
    34
    35
    36
    37
    38
    39
    40
    22-Aug-91  11:54 PM                                                ■
```

Figure 6.12

View the pie chart to see how this change has affected the relative percentages of each pay station. Your screen should look similar to Figure 6.13.

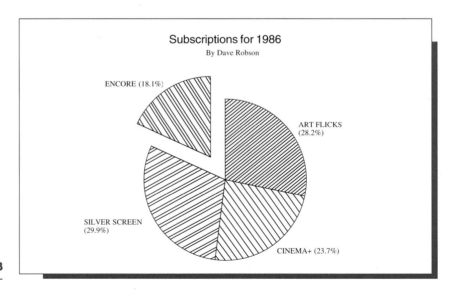

Figure 6.13

Art Flicks now has a much smaller percentage of the total number of subscribers, whereas the other three stations have larger percentages of the total. Changes in worksheet data are immediately reflected in any graphs based on the data. What-if graphing is a very powerful way to visualize the effect of changes in the worksheet.

Return to the worksheet, and then edit cell B29 to redisplay the original data for Art Flicks, 15 million.

Creating Mixed Graphs

Another section of Dave's paper is concerned with recent demographic and financial changes in education. Dave has found data on the percent of families with children under 18 and the cost of education.

To see this data,

Press: `PGDN`

A **mixed graph** combines a bar graph with a line graph. A mixed graph shows different types of data on one chart. 1-2-3 uses the A, B, and C data ranges for the sets of bars and the D, E, and F data ranges for the lines.

The graph settings for the mixed chart are different from the pie graphs. Before you can create the mixed chart, you need to reset the current graph settings.

Issue the following command sequence:

/**G**raph **R**eset **G**raph

Mixed charts use the X data range to label the X axis just as the line and bar charts did. For Dave's chart, the X data range will be the years 1970 through 1988. The A data range will be used to create bars that represent the cost of education; the D data range will be used to graph the line showing the percentage of families with children under 18.

Create the mixed graph as follows:

- Set the graph type to Mixed

- Enter the X range as B49..F49

- Enter the A range as B51..F51

- Enter the D range as B52..F52

- Set the first graph title: Changes in Education (or use cell C45)

- Set the second graph title: For Families with Children under 18 (or use cell B46)

- Set the X-axis graph title: Years

- Set legends: Cost (in thousands) for the A range; Percent of Families for the D range

- Set data labels for range A as B51..F51, and center the labels

- View the graph

Your screen should look similar to Figure 6.14.

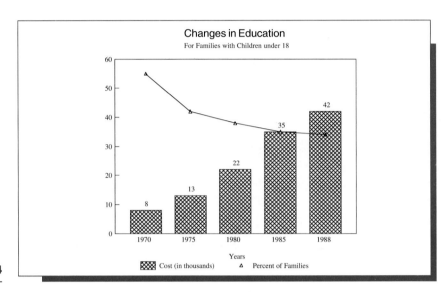

Figure 6.14

The graph shows Dave that as the number of families with children under 18 decreased, the cost of education increased.

Return to the Graph menu and:

- Name the graph MIXED

- Save the graph as MIXED

Recalling Previously Named Graphs

Dave feels that he has enough graphs for his report. Review each of the graphs you have named. After viewing a graph, press SPACEBAR before you issue the following command sequences:

Name Use **BAR** (↵)

Name Use **STACKED** (↵)

Name Use **PIE** ⏎

Name Use **MIXED** ⏎

To leave the Graph menu.

Select: **Q**uit

You are now ready to print the graphs you saved. Before you can start the PrintGraph program, you must save the worksheet containing all the named graphs as GRAPHS.WK1, and then exit 1-2-3 by issuing the following command sequences:

/**F**ile **S**ave **G**raphs ⏎

/**Q**uit **Y**es

You are returned to the DOS prompt.

Using PrintGraph

Load and start PrintGraph as you did in Lab 5. To select the graphs to be printed, issue the following command:

Image-Select

Your screen should look similar to Figure 6.15.

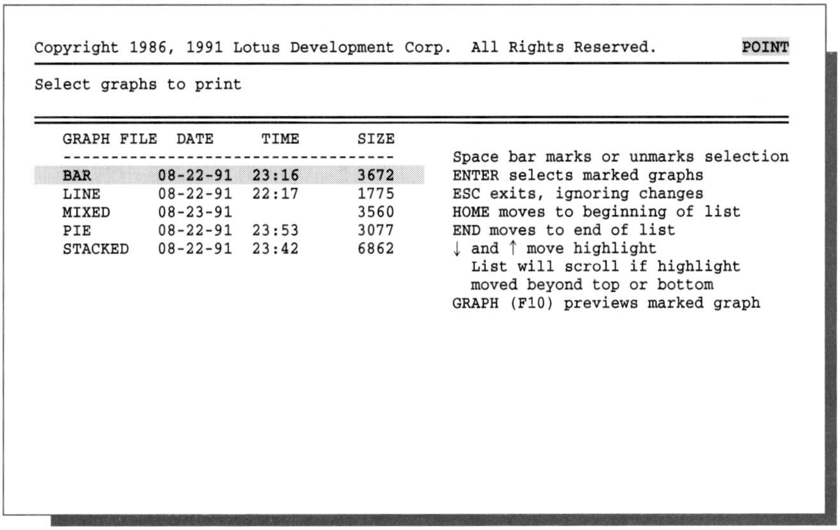

```
Copyright 1986, 1991 Lotus Development Corp.  All Rights Reserved.      POINT

Select graphs to print


  GRAPH FILE  DATE      TIME    SIZE
  ----------------------------------              Space bar marks or unmarks selection
  BAR         08-22-91  23:16    3672              ENTER selects marked graphs
  LINE        08-22-91  22:17    1775              ESC exits, ignoring changes
  MIXED       08-23-91           3560              HOME moves to beginning of list
  PIE         08-22-91  23:53    3077              END moves to end of list
  STACKED     08-22-91  23:42    6862              ↓ and ↑ move highlight
                                                     List will scroll if highlight
                                                     moved beyond top or bottom
                                                  GRAPH (F10) previews marked graph
```

Figure 6.15

For now, you will print the BAR and STACKED graphs. To select or mark the graphs to be printed:

Move to: BAR

Press: SPACEBAR

Move to: STACKED

Press: SPACEBAR

A # sign appears next to the selected graph files. To complete your selections,

Press: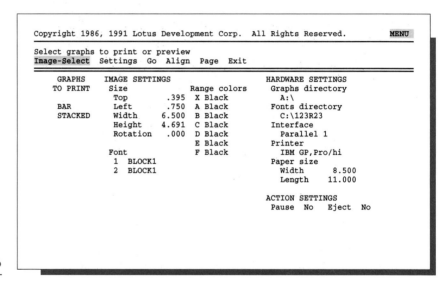

Your screen should look similar to Figure 6.16.

```
Copyright 1986, 1991 Lotus Development Corp.  All Rights Reserved.    MENU

Select graphs to print or preview
Image-Select   Settings  Go  Align  Page  Exit
────────────────────────────────────────────────────────────────────────
   GRAPHS     IMAGE SETTINGS                     HARDWARE SETTINGS
   TO PRINT    Size                 Range colors  Graphs directory
               Top          .395    X Black          A:\
   BAR         Left         .750    A Black       Fonts directory
   STACKED     Width       6.500    B Black          C:\123R23
               Height      4.691    C Black       Interface
               Rotation     .000    D Black          Parallel 1
                                    E Black       Printer
               Font                 F Black          IBM GP,Pro/hi
               1  BLOCK1                          Paper size
               2  BLOCK1                             Width      8.500
                                                     Length    11.000

                                                  ACTION SETTINGS
                                                  Pause  No   Eject  No
```

Figure 6.16

The selected graph file names are displayed. Prepare the printer by turning it on. If you are using continuous form paper, adjust the page so that the perforation is near the first print position. Make sure the printer is on line. Start printing by issuing the following command sequence:

Align **G**o

To advance the paper to the top of the next page and to leave the PrintGraph program, issue the following command sequence:

Page **E**xit **Y**es

Once again, you are returned to the DOS prompt.

Exploded pie chart: A pie chart with one or more slices exploded to emphasize a particular value or values.

Hatch patterns: The display pattern 1-2-3 uses to distinguish among data ranges in bar graphs, stacked bar graphs, and pie charts.

Named graph: A graph whose settings have been assigned a name so that more than one set of graph settings can be created in a worksheet.

Shading values: A range of numbers (1 through 8) that defines the hatch patterns or colors for the corresponding slices of a pie chart.

Start value: The first value 1-2-3 enters in a range during the /Data Fill command.

Step value: The increment between values in a range that is filled using the /Data Fill command.

Stop value: The number 1-2-3 uses as the upper limit for the sequence of values entered using the /Data Fill command.

Matching

1. (F6)

2. #

3. Mixed graph

4. B data range

5. Data Fill

6. 100

7. Pie chart

8. 3-D

9. /GNC

10. /GNU

_____ **a.** the type of graph that compares the parts to the whole

_____ **b.** used to enter a sequence of numbers

_____ **c.** in MENU mode, turns off display of dialog boxes

_____ **d.** makes a named graph current

_____ **e.** enhances a graph

_____ **f.** indicates selection of graph for printing

_____ **g.** names a graph

_____ **h.** combines bar and line graph

_____ **i.** added to explode a pie slice

_____ **j.** indicates shading values for a pie chart

Multiple Choice

1. A _____ compares totals as well as individual values.

   a. pie chart

   b. line graph

   c. bar graph

   d. stacked bar graph

2. The three values used by the /Data Fill command are:

   a. first, middle, and last

   b. start, step, and end

   c. start, step, and stop

   d. first, step, and end

3. To emphasize slice(s) from a pie chart, you would _____ the slice(s).

   a. expand

   b. explode

   c. blast

   d. erupt

4. To view the current graph, use:

   a. F6

   b. F2

   c. F5

   d. F10

5. Data entered in consecutive columns or rows can be graphed using the _____ command.

   a. Set

   b. Group

   c. Collect

   d. Gather

6. To recall a graph and display it on the screen, you must _____ it before creating another graph.

   a. save

   b. name

   c. print

   d. replace

7. There are _____ possible patterns for a pie chart.

   a. four

   b. two

   c. eight

   d. ten

8. To create more than one graph per worksheet, each graph needs to be _____.

   a. printed

   b. named

   c. exploded

   d. grouped

9. To remove a range from a graph, use the _____ command.

   a. Clear

   b. Reset

   c. Erase

   d. Delete

10. To make a graph easier to read, use:

a. grids   c. hatch patterns

b. data labels   d. all of the above

Cases

1. To complete this problem, you first must have completed Practice Case 3 in Lab 5. If you have completed that problem, retrieve the file HWLAB5-3.WK1. Complete the following steps viewing the graph as needed:

a. Change the graph type to bar. Edit the second title line to display the current date. View the graph. Name the graph BAR6-1. Save the graph as BAR6-1.

b. Change the graph type to stacked bar. View the graph. Name the graph STACK6-1. Save the graph as STACK6-1.

c. Donna would like to see the percentage of sales over the four weeks for each person.

1) Reset the graph.

2) Set the graph type to PIE.

3) Set the X range as the four employees' names.

4) Set the A range as the employees' totals.

5) Add an appropriate first title, and add a second title as your name and the current date.

6) Add shading to the pie chart, and explode Thomas's slice of the pie.

7) Name the graph PIE6-1. Save the graph as PIE6-1.

d. Save the worksheet as HWLAB6-1.

e. Print the graphs using PrintGraph.

2. Scott is doing a report on the candy industry for his finance class. While researching this topic, he found the following data:

U.S. Market Share in 1988

Hershey Foods Corp.	20.8
Mars, Inc.	18.5
Jacobs Suchard	7.2
Nestle, S.A.	7.0
RJR Nabisco	4.7
Other	41.8

Source: *The Wall Street Journal,* March 29, 1989, p. B1.

a. Create a worksheet of this data. Put your name in cell A1 and the current date in cell A2.

b. Create a pie chart showing the percentage each company had in the 1988 market.

c. Add an appropriate first title. Add a second title that displays your name and the current date.

d. Add shading to the pie chart, and explode the RJR Nabisco slice.

e. Save the graph for printing as PIE6-2.PIC.

f. Save the worksheet as HWLAB6-2, and then print the worksheet.

g. Print the pie chart using PrintGraph.

3. Kathy Lawrence has been on a strict low-calorie diet for the past few weeks. This morning, however, Kathy attended a breakfast meeting and splurged on her calories. Kathy had two pieces of bacon, two eggs, two links of sausage, two waffles, and a roll.

As soon as Kathy returned home, she felt guilty. She went to her calorie converter and exercise guide to see what she could do to burn off those extra calories. Retrieve the file PROB6-3.WK1 to see how many minutes of each exercise would be required to burn off Kathy's breakfast.

a. Create a bar graph using the Group command to specify the four exercise categories Run, Swim, Bike, and Walk as the X-axis labels and the corresponding data as the A, B, C, D, and E data ranges.

1) Add appropriate titles and legends.

2) Name the graph BAR6-3.

3) Save the graph as BAR6-3.

4) View the graph.

b. Create a stacked bar graph using the same data ranges specified for the bar graph.

    1) Name the graph STACK6-3.

    2) Save the graph as STACK6-3.

    3) View the graph.

c. Reset the graph settings.

d. Create a pie chart to display what percentage of the total calories of Kathy's breakfast is made up of each of the foods she ate.

    1) Use the names of the foods as the X-axis data range.

    2) Use the calories of the foods as the A data range.

    3) Add an appropriate first title. Add a second title displaying your name and the current date.

    4) Add shading to the pie chart, and explode the Bacon slice.

    5) Name the graph PIE6-3. Save the graph as PIE6-3.

    6) View the graph.

e. Save the worksheet as HWLAB6-3.

f. Use the PrintGraph program to print BAR6-3, STAK6-3, and PIE6-3.

4. The following table represents data on the average starting salaries for students with master's degrees.

Years

	1990	1991
Engineering	37800	39400
Other Tech. Fields	36800	38000
MBA W/Tech. B.S.	41200	42100
MBA W/NonTech. B.A.	43600	44300
Accounting	33100	33800

Source: Northwestern University/*Chicago Tribune* graphic. Printed in *After College*, March/April 1991, p. 24.

a. Create a worksheet of the data. Enter your name in cell A1 and the current date in cell A2. Save the worksheet as HWLAB6-4, and then print the worksheet.

b. Create graphs that best represent the data. Enter your name and the current date as the second title line. Save and name the graphs appropriately. Print the graphs.

5. To complete this problem, you must have completed the graph in Practice Case 5 in Lab 5. If you have completed that problem, retrieve the file HWLAB5-5.WK1.

Jay Tucker is not happy with the line graph created in Lab 5.

a. Change it to a bar graph and a stacked bar graph. Which graph shows the best representation of the data? Name the graph as BAR6-5 or STACK6-5. Save the graph BAR6-5 or STACK6-5.

b. Create a pie chart of the data for age 25. Create a pie chart for age 65. How different are the percentages? Name and save the pie charts as PIE256-5 and PIE656-5.

c. Save the worksheet as HWLAB6-5.

d. Print the graphs.

6. Interested in the stock market? Pick four related stocks, and create an HLCO graph. (Use the Help feature to learn more about HLCO graphs.) Save and name the graph HLCO6-6. Save the worksheet as HWLAB6-6 and then print the worksheet. Print the graph.

Lab 7

Creating a Database

In Lab 7, you will learn how to:

- **Create, format, and modify a database**
- **Insert, edit, and delete records**
- **Sort a database**
- **Find selected records**
- **Use the Search and Replace command**

Case Study

The Gallery Print Distribution Co. is a small, newly formed distribution company for independent artists. It specializes in the distribution of limited-edition gallery prints. Karl Konrad, the company's computer analyst, has used 1-2-3 to keep track of many of the company's ventures. He is impressed with 1-2-3's ease of use and ability to perform what-if analysis. Karl recently learned that 1-2-3 can also be used as a database.

This lab will follow Karl as he creates and uses the database Gallery Print Distribution Inventory, shown in Figure 7.1.

Creating a Database

A **database** is a collection of data that consists of fields and records. A **field** is a collection of related characters, such as the name of a city. A **record** is a collection of related fields, such as a vendor's name, location, name of artist, and number of prints purchased. In a 1-2-3 database, each record is a row, and each field is a column. There can be more than one database within a worksheet.

The first row of information in the database contains **field names**. The field name is a label that identifies the contents of each column, or field, of data. Figure 7.1 identifies the parts of a database.

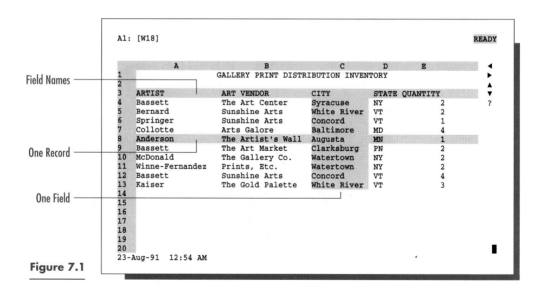

Figure 7.1

The first step in creating a database is to determine the field names and column widths for each field of data. Each column should be large enough to fully display both the field name and the largest possible entry into that field.

Observe the following rules when you are constructing field names:

- Field names must be entered in the first row of the database.
- They must be entered as a label in a single cell.
- They must be unique within the database.
- They should be descriptive of the contents of the field.
- They should not begin or end with a blank space.
- They must not exceed 240 characters.

After reviewing his records, Karl decides to use the field names and column widths shown in Table 7.1.

Field Contents	Field Name	Column Width
Artist's name	ARTIST	18
Name of vendor	ART VENDOR	19
City of vendor	CITY	13
State of vendor	STATE	6
Number of prints sent	QUANTITY	10

Table 7.1

To create the database of prints shipped for The Gallery Print Distribution Co., load 1-2-3.

First, enter a title for the database in the first row of the worksheet.

Move to: B1

Type: **GALLERY PRINT DISTRIBUTION INVENTORY**

Press: ⏎

Next, to enter the field names specified in Table 7.1 in row 3,

Move to: A3

The first field of data, the artist's name, requires a column width of 18 spaces. Increase the column width to 18 spaces by issuing the following command sequence:

/**W**orksheet **C**olumn **S**et-Width **18** ⏎

To enter the first field name,

Type: **ARTIST**

Press: ↵

Beginning in cell B3, complete the other field names by referring to Table 7.1 for the appropriate column widths and field names. If you make an error entering the field names, correct it just like any other worksheet entry.

When you have finished, your screen should look similar to Figure 7.2.

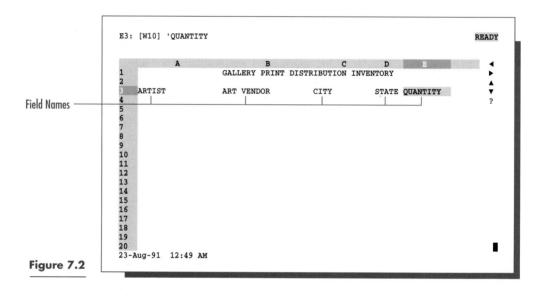

Figure 7.2

Now you are ready to enter the data into the database. Always enter the first record of the database in the row immediately below the field names. Do not leave a blank row below the field names. The data for the first database record are as follows:

ARTIST	:	Bassett
ART VENDOR	:	The Art Center
CITY	:	Syracuse
STATE	:	NY
QUANTITY	:	2

To enter the first record into the database,

Move to: A4

Type: **Bassett**

Move to: B4

Type: **The Art Center**

Move to: C4

Type: **Syracuse**

Move to: D4

Type: **NY**

Move to: E4

Type: **2**

Press: ⏎

Your screen should now look similar to Figure 7.3.

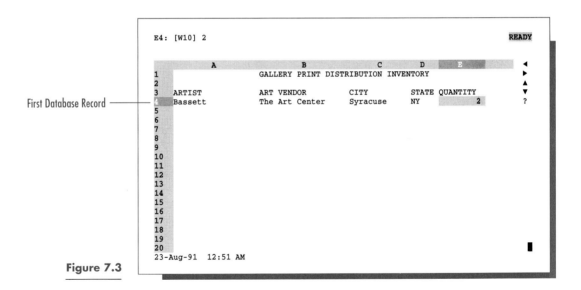

First Database Record

Figure 7.3

The data in a field can be a label, a value, or a formula. However, each field should contain the same type of data (all values or all labels) for each record. It is important to be consistent when you enter data into a database. If a number in a field is defined as a label (for example, if you had included the artists' Social Security numbers), all numbers in that field should be entered as labels. If certain words are abbreviated (for example, St. and Ave.), always abbreviate them the same way. Do not use extra spaces before or after an entry in a field.

Beginning in cell A5, enter the second record into the database.

ARTIST	:	Bernard
ART VENDOR	:	Sunshine Arts
CITY	:	White River
STATE	:	VT
QUANTITY	:	2

Your screen should look similar to Figure 7.4.

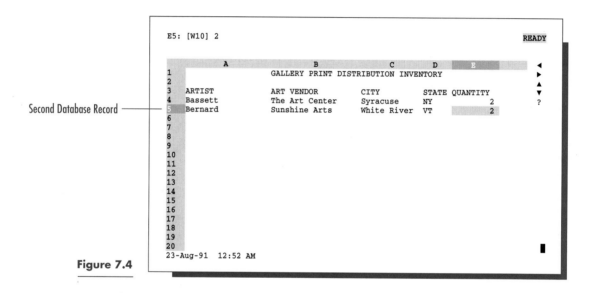

Second Database Record

Figure 7.4

The second record is now entered into row 5 in the database.

After setting up the database and entering the two records, Karl asks his assistant to continue entering more records. To see what has been completed so far, retrieve the file ARTINVNT.WK1. (You do not need to save the current worksheet.)

Your screen should look similar to Figure 7.5.

```
A1: [W18]                                                            READY

                A                B                C       D     E       ◄
                                                                        ►
 1                       GALLERY PRINT DISTRIBUTION INVENTORY           ▲
 2                                                                      ▼
 3      ARTIST           ART VENDOR       CITY      STATE QUANTITY       ?
 4      Bassett          The Art Center   Syracuse    NY        2
 5      Bernard          Sunshine Arts    White River VT        2
 6      Springer         Sunshine Arts    Concord     VT        1
 7      Collotte         Arts Galore      Baltimore   MD        4
 8      Andersun         The Artist's Wall Augusta    MN        1
 9      Bassett          The Art Market   Clarksburg  PN        2
10      McDonald         The Gallery Co.  Watertown   NY        2
11      Winne-Fernandez  Prints, Etc.     Watertown   NY        2
12      Bassett          Sunshine Arts    Concord     VT        4
13      Pilcasso         &*(^&%&^%^&*     Baltimore   MD
14      Kaiser           The Gold Palette White River VT        3
15
16
17
18
19
20
        23-Aug-91  01:57 AM                                        ■
```

Figure 7.5

Modifying a Database

Karl notices few problems in the database. First, Anderson, the artist's name, is misspelled in row 8. Correct it. The record in row 13 should be deleted from the database. Move the cell pointer to any cell in row 13, and use the /**W**orksheet **D**elete **R**ow command to delete the row.

To add another record to the database, move to the row just below the last record in the database, and enter the new record. Insert the record shown below into row 14.

ARTIST	:	Dachsman
ART VENDOR	:	The Art Shop
CITY	:	Richmond
STATE	:	VA
QUANTITY	:	6

Your screen should look similar to Figure 7.6.

```
E14: [W10] 6                                                          READY

         A                    B               C        D        E         ◄
1                    GALLERY PRINT DISTRIBUTION INVENTORY              ►
2                                                                         ▲
3   ARTIST           ART VENDOR       CITY        STATE QUANTITY          ▼
4   Bassett          The Art Center   Syracuse    NY         2           ?
5   Bernard          Sunshine Arts    White River VT         2
6   Springer         Sunshine Arts    Concord     VT         1
7   Collotte         Arts Galore      Baltimore   MD         4
8   Anderson         The Artist's Wall Augusta    MN         1
9   Bassett          The Art Market   Clarksburg  PN         2
10  McDonald         The Gallery Co.  Watertown   NY         2
11  Winne-Fernandez  Prints, Etc.     Watertown   NY         2
12  Bassett          Sunshine Arts    Concord     VT         4
13  Kaiser           The Gold Palette White River VT         3
14  Dachsman         The Art Shop     Richmond    VA         6
15
16
17
18
19
20
23-Aug-91   01:58 AM                                                     ■
```

Figure 7.6

Sorting a Database

After looking at the database of records, Karl wants to change the order of the records. The records currently appear in the order they were entered into the database. 1-2-3 has a sorting feature that lets you re-arrange the order of records alphabetically, numerically, or chronologically. The records can be sorted either in ascending (low to high) or descending (high to low) order.

Karl wants the records arranged in ascending alphabetical order according to the artist's name. All database operations are executed using the Data menu. To see this menu,

Select: /Data

There are eight Data menu commands. The command to rearrange the records in a database is Sort. Obtain help on the Sort command by selecting Sort and then accessing Help for the different options, as you have learned to do using either the keyboard or the mouse.

Your screen should look similar to Figure 7.7.

Data Sort Options

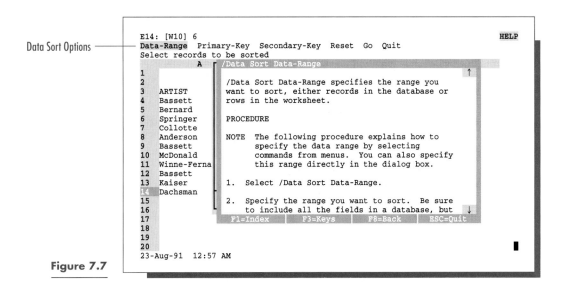

Figure 7.7

The Help screen briefly describes the procedure for specifying the data range. After you have carefully read the Help information, press (ESC) to return to the Sort Settings dialog box.

Your screen should now look similar to Figure 7.8.

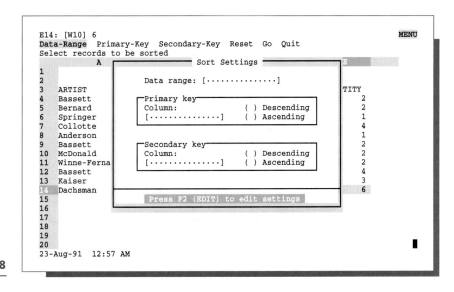

Figure 7.8

The **S**ort command requires that you specify three items: the range to sort, the field(s) to sort by, and the order of the sort. Since it is easier to select these options when viewing the worksheet, you will use the menu to specify the settings. The dialog box will help you keep track of the settings you specify.

The first setting you must specify is the range of data to be sorted.

Select: **D**ata-Range

The Sort Settings dialog box is cleared from the screen to allow you to view the worksheet while you enter the data range. The data range should include all records and fields in the database.

The database records begin in cell A4 (the first field of the first record) and end in cell E14 (the last field of the last record). The field names in row 3 are not included in the data range. If they were included, the field names would be sorted alphabetically within the database records.

Respond to the prompt for the data range by specifying A4 to E14 either using the keyboard or dragging the mouse.

You are returned to the Sort Settings dialog box, and the data range you specified is displayed.

Next you must specify the field to sort by. This is called the **sort key**. The sort key determines the new order for the database records. Two sort keys can be specified, a primary key and a secondary key. To continue the command sequence,

Select: **P**rimary-Key

The **primary key** is the field in the database that will determine the new order of the records. Since Karl wants the records arranged by artist's name, you will specify the ARTIST field as the primary key. To do this, you can enter any cell address in the column, using either the keyboard or the mouse. For this database, use cell A3. If you are using a mouse, click anywhere in column A twice. With the keyboard, in response to the prompt,

Type: **A3**

Press: ⏎

You are returned to the Sort Settings dialog box, and the specified primary key field is displayed. The prompt "Sort order (A or D):" appears on the right side of the control panel. The default **sort order** is descending. The sort order determines whether the records are listed in **descending order** (Z through A or 9 through 0) or **ascending order**

(A through Z or 0 through 9). Since Karl wants the records organized in ascending alphabetical order, in response to the prompt in the control panel,

Type: **A**

Press: ⏎

The change is reflected in the dialog box. To remove the dialog box and see the worksheet,

Press: F6 (WINDOW)

Notice that the database contains three records with the same artist (Bassett). Karl wants these records sorted by art vendor within the artist field. To do this, you will specify a **secondary key.** The secondary key determines the order of records with identical primary key entries. Here, the secondary key will be the ART VENDOR field (cell B3). To specify the secondary key, enter the following command sequence:

Secondary-Key **B3** ⏎ **A**scending ⏎

Then return to the dialog box by pressing F6 (WINDOW).

Your screen should look similar to Figure 7.9.

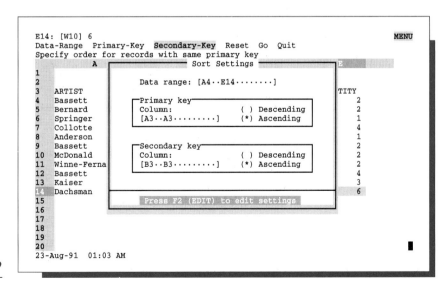

Figure 7.9

The secondary key is an optional sort setting. The data range and primary key are required sort settings.

Finally, to perform the sort,

Select: **G**o

Your screen should now look similar to Figure 7.10.

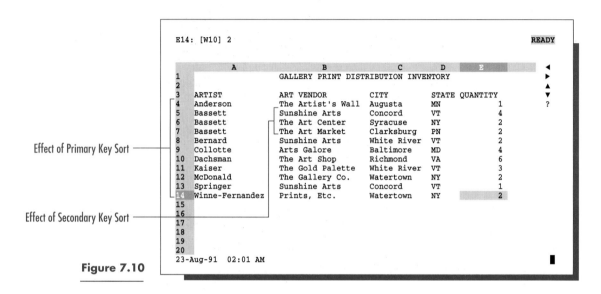

E14: [W10] 2   READY

	A	B	C	D	E
1		GALLERY PRINT DISTRIBUTION INVENTORY			
2					
3	ARTIST	ART VENDOR	CITY	STATE	QUANTITY
4	Anderson	The Artist's Wall	Augusta	MN	1
5	Bassett	Sunshine Arts	Concord	VT	4
6	Bassett	The Art Center	Syracuse	NY	2
7	Bassett	The Art Market	Clarksburg	PN	2
8	Bernard	Sunshine Arts	White River	VT	2
9	Collotte	Arts Galore	Baltimore	MD	4
10	Dachsman	The Art Shop	Richmond	VA	6
11	Kaiser	The Gold Palette	White River	VT	3
12	McDonald	The Gallery Co.	Watertown	NY	2
13	Springer	Sunshine Arts	Concord	VT	1
14	Winne-Fernandez	Prints, Etc.	Watertown	NY	2
15					
16					
17					
18					
19					
20					

23-Aug-91 02:01 AM

Effect of Primary Key Sort

Effect of Secondary Key Sort

Figure 7.10

The database is now sorted alphabetically by artist's name. The three Bassett orders are further sorted by vendor name, as specified by the secondary key.

Once a database is sorted, if any new records are added to the end of the database, the database must be resorted to maintain the correct order. If, in the meantime, no other sorts have been performed, all you need to do after entering the new records is to redefine the data range to include the new records. 1-2-3 stores the most recent sort settings in memory and as part of the worksheet file when you save the file. To clear previous sort settings, use **/D**ata **S**ort **R**eset.

It is always a good idea to save a copy of the worksheet before you sort a file. Then, if you incorrectly specify the sort settings, you can retrieve the original file and try again.

Finding Records in a Database

Next, Karl sees a note on his desk te"ing him that, "The Sunshine Arts Company in White River has changed its order from 2 to 3 prints."

He needs to find Sunshine Arts and change the quantity to 3 prints. Because the Gallery Print Distribution Inventory database is small, you can find the appropriate record just by looking at the database. But what if the database were much larger?

Locating a particular item in a database is a common database operation. The 1-2-3 command that searches or **queries** a database to locate records quickly according to specified requirements, or **criteria**, is /**D**ata **Q**uery. You will use this command to search the database for the Sunshine Arts record.

Before you can use this command, you must specify an open area of the worksheet in which to enter the selection criteria. This area is called the **criteria range** and consists of at least two rows of information. You will use cells A17 and A18 as the criteria range.

> **Move to:** A17

The first row of the criteria range contains one or more field names exactly as they appear in the database. You need to locate a record using the data in the ART VENDOR name field. To ensure that the criteria field name is an exact duplicate of the field name in the database, copy the field name label (ART VENDOR) in cell B3 to cell A17. To do this, issue the following command sequence:

> /**C**opy **B3** ⏎ ⏎

The second row of the criteria range contains the record selection criteria or the entries that you want 1-2-3 to match. In this case, the criteria is Sunshine Arts. The criteria can be entered in uppercase or lowercase letters since 1-2-3 is not case-sensitive when searching the database for matches. The criteria must, however, be spelled exactly as it is entered in the database. To enter the criteria,

> **Move to:** A18
>
> **Type:** **Sunshine Arts**
>
> **Press:** ⏎

Your screen should look similar to Figure 7.11.

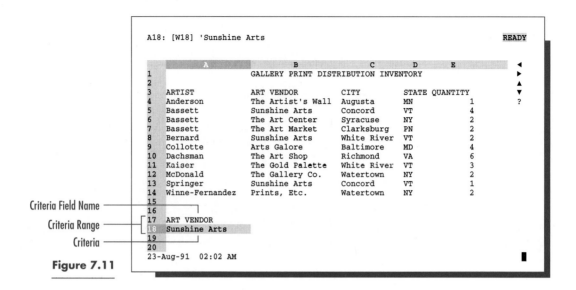

```
A18: [W18] 'Sunshine Arts                                              READY

                      A                B              C        D      E      ◄
         1                        GALLERY PRINT DISTRIBUTION INVENTORY        ►
         2                                                                   ▲
         3     ARTIST            ART VENDOR       CITY      STATE QUANTITY    ▼
         4     Anderson          The Artist's Wall Augusta  MN           1   ?
         5     Bassett           Sunshine Arts    Concord   VT           4
         6     Bassett           The Art Center   Syracuse  NY           2
         7     Bassett           The Art Market   Clarksburg PN          2
         8     Bernard           Sunshine Arts    White River VT         2
         9     Collotte          Arts Galore      Baltimore MD           4
         10    Dachsman          The Art Shop     Richmond  VA           6
         11    Kaiser            The Gold Palette White River VT         3
         12    McDonald          The Gallery Co.  Watertown NY           2
         13    Springer          Sunshine Arts    Concord   VT           1
         14    Winne-Fernandez   Prints, Etc.     Watertown NY           2
         15
         16
         17    ART VENDOR
         18    Sunshine Arts
         19
         20
         23-Aug-91  02:02 AM                                              ▮
```

Criteria Field Name

Criteria Range

Criteria

Figure 7.11

The field name and criteria have been entered into the criteria range A17 through A18, with the field name in the first row of the range and the criteria to search for in the second row of the range.

Once the selection criteria are entered in the criteria range, you are ready to use the /**D**ata **Q**uery command.

Select: /**D**ata

For more information on these commands,

Move to: Query

Press: F1 (HELP)

Your screen should look similar to Figure 7.12.

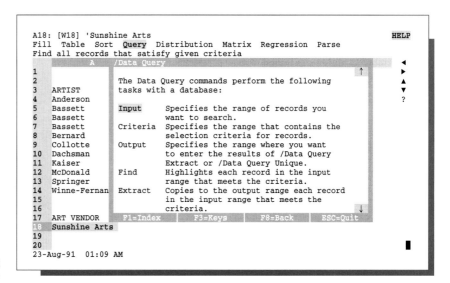

```
A18: [W18] 'Sunshine Arts                                        HELP
Fill  Table  Sort  Query  Distribution  Matrix  Regression  Parse
Find all records that satisfy given criteria
         A        /Data Query                                      ◀
 1                                                            ↑     ▶
 2                    The Data Query commands perform the following ▲
 3    ARTIST         tasks with a database:                        ▼
 4    Anderson                                                      ?
 5    Bassett        Input     Specifies the range of records you
 6    Bassett                  want to search.
 7    Bassett        Criteria  Specifies the range that contains the
 8    Bernard                  selection criteria for records.
 9    Collotte       Output    Specifies the range where you want
10    Dachsman                 to enter the results of /Data Query
11    Kaiser                   Extract or /Data Query Unique.
12    McDonald       Find      Highlights each record in the input
13    Springer                 range that meets the criteria.
14    Winne-Fernan   Extract   Copies to the output range each record
15                             in the input range that meets the
16                             criteria.                       ↓
17    ART VENDOR      F1=Index       F3=Keys       F8=Back     ESC=Quit
18    Sunshine Arts
19
20                                                                  ■
23-Aug-91  01:09 AM
```

Figure 7.12

After you have carefully read the Help information on this topic, press
(ESC) to return to the worksheet. To access the Query submenu,

Select: Query

The Query Settings dialog box is displayed, and the second line of the
control panel shows the nine **/D**ata **Q**uery commands. The first three
commands, **I**nput, **C**riteria, and **O**utput, are the range settings that are
required by the **Q**uery command. The next five commands, **F**ind,
Extract, **U**nique, **D**elete, and **R**eset, are the different **/D**ata **Q**uery operations that can be selected.

You will use the **F**ind command to locate the record in the database. The
Find command requires that you specify a criteria range and an input
range.

Since you just finished entering the criteria, you will specify the **criteria
range** first. This is the range of cells that contains the criteria field name
and the selection criteria (A17..A18). To enter the range, continue the
command sequence as follows:

Criteria **A17..A18** (↵)

Next, you need to specify the **input range,** which is the range of cells in the database to be queried. In this case, it is all database records. This range must include the field names in the first row of the database. To specify the range, continue the command sequence as follows:

Input **A3..E14** ⏎

The Query Settings dialog box reflects the settings you specified for the input and criteria ranges.

Finally, to locate and highlight records in the database that match the selection criteria,

Select: **F**ind

Your screen should now look similar to Figure 7.13.

Matching Record ——

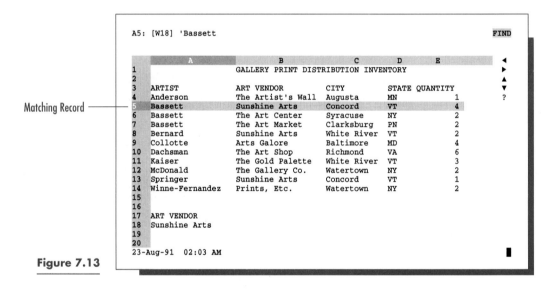

Figure 7.13

The mode indicator has changed from READY to FIND. The cell pointer highlights the record for Bassett prints ordered by Sunshine Arts. This is the first record in the database that matches the criteria.

Press: ⬆

The cell pointer does not move, indicating there are no other records in the database before Sunshine Arts that match the criteria.

Press: ⬇

The cell pointer is now highlighting another Sunshine Arts, the second record that matches the criteria. Each time you press ⬇, the cell pointer moves to the next record meeting the criteria.

Press: ⬇

Now the record for Springer prints ordered by Sunshine Arts is highlighted. Try to move the cell pointer down again. Again, the cell pointer does not move, because this is the last record in the database that matches the criteria.

You can return to the other records by pressing ⬆.

To leave FIND mode,

Press: ↵

To return to READY mode,

Select: **Q**uit

You have found three records for the art vendor Sunshine Arts in the database, but you do not know which one should have the quantity changed. After checking the note again, Karl sees that the store is located in White River.

To increase the accuracy of the **F**ind command, multiple criteria for different fields can be entered in the criteria range. By entering the criteria in the same row, you tell 1-2-3 to search for records that match all the criteria in the row. 1-2-3 treats the criteria as if they were connected by the word *and*.

To modify the criteria range to include two criteria, ART VENDOR name of Sunshine Arts *and* CITY of White River,

Move to: B17

Copy the field name, CITY, in cell C3 to cell B17.

Move to: B18

Type: **White River**

Press: ↵

Your screen should look similar to Figure 7.14.

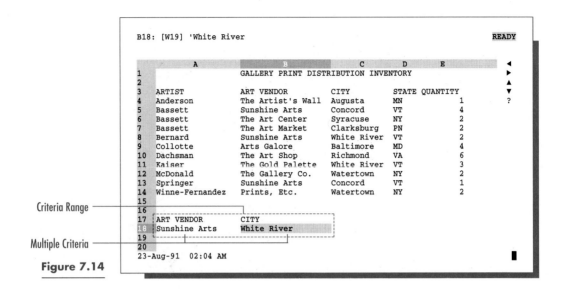

```
B18: [W19] 'White River                                          READY

              A                B              C        D     E       ◄
1                       GALLERY PRINT DISTRIBUTION INVENTORY        ►
2                                                                   ▲
3     ARTIST           ART VENDOR       CITY       STATE QUANTITY    ▼
4     Anderson         The Artist's Wall Augusta   MN        1      ?
5     Bassett          Sunshine Arts    Concord    VT        4
6     Bassett          The Art Center   Syracuse   NY        2
7     Bassett          The Art Market   Clarksburg PN        2
8     Bernard          Sunshine Arts    White River VT       2
9     Collotte         Arts Galore      Baltimore  MD        4
10    Dachsman         The Art Shop     Richmond   VA        6
11    Kaiser           The Gold Palette White River VT       3
12    McDonald         The Gallery Co.  Watertown  NY        2
13    Springer         Sunshine Arts    Concord    VT        1
14    Winne-Fernandez  Prints, Etc.     Watertown  NY        2
15
16
17    ART VENDOR       CITY
18    Sunshine Arts    White River
19
20
      23-Aug-91  02:04 AM                                          ■
```

Criteria Range

Multiple Criteria

Figure 7.14

The criteria range now contains the field names ART VENDOR and CITY, along with the selection criteria, Sunshine Arts and White River.

To define the new criteria range, issue the following command sequence:

/**D**ata **Q**uery **C**riteria **A17..B18** ⏎

The Query Settings dialog box is displayed again. You do not need to specify the input range again because 1-2-3 remembers the range last specified.

To find all the records in the database with ART VENDOR name Sunshine Arts *and* CITY White River,

Select: **F**ind

Your screen should look similar to Figure 7.15.

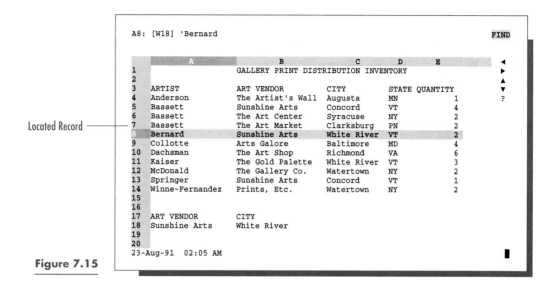

```
A8: [W18] 'Bernard                                                        FIND

                    A                    B                 C         D         E       ◄
            1                      GALLERY PRINT DISTRIBUTION INVENTORY              ►
            2                                                                        ▲
            3    ARTIST            ART VENDOR        CITY       STATE QUANTITY       ▼
            4    Anderson          The Artist's Wall Augusta    MN          1        ?
            5    Bassett           Sunshine Arts     Concord    VT          4
            6    Bassett           The Art Center    Syracuse   NY          2
            7    Bassett           The Art Market    Clarksburg PN          2
            8    Bernard           Sunshine Arts     White River VT         2
            9    Collotte          Arts Galore       Baltimore  MD          4
           10    Dachsman          The Art Shop      Richmond   VA          6
           11    Kaiser            The Gold Palette  White River VT         3
           12    McDonald          The Gallery Co.   Watertown  NY          2
           13    Springer          Sunshine Arts     Concord    VT          1
           14    Winne-Fernandez   Prints, Etc.      Watertown  NY          2
           15
           16
           17    ART VENDOR        CITY
           18    Sunshine Arts     White River
           19
           20
           23-Aug-91  02:05 AM                                                      ∎
```

Located Record ——

Figure 7.15

The cell pointer now highlights the art vendor Sunshine Arts located in White River. Try to move the cell pointer up or down. 1-2-3 will not move the cell pointer because only one record meets the criteria.

While in FIND mode, you can edit the contents of the current record. The blinking cursor within the cell pointer identifies the field. To move the cursor, use ⟶ and ⟵. As the cursor moves, the cell contents are displayed in the control panel.

To change the number of prints ordered to 3, use ⟶ to move the cursor to the QUANTITY field.

Move to: E8

To change the value in this cell to 3, you can either type in the new data and press ⏎ or use the EDIT function key, (F2), to modify the cell contents and press ⏎. Using either approach, change the value to 3.

To leave FIND mode and return to READY mode, issue the following command sequence:

⏎ **Q**uit

Whenever multiple criteria are entered in the same row of the criteria range, 1-2-3 searches for only those records that match all the criteria. If the criteria are entered on separate rows, 1-2-3 searches for all records that match any of the criteria. 1-2-3 treats these criteria as if they were connected by the word *or*.

To demonstrate this, you will find all records that have ART VENDOR name of Sunshine Arts *or* CITY of White River.

To move the criteria in B18 to B19, issue the following command sequence:

/Move **B18** ⏎ **B19** ⏎

Your screen should look similar to Figure 7.16.

Criteria Range ——

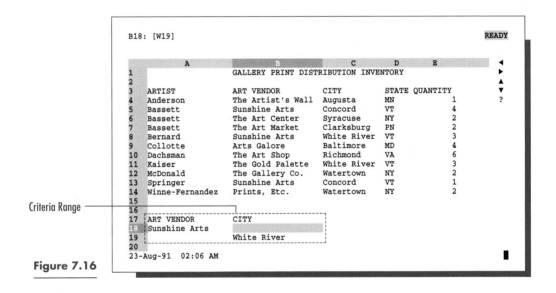

Figure 7.16

Next, to find all records that meet either *or* both of the criteria, issue the following command sequence:

/Data **Q**uery

Notice in the Query Settings dialog box that 1-2-3 automatically adjusted the criteria range to A17..B19 when you used the **/M**ove command. To complete the command sequence,

Select: **F**ind

The first record that meets either of the criteria is highlighted. Use (↓) to find other records that meet the criteria. All records with ART VENDOR name of Sunshine Arts *or* CITY of White River are highlighted.

> (↵) **Q**uit

Next, Karl wants to locate all records with Sunshine Arts as the vendor or a city of Watertown. The only change you need to make in the criteria range is to the city.

To change the city to Watertown in cell B19.

> **Move to:** B19
>
> **Type:** **Watertown**
>
> **Press:** (↵)

Because the criteria and input ranges have not changed, you can use the QUERY function key, (F7), from READY mode to quickly locate all records in the database that match the criteria.

> **Press:** (F7) (QUERY)

The first record that meets the new criteria should be highlighted. Use (↓) to locate all the records that match the criteria.

Another way to end the /**D**ata **Q**uery **F**ind command is to press (F7) (QUERY). When you use this method, the cell pointer remains in the current cell.

> **Press:** (F7) (QUERY)

Using Search and Replace

Karl received a letter from Sunshine Arts informing him that they had changed their name to The Sunny Arts Co. To make changes in the database, you could use the /**D**ata **Q**uery **F**ind command to locate all records in the database that have the ART VENDOR as Sunshine Arts and then individually edit each record to change the ART VENDOR name to The Sunny Arts Co. However, a quicker way is to use the /**R**ange **S**earch command. This command will quickly locate any **string** (combination of characters) within formulas or labels in the worksheet. It will not locate numbers unless they are part of a formula.

> **Select:** /**R**ange **S**earch

The prompt "Enter range to search:" is displayed in the control panel. The range will be the column containing the ART VENDOR field data.

Select: **B4..B14**

Press: ⏎

Next, you must indicate the search string to be specified. It can be entered in either uppercase or lowercase characters since the search string is not case-sensitive. To search for all cell entries of Sunshine Arts,

Type: **Sunshine Arts**

Press: ⏎

Next, you must select **F**ormulas, **L**abels, or **B**oth from the menu. These options have the following meanings:

Formulas	Looks for string in formulas only
Labels	Looks for string in labels only
Both	Looks for string in both formulas and labels

Because the search string is used only as a label entry,

Select: **L**abels

Your choice from the next menu lets you find (locate only) or replace (locate and replace) matches in the search range. Since Karl wants to change all the entries containing the vendor name of Sunshine Arts to The Sunny Arts Co., the **R**eplace option will be used.

Select: **R**eplace

The final piece of information needed is the replacement string. You must enter this exactly as you want it to appear in the worksheet. To enter the replacement string,

Type: **The Sunny Arts Co.**

Press: ⏎

Your screen should be similar to Figure 7.17.

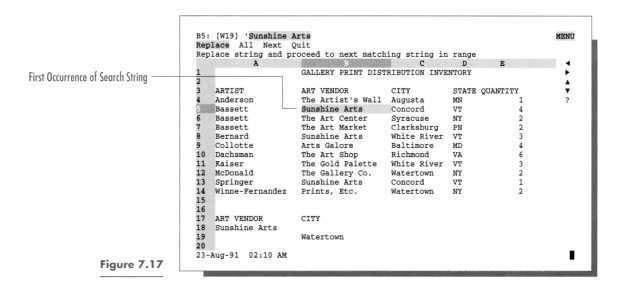

First Occurrence of Search String

```
B5: [W19] 'Sunshine Arts                                              MENU
Replace  All  Next  Quit
Replace string and proceed to next matching string in range
          A                  B              C        D     E           ◄
1                   GALLERY PRINT DISTRIBUTION INVENTORY               ►
2                                                                      ▲
3    ARTIST             ART VENDOR         CITY      STATE QUANTITY     ▼
4    Anderson           The Artist's Wall  Augusta   MN       1         ?
5    Bassett            Sunshine Arts      Concord   VT       4
6    Bassett            The Art Center     Syracuse  NY       2
7    Bassett            The Art Market     Clarksburg PN      2
8    Bernard            Sunshine Arts      White River VT     3
9    Collotte           Arts Galore        Baltimore MD       4
10   Dachsman           The Art Shop       Richmond  VA       6
11   Kaiser             The Gold Palette   White River VT     3
12   McDonald           The Gallery Co.    Watertown NY       2
13   Springer           Sunshine Arts      Concord   VT       1
14   Winne-Fernandez    Prints, Etc.       Watertown NY       2
15
16
17   ART VENDOR         CITY
18   Sunshine Arts
19                      Watertown
20
23-Aug-91  02:10 AM                                                    ■
```

Figure 7.17

The cell pointer highlights the first occurrence of the search string in the search range. The menu offers the following options:

Replace   Replaces the current string with the replacement string and searches for the next matching string in the range

All   Replaces all matching strings in the search range with the replacement string

Next   Does not replace the current string but searches for the next matching string

Quit   Returns 1-2-3 to READY mode

To replace all occurrences of the original vendor name with the new vendor name,

Select: **A**ll

Your screen should be similar to Figure 7.18.

Replaced All ──

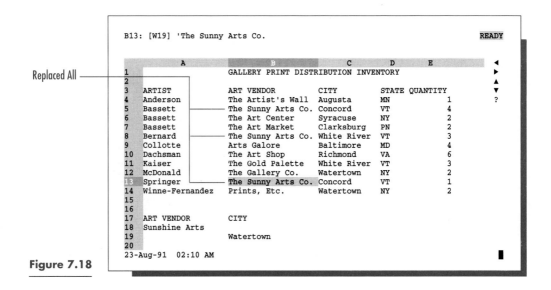

```
B13: [W19] 'The Sunny Arts Co.                                    READY

           A              B                 C       D      E       ◀
   1                GALLERY PRINT DISTRIBUTION INVENTORY           ▶
   2                                                               ▲
   3   ARTIST         ART VENDOR        CITY      STATE QUANTITY    ▼
   4   Anderson       The Artist's Wall Augusta     MN        1    ?
   5   Bassett        The Sunny Arts Co. Concord    VT        4
   6   Bassett        The Art Center    Syracuse    NY        2
   7   Bassett        The Art Market    Clarksburg  PN        2
   8   Bernard        The Sunny Arts Co. White River VT       3
   9   Collotte       Arts Galore       Baltimore   MD        4
  10   Dachsman       The Art Shop      Richmond    VA        6
  11   Kaiser         The Gold Palette  White River VT        3
  12   McDonald       The Gallery Co.   Watertown   NY        2
  13   Springer       The Sunny Arts Co. Concord    VT        1
  14   Winne-Fernandez Prints, Etc.     Watertown   NY        2
  15
  16
  17   ART VENDOR     CITY
  18   Sunshine Arts
  19                  Watertown
  20
       23-Aug-91  02:10 AM                                       ▮
```

Figure 7.18

The new vendor name quickly replaced all occurrences of the original vendor name. 1-2-3 automatically returns to READY mode when no more occurrences are found.

Be careful when you use the **A**ll command to replace character strings, since you may get some unexpected results. You might want to test how this command is working by selecting **R**eplace for the first few occurrences and then changing to **A**ll. If you do get unexpected results and the UNDO feature is on, you can undo the error if you immediately press (ALT)-(F4) (UNDO) after returning to READY mode.

Save the worksheet under the file name ARTS. Print the worksheet, and then exit from 1-2-3.

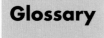

Glossary

Ascending order: Records are sorted in A through Z or 0 through 9 order.

Criteria: The cell entries that 1-2-3 interprets as the tests or requirements for the query.

Criteria range: The range of cells that contains the field names and criteria to be located in a query.

Database: A collection of related information that consists of fields and records.

Data range: The range of cells that contains the data records to be sorted.

Descending order: Records are sorted in Z through A or 9 through 0 order.

Field: A collection of related characters, such as a person's name.

Field name: A label that identifies the contents of each column or field of data.

Input range: The range of cells that contains the field names and the data records to be queried.

Primary key: The column in the data range whose values determine the sort order.

Query: The process of searching the database to locate specific records.

Record: A collection of related fields, such as a person's name, address, Social Security number, and rate of pay.

Secondary key: The field whose entries determine the sort order of records with identical primary key entries.

Sort key: The field that determines the order of the sort.

Sort order: Determines whether records are sorted in ascending or descending order.

String: Any combination of characters.

Practice Problems and Cases

Matching

1. (F7)
2. Field
3. Secondary key
4. Record
5. Data range
6. Criteria range
7. Field name
8. Input range
9. /DQF
10. /DS

___ **a.** contains selection information used in a query

___ **b.** includes all records but no field names

___ **c.** arranges a database in sorted order

___ **d.** a label in the first row of a database

___ **e.** the query key

___ **f.** a collection of related fields

___ **g.** a collection of related characters

___ **h.** finds a record in a database

___ **i.** field used to break ties in a sort

___ **j.** consists of the field names and all records

Multiple Choice

Kevin has been working on a database of his friend's phone numbers. His current screen looks like the figure below. Use this figure to answer the following questions.

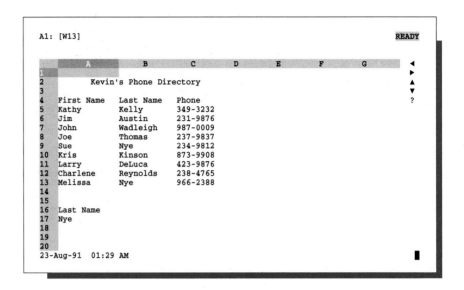

1. Cell A4 contains a:

   a. record

   b. field name

   c. title

   d. field

2. The range A5..C5 contains a:

   a. record

   b. field name

   c. title

   d. field

3. The data range for a sort would be:

   a. A1..C13

   b. A4..C13

   c. A5..C13

   d. A5..A13

4. To list records in order A through Z or 0 through 9, use:

   a. descending order

   b. ascending order

   c. sort order

5. Cell A16 contains:

   a. criteria range

   b. criteria

   c. criteria field name

   d. criteria option

6. The query in A16..A17 will find _____ records.

   a. 1

   b. 2

   c. 3

   d. 4

7. If the database is sorted by last name, _____ will be the first record.

   a. Jim Austin

   b. Kathy Kelly

   c. Charlene Reynolds

   d. Larry DeLuca

8. To begin a search and replace operation, select:

   a. /RCS

   b. /WRS

   c. /RS

   d. /FRS

9. The phone numbers in a database are:

   a. values

   b. labels

   c. formulas

   d. characters

10. The QUERY function key:

    a. sorts the database

    b. executes the last data query command

    c. saves the file

    d. restores deleted records

Cases

1. Tracy Miles is the personnel manager for a large toy store. She needs a database to help her keep track of the employees.

    a. Create a database for Tracy with the field names and column widths shown below. Enter the database field names in row 4. Put your name in cell A1 and the current date in cell A2.

Field Name	Column Width
Last Name	12
First Name	12
Job Title	12
Street	19
City	14
State	6
Zip Code	8
Telephone	10
Pay Rate	8

    b. Insert the following records into the database:

Last Name:	Covey
First Name:	Kelly
Job Title:	Clerk
Street:	458 W. Second St.
City:	Scottsdale
State:	AZ
Zip Code:	84578
Telephone:	555-9834
Pay Rate:	7.50

Last Name:	Hoover
First Name:	Donald
Job Title:	Supervisor
Street:	879 E. Washington
City:	Tempe
State:	AZ
Zip Code:	86542
Telephone:	555-4768
Pay Rate:	10.50
Last Name:	Fuller
First Name:	Mike
Job Title:	Clerk
Street:	89 S. Eastman St.
City:	Mesa
State:	AZ
Zip Code:	86543
Telephone:	555-6578
Pay Rate:	7.25
Last Name:	Havler
First Name:	Mike
Job Title:	Clerk
Street:	44 George St.
City:	Tempe
State:	AZ
Zip Code:	85252
Telephone:	555-1626
Pay Rate:	7.35

c. Sort the records alphabetically by last name as the primary key and by first name as the secondary key. The sort order should be ascending.

d. Enter a fifth record using your name and address information. Your job title is supervisor.

e. Sort the records again using the same settings as in step c. Print a copy of the database.

f. Sort the records by job title as the primary key and by pay rate as the secondary key. The order for both keys should be ascending.

g. Save the worksheet with the file name HWLAB7-1. Print the worksheet.

2. Joanne Pulaski works for the motion picture firm Starfilms. She has started to create a database to keep track of the employees working on films produced by Starfilms.

Retrieve the database file PROB7-2.WK1. Enter your name in cell A1 and the current date in cell A2.

a. Correct Timothy Miller's first name.

b. Sort the database in ascending order by last name.

c. Sort the database again by Film as the primary key in descending order and by Wage as the secondary key in ascending order. Print a copy of the database.

d. Find all records in the database for people who worked on location in Tucson. How many are there?

e. Find all records in the database for employees who earned $10.50 an hour and worked on location in New York. How many are there?

f. Find all records in the database for employees who worked on "Young Billy" or worked on location in Paris. How many are there?

g. Using search and replace, change the name of the film "The Riders" to "The Pony Express."

h. Save the worksheet using the file name HWLAB7-2. Print your worksheet, including the criteria range.

3. The city of Arlington has a summer coed baseball league. Joanne wants a database to keep track of the people joining the baseball league. Joanne would like to have the database started using information from registration applications.

a. Create a database for Joanne with the field names and column widths shown below. Enter the database field names in row 5. Put your name in cell A1 and the current date in cell A2.

Field Name	Column Width
FIRST NAME	18
LAST NAME	18
POSITION	19
SEX	3

b. Insert the following records into the database:

FIRST NAME:	Tim
LAST NAME:	Spear
POSITION:	Catcher
SEX:	M
FIRST NAME:	Anthony
LAST NAME:	Manahan
POSITION:	Shortstop
SEX:	M
FIRST NAME:	Tommy
LAST NAME:	Adams
POSITION:	Right Field
SEX:	M
FIRST NAME:	Lisa
LAST NAME:	Stubert
POSITION:	Pitcher
SEX:	F

c. Sort the records alphabetically by last name as the primary key and by first name as the secondary key. The sort order is ascending.

d. Enter a fifth record using your name. Your position is Pitcher.

e. Sort the records again using the same settings as in step c. Print a copy of the database.

f. Sort the records by position as the primary key and by last name as the secondary key. The order for both keys is ascending.

g. Save the worksheet under the file name HWLAB7-3. Print the worksheet.

4. Retrieve the file PROB7-4.WK1. Enter your name in cell A1 and the current date in cell A2. The file contains a database of employee records. Locate and correct the errors, set the column widths to fully display the entries, and change the format of the cells to display dollar signs and decimal places. Save the corrected database file as HWLAB7-4, and then print the database.

5. Create a database to help you keep track of the classes you have taken. You may want to include the course number, course name, semester taken, and the number of credit hours along with any other data you might like to keep track of. Sort the data in the most appropriate way for your needs. Enter an appropriate title. Enter your name in cell A1 and the current date in cell A2. Save the database as HWLAB7-5. Print the database.

6. Having trouble keeping track of all the new friends you have made in school? Create a database to hold names, addresses, phone numbers, and any other information that might be meaningful. Sort the data in the most appropriate way for your needs. Enter an appropriate title. Enter your name in cell A1 and the current date in cell A2. Save the database as HWLAB7-6. Print the database.

Lab 8

Using a Database

In Lab 8, you will learn how to:

Objectives

- Document a database
- Use @VLOOKUP
- Use @IF
- Use @DAVG, @DMIN, @DMAX, and @DCOUNT
- Extract records from the database

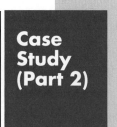

Case Study (Part 2)

Lynne Martinez has just been promoted to Information Systems Manager for the Gallery Print Distribution Co. Her first assignment is to review the existing inventory database.

After looking at the Gallery Print Distribution Inventory database created by Karl Konrad, Lynne has decided to include some more information, such as the selling price of each print. And since the database is getting large, Lynne suggests that Karl provide some written documentation for the database. You will follow Lynne and Karl as they review, revise, and use this database.

Documenting a Database

Load 1-2-3 in the usual manner.

Karl has added some new records to the database he developed previously. To see the updated database, retrieve the file ARTINVN2.WK1.

Your screen should look similar to Figure 8.1.

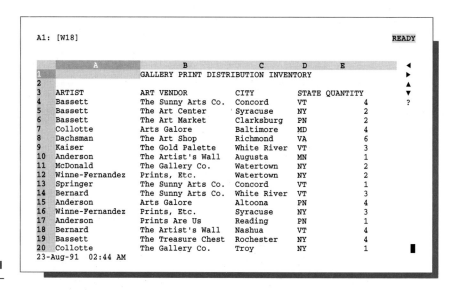

Figure 8.1

After reviewing the database, Lynne wants Karl to modify the database to include the following information: the price per print, a subtotal, the tax when applicable, and a total. Before adding these fields to the database, she also wants Karl to document the structure of the file ARTINVN2 with the new proposed changes. He prepared the documentation shown in Table 8.1. The new fields that will be entered in the database are starred.

Field Name	Column Width	Definition	Label(L) or Value(V)
ARTIST	18	Name of artist	L
ART VENDOR	19	Name of purchasing vendor	L
CITY	13	City location of vendor	L
STATE	6	State of vendor	L
* PRICE	7	Selling price per print	V
QUANTITY	10	Number of prints purchased	V
* SUBTOTAL	11	Subtotal (PRICE * QUANTITY)	V
* TAX	9	State tax, if applicable	V
* TOTAL	11	Total purchase amount	V

Table 8.1

Lynne has filed a copy of Table 8.1 in the Information Systems' central file, along with a disk containing a copy of the database. You will continue to document and modify the worksheet throughout this lab.

To see the rest of the records in the database,

    Press: PGDN

There are 20 print sales records.

    Press: HOME

Using @VLOOKUP

The first new field Karl will enter in the database is price. Insert a new column between STATE and QUANTITY. Set the column width to 7, and enter the label PRICE into cell E3 so that it is right-justified.

This field will contain the price for each print. Each artist charges a standard price for his or her prints. Rather than manually look up and insert the price for each record, Karl decides to create a table in the worksheet that lists the selling price for each type of print. Then, he will use the @VLOOKUP function to locate and copy the appropriate value from the table into the worksheet. This function produces the contents of a cell from a specified column in a vertical lookup table. As you will see, using the @VLOOKUP function automates the entry of standard data into the worksheet.

The first step is to create the table listing the prices of the different artists. After reviewing the database, Karl has prepared the data shown in Table 8.2.

Type	Price
Bassett	225
Collotte	150
Dachsman	100
Kaiser	250
Anderson	325
McDonald	254
Winne-Fernandez	127
Springer	144
Bernard	265

Table 8.2

To enter this table into an open area of the worksheet, use the GOTO command:

Press:	(F5) (GOTO)
Type:	**H1**
Press:	(↵)
Move to:	I3
Type:	**ARTIST**
Move to:	J3
Type:	**UNIT PRICE**
Press:	(↵)

Increase the width of column I to 15. Enter the nine artists and prices from Table 8.2 beginning in cells I4 and J4, respectively. Be sure to enter the names exactly as they appear in the table. Then format cells J4 through J12 as currency with zero decimal places.

Your screen should look similar to Figure 8.2.

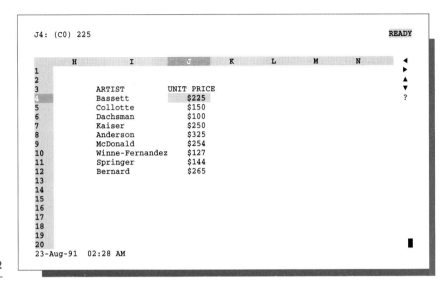

```
J4: (C0) 225                                                    READY

        H              I              J        K      L      M      N    ◄
1                                                                        ►
2                                                                        ▲
3                     ARTIST        UNIT PRICE                           ▼
4                     Bassett          $225                              ?
5                     Collotte         $150
6                     Dachsman         $100
7                     Kaiser           $250
8                     Anderson         $325
9                     McDonald         $254
10                    Winne-Fernandez  $127
11                    Springer         $144
12                    Bernard          $265
13
14
15
16
17
18
19
20                                                                      ■
     23-Aug-91  02:28 AM
```

Figure 8.2

This table contains the data necessary for the @VLOOKUP function to compute the artist's selling price and to enter it into the price field in the database. In order to make the @function easier to write and understand, you will assign the range name PRICE_TABLE to the range I3..J12:

/Range **N**ame **C**reate **PRICE_TABLE** ⏎ **I3..J12** ⏎

The next step is to use the @VLOOKUP function. The format or syntax for this function is:

@VLOOKUP(x,range,column-offset)

The **x** represents the search value that the @function looks for in the first column of the table. In this example, the search value will be an artist's name. Therefore, x will be a label from the artist field of the database. This has to be an exact match. Be sure that the label in the table matches the label in the artist field exactly. The @VLOOKUP function will match the name to an entry in the first column of the table.

The **range** represents the table range itself. In this example, the range is I3..J12, to which you assigned the name PRICE_TABLE.

The **column-offset** is how many columns over from the first column of the table @VLOOKUP goes to get the answer. The column-offset number is determined by assigning the leftmost column in the table range the value 0, the second column the value 1, the third column the value 2, and so forth. In this example, the selling prices in the table (column J) contains the values the @function will use. It is the second column in the table, therefore, the column-offset will be 1.

Enter the @VLOOKUP function as follows:

Press: HOME

Move to: E4

Type: **@VLOOKUP(A4,$PRICE_TABLE,1)**

Press: ⏎

Your screen should look similar to Figure 8.3.

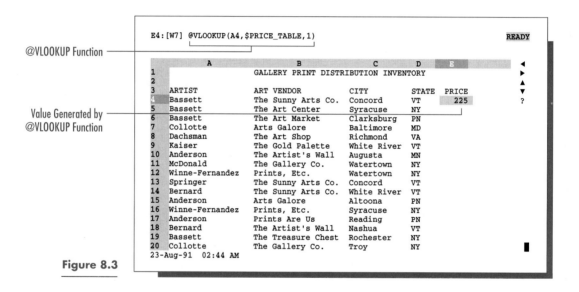

E4:[W7] @VLOOKUP(A4,$PRICE_TABLE,1)   READY

@VLOOKUP Function ─────────────

Value Generated by ─────────
@VLOOKUP Function

	A	B	C	D	E
1		GALLERY PRINT DISTRIBUTION INVENTORY			
2					
3	ARTIST	ART VENDOR	CITY	STATE	PRICE
4	Bassett	The Sunny Arts Co.	Concord	VT	225
5	Bassett	The Art Center	Syracuse	NY	
6	Bassett	The Art Market	Clarksburg	PN	
7	Collotte	Arts Galore	Baltimore	MD	
8	Dachsman	The Art Shop	Richmond	VA	
9	Kaiser	The Gold Palette	White River	VT	
10	Anderson	The Artist's Wall	Augusta	MN	
11	McDonald	The Gallery Co.	Watertown	NY	
12	Winne-Fernandez	Prints, Etc.	Watertown	NY	
13	Springer	The Sunny Arts Co.	Concord	VT	
14	Bernard	The Sunny Arts Co.	White River	VT	
15	Anderson	Arts Galore	Altoona	PN	
16	Winne-Fernandez	Prints, Etc.	Syracuse	NY	
17	Anderson	Prints Are Us	Reading	PN	
18	Bernard	The Artist's Wall	Nashua	VT	
19	Bassett	The Treasure Chest	Rochester	NY	
20	Collotte	The Gallery Co.	Troy	NY	

23-Aug-91 02:44 AM

Figure 8.3

The value 225 was entered into cell E4. The @VLOOKUP function took the label in cell A4 (Bassett) and looked for a match in the first column of the table range, PRICE_TABLE. The column-offset is 1, so the @function took, for the answer, the value one column over from Bassett which is the value 225.

Notice that the table range, PRICE_TABLE, was made absolute. This was done so that the formula could be copied down the price field. All the @VLOOKUP functions in the price field will need to refer to the same range for the table. If PRICE_TABLE were left relative, the table range would shift down one row every time the @function was copied down a row. You will now copy the @function down the price field:

Format the values in the price field as currency format, with no decimal places.

Your screen should look similar to Figure 8.4.

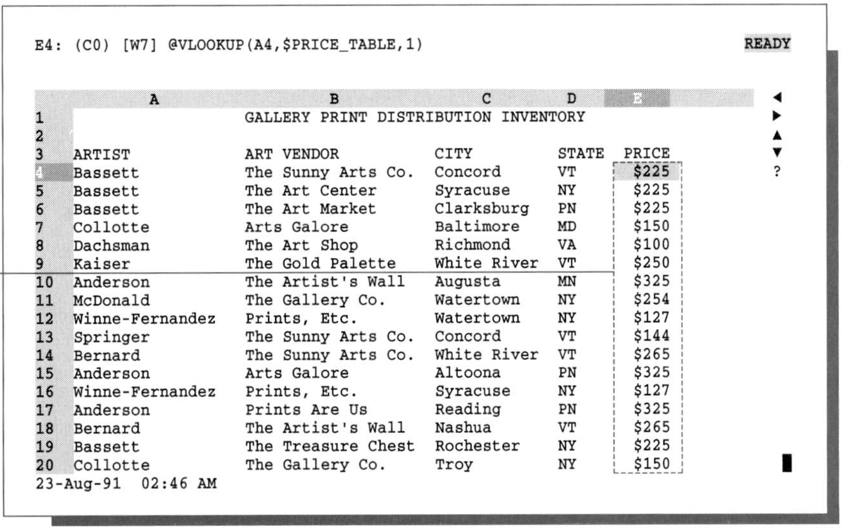

```
E4: (C0) [W7] @VLOOKUP(A4,$PRICE_TABLE,1)                              READY

              A                B                C         D      E        ◄
   1                    GALLERY PRINT DISTRIBUTION INVENTORY             ►
   2                                                                     ▲
   3   ARTIST           ART VENDOR       CITY         STATE  PRICE       ▼
   4   Bassett          The Sunny Arts Co.  Concord      VT   $225       ?
   5   Bassett          The Art Center   Syracuse     NY    $225
   6   Bassett          The Art Market   Clarksburg   PN    $225
   7   Collotte         Arts Galore      Baltimore    MD    $150
   8   Dachsman         The Art Shop     Richmond     VA    $100
   9   Kaiser           The Gold Palette White River  VT    $250
  10   Anderson         The Artist's Wall Augusta     MN    $325
  11   McDonald         The Gallery Co.  Watertown    NY    $254
  12   Winne-Fernandez  Prints, Etc.     Watertown    NY    $127
  13   Springer         The Sunny Arts Co. Concord    VT    $144
  14   Bernard          The Sunny Arts Co. White River VT   $265
  15   Anderson         Arts Galore      Altoona      PN    $325
  16   Winne-Fernandez  Prints, Etc.     Syracuse     NY    $127
  17   Anderson         Prints Are Us    Reading      PN    $325
  18   Bernard          The Artist's Wall Nashua      VT    $265
  19   Bassett          The Treasure Chest Rochester  NY    $225
  20   Collotte         The Gallery Co.  Troy         NY    $150       ∎
  23-Aug-91  02:46 AM
```

Values Generated by @VLOOKUP Function

Figure 8.4

One advantage of using the @VLOOKUP function is that if the unit price for any print changes, Karl needs to make the change only once. For instance, Karl notices that he typed in the wrong value for the price of Anderson prints. The correct price should be $345. Instead of going through the database and correcting the selling price for every Anderson record, the change can be made one time in the price table:

Move to: J8

Type: 345

Press: ⏎

Press: (HOME)

Look at rows 10 and 17. The prices of Anderson prints have been automatically changed.

Next, Karl needs to enter the last three columns for the database. Insert three new columns after QUANTITY. Using Table 8.3 (on the next page), enter the field names so that they are right-justified.

Cell	Field Name	Column Width
G3	SUBTOTAL	11
H3	TAX	9
I3	TOTAL	11

Table 8.3

Each of these fields will contain a formula. You will enter each of these formulas and then copy them down for all the records.

The formula for the SUBTOTAL field is the number of prints multiplied by the price. To enter this formula:

Move to: G4

Type: +E4*F4

Press: ⏎

The subtotal for the first record should be 900. Copy the formula down the column, and format the column as currency with no decimal places.

Your screen should look similar to Figure 8.5.

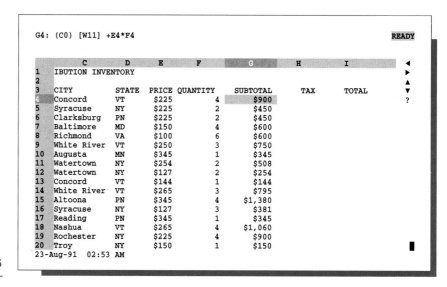

Figure 8.5

Lab 8 Using a Database

Using @IF

The TAX field is more complicated. Since The Gallery Print Distribution Co. is located in New York, they must charge sales tax to those vendors located in New York. However, vendors located outside New York do not pay this sales tax. Karl decides to use the @IF function to determine whether sales tax is required. This function will check to see if certain conditions are met and then takes action based upon the results of the check.

The @IF function uses the following syntax:

@IF(condition,x,y)

The @IF function makes a decision based on the **condition**. Usually the condition is a formula that compares values by determining whether one value is equal to another (=), greater than another (>), less than another (<), greater than or equal to another (>=), or less than or equal to another (<=). If the condition is true, the value of **x** is the answer. If the condition is false, the value of **y** is the answer. In this example, the function will determine whether or not the state field is equal to NY. If it is, the tax will be calculated as 7 percent of the subtotal, which is the standard sales tax for the part of New York where the Gallery Print Distribution Co. sells its prints. If the state is not NY, the tax will be 0. Enter the following @IF function into the worksheet:

Move to: H4

Type: **@IF(D4="NY",G4*.07,0)**

Press: ⏎

Notice that NY appears in quotation marks in the function. This is because NY is a label or string. Any time strings are used in a formula, they must be entered in quotation marks. A value of 0 appears in cell H4 because the order for the first record was not from a New York vendor.

Copy the formula down the column for the rest of the records in the database. Then format the column as currency with two decimal places.

Your screen should look similar to Figure 8.6.

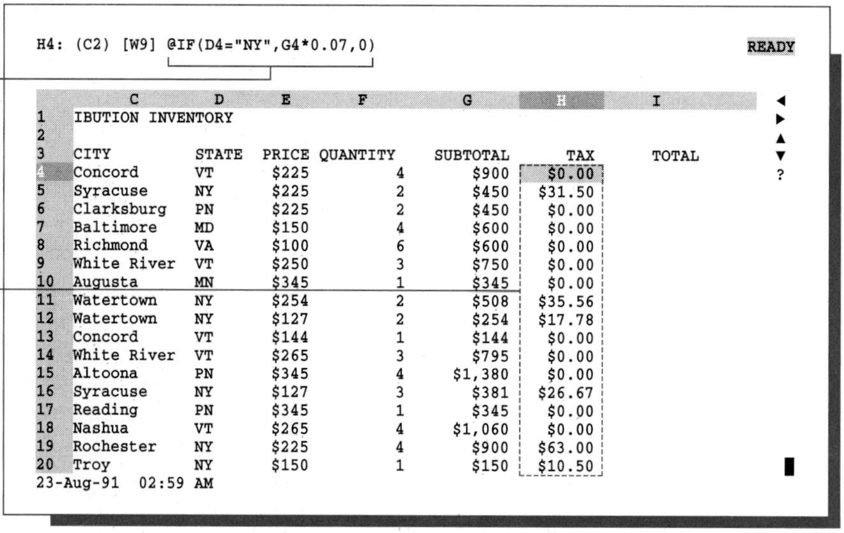

```
H4: (C2) [W9] @IF(D4="NY",G4*0.07,0)                                    READY
```

@IF Function ────────────

```
              C            D       E       F            G           H          I      ◄
        1  IBUTION INVENTORY                                                            ►
        2                                                                               ▲
        3  CITY          STATE   PRICE QUANTITY     SUBTOTAL        TAX      TOTAL       ▼
        4  Concord       VT      $225      4          $900        $0.00                  ?
        5  Syracuse      NY      $225      2          $450       $31.50
        6  Clarksburg    PN      $225      2          $450        $0.00
        7  Baltimore     MD      $150      4          $600        $0.00
        8  Richmond      VA      $100      6          $600        $0.00
        9  White River   VT      $250      3          $750        $0.00
       10  Augusta       MN      $345      1          $345        $0.00
       11  Watertown     NY      $254      2          $508       $35.56
       12  Watertown     NY      $127      2          $254       $17.78
       13  Concord       VT      $144      1          $144        $0.00
       14  White River   VT      $265      3          $795        $0.00
       15  Altoona       PN      $345      4        $1,380        $0.00
       16  Syracuse      NY      $127      3          $381       $26.67
       17  Reading       PN      $345      1          $345        $0.00
       18  Nashua        VT      $265      4        $1,060        $0.00
       19  Rochester     NY      $225      4          $900       $63.00
       20  Troy          NY      $150      1          $150       $10.50
       23-Aug-91  02:59 AM
```

Values Generated by ────────── (points to row 10/11 area)
@IF Function

Figure 8.6

Sales tax values appear only for those vendors who are located in New York.

The formula for the TOTAL field is simply SUBTOTAL plus TAX. To enter the formula:

Move to: I4

Type: +G4+H4

Press: ⏎

Now the cell I4 displays the value 900. Copy the formula down the column for the other records, and format the column as currency with two decimal places.

Karl has finished updating and expanding the database. He makes a copy of the database and sends it to Lynne. Now we will follow Lynne as she uses the database to perform some statistical analysis.

Using @DAVG, @DMIN, @DMAX, @DCOUNT

To begin her analysis of the Gallery Print Distribution Inventory database, Lynne wants to compare sales in New York to those in Vermont.

Specifically, she wants to calculate the average, the minimum, and the maximum sale for each state. She also wants to determine the total number of prints sold in each state.

To obtain these comparisons, you will use some of 1-2-3's database statistical @functions. These functions require that you create a criteria range that specifies the requirements for the @function to use with the computation.

You will begin by calculating the average sales for New York using the @DAVG function. The syntax for this @function is

@DAVG(input,field,criteria)

The first step is to enter the criteria in any open area of the worksheet. You will use the area to the right of the database and the price table. To move to this area,

Press: (F5) (GOTO)

Type: **P1**

Press: (↵)

Because this worksheet will contain many different items, it is a good procedure to document the different areas of the worksheet with descriptive labels. These labels identify the contents of each area of the worksheet. This area of the worksheet will contain the criteria for the @functions. To enter a descriptive label to document this area of the worksheet,

Type: **CRITERIA: New York Sales**

Press: (↵)

The next step is to enter the criteria field name. This field name must be an exact duplication of the field names in the database. You can enter the field name either by typing or by copying from the database. We will use the second approach because there is less chance for an error.

To enter the criteria field name, STATE,

Move to: Q3

Copy the field name STATE from cell D3 to cell Q3.

To enter the selection criteria, NY, for New York,

Move to: Q4

Type: **NY**

Press: (↵)

Your screen should look similar to Figure 8.7.

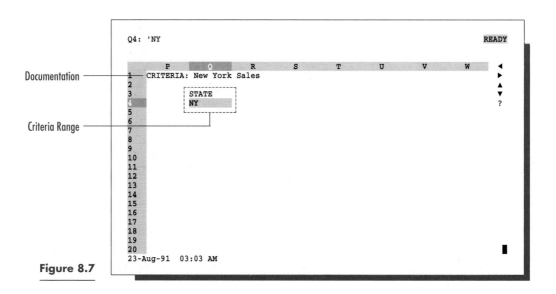

Documentation

Criteria Range

```
Q4: 'NY                                                                  READY

         P          Q          R       S        T        U       V       W    ◄
    1──── CRITERIA: New York Sales                                             ►
    2                                                                          ▲
    3             ┌─────────────┐                                             ▼
    4             │ STATE       │                                             ?
    5             │ NY          │
    6             └─────────────┘
    7
    8
    9
   10
   11
   12
   13
   14
   15
   16
   17
   18
   19
   20                                                                         ■
    23-Aug-91  03:03 AM
```

Figure 8.7

You are now ready to enter the database statistical @functions to calculate the sales for New York.

Move to: P6

Again, document this area of the worksheet by adding a descriptive label.

Type: **STATISTICS: New York Sales**

Move to: Q8

Type: **AVG. SALE**

Press: ⏎

Set the width of column Q to 11 spaces.

Your screen should look similar to Figure 8.8.

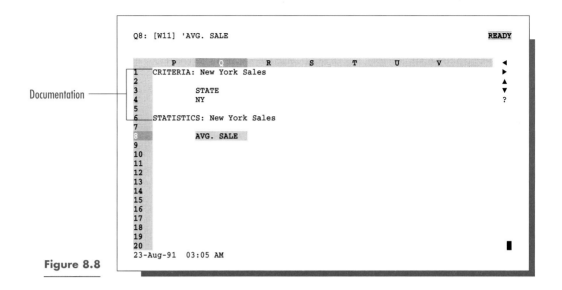

Documentation

```
Q8: [W11] 'AVG. SALE                                        READY

        P        Q        R        S        T        U        V      ◄
  1  CRITERIA: New York Sales                                          ►
  2                                                                    ▲
  3            STATE                                                   ▼
  4            NY                                                      ?
  5
  6  STATISTICS: New York Sales
  7
  8            AVG. SALE
  9
 10
 11
 12
 13
 14
 15
 16
 17
 18
 19
 20
 23-Aug-91   03:05 AM                                           ■
```

Figure 8.8

To enter the @function to calculate the average sales for New York,

Move to: R8

Type: **@DAVG(**

The first argument you need to enter is the input range. This range specifies the records in the database to be used in the calculation. The range
must include the field names. To specify all records,

Type: **A3..I23**

To separate this argument from the next,

Type: **,** (comma)

The second argument is the field in the database that the function should
perform the average on. The field is identified by an **offset-number**.
The first column in the database is counted as column 0, the second
column is 1, the third column is 2, and so forth. This is similar to the
offset used by the @VLOOKUP function. The offset number specifying
the field TOTAL is 8.

Type: **8,**

The last argument you need to enter is the criteria range.

Type: **Q3..Q4)**

Press: ⏎

Your screen should look similar to Figure 8.9.

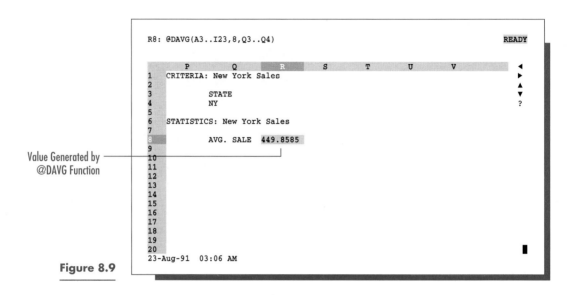

Value Generated by
@DAVG Function

Figure 8.9

The value 449.8585 generated by the @DAVG function is displayed in cell R8. If the value in cell R8 is not 449.8585, check the function. It should be @DAV(A3..I23,8,Q3..Q4).

You will use the @DMAX, @DMIN, and @DCOUNT @functions to calculate the maximum and minimum sales for New York and the total number of New York sales in the database. The input, field, and criteria for each of these @functions are identical to those specified in the @DAVG function.

To document the worksheet,

Move to: Q9

Type: **MIN. SALE**

Move to: Q10

Type: **MAX. SALE**

Move to: Q11

Type: **NUM. SALES**

Press: ⏎

To enter the @functions,

Move to: R9

Type: **@DMIN(A3..I23,8,Q3..Q4)**

Move to: R10

Type: **@DMAX(A3..I23,8,Q3..Q4)**

Move to: R11

Type: **@DCOUNT(A3..I23,8,Q3..Q4)**

Press: ⏎

The average, minimum, maximum, and number of sales for New York are now calculated. Format the values in R8..R10 to be displayed as currency with zero decimal places.

Your screen should look similar to Figure 8.10.

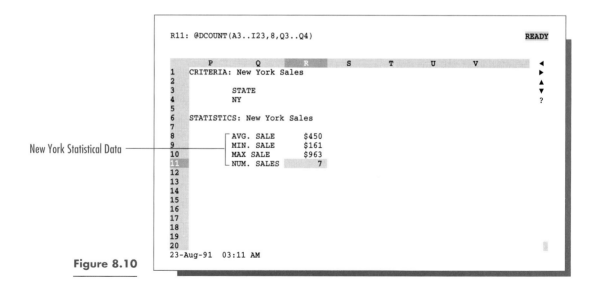

New York Statistical Data

Figure 8.10

Lynne created similar statistics for Vermont. To see the Vermont statistics, retrieve the worksheet ARTINVN3.WK1. You do not need to save ARTINVN2.

Your screen should look similar to Figure 8.11.

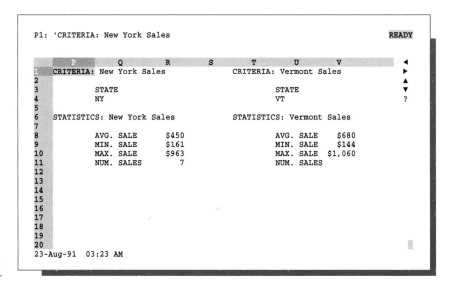

```
P1: 'CRITERIA: New York Sales                                     READY


        P        Q         R        S        T        U        V      ◄
1   CRITERIA: New York Sales              CRITERIA: Vermont Sales      ►
2                                                                      ▲
3            STATE                                 STATE               ▼
4            NY                                    VT                  ?
5
6   STATISTICS: New York Sales            STATISTICS: Vermont Sales
7
8            AVG. SALE      $450                   AVG. SALE      $680
9            MIN. SALE      $161                   MIN. SALE      $144
10           MAX. SALE      $963                   MAX. SALE  $1,060
11           NUM. SALES       7                    NUM. SALES
12
13
14
15
16
17
18
19
20
    23-Aug-91   03:23 AM
```

Figure 8.11

Lynne has not entered the @DCOUNT function for cell V11. To complete the Vermont statistics:

Move to: V11

Type: **@DCOUNT(A3..I23,8,U3..U4)**

Press: ⏎

The number of sales in Vermont is 6. Lynne can now easily compare the average, minimum, and maximum sales and the number of sales that have occurred in New York and Vermont.

Using the Data Query Extract Command

Finally, Lynne wants to create two separate lists that show the ARTIST, CITY, and TOTAL data for all New York and Vermont sales. To do this, you will use the **/D**ata **Q**uery **E**xtract command. This command requires a criteria range, an input range, and an **output range.** The only new range that you need to specify is output.

The output range is where the specified fields of data meeting the criteria will be displayed. You will use the worksheet space to the right of the statistics for the output range. To document this area of the worksheet, begin with the GOTO command:

Press: (F5) (GOTO)

Type: **X1**

Press: (↵)

Type: **OUTPUT: New York**

Press: (↵)

The first row of the output range must contain the field names from the database of each field you want to be displayed. Lynne wants only the data in the ARTIST, CITY, and TOTAL fields to appear in the list.

Like the criteria range, the field names in the output range must be exact duplicates of the field names in the database. You will use the /Copy command to reduce the chance of an error.

Move to: X3

To enter the output field names: copy the field name ARTIST from cell A3 of the database to cell X3, copy the field name CITY from cell C3 to cell Y3, and copy the field name TOTAL from cell I3 to cell Z3. Set the column width of columns X and Y to 16.

Your screen should look similar to Figure 8.12.

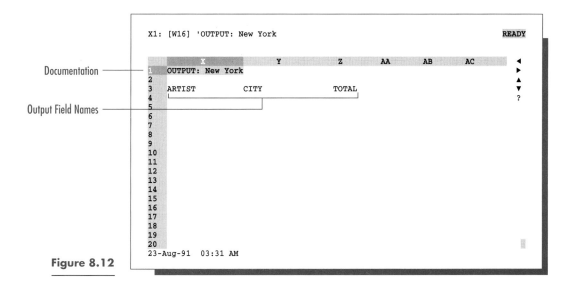

Figure 8.12

You are now ready to use the **/Data Query** command to **extract** the data for New York sales to the output range. Issue the following command sequence:

/Data Query

The Query Settings dialog box is displayed.

First, specify the input range. The input range must begin with the row of field names in the database and end with the last record to be queried.

To specify the input range as the entire database from cell A3 through cell I23, continue the command sequence as follows:

Input A3..I23 ⏎

Next, to specify the criteria range for New York as Q3 through Q4,

Select: Criteria **Q3..Q4**

Press: ⏎

The final setting to specify is the output range, where the records meeting the criteria will be displayed.

You can specify the output range in two different ways. One way is to specify a single-row output range. The output range would consist of only the row containing the output field names. When the data meeting the criteria is copied from the database, it will be displayed below the appropriate field names. 1-2-3 will use as many rows as it needs below the output field names to display the data meeting the criteria. If necessary, it will copy over any existing data.

The other way is to specify a multiple-row output range consisting of the field names in the first row and a number of rows below the field names to display the extracted data. 1-2-3 will display as many rows of data below the field names as there are rows in the specified range. However, if the range is not large enough, the error message "Too many records for Output range" will appear, and you must respecify the output range.

You will specify a single-row output range because there is nothing below this area in the worksheet. Issue the following command sequence:

Output X3..Z3 ⏎

Now you are ready to extract the artists, cities, and totals for all the New York sales in the database. Issue the following command:

Extract Quit

Your screen should look similar to Figure 8.13.

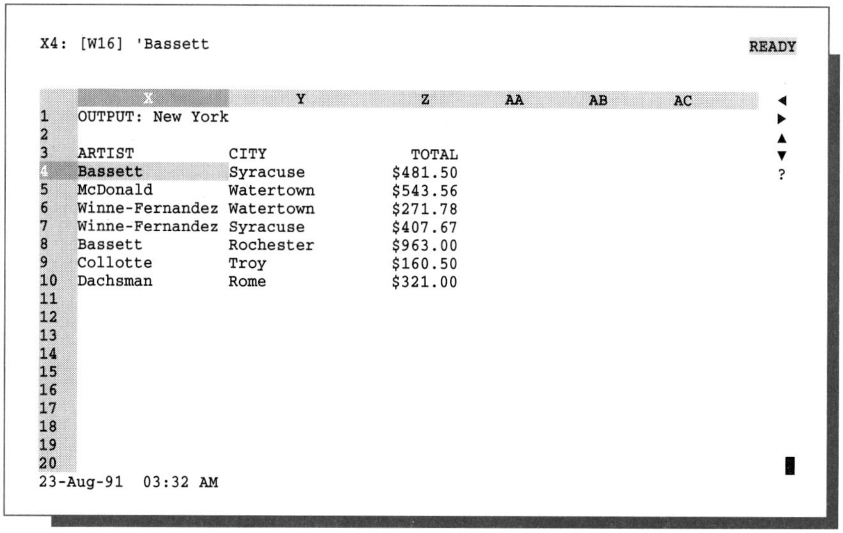

```
X4: [W16] 'Bassett                                                    READY

        X              Y           Z        AA      AB      AC       ◄
 1  OUTPUT: New York                                                 ►
 2                                                                   ▲
 3  ARTIST         CITY           TOTAL                              ▼
 4  Bassett        Syracuse      $481.50                             ?
 5  McDonald       Watertown     $543.56
 6  Winne-Fernandez Watertown    $271.78
 7  Winne-Fernandez Syracuse     $407.67
 8  Bassett        Rochester     $963.00
 9  Collotte       Troy          $160.50
10  Dachsman       Rome          $321.00
11
12
13
14
15
16
17
18
19
20
    23-Aug-91  03:32 AM                                              ■
```

Figure 8.13

Look at the contents of cells X4 through Z10. The selected field data, ARTIST, CITY, and TOTAL, for all records meeting the criteria have been copied into these cells.

Next, you need to extract the same fields of information for Vermont sales from the database.

To extract this information, enter in cell AB1 the descriptive label OUTPUT: Vermont. Then copy the field names from cells X3 through Z3 to cells AB3 through AD3. Change the column width of column AA to 5, column AB to 16, column AC to 16, and column AD to 10.

Issue the following command sequence:

/**D**ata **Q**uery **C**riteria **U3..U4** ⏎

To specify the new output range,

Select: **O**utput **AB3..AD3**

Press: ⏎

To copy the selected data into the output range and return to READY mode, issue the following command sequence:

Extract **Q**uit

Your screen should now look similar to Figure 8.14.

```
AB4: [W16] 'Bassett                                              READY

           Y            Z          AA          AB          AC          AD      ◄
1                                        OUTPUT: Vermont                        ►
2                                                                               ▲
3   CITY            TOTAL             ARTIST      CITY            TOTAL          ▼
4   Syracuse        $481.50           Bassett     Concord         $900.00       ?
5   Watertown       $543.56           Kaiser      White River     $750.00
6   Watertown       $271.78           Springer    Concord         $144.00
7   Syracuse        $407.67           Bernard     White River     $795.00
8   Rochester       $963.00           Bernard     Nashua        $1,060.00
9   Troy            $160.50           Springer    Claremont       $432.00
10  Rome            $321.00
11
12
13
14
15
16
17
18
19
20
23-Aug-91  03:35 AM                                                            ■
```

Figure 8.14

Save the worksheet as ARTINVN4.

To print the extracted data, use compressed printing to print the range X1..AD24.

When you are finished printing, exit 1-2-3.

Glossary

Column-offset: The number of columns over from the first column of the table to which @VLOOKUP goes to get the answer.

Condition: A formula that compares the value in two cells to determine if one is less than, greater than, or equal to another or that checks the result of a specified formula.

Extract: Finds the records in a database that meet specified criteria and copies the specified fields of each located record to the output range.

Offset number: A number assigned to the column in the input range required by the database @function field argument.

Output range: The area specified in the worksheet where the records meeting the criteria are copied during the /Data Extract command.

Practice Problems and Cases

Matching

1. @VLOOKUP
2. @IF
3. @DAVG
4. @DMAX
5. Condition
6. Offset number
7. Output range
8. Table range
9. @DCOUNT
10. /DQE

_____ **a.** area of the worksheet to which extracted data is copied

_____ **b.** argument for @VLOOKUP

_____ **c.** argument for @IF

_____ **d.** calculates an average value from a database field

_____ **e.** a command used to copy records meeting criteria to a separate area of the worksheet

_____ **f.** evaluates a condition and takes one of two actions

_____ **g.** finds largest value in a database field

_____ **h.** indicates the location of the column containing the field in the input range that the @function will operate on

_____ **i.** calculates how many values match criteria

_____ **j.** finds a value in a specific column of a vertical table

Multiple Choice

1. The /Data Query Extract command requires an:

   a. input range   c. criteria range

   b. output range   d. all the above

2. The command that finds the records in a database that meet specified criteria and copies the specified fields to an output range is:

   a. Extract   c. Find

   b. Locate   d. Output

3. @VLOOKUP requires _____ arguments.

   a. 1   c. 3

   b. 2   d. 4

4. The correct form of an @DAVG function is:

   a. @DAVG(field,input,criteria)

   b. @DAVG(input,field,criteria)

   c. @DAVG(criteria,input,field)

   d. @DAVG(input,criteria,field)

5. An @IF is most useful in decision making involving _____ possible outcome(s).

   a. one   c. three

   b. two   d. four

6. If there are seven columns in a database and you are using column 5 in a database function, the offset number would be:

   a. 7   c. 4

   b. 5   d. 6

7. The format of an @IF is @IF(condition,x,y). The x represents a:

   a. true condition

   b. false condition

8. An output range can be:

   a. one row

   b. multiple rows

   c. either one row or multiple rows

   d. all cells in a field of selected records

9. The @DMIN function finds the:

   a. largest value in a given field of selected records

   b. largest value in a database

   c. smallest value in a given field of selected records

   d. smallest value in a database

10. The first argument in a database function is:

   a. criteria range   c. field name

   b. data range   d. input range

Cases

1. Tracy Miles, the personnel manager for a large toy store, has continued to enter data into her personal database. Retrieve the file PROB8-1.WK1. This file has the same database structure as the file created in Practice Case 1 in Lab 7 and saved as HWLAB7-1. The file now contains 30 records.

   a. Enter your name in cell A1 and the current date in cell A2.

   b. Add a new column between Telephone and Pay Rate. Title the column Hours, and set the column width to 6. All the employees at the toy store work 40 hours a week. Enter 40 in cell I5, and copy it down the column.

   c. In the column after Pay Rate, enter the title Weekly Pay. Enter the formula to multiply Hours by Pay Rate. Format the cell as currency with two decimal places. Copy the formula down the column.

      Tracy would like to compare the average pay of employees who work in the stock room with those who work on the loading dock.

   d. In an open area to the right of the worksheet, enter the labels CRITERIA: Stock Room and CRITERIA: Loading Dock.

   e. Enter the criteria field name as Job Title below both description labels. Then enter the selection criteria below each field name.

   f. Below the criteria fields, enter the descriptive titles STATISTICS: Stock Room and STATISTICS: Loading Dock.

   g. Below the titles, enter the label AVERAGE PAY and then the @DAVG function to find the average weekly pay for the two departments. Format the cells as currency with two decimal places.

   h. Continue the statistics for the employees in the stock room and loading dock by calculating the MAX pay rate, MIN pay rate, and the number of employees.

   i. Save the worksheet as HWLAB8-1. Print the worksheet.

2. To complete this problem, you must have completed Practice Case 1.

   The toy store has just started a new insurance program. Employees who earn less than $300 a week pay $15 a week for insurance, and employees who earn $300 or more pay $30 a week.

   a. Retrieve the file HWLAB8-1.WK1.

   b. Insert a new column after Weekly Pay. Title the column Insurance. Enter an @IF function to display the amount paid based on the employee's weekly pay.

c. Format the column to display currency with two decimal places. Copy the @IF function down the column.

d. Enter the criteria, and calculate the MIN, MAX, and COUNT statistics for insurance for employees with the job title Clerk and Supervisor. (*Hint:* You can copy the information for the stock room and adjust it.)

e. Save the worksheet as HWLAB8-2.

f. Print the worksheet.

3. Sam Walker owns Sam's Fish Shop. Sam is using 1-2-3 to keep track of his inventory. Complete the following steps.

a. Retrieve the file PROB8-3.WK1. Enter your name in cell A1 and the current date in cell A2.

b. Name the table in cells I5 through J12 PRICE_TABLE.

c. Use an @VLOOKUP function to enter the price in column F. Format the column to display dollar signs with two decimal places. Copy the formula down column F.

d. Complete the total column by multiplying QUANTITY * PRICE. Format the cell to display dollar signs with two decimal places. Copy the formula down the column.

e. Sam has been having trouble with deliveries from Everett Shipping, and he wants to see their records. Extract all the records from Everett Shipping. Print the records.

f. Save the database as HWLAB8-3. Print the entire worksheet.

4. To complete this problem, you first must have completed Practice Case 6 in Lab 7. If you have completed that problem, retrieve the file HWLAB7-6.WK1.

Complete the worksheet by entering a column to display total weekly pay; statistics for average, maximum, and minimum pay; and number of employees from each city. Enter the current date in cell A2. Save the worksheet as HWLAB8-4, and print the worksheet.

5. Create an inventory database for a toy store. Include a description of each item, the vendor, the state where the vendor's factory is located, the price, the number on hand, the subtotal, the tax, and the total price. Use an @VLOOKUP table to enter the price paid per item. Enter your name in cell A1 and the current date in cell A2. Save the worksheet as HWLAB8-5 and print the worksheet.

6. Joanne has completed her database for the Arlington summer coed baseball league. She has divided the players into teams. Retrieve the file PROB8-6.WK1. This file contains information for the team called the Road Runners.

Calculate the batting average AVG, MAX, MIN, and COUNT statistics for both male and female players.

Lab 9

Creating and Using Macros

In Lab 9, you will learn how to:

- Create, edit, run, and debug macros
- Create interactive macros
- Use a repetition factor
- Use LEARN mode
- Use STEP mode

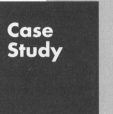

Case Study

Susan Chang is the owner of a concession stand that serves sandwiches, drinks, and side orders. Susan would like to keep track of daily sales using a 1-2-3 worksheet with macros.

You will follow Susan as she creates a daily sales report form. This report will specify the product, price, number sold, total sales, and percent of sales for each item sold by the concession stand. Susan will use some basic macro commands to help her create the report and several other macro commands to help her enter the data.

Introducing Macros

A **macro** is a set of instructions for automating a 1-2-3 task, consisting of a sequence of keystrokes and commands that you type into a worksheet as cell entries. The commands are performed whenever you invoke (run) the macro.

You can use a macro to issue commands or to enter data into a worksheet. More complex macros can accept user entries from the keyboard, perform conditional tests, or display user-defined menus. Macros are particularly useful in automating frequently used 1-2-3 commands, performing repetitive procedures, and developing customized worksheets.

The simplest type of macro represents keys on the keyboard. The macro commands consist of **keystroke instructions**, which can be a single character key or key names enclosed in braces ({key name}). The single-character keystroke instructions represent typewriter keys on the keyboard and are identical to the keys they represent. The only exception to this is the ⏎ key. The single character key that represents ⏎ is the ~ (tilde). Table 9.1 shows many of the keystroke instructions that consist of a key name enclosed in braces.

Macro Key	Description
{U} or {UP}	Move pointer up (↑)
{D} or {DOWN}	Move pointer down (↓)
{R} or {RIGHT}	Move pointer right (→)
{L} or {LEFT}	Move pointer left (←)
{HOME}	Move pointer to upper left cell of worksheet (HOME)
{END}	End key (END)
{PGUP}	Page Up key (PGUP)
{PGDN}	Page Down key (PGDN)
{BIGLEFT}	Move pointer one page left (CTRL)-(←)

Table 9.1

Macro Key	Description
{BIGRIGHT}	Move pointer one page right (CTRL)-(→)
{BACKSPACE} or {BS}	BACKSPACE key
{DELETE} or {DEL}	Delete key (DEL)
{ESCAPE} or {ESC}	Escape key (ESC)
{HELP}	(F1)
{EDIT}	(F2)
{NAME}	(F3)
{ABS}	(F4)
{GOTO}	(F5)
{WINDOW}	(F6)
{QUERY}	(F7)
{TABLE}	(F8)
{CALC}	(F9)
{GRAPH}	(F10)
{?}	Wait for keyboard entry (pause)
~ (tilde)	(↵)
{APP1}	(ALT)-(F7)
{APP2}	(ALT)-(F8)
{APP3}	(ALT)-(F9)
{APP4}	(ALT)-(F10)
/, < , or {MENU}	/ (slash) or < (less than symbol)
{{}	{ (open brace)
{}}	} (close brace)

Table 9.1 Continued

Susan wants to create a daily sales report form so that she can easily record the sales on nine specific products. She has already started the report using 1-2-3. To view the report, load 1-2-3, and retrieve the file SALES1.WK1.

Your screen should look similar to Figure 9.1.

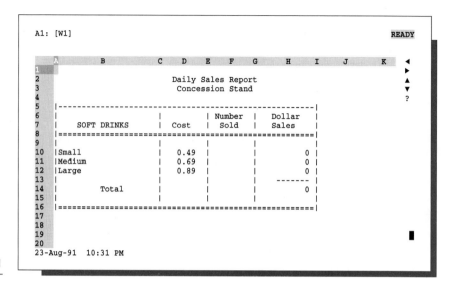

```
A1: [W1]                                                          READY

      A        B           C    D   E    F    G    H    I    J    K    ◄
  1                                                                    ►
  2                          Daily Sales Report                       ▲
  3                          Concession Stand                         ▼
  4                                                                    ?
  5   |------------------------------------------------------|
  6   |                        |        | Number  |  Dollar  |
  7   |    SOFT DRINKS         |  Cost  | Sold    |  Sales   |
  8   |========================================================|
  9   |                        |        |         |          |
 10   |Small                   |  0.49  |         |        0 |
 11   |Medium                  |  0.69  |         |        0 |
 12   |Large                   |  0.89  |         |        0 |
 13   |                        |        |         |  ------- |
 14   |          Total         |        |         |        0 |
 15   |                        |        |         |          |
 16   |========================================================|
 17
 18
 19
 20                                                               ■
      23-Aug-91  10:31 PM
```

Figure 9.1

The completed sales report will have three sections. Susan has created only the first section of the sales report, Soft Drinks. The cost of each item is listed next to the appropriate drink size. She will enter the daily sales in the Number Sold column.

The Dollar Sales column is computed by taking the value in the Number Sold column and multiplying it by the figures in the Cost column.

Susan has entered the formula to calculate the Dollar Sales for small drinks and copied the formula down for the other two sizes. She has also entered the @SUM function to calculate the Total Dollar Sales.

To see the formula used to calculate Dollar Sales, use the pointer-movement keys to

    Move to: H10

The first line in the control panel now displays the formula. Cells H11 and H12 contain similar formulas.

Creating Macros

Susan wants to format the three values in the Cost column as currency with two decimal places. Likewise, the three values in the Dollar Sales column need to be formatted. You will create a macro to perform this operation by following three basic steps: planning, entering, and naming the macro.

Step 1 Plan the macro. You must determine the exact steps necessary to format three continuous cells in a column as currency, with two decimal places.

With the cell pointer in D10, the command sequence that would format cell D10, and the two cells below it as currency with two decimal places, would be **/R**ange **F**ormat **C**urrency ⊙ **D10..D12** ⊙.

Alternatively, an equivalent command sequence using pointing would be **/R**ange **F**ormat **C**urrency ⊙ ⊙ ⊙ ⊙. The advantage to using this sequence as a macro is that it could be used any place in the worksheet where three continuous numbers down a column need to be formatted.

By using only the first letter of the command and the macro keys shown in Table 9.1, this same command sequence using pointing expressed as a macro is **/RFC~{D}{D}~**.

The ~ is equivalent to ⊙, and the **{D}** is equivalent to ⊙.

Step 2 Enter the macro. A macro is entered as a label. If the macro begins with a /, \, (, or one of the numeric symbols, you must begin the macro with a label-prefix character. In the macro you will enter, the first character you will type is a /. If you do not begin the macro with a label-prefix character, the 1-2-3 main menu will be displayed, and you will be unable to enter the macro as a label in the cell.

The macro can be entered in either uppercase or lowercase characters. Be careful not to enter blank spaces in the macro instructions.

A macro is entered in any blank area of the worksheet. It can be entered in a single cell or a continuous range of vertical cells. You will enter this macro in a single cell.

To enter the macro instructions to format three continuous cells in a column as currency with two decimal places,

Move to: D18

Type: '/RFC~{D}{D}~

Press: ⊙

Your screen should look similar to Figure 9.2.

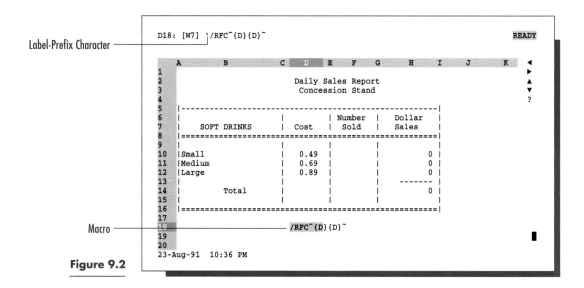

Label-Prefix Character

Macro

Figure 9.2

```
D18: [W7]  /RFC~{D}{D}~                                              READY

         A        B         C     D    E    F    G    H    I    J    K    ◄
1                                                                         ►
2                             Daily Sales Report                          ▲
3                             Concession Stand                            ▼
4                                                                         ?
5        |---------------------------------------------------|
6        |                      |      | Number |  Dollar   |
7        |    SOFT DRINKS       | Cost |  Sold  |  Sales    |
8        |===================================================|
9        |                 |          |        |           |
10       |Small            |    0.49  |        |         0 |
11       |Medium           |    0.69  |        |         0 |
12       |Large            |    0.89  |        |         0 |
13       |                 |          |        |  ------- |
14       |        Total    |          |        |         0 |
15       |                 |          |        |           |
16       |===================================================|
17
18                              /RFC~{D}{D}~
19
20
23-Aug-91  10:36 PM
```

The commands entered in cell D18 duplicate the keystrokes that you would use to format cells D10, D11, and D12 using pointing.

Be sure you have entered the macro into cell D18 exactly as it appears in Figure 9.2. If yours is not the same, correct the entry by editing the cell.

Step 3 Name the macro. To define cell D18 as a macro, it must be named. To do this, use the **/R**ange **N**ame **C**reate command.

> **Select:** /**R**ange **N**ame **C**reate

The prompt to enter a name is displayed in the control panel. There are two ways to name a macro. The first method consists of a backslash (\) followed by a single letter A to Z. The second method follows the same rules for naming a range. That is, it can consist of any combination of up to 15 characters.

We will use the first method to name this macro. When assigning a macro a single-letter name, it is a good idea to use a letter that is descriptive of the action of the macro. For example, because this macro formats a group of cells as currency, you will name the macro \C for Currency.

In response to the prompt,

> **Type:** \C
>
> **Press:** ⏎

To accept cell D18 as the range,

Press: ⏎

Executing Macros

After a macro has been created, it should be run and tested. To run, or execute, a macro whose name consists of a \ and a single letter, hold down (ALT) and press the letter of the name of the macro (in this case, C).

First, to position the cell pointer in the cell that contains the first value in the column to be formatted,

Move to: D10

Then, to run the macro,

Press: (ALT)-**C**

Your screen should look similar to Figure 9.3.

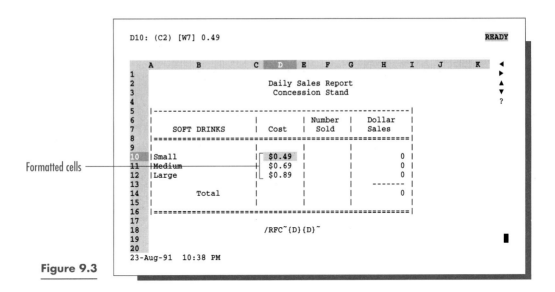

Formatted cells

Figure 9.3

The macro you just executed should have formatted cells D10, D11, and D12 as currency with two decimal places. If this did not happen, your macro probably contains an error. The next section will help you **debug**, or locate and correct, errors in a macro.

Debugging Macros

Common errors to look for when you are debugging a macro are misspelled words, misplaced spaces and tildes, and missing commands.

To demonstrate, you will enter the same macro instructions in cell D20 with an intentional error. To do this,

Move to: D20

Type: '/RFC~{DN}{D}~

Press: ⏎

Note that the first key name, {D}, has been incorrectly entered as {DN}.

Name this macro \W (for wrong) using the following command sequence:

/Range **N**ame **C**reate **\W** ⏎ **D20** ⏎

To test the macro on the dollar sales column, position the cell pointer, and run this macro as follows:

Move to: H10

Press: (ALT)-**W**

Your screen should now look similar to Figure 9.4.

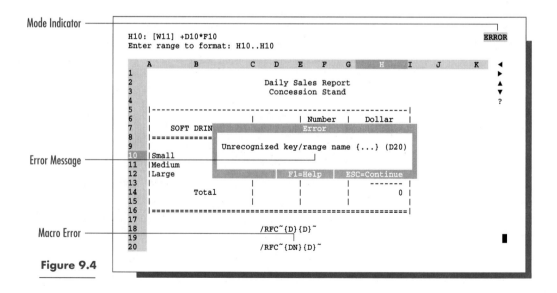

Mode Indicator

Error Message

Macro Error

Figure 9.4

The mode indicator flashes ERROR, and the error message "Unrecognized key/range name {...} (D20)" is displayed in the pop-up error message box in the middle of the screen. The message tells you the type and the location of the error.

To clear the error message and return to READY mode,

Press: ESC

You edit and correct macros just like any other cell entry. They can be edited in EDIT mode or READY mode.

Correct the entry in cell D20 by changing {DN} to {D}.

Because 1-2-3 records the range where the keystrokes are stored, not the actual keystrokes, it is not necessary to rename the macro.

Next, to position the cell pointer and invoke the \W macro again,

Move to: H10

Press: (ALT)-**W**

Cells H10, H11, and H12 should now be displayed as currency format.

If your macro in cell D20 did not execute properly, go back and correct the macro, and then execute the macro in cell H10 again.

The total sales amount in cell H14 was not formatted because the macro specifies that only three cells be formatted. Later in this lab, you will modify this macro so that all the numbers in the column will be formatted.

Creating Interactive Macros

Next Susan wants to create a macro to help her insert data into the worksheet. During execution, this macro will temporarily pause to allow her to enter data directly from the keyboard into the worksheet. This is called an **interactive macro.**

To create an interactive macro, the {?} (pause) macro keystroke instruction is used to stop macro execution temporarily to allow user entry. Execution continues when the user presses ⏎.

Without a macro, Susan would begin by moving the cell pointer to cell F10. She would then enter the number of small drinks sold, press ↓ once, enter the number of medium drinks sold, press ↓ once, enter the number of large drinks sold, and press ⏎.

You will enter the macro to perform this operation, beginning in cell H18 and continuing down the column. You will recall that a macro can be entered in a single cell of a continuous range of cells.

Move to: H18

The first macro command will move the cell pointer to cell F10 using the GOTO feature. The macro key name for this feature is {GOTO}.

Type: **{GOTO}F10~**

Move to: H19

The next macro instruction tells 1-2-3 to pause execution to allow the entry of data, move down one cell, and pause again. The macro key name to pause execution is {?}.

Type: **{?}{D}{?}**

Move to: H20

The instructions in cell H20 will move the cell pointer down one row and then wait for user entry. The data is entered into the cell by the ~ (enter) macro instruction. Complete the macro instructions as follows:

Type: **{D}{?}~**

Press: ⏎

Your screen should look similar to Figure 9.5.

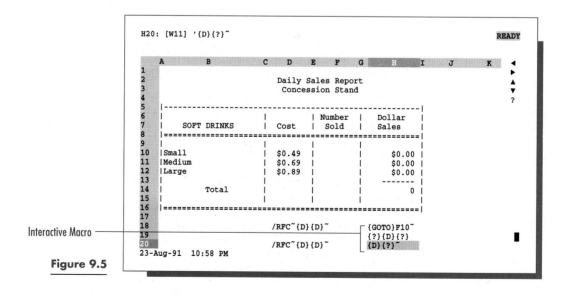

The macro instructions begin in cell H18 and continue through cell H20. When the macro is executed, 1-2-3 will read and perform the instructions in cell H18 from left to right. It will continue execution by performing the instructions in the next cell in the same column. Whenever it reads the {?} key name, it will pause execution to allow the user to enter data. To continue macro execution after a pause, you must press ⏎. The macro will stop running when it encounters a blank cell, a numeric cell, or a {QUIT} command.

Now you are ready to name the macro. The second method of naming a macro lets you assign a name up to 15 characters long. Again, the name should be descriptive of the function of the macro. You will name the macro ENTRY. To do this, move to H18, and issue the following command sequence:

/Range **N**ame **C**reate **ENTRY** ⏎

If the macro is longer than a single cell, it is necessary to specify only the cell beginning the macro as the range. To complete the command sequence,

Type: **H18**

Press: ⏎

Now you are ready to run the macro. To run a macro that has been named using the second method, you must use the (ALT)-(F3) (RUN) key. You can use the (ALT)-(F3) (RUN) key to run any macros, including those named with the backslash character. Since this macro will position the cell pointer for data entry, you do not need to move the cell pointer. To run the macro,

Press: (ALT)-(F3) (RUN)

The prompt "Select the macro to run:" is displayed in the second line of the control panel, and the names of the macros are listed in the third line. The mode indicator displays NAMES. If there are other named ranges in the worksheet, they will be displayed along with the macro names. For this reason, you may want to begin all macro names in a worksheet with the same character, such as a backslash, to distinguish the macro names from the range names.

Since the highlight bar is already over the macro name we want to use (ENTRY), to select it,

Press: ⏎

The cell pointer is positioned in cell F10. The status indicator, CMD, at the bottom of the screen indicates that the macro is executing. Macro execution is interrupted to accept the number of small drinks sold. As soon as an entry is made and ⏎ is pressed, the macro will continue execution. To enter 27 as the number of small drinks sold,

Type: **27**

Press: ⏎

The cell pointer has now moved down one cell to cell F11. The number 27 was entered in cell F10. The macro pauses again to accept the number of medium drinks sold.

Type: **43**

Press: ⏎

Again, the number 43 was entered in cell F11, the cell pointer moved down one cell, and the macro paused to accept the number of large drinks sold.

Type: **62**

Press: ⏎

Your screen should look similar to Figure 9.6.

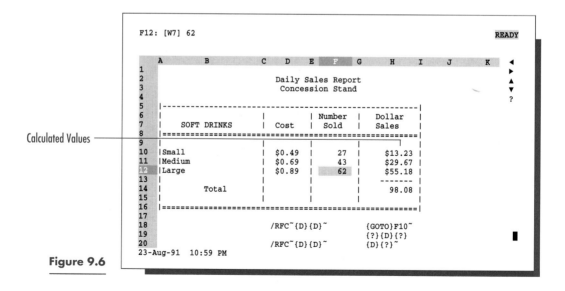

Figure 9.6

Lab 9   Creating and Using Macros

The worksheet automatically calculated the Dollar Sales and Total Dollar Sales as the values were entered into the worksheet.

In summary, to develop a macro, follow these steps:

1. Plan the macro. Whenever you create a macro, you should actually perform and then write down the keystrokes that the macro will perform.

2. Enter the macro. The macro instructions are entered as a label in a single cell or in a series of continuous cells in a single column. You should enter the macro in a convenient and open area of the worksheet. The macro should not contain any blank spaces.

3. Name the macro. The /**R**ange **N**ame **C**reate command assigns a macro a name. A macro name can consist of a \ (backslash) followed by a single letter or any combination of up to 15 characters.

4. Run the macro. If the macro name consists of a backslash and a single letter, you can use (ALT) followed by the letter name of the macro to run it. If the macro name consists of any other combination of up to 15 characters, you must use (ALT)-(F3) (RUN) to run the macro. The first time you execute a macro, it is a good idea to test it. Save your worksheet first so that you don't lose any valuable data. Then, test the macro in an area of the worksheet that will not be affected if the macro performs incorrectly.

5. Edit the macro. Because a macro is interpreted exactly as it appears, any misspelled or misplaced commands will result in an error message. If an error message appears, use (ESC) key to return to READY mode, then edit the macro. If during execution you notice that the macro is not performing its intended task, you can press (CTRL)-(BREAK) to stop macro execution, press (ESC) to return to READY mode, and correct the macro. Then repeat step 4.

Modifying Macros

Susan thought this macro would help her enter her daily report. She modified and extended the worksheet to include the other two categories, sandwiches and side orders. Retrieve the file SALES2.WK1. You do not need to save the current worksheet.

This file contains all the information from the previous worksheet plus two more product categories. Susan has also added a new column, Percent Sales, to the worksheet. To see the formula for Percent Sales,

Move to: J12

The formula should be displayed in the control panel. This formula calculates the percentage of small drink sales relative to total drink sales. When the formula was written, an absolute cell reference was used so that it could be copied down for the other two drink sizes. Use ⬇ to examine the other two formulas. Soon you will write a macro to format these cells with percent signs.

To see the other two product categories, use the arrow keys to

Move to: A38

Your screen should look similar to Figure 9.7.

```
A38: [W1] |                                                         READY

        A          B          C    D     E    F    G    H    I    J    K    ◄
   19   |                      |          |         |         |         |    ►
   20   |      SANDWICHES      |          |         |         |         |    ▲
   21   |                      |          |         |         |         |    ▼
   22   |Tuna                  |    1.99  |         |       0 |     ERR |    ?
   23   |Pastrami              |    2.39  |         |       0 |     ERR |
   24   |Chicken               |    2.49  |         |       0 |     ERR |
   25   |                      |          |         | ------- | ------- |
   26   |            Total     |          |         |       0 |     ERR |
   27   |                      |          |         |         |         |
   28   |========================================================================|
   29   |                      |          |         |         |         |
   30   |      SIDE ORDERS:    |          |         |         |         |
   31   |                      |          |         |         |         |
   32   |Potato Chips          |    0.59  |         |       0 |     ERR |
   33   |Potato Salad          |    0.79  |         |       0 |     ERR |
   34   |Onion Rings           |    0.89  |         |       0 |     ERR |
   35   |                      |          |         | ------- | ------- |
   36   |            Total     |          |         |       0 |     ERR |
   37   |                      |          |         |         |         |
   38   |========================================================================|
   23-Aug-91  11:02 PM
```

Figure 9.7

The prices for the sandwiches and side orders are already entered in column D. Columns H and J contain the formulas. The ERR messages in column J will be replaced with percentages once data is entered into the Number Sold column.

Next, to see the macros,

Move to: A48

Your screen should look similar to Figure 9.8.

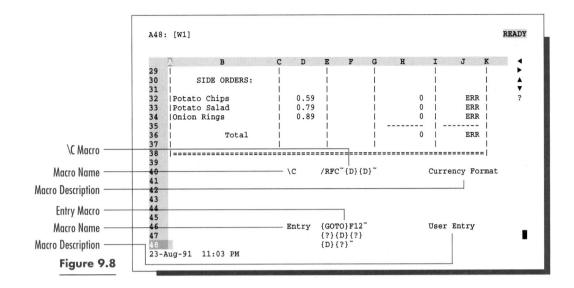

```
A48:  [W1]                                                                   READY

        A           B             C    D     E     F     G     H     I    J    K       ◄
      29  |                       |          |           |           |          |       ►
      30  |     SIDE ORDERS:      |          |           |           |          |       ▲
      31  |                       |          |           |           |          |       ▼
      32  |Potato Chips           |   0.59   |           |        0  |     ERR  |       ?
      33  |Potato Salad           |   0.79   |           |        0  |     ERR  |
      34  |Onion Rings            |   0.89   |           |        0  |     ERR  |
      35  |                       |          |           |  -------- | -------- |
      36  |            Total      |          |           |        0  |     ERR  |
      37  |                       |          |           |           |          |
\C Macro ─────────── 38  |===========================================================|
      39
Macro Name ───────── 40                    \C    /RFC~{D}{D}~            Currency Format
      41
Macro Description ── 42
      43
Entry Macro ──────── 44
      45
Macro Name ───────── 46                  Entry  {GOTO}F12~             User Entry        ▮
      47                                         {?}{D}{?}
Macro Description ── 48                          {D}{?}~
      23-Aug-91  11:03 PM
```

Figure 9.8

The two macros created earlier have been moved to the bottom of this new worksheet. Following good documentation procedures, Susan added some descriptive labels to document the worksheet.

She placed the name of the macros in the cells to the left of the macro commands and a brief description of the functions of the macros in the cells to the right.

Documenting macros is particularly important when several macros are used within one worksheet and when macros become more complex.

In the previous worksheet, the \C macro was used to format a three-cell range as currency. In this worksheet, Susan needs to format several ranges as currency, but some of the ranges are larger than three cells.

You will modify the \C macro to format the contents of a contiguous range of cells, no matter how long it is. The macro will work the same as before, but instead of specifying the number of times to move down when indicating the format range, the macro will use the (END) key to automatically find the bottom of the column. Whenever the cursor is positioned on data and (END) is pressed, contiguous followed by one of the four arrow keys, the cursor will move to the last cell containing data in the column or row. You will replace the {D} commands with the {END}{D} combination. This will format all the contiguous cells below the current cell location as currency format.

To change this macro,

Move to: E40

Using (F2) EDIT,

Change the \C macro to: '/RFC~{END}{D}~

Press: (↵)

The \C macro has already been named. Your screen should look similar to Figure 9.9.

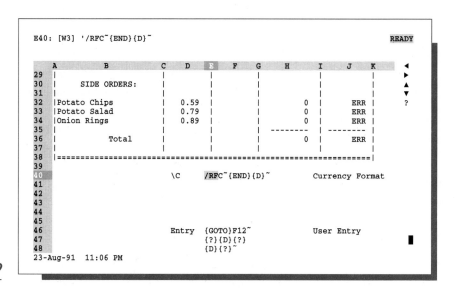

Figure 9.9

To test the macro, position the cell pointer at the beginning of the range to be formatted, and run the macro as follows.

Move to: H12

Press: (ALT)-**C**

The cells from H12 through H16 should now be displayed in currency format. The macro now formats the contiguous values in the column, including the total. If the cells are not displayed with currency format, correct your macro and try again.

The \C macro can now be used to format any contiguous column of numbers, regardless of the length of the column. In order for the macro to work correctly, however, the cursor must be positioned at the first number, and there must be no empty cells within the column of numbers. To format the cost amounts for drinks,

Move to: D12

Press: (ALT)-**C**

The three cells should be formatted as currency with two decimal places.

Using LEARN Mode

Susan needs to enter a similar macro to format a range of cells as percents. You could type in a macro similar to the \C macro. However, Susan wants to use **LEARN mode** to enter the percent format macro. LEARN mode is a 1-2-3 feature that records your keystrokes as a macro at the same time you are using the program to perform a task.

Before using this feature, you must define a range in the worksheet where the macro commands will be recorded. This is called the **learn range**. This range is a single-column range that should be large enough to contain all the macro instructions. To enter the macro below the \C macro instructions, you will define the range as E42 through E44. To define the range, issue the following command sequence:

/**W**orksheet **L**earn **R**ange **E42..E44** (↵)

To have 1-2-3 record your keystrokes as a macro, you must turn on LEARN mode by pressing (ALT)-(F5), the LEARN key. First, you need to position the cell pointer in the first cell range to be formatted.

Move to: J12

To turn on the LEARN mode,

Press: (ALT)-(F5) (LEARN)

Your screen should look similar to Figure 9.10.

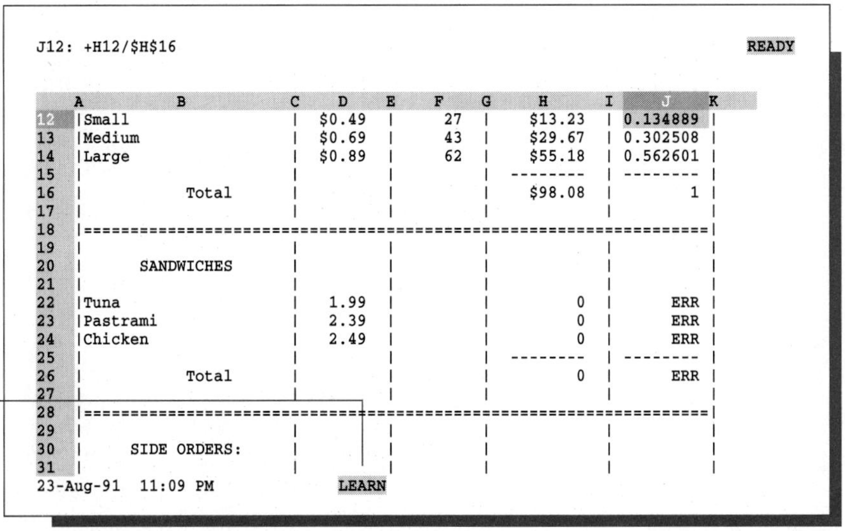

```
J12: +H12/$H$16                                                    READY

       A          B          C     D     E    F    G      H      I      J      K
  12  |Small                 |   $0.49  |     27  |   $13.23  |  0.134889 |
  13  |Medium                |   $0.69  |     43  |   $29.67  |  0.302508 |
  14  |Large                 |   $0.89  |     62  |   $55.18  |  0.562601 |
  15  |                      |          |         |  -------- | -------- |
  16  |          Total       |          |         |   $98.08  |        1 |
  17  |                      |          |         |           |          |
  18  |=====================================================================|
  19  |                      |          |         |           |          |
  20  |        SANDWICHES    |          |         |           |          |
  21  |                      |          |         |           |          |
  22  |Tuna                  |   1.99   |         |         0 |      ERR |
  23  |Pastrami              |   2.39   |         |         0 |      ERR |
  24  |Chicken               |   2.49   |         |         0 |      ERR |
  25  |                      |          |         |  -------- | -------- |
  26  |          Total       |          |         |         0 |      ERR |
  27  |                      |          |         |           |          |
  28  |=====================================================================|
  29  |                      |          |         |           |          |
  30  |    SIDE ORDERS:      |          |         |           |          |
  31  |                      |          |         |           |          |
  23-Aug-91  11:09 PM                      LEARN
```

LEARN Indicator ─────────

Figure 9.10

Notice that the status indicator displays LEARN. Now anything you type or any commands you enter will be recorded as a macro. To format the range as percent, and record the command sequence as a macro in the learn range,

Select: /**R**ange **F**ormat **P**ercent

To enter the number of decimal places,

Type: **1**

Press: (↵)

Finally, to define the range to format,

Press: (END) (↓)

Press: (↵)

The cells have been formatted as percent with one decimal place. To turn off LEARN mode,

Press: (ALT)-(F5) (LEARN)

The LEARN indicator is no longer displayed. To see the macro instructions as they were recorded using LEARN mode,

Move to: J44

Your screen should look similar to Figure 9.11.

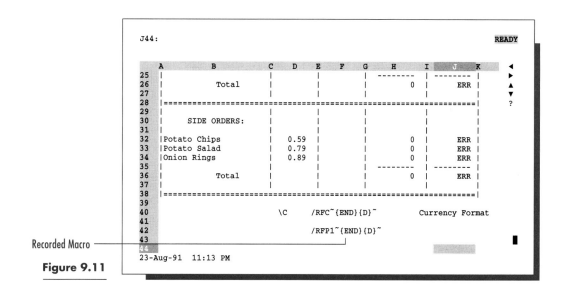

Recorded Macro

Figure 9.11

The macro commands are displayed in the first cell of the learn range. If you enter more characters than your learn range can hold, 1-2-3 will turn off LEARN mode and tell you that the learn range is full. The learn range will contain all the macro instructions entered up to that point. You can either erase the contents of the range, define a larger range and begin again, or define a larger range and begin again where you left off.

Before you can use this macro to format the rest of the percent figures in column J, the macro has to be named. To name the macro \P (for percent),

Move to: E42

Then issue the following command sequence:

/Range **N**ame **C**reate **\P** ⤶ ⤶

To add documentation in cells D42 and I42 similar to the documentation for the currency macro,

Move to: D42

Type: '\P

Move to: I42

Type: **Percent Format**

To position the cell pointer at the beginning of the range to be formatted and to run the macro,

Move to: J22

Press: (ALT)-**P**

Your screen should look similar to Figure 9.12.

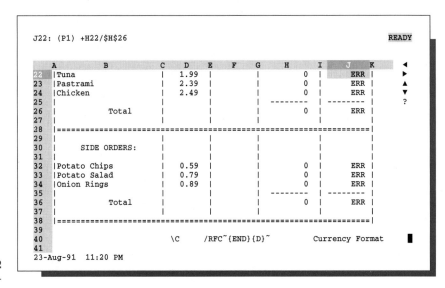

```
J22: (P1) +H22/$H$26                                                    READY

        A          B        C    D    E    F    G    H    I    J    K    ◄
   22 |Tuna               |   1.99 |      |      |    0 |    ERR |     ►
   23 |Pastrami           |   2.39 |      |      |    0 |    ERR |     ▲
   24 |Chicken            |   2.49 |      |      |    0 |    ERR |     ▼
   25 |                   |      |      |      | -------- | -------- |   ?
   26 |          Total    |      |      |      |    0 |    ERR |
   27 |                   |      |      |      |      |      |
   28 |=============================================================|
   29 |                   |      |      |      |      |      |
   30 |    SIDE ORDERS:    |      |      |      |      |      |
   31 |                   |      |      |      |      |      |
   32 |Potato Chips       |   0.59 |      |      |    0 |    ERR |
   33 |Potato Salad       |   0.79 |      |      |    0 |    ERR |
   34 |Onion Rings        |   0.89 |      |      |    0 |    ERR |
   35 |                   |      |      |      | -------- | -------- |
   36 |          Total    |      |      |      |    0 |    ERR |
   37 |                   |      |      |      |      |      |
   38 |=============================================================|
   39
   40                 \C       /RFC~{END}{D}~            Currency Format   ▮
   41
   23-Aug-91  11:20 PM
```

Figure 9.12

Nothing seemed to happen because the cells currently display ERR. This is because the formula for computing percent sales divides by the total sales, which is currently zero. The command line, however, indicates that the format is (P1), or percent format with one digit after the decimal place.

Confirm that cells J22 through J26 have been formatted as percent with one decimal place (P1). If they have not, correct the macro and try again.

Using STEP Mode

Finding errors in a macro (especially a large one) can be difficult. **STEP mode** helps you locate errors by slowing down the macro execution to one keystroke at a time.

You will use STEP mode macro execution on the \C macro to demonstrate this procedure. To use STEP mode,

Press: (ALT)-(F2) (STEP)

The STEP indicator appears at the bottom of the screen.

To run the macro,

   Move to: H22

   Press: (ALT)-**C**

The STEP indicator is no longer displayed. Instead the macro commands are executed, their cell address and cell contents are displayed on the status line. The macro instruction (/) to be executed next is highlighted. To execute the first macro instruction,

   Press: any key (SPACEBAR is recommended)

Your screen should look similar to Figure 9.13.

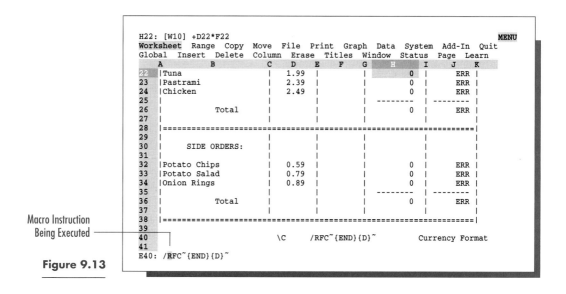

Macro Instruction
Being Executed

Figure 9.13

The first keystroke in the macro, /, has been executed, and the 1-2-3 main menu should be displayed in the control panel. The next macro instruction to be executed (R) is highlighted. To continue,

   Press: SPACEBAR

Your screen should now look similar to Figure 9.14.

Range Menu —

```
H22: [W10] +D22*F22                                                MENU
Format  Label  Erase  Name  Justify  Prot  Unprot  Input  Value  Trans  Search
Fixed   Sci   Currency  ,  General  +/-  Percent  Date  Text  Hidden  Reset
     A          B          C    D    E    F    G    H       I    J    K
22  |Tuna               |   1.99 |         |         0  |      ERR |
23  |Pastrami           |   2.39 |         |         0  |      ERR |
24  |Chicken            |   2.49 |         |         0  |      ERR |
25  |                   |        |         |  -------- | -------- |
26  |         Total     |        |         |         0  |      ERR |
27  |                   |        |         |         |         |
28  |================================================================|
29  |                   |         |         |         |         |
30  |    SIDE ORDERS:    |         |         |         |         |
31  |                   |         |         |         |         |
32  |Potato Chips       |   0.59 |         |         0  |      ERR |
33  |Potato Salad       |   0.79 |         |         0  |      ERR |
34  |Onion Rings        |   0.89 |         |         0  |      ERR |
35  |                   |        |         |  -------- | -------- |
36  |         Total     |        |         |         0  |      ERR |
37  |                   |        |         |         |         |
38  |================================================================|
39
40                            \C     /RFC~{END}{D}~          Currency Format
41
E40: /RFC~{END}{D}~
```

Figure 9.14

The macro has executed the **R**ange command, and the control panel now displays the Range menu. Each time you press a key, a command is executed, and the macro advances one step to the next macro instruction.

Once you locate an error, you can stop the macro execution by pressing (CTRL)-(BREAK) followed by (ESC). Then you can edit and rerun the macro. STEP mode is still on when the macro runs again to let you continue testing your macro commands.

Continue to run the \C macro using STEP mode until the execution of the macro is complete and you return to READY mode. The STEP indicator is redisplayed to tell you that STEP mode is still on.

To turn off STEP mode,

Press: (ALT)-(F2) (STEP)

Use the \C macro to format the last group of numbers in column H as currency and the cost amounts for sandwiches and side orders in column D. Use the \P macro to format the last group of numbers in column J for percent format.

Using a Repetition Factor

The report is almost complete. However, Susan still needs to modify the ENTRY macro located in cell E46. After the numbers sold for the three drinks have been entered, the macro needs to skip down eight cells to the next product category (sandwiches), allow the user to enter the number sold in that category, move down eight more cells to the next category (side orders), and allow the user to enter the number sold in that category.

To add these new instructions to the macro,

Move to: E49

Type: {D 8}{?}{D}{?}{D}{?}

Press: ⏎

Notice the {D 8}. To make it easier to enter consecutive uses of the same macro key name, 1-2-3 lets you enter a **repetition factor** within the key name. The repetition factor is a number that tells 1-2-3 how many times to repeat the key name. It is separated from the key name by a single space. For example, {D 4} is equivalent to {D}{D}{D}{D} or pressing ⬇ four times.

Completing the Macro

To continue the macro instructions to allow entry of data in the category for side orders, the same sequence of keys as in the macro instructions in cell E49 needs to be used. A macro, like any other worksheet entry, can be copied.

To copy the macro instructions in cell E49 to cell E50, issue the following command sequence:

/Copy **E49** ⏎ **E50** ⏎

To enter the data in the last cell of that category, an enter (~) symbol needs to be added to this macro. To do this,

Move to: E50

Press: (F2) (EDIT)

Type: ~

Press: ⏎

To execute your modified macro,

Press: (ALT)-(F3) (RUN)

Select: ENTRY

Your screen should look similar to Figure 9.15.

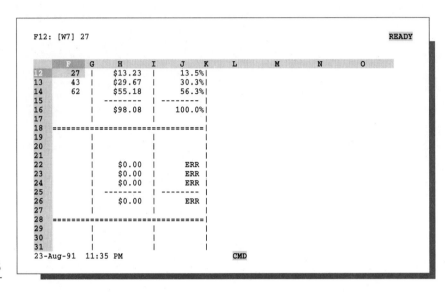

```
F12: [W7] 27                                                    READY

        F    G      H       I      J    K     L      M      N      O
12      27  |     $13.23  |     13.5%|
13      43  |     $29.67  |     30.3%|
14      62  |     $55.18  |     56.3%|
15          |     --------|     --------|
16          |     $98.08  |    100.0%|
17          |            |            |
18      ============================|
19          |            |            |
20          |            |            |
21          |            |            |
22          |      $0.00 |      ERR |
23          |      $0.00 |      ERR |
24          |      $0.00 |      ERR |
25          |     --------|     --------|
26          |      $0.00 |      ERR |
27          |            |            |
28      ============================|
29          |            |            |
30          |            |            |
31          |            |            |
     23-Aug-91  11:35 PM                   CMD
```

Figure 9.15

The macro should have moved the cell pointer to cell F12. However, the product categories and column labels are not visible in the current window. The window is not positioned properly over the worksheet.

Whenever {GOTO} references a cell outside the current window, the window is shifted to position the referenced cell in the upper left corner.

To correct this problem, you must interrupt execution of the ENTRY macro.

Press: (CTRL)-(BREAK)

The mode indicator flashes ERROR, and the error message "Break" is displayed. The ERROR mode indicator appears because the regular functioning of the macro has been stopped, even though an actual error has not occurred. To return to READY mode,

Press: (ESC)

To properly frame the worksheet in the window, you need modify the macro by entering {HOME} as the first instruction in the macro.

Move to: E46

Press: (F2) (EDIT)

Press: (HOME)

Press: (→)

Type: **{HOME}**

Press: (↵)

To see the entire macro,

Move to: E50

Your screen should look similar to Figure 9.16.

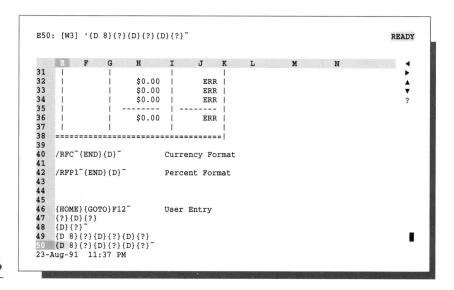

```
E50: [W3]  '{D 8}{?}{D}{?}{D}{?}~                                        READY

      E   F     G     H         I     J     K     L     M     N          ◄
  31  |         |               |           |                           ►
  32  |         |     $0.00     |     ERR   |                           ▲
  33  |         |     $0.00     |     ERR   |                           ▼
  34  |         |     $0.00     |     ERR   |                           ?
  35  |         |     --------  |  --------  |
  36  |         |     $0.00     |     ERR   |
  37  |         |               |           |
  38  |=====================================|
  39
  40  /RFC~{END}{D}~           Currency Format
  41
  42  /RFP1~{END}{D}~          Percent Format
  43
  44
  45
  46  {HOME}{GOTO}F12~         User Entry
  47  {?}{D}{?}
  48  {D}{?}~
  49  {D 8}{?}{D}{?}{D}{?}                                               ▮
  50  {D 8}{?}{D}{?}{D}{?}~
      23-Aug-91  11:37 PM
```

Figure 9.16

To run the macro again,

Press: (ALT)-(F3) (RUN)

Select: ENTRY

Your screen should look similar to Figure 9.17.

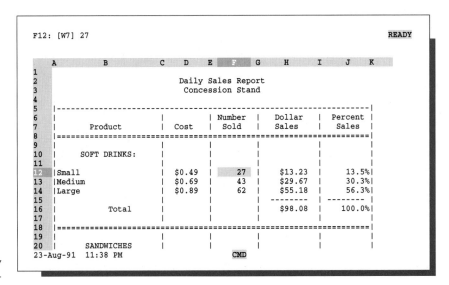

```
F12: [W7] 27                                                                READY

        A        B        C    D    E    F    G    H    I    J    K
 1
 2                              Daily Sales Report
 3                               Concession Stand
 4
 5  |-----------------------------------------------------------------|
 6  |                   |       | Number |   Dollar   |  Percent  |
 7  |      Product      |  Cost |  Sold  |    Sales   |   Sales   |
 8  |===================================================================|
 9  |                   |       |        |            |           |
10  |    SOFT DRINKS:   |       |        |            |           |
11  |                   |       |        |            |           |
12  |Small              | $0.49 |    27  |   $13.23   |    13.5%  |
13  |Medium             | $0.69 |    43  |   $29.67   |    30.3%  |
14  |Large              | $0.89 |    62  |   $55.18   |    56.3%  |
15  |                   |       |        | --------   | --------  |
16  |          Total    |       |        |   $98.08   |   100.0%  |
17  |                   |       |        |            |           |
18  |===================================================================|
19  |                   |       |        |            |           |
20  |     SANDWICHES    |       |        |            |           |
23-Aug-91  11:38 PM                            CMD
```

Figure 9.17

The window now correctly frames the worksheet. If your screen is not similar to Figure 9.17, interrupt execution of the macro again, and correct your macro before proceeding.

Enter some hypothetical data to test the macro. Remember to press ⏎ after each entry. Do not use ↓ to enter the numbers because the macro will automatically move the cursor down after each entry. If your macro does not operate correctly, you may want to use STEP mode to locate the problem.

When your ENTRY macro operates correctly, run the macro again, and enter the following values for the Number Sold column.

Small drinks	40
Medium drinks	50
Large drinks	120
Tuna sandwich	24
Pastrami sandwich	56
Chicken sandwich	43
Potato chips	22
Potato salad	35
Onion rings	78

Your screen should look similar to Figure 9.18.

```
F34: [W7] 78                                                    READY

        A        B          C    D    E    F    G    H      I    J    K     ◄
   15  |                    |         |         |  -------- |  -------- |    ►
   16  |         Total      |         |         |  $160.90  |  100.0%|        ▲
   17  |                    |         |         |           |        |        ▼
   18  |==================================================================|  ?
   19  |                    |         |         |           |        |
   20  |    SANDWICHES       |         |         |           |        |
   21  |                    |         |         |           |        |
   22  |Tuna                | $1.99   |    24   |  $47.76   |  16.5%|
   23  |Pastrami            | $2.39   |    56   |  $133.84  |  46.4%|
   24  |Chicken             | $2.49   |    43   |  $107.07  |  37.1%|
   25  |                    |         |         |  -------- |  -------- |
   26  |         Total      |         |         |  $288.67  |  100.0%|
   27  |                    |         |         |           |        |
   28  |==================================================================|
   29  |                    |         |         |           |        |
   30  |    SIDE ORDERS:     |         |         |           |        |
   31  |                    |         |         |           |        |
   32  |Potato Chips        | $0.59   |    22   |  $12.98   |  11.8%|
   33  |Potato Salad        | $0.79   |    35   |  $27.65   |  25.1%|      ■
   34  |Onion Rings         | $0.89   |    78   |  $69.42   |  63.1%|
   23-Aug-91  11:40 PM
```

Figure 9.18

The values for the Number Sold have been entered into the appropriate cells, and the Total Dollar Sales and Percent Sales for each category have been recalculated. If your macro did not execute properly, correct it and try again.

The interactive macro should make it easy for Susan to enter the daily sales data into the worksheet.

Save the worksheet as SALES3.

Print the worksheet including the macro commands, and then exit from 1-2-3.

Glossary

Debug: To locate and correct errors in a macro.

Interactive macro: A macro that combines macro execution with manual entries by inserting a pause in the macro instruction sequence.

Keystroke instruction: An instruction in a macro that represents a key on the keyboard.

LEARN mode: A feature that will record your keystrokes as a macro while performing the task or command.

Learn range: The area in a worksheet where 1-2-3 will record the macro instructions when LEARN mode is in use.

Macro: A set of instructions that automates a 1-2-3 task. A macro consists of a sequence of keystrokes and commands that you type into a worksheet, name, and run to perform a task automatically.

Repetition factor: A number used to specify two or more consecutive uses of the same key in a macro key symbol.

STEP mode: A feature that helps you locate errors in a large macro by slowing down the macro execution to one keystroke at a time.

<table>
<tr><td rowspan="11">

Practice Problems and Cases

</td><td colspan="2">

Matching A

</td></tr>
<tr><td>1. (ALT)-(F2) _____</td><td>**a.** used with a single letter to run a macro</td></tr>
<tr><td>2. (ALT)-(F3) _____</td><td>**b.** command to name a macro</td></tr>
<tr><td>3. (ALT)-(F5) _____</td><td>**c.** pauses macro execution</td></tr>
<tr><td>4. (ALT) _____</td><td>**d.** command to define a learn range</td></tr>
<tr><td>5. {?} _____</td><td>**e.** turns STEP mode on and off</td></tr>
<tr><td>6. {GOTO} _____</td><td>**f.** macro instructions for ⏎</td></tr>
<tr><td>7. {D 6} _____</td><td>**g.** activates LEARN mode</td></tr>
<tr><td>8. ~ _____</td><td>**h.** macro instruction to move to a particular cell</td></tr>
<tr><td>9. /RNC _____</td><td>**i.** the RUN key</td></tr>
<tr><td>10. /WLR _____</td><td>**j.** macro instruction to move six cells down</td></tr>
</table>

Matching B

Karen has created ten macros. Match the macros to the functions they perform.

1. /WGC12~	_____ **a.** names a range
2. /FS~	_____ **b.** sets a graph type and waits for a range
3. /RFC0~{END}{D}~	
4. /RNC{?}~~	_____ **c.** moves cell pointer to F15
5. {HOME}{GOTO}F15~	_____ **d.** moves to a specific cell and enters a statement
6. /C{D 4}~{D 10}.{D 4}~	_____ **e.** globally sets column width to 12
7. /GT~G{?}~	
8. /M{END}{D}~{?}~	_____ **f.** waits for entry of two columns

9. {?}{D}{?}{D}{?}{D} ———— **g.** formats a column to currency
{L 2}{U 3}{?}{D}{?}~   with zero decimal places

10. {GOTO}G3~LEARNING ———— **h.** saves a file
     MACROS IS FUN

———— **i.** copies a range of cells

———— **j.** moves a column of
         information

Cases

1. Rose Stevens created a worksheet to help her keep track of daily
supply requests. She created three macros to help her use the worksheet more efficiently. Retrieve the file PROB9-1.WK1. This file contains Rose's worksheet and macros; however, the macros need to be
edited before they will run.

a. Enter your name in cell A1 and the current date in cell A2.

b. Move the cell pointer to E6. Run the first macro ((ALT)-C). Locate the
error, correct it, and rerun the macro.

c. Move the cell pointer to F6. Run the first macro again, formatting
for all the relevant cells.

d. Enter a formula to multiply ITEMS by COST PER ITEM in cell F6.
Run the second macro ((ALT)-F), locate any errors, correct them,
and rerun the macro.

e. Rose did not finish the macro in cell B19..B20. Complete the entry.
Run the macro ((ALT)-E) entering test data.

f. Save the worksheet as HWLAB9-1. Print the worksheet, including
the macros.

2. Barbara Ramage has started a weekly sales report form for Entertainment Now, Inc. Retrieve the file PROB9-2.WK1 to see what
Barbara has completed. To finish the worksheet, complete the following steps:

a. Create and document a macro to enter your name in cell B1 and
the current date in cell B2. Name the macro \N (for name).
Execute the macro, and then edit it if necessary.

b. Create, name, and document a macro that will copy the formula in
cell J14 to the other appropriate cells in the column. Execute the
macro, and then edit it if necessary.

c. Create, name, and document a macro that will format a group of
cells as currency with two decimal places. Execute the macro, and
edit it if necessary. Use the macro to format columns D, H, and J.

d. Create and document a macro to enter values in column F. Name the macro ENTRY. Enter some hypothetical data to test the macro. If your macro does not operate correctly, you may want to use STEP mode to locate the problem.

e. Save the current worksheet as HWLAB9-2. Print the worksheet, including the macros.

3. To complete this problem, you first must have finished the worksheet as specified in Practice Case 2. Barbara has decided she would like to add a few more macros to the weekly sales report worksheet. Retrieve the file HWLAB9-2.WK1.

a. Edit the Name macro to erase the contents of cell A2. Then have the macro enter the function (@NOW) to calculate the current date, and format the cell to display the date as mm/dd/yy. Execute the macro, and then edit it if necessary.

b. Create and document a macro that will print only the sales report portion of the worksheet. Name this macro PRINT. Execute the macro, and edit it if necessary.

c. Create and document a macro that will save the current worksheet file as HWLAB9-3. Name the macro SAVE. Execute the macro, and edit it if necessary.

d. Modify the SAVE macro to save and replace the file name. Execute the macro, and edit it if necessary.

e. Modify the PRINT macro to print the entire worksheet, including the macro commands. Execute the macro.

f. Save the current worksheet using your SAVE macro, and then exit from 1-2-3.

4. Create a weekly sales report worksheet for The Ace Video Store. Enter macros to format cells, enter data, print and save the worksheet. Enter your name in cell A1 and the current date in cell A2. Save the worksheet as HWLAB9-4. Print the worksheet, including the macros.

5. Most worksheets require numeric input. The pointer-movement area of the IBM PC keyboard, as well as many others, doubles as a numeric keypad when you press the (NUM LOCK) key. Switching back and forth with the (NUM LOCK) key often frustrates those accustomed to a numeric keypad.

Create macros that will control cell-pointer movements. These macros will allow the numeric keypad to enter data exclusively. Enter your name in cell A1 and the current date in cell A2. After you have created, executed, tested, and documented the macros, save the worksheet as HWLAB9-5. Print the worksheet.

6. Many worksheets can use the same macros. Instead of writing the same macro many times, you can create a file of macros. In a blank worksheet, create and document ten macros that you can copy and use in another worksheet. Some examples are macros to change column widths, format a cell, enter lines, and enter month names in a row. Be sure to have at least one macro for printing a worksheet, saving a worksheet, entering your name in a specific cell, and formatting cells. Execute each macro separately, and edit them if necessary. When all the macros work, save the worksheet as HWLAB9-6, and then print the worksheet.

Lab 10

Advanced Macros

In Lab 10, you will learn how to:

- **Use macro subroutines**
- **Build a custom menu system**
- **Create a print macro**
- **Create a looping macro**
- **Control the screen with a macro**
- **Create an autoexecuting macro**

Objectives

In Lab 9, Susan Chang developed some basic macros to help her enter the daily sales figures into a worksheet. She would like to delegate the responsibility of entering the figures to other employees. Since the other employees have limited experience with 1-2-3, Susan will simplify the process of entering the data and printing the report by creating a custom menu. You will help Susan develop the necessary macros and the menu system.

Retrieve the file SALES3A.WK1.

Your screen should look similar to Figure 10.1.

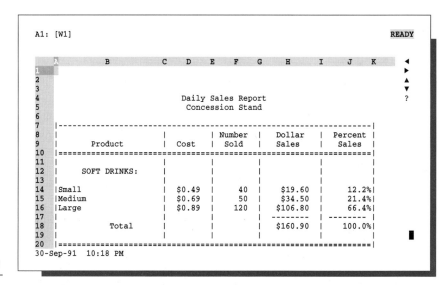

```
A1: [W1]                                                            READY

        A        B         C   D    E    F    G    H     I   J    K      ◄
     1                                                                   ►
     2                                                                   ▲
     3                                                                   ▼
     4                         Daily Sales Report                       ?
     5                          Concession Stand
     6
     7   |-----------------------------------------------------------|
     8   |                      | Number  |   Dollar   |  Percent  |
     9   |      Product    | Cost | Sold   |   Sales    |   Sales   |
    10   |===========================================================|
    11   |                 |      |        |            |           |
    12   |    SOFT DRINKS:  |      |        |            |           |
    13   |                 |      |        |            |           |
    14   |Small            |$0.49 |   40   |   $19.60   |   12.2%|
    15   |Medium           |$0.69 |   50   |   $34.50   |   21.4%|
    16   |Large            |$0.89 |  120   |  $106.80   |   66.4%|
    17   |                 |      |        |  --------  |  -------- |
    18   |        Total    |      |        |  $160.90   |  100.0%|
    19   |                 |      |        |            |           ■
    20   |===========================================================|
        30-Sep-91   10:18 PM
```

Figure 10.1

This worksheet is very similar to the worksheet that you developed in Lab 9, except the entry macro has been removed. You will create a more efficient entry macro using macro subroutines.

Using Subroutines

A **subroutine** contains a set of macro instructions that may need to be repeated several times during the execution of another macro. It can also be used by different macros that require the same set of instructions. In this section, you will create a new entry macro that uses a subroutine three times.

In Lab 9, the purpose of the entry macro was to position the cell pointer at each category — soft drinks, sandwiches, and side orders — and allow the user to enter the appropriate values. Each category itself has three items. Therefore, for each of the three categories, the macro pauses three times to allow entry. The process of pausing three times for entry into a category will become a subroutine.

The main macro should be created first; then you will create the subroutine. You will enter all the macros in one area of the worksheet. To move to this area,

Press: (F5) (GOTO)

Type: **M50**

Press: (↵)

The first instruction the macro will perform is to position the cell pointer in cell F14 for entering drink sales. Then it will call an entry subroutine.

Move to: N55

Type: **{GOTO}F14~**

Press: (↓)

Type: **{ENTRY}**

Press: (↓)

Your screen should look similar to Figure 10.2.

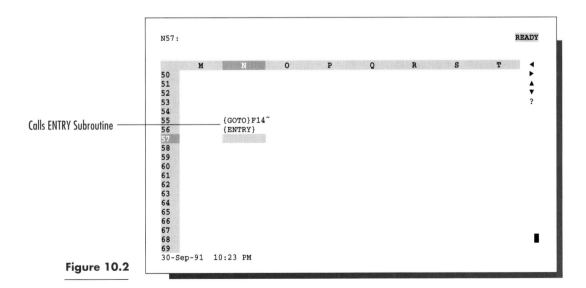

Calls ENTRY Subroutine

Figure 10.2

ENTRY will be the name of the subroutine that you will create and name. When a macro is to **call** (use) a subroutine, the name of the subroutine is simply enclosed in brackets. The ENTRY subroutine will make the macro pause for data entry, move down one cell, pause again for entry, move down another cell, and pause a final time for entry. Once the subroutine has completed, execution will return to the **calling macro**, which is the macro containing the subroutine. Specifically, execution returns to the next instruction after the subroutine call.

To continue with the next instruction and complete the calling macro, with the cell pointer in N57,

Type:	{D 8}
Press:	⬇
Type:	{ENTRY}
Press:	⬇
Type:	{D 8}
Press:	⬇
Type:	{ENTRY}
Press:	⬇
Type:	{HOME}
Press:	⏎

You will recall from Lab 9 that the instruction {D 8} moves the cursor down eight rows.

Your screen should look similar to Figure 10.3.

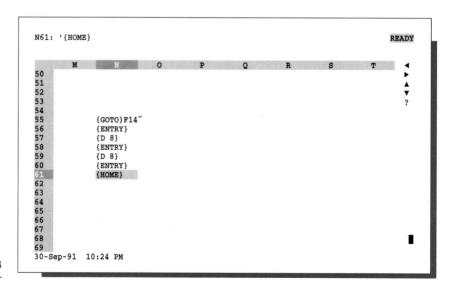

Figure 10.3

Check your macro against Figure 10.3. If you see any errors correct them by editing the cell entry. The ENTRY subroutine will be called three times during the execution of this macro. Now you will create the ENTRY subroutine:

Move to:	N64
Type:	**{?}{D}{?}**
Press:	⬇
Type:	**{D}{?}~**
Press:	⬇
Type:	**{RETURN}**

RETURN is a special macro command, provided by 1-2-3, that tells the subroutine to return to the calling macro. Commands like RETURN do not represent keystrokes; they are part of 1-2-3's macro command language and work only in macros. You will learn about more of these commands later in this lab.

Before you can test the macro, both the calling macro and the subroutine need to be named. The subroutine will be named ENTRY, and the calling macro will be named \E. When you name them, you will also have to specify their ranges in the worksheet.

To document and name the subroutine and macro,

Move to:	M64
Type:	**ENTRY**
Move to:	N64
Select:	**/R**ange **N**ame **C**reate **ENTRY** ⏎ **N64** ⏎
Move to:	M55
Type:	**'\E**
Move to:	N55
Select:	**/R**ange **N**ame **C**reate **\E** ⏎ **N55** ⏎

Your screen should look similar to Figure 10.4.

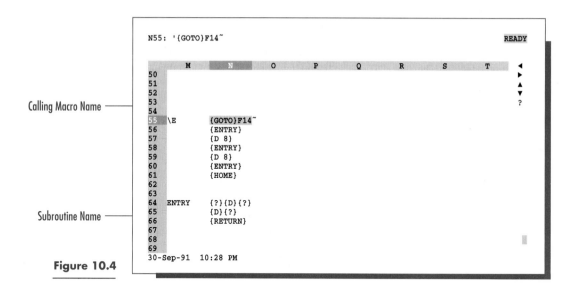

Calling Macro Name —————

Subroutine Name —————

Figure 10.4

```
N55:  '{GOTO}F14~                                          READY

          M          N          O      P      Q      R      S      T    ◄
    50                                                                   ►
    51                                                                   ▲
    52                                                                   ▼
    53                                                                   ?
    54
    55   \E         {GOTO}F14~
    56               {ENTRY}
    57               {D 8}
    58               {ENTRY}
    59               {D 8}
    60               {ENTRY}
    61               {HOME}
    62
    63
    64   ENTRY       {?}{D}{?}
    65               {D}{?}
    66               {RETURN}
    67
    68
    69
    30-Sep-91  10:28 PM
```

To return to the report area of the worksheet and test the macro,

Press: (HOME)

Press: (ALT)-**E**

Enter any nine values for Number Sold. Remember to press ⏎ after each entry. After entering the nine numbers, the cell pointer should return to cell A1. If your entry macro did not work properly, recheck the macro and subroutine carefully, and correct them before continuing.

Building a Custom Menu

Susan wants to create a customized menu to help the other employees enter data and print the worksheet. Once the **custom menu** is created, it will display a list of options and descriptions in the control panel where the regular 1-2-3 menu displays.

A custom menu may have up to eight options. If each menu option begins with a different first letter, an option can be selected by typing the first letter. If two or more options begin with the same letter, the option will have to be highlighted to be selected. Susan's menu will have three options: Sales_Entry, Print, and Quit. In this menu, each option will begin with a different letter.

The menu options need to be entered into a row of continuous cells in the worksheet. The menu descriptions are entered into the row directly beneath the option names. The macro that will execute when an option is selected must begin in the row just below the option description.

To move to the macro area,

Press: (F5) (GOTO)

Type: **M50**

Press: (↵)

To accommodate the long menu option names and descriptions, column N must be set to 28 spaces and column O to 18 spaces:

Move to: N50

Select: /**W**orksheet **C**olumn **S**et-Width **28** (↵)

Move to: O50

Select: /**W**orksheet **C**olumn **S**et-Width **18** (↵)

To enter the option names on row 53 and their descriptions in row 54,

Move to: N53

Type: **Sales_Entry**

Move to: N54

Type: **Enter Daily Sales Figures**

Move to: O53

Type: **Print**

Move to: O54

Type: **Print the Report**

Move to: P53

Type: **Quit**

Move to: P54

Type: **Leave the Menu**

Press: (↵)

Your screen should look similar to Figure 10.5.

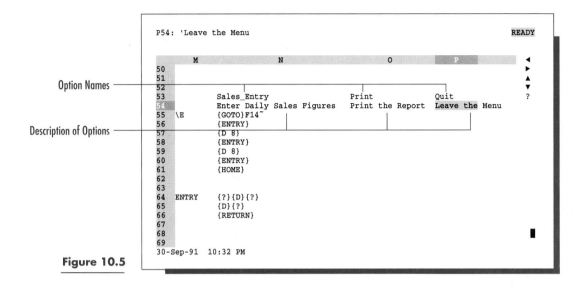

Option Names

Description of Options

Figure 10.5

```
P54: 'Leave the Menu                                                    READY

           M                    N                    O           P          ◄
     50                                                                      ►
     51                                                                      ▲
     52                                                                      ▼
     53               Sales_Entry              Print         Quit           ?
     54               Enter Daily Sales Figures Print the Report  Leave the Menu
     55    \E         {GOTO}F14~
     56               {ENTRY}
     57               {D 8}
     58               {ENTRY}
     59               {D 8}
     60               {ENTRY}
     61               {HOME}
     62
     63
     64    ENTRY      {?}{D}{?}
     65               {D}{?}
     66               {RETURN}
     67
     68                                                                      ▮
     69
     30-Sep-91  10:32 PM
```

Notice that the \E macro begins directly beneath the first menu option
and description. This is essential. When a menu option is selected, 1-2-3
executes the macro directly beneath the option. Soon you will place
macros beneath the Print and Quit options.

Before this menu can be used, it must be assigned a range name. Any
range name up to 15 characters can be used; you will use the name
MENU. Although the name could be assigned to the entire menu range,
only the first cell (upper left corner) of the menu needs to be named.
Since the menu begins in N53, assign the range name MENU to cell N53
by issuing the following command sequence:

/**R**ange **N**ame **C**reate **MENU** ⏎ **N53** ⏎

Now a macro needs to be created that will display the menu. This macro
will use the MENUBRANCH command. Like RETURN, this command is
part of 1-2-3's macro command language. The format of the command is:

{MENUBRANCH location}

Location is the name of the menu you want the MENUBRANCH command to display in the control panel. Since you named the menu MENU,
the command in this case will be {MENUBRANCH MENU}. It is important
that you include a space after the word MENUBRANCH.

This macro will also position the cell pointer home before displaying the menu. To enter this macro,

Move to: N50

Type: {HOME}

Move to: N51

Type: {MENUBRANCH MENU}

Press: ⏎

To document the macro and to assign the range name \M,

Move to: M50

Type: '\M

Move to: N50

Select: /Range Name Create \M ⏎ N50 ⏎

Your screen should look similar to Figure 10.6.

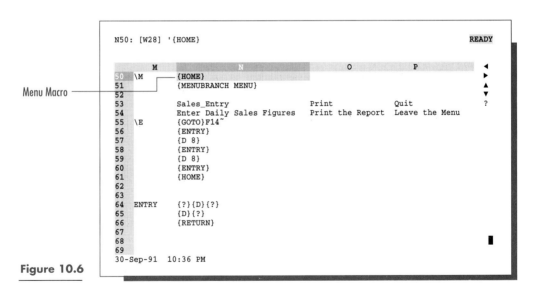

Figure 10.6

To see the menu and execute the \M macro,

Press: ALT-M

Your screen should look similar to Figure 10.7.

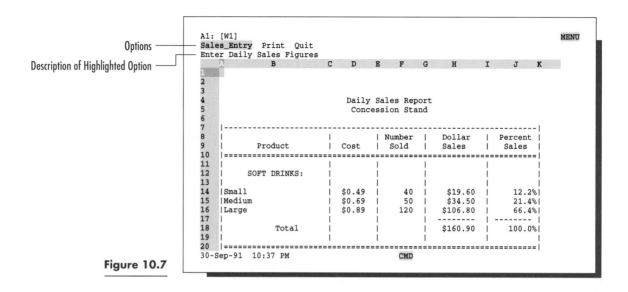

Options ——

Description of Highlighted Option ——

```
A1: [W1]                                                              MENU
Sales_Entry  Print  Quit
Enter Daily Sales Figures
      A           B          C    D    E    F    G    H    I    J    K
1
2
3
4                              Daily Sales Report
5                              Concession Stand
6
7    |---------------------------------------------------------------------|
8    |                        |       | Number |    Dollar   |   Percent   |
9    |       Product          | Cost  |  Sold  |    Sales    |   Sales     |
10   |=====================================================================|
11   |                        |       |        |             |             |
12   |     SOFT DRINKS:       |       |        |             |             |
13   |                        |       |        |             |             |
14   |Small                   | $0.49 |   40   |   $19.60    |    12.2%|
15   |Medium                  | $0.69 |   50   |   $34.50    |    21.4%|
16   |Large                   | $0.89 |  120   |  $106.80    |    66.4%|
17   |                        |       |        |  --------   |  -------- |
18   |           Total        |       |        |  $160.90    |   100.0%|
19   |                        |       |        |             |             |
20   |=====================================================================|
30-Sep-91  10:37 PM                         CMD
```

Figure 10.7

This menu works like a regular 1-2-3 menu. Moving the highlight bar to an option changes the description on the second line of the command panel. Use → to move to the different options and read the descriptions.

The only option that can be selected at this time is Sales_Entry since we have not yet written the macros for Print or Quit.

Select: **S**ales_Entry

This executes the entry macro you created earlier. Enter some sample data. When the macro is finished, the cell pointer should return to A1. If you want to try the menu macro again, press (ALT)-**M** to display the menu.

If your macros did not work properly, carefully recheck and correct them before continuing to the next section.

Creating a Print Macro

The Print macro will print a copy of the completed report. Before you create the macro, assign the range name REPORT to the print range by issuing the following command sequence:

/Range **N**ame **C**reate **REPORT** ⏎ **A1..K40** ⏎

To print the worksheet, the commands would be **/P**rint **P**rinter **R**ange **REPORT** ⏎ **A**lign **G**o **P**age **Q**uit. You may wish to try these commands manually before creating the macro.

The Print macro needs to be entered directly under the Print option and description. To return to the macro area,

Press: (F5) (GOTO)

Type: **M50**

Press: (↵)

To enter the Print macro,

Move to: O55

Type: **'/pprREPORT~agpq**

Press: (↵)

Your screen should look similar to Figure 10.8.

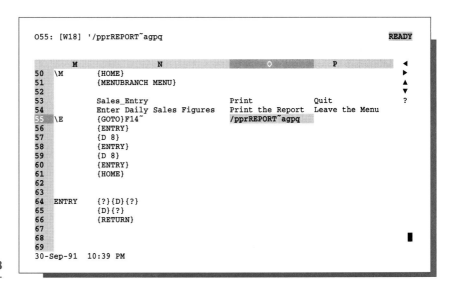

```
O55: [W18] '/pprREPORT~agpq                                          READY

          M              N                        O              P        ◄
50  \M          {HOME}                                                    ►
51              {MENUBRANCH MENU}                                         ▲
52                                                                        ▼
53              Sales_Entry              Print          Quit             ?
54              Enter Daily Sales Figures Print the Report Leave the Menu
55  \E          {GOTO}F14~               /pprREPORT~agpq
56              {ENTRY}
57              {D 8}
58              {ENTRY}
59              {D 8}
60              {ENTRY}
61              {HOME}
62
63
64  ENTRY       {?}{D}{?}
65              {D}{?}
66              {RETURN}
67
68
69                                                                        ■
30-Sep-91   10:39 PM
```

Figure 10.8

Notice the capitalization in the Print macro. Although it is not necessary to capitalize any part of a macro, capitalization of range names in a macro will make the macro easier to read and debug.

Since this macro is part of a custom menu system, it doesn't need to be individually named. It will work when it is selected from the menu because it has been placed directly under the menu option and description. To test the macro (be sure your printer is turned on),

Press: (ALT)-**M**

Select: **P**rint

The report is printed. If your macro does not work properly, check the Print macro and the range defined by REPORT. Correct them before continuing.

Using the QUIT Macro Command

When 1-2-3 encounters a blank cell in a macro, execution of the macro is ended. Therefore, the Quit option will work if the cell beneath the description is left blank. However, the conventional way to tell 1-2-3 to end a macro and leave a menu is by using the 1-2-3 macro command {QUIT}.

To move to the macro area,

Press: (F5) (GOTO)

Type: **M50**

Press: (↵)

To enter the Quit macro,

Move to: P55

Type: **{QUIT}**

Press: (↵)

Your screen should look similar to Figure 10.9.

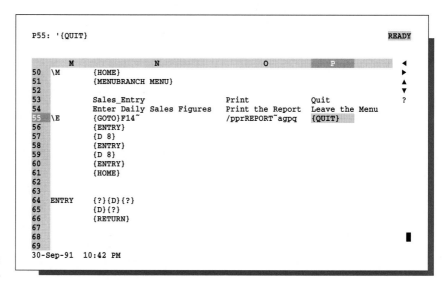

P55: '{QUIT}   READY

```
        M                N                      O               P
50  \M      {HOME}                                                       ◄
51          {MENUBRANCH MENU}                                            ►
52                                                                       ▲
53          Sales_Entry              Print           Quit                ▼
54          Enter Daily Sales Figures Print the Report Leave the Menu    ?
55  \E      {GOTO}F14~               /pprREPORT~agpq  {QUIT}
56          {ENTRY}
57          {D 8}
58          {ENTRY}
59          {D 8}
60          {ENTRY}
61          {HOME}
62
63
64  ENTRY   {?}{D}{?}
65          {D}{?}
66          {RETURN}
67
68
69
    30-Sep-91  10:42 PM
```

Figure 10.9

To run the macro and test the Quit option,

Press: (ALT)-**M**

Select: **Q**uit

The menu disappears, and the cell pointer is in cell A1, with the mode indicator in READY mode. If your macro did not work properly, recheck and correct it.

Creating a Looping Menu

When an option is selected from the menu the selected macro executes, but on completion of the macro the custom menu does not reappear. Susan wants the menu to keep reappearing until the Quit option is selected. This will make it more convenient for the employees to enter the sales data and then print the report.

The macro command that displays the menu is {MENUBRANCH MENU}. To have the menu reappear after the Sales_Entry or Print option is selected, Susan needs to place {MENUBRANCH MENU} at the end of the Sales_Entry and Print macros.

To move to the macro area and add the new commands,

Press: (F5) (GOTO)

Type: **M50**

Press: (↵)

Move to: N62

Type: **{MENUBRANCH MENU}**

Move to: O56

Type: **{MENUBRANCH MENU}**

Press: (↵)

Your screen should look similar to Figure 10.10.

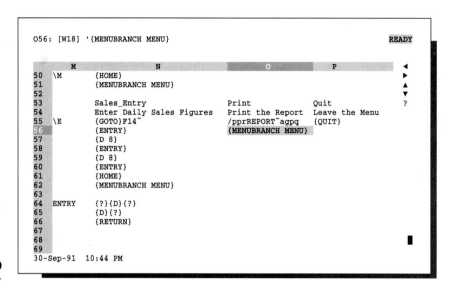

```
O56: [W18] '{MENUBRANCH MENU}                                          READY

          M              N                    O              P          ◄
  50  \M        {HOME}                                                  ►
  51            {MENUBRANCH MENU}                                       ▲
  52                                                                    ▼
  53            Sales_Entry               Print          Quit          ?
  54            Enter Daily Sales Figures Print the Report Leave the Menu
  55  \E        {GOTO}F14~                /pprREPORT~agpq  {QUIT}
  56            {ENTRY}                   {MENUBRANCH MENU}
  57            {D 8}
  58            {ENTRY}
  59            {D 8}
  60            {ENTRY}
  61            {HOME}
  62            {MENUBRANCH MENU}
  63
  64  ENTRY     {?}{D}{?}
  65            {D}{?}
  66            {RETURN}
  67
  68                                                                    ■
  69
      30-Sep-91  10:44 PM
```

Figure 10.10

Execute the \M macro. Test the Sales_Entry and Print options to make sure the menu returns. Finally, choose Quit to leave the menu. If your macros did not work properly, recheck and correct them before proceeding to the next section.

Controlling the Screen with a Macro

Susan likes the new menu system but thinks that the appearance of the screen as the macro executes could be improved.

She notices that as the Sales_Entry option is executed, the column headers run off the top of the screen. To prevent this, she would like to have the macro freeze the rows above row 11. Since the titles need to be frozen only once before any data is entered, she decides to put the commands to freeze the titles in the \M macro.

To move to the macro area,

Press: (F5) (GOTO)

Type: **M50**

Press: (↵)

Recall that in order to freeze titles the cursor needs to be placed one row beneath the rows to be frozen. You will modify the \M macro so that the cursor is positioned at A11 and the titles are frozen horizontally. You may wish to try freezing the titles manually first.

The new commands will be inserted between {HOME} in N50 and {MENUBRANCH MENU} in N51. To make room for these new commands, all the macros below row 51 will be moved down two rows by issuing the following command sequence:

/Move **M51..P66** ⏎ **M53** ⏎

To insert the macro commands,

Move to: N51

Type: {GOTO}A11~

Move to: N52

Type: '/wth

Press: ⏎

Your screen should look similar to Figure 10.11.

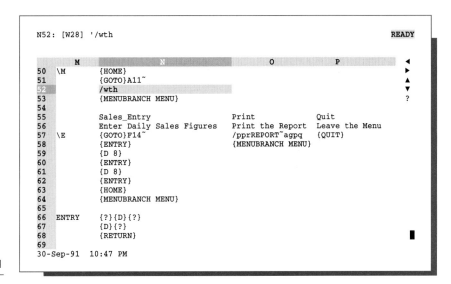

```
N52: [W28] '/wth                                                    READY

         M              N                    O              P        ◄
50  \M        {HOME}                                                 ►
51            {GOTO}A11~                                             ▲
52            /wth                                                   ▼
53            {MENUBRANCH MENU}                                      ?
54
55            Sales_Entry          Print          Quit
56            Enter Daily Sales Figures  Print the Report  Leave the Menu
57  \E        {GOTO}F14~           /pprREPORT~agpq  {QUIT}
58            {ENTRY}              {MENUBRANCH MENU}
59            {D 8}
60            {ENTRY}
61            {D 8}
62            {ENTRY}
63            {HOME}
64            {MENUBRANCH MENU}
65
66  ENTRY     {?}{D}{?}
67            {D}{?}
68            {RETURN}                                               ■
69
30-Sep-91  10:47 PM
```

Figure 10.11

Execute the \M macro, and test the Sales_Entry option. The column headers should remain on the screen while the entries are made. Leave the menu by selecting the **Q**uit option.

Press: (HOME)

The cell pointer is in cell A11 rather than A1. That is because the titles are still frozen. To change this, the Quit macro will be modified.

To clear the frozen titles and move to the macro area,

Select: /**W**orksheet **T**itles **C**lear

Press: (F5) (GOTO)

Type: **M50**

Press: (↵)

To modify the Quit macro, the command to clear the titles will be inserted just above the {QUIT} command in cell P57. To make room for this new command,

Select: /**M**ove **P57** (↵) **P58** (↵)

Move to: P57

Type: **'/wtc**

Press: (↵)

Your screen should look similar to Figure 10.12.

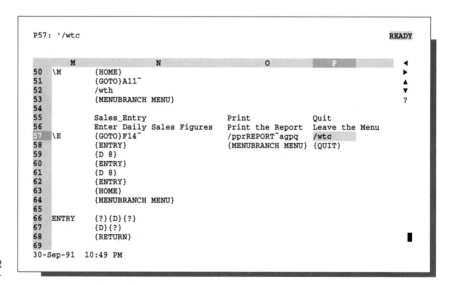

```
P57: '/wtc                                                    READY

          M              N                  O              P        ◄
    50  \M         {HOME}                                            ►
    51             {GOTO}A11~                                        ▲
    52             /wth                                              ▼
    53             {MENUBRANCH MENU}                                 ?
    54
    55             Sales_Entry             Print         Quit
    56             Enter Daily Sales Figures  Print the Report  Leave the Menu
    57  \E         {GOTO}F14~              /pprREPORT~agpq  /wtc
    58             {ENTRY}                 {MENUBRANCH MENU} {QUIT}
    59             {D 8}
    60             {ENTRY}
    61             {D 8}
    62             {ENTRY}
    63             {HOME}
    64             {MENUBRANCH MENU}
    65
    66  ENTRY      {?}{D}{?}
    67             {D}{?}
    68             {RETURN}                                          ■
    69
    30-Sep-91  10:49 PM
```

Figure 10.12

To execute and test the Quit macro,

Press: (ALT)-**M**

Select: **Q**uit

Press: (HOME)

The cell pointer is in cell A1, and the titles are unfrozen. If your macros did not work properly, recheck and correct them before continuing.

Susan will add two advanced 1-2-3 macro commands, {PANELOFF} and {FRAMEOFF}, to the \M macro. {PANELOFF} will freeze the control panel while the macro is executing. This will prevent the menus and prompts that result from the macro from appearing in the control panel. {FRAMEOFF} suppresses the display of the row numbers and column letters during macro execution. These two commands are optional and will not affect what the macros do; they will simply make the screen less cluttered during macro execution. These two commands will be inserted into the \M macro.

To move to the macro area,

Press:	(F5) (GOTO)
Type:	**M50**
Press:	(↵)

To make room for the two new commands, all the macros below row 51 will be moved down two rows.

Select:	/Move **M51..P68** (↵) **M53** (↵)
Move to:	N51
Type:	**{PANELOFF}**
Move to:	N52
Type:	**{FRAMEOFF}**
Press:	(↵)

Now you need to tell the Quit option to turn the panel and frame back on when the macros are not executing. To make room for these commands, issue the following command sequence:

/Move **P60** (↵) **P62** (↵)

Then,

Move to:	P60
Type:	**{PANELON}**
Move to:	P61
Type:	**{FRAMEON}**
Press:	(↵)

Your screen should look similar to Figure 10.13.

```
P61: '{FRAMEON}                                                      READY

         M               N                    O              P        ◄
   50  \M     {HOME}                                                  ►
   51         {PANELOFF}                                              ▲
   52         {FRAMEOFF}                                              ▼
   53         {GOTO}A11~                                              ?
   54         /wth
   55         {MENUBRANCH MENU}
   56
   57         Sales_Entry            Print         Quit
   58         Enter Daily Sales Figures  Print the Report  Leave the Menu
   59  \E     {GOTO}F14~             /pprREPORT~agpq  /wtc
   60         {ENTRY}                {MENUBRANCH MENU}  {PANELON}
   61         {D 8}                                  {FRAMEON}
   62         {ENTRY}                               {QUIT}
   63         {D 8}
   64         {ENTRY}
   65         {HOME}
   66         {MENUBRANCH MENU}
   67
   68  ENTRY  {?}{D}{?}                                               ■
   69         {D}{?}
30-Sep-91   10:54 PM
```

Figure 10.13

Execute the \M macro, try the Sales_Entry and the Print options, and then select the Quit option. Notice how much "cleaner" the macros now run.

Creating an Autoexecuting Macro

An **autoexecuting macro** is simply a macro that automatically runs when a worksheet is retrieved. Each worksheet can have an autoexecuting macro. Susan would like to have the custom menu appear as soon as the sales report is retrieved.

To have a macro autoexecute, you assign it the range name \0 (zero). However, you cannot invoke the macro by pressing (ALT)-**0**, so the macro should have another name as well.

The macro that displays the menu has been named \M. To make this an autoexecuting macro, assign cell N50 a second range name of \0. Issue the following command sequence:

/**R**ange **N**ame **C**reate **\0** ↩ **N50** ↩

Save the worksheet as SALES4. Then retrieve SALES4.WK1 so that you can see how the autoexecuting macro works once the file is retrieved.

The custom menu appears in the control panel. If the autoexecution did not work properly, enter the command to name the cell N50 as **\0.**

Try the Sales_Entry and the Print options, and then select the Quit option. If your macros did not work properly, carefully recheck all the commands in the menu area.

Susan has accomplished her goal of simplifying the report for her employees.

Save your worksheet and print it. Then exit 1-2-3.

Glossary

Autoexecuting macro: A macro that automatically runs when a worksheet is retrieved.

Call: The name of the subroutine enclosed in brackets.

Calling macro: The original macro that contains the subroutine.

Custom menu: User-created display of options and descriptions on the control panel where the regular 1-2-3 menu displays.

Location: The name of the menu the MENUBRANCH command displays on the control panel.

Subroutine: A set of macro instructions that may be repeated several times during the execution of another macro.

Practice Problems and Cases

Matching A

1. Menu options
2. Custom menu
3. Autoexecute
4. {RETURN}
5. Subroutines
6. {MENUBRANCH}
7. '\P
8. (ALT)-M
9. /WCS18
10. Calling macro

_____ **a.** set of macro instructions repeated during the execution of another macro

_____ **b.** displays a custom menu

_____ **c.** contains a subroutine

_____ **d.** menu created to ease the use of macros

_____ **e.** key combination to run a macro

_____ **f.** a series of choices that appear on the control panel after accessing a menu

_____ **g.** command to set column width

_____ **h.** a special macro command that tells a subroutine to go back to the calling macro

_____ **i.** macro name

_____ **j.** macro that runs as soon as a file is opened

Matching B

Eric is helping his friend Carl debug the macros that appear in Carl's worksheet. Carl's current screen looks like the one below and still contains some errors. Use the worksheet to match the letter with their descriptions.

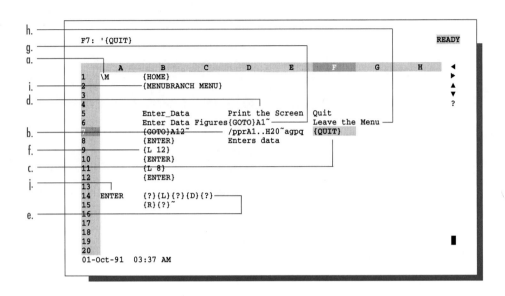

_____ **1.** macro to leave custom menu

_____ **2.** name of menu macro

_____ **3.** subroutine to enter data

_____ **4.** descriptive label for custom menu option

_____ **5.** a menu option

_____ **6.** command to return to A1

_____ **7.** macro to print designated range

_____ **8.** command to move 12 cells to the left

_____ **9.** command to display custom menu

_____ **10.** command to stop and wait for input

Cases

1. Barbara Ramage liked the macros written in PROB9-3 for her weekly sales report form for Entertainment Now, Inc. She has delegated the updating to Kevin. However, Kevin has limited experience with 1-2-3. Retrieve the file PROB10-1.WK1 to see the worksheet. To finish the worksheet, complete the following steps.

   a. Enter your name in cell A1 and the current date in cell A2.

   b. Create and document a macro using subroutines to enter the values in column F. Name the macros. Enter some hypothetical data to test the macro. If your macro does not operate correctly, you may want to use STEP mode to locate the problem.

   c. Create a macro to print the worksheet. Name the macro. Execute the macro, and edit it if necessary.

   d. Save the worksheet as HWLAB10-1. Print the worksheet, including the macros.

2. To complete this problem, you first must have completed Practice Case 1. Barbara would like to make the worksheet even easier for Kevin to use. Complete the following steps to improve the worksheet.

   a. Create a custom menu that can be used to enter the data, print the worksheet, and quit the custom menu.

   b. Modify the enter macro to freeze the titles on the screen. Change the macro to also turn the frame and panel off.

   c. Modify the quit macro to unfreeze the titles. Then modify the macro to turn the frame and panel on.

   d. Set the custom menu to execute as soon as the file is retrieved. Test the macro, and edit if necessary.

   e. Use the custom menu print selection to print the worksheet.

   f. Save the worksheet as HWLAB10-2.

3. To complete this problem, you first must have built the worksheet as specified in Practice Case 1 of Lab 9. If you have completed that problem, retrieve the file HWLAB9-1.WK1. Complete the following steps.

   a. Enter the current date in cell A2.

   b. Create a custom menu to display the names of the macros.

   c. Enter a macro to print the worksheet. Add the print macro to the custom menu.

d. Test the macros and custom menu.

e. Set the custom menu to autoexecute when the worksheet is opened.

f. Save the worksheet as HWLAB10-3. Print the worksheet, including the macros.

4. To complete this problem, you first must have built the worksheet as specified in Practice Case 4 of Lab 9. Create a custom menu to reflect the macros. Turn the frame and panel off and back on with the proper macros. The macro to enter data should autoexecute when the file is retrieved. Execute the macros, and make corrections as necessary. Enter the current date in cell A2. Save the worksheet as HWLAB10-4. Print the worksheet, including the macros.

5. Create a database of employees for The Aloha Travel Agency. Create a macro to help you enter data into the database more effectively. Create macros to print the database, change employee wages, and change employees' hours. Create an autoexecuting custom menu for the database. Save the worksheet as HWLAB10-5. Print the worksheet, including the macros.

6. Create a worksheet to keep track of your work and class schedule. List the number of hours you spend daily at work or school. Create a custom menu to help you use the worksheet more efficiently. Use any of the functions and features you feel enhance the worksheet. Save the worksheet as HWLAB10-6. Print the worksheet, including any macros you have written.

1-2-3

Reference

Chapter 1

Basic Skills

The 1-2-3 Screen   Figure 1.1 shows the 1-2-3 screen. 1-2-3 divides the screen into three areas: the worksheet area, the control panel, and the status line.

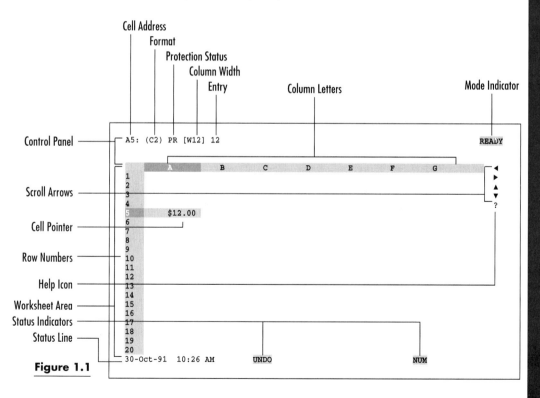

Figure 1.1

The Worksheet Area

The **worksheet area,** which occupies the largest section of the screen, is where you enter and calculate data. It displays a section of the worksheet you are currently working on. The worksheet is a grid made up of horizontal rows and vertical columns. The worksheet contains 8,192 rows and 256 columns. Each intersection of a row and column forms a cell, in which you can store data (a value or a label).

A row number identifies a row in the worksheet. It appears in the left border of the worksheet. Rows are numbered consecutively from 1 to 8192.

A column letter identifies a column in the worksheet. It appears in the top border of the worksheet. Columns are lettered A–Z, then AA–AZ, then BA–BZ, and so on to IV.

A **cell** is a unit of the worksheet that stores data. It is formed by the intersection of a column and a row, and has a unique address that consists of its column letter and row number. For example, B6 identifies the cell at the intersection of column B and row 6.

The **cell pointer** is a rectangular highlight that appears on one cell in the worksheet and identifies it as the current cell. You can move the cell pointer to any cell in the worksheet.

The **current cell** contains the cell pointer, which indicates that your next entry or procedure affects this cell. For example, typing an entry or selecting certain commands affects the current cell.

The Control Panel

The **control panel** consists of three lines at the top of the screen that display information about the current cell and commands (actions you tell 1-2-3 to perform).

The first line of the control panel displays the cell address, the contents of the current cell, and information about the current cell and the current mode. This consists of information about the **cell format,** which controls the way 1-2-3 displays values in a cell; the cell **protection status** (U if the cell is unprotected, PR if the cell is protected and protection is on, or nothing if protection is off); the cell's **column width,** or number of characters 1-2-3 displays in the cell if you have changed the initial setting; and the **mode indicator,** which indicates the mode or state of 1-2-3.

The second line of the control panel displays the current entry when you enter or edit data. It displays the **main menu,** a list of commands that appears if you press / (slash) or < (less than symbol) in READY mode, as well as the **submenus** that appear after you make a selection from the main menu. The second line of the control panel also displays **prompts,** or requests for information that 1-2-3 needs to complete a command.

The third line of the control panel displays either submenu commands for the highlighted command or a description of the highlighted command. The **icon panel** contains **scroll arrows** and **? (Help icon)** for moving around the worksheet and getting help using the mouse.

The Status Line

The **status line** is at the bottom of the screen. 1-2-3 uses the status line to display the date-and-time (or the file name) indicator and status indicators such as CAPS when the (CAPS LOCK) key is on.

1-2-3 Indicators

An indicator is a highlighted word that 1-2-3 displays to provide you with information about the program or special keys. 1-2-3 has two types of indicators: mode and status.

Mode Indicators

The mode indicator is located at the far right of the first line of the control panel. It tells you what mode or state 1-2-3 is currently in. Table 1.1 lists and describes the mode indicators.

Mode Indicator	Meaning
EDIT	You pressed (F2) (EDIT) to edit a cell entry, you are editing settings in a dialog box, or you entered a formula incorrectly.
ERROR	1-2-3 has encountered an error. An error message appears in a dialog box. Press (F1) (HELP) for further information.
FILES	1-2-3 is displaying a menu of file names in the control panel. Press (F3) (NAME) or click List to display a full-screen menu of file names.
FIND	You selected **/D**ata **Q**uery **F**ind or pressed (F7) (QUERY) to repeat the last **/D**ata **Q**uery **F**ind you specified, and 1-2-3 is highlighting a database record that matches your criteria.
FRMT	You selected **/D**ata **P**arse **F**ormat-Line **E**dit to edit a format line.
HELP	You pressed (F1) (HELP) and 1-2-3 is displaying a Help screen.
LABEL	You are entering a label.
MENU	You pressed / (slash) or < (less than symbol), and 1-2-3 is displaying a menu of commands.
NAMES	1-2-3 is displaying a menu of range names, graph names, or names of attached add-ins.
POINT	1-2-3 is prompting you to specify a range, or you are creating a formula by highlighting a range.
READY	1-2-3 is ready for you to enter data or select a command.
SETTINGS	1-2-3 is displaying an active dialog box.
STAT	You selected **/W**orksheet **S**tatus or **/W**orksheet **G**lobal **D**efault **S**tatus, and 1-2-3 is displaying the corresponding status screen.
VALUE	You are entering a value (a number or a formula).
WAIT	1-2-3 is in the middle of a command or process.

Table 1.1

Status Indicators

Status indicators appear in the status line at the bottom of your screen. They appear when you use certain 1-2-3 keys and when a particular program condition exists. Table 1.2 lists and describes the status indicators.

Status Indicator	Meaning
CALC	Formulas in the worksheet need to be recalculated. Press (F9) (CALC).
CAPS	The (CAPS LOCK) key is on.
CIRC	The worksheet contains a formula that refers to itself. Use /Worksheet Status to get information about the circular reference.
CMD	1-2-3 is running a macro.
END	The (END) key is on.
LEARN	You pressed (ALT)-(F5) (LEARN) to turn on the Learn feature, and 1-2-3 is recording your keystrokes in the learn range.
MEM	The amount of available memory has fallen below a minimum number of bytes. You may soon get a "Memory full" error message if you continue to enter data without increasing the amount of available memory.
NUM	The (NUM LOCK) key is on.
OVR	The (INS) key is on. Instead of inserting the character you type to the left of the cursor, 1-2-3 replaces the character at the cursor with the character you type.
RO	The worksheet has read-only status, which means you cannot save any changes you make unless you get the file reservation or you save the worksheet with a new file name. This indicator appears when you are using 1-2-3 on a network.
SCROLL	The (SCROLL LOCK) key is on. Using the pointer-movement keys scrolls the worksheet in the direction indicated, instead of moving the cell pointer.
SST	A macro is being executed in single-step mode and is waiting for user input.
STEP	Single-step mode is turned on. Once invoked, macros are processed one step at a time.
UNDO	You can press (ALT)-(F4) (UNDO) to cancel any changes made to your worksheet since 1-2-3 was last in READY mode.

Table 1.2

Function Keys

You use the function keys on your keyboard to perform special operations. Each function key, except (F6), performs two operations: one when you press only the function key and another when you hold down (ALT) and then press the function key. Table 1.3 briefly describes the 1-2-3 function keys.

Key	Description
(F4) **(ABS)**	In POINT and EDIT modes, cycles a cell or range address between relative, absolute, and mixed.
(ALT)-(F7) **(APP1)**	Starts an add-in program assigned to the key.
(ALT)-(F8) **(APP2)**	Starts an add-in program assigned to the key.
(ALT)-(F9) **(APP3)**	Starts an add-in program assigned to the key.
(ALT)-(F10) **(APP4)**	If no add-in program is assigned to the key, displays the Add-In menu, which lets you attach, detach, invoke, or clear add-in programs.

Table 1.3

Key	Description
(CTRL)-(F1) **(BOOKMARK)**	Displays the last Help screen you viewed.
(F9) **(CALC)**	In READY mode, recalculates all worksheet formulas. In VALUE and EDIT modes, converts a formula to its current value.
(ALT)-(F1) **(COMPOSE)**	Creates characters in 1-2-3 that you cannot enter directly from the keyboard.
(F2) **(EDIT)**	Puts 1-2-3 in EDIT mode so that you can edit the entry in the current cell.
(F5) **(GOTO)**	Moves the cell pointer directly to a specified cell or named range.
(F10) **(GRAPH)**	Displays the current graph.
(F1) **(HELP)**	Displays the 1-2-3 on-line Help screens.
(ALT)-(F5) **(LEARN)**	Turns the Learn feature on or off.
(F3) **(NAME)**	In POINT mode, displays a menu of named ranges. In FILES and NAMES modes, displays a full-screen menu of names.
(F7) **(QUERY)**	Repeats the last /Data **Q**uery command you selected or, during a /Data **Q**uery **F**ind command, switches 1-2-3 between FIND mode and READY mode.
(ALT)-(F3) **(RUN)**	Selects a macro to run.
(ALT)-(F2) **(STEP)**	Turns STEP mode on or off.
(F8) **(TABLE)**	Repeats the last /Data **T**able command you selected.
(ALT)-(F4) **(UNDO)**	In READY mode, reverses any changes made to your worksheet since 1-2-3 was last in READY mode. Press (ALT)-(F4) (UNDO) again to restore those changes.
(F6) **(WINDOW)**	In READY mode, moves the cell pointer between the two windows created with /**W**orksheet **W**indow. Also turns display of dialog boxes on and off.

**Table 1.3
Continued**

Special Keys

Table 1.4 briefly describes the 1-2-3 special keys. To determine which keys on your computer's keyboard are equivalent to these keys, see the keyboard template.

Key	Description
(ALT)	Invokes a macro when used in combination with a single-letter macro name.
BACKSPACE	Erases the character to the left of the cursor in EDIT mode; if a range is selected, erases the current range.
(CAPS LOCK)	Makes letter keys produce only uppercase letters; number and punctuation keys are not affected.
(CTRL)	When used in combination with certain keys, changes the function of those keys.
(CTRL)-(BREAK)	Cancels the current procedure; in MENU mode returns you to READY mode.
(DEL)	Erases the current character in EDIT mode; deletes the cell entry in READY mode.
(↵)	Completes an entry, command, or part of a command.
(ESC)	Cancels the current entry or range or returns to the previous menu or command step.

Table 1.4

Key	Description
(INS)	Switches between inserting the text by moving existing text to the right and writing over existing text.
< (less than symbol)	Displays the 1-2-3 main menu in READY mode.
(NUM LOCK)	Switches between the number keys and pointer-movement keys on the numeric keypad.
. (period)	When entering a range in POINT mode, anchors the cell pointer if unanchored or cycles the anchor cell and free cell in range.
(SCROLL LOCK)	Switches the pointer-movement keys between moving the cell pointer and moving the window.
(SHIFT)	When used in combination with another key on the typewriter section of the keyboard, produces the upper symbol of the key.
/ (slash)	In READY mode, displays the 1-2-3 main menu.
SPACEBAR	Inserts a space in LABEL, VALUE, and EDIT modes; moves the menu pointer right one item in MENU mode.
(TAB)	In READY mode, moves the pointer one screen to the right; in EDIT mode, moves the cursor five characters to the right.

Table 1.4 Continued

Using the Mouse

In 1-2-3 Release 2.3, you can use a mouse for many tasks, including selecting commands from a menu, specifying ranges, selecting and marking items in dialog boxes, selecting Help topics, and moving the cell pointer. To use a mouse, you must be familiar with the following terms:

- **Click** — Press the mouse button and release it. Do not hold the mouse button down for longer than a fraction of a second. Click the left button to select something; click the right button to cancel (equivalent to pressing (ESC)).

- **Drag** — Hold down the mouse button and move the mouse; then release the mouse button.

- **Press** — Click and hold the mouse button without moving the mouse.

- **Double-click** — Press the mouse button twice in rapid succession.

This book assumes you use the left button to select items unless the right button is specified. If you switched mouse buttons when you installed 1-2-3, use the right button when the instructions do not specify a button or when the left button is specified; use the left button when the instructions specify the right button.

Selecting a Command

To tell 1-2-3 what you want to do, you select a series of commands from menus. You select commands by highlighting (with the rectangular highlight called the menu pointer), by typing the first character of the command, or by clicking the command.

When you press / (slash) or < (less than symbol), or move the mouse pointer to the control panel, the 1-2-3 main menu appears. If you want to cancel a menu selection without selecting an option, you can press (ESC) as many times as you need to in order to back out of the menu, click the right mouse button as often as necessary to leave the menu, or click CANCEL in a dialog box to back up one menu level at a time. To completely stop a procedure and return to READY mode, press (CTRL)-(BREAK).

Responding to Prompts

Often when you select a command, 1-2-3 requires you to supply more information. In many cases, 1-2-3 displays a prompt, or message, that asks you to enter specific information. You may have to supply this information in one of several ways:

- If 1-2-3 displays a menu of names, for example, when you select **/G**raph **N**ame **U**se, move the menu pointer to the name and press (↵), type the name and press (↵), or click the name. To display a full-screen list of names, either press (F3) (NAME) or click List in the first line of the control panel.

- If 1-2-3 suggests a response to the prompt and you want to accept the suggestion, press (↵) or click the control panel.

- If 1-2-3 suggests a response to a prompt and you want to enter a new response, type the response and press (↵) or type the response and click the control panel. (You may need to press (ESC) to clear a suggested response before you can type a new one.)

Dialog Boxes

A dialog box is a special status screen that helps you keep track of the choices you are making (see Figure 1.2). It shows you the current settings for all the options associated with a task. You can specify settings in the dialog box directly with the keyboard or the mouse, or you can select commands from the menu above the dialog box. If you prefer to use the menu and do not want to use the dialog box, you can press (F6) (WINDOW) to turn off the display of a dialog box when it appears. To redisplay the dialog box, press (F6) (WINDOW) again.

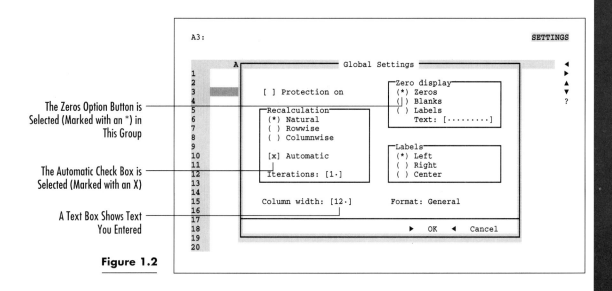

The Zeros Option Button is Selected (Marked with an *) in This Group

The Automatic Check Box is Selected (Marked with an X)

A Text Box Shows Text You Entered

Figure 1.2

Instead of commands in menus, dialog boxes use the following components to let you select settings:

- **Option buttons** and **check boxes** offer choices: You can select one option from a group of option buttons and one or more options (or none) if the options appear with check boxes. An option button is selected, or marked, when an * (asterisk) appears next to the option; a check box is selected, or marked, when an x appears next to the option.

- **Text boxes** accept whatever type of entry is required, including numbers, cell addresses, range names, or text.

- **Popup dialog boxes** appear over a dialog box when a selection in a dialog box leads to further options (see Figure 1.3).

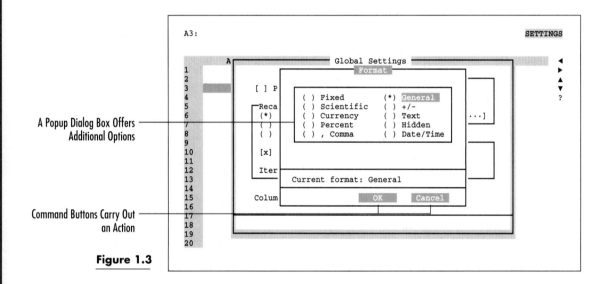

A Popup Dialog Box Offers Additional Options

Command Buttons Carry Out an Action

Figure 1.3

- Dialog boxes include at least one **command button.** Command buttons appear when the dialog box is active, and they carry out the action of the command. OK is the most common command button; it confirms the current selections and completes the command. Some command buttons are followed by ... (ellipsis); these command buttons produce another dialog box.

- **List boxes** let you select from many choices, such as a list of range names.

To use a dialog box, you must first activate it. You do this by pressing (F2) (EDIT) or by clicking anywhere in the box with the mouse (the mode indicator changes to SETTINGS). Then select dialog box components with the pointer-movement keys, by typing the highlighted character, or by clicking the component with the mouse.

Moving Around the Worksheet

You move around in 1-2-3 with either the pointer-movement keys or the mouse. Table 1.5 describes how to move within the worksheet.

To	Press	Or Do This with the Mouse
Move the cell pointer left or right one column or up or down one row	(←) (→) (↑) (↓)	Click the cell or the scroll arrow to the right of the worksheet border
Move the cell pointer left one screen	(SHIFT)-(TAB) or (CTRL)-(←)	
Move the cell pointer right one screen	(TAB) or (CTRL)-(→)	
Move the cell pointer to the intersection of a blank and a nonblank cell (a blank cell contains no data or label prefixes)	(END)-(←) (END)-(→) (END)-(↑) (END)-(↓)	
Move the cell pointer to the lower right corner of the active area (the rectangular area between cell A1 and the lowest and rightmost nonblank cell in the worksheet)	(END)-(HOME)	
Move the cell pointer to cell A1	(HOME)	Click the empty cell above the first visible row and to the left of the first visible column
Move the cell pointer up or down one screen	(PGUP) or (PGDN)	Click the up or down scroll arrow (moves the cell pointer one row at a time)
Move the view of the worksheet without moving the cell pointer	(SCROLL LOCK) and then press a pointer-movement key	
Move the cell pointer directly to a cell or a named range	(F5) (GOTO) and enter the cell address or press (F5) (GOTO) and then press (F3) (NAME) and select the name of the cell or range	Click the cell. If the cell is not visible, click a scroll arrow until the cell is visible, and then click the cell
Scroll the worksheet left, right, up, or down	Hold down (←)(→)(↑)(↓)	Click a scroll arrow

Table 1.5

Entering and Editing Data

You can enter any kind of data in a cell by typing. You can edit an entry as you type it or return to a completed entry and revise it.

Typing Entries

The simplest method of entering data in a cell is by typing. Move the cell pointer to a cell, type the entry, and then press (↵) or a pointer-movement key. The entry appears in the cell after you press (↵). When you press a pointer-movement key, 1-2-3 completes the entry and moves the cell pointer to another cell in the direction of the pointer-movement key.

When you press ⏎ or a pointer-movement key to complete an entry, several things occur:

- 1-2-3 checks for errors in the entry. If it finds an error, it beeps, places the cursor at the location of the problem, and switches to EDIT mode.

- If 1-2-3 finds no error, it stores the entry in the current cell. The previous entry, if any, disappears from the cell.

- The entry disappears from the second line of the control panel. After you press ⏎, the entry appears on the first line of the control panel. After you press a pointer-movement key, the entry disappears completely from the control panel.

- If the **R**ecalculation setting is **A**utomatic, 1-2-3 recalculates every formula in the worksheet that is affected by the change. (See the section on the **/W**orksheet **G**lobal **R**ecalculation command in Chapter 2.)

- 1-2-3 returns to READY mode.

Editing Entries

Editing an entry means altering existing data rather than replacing it with entirely new data. You can edit an entry as you type it or after you have entered it in a cell. To edit an entry, 1-2-3 must be in EDIT mode. 1-2-3 automatically changes to EDIT mode if you try to complete an entry that contains an error. Table 1.6 describes how to edit an entry under various conditions.

To	Do This
Edit as you type	Press BACKSPACE to erase previous characters, or press ⌷F2⌷ (EDIT) to start EDIT mode. Type replacement characters and press ⏎, or click the control panel.
Cancel the entry you are typing	Press ⌷ESC⌷. (In EDIT mode, press ⌷ESC⌷ twice.)
Edit a short entry	Move to the cell. Type the new entry, and confirm it by pressing ⏎ or a pointer-movement key or by clicking the control panel.
Change an entry	Move to the cell. Press ⌷F2⌷ (EDIT) to start EDIT mode. Move the cursor to where you want to edit the entry. Press BACKSPACE to delete characters to the left of the cursor, ⌷INS⌷ to replace characters with new characters as you type, or ⌷DEL⌷ to delete characters at the cursor. Type new characters to insert them. Press ⏎ or click the control panel when you finish editing the entry.
Erase a single entry	Move to the cell you want to erase, and press ⌷DEL⌷.
Erase several entries	Select **/R**ange **E**rase. Specify the range to erase. Press ⏎, or click the control panel.
Find an entry	Select **/R**ange **S**earch. Specify the range that contains the entry you want to find. Enter the characters to find at the prompt; you can use the wildcard characters ? (question mark) or * (asterisk) to search for several similar entries (for example, h?t finds hat and hot, and h* finds hat, hot, head, and so on). Select **F**ormulas (to search in formulas only), **L**abels (to search in labels only), or **B**oth (to search in both). Select **F**ind. Select **N**ext (to find the next occurrence) or **Q**uit (to stop **/R**ange **S**earch).

Table 1.6

To	Do This
Replace an entry	Select **/R**ange **S**earch. Specify the range that contains the entry you want to replace. Enter the characters to find at the prompt. Select **F**ormulas (to search in formulas only), **L**abels (to search in labels only), or **B**oth (to search in both). Select **R**eplace. Enter the new characters after the prompt. Select **R**eplace (to replace the current instance and find the next), **A**ll (to replace all occurrences of the characters), **N**ext (to find the next occurrence, leaving the current occurrence unchanged), or **Q**uit (to stop **/R**ange **S**earch).

Table 1.6 Continued

The pointer-movement keys work differently in EDIT mode. Table 1.7 lists the keys you can use in EDIT mode.

Press	To
←	Move the cursor left one character.
→	Move the cursor right one character.
↑	Complete editing and move the cell pointer up one row.
↓	Complete editing and move the cell pointer down one row.
BACKSPACE	Erase the character to the left of the cursor.
ALT-F1 **(COMPOSE)**	Create characters that are not available on the keyboard.
CTRL-→ **or** TAB	Move the cursor right five characters.
CTRL-← **or** SHIFT-TAB	Move the cursor left five characters.
DEL	Erase the current character.
END	Move to the right of the last character in the entry.
↵	Complete editing.
ESC	Clear the entry from the control panel.
F2 **(EDIT)**	Switch to VALUE or LABEL mode.
F9 **(CALC)**	Convert a formula to its current value.
HOME	Move to the first character in an entry.
INS	Switch between inserting text by moving existing text to the right (INS mode) and writing over existing text (OVR mode).
PGUP	Complete editing and move the cell pointer up one screen.
PGDN	Complete editing and move the cell pointer down one screen.

Table 1.7

If the Undo feature is on and you edit an entry and then change your mind, press ALT-F4 (UNDO) immediately to restore the entry.

Types of Data

1-2-3 recognizes two types of data: values and labels. A value is any number or a formula or @function that returns a value. Formulas calculate or combine numbers or text. @Functions are built-in formulas that calculate with text and numbers. A label is a text entry.

The first character of an entry tells 1-2-3 the entry type. Numbers and the symbols + − (. @ $ # or any currency symbol signal a value. All other characters signal a label, and 1-2-3 inserts a label-prefix character to control alignment.

Values

A value entry must conform to these rules:

- Cannot be longer than 240 characters

- Must be between 10^{-99} and 10^{99}, inclusive; however, 1-2-3 can store a number as a result of calculations, ranging from 10^{-308} to 10^{308}

- Cannot include spaces or commas; you can change the cell format later to include commas (see the section on the /Range Format command in Chapter 2)

- Can contain no more than one decimal point

- Can end with a percent sign to indicate a percentage

- Can be entered in scientific format, as shown in Figure 1.4

When you enter the first character of a value entry, the mode indicator changes from READY to VALUE. When you complete the entry, the mode indicator changes back to READY.

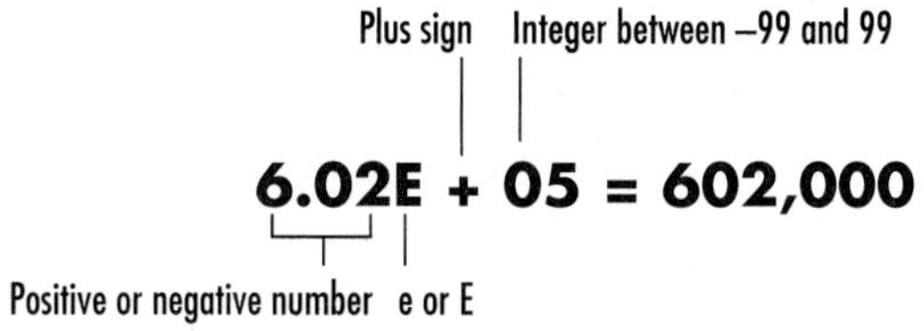

Plus sign   Integer between −99 and 99

$$6.02E + 05 = 602{,}000$$

Figure 1.4

Positive or negative number   e or E

Alignment of a Value A value aligns on the right edge of a cell. You cannot change the alignment of a value entry.

Format of a Value You can change the format, or appearance, of a value entry in a cell without changing the way 1-2-3 stores the entry. For example, you can format the entry 65.3 so that it appears as $65.30, 65.3%, or 65. (See the sections on the /Range Format and /Worksheet Global Format commands in Chapter 2.)

Long Values If a value contains too many characters to fit in a cell, and the cell format is General, 1-2-3 displays the number in scientific notation. If the format of the cell that contains the number is not General, 1-2-3 displays asterisks (*****) in the cell instead of the entry. This does not affect the way 1-2-3 stores the entry. When you make the column wide enough, the entire value appears in the worksheet. (See the sections on the /**W**orksheet **C**olumn **S**et-Width and /**W**orksheet **G**lobal **C**olumn-Width commands in Chapter 2.)

Decimal Places 1-2-3 can store a value with up to 15 decimal places. The control panel, however, displays a maximum of 9 decimal places. If you enter a value with 12 decimal places, for example, 1-2-3 calculates the entry using 12 decimal places although you can see only 9 decimal place numbers on the control panel.

Labels

Any entry that 1-2-3 determines is not a number or a formula is a label. Often label entries are descriptive text, such as May Sales or Principal. A label can consist of any characters in the Lotus International Character Set (LICS). LICS is an extension of the ASCII character set.

A label must conform to these rules:

- Must begin with either a label-prefix character or any character that does not indicate the start of a number or a formula

- Cannot be longer than 240 characters

- Can contain number characters as long as the first character is a label-prefix character

When you enter the first character of a label, the mode indicator changes from READY to LABEL. When you complete a label entry, the mode indicator changes back to READY.

Label-Prefix Characters Beginning an entry with a label-prefix character determines how the entry is aligned in the cell. There are three choices for labels: right-aligned, left-aligned, and centered. If you do not enter a label-prefix character, 1-2-3 automatically aligns the label entry according to the default worksheet alignment, which unless you change it, is left. (See the section on the /**W**orksheet **G**lobal **L**abel-Prefix command in Chapter 2.)

A label-prefix character does not appear in the worksheet cell; it appears on the first line of the control panel when the cell pointer is on the cell.

The label-prefix characters are described as follows:

Prefix:	Example:	Result:	
'(single quote)	'TOTAL	left-aligned	[TOTAL]
"(double quote)	"TOTAL	right-aligned	[TOTAL]
^(caret)	^TOTAL	centered	[TOTAL]

You can also type the \ (backslash) as the first character of a label entry. Characters you type after the backslash repeat across the worksheet cell. For example, \ * creates a cell filled with asterisks. The ¦ (split vertical bar) is also a label prefix. If you use it as a label prefix for a label that is located in the first column of a print range, the ¦ tells 1-2-3 not to print the row.

Entering Numbers as Labels

To enter a label that starts with a digit or a number symbol, begin the entry with a label-prefix character. A label-prefix character identifies the entry as a label no matter what characters the entry contains. For example, you would use a label-prefix character at the beginning of the entry 96 Lake St. If you omit the label-prefix character in such an entry, 1-2-3 beeps and changes to EDIT mode so that you can correct the entry.

Long Labels

If you enter a label entry that is too long to appear in one cell, the entry extends into the blank cells to the right. If the cells to the right are filled, 1-2-3 cuts off the entry at the right edge of the cell.

1-2-3 stores the entire entry even if it cannot display the entry in a worksheet cell. To make the complete entry appear in the worksheet cell, erase the cell entries to the right or widen the column that contains the entry.

Ranges

A range is a rectangular block of adjacent cells. It can be a single cell, several cells that are in adjacent rows and columns, a row, a column, or several adjacent rows and columns.

1-2-3 prompts you to enter a range during many commands. For example, 1-2-3 prompts you to enter a range when you use the **/M**ove command to move a group of cells to another part of the worksheet. You can also enter a range in an @function. You use ranges in commands and formulas to perform operations on more than one cell at the same time. To use a range, you need to identify, or specify, it. In most cases, you use either the keyboard or the mouse to specify ranges.

Specifying a Range

You can specify a range in three ways:

- Type the range address in a formula or in response to a prompt. A range address consists of the cell addresses of the upper left and lower right cells in the range, separated by one or two periods. After you enter a range address, 1-2-3 always displays it in uppercase letters as the upper left and lower right cells (except in a formula), separated by two periods.

- Highlight a range with the mouse or the keyboard before you select a command. You can also highlight a range when 1-2-3 is in POINT mode. 1-2-3 enters POINT mode when you press (F4) (ABS), when you hold down the left mouse button, when you must specify a range for a command, or when you are highlighting a range for a formula or an @function. (To enter POINT mode in a dialog box, press F4 (ABS).) Moving the cell pointer or pressing ESC in READY mode cancels the preselected range.

• Use a range name in a formula, in the **R**ange text box in a dialog box, or in response to a prompt. Pressing F3 (NAME) displays a list of all range names in the worksheet. Using a range name simplifies specifying a range in dialog boxes, formulas, and @functions. Name a range if you will frequently need the data it contains, if it is large, or if you will need to specify the range often.

Table 1.8 describes the keys you use to highlight a range in POINT mode. When a range is anchored, a pointer-movement key expands the highlight; when a range is unanchored, a pointer-movement key moves the cell pointer (and the anchor cell, the cell from which you start highlighting the range).

Key	Unanchored Range	Anchored Range
.(period)	Makes the current cell the anchor cell.	Moves the anchor cell clockwise from one corner to next of the highlighted range.
ESC	If you are using a command, returns you to the previous menu. If you are entering a formula, clears the last cell address in the formula and returns 1-2-3 to VALUE or EDIT mode.	Removes the range highlight and unanchors the cell pointer.
BACKSPACE	Returns the cell pointer to original location (before 1-2-3 entered POINT mode).	Removes the range highlight, unanchors the cell pointer, and returns the cell pointer to wherever it was before 1-2-3 entered POINT mode.
Pointer-movement keys	Moves the cell pointer and anchor cell.	Extends the range highlight.

Table 1.8

Using a Range Name

To refer more easily to a range, you can name it. Range names are names of up to 15 characters that you use in commands and formulas instead of cell or range addresses. For example, if you assign the name Sales to A5..D9, you can move the cell pointer to A5 by pressing F5 (GOTO), typing **Sales**, and pressing ↵; you can add the values in A5..D9 with the formula @SUM(SALES).

A range name is often easier to remember than a range address because the name can describe the contents of a range. (For details on naming a range, see the section on the **/R**ange **N**ame **C**reate command in Chapter 2.)

Working with Formulas

A formula is an entry that performs a calculation using numbers, other formulas, or strings. The calculation can be a simple mathematical operation, such as subtracting one number from another, or a more complicated operation, such as determining the net present value of a series of future cash flows.

When you enter a formula, 1-2-3 displays the value that results from the calculation in the cell. For example, if you enter the formula 25+5, 1-2-3 displays the value 30 in the cell. When the cell pointer is on the cell, however, 1-2-3 displays 25+5 in the first line of the control panel. 1-2-3 lets you enter three types of formulas: numeric, string, and logical.

- Numeric formulas calculate numeric values using the arithmetic operators (+ − * / and ^) or @functions. 1-2-3 can calculate any numeric formula whose value is between 10^{-308} and 10^{308}, but the value must be between 10^{-99} and 10^{99} for 1-2-3 to display it in the worksheet (otherwise 1-2-3 displays asterisks across the cell that contains the formula). For example, the formula 2*H16 calculates a numeric value by multiplying the value in cell H16 by 2 (see Table 1.9).

- String formulas calculate string values using the string operator, the ampersand (&), or @functions. For example, if D4 contains the label Robinson, the formula +"Dear**o**Mr.**o**and**o**Mrs.**o**"&D4 produces the string value Dear Mr. and Mrs. Robinson by concatenating (joining together) the text in quotation marks (called a literal string) with the contents of D4. (Each **o** represents one space.)

- Logical formulas are statements that return either 1 (meaning the statement is true) or 0 (meaning the statement is false). Logical formulas use the logical operators (=, <, >, <=, >=, <>, #AND#, #OR#, and #NOT#) or @functions. For example, +A12>=500 returns 1 (true) if the value in A12 is greater than or equal to 500; otherwise, it returns 0 (false).

Use the following guidelines when entering a formula:

- A formula can begin with a number or one of the numeric symbols + − . @ ($. In addition, the # (pound symbol) can be used to begin a logical formula.

- When the first element in a formula is a cell address, range name, or file reference, begin the formula with + − (or $. For example, +B7/B8, −B7*B8, $SALES/12, (SALES-EXPENSES), and +<<BUDGET.WK1>>B7 are all valid formulas.

- When a string formula starts with a literal string, begin the formula with + or (. For example, +"Ms. "&LAST and ("Ms. "&LAST) are both valid formulas.

- A formula can contain up to 240 characters.

- A formula cannot contain spaces, except within literal strings in string formulas.

You can use the following types of data in a formula:

- Numbers (for example, 450, −92, 7.1E12, date numbers, and time numbers)

- Literal strings (for example, "Budget for" or "TOTAL")

- @Functions (for example, @SUM(A4..A8))

- Cell and range addresses (for example, B12, F23..H35)

- Range names (for example, JANSALES, BUDGET_90)

Order of Precedence

Table 1.9 shows the operators you can use in formulas and their precedence numbers. Precedence numbers represent the order in which 1-2-3 performs operations in a formula. The lower the precedence number, the earlier 1-2-3 performs the operation. Operators with the same precedence number are performed sequentially from left to right.

Operator	Operation	Precedence Number
^	Exponentiation	1
− +	Negative, positive	2
+ /	Multiplication, division	3
+ −	Addition, subtraction	4
= <>	Equal, not equal	5
< >	Less than, greater than	5
<=	Less than or equal	5
>=	Greater than or equal	5
#NOT#	Logical NOT	6
#AND#	Logical AND	7
#OR#	Logical OR	7
&	String concatenation	7

Table 1.9

Overriding Precedence Numbers

You can override the order of precedence by putting parentheses around an operation. 1-2-3 performs operations in parentheses first. Within each set of parentheses, precedence numbers apply. You can nest one set of parentheses within another set of parentheses and create as many nesting levels as you want.

Figure 1.5 shows how 1-2-3 performs the operations in a formula according to precedence number.

Figure 1.5

1-2-3 performs the operations in this order:

$$450 + ((5000 + A20)*.145)/12\text{-}J30$$

4th   1st   2nd   3rd   5th

Using Cell and Range References in Formulas

Cell addresses in formulas can be relative, absolute, or mixed. The difference between relative, absolute, and mixed cell references is important when you copy or move formulas.

Use a relative reference to refer to a position of a cell in relation to the cell that contains the formula. A relative reference is not a permanent reference to a particular cell. To create a relative reference in a formula, you simply type the address or range name, such as B1, D25..D30, or PROFITS. For example,

Cell reference	Meaning in a formula in H11
G5	the cell one column left and six rows above this one

Use an absolute reference to refer to the same cell no matter where you copy the formula to. An absolute reference is a permanent reference to a particular cell. To create an absolute reference, type a $ (dollar sign) in front of both the column letter and row number of the address (for example, $F$2 or $A$5..$B$10). To create an absolute range name, type a $ in front of the range name ($RATE). For example,

Cell reference	Meaning in a formula in H11
$G$5	cell G5

Use a mixed reference to make a cell reference that is part relative and part absolute — either the column letter or the row number remains constant. To create a mixed reference, precede the column letter or the row number with a $ (dollar sign), for instance, $C4 or C$4. For example,

Cell reference	Meaning in a formula in H11
$G5	the cell in column G, six rows above this one
G$5	the cell one column left of this one, in row 5

Cell references are relative by default.

Using F4 (ABS) to Change Reference Types

When entering or editing a formula, press F4 (ABS) when the cursor is on or immediately to the right of a cell or range address. 1-2-3 cycles the address through the different reference types. 1-2-3 always cycles through the types of cell reference in the same order regardless of whether the original reference type is relative, absolute, or mixed.

Table 1.10 shows how pressing F4 (ABS) changes the address C5 after you type +C5.

You can also indicate absolute, mixed, and relative addresses when pointing. After you point to a cell or a range and before you type the next character, press F4 (ABS) repeatedly. The cell or range address on the control panel cycles through absolute, mixed, and relative.

You can edit an existing cell or range address by moving to the cell that contains the formula and pressing (F2) (EDIT). Move the cursor to the address you want to change, and press (F4) (ABS) repeatedly to cycle through relative, absolute, and mixed.

When Control Panel Displays	Press (F4) (ABS) to Get This
+C5	$C$5 (absolute address)
+$C$5	C$5 (mixed address with absolute row reference)
+C$5	$C5 (mixed address with absolute column reference)
+$C5	C5 (relative address)

Table 1.10

Entering References in Formulas

You can include a cell or range reference in a formula by typing it or by pointing to it.

You can use the mouse or the pointer-movement keys to point to a cell. (You use the mouse in conjunction with the triangle icons in the icon panel.) First type an operator. Then move the cell pointer to the cell whose address you want to include. The cell address appears on the control panel. Type the next operator, or press (←) to complete the formula. The pointer returns to the cell in which you are entering the formula.

If the specified cell or range is a named range, 1-2-3 automatically substitutes the name for the address in the formula. If the specified cell or range has more than one range name, 1-2-3 displays the range name that comes first alphabetically. (See "Specifying a Range" earlier in this chapter.)

@Functions

1-2-3 has a special set of built-in formulas, called @functions. @Functions are different from regular formulas because you supply the values but not the operators.

Format of an @Function

An @function contains specific elements: the @function name and the values or data 1-2-3 needs to complete the @function calculation, which are enclosed in parentheses. Values in @functions are called arguments. An @function can have no arguments, one argument, or several arguments (see Figure 1.6).

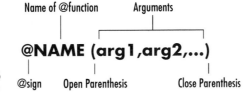

Figure 1.6

Many @functions allow you to perform common calculations more easily than standard formulas. For example, the @function @SUM(B4..B10) performs the same task as the formula +B4+B5+B6+B7+B8+B9+B10, but the @function is easier to enter.

Other @functions perform complex calculations efficiently. For example, the @function @PV calculates the present value of an annuity, which would otherwise require a complicated formula. (For more details about @functions, see Chapter 4.)

The Undo Feature

The Undo feature is an important safeguard against time-consuming mistakes. When the Undo feature is on, you can press (ALT)-(F4) (UNDO) almost any time when 1-2-3 is in READY mode to cancel the most recent operation that changed worksheet data or settings. When you use (ALT)-(F4) (UNDO), 1-2-3 automatically restores whatever worksheet data and settings existed the last time 1-2-3 was in READY mode. In addition, if you change your mind about what you just undid, you can press (ALT)-(F4) (UNDO) again, and 1-2-3 will undo the effect of the undo operation.

You can cancel the previous action or command if the Undo feature is on. Initially Undo is off; to be able to undo actions, you must select **/W**orksheet **G**lobal **D**efault **O**ther **U**ndo **E**nable. If you want Undo to be on by default, then select **U**pdate. When Undo is on, the UNDO indicator appears in the status line at the bottom of your screen when 1-2-3 is in READY mode. If the UNDO indicator is not displayed, pressing (ALT)-(F4) (UNDO) will have no effect.

Using Undo

Although the Undo feature is a valuable tool, you should not use it until you are familiar with how it works; otherwise, you may get unexpected results.

- The Undo feature works only when you are working in 1-2-3 and 1-2-3 is in READY mode. You cannot use the Undo feature with any of the 1-2-3 utility programs (PrintGraph and Install) or while add-in programs (such as the Macro Library Manager) are invoked. You can, however, use Undo while the add-ins are attached.

- Any series of 1-2-3 commands performed after you press / (slash) to display the main menu and before 1-2-3 returns to READY mode is a single undoable operation. For example, if you select **/G**raph, complete a series of **G**raph commands without leaving the Graph menu, and then return 1-2-3 to READY mode, pressing (ALT)-(F4) (UNDO) cancels the entire series of **G**raph commands you completed.

- If you press (ALT)-(F4) (UNDO) after running a macro that changes worksheet data or settings, 1-2-3 returns your worksheet data and settings to the state they were in prior to running the macro regardless of how many individual changes the macro made.

- To undo your last operation, 1-2-3 must reserve a portion of memory to keep a copy of the worksheet. This reduces the amount of available memory.

When Does 1-2-3 Back Up the Worksheet?

1-2-3 creates a temporary backup copy of the worksheet when you press any key that might lead to a worksheet change. This allows 1-2-3 to restore your work to its previous state if you press (ALT)-(F4) (UNDO). For example, 1-2-3 backs up the worksheet when you press / (slash) to display the main menu, press a character that begins a label or value, or press the (F8) (TABLE) or (F9) (QUERY) key. 1-2-3 does not wait for you to complete a command or cell entry before backing up the worksheet. Therefore, if you press / to select a new command but then press (ESC) because you decide you want to undo your previous operation, you will not be able to undo the previous operation because 1-2-3 backed up the worksheet again as soon as you pressed /.

1-2-3 does not back up the worksheet when the key you press cannot lead to worksheet changes. For example, 1-2-3 does not back up the worksheet when you press a pointer-movement key, such as (←) or (PGUP), or when you press a function key that cannot change the worksheet, such as (F5) (GOTO).

1-2-3 also does not back up the worksheet if you press any of the following keys in READY mode: BACKSPACE, (CTRL)-(F1) (BOOKMARK), (CTRL)-(BREAK), (↵), (ESC), (F5) (GOTO), (F10) (GRAPH), (F1) (HELP), (INS), (ALT)-(F5) (LEARN) (when pressed to turn off the Learn feature), (F3) (NAME), (ALT)-(F2) (STEP), (F6) (WINDOW).

What Operations Can't You Undo?

1-2-3 cannot undo the following operations:

- If you suspend a 1-2-3 session so that you can use the operating system (/**S**ystem or {SYSTEM})
- If you instantly change the default directory (/**F**ile **D**irectory or /**W**orksheet **G**lobal **D**efault **D**irectory)
- If you change the Help access method (/**W**orksheet **G**lobal **D**efault **O**ther **H**elp)
- If you attach, invoke, or detach an add-in
- If you change data on a disk with /**F**ile **S**ave, /**F**ile **E**rase, or /**F**ile **X**tract
- If you change a file's reservation status

The Help Facility

1-2-3 provides context-sensitive help that describes your current action. Help includes a series of procedures (How Do I . . . ?) and a glossary of 1-2-3 terms. For example, if you highlight a command or type an @function name and then press (F1) (HELP) or click ? (Help icon), 1-2-3 displays Help text about that command or @function.

The Help index provides access to any topic. Within Help, cross-references to additional Help topics appear in a brighter intensity or in a different color. When you finish using Help, press (ESC) or click the right mouse button or the ESC box at the bottom of the Help window. Table 1.11 describes how to use the online Help system.

To	Press	Click
Start Help	(F1) (HELP)	? (HELP icon)
Display the last Help topic you used (without starting Help)	(CTRL)-(F1) (BOOKMARK)	
Display the Help Index (when Help is active)	(F1) (HELP)	F1=Index button
Display a list of Help keys	(F3)	F3=Keys button
Display Help text for highlighted topic	(↵)	The topic
Display previous Help topic	(F8) or BACKSPACE	F8=Back button
Leave Help	(ESC)	Right mouse button or ESC=Quit button
Scroll through the Help topic and cross-references	(←)(→)(↑)(↓)(PGUP) (PGDN)(TAB)(SHIFT)-(TAB)	Scroll arrow
Table 1.11 Move to beginning or end of current Help screen	(HOME)(END)	

The Access System*

You can start 1-2-3 from the operating system prompt or from the Lotus Access system. The Access system lets you start 1-2-3 by selecting the program's name from the Access menu. Access makes it easy to switch between 1-2-3 and the 1-2-3 utility programs (Install, Translate, and PrintGraph). When you start 1-2-3 from the Access system, you return to the Access system when you end 1-2-3.

Note Starting 1-2-3 directly from the operating system prompt gives you more of your computer's memory for work (about 2KB). Remember, though, that when you start 1-2-3 from the operating system, you return to the operating system prompt when you end 1-2-3. If you want to use one of the 1-2-3 utility programs, you need to start it directly from the operating system or start the Access system.

To start 1-2-3 from the Access system:

1. Make sure your computer is turned on and the operating system prompt is displayed. Remove any disks from the disk drives.

2. At the operating system prompt,

   Type: **CD\123R23**

   Press: (↵) to make the 1-2-3 Release 2.3 program directory the current directory

*The Access system is not included in the Addison-Wesley Lotus 1-2-3 Release 2.3 Educational Software Series software.

3. Type: **LOTUS**

   Press: ⏎

   The Access menu appears at the top of the screen.

   The Access system contains the five menu options shown in Table 1.12.

Option	Description
1-2-3	Starts 1-2-3
PrintGraph	Starts the PrintGraph utility through which you print 1-2-3 graph files
Translate	Starts the Translate utility with which you can transfer data between 1-2-3 and other programs
Install	Starts the Install utility with which you set up 1-2-3
Exit	Leaves the Access menu and returns you to the operating system

Table 1.12

To select a menu option from the Access system menu, move the highlight to that option and press ⏎.

Chapter 2

Commands

This chapter is divided into nine sections. The sections are **W**orksheet commands, **R**ange commands, the **C**opy command, the **M**ove command, **F**ile commands, **P**rint commands, **G**raph commands, **D**ata commands, and the **S**ystem command. At the beginning of each section, a functional summary describes the tasks you can perform with each command by choosing different options or command sequences from the command menu.

The command sequences for each procedure are printed in the left margin. The first letter of each command option is in boldface type, indicating that the option can be selected by typing the boldface letter if appropriate. Settings and options for a procedure (as they appear on the submenu) are printed to the right of the command sequences outlined in a rectangle. The first letter of each submenu option is in boldface type, again indicating that it can be selected by typing the boldface letter. The following pages illustrate the 1-2-3 menu structure; you may find it useful to refer to these command charts in conjunction with the command descriptions.

File Commands

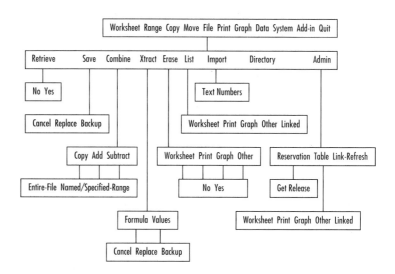

Worksheet Range Copy Move File Print Graph Data System Add-in Quit

Retrieve   Save   Combine   Xtract   Erase   List   Import   Directory   Admin

No Yes

Cancel Replace Backup

Copy Add Subtract

Entire-File Named/Specified-Range

Text Numbers

Worksheet Print Graph Other Linked

Worksheet Print Graph Other

No Yes

Reservation Table Link-Refresh

Get Release

Worksheet Print Graph Other Linked

Formula Values

Cancel Replace Backup

Print Commands

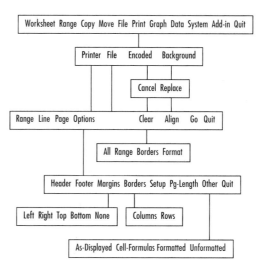

Worksheet Range Copy Move File Print Graph Data System Add-in Quit

Printer   File   Encoded   Background

Cancel Replace

Range Line Page Options   Clear   Align   Go   Quit

All Range Borders Format

Header Footer Margins Borders Setup Pg-Length Other Quit

Left Right Top Bottom None   Columns Rows

As-Displayed Cell-Formulas Formatted Unformatted

Range
Commands

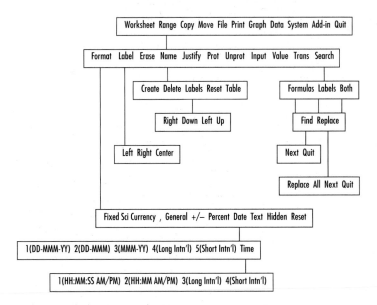

Worksheet Range Copy Move File Print Graph Data System Add-in Quit

Format Label Erase Name Justify Prot Unprot Input Value Trans Search

Create Delete Labels Reset Table

Right Down Left Up

Formulas Labels Both

Find Replace

Next Quit

Replace All Next Quit

Left Right Center

Fixed Sci Currency , General +/− Percent Date Text Hidden Reset

1(DD-MMM-YY) 2(DD-MMM) 3(MMM-YY) 4(Long Intn'l) 5(Short Intn'l) Time

1(HH:MM:SS AM/PM) 2(HH:MM AM/PM) 3(Long Intn'l) 4(Short Intn'l)

Data Commands

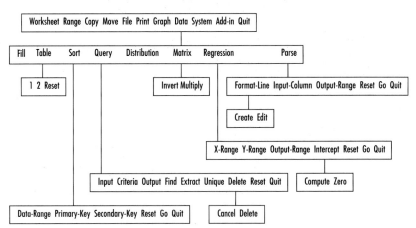

Worksheet Range Copy Move File Print Graph Data System Add-in Quit

Fill   Table   Sort   Query   Distribution   Matrix   Regression   Parse

1 2 Reset

Invert Multiply

Format-Line Input-Column Output-Range Reset Go Quit

Create Edit

X-Range Y-Range Output-Range Intercept Reset Go Quit

Input Criteria Output Find Extract Unique Delete Reset Quit

Compute Zero

Data-Range Primary-Key Secondary-Key Reset Go Quit

Cancel Delete

Graph
Commands

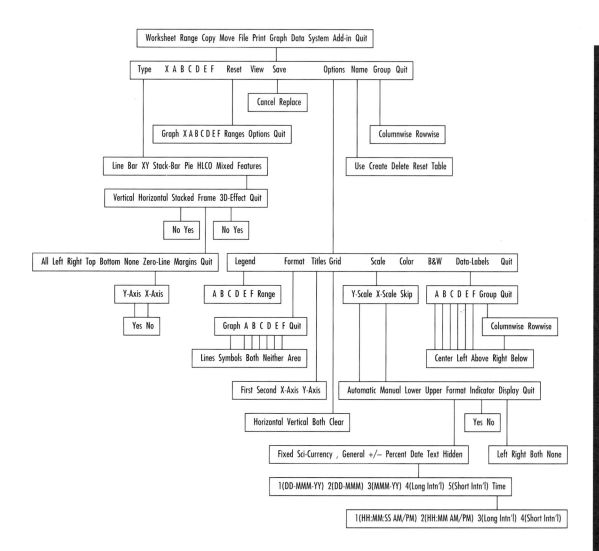

Worksheet Commands

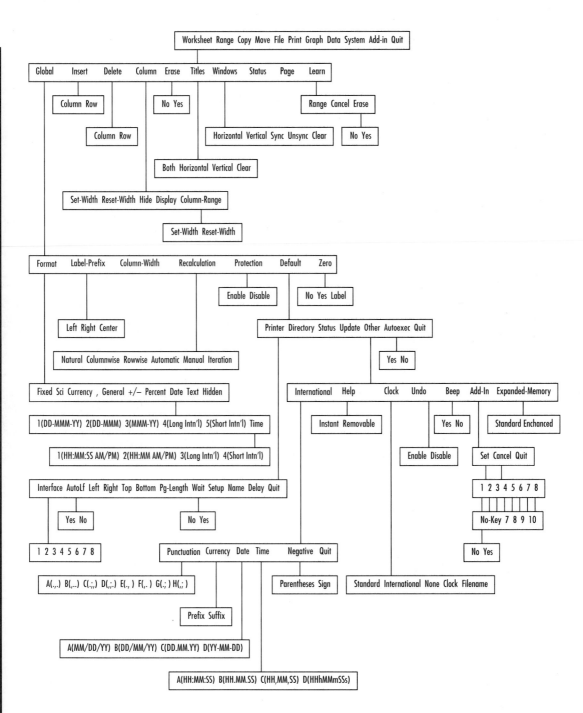

Setting Defaults

A 1-2-3 worksheet has many settings, or defaults, when you start working in it. There are three different kinds of defaults:

- An **initial setting** is one that 1-2-3 uses unless you specify a different setting. For example, the default currency sign is $ (dollar sign) as a prefix unless you change it.

- A **global setting** is one that affects the entire worksheet or the entire 1-2-3 program. When you save a worksheet, you save its global settings, with the exception of the zero display setting. You can override many global settings on the local level (see the section on "Range Commands").

- A **configuration setting** is one that 1-2-3 uses each time you begin a session, for example, the collating sequence, the default directory, the Help access method, and printer instructions. Configuration settings are stored in a file named 123.CNF and appear in the Default Settings dialog box.

The /Worksheet Global commands let you change the default settings of the worksheet for the current 1-2-3 session and the configuration settings that 1-2-3 uses every time you start a 1-2-3 session.

Worksheet Commands

The /Worksheet commands let you control the display and organization of your work. They also let you establish global settings, which are 1-2-3 settings that affect the entire worksheet and the 1-2-3 program.

The /Worksheet commands perform these tasks:

/Worksheet Global	Lets you change the default settings of the worksheet for the current 1-2-3 session and the configuration settings that 1-2-3 uses every time you begin a 1-2-3 session.
/Worksheet Insert	Inserts blank columns or rows in the worksheet.
/Worksheet Delete	Deletes columns and rows from the worksheet.

/Worksheet **C**olumn	Establishes the width for one or more columns, resets column width, and hides and redisplays columns.
/Worksheet **E**rase	Removes the current worksheet from memory.
/Worksheet **T**itles	Freezes row or column headings so that they remain visible while you scroll through the worksheet.
/Worksheet **W**indow	Splits the worksheet into two horizontal or vertical views, which you can scroll independently or together.
/Worksheet **S**tatus	Displays information in a dialog box about memory, hardware, and circular references.
/Worksheet **P**age	Places a page break in a worksheet for printing.
/Worksheet **L**earn	Specifies a range in which keystrokes are recorded when the Learn feature is turned on.

/Worksheet **G**lobal

/Worksheet **G**lobal lets you change the default settings for the current 1-2-3 session and the configuration settings that 1-2-3 uses every time you begin a 1-2-3 session. When you select /Worksheet **G**lobal, the following menu appears:

Menu Item	Description
Format	Sets the global display format for numeric values and formulas.
Label-Prefix	Sets global alignment for text labels.
Column-Width	Sets global column width.
Recalculation	Sets how and how many times a worksheet recalculates.
Protection	Turns on global protection.
Default	Specifies the 1-2-3 configuration settings.
Zero	Specifies the display for zeros.

When you select /Worksheet **G**lobal, 1-2-3 displays the Global Settings dialog box. You can change settings by selecting options in the dialog box or by selecting the corresponding commands from the menu above the dialog box. Press ⒡
(EDIT) or click the dialog box to activate it.

/Worksheet **G**lobal **F**ormat

Fixed Sci Currency , General +/- Percent Date Text Hidden

/Worksheet **G**lobal **F**ormat sets the way numeric values and formulas are displayed for the entire worksheet. It does not affect the data itself. Labels are unaffected by the command.

If you choose **F**ixed, **S**ci, **C**urrency, **,** (comma), or **P**ercent, you need to specify the number of decimal places. Press ⏎ to accept the default setting of 2, or type a different number (0–15) and press ⏎.

If you choose **D**ate, select one of the five date formats, or select **T**ime and one of the four time formats.

In date formats, a positive number (rounded off to an integer) is defined as the serial number of a date from 1 (1 January 1900) to 73050 (31 December 2099). Use the @DATE and @NOW functions to generate these serial numbers.

In time formats, fractional parts of serial numbers represent time (.000 = midnight, .5 = noon, 15/24 = 3:00 PM, and so on). Use the @TIME and @NOW functions to generate these serial numbers.

See Table 2.6, in the "Range Commands" section in this chapter, for a description of each format.

If a value's formatted display does not fit within its column width, asterisks appear in the cell. 1-2-3 retains values with a precision of 15 decimal places regardless of format.

/Worksheet **G**lobal **L**abel-Prefix

Left Right Center

/Worksheet **G**lobal **L**abel-Prefix sets the alignment of labels for the entire worksheet. Labels can be left-aligned, right-aligned, or centered.

The default label alignment is **L**eft. All labels subsequently entered into the worksheet without a label-prefix character are aligned according to the alignment set with this command. This command does not affect existing label entries or values.

You can override the global label alignment setting either by using **/R**ange **L**abel after you enter a label or by typing a label prefix as the first character in a label you are entering.

/Worksheet **G**lobal **C**olumn-Width

/Worksheet **G**lobal **C**olumn-Width sets the width for all worksheet columns but does not affect those columns whose widths you set individually with **/W**orksheet **C**olumn.

Column width can be from 1 to 240 characters. Initially, the default setting is 9. Use → or ← to increase or decrease the width (the screen displays the effect of each change), or enter a number. To see the current global column width setting, select **/W**orksheet **G**lobal.

/Worksheet **G**lobal **R**ecalculation

Natural Columnwise Rowwise Automatic Manual Iteration

/Worksheet **G**lobal **R**ecalculation controls when, in what order, and how many times formulas in the worksheet are recalculated (see Table 2.1).

Menu Item	Description
Recalculation Order:	
Natural	Before recalculating a particular formula, 1-2-3 recalculates any other formulas that it depends on. For example, if the formula in cell B7 depends on the formula in cell C28, 1-2-3 recalculates the formula in C28 before it calculates the one in B7. This is the initial default order of recalculation.
Columnwise	1-2-3 begins recalculating at the top of column A and proceeds to the bottom of the column. It then recalculates columns B, C, and so on.
Rowwise	1-2-3 begins recalculating at the beginning of row 1 and proceeds to the end of the row. It then recalculates rows 2, 3, and so on.
Recalculation Method:	
Automatic	1-2-3 recalculates any formulas that are affected each time you change the contents of a cell. **A**utomatic is the default setting.
Manual	1-2-3 recalculates formulas only when you press (F9) (CALC). The CALC indicator appears in the lower right corner of the screen whenever any cell entries have changed since the last recalculation. Press (F9) (CALC) when you want to update the worksheet.
Recalculation Passes:	
Iteration	Sets the number of times (1 through 50) 1-2-3 recalculates formulas when the recalculation method is set to **C**olumnwise or **R**owwise, or when recalculation is set to **N**atural and there is a circular reference. The default setting is 1. This setting has no effect if recalculation is set to **N**atural and there are no circular references.

Table 2.1

- Use **M**anual recalculation when 1-2-3 takes a long time to calculate a large or complex worksheet or to speed up macro execution.

- Use **C**olumnwise or **R**owwise when you need to control the order in which 1-2-3 recalculates formulas.

- When the recalculation order is **N**atural, 1-2-3 recalculates only those cells that have changed since the worksheet was last recalculated and the cells that depend on them. This feature is called minimal recalculation. If you change the recalculation order to a setting other than **N**atural, 1-2-3 does not use minimal recalculation and will recalculate all the formulas in the worksheet when you make a change.

Note There are several @functions that 1-2-3 updates each time it recalculates the worksheet — even when minimal recalculation is in effect — because their values may change even if you do not modify the worksheet. 1-2-3 also recalculates cells that depend on cells that contain these @functions: @@, @CELL, @CELLPOINTER, @DATEVALUE, @ISAAF, @ISAPP, @NOW, @RAND, @STRING, @TIMEVALUE, @VALUE.

/Worksheet **G**lobal **P**rotection

Enable Disable

/**W**orksheet **G**lobal **P**rotection works in conjunction with /**R**ange **P**rot and /**R**ange **U**nprot to prevent changes to particular cells.

When the Protection facility is turned on with /Worksheet Global Protection Enable, you cannot make changes to any cells in the worksheet. PR is displayed in the control panel when the cell pointer is on a protected cell.

Once the Protection facility is turned on, you can use /Range Unprot if you want to make changes to specific cells. U is displayed in the control panel when the cell pointer is on an unprotected cell and protection is enabled.

While protection is enabled, you cannot delete columns or rows that include protected cells or make cells visible whose contents you have hidden with /Range Format Hidden. You can, however, still erase the entire worksheet with the /Worksheet Erase command. Choosing Disable turns off global protection and allows you to change any cell entry, even if it has been protected with /Range Prot.

/Worksheet Global Default

Printer Directory Status Update Other Autoexec Quit

The /Worksheet Global Default commands allow you to specify global defaults that affect the current 1-2-3 session. You can also save these global settings as configuration settings, which means 1-2-3 uses them in future 1-2-3 sessions. To specify global worksheet settings that you can save as configuration settings, select /Worksheet Global Default. Press (F2) (EDIT) or click the dialog box to activate it.

Default settings you can establish for yourself with these commands include the following:

- Type of printer and its connection, as well as the printed page format
- Directory that 1-2-3 automatically uses when searching for files
- International and clock display formats
- Method of using the Help facility
- Autoexecuted macros and autoattached add-ins

These settings are preset in 1-2-3. You can change these settings and establish your own defaults for future sessions by using the /Worksheet Global Default Update command.

/Worksheet Global Default Printer

Interface AutoLF Left Right Top Bottom Pg-Length Wait Setup Name Delay Quit

/Worksheet Global Default Printer specifies the default printer and interface settings and the default settings for printed pages.

Table 2.2 shows the initial default settings supplied by 1-2-3.

Menu Item	Description	Choices
Interface	Specifies the connection between 1-2-3 and your printer as parallel or serial. If you select a serial interface, you must also supply a baud rate (speed of transmission) and set your printer to 8 bits, no parity, and 1 stop bit (except 2 stop bits at 110 baud). Choices 5 through 8 refer to devices accessed through DOS on a local area network.	(1) Parallel 1 (default) (2) Serial 1 (3) Parallel 2 (4) Serial 2 (5) DOS Device LPT1 (6) DOS Device LPT2 (7) DOS Device LPT3 (8) DOS Device LPT4
AutoLF	Specifies whether your printer automatically issues a linefeed after a carriage return. If what you print is double spaced, set AutoLF to Yes; if the paper does not advance, set AutoLF to No.	Yes No (default)
Left	Sets left margin (number of spaces) on printed page.	0–240 (default is 4)
Right	Sets right margin (number of spaces) on printed page.	0–240 (default is 76)
Top	Sets top margin (number of lines) on printed page.	0–32 (default is 2)
Bottom	Sets bottom margin (number of lines) on printed page.	0–32 (default is 2)
Pg-Length	Sets length (number of lines) of printed page.	1–100 (default is 66)
Wait	Allows you to insert a pause at the end of each printed page to change paper in single-sheet feed printers.	Yes No (default)
Setup	Specifies a string of blank control characters to be sent to your printer before printing begins. (Some printers need to be initialized.) The default setting is blank for no setup string. (See the printer control codes in your printer manual for a description of how to enter setup strings.)	
Name	Specifies which printer to use. If you selected more than one text printer when you installed 1-2-3, a list of the printers appears when you choose this menu item.	The default is the first printer you selected when installing 1-2-3.
Delay	Specifies the amount of time (in minutes) that 1-2-3 waits for your printer to print before it displays an error message.	0–30 (default is 2)
Quit	Returns you to the Worksheet Global Default menu.	

Table 2.2

*/**W**orksheet **G**lobal **D**efault **D**irectory*

/Worksheet Global Default Directory specifies the directory that 1-2-3 will automatically search (when you retrieve a file) and write to (when you save a file) if you do not specify a directory at the time. If necessary, press (ESC) to clear the current directory before entering the new directory.

If you execute the command and clear the existing setting without providing a new directory, 1-2-3 uses the directory that was current when you started the program.

When you use /Worksheet Global Default Directory, you can enter ¦ (split vertical bar) as the first character of the default directory name to specify that 1-2-3 should not expand the entry to a full path or convert it to uppercase.

You can always override the default directory by typing in a directory when you specify a file with the /File commands.

/Worksheet Global Default Status

/Worksheet Global Default Status displays the current settings established by the other /Worksheet Global Default commands.

To clear the status screen and return to the worksheet, choose Quit. Use the other /Worksheet Global Default commands to change the settings.

/Worksheet Global Default Update

/Worksheet Global Default Update saves the current settings established by the other /Worksheet Global Default commands in a configuration file (123.CNF). The next time you start 1-2-3, the new default settings will be read from the configuration file.

/Worksheet Global Default Other

/Worksheet Global Default Other provides options for the following seven settings.

/Worksheet Global Default Other International

Punctuation Currency Date Time Negative Quit

/Worksheet Global Default Other International specifies display for punctuation, currency, date, time, and negative number formats. Choose Quit to return to the previous menu.

Table 2.3 describes the options for this command.

Menu Item	Description	Choices
Punctuation	Specifies which characters 1-2-3 uses as the point and thousands separators on numbers and as the argument separator in @functions and macro keywords. The eight settings (A through H) provide fixed combinations of period, comma, and space separators and are listed in the order of decimal point separator, argument separator, and thousands separator.	(A) (.,,) (initial) (B) (,..) (C) (.;,) (D) (,;.) (E) (.,) (F) (,.) (G) (.;) (H) (,;)
Currency	Specifies the alphanumeric sequence to use as the currency sign. It also specifies whether the currency sign precedes or follows the value. You can use any Lotus International Character Set (LICS) character.	Alphanumeric sequence (initially $) preceding value
Date	Specifies the international date format setting (D4 and D5). The D4 format setting displays month, day, and year; D5 displays only month and day. 1-2-3 uses the D4 setting when it displays the date at the bottom of the screen if Clock is set to International. This setting affects how you enter the argument for @DATEVALUE. If you use this @function with either of the international formats, you must use the form specified here.	(A) MM/DD/YY (initial) (B) DD/MM/YY (C) DD.MM.YY (D) YY-MM-DD

Table 2.3

Menu Item	Description	Choices
Time	Specifies the international time format settings (D8 and D9). The D8 format setting includes hours, minutes, and seconds; D9 includes only hours and minutes. All the international time formats are 24 hour instead of 12 hour. 1-2-3 uses the D9 setting when it displays the time at the bottom of the screen if **Clock** is set to **International**. This setting affects how you enter the argument for @TIMEVALUE. If you use this @function with either of the international formats, you must use the form specified here.	(A) HH:MM:SS (initial) (B) HH.MM.SS (C) HH,MM,SS (D) HHhMMmSSs
Negative	Specifies whether 1-2-3 uses parentheses (default) or a minus sign for negative values in cells formatted as **,** (comma) or **Currency**.	Parenthesis or Sign
Quit	Returns you to the Worksheet Global Default menu.	

Table 2.3 Continued

/Worksheet **G**lobal **D**efault **O**ther **H**elp

Instant Removable

/**W**orksheet **G**lobal **D**efault **O**ther **H**elp specifies the way 1-2-3 accesses the Help facility.

If you choose **I**nstant, 1-2-3 opens the Help file when you press the (F1) (HELP), and the file remains open throughout the session. When you press (F1) (HELP) again, 1-2-3 reads the file instantly. If you choose **R**emovable, 1-2-3 closes the Help file when you leave the Help facility.

/Worksheet **G**lobal **D**efault **O**ther **C**lock

Standard International None Clock Filename

/**W**orksheet **G**lobal **D**efault **O**ther **C**lock specifies the display for the date-and-time indicator.

Standard displays the date in DD-MMM-YY format and the time in HH:MM AM/PM format. **I**nternational displays the formats specified in **D**efault **I**nternational **S**ettings. **N**one means nothing is displayed in the date-and-time indicator. **C**lock displays the date and time in the most recently selected format. **F**ilename displays the current worksheet's file name instead of the date and time.

/Worksheet **G**lobal **D**efault **O**ther **U**ndo

Enable Disable

/**W**orksheet **G**lobal **D**efault **O**ther **U**ndo lets you turn the Undo feature on and off. When the Undo feature is on, you can press (ALT)-(F4) (UNDO) to cancel any changes made to the worksheet since 1-2-3 was last in READY mode.

Enable turns on the Undo feature; **D**isable turns it off.

/Worksheet **G**lobal **D**efault **O**ther **B**eep

Yes No

/Worksheet **G**lobal **D**efault **O**ther **B**eep lets you control whether 1-2-3 sounds the computer's bell when an error occurs and during {BEEP} commands in a macro.

If you choose **Y**es, 1-2-3 will sound the bell. If you choose **N**o, 1-2-3 will not sound the bell.

/Worksheet **G**lobal **D**efault **O**ther **A**dd-In

Set Cancel Quit

/Worksheet **G**lobal **D**efault **O**ther **A**dd-In lets you configure 1-2-3 to automatically attach an add-in whenever you start 1-2-3. You can specify up to eight autoattach add-ins. You can also specify whether you want 1-2-3 to automatically invoke one of the autoattach add-ins.

Choosing **S**et sets and attaches an autoattach add-in. Choosing **C**ancel cancels and detaches an autoattach add-in. Choosing **Q**uit returns you to the Worksheet Global Default menu.

/Worksheet **G**lobal **D**efault **O**ther **E**xpanded-Memory

Standard Enhanced

/Worksheet **G**lobal **D**efault **O**ther **E**xpanded-Memory lets you specify how you want 1-2-3 to use available expanded memory. Choose **S**tandard if you want to maximize processing speed. Choose **E**nhanced if you are working with a large worksheet.

/Worksheet **G**lobal **D**efault **A**utoexec

Yes No

/Worksheet **G**lobal **D**efault **A**utoexec lets you tell 1-2-3 whether to run autoexecute macros, macros named \0 (zero), when it retrieves a file that contains one.

Choosing **Y**es automatically executes macros named \0 (zero). Choosing **N**o does not automatically execute macros named \0 (zero).

/Worksheet **G**lobal **Z**ero

No Yes Label

/Worksheet **G**lobal **Z**ero specifies whether 1-2-3 displays a zero, a label, or nothing in cells that contain either the number zero or a formula that evaluates to zero.

Choosing **N**o displays zero in cells whose value is zero (the default setting).

Choosing **Y**es causes cells whose value is zero to appear blank. 1-2-3 continues to display the contents of these cells in the control panel.

Choosing **L**abel displays a label in cells whose value is zero. Type the label you want in the text box. 1-2-3 continues to display the contents of these cells in the control panel.

If you select **/W**orksheet **G**lobal **Z**ero **Y**es, it is a good idea to enable worksheet protection (**/W**orksheet **G**lobal **P**rotection **E**nable) so that you do not inadvertently write over data in cells that appear empty.

/Worksheet **I**nsert

Column Row

/Worksheet **I**nsert inserts one or more blank columns or rows in the worksheet.

When you insert rows or columns, existing rows or columns move down or over to make room for the new rows or columns, and 1-2-3 adjusts any formulas so that they continue to refer to the same data. If you insert rows or columns into a named range or a range that appears in a formula, the size of the range increases. Inserted rows or columns assume the global formats and column width of the worksheet.

CAUTION   Inserting rows may insert blank cells in macros that invalidate the macros.

/Worksheet **D**elete

Column Row

/Worksheet **D**elete permanently removes one or more rows or columns from the worksheet.

All columns to the right of a deleted column shift to the left, and all rows below a deleted row shift up. Deletions inside ranges make the range smaller. Deleting a corner of a range invalidates the range.

Formulas that refer to a deleted cell or to a range with a deleted corner now have the value ERR. 1-2-3 adjusts all other formulas and named ranges so that they continue to refer to the same data.

CAUTION   **/W**orksheet **D**elete permanently deletes rows and columns from the worksheet. To avoid possible data loss, be sure these rows or columns do not contain important data. If you make a mistake and the Undo feature is on, press (ALT)-(F4) (UNDO) immediately to restore the worksheet to its original state.

/Worksheet **C**olumn

Set-Width Reset-Width Hide Display Column-Range

/Worksheet **C**olumn sets the width of one or more columns, resets columns to the global column width, and hides or redisplays columns. Table 2.4 describes the options for this command.

Menu Item	Description
Set-Width	Changes the width of the current column (overrides the global default column width).
Reset-Width	Resets the current column width to the global default column width (nine characters).
Hide	Hides one or more columns without erasing the data.
Display	Redisplays one or more hidden columns.
Column-Range	Changes the column width of a range of columns (overriding the global default column width) or resets a range of columns to the global default column width (nine characters).

Table 2.4

Use **/W**orksheet **C**olumn **S**et-Width if a cell displays asterisks because it is too narrow for the values it contains.

/Worksheet **E**rase

No Yes

/Worksheet **E**rase removes the current worksheet from memory and replaces it with a blank worksheet. If you want to keep the current worksheet, save it with **/F**ile **S**ave before you use **/W**orksheet **E**rase.

If you choose **N**o, 1-2-3 returns to READY mode without erasing the worksheet. If you choose **Y**es, 1-2-3 erases the worksheet.

/Worksheet **T**itles

Both Horizontal Vertical Clear

/Worksheet **T**itles freezes one or more rows or columns along the top and left edges of a worksheet so that they remain in view as you scroll through the worksheet.

Position the cell pointer one row below the rows you want to freeze, in the column to the right of the columns you want to freeze, or one row below and one column to the right of the rows and columns you want to freeze.

Both freezes the rows above and the columns to the left of the cell pointer. **H**orizontal freezes the rows above the cell pointer. **V**ertical freezes the columns to the left of the cell pointer. **C**lear unfreezes all title rows and columns.

/Worksheet **W**indow

Horizontal Vertical Sync Unsync Clear

/Worksheet **W**indow splits the screen into two horizontal or vertical windows, turns synchronized scrolling on or off, and restores single-window display. Table 2.5 describes the options for this command.

When you create two windows, you can use one to display one part of the worksheet and the second to display the same or a different part of the worksheet.

Press (F6) (WINDOW) or click the window to move the cell pointer from one window to the other.

Menu Item	Description
Horizontal	Creates two windows with the screen split horizontally. Move the cell pointer to the row you want to use as the top edge of the second window, and select /Worksheet Window Horizontal.
Vertical	Creates two windows with the screen split vertically. Move the cell pointer to the column you want to use as the left edge of the second window, and select /Worksheet Window Vertical.
Sync	Synchronizes window scrolling. For horizontal windows, the same columns are visible in both windows. For vertical windows, the same rows are visible in both windows. This is the default setting.
Unsync	Causes windows to scroll independently in all directions.
Clear	Restores to single-window display.

Table 2.5

Commands that change the worksheet display affect both windows, except for /Worksheet Column, /Worksheet Global Column-Width, and /Worksheet Titles, which affect only the current window.

When you select Clear, the single window uses the titles, column widths, global formats, and global label prefixes of the window that was on top or on the left.

/Worksheet Status

/Worksheet Status displays information in a dialog box about available conventional memory, available expanded memory, EMS (Expanded Memory System) memory, type of memory in which cell pointers are stored, math coprocessor, and circular references.

Circular reference displays the address of a cell where the formula refers to the cell itself. If you eliminate the circular reference in the cell, select /Worksheet Status again to see if another cell has a circular reference. The status screen displays only one circular reference at a time.

/Worksheet Page

/Worksheet Page inserts a row and creates a page break (::) in a worksheet, which causes 1-2-3 to begin a new page when you print the worksheet.

Before you use the command, move the cell pointer to the leftmost column of the range you want to print and to the row where you want the page to begin. To remove a page break symbol, use /Range Erase, /Worksheet Delete Row, or (DEL).

/Worksheet Learn

Range Cancel Erase

/Worksheet Learn specifies a range in which to record keystrokes to run as a macro. (For more information about the Learn feature, see Chapter 3.)

Range specifies the range where 1-2-3 will record keystrokes as labels. **C**ancel cancels the current learn range. **E**rase clears the contents of all cells in the current learn range without canceling the learn range.

Range Commands

The **/R**ange commands help you work with data quickly and efficiently by letting you work with a group of cells rather than a single cell at a time. A range is any rectangular block of cells (including a single cell), such as part of a row or column, a whole row or column, parts of several rows and columns, or an entire worksheet.

The **/R**ange commands perform these tasks:

/Range **F**ormat	Changes how 1-2-3 displays data in a range.
/Range **L**abel	Left-aligns, right-aligns, or centers labels in a range.
/Range **E**rase	Erases data in a range without changing the format or protection status.
/Range **N**ame	Creates, modifies, deletes, or generates tables of range names.
/Range **J**ustify	Rearranges a column of labels as a paragraph to fit within a specified width.

CAUTION   Do not use **/R**ange **J**ustify on a column whose contents are used in macros or text formulas; if you do, the macros may not work.

/Range **P**rot	Reprotects cells in a range (that have been unprotected with **/R**ange **U**nprot) when global worksheet protection is on.
/Range **U**nprot	Unprotects and allows changes to cells in a range when global worksheet protection is on; allows changes to cells in a range that will be used with **/R**ange **I**nput.
/Range **I**nput	Restricts cell-pointer movement and data entry to unprotected cells in a range used along with **/R**ange **U**nprot.
/Range **V**alue	Copies a range of data, replacing any copied formulas with their current values.
/Range **T**rans	Copies a range of data to a new location and transposes it from rows to columns, replacing any copied formulas with their current values.
/Range **S**earch	Finds or replaces a specified string in a range.

/Range **F**ormat

Fixed Sci Currency **,** General +/- Percent Date Text Hidden Reset

/Range **F**ormat sets the numeric format for a range of cells, overriding the default numeric format. The numeric format determines the appearance of numbers but does not affect the display of labels.

- The numeric format changes the appearance of numbers, not their actual value. You may, for example, choose to display a number without its decimal places. However, 1-2-3 still stores the number with its decimal places for calculations.

- A numeric format you choose with /Range Format overrides the default numeric format in which numbers automatically appear. (The default numeric format is initially General, but you can change the default with /Worksheet Global Format.) Changing the format has no effect on the way you enter numbers.

- A numeric format affects the appearance of numbers and formula values but has no effect on labels unless you choose the Hidden format. You can hide any kind of cell entry with the Hidden format.

- To use date and time formats, you must first generate serial numbers that represent dates and times. You produce serial numbers with @functions (@DATE, @DATEVALUE, @TIME, @TIMEVALUE, and @NOW). (See Chapter 4.)

- Global default settings determine certain date and time formats. You can set these defaults with the /Worksheet Global Default Other International command. Global default settings also determine the currency sign and its position and the separator used to separate thousands. You can set these defaults with the /Worksheet Global Default Other International command.

Table 2.6 describes the command options.

Menu Item	Description	Examples
Fixed	Constant number of decimal places (0 to 15). Leading zero integers always appear.	12 −125.00 0.567
Sci	Scientific (exponential) notation with a specified number of decimal places (0 to 15) in the multiplier. Exponent of 10 from -99 to +99.	−43E + 1.2E + 01 1.245E + 22 6.24E − 24
Currency	Displays numbers with a currency symbol. Separators between thousands. Negative values displayed with a minus sign or in parentheses. Leading zero integers always appear. Decimal places (0 to 15).	$12.43 ($4.25) −.246 $8.999 $0.67
, (comma)	Separators between thousands. Negative values in parentheses. Leading zero integers always appear. Decimal places (0 to 15).	8,999.00 (15,000) −15,000 0.55
General	Trailing zeros suppressed (after decimal pointer). Leading zero integers always appear. No thousands separator. Negative values displayed with a minus sign. This is the default numeric format. Very large and very small numbers appear in scientific (exponent) format.	12.427 0.45 −4.25 1.3E + 12 2E − 07

Table 2.6

Menu Item	Description	Examples
+/−	Horizontal bar graph. Each symbol equals one integer. Symbols: + for positive values, - for negative values, . for zero and values between −1 and +1. Limited by column width.	+ + + − − −
Percent	Percentage, with specified number of decimal places (0 to 15). Displays the value times 100, followed by a percent sign.	1242.7% −4.25%
Date	1 DD-MMM-YY 2 DD-MMM 3 MMM-YY 4 MM/DD/YY (long international) 5 MM/DD (short international	06-Jan-90 06-Jan Jan-90 01/06/90 01/06
Time	1 HH:MM:SS AM/PM 2 HH:MM AM/PM 3 HH:MM:SS 24-hour (long international) 4 HH:MM 24 (short international)	12:03:14 PM 04:23 AM 14:05:10 20:15
Text	Formulas (not their values) appear as entered; any numbers in the range appear in General format.	.2456 12.427 +C22/4
Hidden	Contents of the specified range do not appear on the screen although they still exist.	
Reset	Restores default numeric format for specified range. Redisplays all or part of hidden range of cells.	

Table 2.6 Continued

When the cell pointer is on a cell that you have formatted, the first letter of the format name and the number of decimal places you chose appear in parentheses before the cell contents on the control panel. For example, (CO) means **C**urrency format with 0 decimal places.

In a format other than **G**eneral, if a number is too large to fit in a cell, 1-2-3 displays asterisks in the cell instead of the number. Use **/W**orksheet **C**olumn **S**et-Width or **/W**orksheet **G**lobal **C**olumn-Width to widen the column so that the number can be displayed. In **G**eneral format, 1-2-3 displays a large number in scientific notation.

A cell retains the numeric format that you assign to it with **/R**ange **F**ormat, even if you subsequently erase its contents with **/R**ange **E**rase.

If you move the contents of a range that you have formatted, the moved data retain their numeric format. The area you moved the range from, however, reverts to the default numeric format.

When you copy data in a formatted range, 1-2-3 copies cell formats with the date. When you move data from a formatted range, 1-2-3 moves the cell format with the data. The original range reverts to the global cell format.

/Range **L**abel

Left Right Center

/Range Label aligns existing labels in a range of cells. 1-2-3 can position labels at the left edge, the right edge, or in the center of cells in a range. You cannot "preformat" a range before entering labels in it; /Range Label affects only existing labels and has no effect on numbers, which are always right-aligned.

1-2-3 displays all the labels in the specified range according to the alignment you selected. Any labels you subsequently enter in this range, however, are unaffected by the alignment you chose.

/Range Erase

/Range Erase removes the contents of cells in a range without changing the format or protection status. Before you use this command, be sure you do not need the data. If necessary, first save the worksheet with /File Save.

/Range Name

/Range Name creates, modifies, deletes, or generates tables of range names. When you select /Range Name, the following menu appears:

Create — Creates or modifies a range name. If you enter a range name that is identical to an existing range name, 1-2-3 reassigns the range name to the new range.

Delete — Deletes a range name. The data in the range remains unchanged.

Labels — Creates range names for single-cell ranges, using labels in adjacent cells as the range names.

Reset — Deletes all range names in the current worksheet. The data in the ranges remains unchanged.

CAUTION All named macro labels are deleted with /Range Name Reset.

Table — Creates a two-column table in the worksheet that alphabetically lists range names and their corresponding addresses.

/Range Name Create

/Range Name Create creates or modifies a range name. If you enter a range name that is identical to an existing range name, 1-2-3 reassigns the range name to the new range.

A range name can be up to 15 characters long. To prevent confusion when using range names in formulas and advanced macro commands, do not use spaces, commas, semicolons, or the characters + * − / & > < { @ and # in a range name. Also avoid names that look like cell addresses, such Q2. Do not create range names that begin with a number or consist entirely of numbers. 1-2-3 does not distinguish between uppercase and lowercase letters.

To change the cells an existing range name refers to or to view the current location of a named range, select a name from the menu of range names 1-2-3 displays, and press ⏎.

If you are just viewing the range, press ⏎ to get back to READY mode; otherwise, specify the range you are naming or whose definition you are changing, and press ⏎.

If you move data or insert or delete columns or rows so that either the upper left or lower right corner of a named range is affected, 1-2-3 modifies the named range.

If you are unsure of the name you assigned when 1-2-3 requests a range, press ⒡⒊ (NAME) to see a list of range names you have assigned, and select the one you want.

When writing a macro, name the macro by assigning a range name to the first cell in the range that contains the macro.

1-2-3 saves range names as part of the worksheet when you save the worksheet with **/F**ile **S**ave.

/Range **N**ame **D**elete

/Range **N**ame **D**elete removes a range name but leaves the contents of the range unchanged.

1-2-3 deletes the name that you specify. You can no longer use this name in formulas or in commands that require a range specification. If a formula previously used this name, however, it continues to refer to the same cells by cell address rather than by name.

/Range **N**ame **L**abels

Right Down Left Up

/Range **N**ame **L**abels names single-cell ranges, using existing labels located in adjacent cells for the range names.

When you have labels that can serve as range names next to the cells you want to name, **/R**ange **N**ame **L**abels is useful. You can use **/R**ange **N**ame **L**abels to assign names to the fields of the first record of a database. 1-2-3 does not assign numbers as range names and uses only the first 15 characters of a label for the range name.

Position the cell pointer on one of the corner cells in a range of labels you want to use, then select **/R**ange **N**ame **L**abels. Choose **R**ight, **D**own, **L**eft, or **U**p, depending on the direction of the cells you are naming in relation to the labels, then specify the range of labels you are using to name the adjacent cells.

1-2-3 names each cell in the direction you indicated with the corresponding label in the cell in the range you specified.

If a label you used to name a range duplicates an existing range name, 1-2-3 erases the previous range address and uses the new cell address. 1-2-3 does not warn you of this change. If a formula referred to the named range as it was previously defined, it continues to refer to the same range, but by range address not by range name.

/Range **N**ame **R**eset

/Range **N**ame **R**eset deletes all the range names in the current worksheet but leaves the content unchanged. Formulas that used range names continue to refer to the same ranges, but by range addresses not by range names.

CAUTION   All named macro labels are deleted with **/R**ange **N**ame **R**eset. To delete individual range names, use **/R**ange **N**ame **D**elete.

/Range Name Table   /Range Name Table lists alphabetically all the range names and their corresponding addresses in a two-column table in the worksheet.

Decide on a location for the range name table before you select the command. Then select **/R**ange **N**ame **T**able, and specify the upper left cell of the location.

CAUTION   1-2-3 will write over existing data in the range when it creates the table, which is two columns wide and as many rows long as there are range names, plus one. If the Undo feature is on, you can press (ALT)-(F4) (UNDO) to restore the worksheet if necessary.

/Range Justify   /Range Justify rearranges a column of labels as a paragraph to fit within a specified width.

CAUTION   Do not use this command on a column whose contents are used in macros or text formulas; if you do, the macros and formulas may not work properly.

Move the cell pointer to the first cell in the column of labels you want to justify, then select **/R**ange **J**ustify. You will be prompted to specify a single-row or multiple-row range of the width you want the text to occupy.

The width and length of the justify range control the way 1-2-3 performs the justification. The total width of the columns in the justify range determines the maximum width of the justified labels (to a limit of 240 characters). The total number of rows in the justify range affects the result of **/R**ange **J**ustify.

If you specify a single-row range, 1-2-3 justifies the entire column of labels to fill the width of the justify range using as many rows as necessary. If the justified labels occupy more rows than the original labels, 1-2-3 moves down any subsequent data in the column (data below the justified labels). If the justified labels occupy fewer rows than the original labels, 1-2-3 moves up any subsequent data. Use a single-row justify range only if all cells below the labels you are justifying are blank or if movement of data below the labels is acceptable.

If you specify a multiple-row range, 1-2-3 restricts the justification to the exact area you have specified and does not move data below the justify range. Be sure the range is wide and deep enough to hold the entire series of justified labels.

/Range **J**ustify rearranges only one column of labels at a time. (A blank cell or numeric value marks the end of a column of labels.)

/Range Prot   /Range Prot restores protection status to a range of cells, preventing changes and deletions. **/R**ange **U**nprot lets you make changes to cells in a worksheet where global protection is enabled.

Protecting cells is particularly useful when you create a worksheet for others to use so that they cannot change or delete data in specified ranges of cells.

/Range **P**rot has no effect unless you have first enabled global protection using **/W**orksheet **G**lobal **P**rotection **E**nable, or unless the protected cells are part of the range you are working with while using the **/R**ange **I**nput command, which limits cell pointer movement to unprotected cells.

Once global protection is enabled, to change or add data, unprotect specific cells with **/R**ange **U**nprot.

When worksheet global protection is on, 1-2-3 displays PR in the control panel when the cell pointer is on a protected cell. When the cell pointer is on an unprotected cell, 1-2-3 displays U in the control panel.

/Range **U**nprot   **/R**ange **U**nprot allows changes to a range of cells when global protection for the worksheet is enabled.

Specify the range to unprotect so that you can make changes to its contents. When the cell pointer is on an unprotected cell, 1-2-3 displays U in the control panel.

If you are using the **/R**ange **I**nput command, you can move the cell pointer only to the unprotected cells in the specified range.

/Range **I**nput   **/R**ange **I**nput limits the movement of the cell pointer to unprotected cells within a specified range.

/Range **I**nput helps you set up fill-in-the-blanks entry forms to facilitate data entry. With the cell pointer limited to unprotected cells, protected cells can contain information you do not want modified. The **/R**ange **I**nput command is especially useful in conjunction with macros.

Begin by typing labels or values into the worksheet to identify the information you will be entering. Then select **/R**ange **U**nprot to remove protection from the cells in which you want to enter data. Select **/R**ange **I**nput, and specify the range you want to serve as the entry-form area. Press ⏎. The entire input range moves to the upper left corner of the screen. You can move the cell pointer only to the unprotected cells in the range.

You can now enter or edit the data in these cells using the following keys: ⏎, F1 (HELP), F2 (EDIT), BACKSPACE, HOME, END, ←, →, ↑, and ↓. To end the **/R**ange **I**nput command, press ⏎ or ESC when 1-2-3 is in READY mode.

After you finish using **/R**ange **I**nput, the cell pointer returns to its initial position.

If you use **/R**ange **I**nput as part of a macro, 1-2-3 suspends all macro activity to process data input. When you end the **/R**ange **I**nput command, 1-2-3 returns control to the macro.

/Range **V**alue   **/R**ange **V**alue converts formulas in a range to their values. **/R**ange **V**alue is useful if you want to copy only the displayed values of formulas, not the formulas themselves, to another part of the worksheet.

You specify the range of cells with the entries you want to convert (the source range) at the "Convert what?" prompt and specify the location in the worksheet where you want the values displayed (the destination range) at the "To where?" prompt.

1-2-3 copies cell values to the destination range. The copied entries include the cell format of the source range. Only the upper left corner cell of the destination range needs to be entered. 1-2-3 will use rows below this cell and columns to the right of this cell to display the values. Be sure you specify the destination range in an empty area of the worksheet since 1-2-3 will write over any data in the range.

If you specify the destination range to be the same as the source range, **/R**ange **V**alue converts the formulas to their values but overwrites the formulas in the process, so they are lost permanently.

/Range **T**rans | **/R**ange **T**rans reorders ranges from columns to rows or from rows to columns. Transposing a range leaves the original range as it was; the operation results in a rearranged copy of the original range. Any copied formulas are replaced with their current values.

You specify the range that contains the cells you want to transpose (the source range) at the "Transpose what?" prompt and specify the location in the worksheet where you want to place the transposed range (the destination range) at the "To where?" prompt. You need to specify only the upper left corner cell of the destination range. **/R**ange **T**rans may produce unexpected results if the source and destination ranges overlap.

CAUTION   If you transpose a range to a location whose cells already contain data, 1-2-3 replaces their contents with the transposed range. Formulas that depend on the previous contents of the destination range will now refer to the transposed cell entries.

/Range **S**earch

Formulas Labels Both

/Range **S**earch finds or replaces a specified string in a range. You can use either uppercase or lowercase text when searching for a string, but you must type replacement text as you want it to appear.

To search for a string, select **/R**ange **S**earch. Specify the range that contains the entry you want to find. Enter the characters to find at the prompt; you can use the wildcard characters ? or * to search for several similar entries (for example, h?t finds hat and hot, and h* finds hat, hot, head, and so on). Select **F**ormulas to search in formulas only, **L**abels to search in labels only, and **B**oth to search in both formulas and labels.

Select **F**ind to highlight the first occurrence of the search string. Then select **N**ext to highlight the next occurrence, or select **Q**uit to return to READY mode.

To replace an entry, select **/R**ange **S**earch. Specify the range that contains the entry you want to replace. Enter the characters to find at the prompt. Select **F**ormulas to search in formulas only, **L**abels to search in labels only, and **B**oth to search in both formulas and labels. Select **R**eplace (to replace the current string and search for the next occurrence), **A**ll (to replace all strings without confirmation), **N**ext (to search for the next occurrence without replacing the current string), or **Q**uit (to return to READY mode).

Copy Command

The /Copy command lets you copy data from one location to another, leaving the data in the location you copied from unchanged. You can copy a single cell entry to other cells or ranges, copy ranges to ranges, or copy formulas to other cells or ranges. When you copy a formula, the formula in the destination depends on the type of cell address used in the original formula. For example, if you copy a formula from H12 to J15, and H12 contains the relative reference +H10 ("two cells up"), the contents of cell J15 will contain the relative reference +J13, that is, still "two cells up" from its current location. (The relative reference remains intact.)

CAUTION   1-2-3 writes over existing data when it copies data to the range you specify. To avoid possible data loss, save the worksheet before you use this command. (If you accidentally write over existing data and the Undo feature is on, press (ALT)-(F4) (UNDO) immediately to restore the worksheet to its previous state.)

/Copy   /Copy copies a cell or range of data and its cell formats to another cell or range in the worksheet. You can also use this command to duplicate data in one cell so that it fills a range. /Copy makes one copy or multiple copies of a cell or range of data. It applies a formula that refers to a single column or row to multiple columns or rows.

You specify the range that contains the cells you want to copy (the source range) at the "Copy what?" prompt and specify the location in the worksheet where you want to place the copied range (the destination range) at the "To where?" prompt. You need to specify only the upper left corner cell of the destination range.

CAUTION   Avoid specifying overlapping source and destination ranges. If they overlap, some of the original cell contents will be erased.

Move Command

The /Move command lets you transfer a range of data, formulas, range names, and cell formats to another range in the worksheet. Use /Move to reorganize data.

CAUTION   The range to which you move data can be any unprotected area of the worksheet. To avoid possible data loss from writing over existing data, save the worksheet before you use /Move. If you make a mistake and the Undo feature is on, press (ALT)-(F4) (UNDO) immediately to restore the worksheet to its previous state.

/Move   /Move removes data from one location and enters it in another location in the same worksheet.

/Move lets you rearrange data in the worksheet while maintaining all the functional relationships among the cells that contain the data. 1-2-3 automatically adjusts all formulas in the worksheet to account for moved data. As a result, /Move is a powerful tool for redesigning the worksheet.

If you move a cell that contains a formula, the formula stays the same. If you move the contents of a cell to which a formula refers, 1-2-3 changes the formula to reflect the new location of the data.

You specify the range that contains the data you want to move (the source range) at the "Move what?" prompt and specify the location in the worksheet where you want to place the data (the destination range) at the "To where?" prompt. You need to specify only the upper left corner cell of the destination range.

If you move a cell that is the upper left or lower right corner of a named range, 1-2-3 adjusts the definition of the named range. Moving any other cell in a named range effectively moves it out of the range but does not alter the range named definition.

File Commands

A file is a named collection of data stored on a disk. As you work with 1-2-3, you use the /File commands to manage data in several ways:

- To save a worksheet by copying it from memory to a file on disk to keep a permanent record of the work you do during a 1-2-3 session. You can save an entire worksheet with /File Save or only part of it with /File Xtract.

- To retrieve a file by copying it from disk into memory. When you do, 1-2-3 displays the file exactly as it was when you last saved it. You retrieve files with /File Retrieve or with the Viewer add-in.

- To restrict access to a file with a password.

- To erase files on disk.

- To combine all or parts of a file with another file.

- To use files that are shared on a network.

CAUTION Some of the changes you make when you manage files change information on disks. You cannot undo these changes, even if the Undo feature is on. All the commmands you use to manage files prompt you when data may be lost; select responses to these prompts with care to avoid replacing or changing data you want to keep.

Before you work with files, you need to be familiar with the following terms:

- The path supplies two pieces of information: the drive name (if it is different from the current drive) and the directory (and subdirectory) where the file is located.

- The drive tells 1-2-3 where the disk that stores the file is located. A drive name always consists of a letter followed by a colon, for example, C:. If the file is located on a disk in the current drive, you do not need to specify a drive name.

- A directory is a subdivision of a disk used for organizing files. When you specify a file, use the directory name to tell 1-2-3 in which directory on the specified drive the file is located. If you are specifying a file in a sub-directory (a directory that is included in another directory), you must use a \ (backslash) to separate each directory name from the next. Further, you must use a backslash to separate the last directory name from the file name.

For example, C:\BUDGETS\1992\RESEARCH.WK1 specifies a file called RESEARCH.WK1 that is on the C: drive, in a directory called BUDGETS, in a subdirectory called 1992. (The extension .WK1 is explained later.)

If the file is in the current directory (the directory specified with /File Directory or /Worksheet Global Default Directory), you do not need to specify a directory name. Refer to your operating system documentation for information about creating and maintaining directories.

File Names and Extensions

Every file in a directory has a unique file name, which you assign when you first create the file. Each operating system has its own guidelines for naming files, which are described in your operating system documentation, but the following general guidelines apply to file names: Use any combination of eight letters, numbers, - (hyphens), and _ (underscores). Do not use spaces. If you enter more than eight characters, 1-2-3 ignores the extra characters. Do not use the name AUX, CON, COM1, COM2, LPT1, NUL, or PRN. Uppercase and lowercase letters are treated as the same letter.

A file name extension is a suffix to a file name. It consists of a . (period) followed by three characters. Extensions group files into categories. If you do not specify an extension, 1-2-3 automatically adds one that is appropriate to the type of file you are naming. Uppercase and lowercase letters are treated as the same letter.

Table 2.7 lists some of the file types that 1-2-3 creates.

File Type	Description
.WK1	A worksheet file created with /File Save or /File Extract, which stores the data you have entered in 1-2-3.
.BAK	A backup worksheet file created with /File Save Backup or /File Xtract, which stores the previously saved version of a worksheet file.
.ENC	An encoded file created with /Print Encoded or /Print Background, which stores printer codes, text, and other information for printing a formatted worksheet.
.PRN	A text or print file created with /Print File, which stores worksheet data in ASCII format.
.PIC	A graph file created with /Graph Save, which stores a 1-2-3 graph in a picture format for use with PrintGraph and other programs.
.CNF	A configuration file created with /Worksheet Global Default Update, which stores default settings that affect every 1-2-3 session.

Table 2.7

Responding to File Name Prompts

When you select a command that requires a file name, such as /File Retrieve, 1-2-3 displays a list of files and subdirectories in the current directory. You can specify a file by selecting a file name from the menu or by typing the file name. If you want to display available file names in a full-screen list, either press

(F3) (NAME) or click List in the first line of the control panel. If you need to display files from a different drive or directory, press (ESC) or click the right mouse button to clear the file names (and directory if necessary), edit the drive or directory, and then press (↵). You can also click a drive letter in the control panel to specify a different drive.

Using Wildcard Characters in File Names and Extensions

You can use * (asterisk) as a wildcard character in a file name to represent any number of sequential characters. *.WK1 tells 1-2-3 to list the name of every file with a .WK1 extension in the current directory. *.PIC tells 1-2-3 to list the name of every file with a .PIC extension.

You can also use ? (question mark) as a wildcard character, but it represents any single character in a file name or extension.

Limiting Access to Files

You can limit access to a worksheet file by saving or extracting it with a password. When you save a file with a password, no one can retrieve the file without knowing and specifying the password. To create a password, use /File Save. Passwords can be up to 15 characters long, and they can contain spaces. Passwords are case sensitive. When you save a file with a password, you can retrieve the file again only if you enter the correct password.

Retrieving a File When You Start 1-2-3

You can retrieve a file when you start 1-2-3 by typing **123 -w** followed by the name of the file on the operating system command line. For example, to retrieve a file named DATA.WK1 in the default directory, you would type **123 -wdata.** You can also specify a different drive or directory, such as **-wc:\sales\data.**

Automatic File Retrieval

When you start a 1-2-3 session, a blank worksheet appears on the screen. Instead of displaying a blank worksheet, 1-2-3 can retrieve a particular worksheet automatically every time you start the program. Name the worksheet that you want to retrieve automatically AUTO123.WK1, and save it in the default directory. 1-2-3 will automatically retrieve that worksheet every time you start a session.

Linking Files

File linking saves you the effort of manually updating every worksheet affected by a change in another worksheet. One of the most useful applications of file linking is the consolidation of data from a number of worksheets in a summary worksheet.

The 1-2-3 file-linking feature lets you use values from cells in other worksheets in the current worksheet. You create a link between two files by entering a linking formula in one file that refers to a cell in the other file. The file in which you enter the formula is called the target file because it receives the data. The file that the formula refers to is called the source file because it supplies the data.

Once the two files are linked, 1-2-3 copies the value of the cell in the source file (the source cell) to the cell in the target file (the target cell). If the value of a source cell is changed, the value of the target cell is automatically updated whenever you retrieve the target file or select **/F**ile **A**dmin Link-Refresh while you are working in the target file.

If the data you are linking to depends on linked cells, you can get incorrect results. For example, if worksheet A depends on worksheet B, and worksheet B depends on worksheet C, the changes you make in worksheet C are not reflected when you retrieve worksheet A. After you save the changes in worksheet C, you must retrieve and save worksheet B before you can retrieve worksheet A.

Creating a Link   Follow these steps to create a linking formula:

1. Move the cell pointer to the target cell.

2. Type a + (plus sign) to begin the formula.

3. Enter a file reference enclosed in << >> (double angle brackets).

   A file reference must always include the name of the source file. In some cases, however, it may also be necessary for you to supply other information:

   - If the source file does not have the default file extension .WK1, you must include the appropriate file extension.

   - If the source file is not in the default directory (the directory specified with **/F**ile **D**irectory), you must include a directory name to tell 1-2-3 where to look for the file.

   - If the source file is not on the disk in the default drive (the drive specified with **/F**ile **D**irectory), you must include a drive name to tell 1-2-3 where to look for the file.

4. Enter a cell reference, either the address of the source cell or its range name.

   - If you enter a range address, 1-2-3 uses only the cell in the upper left corner of the range as the source cell.

   - If you enter a range name that represents a multiple-cell range in the source file, 1-2-3 uses only the cell in the upper left corner of the range as the source cell although it always displays the range name in the formula.

5. Press ⏎ to complete the formula.

   When you press ⏎ to complete the linking formula, 1-2-3 checks to make sure the source file you referenced exists. If any of the following conditions exist, 1-2-3 displays an error message and will not enter the formula in the worksheet:

   - The source file does not exist.

- The specified directory does not exist, so 1-2-3 cannot find the source file.
- The specified drive is not ready (for example, you have not closed the door on a disk drive).
- The specified range name does not exist in the source file.
- The source file is a password-protected worksheet.
- The data in the file cannot be read by 1-2-3.
- You are sharing files on a network, and the source file is being retrieved or saved by another user.

If 1-2-3 is able to locate the source file and cell, it copies the value of that cell into the target cell.

6. To make a link permanent, use **/F**ile **S**ave to save the worksheet.

The **/F**ile commands perform these tasks:

/File **R**etrieve	Reads a worksheet file into memory. The retrieved file replaces the current worksheet.
/File **S**ave	Saves the current worksheet to a worksheet file on disk; creates new files on disk and replaces existing files.
/File **C**ombine	Incorporates data from a worksheet file on disk into the current worksheet.
/File **X**tract	Copies a range of data, including labels, numbers, and formulas, or copies a range of data, including labels, numbers, and the values of formulas, from the current worksheet and saves it in a worksheet file on disk. All settings associated with the worksheet are saved.
/File **E**rase	Deletes a worksheet file, text file, graph file, or any other file on disk; erases the current file in memory.

CAUTION Once you erase a file on disk, you cannot retrieve the data in that file or use (ALT)-(F4) (UNDO) to recover the file.

/File **L**ist	Displays a list of information about worksheet, text, graph, linked, or all files currently on disk.
/File **I**mport	Copies data (text or numbers) from an ASCII file on disk (created with 1-2-3 or another program) into the current worksheet.
/File **D**irectory	Changes the default directory for the current 1-2-3 session.
/File **A**dmin	Creates a table of information about files, updates file links in the current worksheet, and controls access to a worksheet file reservation.

/File Retrieve	**/File Retrieve** loads a worksheet file from a disk into the computer's memory and displays it on the screen. 1-2-3 retrieves a file only from the current directory. Select a file from the list or type the file name. If you want to display a full-screen list of file names, press (F3) (NAME) or click List in the first line of the control panel.

1-2-3 replaces the current worksheet when you use the **/File Retrieve** command. If you retrieve a protected worksheet file, 1-2-3 prompts you to enter the file's password. You must enter the exact combination of uppercase and lowercase letters in the password.

/File Save

Cancel Replace Backup

/File Save saves the current worksheet and the settings associated with it in a worksheet file.

At the prompt, select the current file. To use a new file name, type the file name and press (↵) or click the control panel. If you choose **Cancel**, you return to the current worksheet in READY mode; nothing is saved. If you choose **Replace**, you write over the file of the same name on disk with the contents from the current worksheet. If you choose **Backup**, 1-2-3 saves the current worksheet and keeps a copy of the previous version of the file with the extension .BAK.

Saving a File with a Password

You can save and protect any 1-2-3 file by entering a password during the **/File Save** command.

Type the file name, press SPACEBAR, and type **P**. You will be prompted to enter and then verify the password. You do not see your password on the screen. Your password can be up to 15 characters long, and you can use any LICS characters except spaces.

To change or delete a password, select **/File Save**. The current file name is displayed, followed by the message "[PASSWORD PROTECTED]." To clear this message, press (ESC) or BACKSPACE, then press SPACEBAR and type **P** to display the password prompt. To change the password, enter and verify the new password. To delete the password, press (↵) at the password prompts. Select **Replace** to save the worksheet.

CAUTION   When you save a file with a password, you can retrieve it only if you enter the correct password. If you forget the password, there is no way to retrieve the file.

/File Combine

Copy Add Subtract

/File Combine incorporates all or part of a worksheet file into the current worksheet at the location of the cell pointer. 1-2-3 uses the cell pointer as the upper left corner cell for the incoming data. All other entries fall into corresponding cells to the right and below the cell pointer.

Position the cell pointer in the upper left corner of the area of the worksheet where you want to incorporate the incoming data. Select **C**opy, **A**dd, or **S**ubtract from the menu (see Table 2.8 for a description of these options). You will be prompted to choose **E**ntire-File or **N**amed/Specified-Range from the menu. If you choose **E**ntire-File, select a name from the menu or enter a new file name. Include a drive or a directory in the path name if you want 1-2-3 to read files from another directory. If you choose **N**amed/Specified-Range, type the name of the range to extract from the worksheet.

Menu Item	Description
Copy	Replaces the entries in the current worksheet with incoming data.
Add	Adds incoming numeric data to the values in the current worksheet. If an incoming value overlays a cell that contains a number, 1-2-3 adds the two values. Incoming values replace blank cells. If an incoming value overlays a label or formula cell, 1-2-3 discards the incoming value and retains the label in the current worksheet.
Subtract	Subtracts incoming numeric data from values in the current worksheet file. A positive number subtracted from a blank cell produces a negative result. The incoming data has no effect on labels or formulas in the current worksheet.

Table 2.8

1-2-3 combines only cell entries. No worksheet or print settings are incorporated into the current worksheet. Avoid any loss of data from combining a file incorrectly by saving the current worksheet before you use **/F**ile **C**ombine. If you make a mistake when combining files and the Undo feature is on, press (ALT)-(F4) (UNDO) immediately to restore the worksheet to its original state.

/File **X**tract

Formulas Values

/File **X**tract extracts and saves a portion of the current worksheet in a separate worksheet file. **/F**ile **X**tract does not change any data in the current worksheet.

Select **F**ormulas to copy a range of data in the current worksheet to a file on disk, including labels, formulas, numbers, and all worksheet settings. Select **V**alues to copy a range of data in the current worksheet to a file on disk, including labels, numbers, the value of formulas, and all worksheet settings. Then specify the range of cells to extract. Select a file name from the menu, or enter a new file name at the prompt.

If you specified a file name that already exists, you can select one of the following: **C**ancel returns 1-2-3 to READY mode without extracting the range; **R**eplace writes over the file on disk with the extracted range; **B**ackup renames the previously extracted file on disk with the extension .BAK and saves the extracted range with the existing file name and the extension .WK1.

When you select a range to extract, it cannot contain formulas that reference cells outside the extracted range or range names that refer to ranges outside the extracted range.

The global settings in the current worksheet (such as named ranges, graphs, and formats) are saved in the new file with the extracted range.

Use **/File X**tract to split a large worksheet into smaller parts or to use one part of a worksheet in another worksheet.

/File **E**rase

Worksheet Print Graph Other

/File **E**rase removes a file from disk.

Worksheet displays all .WK1, .WKS, and .WK3 files. **P**rint displays all .PRN files. **G**raph displays all .PIC files. **O**ther displays all files in the current directory. Select the name of the file you want to erase and press ⏎, or type in a file name.

CAUTION   Once you erase a file on disk, you cannot retrieve the data in that file or use [ALT]-[F4] (UNDO) to recover the file. Therefore, before using this command, make certain that you no longer need the data in the file you are erasing.

/File **L**ist

Worksheet Print Graph Other Linked

/File **L**ist displays the names of all files of a particular type stored in the current directory. When you select a file name in the list, 1-2-3 displays the date and time the file was last saved and the file size in bytes.

Worksheet displays all .WK1, .WKS, and .WK3 files. **P**rint displays all .PRN files. **G**raph displays all .PIC files. **O**ther displays all files in the current drive and directory.

The list of file names temporarily replaces the current worksheet on the screen. If no files of the specified file type are on the disk, 1-2-3 puts you in EDIT mode so that you can enter a new file extension. Use **/File L**ist after you erase a file to see if it is erased from the list of current files.

Linked displays all files on disk that are linked to the current worksheet by formula references. When you highlight a file name, 1-2-3 displays the full path in the control panel. Characters you typed when you linked the file are displayed in color or brighter intensity; 1-2-3 completes the path if necessary with characters displayed in normal color or intensity.

/File **I**mport

Text Numbers

/File **I**mport copies a print file from the current directory into the current worksheet at the location of the cell pointer. You can import text or numbers. **/File I**mport imports standard ASCII files.

There are two types of text files from which you can import data. A delimited text file contains characters (delimiters) that separate data. For 1-2-3 to import a delimited text file correctly, labels must be enclosed in quotation marks, and all labels and numbers must be separated by commas, spaces, colons, or semicolons. Numbers must not be formatted with commas for thousands separators because the commas will act as delimiters. A nondelimited text file does not separate data. For 1-2-3 to import a nondelimited text file correctly, each line in the file must end with a carriage return or a line feed, and each line must not exceed 240 characters.

CAUTION   Many word processors produce files that contain special characters. If you try to import these files with the **/F**ile **I**mport command, you may get unpredictable results. Most word processors, however, produce standard ASCII files, which should be compatible with 1-2-3.

Before you initiate the command sequence, move the cell pointer to the top left corner of the range where you want the imported file to be displayed. Table 2.9 describes the command options.

Menu Item	Description
Text	Imports labels and numbers from a nondelimited text file; do not use with a delimited text file. 1-2-3 imports each line of data as a long label, entering it in a single cell in the current worksheet beginning at the cell pointer location. 1-2-3 enters each successive line from the text file in the same column, one cell below the other.
Numbers	Imports only numbers from a nondelimited text file; imports numbers and labels from a delimited text file. 1-2-3 places each entry in a separate cell in the current worksheet beginning at the current cell pointer location.

Table 2.9

/File **D**irectory   /**F**ile **D**irectory changes the directory for the current 1-2-3 session.

/File **A**dmin

Reservation Table Link-Refresh

/**F**ile **A**dmin creates a table of information about files, updates file links in the current worksheet, and controls access to a worksheet file's reservation on a network.

Selecting **R**eservation lets you get and release a file's reservation, or lock. You use this command when you share worksheet files on a network and want to save files or allow other people to save files. Selecting **T**able creates a table of information about files on disk. The table can be placed in any unprotected area of the worksheet. However, make sure that the worksheet location is blank or contains unimportant data since 1-2-3 will write over existing data when it creates the table. Selecting **L**ink-Refresh recalculates formulas in the current worksheet that include references to files on disk by retrieving the current contents of the linked cells.

Print Commands

The /**P**rint commands control basic printing operations such as specifying a range to print or advancing the paper in the printer by a line or a page. You can also use the /**P**rint commands to enhance printed worksheets. For example, you can add headers, footers, and borders. The /**P**rint command provides print options on the Print Settings dialog box or through corresponding commands in the menu above the dialog box. Press ⒡ (EDIT) or click the dialog box to activate it. You can also use the /**P**rint commands to create a text file or an encoded file on a disk, so you can import the data into another program or print the file using an operating system command.

Selecting a Destination

Before you can use /**P**rint, you must select the destination for your worksheet print output. 1-2-3 offers you four choices of how to print your data:

- Directly on a printer
- To a text file on a disk
- To an encoded file on a disk
- In the background while you do other work

Printing Directly on a Printer

You use /**P**rint **P**rinter to print your work on a printer. Be sure you used the Install program to install that printer for use with 1-2-3. You can select /**W**orksheet **G**lobal **D**efault **P**rinter to check the printer name setting in the dialog box.

Printing Data to a Text File

When you use /**P**rint **F**ile to create a text file from a worksheet range, 1-2-3 assigns the default extension .PRN to the file. You can use the text file in another program (for example, a word processing program), or you can print the text file later with an operating system command. When you select /**P**rint **F**ile, 1-2-3 prompts you to enter a name for the text file. 1-2-3 creates the text file when you select **Q**uit to leave the Print menu.

Printing Data to an Encoded File

When you use /**P**rint **E**ncoded to create an encoded file, 1-2-3 assigns the default extension .ENC to the file. You can print the encoded file later with an operating system command. (Be sure the current printer listed in the Print Settings dialog box is the one you will use to print the encoded file.) When you select /**P**rint **E**ncoded, 1-2-3 prompts you to enter a name for the encoded file.

Printing Data in the Background

/**P**rint **B**ackground prints worksheet data to an encoded file and then prints the encoded file on a printer while you continue to work with 1-2-3, or even quit 1-2-3. Before you can select /**P**rint **B**ackground, however, you must leave 1-2-3 and run a program called BPrint. BPrint is a terminate-and-stay-resident (TSR) program. To run BPrint, you use /**Q**uit (not /**S**ystem) to leave 1-2-3, and then type **bprint** at the operating system prompt. (If you have not started BPrint when you select /**P**rint **B**ackground, 1-2-3 displays an error message.)

You can also print directly from the operating system prompt instead of printing with the /**Print** command. In this case, you type **bprint** followed by the name of the file you want to print. Precede bprint with the appropriate directory information if the current directory is not 1-2-3 and 1-2-3 is not in your path (for example, **c:\123r23\bprint**). Printing files with BPrint from the operating system command line provides options that are not available when you print from 1-2-3.

After you type bprint, you can enter one or more arguments, using the format illustrated below. Only one file operation is performed by each BPrint command, however. Enter arguments in any order, but separate them with spaces.

*[path]*BPrint*[argument1 argument2 argumentn]*

Table 2.10 describes each BPrint argument.

Argument	What it Does
filename	Sends *filename* to the printer. *filename* is a file with the extension .ENC or a text file. (After you print a text file, you need to manually position the paper in your printer to the top of the page.)
-p=*number*	Directs printing to a parallel port. *number* is the value 1 or 2. The default printer port is parallel port 1.
-s=*number*	Directs printing to a serial port. *number* is the value 1 or 2.
-pa	Pauses background printing.
-r	Continues printing 1-2-3 print jobs that were temporarily suspended with -pa.
-c *filename*	Cancels the print job you specify and removes it from the print queue. *filename* must include a path and cannot be the file that is currently printing.
-t	Stops the current 1-2-3 print job and cancels any other 1-2-3 print jobs waiting to be printed.

Table 2.10

If you omit the -p or -s argument, BPrint attaches to parallel port 1.

When you run BPrint, follow these guidelines:

- Make sure that BPrint is the last TSR that you load before you start 1-2-3.

- If you have already loaded PRINT.COM, you will not be able to start BPrint.

- Once you start BPrint, you cannot detach it from one port and attach it to another port.

- If you are using BPrint on a network, make sure you load your network software first. BPrint must be in your personal directory on the network. BPrint prints only to your local printer, not to a shared network printer.

To Print a Range

After you select the print destination, 1-2-3 displays the Print Settings dialog box, which lists all the print settings and the settings for what you are currently printing. Press (F2) (EDIT) or click the dialog box to activate it. You can change settings in the dialog box directly, or you can select commands from the menu. Whether you are printing on a printer or to a file on a disk, you must specify the print range (the cells you want 1-2-3 to print when you select **G**o). It is important to save your file before beginning any printing. Follow these steps to print a range.

1. (Optional) To use background printing, run BPrint first.

2. Select **/P**rint.

3. Select a destination from **B**ackground, **E**ncoded, **F**ile, or **P**rinter.

4. If you select **F**ile, **E**ncoded, or **B**ackground, specify the name of the text file or encoded file you want 1-2-3 to create. 1-2-3 displays the names of files in the current directory with the extension .PRN if you selected **F**ile, or .ENC if you selected **E**ncoded. Change the drive, directory, or extension if necessary.

5. If you select **F**ile, **E**ncoded, or **B**ackground, and you specify the name of a file that already exists, select **C**ancel to return to READY mode or **R**eplace to write over the existing file on disk.

6. Specify the range you want to print. Press (F2) (EDIT) or click the Print Settings dialog box to activate it and specify the range name or address in the Range text box, or select **/P**rinter [**P**rinter, **F**ile, **E**ncoded, **B**ackground] **R**ange and specify the range at the prompt.

7. (Optional) Change the current print settings. If you do not make any changes in the individual or global page format, 1-2-3 uses the following settings when you print a worksheet on standard 8 1/2-by-11-inch paper:

Left margin	4 characters from the left edge of the paper
Right margin	76 characters from the left edge of the paper
Top margin	2 lines from the top of the paper
Bottom margin	2 lines from the bottom of the paper
Page length	66 lines

You can change any of these settings for all worksheets with **/W**orksheet **G**lobal **D**efault **P**rinter. You can change them for a single worksheet with **/P**rint **P**rinter **O**ptions.

The default printer port is Parallel 1. If you are using a serial printer or a printer on a DOS network, select **/W**orksheet **G**lobal **D**efault **P**rinter **I**nterface, and then choose the appropriate port. Select **Q**uit and then **U**pdate to store this change for future 1-2-3 sessions.

8. Select OK.

9. Select **Q**uit if necessary to return to the **P**rinter [**P**rinter, **F**ile, **E**ncoded, **B**ackground] menu.

10. Select **A**lign.

11. Select **G**o to print the range.

12. Select **Q**uit. If you are printing on a network printer, to a text file, or in the background, nothing happens until you select **Q**uit.

The **/P**rint commands perform these tasks:

/Print [**P**rinter, **F**ile, **E**ncoded, or **B**ackground] **R**ange	Specifies the range to print either to a printer or to a file.
/Print [**P**rinter, **F**ile, **E**ncoded, or **B**ackground] **L**ine	Advances the paper in the printer by one line.
/Print [**P**rinter, **F**ile, **E**ncoded, or **B**ackground] **P**age	Advances the paper in the printer to the top of the next page or inserts blank lines in a text file on disk.
/Print [**P**rinter, **F**ile, **E**ncoded, or **B**ackground] **O**ptions	Establishes printing settings, including the header, footer, margins, borders, setup string, page length, and range format.
/Print [**P**rinter, **F**ile, **E**ncoded, or **B**ackground] **C**lear	Resets some or all of the current print settings and returns them to the default settings.
/Print [**P**rinter, **F**ile, **E**ncoded, or **B**ackground] **A**lign	Tells 1-2-3 that the paper in the printer is correctly positioned at the top of a page and ready for printing; resets the page number to 1.
/Print [**P**rinter, **F**ile, **E**ncoded, or **B**ackground] **G**o	Starts printing. Sends worksheet data to a printer or to a file on disk.
/Print [**P**rinter, **F**ile, **E**ncoded, or **B**ackground] **Q**uit	Ends the current print job and returns 1-2-3 to READY mode; tells 1-2-3 to send the print job to a network printer. (You cannot print until you select **Q**uit.)

/Print [**P**rinter, **F**ile, **E**ncoded, or **B**ackground] **R**ange

/Print [**P**rinter, **F**ile, **E**ncoded, or **B**ackground] **R**ange specifies the range to print either to a printer or to a file.

If the print range includes a long label, you must specify the range to include the cell(s) the long label overlaps as well as the cell that contains the long label. For example, to print a long label entered in A1 that overlaps B1 and C1, include cells A1, B1, and C1 in the print range. If 1-2-3 cannot display a long label entirely, it prints only what appears in the worksheet.

1-2-3 remembers the last range you specified. To print the same range again, select **G**o without respecifying a range. To clear the current print range, select **C**lear **R**ange.

/Print [Printer, File, Encoded, or Background] **Li**ne advances the paper in the printer one line.

/Print [Printer, File, Encoded, or Background] **P**age advances the paper in the printer to the top of the next page or inserts blank lines in a text file on disk.

> Header Footer **M**argins Borders Setup Pg-Length **O**ther **Q**uit

/Print [Printer, File, Encoded, or Background] **O**ptions changes the margins, borders, and page length of your printed documents; adds headers and footers; and indicates font size and style. Table 2.11 describes the command options. The settings will appear in the Print Settings dialog box.

Menu Item	Description
Header	Prints one line of text just below the top margin of every page. You can type up to 240 characters (limited by your paper width and margins). Use a number sign (#) to generate sequential page numbers, starting with 1. Use an at sign (@) to produce the current date. Type \ (backslash) followed by a cell address or range name to use the contents of a cell as a header.
Footer	Prints one line of text just above the bottom margin of every page. You can type up to 240 characters (limited by your paper width and margins). Use a number sign (#) to generate sequential page numbers, starting with 1. Use an at sign (@) to produce the current date. Type \ (backslash) followed by a cell address or range name to use the contents of a cell as a footer.
Margins	Sets margins for the printed page. Select **L**eft, **R**ight, **T**op, **B**ottom, or **N**one. 1-2-3 displays the current margin setting. To change the setting, type a number up to 240 (for left or right margin) or 32 (for top or bottom margin), and then press (⏎). To clear the current margins and reset the top, left, and bottom margins to 0 and the right margin to 240 in one step, select **N**one.
Borders	Prints specified rows or columns on every page, above or to the left of the range you are printing. Choose **R**ows or **C**olumns, and specify the range you want to print as borders. Do not include the area specified for the borders in your print range, or you will get two copies of the same information.
Setup	Specifies font size and style for the printer. Type a setup string of up to 39 characters and press (⏎). If 1-2-3 displays an existing setup string, press (ESC) first. Setup strings come from printer control codes, which you can find in your printer manual. You generally use a three-digit or four-digit code, prefaced with a backslash (\).
Pg-Length	Indicates the number of printed lines to be printed on a page. Press (⏎) d to use the current page length, or type a number between 10 and 100.
Other	This command is described in the /Print [Printer, **B**ackground, **E**ncoded, or **F**ile] Options **O**ther section.
Quit	Select **Q**uit to return to the Print menu.

Table 2.11

1-2-3 always leaves two blank lines between the text and the headers or footers. Headers and footers can have up to three parts: left-aligned, centered, and right-aligned segments. Use the split vertical bar (|) to separate segments. The following examples illustrate page 15 of a document printed February 23, 1992:

Enter:	Result:		
ABC Company	ABC Company		
|ABC Company		ABC Company	
ABC Company||Page #	ABC Company		Page 15
@|ABC Company|Page #	2/23/92	ABC Company	Page 15

The initial default page length is 66, which is appropriate for type that uses 6 lines per inch on 11-inch paper. With a page length of 66, you can print 56 lines from the worksheet.

To indicate a setup string, use your printer's control codes in the form *nnn*. (Refer to your printer's manual.) If you change from one setup string to another, you usually have to turn your printer off and then on again for the change to take effect.

The following examples work for many printers:

Setup string:	Result:	Note:
\015	Turns on compressed print	Maximum right margin of 132
\018	Turns off compressed print	Maximum right margin of 80
\270	Sets line spacing to 8 lines per inch	Set Pg-Length to 88
\072	Sets line spacing to 6 lines per inch	Set Pg-Length to 66

You can enter certain setup strings in worksheet cells to switch from one print style to another within a single worksheet. Place two split vertical bars (\|\|) before the setup string. For example, on some printers, you can use \|\|\015 to print a section of the worksheet in compressed print. Use \|\|\018 at the point where you want to return to standard print.

/**P**rint [**P**rinter, **F**ile,
Encoded, or **B**ackground]
Options **O**ther

As-Displayed Cell-Formulas Formatted Unformatted

/**P**rint [**P**rinter, **F**ile, **E**ncoded, or **B**ackground] **O**ptions **O**ther changes the printing format and the information contained in the document. Table 2.12 describes the command options.

Menu Item	Description
As-Displayed	1-2-3 prints the range as it appears on the screen. Use this option to restore standard output after you have chosen **C**ell-Formulas.
Cell-Formulas	1-2-3 prints the contents of each filled cell in the print range, one cell per line. Each line contains exactly what appears on the first line of the control panel when the cell pointer is on the cell: the cell address, the format, the protection status (P or U), and the value or formula in the cell.
Formatted	Restores any page breaks, headers, or footers after you have chosen **U**nformatted.
Unformatted	1-2-3 prints ranges without page breaks, headers, or footers. This is useful if you are printing a range to a file or if you are trying to print a very full page.

Table 2.12

/**P**rint [**P**rinter, **F**ile,
Encoded, or **B**ackground]
Clear

All Range Borders Format

/**P**rint [**P**rinter, **F**ile, **E**ncoded, or **B**ackground] **C**lear resets some or all of the current print settings.

All clears the current print range; clears all borders, headers, and footers; and resets all formats and options to their default settings. **R**ange clears the current print range. **B**orders clears all borders (column and row ranges). **F**ormat resets margins, page length, and setup strings to default values.

/**P**rint [**P**rinter, **F**ile,
Encoded, or **B**ackground]
Align

/**P**rint [**P**rinter, **F**ile, **E**ncoded, or **B**ackground] **A**lign tells the printer that you have positioned the paper at the top of a new page. You do not see any change on your screen. Use this command to reset the page number to 1.

Select **A**lign each time you print a worksheet. If you do not use this command, you may get gaps in the middle of your printed page.

/**P**rint [**P**rinter, **F**ile, **E**ncoded, or **B**ackground] **G**o starts the process of printing and sends worksheet data to a printer or to a file on a disk.

If your printer is off or disconnected when you select **G**o, 1-2-3 beeps and displays a printer error message at the bottom of the screen. Press (ESC), check your printer, and try again. Select **Q**uit to return to READY mode.

With some systems, you can interrupt printing and return to the Print menu by pressing (BREAK) and then (ESC). The printer may not stop immediately because it still has characters in its memory. To clear the printer's memory, turn it off. When you turn it back on, reposition the paper, and then select /**P**rint **P**rinter **A**lign **G**o.

Printing Using a Driver Set Other Than 123.SET

Unless you specify a different driver set name when you start a work session, 1-2-3 assumes you are using printer drivers that you saved in 123.SET and automatically uses this file to print your documents. To use a driver set with a different name, at the operating system prompt,

Type: **123** *Driver set name*

For example, to use a driver set named LASER.SET,

Type: **123 LASER**

You do not need to include the driver set extension.

Graph Commands

You can represent numeric data you enter into a worksheet as a graph. The **/G**raph commands can create seven different types of graphs: line graphs, bar graphs, XY graphs, stacked bar graphs, high-low-close-open (HLCO) graphs, mixed graphs, and pie charts.

Line graphs show changes in data over time; bar and stacked bar graphs emphasize differences between data items; XY graphs show relationships between two sets of data; HLCO graphs track changes in data over a specific period, such as the high, low, closing, and opening prices of stock; mixed graphs combine line and bar graphs; and pie charts compare parts to the whole.

Creating a Graph

You create graphs from worksheet data and view them on your computer's screen if your system has graphics capability. Even if you cannot view the graphs on your computer's screen, you can create a file to print graphs on a printer or plotter using the 1-2-3 PrintGraph program. (See Chapter 5.)

Each group of worksheet values to be graphed is called a data range. Data ranges are columns or rows of numbers in the worksheet that you want to view for comparison or presentation. When you create a graph, you create a link between the worksheet data and the graph. This link is dynamic; if you change the worksheet data, 1-2-3 automatically changes the graph to reflect the changes to the data. If the data that you want to graph is located in consecutive columns or rows of a range that also contains X-axis labels, you can use **/G**raph **G**roup to create a graph quickly.

When you select **/G**raph, 1-2-3 displays the Graph Settings dialog box. This dialog box lets you see the basic settings for the current graph. You can change any of the settings directly in the Graph Settings dialog box, or you can select commands from the menu above the dialog box. 1-2-3 uses the settings in the Graph Settings dialog box each time you display a graph with **/G**raph **V**iew or press (F10) (GRAPH).

The /Graph commands perform these tasks:

/Graph Type	Specifies the kind of graph to create and adds features (stacked data ranges, frames, margins, 3-D effects, and choice of horizontal or vertical graph orientation).
/Graph X A-F	Specifies the range that contains the X-axis labels, the X-axis values for an XY graph, or the pie slice labels; specifies ranges that contain the numeric data you want to graph.
/Graph Reset	Resets some or all of the current graph settings to the default graph settings.
/Graph View	Temporarily removes the current worksheet from the screen to display the current graph.
/Graph Save	Saves the current graph in a graph file (.PIC) for use with PrintGraph or other programs.
/Graph Options	Adds enhancements such as titles, legends, colors, and grid lines to a graph and determines the scaling method for the axes of the graph.
/Graph Name	Creates, modifies, or deletes named graphs in the current worksheet and creates tables of the named graphs.
/Graph Group	Specifies multiple graph data ranges (X and A–F) at once, when the ranges are located in consecutive columns or rows.
/Graph Quit	Returns 1-2-3 to READY mode.

/Graph Type

Line Bar XY Stack-Bar Pie HLCO Mixed Features

Line Graph A line graph represents each value in a category as a point on a line. You can create up to six lines on a single graph. 1-2-3 uses different symbols to identify the points on each line.

Use the A range to indicate the set of values you want to represent with your first line or with one single line. Use the B through F ranges to indicate the sets of values you want to represent with each additional line. Use the X range to indicate labels for the points along the horizontal X axis. 1-2-3 automatically indicates a numeric scale along the vertical Y axis.

Bar Graph A bar graph represents the values in a range with bars of varying heights. You can create a single-range bar graph, which compares values in one set of data to one another, or a multiple-range bar graph, which displays comparable values for up to six sets of data at each point along the X axis. In a multiple-range bar graph, 1-2-3 uses a variety of shadings (hatch patterns) or colors to identify the bars for each data range.

For a single-range bar graph, use the A range to indicate the range of values you want each bar to represent. For a multiple-range bar graph, use the A through F ranges to indicate the ranges of values you want to represent simultaneously. You should use the X range to indicate labels for the points along the X axis. 1-2-3 automatically indicates a numeric scale along the Y axis.

XY Graph   In an XY graph (also called a scatter chart), 1-2-3 pairs each value from the X range with the corresponding value from each of the A through F ranges to plot points on the graph. You can create up to six lines on a single XY graph. 1-2-3 uses different symbols to identify the points on each line.

Use the X range to indicate the set of values you want to plot on the X axis. Use the A range to indicate the set of values you want to plot on the Y axis in your first line or in one single line. Use the B through F ranges to indicate the sets of values you want to plot on the Y axis in each additional line. 1-2-3 automatically indicates numeric scales along both the X and the Y axes.

Stacked Bar Graph   In a stacked bar graph, 1-2-3 displays the corresponding value from each data range stacked above the preceding value in each bar. You can create stacked bar graphs that show up to six corresponding values at each point along the X axis. 1-2-3 uses different shadings (hatch patterns) or colors to represent each data range.

You should use the A through F ranges to indicate each set of values you want to represent. The A range is the lowest portion of each bar. The B through F ranges are stacked successively above the A range. You should use the X range to indicate labels along the X axis. 1-2-3 automatically indicates a numeric scale along the Y axis.

Pie Chart   A pie chart compares parts to the whole, so each value in the range is a slice of the pie.

Use the A range to indicate the set of values that 1-2-3 will represent as slices of the pie. You can indicate shadings or colors for the individual pie slices. In addition, you can explode (separate) one or more slices of the pie to emphasize a particular value or values. 1-2-3 displays the exploded sections slightly apart from the rest of the pie chart.

Use the B range to indicate the range where you enter shading or color and exploding codes for the pie slices. The B range can be any blank range of your worksheet that is the same size as the A range. Enter a number between 1 and 7 to indicate the desired shading (hatch pattern) or color for each corresponding pie slice. The number codes 0 and 8 indicate unshaded slices.

Indicate the section you want to explode by adding 100 to its corresponding shading or color code. For example, the code 106 in the seventh cell of the B range will explode a slice representing the seventh cell of the A range and display it with type 6 shading or color.

Use the X range to indicate labels for each pie slice. 1-2-3 automatically indicates the percentage value of each slice of the pie.

HLCO Graph   An HLCO graph tracks changes in data over a specific period, such as the high, low, closing, and opening prices of stock. Use the X data range for the X-axis labels, and use the A, B, C, and D data ranges to indicate high, low, closing, and opening values, respectively.

Mixed Graph   A mixed graph combines lines and bars in the same graph. Use the A, B, and C data ranges to indicate the ranges of values to be represented as bars. Use the D, E, and F data ranges to indicate the ranges of values to be represented as lines. Use the X data range to indicate X-axis labels.

Features   Selecting **F**eatures provides the following options for enhancing the appearance of your graphs:

Menu Item	Description
Vertical	Displays the Y axis vertically (the default).
Horizontal	Displays the Y axis horizontally.
Stacked	Use this option with line, bar, XY, and mixed graphs that contain two or more data sets. Choices are **N**o, which plots values separately (the default), or **Y**es, which stacks values.
Frame	Puts a frame around all or part of a graph.
3D-Effect	Adds a shadow to bar, stacked bar, and mixed graphs so that they appear three-dimensional.
Quit	Returns you to the **/G**raph menu.

After you have indicated the data you want to graph, select **V**iew to see the graph.

/Graph **R**eset

Graph X A B C D E F Ranges Options Quit

/Graph **R**eset resets some or all of the current graph settings to the default settings. Use **/G**raph **R**eset to start over again on the current graph. Select **G**raph to cancel the settings for the current graph. This command does not affect named graphs.

Select **X, A, B, C, D, E,** or **F** to change an individual data range. Resetting the X range removes the label entries, except on XY graphs. Select **R**anges to clear all data ranges but not graph options. Select **O**ptions to clear all graph options but not data ranges. Select **Q**uit to return to the previous menu.

/Graph **V**iew   You can select **V**iew to see the current graph any time you are in the top-level Graph menu.

You can view your current graph from READY mode by pressing (F10) (GRAPH). Your most recently specified graph type and data ranges remain with the worksheet. The next time you create a graph, these specifications will appear if you saved the worksheet.

You can change the type of graph you create without altering the data ranges if you want to experiment to see which type of graph represents your data most effectively. Select and specify the graph type, and then view the graph.

/Graph **S**ave

Cancel Replace

/Graph **S**ave saves the current graph in a graph file (.PIC) for use with PrintGraph or other programs.

Use **/G**raph **S**ave to generate a graph file that you print later with PrintGraph. This command saves the graph only for printing. You cannot bring the graph back to the screen to modify it. When you save a graph for printing, 1-2-3 stores the graph's image in the current directory unless you specify a different directory as part of the file name. If you save a graph under an existing graph file name, 1-2-3 writes over the contents in that file. Use the **/F**ile **S**ave command to save the graph settings and file before you end your work session. If you want to use a graph again or modify it later, you must create a name for it using the **/G**raph **N**ame **C**reate command.

Select **C**ancel to end the **/G**raph **S**ave command without saving the current graph. Select **R**eplace to complete the **/G**raph **S**ave command, replacing the graph file on disk with the current graph.

/Graph **O**ptions

Legend Format Titles Grid Scale Color B&W Data-Labels Quit

The **/G**raph **O**ptions commands add enhancements such as titles, legends, colors, and grid lines to a graph and determine the scaling method for the graph's axes.

/Graph **O**ptions **L**egend

A B C D E F Range

/Graph **O**ptions **L**egend creates a legend for data ranges A–F. The legends identify the data range represented by each symbol, color, or hatch pattern in the graph.

Choose **A, B, C, D, E,** or **F** to assign a legend to an individual data range. 1-2-3 displays the most recent legend, if any, for that range. Press (↵) to reselect it or (ESC) to cancel it and specify a new legend. Choose **R**ange to assign legends to all data ranges at once.

To use the cell contents as a legend, type a backslash (\) followed by the cell address or range name. If you enter a range name, 1-2-3 uses the contents in the upper left cell as the legend.

Legends should be no more than 19 characters long. Legends will wrap to a second line if necessary. 1-2-3 truncates legends that extend beyond the graph frame and does not display legends that, because of their specified placement, would appear outside the graph frame.

When you use a cell address in a legend, 1-2-3 does not adjust the address if the referenced cells are relocated with the /Move, /Worksheet Insert, or /Worksheet Delete command.

/Graph Options Format

Graph A B C D E F Quit

/Graph Options Format controls data display for line and XY graphs.

Use /Graph Options Format to change the appearance of line and XY graphs.

1. Select /Graph Options Format.
2. Select Graph to change the format of the entire graph.
   - Select A through F to format each data range individually.
   - Choose Lines to connect each range data point with a straight line.
   - Choose Symbols to display each range data point with the same symbol; there is a different symbol for each range.
   - Choose Both to set lines and symbols (the default).
   - Choose Neither if you do not want symbols or lines to appear in the screen display. In this case, select Data-Labels to label the specified line.
   - Choose Area to fill the space below a line with color or a hatch pattern.
   - Select Quit to return to the previous menu.

If you reset a data range, 1-2-3 saves the associated format settings and reuses them whenever you specify a new range.

/Graph Options Titles

First Second X-Axis Y-Axis

/Graph Options Titles assigns a title (of up to 39 characters in length) to each axis or to an entire graph. Use this command in addition to the /Graph Options Legend and /Graph Options Data-Labels commands to expand the descriptions of your graph data.

If you select First and Second, lines in the graph titles appear centered at the top of the graph. First and second lines are independent of the names you use with /Graph Name and /Graph Save. With X-Axis, titles appear below the horizontal axis. With Y-Axis, titles appear on the side to the left of the vertical axis.

To use the contents of a cell in the worksheet as a title, type a backslash (\) followed by the cell address or the range name. If you use a range name, 1-2-3 uses the contents from the upper left cell in the range as the title.

For printed graphs made with the PrintGraph program, the first title line is printed larger than the second. The second title line can be in a different font style. In some cases, the screen displays more characters than the printer can print, depending on the font you select and the total number of characters in the title.

/Graph Options Grid

Horizontal Vertical Both Clear

/Graph Options Grid adds or removes grid lines in a graph. You cannot use grid lines with pie charts.

If you use **Horizontal**, horizontal grid lines appear across the graph. With **Vertical**, vertical grid lines appear across the graph. With **Both**, horizontal and vertical grid lines appear across the graph. **Clear** erases all grid lines.

/Graph Options Scale

Y-Scale X-Scale Skip

/Graph Options Scale determines the axis scaling method and sets the format of the numbers that appear along each axis; sets which entries in data range X appear along the X axis in line, bar, stacked bar, mixed, and HLCO graphs; sets the display of Y-axis labels and tick marks on the left, right, both sides, or no sides of the graph frame; formats the X axis for XY graphs and Y-axis labels in graphs. (The Graph Scale Settings dialog box appears when you select this command.)

Y-Scale alters the scale of the Y axis. **X**-Scale alters the scale of the X axis. **Skip** determines how 1-2-3 displays labels on the X axis. Specify the skip factor. For a skip factor of n, 1-2-3 plots every nth entry from the X range on the horizontal axis in line, bar, stacked bar, mixed, and HLCO graphs. For example, if $n=10$, the 1st, 11th, and 21st X-range entries appear on the x-axis, and so on.

Select one of the options in Table 2.13 after you choose **Y**-Scale or **X**-Scale.

Option	Description
Automatic	When you select **View**, 1-2-3 displays all the data points, using scale limits that let the graph fill the screen. 1-2-3 uses round numbers for the scale limits. This option overrides the other scale options and is the default setting.
Manual	When you select **View**, 1-2-3 displays the data points that fall within the limits you specify. You must specify upper and lower limits. Depending on the limits you choose, some data points may not be displayed. Further, when a data range includes values that vary widely (for instance, 10, 20, 30, 1,000,000, and 2,000,000), bars representing the larger values may not be displayed. If you set a scale to a limit smaller than the spread of data values, 1-2-3 expands the graph of the specified area to fill the screen.

Table 2.13

Option	Description
Lower	Determines the lower scale limit 1-2-3 uses when displaying a graph. 1-2-3 adjusts the limit you set to a round number. This limit is used only after you select /Graph Options Manual. Maximum values may be rounded off slightly. The default value is 0. 1-2-3 ignores a positive upper limit for bar and stacked bar graphs.
Upper	Determines the upper scale limit 1-2-3 uses when displaying a graph. 1-2-3 adjusts the limit you set to a round number. This limit is used only after you select /Graph Options Manual. Maximum values may be rounded off slightly. The default value is 0. 1-2-3 ignores a positive upper limit for bar and stacked bar graphs.
Format	Lets you change the format of numbers in the graph scale. Select a format from the options in Table 2.6 in the "Range Commands" section of this chapter.
Indicator	Determines whether 1-2-3 displays scale indicators such as (thousands) or (millions) on a graph when you select View. Choose Yes to use indicators or No not to use them. The default setting is Yes.
Display	Specifies where the Y axis will appear. Choices are on the Right, Left, Both sides, or None.
Quit	Returns you to Graph Options menu.

Table 2.13 Continued (for Display and Quit rows)

/Graph Options Color

/Graph Options Color sets the graph display to color. 1-2-3 displays bars, pie slices, graph lines, and symbols in contrasting colors if your monitor can display color.

You can save a graph for printing with color settings even if your monitor cannot display colors. When you save a graph, 1-2-3 assigns a different color to each data range so that PrintGraph can draw each data range with a different color even if the graph was made with the /Graph Options B&W command. (However, do not use this command with a black and white printer because the printer will print all ranges in solid blocks of black.) Bar and stacked bar graphs print out as solid bars of different colors.

/Graph Options B&W

/Graph Options B&W sets graph display to black and white (monochrome) if you previously selected /Graph Options Color.

1-2-3 displays bars and pie slices (if you specified a B data range for the pie chart) in contrasting hatch patterns.

/Graph Options Data-Labels

A B C D E F Group Quit

/Graph Options Data-Labels uses the contents of a range as labels for the points or bars in a graph. The labels come from the ranges you specify as the data-label ranges A–F.

Use /Graph Options Data-Labels to include detailed data value information in your graph.

Select A, B, C, D, E, or F to assign a data-label range of the same size as the selected data range. Select Group to assign a data-label range of the same size to all data ranges at once and to clear any settings previously set. If you select

Group and then specify a range, you can select **C**olumnwise to divide the data-label range into individual ranges by columns, or you can select **R**owwise to divide the data-label range into individual ranges by rows. **Q**uit returns you to the Graph Options menu.

In line and XY graphs, you must indicate how you want the data labels to align—centered, left, above, right, or below—in relation to their data points. For bar and stacked bar graphs, data labels are centered above positive bars and below negative bars. Pie charts cannot have data labels.

1-2-3 displays the specified range contents as data point labels the next time you view the graph. If a data-label cell contains a number or a formula, 1-2-3 displays the cell value as a label in the graph. If you reset a data range, 1-2-3 also resets the corresponding data-label range.

/Graph Name

Use Create Delete Reset Table

/Graph **N**ame creates, modifies, and deletes named graphs in the current worksheet and creates tables of the named graphs.

/Graph **N**ame **U**se makes a named graph the current graph so that you can view and use it.

CAUTION   When you use a named graph, you lose all previous graph settings. To preserve these settings, assign a name to them with **/G**raph **N**ame **C**reate before you select **/G**raph **N**ame **U**se.

/Graph **N**ame **C**reate creates or modifies a named graph by storing the current graph settings with the name you specify. If you enter a name that is identical to an existing graph name, 1-2-3 reassigns the graph name to the new graph setting.

Use **/G**raph **N**ame **C**reate to save more than one graph within a worksheet or to shift quickly from one graph to another during a 1-2-3 session. A graph name can be up to 15 characters long.

You must also use the **/F**ile **S**ave command to attach the named settings to the current worksheet. If you make any changes to the graph, select **/G**raph **N**ame **C**reate, and then save the worksheet file.

/Graph **N**ame **D**elete erases a named graph.

CAUTION   When you select **/G**raph **N**ame **D**elete, 1-2-3 erases the graph settings for the selected graph and automatically returns you to the Graph Options menu. There is no confirmation step. However, if the Undo feature is on, select **Q**uit to return to the worksheet, and then press (ALT)-(F4) (UNDO) immediately to restore the named graph.

/Graph Name Reset   /Graph Name Reset deletes all named graphs in the worksheet.

CAUTION   When you select /**G**raph **N**ame **R**eset, 1-2-3 erases all named graphs and automatically returns you to the Graph Options menu. There is no confirmation step.

/**G**raph **N**ame **T**able creates a three-column table that alphabetically lists all named graphs, graph types, and titles. The table can be placed in any blank and unprotected area of the worksheet.

CAUTION   The table will occupy three columns and as many rows as there are named graphs plus one blank row. To avoid possible data loss, save the worksheet before you use /**G**raph **N**ame **T**able. If you make a mistake when placing the table, and the Undo feature is on, press (ALT)-(F4) (UNDO) immediately.

/**G**raph **G**roup	Columnwise Rowwise

/**G**raph **G**roup specifies multiple graph data ranges (**X** and **A–F**) at once, when the ranges are located in consecutive columns or rows.

Columnwise divides the group range into data ranges by columns. **R**owwise divides the group range into data ranges by rows.

1-2-3 uses the first column or row of the group range as the X data range and subsequent columns or rows as the A–F data ranges. If the range includes more than seven columns or rows, 1-2-3 stops assigning data ranges after the seventh column or row.

Data Commands

The /**D**ata commands let you analyze and manipulate data in ranges and in 1-2-3 databases.

Database

A 1-2-3 database is a range of related data organized in rows and columns in a worksheet. A worksheet may contain many different databases. In a database, each column is a field, and each row is a record. The top cell of each column contains a field name that identifies the contents of the field. Field names are the basis for the database. They determine how data is organized and how you will use it. When you create field names, follow these rules:

- Field names must be labels, not numbers or formulas. To enter a field name that begins with a number or other nonalphabetic character, precede the name with a label prefix (', ", or ^).
- Each field name must be unique.

When you create a database, follow these rules:

- Do not leave any blank rows or divider lines below the field names or between records.

- Fields contain either labels or numeric data. Do not mix labels and values within a single field.

- A database may contain up to 256 fields.

The **/D**ata commands perform these tasks:

/Data **F**ill	Enters a sequence of values, column by column, from left to right, in a specified range. (The values you enter can be numbers, percentages, or formulas.)
/Data **T**able	Records the effect of changing the values of one or more variables in one or more formulas; performs what-if analysis; cross-tabulates the information in a 1-2-3 database.
/Data **S**ort	Rearranges the data in a range in the order you specify.
/Data **Q**uery	Locates and edits selected records in a 1-2-3 database based on criteria you specify.
/Data **D**istribution	Calculates the frequency with which values in a range fall within specified numeric intervals.
/Data **M**atrix	Inverts or multiplies matrices to solve problems that involve simultaneous equations.
/Data **R**egression	Produces statistics that describe the association between one data range and another.
/Data **P**arse	Separates a single column of long labels into multiple columns and assigns data types to each column.

*/**D**ata **F**ill*   **/D**ata **F**ill enters an ascending or descending sequence of numbers into a specified range of cells. The values you enter can be numbers, percentages, or formulas.

Use **/D**ata **F**ill with a 1-2-3 worksheet or a 1-2-3 database. This command is often used to assign a unique record number to each record in a database.

Before you use this command, position the cell pointer in the upper left corner cell of the range you want to fill. After you initiate the command, 1-2-3 will prompt you to specify the fill range (the range of cells to fill), the start value (the beginning number) of your sequence, the step value (the increment between each of the numbers), and the stop value (the final number) of the sequence. Stop value is an optional setting.

*/**D**ata **T**able*

1 2 Reset

The **/D**ata **T**able commands record the effect of changing the values of one or more variables in one or more formulas. They let you perform what-if analysis and cross-tabulate the information in a 1-2-3 database.

/Data **T**able **1** produces a table that calculates the results of one or more formulas, each of which uses one variable. The command also lets you analyze or cross-tabulate the data in a database.

Before you select **/D**ata **T**able **1**, you must set up the data table in a table range, which can be in any unused part of the worksheet. Use the following guidelines to set up a Data Table 1:

- Choose a blank area of the worksheet for your table range.
- Choose any cell outside the table range to use as input cell 1. You will use the cell address of this cell to represent the changing value in each of the formulas the data table will calculate.
- Leave the upper left cell of the table range blank.
- Enter formulas into the top cell of the second column of the data table. You can enter one or more formulas that contain values, strings, or cell addresses. You must use the cell address of input cell 1 as the variable in each of the formulas.
- Enter the values for the input cell address into the column of the table range directly below the blank cell.

Once the data table is set up, you can issue this command to generate the table.

1. Position the cell pointer in the blank cell in the upper left corner of the table range.
2. Select **/D**ata **T**able **1**.
3. At the prompt, enter the table range. The table range contains the blank cell, all the formulas in the first row, and all the values in the column below the blank cell.
4. At the prompt, enter the cell address of the input cell 1.

1-2-3 places each value from the first column into the input cell, one at a time, and uses that value to calculate the formulas in the first row. The result of each calculation appears in the data table in the cell below the appropriate formula and to the right of the appropriate value.

1-2-3 does not automatically recalculate the results area of a data table if you change any of the formulas or value entries in the table. You can recalculate your most recent data table from READY mode by pressing (F8) (TABLE). 1-2-3 uses the most recently specified table range and input cell. To cancel the current table range and input cell specifications, use **R**eset.

If you are using **/D**ata **T**able **1** in conjunction with a database, you can use the database statistical @functions as formulas in the top row of the data table. These @functions let you perform calculations using data from only those records that meet your criteria. (See Chapter 4 for detailed information about @functions.)

/Data **T**able **2** produces a table that calculates the results of one formula that uses two variables. Before you select **/Data** **T**able **2**, you must set up the data table in a table range, which can be in any unused part of the worksheet. Use the following guidelines to set up a Data Table 2:

- Choose a blank area of the worksheet for your table range.

- Choose any two cells outside the table range to use as input cell 1 and input cell 2. You will use the cell addresses of these cells to represent the two changing values in the formula that the data table will calculate.

- Enter the formula in the upper left cell of the table range. The formula can contain values, strings, or cell addresses. You must use the cell addresses of input cell 1 and input cell 2 as the two variables in the formula.

- Enter the first set of values into the column of the table range directly below the cell where you entered the formula. These are the values that 1-2-3 uses, one at a time, in place of the cell address of input cell 1 in the formula.

- Enter the second set of values into the top row of the table range to the right of the cell containing the formula. These are the values that 1-2-3 uses, one at a time, in place of the cell address of input cell 2 in the formula.

Once the data table is set up, you can issue the command to generate the table.

1. Position the cell pointer in the cell that contains the formula, the upper left cell of the table range.

2. Select **/Data** **T**able **2**.

3. Enter the table range at the prompt. (The table range contains the cell with the formula, all the values in the column below that cell, and all the values in the top row to the right of that cell.)

4. At the prompt, enter the cell address of input cell 1.

5. At the prompt, enter the cell address of input cell 2.

The result of each calculation appears in the data table in the cell below the appropriate row value and to the right of the appropriate column value. The input cells themselves are unaffected.

1-2-3 does not automatically recalculate the results area of a data table if you change the formula or the value entries in the table. You can recalculate your most recent data table from READY mode by pressing (F8) (TABLE). 1-2-3 uses the most recently specified table range and input cells.

If you are using **/Data** **T**able **2** in conjunction with a database, you can use any database statistical @function as your formula. These @functions let you perform calculations using data from only those records that meet your criteria. (See Chapter 4 for detailed information about @functions.)

/Data **T**able **R**eset clears all the table ranges and input cells you specified in the worksheet. Use this command before you save a file if you do not want to save table range and input cell settings with the file.

/Data **S**ort rearranges the data in a range in the order you specify. The range can be records in a database or rows in the worksheet. (The Sort Settings dialog box appears when you select this command.)

Data-Range specifies the range you want to sort, either records in a database or rows in a worksheet. Include all fields, but do not include the row of field names. **P**rimary-Key determines the primary field for sorting records or rows. (The data can be in either ascending or descending order.) You must specify a primary key and sort order before you can perform a sort.

When prompted for the primary sort key, enter the cell address of any cell in the field you want 1-2-3 to use to determine the new order for your records. At the prompt for the primary sort order, select either **A** for ascending order or **D** for descending order. (See the section below on Sort Order for further information.)

The **S**econdary-Key is the field that 1-2-3 uses to break ties that occur when two or more records have the same entries in the primary key field. **S**econdary-Key is an optional setting. Respond to the prompts for the secondary sort key and secondary sort order following the same procedure as for the **P**rimary-Key.

Reset clears range address settings and sort keys. Select **G**o to sort the data and return to READY mode. **Q**uit returns you to READY mode before a sort is completed.

Avoid formulas with references to cells in different rows of the data range. Use relative cell references in formulas to refer to cells in other fields in the same record. Use absolute cell references in formulas to refer to any cells outside the data range.

Sort Order

Ascending sorts arrange data in the following order, using the collating sequence you choose during the Install program:

- Numbers last: blank cells, labels beginning with letters in alphabetic order, labels beginning with numbers in numeric order, labels beginning with other characters. This sort ignores capitalization and most accent marks.
- Numbers first: blank cells, labels beginning with numbers in numeric order, labels beginning with letters in alphabetic order, labels beginning with other characters. This sort ignores capitalization and most accent marks.
- ASCII blank cells: all labels using their ASCII values.

Descending sorts reverse the above order. All sorts place numeric values or formulas after any label. The sort order of records whose primary- and secondary-key entries are equal is not predictable.

Data Query Commands

The **/D**ata **Q**uery commands let you search a database for specific records, copy records from a database to a separate part of the worksheet, extract records eliminating duplicates, and remove selected records.

Before you can use **/D**ata **Q**uery, you must set up an input range (the range that contains the records to search), a criteria range (the range that contains the conditions to match), and an output range (the range where 1-2-3 will place copies of records that meet the criteria).

Input Range   The input range is the range of a database that you want 1-2-3 to search when you select a **/D**ata **Q**uery command. The input range includes the database field names and all the records you want to search.

Criteria Range   The criteria range tells 1-2-3 which records to search for in the input range. To set up a criteria range, use the following guidelines:

- Choose a blank range in your worksheet, either several rows below your database or to the right of the database. This area will serve as your criteria range.

- In the first row of the criteria range, copy one, some, or all of the field names in the database. You must enter each field name exactly as it appears in the database.

- Enter your criteria in the second row (and subsequent rows) of the criteria range. Enter each criterion below the copy of the appropriate field name. You can enter a label or a value exactly as it appears in the database if you want 1-2-3 to search for records that match the criteria exactly. You can also enter formulas.

- Enter several criteria in the same row if you want 1-2-3 to search only for records that satisfy every criteria.

- Enter multiple criteria one per row if you want 1-2-3 to search for records that satisfy any of the criteria. (See the section "Writing Criteria" for more information.)

Output Range   The output range is required for /Data **Q**uery Extract and /Data **Q**uery Unique. You specify a single-row output range that contains just the field names if you have a lot of empty space below the field names and are not concerned about any existing entries being written over. 1-2-3 will use as many rows below the field names as it needs.

Writing Criteria

You can write criteria that match label or value entries, and you can use more than one criterion.

Searching for Labels

To search for exact matches, enter the label as the criterion. Two special characters allow you to search for similar label entries:

- ? matches any single character. For example, h?t matches hat, hot, and hut, but not huts; h??d matches head and hood, but not heel.

- * matches all characters to the end of the label. For example, cat* matches cat, catsup, and catechism, but not cutthroat.

Precede a label with a tilde (~) to search for all labels except that one. (Empty cells, however, are never selected by any label-match criteria.) For example, ~Smith matches all records with an entry in that field other than Smith. ~S* matches all records with an entry in the field that do not begin with S.

Searching for Values

To search for exact matches, enter the value as the criterion.

To search for all values that meet a condition you set (such as all entries greater than 150), enter the condition as a logical expression, using the cell address of the appropriate field of the first record in the database. Use a logical operator (<, <=, >, >=, <>) in your formula to compare this cell entry to some value.

The logical formula generates a value of 1 if the condition is true or a value of 0 if it is false.

Using Multiple Criteria

Enter multiple criteria for different fields into the same row to search for only those records that match all these criteria at once. 1-2-3 treats criteria in the same row as if they are linked by the word *AND*.

Enter multiple criteria for different fields into separate rows to search for records that match any of the criteria. 1-2-3 treats criteria in separate rows as if they are linked by the word *OR*.

Use compound logical formulas if you want to create compound criteria that match more than one condition in the same field. Use #AND#, #NOT#, or #OR# in the formula to tie together the two conditions. For example, +D2>1500#AND#+D2<2200 will search for all records with entries greater than 1500.00 but less than 2200.00.

Querying a Database

To query a 1-2-3 database, follow these steps:

1. Select /Data Query.

   The Query Settings dialog box appears. Press (F2) (EDIT) or click the dialog box to activate it.

   The dialog box lists the location of the input, criteria, and output ranges. You must specify an input range and a criteria range for all /Data Query commands; an output range is necessary only for /Data Query Extract or /Data Query Unique.

2. Specify the input range.

   Specify the range name or range address. Be sure to include the field names in the first row.

3. Specify the criteria range.

Specify the range name or range address. The criteria range must include a top row that contains the field names of the fields you want to query, and one or more rows below that contain the criteria.

4. For **/D**ata **Q**uery **E**xtract and **/D**ata **Q**uery **U**nique specify the output range as either a single-row or multiple-row range.

CAUTION   If you specify a single-row output range, 1-2-3 will erase all data in the columns below the field names to the bottom row of the worksheet. Then 1-2-3 creates an output range that contains as many rows as needed to contain the data. To avoid possible data loss, save the worksheet before using **/D**ata **Q**uery **E**xtract or **/D**ata **Q**uery **U**nique. If you make a mistake and the Undo feature is on, press (ALT)-(F4) (UNDO) immediately to restore the worksheet to its original state.

Specify a multiple-row output range with the field names as the first row if you want to be certain that 1-2-3 does not write over existing entries. 1-2-3 will write only to the multiple-row range you specify. If the range is not large enough to accommodate all the records that match your selection criteria, 1-2-3 will display the error message "Too many records for the Output range." Press (ESC) to return 1-2-3 to READY mode and then specify an output range with more rows, or specify the row that contains the field names as the output range.

5. Select OK.

1-2-3 returns to the Data Query menu.

6. Select a query operation.

Select **F**ind to highlight records that match criteria. 1-2-3 highlights the first record in the input range that matches the criteria. You can edit the records selected. If there are no matching records, 1-2-3 returns to the Data Query menu.

Select **E**xtract to copy records that match criteria to the output range. 1-2-3 copies formats as well as entries. The records are in the same order as they were in the input range. 1-2-3 copies only the fields included in the output range.

Select **U**nique to copy records that match criteria to the output range. If two or more records are the same, this command eliminates duplicates in the output range. 1-2-3 copies formats as well as entries. The records in the output range are in the same order as they were in the input range.

Select **D**elete to delete records in the input range that match criteria in the criteria range. You must confirm the deletion by selecting **D**elete, or select **C**ancel to cancel the command.

If you select **/D**ata **Q**uery **F**ind, use the following keys to move among the matching records in the input range:

- Press ⬇ or ⬆ to move the cell pointer to other records that match the criteria. If there are no more matching records in those directions, 1-2-3 beeps.

- Press ⬅ or ➡ to move the cell pointer from field to field within a highlighted record.

- Press (HOME) to move the cell pointer to the first record in the input range or (END) to move the cell pointer to the last record in the input range, even if the records do not match the criteria.

- Press ⏎ or (ESC) to end the **/D**ata **Q**uery **F**ind command and return to the Query menu.

- Press (F2) (EDIT) to edit the field displayed in the current record. Press ➡ or ⬅ to move from field to field. Press ⏎ to save the changes and continue using **/D**ata **Q**uery **F**ind. Press (ESC) to cancel changes and continue with the command.

- Press (F7) (QUERY) to end the **/D**ata **Q**uery **F**ind command, leave the cell pointer in the current cell, and return 1-2-3 to READY mode.

7. Select **Q**uit to return to READY mode.

   Select **R**eset to clear the range specifications for the input and criteria ranges.

/Data **D**istribution

/Data **D**istribution calculates the frequency distribution of values in a range. A frequency distribution tells you how many values in a range (the values range) fall within specified numeric intervals (the bin range).

Before you begin the command, choose two adjacent blank columns. The left column serves as the bin range. The right column serves as the output range. Enter the values you want to use as intervals into the bin range column in ascending order with the smallest value at the top.

Initiate the command sequence, and enter the values range at the prompt (the range that contains the values you want to analyze). Next, enter the bin range at the prompt (the range that contains the intervals for the distribution).

The frequency values appear in the output range column to the right of the bin range. The numbers in the output range represent how many values in the value range are less than or equal to the adjacent value in the bin range but greater than the preceding value in the bin column. Blank and label cells have a count value of zero.

The output range always contains a value one row beyond the end of the bin column. This last value is the frequency of values that are greater than the last bin value.

Invert Multiply

/Data **M**atrix multiplies and inverts matrices formed by rows and columns of cell entries.

To invert a matrix:

1. Select **/D**ata **M**atrix.

2. Select **I**nvert.

3. Specify the matrix range you want to invert. The matrix range must have the same number of columns and rows and can contain up to 80 columns and 80 rows.

4. Specify the output range (the range in which you want 1-2-3 to enter the results of the inversion). You can specify either the entire range or only the upper left cell of the range.

To multiply matrices:

1. Select **/D**ata **M**atrix.

2. Select **M**ultiply.

3. Specify the first range you want to multiply. 1-2-3 can multiply any matrix of values up to a maximum of 80 rows by 80 columns.

4. Specify the second range you want to multiply.

5. Specify the output range (the range in which you want 1-2-3 to enter the results of the multiplication). You can specify either the entire range or only the upper left cell of the range.

/Data **R**egression

X-Range Y-Range Output-Range Intercept Reset Go Quit

/Data **R**egression produces statistics that describe the association between one data range and another. It calculates the slope of the line that best illustrates the data or predicts future trends based on current data. The Regression Settings dialog box appears when you select this command.

Use **/D**ata **R**egression if you have several sets of values and you want to see how and whether one set is dependent on the other(s). You can also use **/D**ata **R**egression to determine the slope(s) and the Y intercept(s) of the best-fitting line(s) for a set of data points.

Regression analysis allows you to predict a value for a dependent variable based on other values for one or more independent variables. In the results, the Y-axis intercept appears as the constant, and the X coefficient(s) are the slopes.

The **X**-Range is the range that contains all the columns of data to be analyzed as independent variables. You can specify up to 16 independent variables for multiple regression.

The **Y**-Range is the range that contains the column of data to be analyzed as dependent variables. The X range and the Y range must have the same number of rows.

When entering the **O**utput-Range, you can specify a single cell (the upper left cell of the range), the entire range, or the range name. The range must be at least nine rows long and two columns wider than the number of independent variables. It must be at least four columns wide.

The **I**ntercept option allows you to choose between **C**ompute, computing the Y intercept, and forcing it to be **Z**ero. The default is to compute the Y intercept.

1-2-3 enters the following information into the output range: the constant, the standard error of the Y estimate, the r-squared value, the number of observations, the degrees of freedom, the X coefficients (for each of the independent variables), and the standard error of each of these coefficients.

Reset cancels all the current regression settings.

Go begins the analysis.

Use **Q**uit to return to READY mode before completing the data regression.

To graph a regression line of estimated Y values against the actual Y values, select the XY graph type. Then assign the range of estimated Y values to both the X and A ranges of the graph. Assign the actual Y values to the B range of the graph. Set the format for the B range of the graph to symbols only. The resulting graph shows the regression line with real Y values as points.

/Data **P**arse

Format-Line Input-Column Output-Range Reset Go Quit

/Data **P**arse separates a single column of long labels into several columns and assigns data types to each column.

When you select **/D**ata **P**arse, 1-2-3 displays the Parse Settings dialog box. You can specify the input column range and the output range in the dialog box, or you can use the menu.

Use **/D**ata **P**arse to convert an ASCII text file you have imported into your worksheet with **/F**ile **I**mport **T**ext into a standard 1-2-3 worksheet or database.

1-2-3 treats data imported with **/F**ile **I**mport **T**ext as long labels of text contained in a single column. You must parse this data, breaking up the long labels into individual cell entries that 1-2-3 can use, if you want to perform any other 1-2-3 task, such as numeric analysis or graphing, with the data.

- Before you use this command, position the cell pointer in the top cell of the column you want to parse. Select **/D**ata **P**arse then select **F**ormat-Line **C**reate. Format lines determine how 1-2-3 parses the label below the format line into individual entries, separating the label wherever there are spaces.

1-2-3 analyzes the label at the current position of the cell pointer and inserts a format line of the same length above it in a new row. The format line that is created is 1-2-3's best guess of how the label should be parsed.

The format line is a label preceded by a split vertical bar (¦). 1-2-3 inserts a format line in the cell above the previous position of the cell pointer. The characters in the format line reflect the data type and the width of each block of data in the cell below.

Format lines can contain the following symbols:

L	The first character of a label block
V	The first character of a value block
D	The first character of a date block
T	The first character of a time block
S	Skip the character below when parsing
>	Characters in a data block
*	Blank space immediately below, currently undefined, but can become part of a block of data in following cells

1-2-3 creates the following format line for the long label in the cell below it:

```
¦L>> >>*******************V >>>*********V>>****V>>>
'Costs                     1500       950  1200
```

/**D**ata **P**arse will enter Costs as a label in one column, 1500 as a value in a second column, 950 as a value in a third column, and 1200 as a value in a fourth column.

- An optional step is to edit the format line. Edit format lines if any block (including adjacent * characters) is not wide enough to accommodate any of the data that will be parsed in the rows beneath it, if any of the block widths or data type characters are incorrect, or if any single block contains a space since the format line treats it as two shorter blocks. (See the next section, "Editing a Format Line," for more information.)

The Skip symbol (S) can be entered only manually. You can replace a symbol with an S when you edit the format line. If you begin a block with an S, 1-2-3 does not copy that block into the output range when it passes the line below.

- Another optional step is to create one or more additional format lines. Create an additional format line if any cell below the format line contains a block whose data type does not match that indicated in the format line or if any cell below the format line contains a block whose width should be different from that indicated in the format line.

To create each additional format line, select **Q**uit to return to READY mode, position the cell pointer in the next cell in the column requiring a new format line, and select /**D**ata **P**arse **F**ormat-Line **C**reate. Edit each new line if necessary.

- Select Input-Column to enter the range that contains the column of format lines and the cells you want to parse at the prompt. Be sure to include the format lines. Remember that the range includes only one column.

- Select Output-Range to enter the cell address of the upper left corner of a blank range in the worksheet large enough to hold your rows and columns of parsed data.

- After specifying Format-Line, Input-Column, and Output-Range, select Go.

1-2-3 produces a parsed copy of the imported data in the output range. Each block of data has been entered in an individual cell as a value, date, time, or label.

Editing a Format Line

To edit a format line, position the cell pointer in the cell that contains the format line you want to edit. Select **/D**ata **P**arse **F**ormat-Line **E**dit.

The cell pointer disappears. You can edit the format line on the worksheet itself. The cursor is below the first character of the format line, and the status indicator reads OVR. This tells you that the overstrike editing feature is activated. Use (→) or (←) to move through the format line to the characters you want to edit. Then type new characters in place of the incorrect ones. You can also use (DEL), BACKSPACE, (CTRL)-(←), (CTRL)-(→), and (INS) as you would in EDIT mode.

Press (↓), (↑), (PGDN), or (PGUP) to scroll the rows below the format line to see rows not currently visible on your screen. You can also move a row directly below the format line temporarily so that you can check the format of that row more easily. You do not have to undo scrolling before you press (↵) to finish editing the format line.

Press (ESC) to erase the entire format line. This does not delete the row. Press (HOME) to return the cursor to its initial position in the format line and to undo any scrolling. Press (BREAK) to cancel the format line edit and to return to READY mode with the format line as it was before you began to edit it. Press (↵) when you have completed editing the format line.

After you have edited the format line, the new format line appears in your worksheet, and 1-2-3 returns you to the Data Parse menu so that you can continue with the parse procedure.

System Command

The **/S**ystem command lets you suspend the current 1-2-3 session temporarily and return to the operating system without clearing the worksheet from memory. Select **/S**ystem when you want to use the operating system commands without ending the current 1-2-3 session. When you finish using the operating system commands, type **exit,** and then press (↵) to return to 1-2-3.

/System

/System lets you leave 1-2-3 temporarily, use a DOS command, and then return to your 1-2-3 session.

CAUTION Before you use **/S**ystem, it is recommended that you use **/F**ile **S**ave to save your work.

You can use any DOS command except commands that load another program into memory, such as BPRINT and SETCLOCK. If you load another program into memory, you will not be able to return to the 1-2-3 program.

Chapter 3

Macros

You can use macros to speed up repetitive or complex tasks. A macro is a set of instructions that automate tasks in 1-2-3. You can automate procedures you normally perform from the keyboard, such as using menu commands. You can also use macros to perform complex tasks and programming procedures, such as for loops and if-then-else statements. You use a macro from the worksheet or a macro library. A macro can include procedures entered from the keyboard as well as macro commands.

Note Mouse actions are not acceptable as macro instructions. You must use keystrokes to select commands and data in a macro.

The information in this chapter is divided into three sections. The "Macro Basics" section presents the basic concepts and procedures for creating and using 1-2-3 macros. Section two, "Using the Learn Feature to Create Macros," describes this alternative method of entering macro instructions. The third section, "Advanced Macro Commands," introduces a more advanced way of automating 1-2-3. You should not attempt to use these advanced macro capabilities unless you are an experienced 1-2-3 user or familiar with programming concepts and techniques.

Macro Basics

A macro is a series of cell entries typed in one or more cells in a single column. A macro cell entry must appear in the form of a label, whether it is a command, a number, or a formula.

A macro can include advanced macro commands and keystroke instructions. Advanced macro commands cause 1-2-3 to perform built-in programming functions. (See "Advanced Macro Commands" later in this chapter.) Keystroke instructions represent keys on the keyboard and cause 1-2-3 to perform as it does when you press those keys. They can be divided into two groups: instructions that consist of a single character, such as / (slash), w, and ~ (tilde), and instructions that consist of a key name within {} (braces), such as {RIGHT}.

The single-character keystroke instructions represent the typewriter keys on your keyboard. Most of these instructions duplicate the character on the key they represent. For example, the keystroke instruction that displays the 1-2-3 main menu is / (slash), and the keystroke instruction that selects **W**orksheet from the main menu is **w**.

The keystroke instructions that consist of a key name within {} (braces) represent the pointer-movement keys, function keys, and a few other keys. (See "Keystroke Instructions" in this section.)

Creating a Macro

You can create a macro in five steps:

1. Plan your macro, and go through the steps of your task manually.
2. Enter the macro as one or more labels.
3. Name the macro.
4. Document the macro.
5. Run the macro.

Planning a Macro   Before you write a macro, plan the steps necessary to accomplish the desired task. When you have a good grasp of the required steps, go through each keystroke manually, carefully noting each key that you press. After confirming that the sequence of keystrokes is correct, you are ready to enter the macro.

Entering a Macro   Some guidelines for entering a macro, as well as some rules on macro structure, follow:

- If you enter macros in the same worksheet as data, use a blank area of the worksheet so that the macro does not affect any data that already exist.

- Type the entries for a macro in any column of cells. You can type more than one instruction or command sequence in the same cell.

- The instructions you type in a macro can include any of the standard keyboard characters (for example, h, 9, +), keystroke instructions, and advanced macro commands.

- The instructions in each cell can be as short as a single keystroke or as long as 240 characters. If the keystroke sequence is very long, divide it into more than one cell in a column for easier reading and editing.

- Type all cell entries for a macro in the form of labels. When entering commands (beginning with a /), numbers, or formulas, you must begin the macro entry with a label-prefix character, such as a single quote (').

- Leave the cell below the macro instructions blank so that 1-2-3 does not include any information immediately below the macro as part of the macro's instructions.

- You can use the Learn feature to create macros by entering the keystroke instructions and testing them at the same time. (See "Using the Learn Feature to Create Macros.")

- You can also save the macros in a macro library, a special file that contains only macros. (See "Creating and Using the Macro Library Manager" in Chapter 7.)

Keystroke Instructions You can enter most keystrokes in a macro simply by typing the appropriate key; however, you must type the keystroke instructions, which represent keys on the keyboard, as they appear in Table 3.1.

Keystroke Instruction	1-2-3 Key
~ (a tilde)	⏎
{D} or {DOWN}	↓
{U} or {UP}	↑
{L} or {LEFT}	←
{R} or {RIGHT}	→
{APP1}	ALT-F7 (APP1)
{APP2}	ALT-F8 (APP2)
{APP3}	ALT-F9 (APP3)
{APP4}	ALT-F10 (APP4)
{HOME}	HOME
{END}	END
{PGUP}	PGUP (move up one screen)
{PGDN}	PGDN (move down one screen)
{BIGLEFT}	CTRL-← (move left one screen)
{BIGRIGHT}	CTRL-→ (move right one screen)
{HELP}	F1 (HELP)
{EDIT}	F2 (EDIT)
{NAME}	F3 (NAME)
{ABS}	F4 (ABS)
{GOTO}	F5 (GOTO)
{WINDOW}	F6 (WINDOW)

Table 3.1

Keystroke Instruction	1-2-3 Key
{QUERY}	F7 (QUERY)
{TABLE}	F8 (TABLE)
{CALC}	F9 (CALC)
{GRAPH}	F10 (GRAPH)
{INSERT} or {INS}	INS
{ESCAPE} or {ESC}	ESC
{BACKSPACE} or {BS}	BACKSPACE
{DELETE} or {DEL}	DEL
/ <, or {menu}	/ (slash) or < (less than symbol)
{~}	to have tilde appear as ~
{{} and {}}	to have braces appear as { and }

Table 3.1 Continued

You must enclose all the keystroke instructions (with the exception of the ⏎ symbol) in braces ({ and }). You can type uppercase or lowercase letters interchangeably when entering the key names.

Note   To specify two or more consecutive uses of the same key, you can enter a number following the key name. Separate the number from the key name with a space.

Naming a Macro   After you enter a macro, you must assign the macro a range name. To name a macro, name the first cell of the macro with **/R**ange **N**ame **C**reate or **/R**ange **N**ame **L**abels. You use the range name to run the macro. To name the macro range, follow these steps:

1. Select **/R**ange **N**ame **C**reate.

2. Specify the macros name (up to 15 characters) as the range name. 1-2-3 accepts two kinds of macro names:

   • Backslash names consist of a backslash followed by a single letter, such as \D. You start this macro by pressing ALT and the name that follows the backslash.

   • Multiple-character names are ordinary range names. It is a good idea to specify a name that reminds you of what the macro does.

3. Specify the first cell of the macro as the range to name.

(For more details about naming a macro, see the discussion of the **/R**ange **N**ame command in Chapter 2.)

Documenting a Macro After writing a macro, you may want to write a description of the step-by-step instructions for the macro to the right of the cell or cells that contain the macro and the macro's range name as a label to the left of the first cell of macro instruction. Make sure that the descriptions are not in the same cells as the macro, so 1-2-3 does not confuse your notes with the macro instructions. Documenting a macro clarifies the macro's purpose, describes the steps of the macro procedure, and identifies the range name that belongs to the macro.

Running a Macro Running a macro means starting the macro so that it carries out the task it automates. You run a macro in one of two ways: with (ALT) or with (ALT)-(F3) (RUN). The method you use depends on the macro's name.

CAUTION   Use **/F**ile **S**ave to save your work before you run the macro. If the macro produces unexpected results, you can use **/F**ile **R**etrieve to retrieve the original version of the worksheet. If the Undo feature is on, and no add-in programs are attached, you can press (ALT)-(F4) (UNDO) immediately after the macro is finished to restore your original worksheet.

To run a backslash macro, hold down (ALT) and press the letter of the macro range name. For example, to run a macro named \N, press (ALT)-n.

To run a range name macro:

1. Make sure 1-2-3 is in READY mode.

2. Press (ALT)-(F3) (RUN).

1-2-3 displays a menu of all range names in the worksheet (including macro range names and backslash macros) and in any macro libraries in memory. If you have many range names, press (F3) (NAME) to see a full-screen menu. Highlight a macro range name in the full-screen menu to see the range address or the macro library name (if the range name is in a macro library in memory).

3. To specify the macro to run, do one of the following:

   • Type the macro range name or address, and press (↵).

   • Highlight the macro range name in the list of range names, and press (↵).

   • Click the macro range name in the list of range names.

   • Press (ESC) to switch 1-2-3 to POINT mode, move the cell pointer to the first cell of the macro, and press (↵).

Interrupting a Macro To interrupt a macro at any time during execution, press (CTRL)-(BREAK). Press (ESC) to clear the error message. 1-2-3 returns immediately to READY mode and lets you resume your work session. (CTRL)-(BREAK) is useful for halting a lengthy macro sequence that you want to end early or for ending a macro in an infinite loop. (See the discussion of {BRANCH} in the section "Advanced Macro Commands.")

Interactive Macros You can combine macro execution with manual entries by inserting a pause in the macro instruction sequence.

The {?} keystroke instruction causes the macro to pause for manual entries. You can enter {?} anywhere in the macro instruction sequence. When 1-2-3 reads a {?} keystroke instruction in the macro, it stops executing the macro until you type something and press ⏎.

When you enter {?} in the macro instruction sequence, you must complete the cell entry with a ~ character, which instructs 1-2-3 to continue macro execution after you press ⏎.

Autoexecute Macros An autoexecute macro is a special macro that specifies a task that 1-2-3 implements automatically when you first load the worksheet using the **/File Retrieve** command. Autoexecute macros are useful for worksheets you use often or are preparing for others to use.

You create an autoexecute macro the same way that you create any other macro. However, you give it a special name: \0 (zero). Do not use this name when naming any other macro. A worksheet can contain only one autoexecute macro.

1-2-3 automatically invokes a macro named \0 when you retrieve a worksheet that contains it. To use an auto-execute macro during a 1-2-3 work session, you must assign it an additional macro name, for example, \E.

Dialog Boxes in Macros When you run a macro, 1-2-3 does not display dialog boxes. Dialog boxes appear only if you use {WINDOW} in your macro. 1-2-3 suspends the macro when a dialog box appears if you use {EDIT} to switch to SETTINGS mode. When you select OK or press ⏎, 1-2-3 uses the values you specified in the dialog box and continues to run the macro.

Debugging a Macro

If, when you run a macro, it does not perform as you expected it to, or if 1-2-3 does not finish running it because of an error, you need to debug the macro—find out which macro instructions are causing the problem and edit them.

Some cases in which you would edit a macro are as follows:

- You observe a typing error or an omission of a keystroke. A common missing keystroke is the tilde (~) symbol representing ⏎.

- While the macro is executing, 1-2-3 encounters an error in your keystroke sequence and displays an error message. You need to find and correct the error before you can successfully execute your macro.

- The existing macro, if altered slightly, could be used to perform a similar worksheet procedure, saving you the task of rewriting the entire macro.

To edit a macro, go to the range that contains the macro keystroke sequence and edit the cells as you would any label. As long as the macro begins in the same place as it did previously, you can invoke it using its original name.

Debugging a Macro in STEP Mode

The instructions that are causing an error in a lengthy and complicated macro may not be easy to find. To help you diagnose problems in a macro, 1-2-3 has a feature called STEP mode. This feature allows you to examine a macro one keystroke at a time so that you can locate the error.

To turn on STEP mode, press (ALT)-(F2) (STEP). A STEP indicator appears in the status line. Then invoke the macro as usual.

To proceed through the macro in STEP mode, press any key to execute the macro one step at a time. Each time you press a key to execute another step, 1-2-3 replaces the STEP indicator at the bottom of the screen with the cell address of the cell that contains the macro instructions and the contents of that cell. Keep pressing any key to proceed to the next step.

Note   If you have a {?} command, indicating a pause in the macro, you must press (↵) to continue STEP mode macro execution.

Once you have found the error, end the macro by pressing (CTRL)-(BREAK), and then you can edit it. If you encounter an error that produces an error message, press (↵) or (ESC) both to clear the error and to exit the macro.

You do not need to leave STEP mode to edit a macro. When you quit a macro to edit it, 1-2-3 redisplays the STEP indicator to remind you that STEP mode is still on.

After editing the macro, you can invoke the macro again, remaining in STEP mode. You can then repeat the debugging procedure from the beginning of the macro, if necessary.

To leave STEP mode, press (ALT)-(F2) (STEP) again, and then press any key.

Using the Learn Feature to Create Macros

When you use the Learn feature to create a macro, 1-2-3 automatically records all of your keystrokes in a learn range, a single-column range that you define. To create a macro with the Learn feature, you first specify a learn range for the macro in an empty part of your worksheet. To specify the single-column range, select /Worksheet Learn Range, and then specify a single-column range when prompted. When determining a size for the learn range, it's always better to make it larger than you think you might need so that 1-2-3 doesn't run out of space when recording your keystrokes.

Next, you turn on the Learn feature by pressing (ALT)-(F5) (GOTO). The LEARN indicator appears in the status line. You then perform the task(s) you want to record. As you do so, 1-2-3 records all of your keystrokes in the learn range; you do not enter anything into the learn range directly. 1-2-3 records keystrokes in macro instruction format. For example, when you press (F5) (GOTO), type A5, and then press (↵), 1-2-3 records {GOTO}A5~.

After you finish, press (ALT)-(F5) (LEARN) again to stop 1-2-3 from recording more keystrokes. Move the cell pointer to the learn range, and examine the recorded keystrokes. If you made any mistakes, edit them before you go any further. If you made many mistakes and want to start over, erase the learn range with /Worksheet Learn Erase, and then start again.

If the macro looks correct, assign it a range name. (See "Naming a Macro" earlier in this section.) Depending on how you named the macro, run it by using either (ALT) or (ALT)-(F3) (RUN). (See "Running a Macro" earlier in this section.)

If the macro isn't working as you expected, debug and edit it. (See "Debugging a Macro in STEP Mode" earlier in this section.)

Advanced Macro Commands

In addition to its keystroke instruction feature, 1-2-3 includes advanced macro commands that cause 1-2-3 to perform a built-in programming function. You implement each of these special macro commands with a 1-2-3 advanced macro keyword, such as {IF}, {BRANCH}, and {QUIT}.

This section contains a general explanation of advanced macro commands, including grammar (syntax), arguments, and subroutines; a summary of advanced macro commands by category; and a description of each macro command.

Note This section contains advanced 1-2-3 material. Do not attempt to use the information presented here unless you are an experienced user of 1-2-3 macros or are familiar with programming concepts and techniques.

Advanced Macro Grammar

Each advanced macro command you create must have the correct syntax or grammatical structure. The first word in an advanced macro command is the keyword. You must type the keyword exactly as it appears in this chapter. Uppercase and lowercase letters are interchangeable.

Most of the advanced macro commands require an additional word or two, called arguments. Grammatically speaking, macro keywords are like verbs in a sentence; they tell 1-2-3 what action to perform. Arguments are like direct objects; they complete the command by indicating the what, where, or when of the particular action.

You supply the arguments for advanced macro commands. For example, if you want 1-2-3 to place the number 96.5 in cell B10, use the {LET} command, which has this format:

{LET *location,entry*}

You fill in the arguments as follows:

{LET B10,96.5}

You need to be familiar with several rules of grammar to use advanced macro commands. You must create advanced macro commands as label entries or string-valued formulas (a formula that generates a label). Each command must begin with a left brace ({) character followed by a macro command keyword.

After the keyword, type a single-space character, then one or more arguments. Each argument must be the correct type — number, string, or location (cell address or range). Some macro commands require more than one type of argument. Others require no arguments at all. Multiple arguments are separated from one another with argument separators.

The two valid argument separators are the comma (,) and the semicolon (;). The comma is the default configuration for the argument separator; however, the semicolon is always valid regardless of the default configuration. Do not leave any space characters before or after an argument separator.

Each advanced macro command must end with a right brace (}), and the entire macro command must be within a single cell. You cannot have the beginning brace in one cell and the ending brace in another. The format for writing advanced macro commands is as follows:

{Keyword Arg1,Arg2,...,Argn}

You can store any number of macro commands in a single cell, as long as you do not enter more than 240 characters. You can mix advanced macro commands with individual keystrokes in the same cell.

The following advanced macro commands show the correct syntax, using the {BLANK *location*} command as an example. The {BLANK} command erases the contents of a specified cell or range.

{BLANK A1..G45}	A range as the location argument
{blank G45}	A single-cell address as the location argument

The following commands are incorrect:

{BLANKB45..H56}	Space missing after keyword
{BLANKE A 100}	Keyword misspelled, cell address error

Argument Types

Table 3.2 describes the four types of advanced macro command arguments.

Argument	Description
Value	A number or a formula that results in a number.
String	Text or a formula that results in text.
Location	A range name or address or a formula that results in a range name or address.
Condition	Any logical formula. The macro proceeds depending on the result of a true-false test specified in the condition. It compares the values in two cells to determine if one is less than, greater than, or equal to another or checks the result of a specified formula. The expression can contain any entry, a number, or a string-valued formula.

Table 3.2

Note   In many cases, you must enclose a string argument in quotation marks. Enclose in quotation marks any string or range name that contains a colon, semicolon, or comma.

For example,

> string: {LET A25,"Type a letter; then a number"}

> range name: {BLANK "TOTAL, 5 YEARS"}

In addition, enclose in quotation marks any formula you want to appear as a label or any string argument that may be confused with a range name.

CAUTION   1-2-3 does not adjust cell addresses in macros when you use /**M**ove, /**W**orksheet **I**nsert, and /**W**orksheet **D**elete commands. Therefore, use range names to refer to all individual cells, as well as ranges, in the worksheet. In addition, if the macro contains instructions to insert or delete a row, the results may affect macro execution following those instructions.

Declaring Argument Types   Some commands can process more than one type of argument. For example, a {LET} command can store either a label or a number in a cell. You can use the suffixes :string and :value to explicitly define the argument type.

For example,

{LET A1,12+13} or
{LET A1,12+13:value}   enters the number 25 into cell A1

{LET A1,"12+13"} or
{LET A1,12+13:string}   enters the label '12+13 into cell A1

Macro Subroutines

The section on invoking a macro described the process of starting a macro with the macro key, (ALT). One macro can also invoke another macro. One way to do this is to use a {BRANCH} command.

When 1-2-3 reads a {BRANCH} command, it continues reading macro keystrokes and advanced macro commands at the specified location. In effect, one macro passes control of the 1-2-3 session to another macro.

If you want to use a sequence of macro instructions in several different places in a macro program, you can create a subroutine. Instead of typing the entire macro sequence each time or using a {BRANCH} command to send 1-2-3 somewhere else to get its instructions, you simply put the range name assigned to the sequence in braces at the appropriate location in the macro instructions. This is the subroutine call. When 1-2-3 encounters this subroutine call command, it executes the sequence of instructions you named. When the sequence is finished or it reads a {RETURN} command, 1-2-3 returns to the original routine immediately after the subroutine call.

For example, the macro named MASTER contains the subroutine call command {CLEANUP}. As 1-2-3 executes the commands in MASTER, it will encounter this subroutine call command. This command tells 1-2-3 to stop executing MASTER and begin executing the commands in the macro named CLEANUP. This is known as calling a subroutine. When 1-2-3 comes to the end of CLEANUP, or reads a {RETURN} command, it returns to the macro instructions in MASTER located immediately below the {CLEANUP} command. This is known as returning from a subroutine.

MASTER macro:	**CLEANUP macro:**
XXXX	XXX
XXXXX	XXXX
XXX	XX
{CLEANUP}	XXXXX
XXXX	{RETURN}
XXX	

One macro can call another at any time — in the middle of a range specification, at a file name menu, and so on.

CAUTION   Do not use a subroutine name that is the same as one of the special macro keys in Table 3.1. If a duplication occurs, 1-2-3 performs the subroutine, not the keystroke.

Passing Arguments to Subroutines

In most 1-2-3 advanced macro commands, you specify a keyword followed by one or more arguments. For instance, the command {LET A1,999.5} assigns 999.5 to the location A1. You can also give values to the macro program subroutines that you create. This process is called passing arguments to a subroutine. If you create a subroutine called COMPUTE, you can pass its values by enclosing both the subroutine name and the arguments in braces [COMPUTE 52,G1]. The command is a subroutine call in which two arguments are passed. You may want 1-2-3 to interpret 52 as a number and the argument G1 as a cell address.

For each argument you specify in a subroutine, you must also specify a cell in which to store the value being passed. You may also need to tell 1-2-3 how to interpret the arguments in the subroutine call. To do this, begin a subroutine with a {DEFINE} command.

For more information about the {subroutine} command, see the command description later in this chapter.

Updating Results of Advanced Macro Commands

When you run a macro with the worksheet recalculation method set to **A**utomatic (see /**W**orksheet **G**lobal **R**ecalculation **A**utomatic in Chapter 2), 1-2-3 does not recalculate all data continuously. Automatic recalculation of advanced macro commands occurs if the user enters data in the worksheet in response to a {?} command or if you have followed a command such as {LET} or {GET} with a ~ (tilde) to represent ⏎ (which 1-2-3 interprets as user input). Suppose you have a series of {LET} commands but no user data entry in response to a {?} command. If any other commands in the macro depend on the results of the {LET} command, you'll need to recalculate the worksheet, either by following the last {LET} command with a ~ (tilde) or by including a {RECALC} or {RECALCCOL} command.

Types of Advanced Macro Commands

The advanced macro commands fall into five categories: screen control, interactive, flow of control, data manipulation, and file manipulation.

- Screen control commands control different parts of the screen display, change the contents of the mode indicator, and sound your computer's bell.

- Interactive commands suspend macro execution for keyboard input, control the timing of macro execution, and prevent undesired changes to a worksheet while a macro is running.

- Flow-of-control commands direct the path of macro execution so that you can create a macro that includes for loops, branches, subroutine calls, and conditional processing.

- Data manipulation commands enter data, edit existing entries, erase entries, and clear control panel prompts.

- File manipulation commands work with text files. Text files, also called print files, are files on disk in ASCII format. You can use the file manipulation commands to create a new text file, copy data from a text file to a worksheet, or copy data from a worksheet to a text file.

The following is a description of each advanced macro command by category. Throughout the remainder of this chapter, uppercase words indicate macro keywords. Lowercase *italic* words indicate the type of argument required by a macro keyword. Arguments enclosed by [] are optional. When you enter a macro, you can use either uppercase or lowercase characters. In the examples, range names also appear in uppercase.

Screen Control Commands   The following commands are used to control the screen:

{BEEP}	{INDICATE}
{BORDERSOFF}	{PANELOFF}
{BORDERSON}	{PANELON}
{FRAMEOFF}	{WINDOW}
{FRAMEON}	{WINDOWSOFF}
{GRAPHOFF}	{WINDOWSON}
{GRAPHON}	

BEEP   {BEEP [*tone-number*]} sounds the bell or tone. The *tone-number* argument is optional.

{BEEP} causes 1-2-3 to sound the computer's bell. This command is normally used to signal the end of a macro, to alert you to an error (see {ONERROR}), and to signal the end of a period (see {WAIT}).

The *tone-number* argument specifies the tone of the bell. There are four different beeps, invoked with the arguments 1, 2, 3, and 4. If you do not specify a number argument, 1-2-3 uses the beep invoked by number 1.

BORDERSOFF {BORDERSOFF} suppresses display of the worksheet frame (column letters and row numbers). The worksheet frame remains hidden until 1-2-3 reaches a {BORDERSON} command or the macro ends. When the macro ends, the borders return to their default state of being displayed.

BORDERSON {BORDERSON} restores standard display of the worksheet frame.

FRAMEOFF Identical to {BORDERSOFF}.

FRAMEON Identical to {BORDERSON}.

GRAPHOFF {GRAPHOFF} removes a graph display by {GRAPHON} and redisplays the worksheet.

GRAPHON {GRAPHON} [*named-graph*],[nodisplay] has three possible results, depending on the syntax you use.

{GRAPHON} displays a full-screen view of the current graph while the macro continues to run. {GRAPHON *named-graph*} makes the named-graph settings the current graph settings and displays a full-screen view of *named-graph* while the macro continues to run. {GRAPHON *named-graph*,[nodisplay] makes the named-graph settings the current graph settings without displaying the graph.

INDICATE {INDICATE [*string*]} changes the mode indicator in the upper right corner of the screen. The string argument is optional. 1-2-3 replaces the mode indicator with the indicator string you specify. The new indicator remains on the screen even if the mode subsequently changes when you execute a command or type an entry. The only way to clear the indicator is to execute another {INDICATE} command.

{INDICATE} with no argument restores the READY mode indicator. To remove the mode indicator from the control panel entirely, use the command {INDICATE" "}.

1-2-3 uses only the first five characters of the string. You must type the string into the {INDICATE} command. You cannot use the address of a string-valued cell.

PANELOFF {PANELOFF [clear]} freezes the control panel and status line until 1-2-3 encounters a {PANELON} command or the macro ends. If you include the optional clear argument, 1-2-3 clears the control panel and status line before freezing them. Use {PANELOFF} in interactive macros to suppress activity in the control panel and status line that might be distracting to users.

PANELON	{PANELON} restores standard control panel redrawing. It does not take an argument.
WINDOW	{WINDOW} is equivalent to pressing F6 (WINDOW). Use {WINDOW} to display dialog boxes during a macro. 1-2-3 suspends a macro when a dialog box appears if you use {EDIT} to switch to SETTINGS mode. When you select OK or press ⏎, 1-2-3 uses the values you specified in the dialog box and continues to run the macro.
WINDOWSOFF	{WINDOWSOFF} freezes the screen display, except for the control panel. It does not take an argument.
	{WINDOWSOFF} allows you to manipulate data without having the changes flash on the screen. During normal macro execution, you can see each stage that the macro goes through during its operation. Use this command to suppress macro activity, especially during a long macro. {WINDOWSOFF} also speeds up macro execution since 1-2-3 does not have to keep redrawing the screen.
WINDOWSON	{WINDOWSON} restores normal updating of the screen display, undoing a {WINDOWSOFF} command. It does not take an argument.

Interactive Commands   The following commands are used for keyboard interaction:

{?}	{GETLABEL}
{BREAK}	{GETNUMBER}
{BREAKOFF}	{LOOK}
{BREAKON}	{MENU}
{FORM}	{MENUBRANCH}
{FORMBREAK}	{MENUCALL}
{GET}	{WAIT}

?	{?} halts macro execution temporarily, allowing you to type and move around the worksheet; macro execution continues when you press ⏎. {?} does not take an argument. When you press ⏎, it indicates only that 1-2-3 should resume execution of the macro. If you want 1-2-3 to execute a ⏎, you must include a ~ in the macro.
BREAK	{BREAK} clears the control panel and returns 1-2-3 to READY mode. It does not stop a macro.
BREAKOFF	{BREAKOFF} disables the CTRL-BREAK key during macro execution. It does not take an argument. Unless a macro executes a {BREAKOFF} command, you can always stop the execution of a macro by pressing CTRL-BREAK. If you are preparing an application for others to use but not change, you can make sure they stay under macro control with {BREAKOFF}. When CTRL-BREAK is disabled, others cannot

discontinue or interfere with the macro, either inadvertently or deliberately. {BREAKOFF} stays active until it is canceled with {BREAKON} or until the macro ends.

CAUTION   If {BREAKOFF} is active and the macro goes into an infinite loop, you cannot return to 1-2-3. The only way to stop the macro is to stop and then restart the computer.

BREAKON   {BREAKON} restores the operation of the (CTRL)-(BREAK) key, undoing a {BREAKOFF} command. It does not take an argument.

FORM   {FORM *input-location*,[*call-table*],[*include-list*],[*exclude-list*]} suspends a macro temporarily so that you can enter and edit data in the unprotected cells in *input-location*.

input-location is a range of any size that contains at least one unprotected cell. This is the range where you enter data. It cannot include hidden columns.

call-table is an optional two-column range. Each cell in the first column contains one or more macro names of keyboard keys. Each adjacent cell in the second column contains a set of macro instructions that 1-2-3 performs when you press the key(s) listed in the first column.

include-list is an optional range that lists allowable keystrokes. You can specify any character key and key name. Each cell in the range can contain one or more of the character keys and key names listed in Table 3.1.

exclude-list is an optional range that lists unacceptable keystrokes. Each cell in the range can contain one or more keystrokes. 1-2-3 beeps when you press an excluded key. If you specify an *include-list*, do not specify an *exclude-list*, and vice versa. 1-2-3 uses only one list argument. If you specify both an *include-list* and an *exclude-list*, 1-2-3 uses the *include-list*.

There should be no punctuation between the names of the keyboard keys in *call-table, include-list,* and *exclude-list*. Further, the table and lists are case sensitive. To use {FORM} from a macro library, *input-location* must be a worksheet range. You can specify a *call-table, include-list,* and *exclude-list* from a macro library or the worksheet. Use {FORM} to fill data entry forms. {FORM} is similar to /**R**ange **I**nput, but the three optional arguments give you more control over user entries.

You can nest forms (place one form within another form) by making a call to {FORM}. 1-2-3 lets you nest up to eight forms.

Including {ESC} or ~ (tilde) in a *call-table* subroutine lets you move the cell pointer out of the *input-range*'s unprotected area and use all 1-2-3 keys and menus for the rest of the *call-table* subroutine. To end a macro from within a *call-table* subroutine, use {RESTART} or {QUIT} in the subroutine. To end a {FORM} command from within a *call-table* subroutine and continue the macro, use {FORMBREAK}.

FORMBREAK   {FORMBREAK} ends a {FORM} command canceling the current form. You can also use {FORMBREAK} to end a nested {FORM} command and have 1-2-3 return you to the previous form. 1-2-3 continues at the command that follows the {FORM} command. Use {FORMBREAK} only within a *call-table* subroutine or a subroutine to which you transfer control from a *call-table* subroutine with {BRANCH} or {DISPATCH}. If you use {FORMBREAK} without first using a {FORM} command, 1-2-3 ends the macro and displays an error.

GET {GET *location*} pauses for you to type a single character and then stores in at the specified location. The single character you type can be a standard typewriter key or a 1-2-3 standard key, for instance, (F9) (CALC). The character or standard key is stored as a left-aligned label entry at the upper left corner cell of the location. {GET} makes no provision for a prompt on the control panel. Use {GETLABEL} or {GETNUMBER} when such a prompt is required.

GETLABEL {GETLABEL *prompt,location*} displays *prompt* in the control panel and pauses for you to type a character string and then stores it as a left-aligned label entry at the *location* cell. {GETLABEL} overrides a current {PANELOFF} condition.

You can use any literal string, with as many characters as fit within the control panel edit line, as *prompt*. (Up to 72 characters can be displayed.) *prompt* can also be the range name or address of a cell that contains the prompt string, or a string formula that evaluates to the prompt string.

You can specify a cell or a range as *location*. If you specify a range, 1-2-3 stores your response in the first cell of the range. You can also precede *location* with a + (plus) to indicate it contains the address of a cell where you want to store the label.

The response to the prompt can include up to 240 characters. If you press ⏎ without typing anything, 1-2-3 enters an ' (apostrophe) label prefix in *location*. If you enter a numeric value, it's converted to a label in *location*.

GETNUMBER {GETNUMBER *prompt,location*} pauses for you to type a number and then stores it as a number entry at the location. (See {GETLABEL} for *prompt* and *location* argument details.)

When 1-2-3 encounters a {GETLABEL} or {GETNUMBER} command, it displays the prompt string on the control panel and then pauses.

The response to the prompt must be a number, numeric formula, or reference to a cell containing a number or numeric formula. The response can include up to 240 characters. If you enter a label, string formula, or reference to a cell containing a label or string formula as the response, 1-2-3 enters ERR in *location*. 1-2-3 also enters ERR if you press ⏎ without typing anything.

{GETNUMBER} overrides a current {PANELOFF} condition.

LOOK {LOOK *location*} checks to see if you have typed a character. If you have typed a character since the macro began executing, 1-2-3 stores the first character typed at the specified location. If no characters have been typed, 1-2-3 enters an apostrophe label prefix in the location cell.

While a macro is running, 1-2-3 does not pay attention to the keyboard. If you type something while a macro is running, the operating system stores the characters in its keyboard buffer until 1-2-3 requests them. The keyboard buffer is usually small (for instance, ten characters). When you fill this buffer, the computer beeps each time you press another key.

{LOOK} is similar to {GET}, except that {LOOK} does not suspend macro execution. {LOOK} leaves the character in the keyboard buffer for use by a {?}, {GET}, {GETNUMBER}, or {GETLABEL} command.

MENU {MENU} is equivalent to pressing / (slash) or < (less than symbol) or to moving the mouse pointer to the control panel.

MENUBRANCH {MENUBRANCH *location*} halts execution temporarily to let you select a menu item and then branches accordingly.

MENUCALL {MENUCALL *location*} halts execution temporarily to let you select a menu item and then executes the corresponding macro as a subroutine. When 1-2-3 encounters a {MENUBRANCH} or {MENUCALL} command, it displays a menu on the control panel, based on the contents of the range whose upper left corner is the location. When you choose a menu item, 1-2-3 continues reading macro keystrokes in the column that contains the menu item you select.

{MENUBRANCH} and {MENUCALL} differ in what happens after 1-2-3 executes the last command in the column containing the menu item. Following a {MENUBRANCH} command, 1-2-3 ends the macro after the last command in the column. Following a {MENUCALL} command, 1-2-3 continues macro execution immediately.

To construct a macro menu, follow these steps:

1. Place each menu item in a separate cell in the first row of the menu range. Blank cells are not allowed between menu items. You can include up to eight items in the menu. Keep the total number of characters small to avoid extending beyond the screen. The cell to the right of the final menu item must be blank.

2. Supply brief descriptions (they must be labels) for each item in the second row of the menu range. To create a blank label as a description, use a label that consists only of spaces.

3. Enter the macro instructions for each menu item in the cells immediately below the menu descriptions.

Begin each macro item with a different character so that you can select items by typing the first character. Otherwise, 1-2-3 will select the first entry (reading from left to right) whose first character matches the character you type.

Uppercase and lowercase letters are equivalent when you make a menu selection. For example, you can select **Q**uit by typing q or **Q**. You can always select a menu item by moving the highlight bar and pressing ⏎.

If you press (ESC) at a {MENUBRANCH} or {MENUCALL} menu, 1-2-3 cancels the menu selection process. Execution continues just after the macro command. This is the same point to which control returns after a {MENUCALL}.

{MENUBRANCH} and {MENUCALL} override a current {PANELOFF} condition.

WAIT {WAIT *time-number*} suspends macro execution until the time specified by *time-number*. {WAIT} causes 1-2-3 to halt execution and to display WAIT in the mode indicator. During this time, 1-2-3 will not respond to keystrokes. When the time specified by *time-number* is reached, execution continues. You can interrupt a {WAIT} command by pressing (CTRL)-(BREAK) unless you have executed a {BREAKOFF} command.

time-number can be a number, numeric formula, or reference to a cell that contains a number or numeric formula. The number must represent a future moment in time. If the number represents a nonexistent time or a time that has already passed, 1-2-3 ignores the {WAIT} command and continues to the next macro instruction. In most cases, you will use date and time @functions to specify *time-number*.

Flow-of-Control Commands The following commands control program flow:

{BRANCH}	{ONERROR}
{DEFINE}	{QUIT}
{DISPATCH}	{RESTART}
{FOR}	{RETURN}
{FORBREAK}	{subroutine}
{IF}	{SYSTEM}

BRANCH {BRANCH *location*} continues macro execution at a different cell. 1-2-3 immediately begins reading keystrokes at the new location. You can specify a single cell or a range name as the location. Execution continues at the upper left corner cell of the location.

Note {BRANCH} produces different results from a subroutine call. With {BRANCH}, you cannot return to the original routine except with another {BRANCH} command. A subroutine call returns macro control to the original routine immediately after the subroutine call.

CAUTION Do not confuse {BRANCH} with {GOTO}. {GOTO} moves the cell pointer. {BRANCH} transfers macro execution to the location you specify.

DEFINE {DEFINE *location1,location2,...locationn*} allocates storage locations and declares argument types for arguments to be passed to a subroutine. Use {DEFINE} in subroutines to specify where variables passed to that subroutine are to be stored. It must come before the point in the subroutine where the arguments are used.

The number of arguments in a {DEFINE} command must be the same as in the subroutine call command. Otherwise, 1-2-3 displays an error message when the subroutine is called.

Each location specification can be a single cell, a range, or a range name. If you specify a range, 1-2-3 uses the first cell of the range as the storage location.

1-2-3 has a simple scheme for passing arguments to subroutines. It checks each argument in a subroutine call against the type specified by the {DEFINE} command in the subroutine and then stores the argument in the cell specified by the {DEFINE} command either as a string or as a value.

This is a typical subroutine call:

{SUBR1 45*10,+"Dow"&"Jones",F10}

When the {DEFINE} command in SUBR1 is executed, 1-2-3 checks each argument to see if it should be stored literally as a string or evaluated first. String arguments are always stored as left-aligned labels, regardless of the worksheet's current default label prefix. Value arguments can be stored as numbers or as left-aligned labels, depending on the argument itself.

Declaring a String Argument Type   1-2-3 stores the arguments specified in a {DEFINE} command just as they appear in the command. Thus, 1-2-3 interprets the following {DEFINE} command as a string declaration:

{DEFINE X1,X2,X3}

If this command is the first item in SUBR1, 1-2-3 stores the label 45*10 in cell X1, the label +"Dow"&"Jones" in cell X2, and the label F10 in cell X3.

Declaring a Value Argument Type   As an alternative to the process just described, you can instruct 1-2-3 to evaluate an argument before storing it by typing :value after the cell address in the {DEFINE} command. For example,

{DEFINE X1:value,X2:value,X3:value}

If this command is the first item in SUBR1, 1-2-3 evaluates all three arguments before storing them. Thus, it stores the value of the first argument, 450, as a number in cell X1; the value of the second argument, the string Dow Jones, as a label in cell X2; and the value of the third argument, the contents of cell F10, as either a number or a label in cell X3.

DISPATCH   {DISPATCH *location*} branches to a destination specified in the location cell. The location cell should contain the cell address or the range name of another cell, the branch destination. If the location cell is blank or contains a numeric value, 1-2-3 ends macro execution and returns control to the user.

A typical use of {DISPATCH} would involve setting up the location cell as a variable cell, dependent on continually varying conditions in the worksheet. {DISPATCH} then allows you to branch conditionally to one of many alternative destinations, based on the current contents of the location cell.

Note {DISPATCH} differs from {BRANCH} in that {BRANCH} can execute instructions only in the location cell; it cannot continue to execute instructions at another destination specified in the location cell.

If you use a range name to specify the location cell, make sure the range you name contains only one cell. Specifying a range that contains more than one cell as the location makes {DISPATCH} equivalent to {BRANCH}.

FOR   {FOR *counter,start,stop,step,subroutine*} repeatedly executes the macro that begins at a particular location. {FOR} provides a loop capability (often called FOR-NEXT) similar to that provided by many other programming languages.

The *counter* is a cell in which 1-2-3 keeps track of the repetition of the macro routine it is executing. You do not need to enter anything at the counter location. Initially, the value of the counter cell is the start number value.

The start number is the beginning value of the counter. The stop number indicates the end of the counter. The step number is the value by which the counter increases each time 1-2-3 executes the subroutine. The subroutine is the first cell or range name of the subroutine to be executed.

Processing the Loop   To execute a {FOR} command, 1-2-3 first evaluates the start number, stop number, and step number values. Then (and each subsequent time a repetition is about to begin) 1-2-3 does the following:

1. Enters the start number in counter.

2. Compares the stop number and counter values. If the counter value does not exceed the stop number value, 1-2-3 executes the routine at the subroutine and goes to step 3. Otherwise, 1-2-3 continues reading keystrokes at the cell below the {FOR} command and does not perform the subroutine.

3. Increases the value in the counter cell by the step number value and returns to step 2.

It is possible that 1-2-3 will not perform the routine at all (see the fourth case in Table 3.3) or that the routine will fall into an infinite loop (see the fifth case). In the latter case, you must press (CTRL)-(BREAK) to stop the {FOR} loop.

Table 3.3 lists some typical combinations of start, stop, and step number actions.

Start	Stop	Step	Repetition Count
1	10	1	10
2	10	2	5
2	9	2	5
2	1	1	0 (start value exceeds stop value at beginning)
4	5	0	infinite (counter never exceeds stop value)

Table 3.3

Note   Ending the routine with {RETURN} is acceptable but not necessary. Do not use {QUIT} to end the routine. If you do, the loop will always terminate after the first pass.

1-2-3 stores the start number, stop number, and step number values internally. You cannot have the routine modify these values once it starts.

FORBREAK   {FORBREAK} cancels execution of a {FOR} loop and continues processing at the first character after that {FOR} command.

CAUTION   Use {FORBREAK} only within a subroutine called by a {FOR} command. Using {FORBREAK} anywhere else will result in an error.

{FORBREAK} does not take an argument. {FORBREAK} immediately ends a subroutine called by a {FOR} command and returns processing to the point immediately following the {FOR} command.

IF   {IF *condition*} conditionally executes the command that follows the {IF} command. {IF} allows a macro program to branch depending on the result of a true-false test. 1-2-3 evaluates the condition argument, which can be numeric, string value, or formula.

If the formula does not have the numeric value zero, 1-2-3 considers it to be true. Execution of the macro continues in the same cell immediately after the {IF} command.

If the formula has the numeric value zero, 1-2-3 considers it to be false. Execution of the macro continues in the cell below the one with the {IF} command. A blank cell (but not a cell that contains a blank string), string values, ERR, and NA are zero or false.

The {IF} command implements an if-then-else capability, similar to that in many other programming languages. The instructions in the cell after the {IF} command are the then clause. The instructions in the cell below the {IF} command are the else clause.

Be careful when you compose the then clause. In most instances, you should include a {BRANCH} or {QUIT} command to prevent the else clause from being executed directly after the then clause.

ONERROR   {ONERROR *branch-location*,[*message-location*]} branches to the branch location if a 1-2-3 error message occurs during macro execution. It optionally records the error message that 1-2-3 would have displayed at the message location.

The message-location argument is optional. If you include this argument, 1-2-3 stores the error message it would have displayed in the type of error that occurred because 1-2-3 does not display the message on the screen.

You should structure your macro so that there is no possibility of an error occurring before 1-2-3 encounters the {ONERROR} command.

1-2-3 can use each {ONERROR} command only once. An {ONERROR} condition remains in effect until another {ONERROR} command supersedes it, an error occurs, or macro execution ends. Once an error has occurred, the {ONERROR} condition is canceled. To continue trapping errors, include another {ONERROR} command in the branch-location routine.

CAUTION Pressing (CTRL)-(BREAK) causes an error. {ONERROR} takes effect if you press (CTRL)-(BREAK) unless you have executed a {BREAKOFF} command.

QUIT {QUIT} terminates macro execution, returning control to the keyboard. {QUIT} does not take an argument. {QUIT} is often most useful at the end of an {IF} command or as a result of a {MENUCALL} choice. {QUIT} ends all macro execution, not just the subroutine that may contain it.

RESTART {RESTART} cancels a subroutine and clears the subroutine stack. {RESTART} does not take an argument. {RESTART} is useful only in a subroutine that has been called from at least one other macro or subroutine. Use {RESTART} if your subroutine is nested below the calling routines (the stack) to which you will no longer return. When 1-2-3 encounters a {RESTART}, it continues executing instructions that follow in the subroutine. The macro stops when it encounters a {RETURN} command or a blank cell. It will not return to any of the routines that called it.

RETURN {RETURN} affects flow of control in subroutines. {RETURN} does not take an argument. Use {RETURN} in conjunction with {subroutine} or {MENUCALL} to cause 1-2-3 to immediately return to the calling routine. {RETURN} is not required if a subroutine ends because 1-2-3 encounters a blank or numeric cell. In such cases, control returns automatically to the calling routine.

{RETURN} is not equivalent to {QUIT} in a subroutine. {QUIT} ends macro execution and returns control of the 1-2-3 session to you. {RETURN} causes macro execution to continue just after the location of the last {subroutine} or {MENUCALL} command.

{subroutine} The {*subroutine*[*arg1*],[*arg2*],...[*argn*]} command calls a subroutine, optionally with one or more arguments. Using subroutines allows you to assemble a macro out of a series of modules, each of which can be individually tested and then called from a master routine.

To call a macro subroutine, you enclose the range name assigned to the subroutine's starting cell in braces. For example,

    {SUBR1}

1-2-3 immediately begins reading keystrokes and macro commands at the location specified by the range name {SUBR1}.

When 1-2-3 encounters a {RETURN} command or a cell that is not a label or a string formula, macro execution continues at the point just after the subroutine call. A {QUIT} command also terminates the subroutine and the entire macro program. Control of the 1-2-3 session returns to the keyboard.

You must follow certain guidelines for the {subroutine} command. The {subroutine} location must be a range name assigned to a single cell or a range. Specifying a range does not restrict the size of the subroutine to the size of the range. Only a {RETURN} command, a blank cell, or a nonstring-valued cell (a cell that does not contain a label or a string-valued formula) can indicate the end of a subroutine. Do not use a {subroutine} that is the same as one of the key names in Table 3.1 (for example, NAME). If a duplication occurs, 1-2-3 performs the subroutine, not the keystrokes. Further, do not use a cell address at the {subroutine} location.

You can specify one or more arguments, which 1-2-3 evaluates and stores in separate cells before executing the subroutine. If you include arguments, you must include a {DEFINE} command in the subroutine.

SYSTEM   {SYSTEM command} temporarily suspends the 1-2-3 session and executes the specified operating system command. When the command is completed, the 1-2-3 session automatically resumes and the macro continues. command can be any operating system command, including batch commands or commands to run another program such as an editor, to a maximum of 125 characters. The command must be enclosed in quotation marks.

CAUTION   If you are running 1-2-3 under DOS, do not use {SYSTEM} to load memory-resident programs such as terminate-and-stay-resident programs. If you do so, you may not be able to resume 1-2-3.

Note   To temporarily suspend the 1-2-3 session without specifying an operating system command, use the System command (/S) in the macro instead of {SYSTEM}.

Data-Manipulation Commands   The following macro commands manipulate data:

{APPENDBELOW}	{LET}
{APPENDRIGHT}	{PUT}
{BLANK}	{RECALC}
{CONTENTS}	{RECALCCOL}

APPENDBELOW and APPENDRIGHT   {APPENDBELOW target-location,source-location} copies the contents of the source location to the rows immediately below the bottom row of the target location.

{APPENDRIGHT target-location,source-location} copies the contents of the source location to the columns immediately to the right of the target location.

Source location and target location are named ranges or range addresses. If you specify a named range, 1-2-3 expands the target location after the appended data to include the rows or columns that contain the added data. Use {APPENDBELOW} with **/R**ange **I**nput or {FORM} to transfer records from an entry form to a database. Use {APPENDRIGHT} to add a new field to a database or to add a column of data to a spreadsheet application.

In the following situations, {APPENDBELOW} or {APPENDRIGHT} fails, and the macro stops. 1-2-3 then displays an error message that explains why the macro stopped.

- When you append more rows or columns than can fit between the target location and the worksheet boundaries (column IV or row 8192)
- When appending the source location to the target location would write over data
- When cells below or columns to the right of the target location are protected

When the source location contains formulas, {APPENDBELOW} or {APPENDRIGHT} copies the current values of the formulas to the target location, not the formulas themselves. In {APPENDBELOW}, if any range's last row is also the last row of the target location, that range will be expanded to accommodate the appended data. In {APPENDRIGHT}, if any range's right column is also the right column of the target location, that range will be expanded to accommodate the appended data.

To use {APPENDBELOW} or {APPENDRIGHT} from a macro library, the source location and target location must be worksheet ranges.

BLANK   {BLANK *location*} erases the contents of cells in a range (location). {BLANK} produces the same results as the /**R**ange **E**rase command. 1-2-3 erases the entry from every cell in the specified range. {BLANK} does not affect numeric format and protection settings.

{BLANK} is often more convenient to use than the /**R**ange **E**rase command. For example, use {BLANK} to erase a cell or a range in the middle of a menu command sequence in a macro.

CONTENTS   {CONTENTS *target-location,source-location,[width],[cell-format]*} copies the contents of *source-location* to *target-location* as a label. Use {CONTENTS} to store a numeric value as a string so that you can use it in a string formula.

Although the {CONTENTS} command is similar to the {LET} command, {LET} stores either a number or a label in a specified cell, and {CONTENTS} stores a label that looks like a number in a cell.

When it executes a {CONTENTS} command, 1-2-3 evaluates the contents of the source-location. If you specify a range, 1-2-3 uses the first cell of the range. 1-2-3 then stores this value in the target-location as a label.

If you do not specify the optional arguments, 1-2-3 uses the current column width and numeric format of the source-location cell.

If you specify the optional width argument, 1-2-3 treats the source-location cell as having that column width; it does not actually change its column width. *Width* can be a number, numeric formula, or reference to a cell that contains a number or formula whose value is from 1 to 240. If you specify the optional cell format, 1-2-3 treats the source-location cell as having the corresponding numeric format. *Cell-format* must be one of the code numbers shown in Table 3.4, a formula that evaluates to a code number, or a cell reference that contains a code number. The resulting display (incorporating a number, a width, and a format) is stored as a left-aligned label in the target-location cell.

Code	Corresponding Numeric Format
0 to 15	Fixed, 0 to 15 decimal places
16 to 31	Scientific, 0 to 15 decimal places
32 to 47	Currency, 0 to 15 decimal places
48 to 63	%, 0 to 15 decimal places
64 to 79	, (comma), 0 to 15 decimal places
112	+/− (horizontal bar graph)
113	General
114	D1 (DD-MMM-YY)
115	D2 (DD-MMM)
116	D3 (MMM-YY)
121	D4 (full international; varies with configuration settings)
122	D5 (partial international; varies with configuration settings)
119	D6 (HH:MM:SS AM/PM)
120	D7 (HH:MM AM/PM)
123	D8 (full international; varies with configuration settings)
117	Text display (formulas shown as entered)
118	Hidden (prevents the cell's contents from appearing on the screen)
127	Worksheet's global cell format

Table 3.4

Using {CONTENTS} with the text display format number 117 provides a quick way to retrieve the text of a formula.

LET {LET *location,entry*} enters a number or label entry at the cell location. {LET} stores an entry in a specified cell location. *Entry* can be a number, literal string, formula, or reference to a cell that contains a number, label, or formula. If you specify a range as the location, 1-2-3 stores the entry in the first cell of the range.

{LET} can create either a label entry or a number entry. This is one of the few commands in which you can specify a string-valued expression. For example,

{LET ss   stores the label Hello, Denise in cell G34 if cell X22 contains the label Denise

If you do not specify the :string or the :value suffix, 1-2-3 attempts to evaluate the argument as a numeric or string expression. If successful, 1-2-3 creates a number or label entry at the location. Otherwise, 1-2-3 creates a label entry that contains the characters in the argument.

PUT   {PUT *location,column-offset,row-offset,entry*} stores the number or label at a cell within a location.

{PUT} is a variant of {LET}. {LET} stores a label or number in a specified cell. {PUT} processes a label or a number in exactly the same way. However, instead of storing the result in a particular cell, it stores the result at a particular column and row of a specified location.

You should specify a range as the location that includes the cell in which you are entering data. If you specify a single cell, an error results unless both the column number and the row number equal zero. The first column of the location range is numbered 0, as is the first row.

Note   Specifying a row or column location outside the location causes an error, which you cannot trap with the {ONERROR} command.

RECALC   {RECALC *location*,[*condition*],[*iterations*]} recalculates the formulas in a specified location, proceeding row by row. Use {RECALC} to recalculate formulas located below and to the left of cells on which they depend.

RECALCCOL   {RECALCCOL *location*,[*condition*],[*iterations*]} recalculates the formulas in a specified location, proceeding column by column. Use {RECALCCOL} to recalculate formulas above and to the right of cells on which they depend.

{RECALC} and {RECALCCOL} are helpful for recalculating sections of a large worksheet. They save you time by recalculating only a small, specified region of the worksheet.

1-2-3 evaluates the condition after it executes the range-location calculation. If the condition is false, it calculates the range again. The iteration argument specifies the number of times 1-2-3 recalculates the range. This argument is reduced and compared once each time the range is calculated. Recalculation will continue until the condition is true or until the iteration count is false, whichever comes first. You need to include both optional arguments.

Location can be any cell or range. You can also precede *location* with a + (plus) to indicate it contains the address of a cell or range where you want recalculation to take place. *Condition* is typically a logical formula or reference to a cell containing a logical formula, but it can be any formula, number, literal string, or cell reference. 1-2-3 evaluates any *condition* that does not equal zero as true and any *condition* that does equal zero as false. Blank cells, strings, and ERR and NA values all equal zero when used as *condition*. *Iterations* can be a number, numeric formula, or reference to a cell that contains a number or numeric formula. You cannot use the *iterations* argument without the *condition* argument.

You may need to use {RECALC} or {RECALCCOL} after macro commands that change the data in the worksheet, such as {LET} and {GETNUMBER}. You do not need to use these commands after invoking 1-2-3 commands, such as /Copy and /Move. 1-2-3 automatically recalculates the worksheet after such commands, even during macro execution.

To redraw the screen to reflect the recalculation, include {WINDOWSOFF} and {WINDOWSON} following {RECALC} or {RECALCCOL} in a macro. Otherwise, any subsequent cell entry will redraw the screen.

CAUTION   Recalculating a portion of the worksheet can cause some formulas—the ones you do not process with {RECALC} or {RECALCCOL}—to fail to reflect the current data. Be sure to perform a general recalculation at the end of the macro routine that uses {RECALC} or {RECALCCOL} by including a {CALC} instruction in the macro.

File Manipulation Commands

The following commands are used for working with files:

{CLOSE}	{READLN}
{FILESIZE}	{SETPOS}
{GETPOS}	{WRITE}
{OPEN}	{WRITELN}
{READ}	

Note   Use these commands only when you are working with ASCII (text) files.

CLOSE

{CLOSE} closes the text file that was opened with the {OPEN} command. {CLOSE} does not take an argument. Read and write access to the currently open file is terminated. Any macro instruction that follows {CLOSE} in the same cell is not executed, so you should keep {CLOSE} on a separate line.

Note   If no file is open, {CLOSE} has no effect, 1-2-3 continues executing the macro as though the command is not there.

FILESIZE

{FILESIZE *location*} determines the number of bytes in a currently open text file and then records the number of bytes in the cell specified by the location. You must {OPEN} a text file first.

The location is a cell address or a range name where 1-2-3 should display the file size. The total size of the currently open file is placed as a numeric value in the specified cell location.

Macro execution continues after completion of the {FILESIZE} command in the next cell of the macro. If no file is currently open, 1-2-3 ignores {FILESIZE}, and macro execution continues in the current cell.

GETPOS {GETPOS *location*} determines the current position of the byte pointer in an open file and displays it in the location cell. You must {OPEN} a text file first. The location can be a cell address or a range name. The current position of the byte pointer in the open file appears as a number in the location. (The first position in a file is 0, not 1.)

Macro execution continues after completion of the {GETPOS} command in the next cell of the macro. If a file is not currently open, 1-2-3 ignores {GETPOS}, and macro execution continues in the current cell.

OPEN {OPEN *file-name, access-type*} opens a specified text file for reading, writing, or both. You must open a file with {OPEN} before you can use any of the other file manipulation commands. *File-name* is a full name (including the extension) of a text file or a range name that refers to a single cell containing the full file name. The string cannot exceed 64 characters. If the file you want to open is not in the current directory, the file name should specify a drive location and a subdirectory path, and enclose the argument in quotation marks.

The *access-type* is a single-character string that indicates the type of file access you want:

- R (Read access) opens an existing file with the specified name and allows access with the {READ} and {READLN} commands. You cannot write to a file opened with a Read access mode.

- W (Write access) opens a new file, assigns it the specified name, and allows access with the {WRITE} and {WRITELN} commands, as well as the {READ} and {READLN} commands. 1-2-3 erases and replaces any existing file with the specified name with the new file.

- M (Modify access) opens an existing file with the specified name and allows access with both read ({READ}, {READLN}) and write ({WRITE}, {WRITELN}) commands.

- A (Append access) opens an existing file for reading and writing, placing the byte pointer at the end of the file. You can use {READ}, {READLN}, {GETPOS}, {SETPOS}, {WRITE}, and {WRITELN} with a file opened with Append access.

{OPEN} succeeds if the correct conditions for the desired access mode exist. When successful, if you try to open a file with Read or Modify access and the file does not exist, the {OPEN} command fails, and macro execution continues in the current cell. If you try to open a read-only file for writing, an error may occur.

{OPEN} with Write access always succeeds (unless you specify a nonexistent drive or directory) because it opens a new file. When successful, macro execution continues in the cell immediately following the {OPEN} command.

Note Only one text file can be open at a time. If a text file is open when 1-2-3 performs an {OPEN} command, 1-2-3 automatically closes that text file before opening the new one. If a text file is open when a macro ends, 1-2-3 does not automatically close the text file. You must include a {CLOSE} command in the macro to close the file.

READ   {READ *byte-count,location*} reads the characters from a file into the cell specified as the location. Beginning at the current position of the byte pointer in the file, {READ} copies the specified number of characters (*byte-count*) from the file to the worksheet, placing them into a left-aligned label at the specified cell location. If the byte count is larger than the number of characters left in the file, 1-2-3 reads the remaining characters.

The *byte-count* must be a value, the address or name of a cell that contains a value, or a formula that returns a value from 0 through 240. A negative byte count is equivalent to the maximum positive byte count of 240.

The location can be a cell address or a range name. Using a range name is equivalent to specifying the first cell of the range.

The byte pointer advances by the number specified as the byte count, so a subsequent {READ} command begins at the next character.

If the file is not currently open, {READ} is ignored, and macro execution continues in the same cell. Otherwise, when {READ} is completed, macro execution continues in the next cell.

READLN   {READLN *location*} copies a line of characters from the currently open file into the specified location.

{READLN} works the same way {READ} does, except that instead of reading a specified number of characters, {READLN} reads a whole line beginning with the current position of the byte pointer and ending with a carriage-return line feed. Thus, a byte-count argument is not needed for this command.

Because the file pointer advances to the beginning of the next line, a subsequent {READLN} command begins there. The carriage return is not copied with the line of text.

SETPOS   {SETPOS *offset-number*} sets a new position for the file pointer in the currently open text file. The offset number is a number or a formula that results in a number that specifies the character at which you want to position the pointer. The first character in the file is at position 0, the second at position 1, and so on.

If a file is not currently open, {SETPOS} is ignored, and macro execution continues in the same cell. Otherwise, when {SETPOS} is completed, macro execution continues in the next cell.

CAUTION   1-2-3 does not prevent you from placing the byte pointer past the end of the file. Use the {FILESIZE} command to determine the number of the last character in your file.

WRITE   {WRITE *string*} copies characters into an open file.

{WRITE} copies a string from the worksheet into the current position of the byte pointer in a file that was opened with either the Write, Append, or Modify access type. The string can be text, a text formula, or the address or name of a cell that contains a label or a text formula.

1-2-3 evaluates the argument to produce a character string and then converts each character to a DOS code before sending it to the open file. If necessary, 1-2-3 extends the length of the file to accommodate the incoming string. The byte pointer advances to just beyond the last character written. A subsequent {WRITE} command picks up where this one leaves off unless you reset the pointer with the {SETPOS} command.

WRITELN   {WRITELN *string*} adds a carriage-return line-feed (CR-LF) sequence to a string of characters and writes the string to a file. {WRITELN} works the same as {WRITE}, except that it adds a CR-LF sequence to the end of the string in the file.

As with {WRITE}, the string can be text, a text formula, or the address or name of a cell that contains a label or a text formula. You can use {WRITELN} with an empty string ("") argument to add a CR-LF sequence to the end of a line: {WRITELN ""}.

Chapter 4

@Functions

An @function is a built-in formula in 1-2-3 that performs a specialized calculation automatically. For example, instead of adding a range of numbers (+A5+A6+A7+A8+A9+A10+A11), you can use the function @SUM(A5..A11) to do the work for you. Other @functions replace complex formulas. For example, @NPV calculates the net present value of a series of future cash-flow values. You can use an @function by itself as a formula, combine it with other @functions, or use it in a macro.

Most of 1-2-3's @functions calculate numeric values. Some @functions, however, manipulate sequences of text, called strings. For example, @LENGTH(B9) counts the number of characters in cell B9 when B9 contains text.

The first section of this chapter presents general information about @functions and their arguments. The remainder of the chapter is divided into nine sections that contain descriptions and examples of each @function. Each section begins with a list of specific rules and procedures for that group of @functions. The @functions within each section are organized alphabetically.

@Function Format

The general format of an @function is as follows:

@function name(*argument1,argument2,...*)

The @function name tells 1-2-3 which calculation to perform. The arguments you enter are the values 1-2-3 uses in the function's calculations. In the @function @SUM(A5..A11), @SUM is the @function name, and A5..A11 is the @function's argument. Every @function produces, or returns, a single value, depending on the arguments you give it to evaluate. In this chapter, @function names are in upper-case letters, and argument names are in lowercase *italic* letters. You can type an @function name in uppercase or lowercase letters. 1-2-3 automatically converts @function names to uppercase.

Arguments

There are four argument types: values, strings, locations (cells or ranges), and conditions. Different @functions require different types of data as arguments. The @function @INT(*x*) asks you to substitute a numeric value for *x*. The @function @SUM(*list*) asks you to substitute one or more ranges of numeric values for *list*. The @function @LENGTH(*string*) asks you to substitute a text string value for *string*. The @function @IF(*condition,x,y*) evaluates a condition (usually a logical formula).

You can enter arguments as actual numeric or string values or as cells or ranges that contain the values you want to use. Table 4.1 gives examples of the ways you can enter arguments in @functions.

Types of Arguments	Examples
Numeric values by	
Actual value	@INT(375.68)
Cell address	@INT(D6)
Cell range name	@INT(TOTAL)
Formula	@INT((25 + 47)/5)
@Function	@INT(@SUM(A5..A11))
Combination	@INT(@SUM(D2..D*) + TOTAL + 33.5)
Range values by	
Range address	@SUM(A5..A11)
Range name	@SUM(RANGE2)
Combination	@SUM(RANGE2,D2..D8,TOTAL)
String values by	
Actual value	@LENGTH("Monthly Profits")
Cell address	@LENGTH(B9)
Cell name	@LENGTH(TITLE)
Formula	@LENGTH("Monthly"&"Profits")

Table 4.1

Entering Arguments in @Functions

Use the following guidelines when you write @functions:

- Begin every @function with the @ sign.

- Enclose an @function's argument in parentheses.

- Do not include any spaces between the @function's name and its arguments.

- Separate multiple arguments in an @function with argument separators. The default valid argument separators are a comma (,) or a semicolon (;). Do not use spaces between arguments.

- When you use an @function as an argument, enclose its arguments in parentheses, and enclose the @function, including its arguments, in another set of parentheses. For example, in @INT(@SUM(A5..A11)), the range A5..A11 is the argument for the @SUM function, and the @function @SUM(A5..A11) is the argument for the @INT function.

- Use a pair of double quotes (" ") around the actual string values you use as arguments.

- Seven @functions do not require arguments: @RAND, @PI, @FALSE, @TRUE, @ERR, @NA, and @NOW. Write them without parentheses.

- The @functions @CELL, @N, and @S take single-cell values as arguments but require you to enter these values as ranges. You can enter single-cell ranges in two ways: with the range address format @N(G5..G5) or with the cell address preceded by an exclamation point, such as @N(!G5).

- Use only the required argument type in an @function. For example, you cannot use a string value in an @function that requires a numeric value.

- If you make an error in entering any @function argument, 1-2-3 returns the value ERR in the cell in which you entered the @function.

- If you type an @function name incorrectly or enter an @function in an incorrect format, 1-2-3 beeps and puts you in EDIT mode.

Mathematical @Functions

Mathematical @functions simplify various mathematical operations, such as calculating square roots and complex trigonometric functions. Some mathematical @functions return new values, whereas others affect values calculated by other formulas or @functions.

All angles that you enter for the sine, cosine, and tangent @functions must be expressed in radians. To convert degrees to radians, multiply the number of degrees by @PI/180.

The arc sine, arc cosine, and arc tangent @functions return all angles in radians. To convert radians to degrees, multiply the number of radians by 180/@PI.

Mathematical @functions use only values (a value, a special value such as ERR or NA, a cell address, or a single-cell range name) as arguments. These @functions do not accept multiple-cell ranges. Except as otherwise noted, any mathematical

@function accepts a blank cell or empty string (a string with a length of 0). The result is the same as applying the @function to the value 0.

@ABS   @ABS(x) returns the absolute, or positive, value of x.

> **Example:** @ABS(–6.2) = 6.2

@ACOS   @ACOS(x) calculates the arc cosine (inverse cosine) of a value. It returns the angle, in radians, whose cosine is x. The result always lies between 0 and π, representing a quadrant I or II angle.

Argument x must be between –1 and 1, inclusive.

> **Example:** @ACOS(.5) = 1.047197 (radians)

@ASIN   @ASIN(x) calculates the arc sine (inverse sine) of a value. It returns the angle, in radians, whose sine is x. The result always lies between $\pi/2$ and $-\pi/2$, representing a quadrant I or IV angle.

Argument x must be between –1 and 1, inclusive.

> **Example:** @ASIN(1) = 1.570796 (radians)

@ATAN   @ATAN(x) calculates the arc tangent (inverse tangent) of a value. It returns the angle, in radians, whose tangent is x. The result always lies between $\pi/2$ and $-\pi/2$, representing a quadrant I or IV angle.

There is no restriction on the value of argument x.

> **Example:** @ATAN(1) = 0.785398 (radians)

@ATAN2 @ATAN2(x,y) calculates the arc tangent (inverse tangent) using the tangent y/x of an angle.

Arguments x and y can be any numeric value. If y is 0, the @function returns 0. If both x and y are 0, the result is ERR.

@ATAN2 differs from @ATAN in that its result lies anywhere between $-\pi$ and π, representing any quadrant. The possible ranges of values of @ATAN2 are the following:

If x is:	And y is:	@ATAN2(x,y) returns:
Positive	Positive	Between 0 and $\pi/2$
Negative	Positive	Between $\pi/2$ and π
Negative	Negative	Between $-\pi$ and $-\pi/2$
Positive	Negative	Between $-\pi/2$ and 0

> **Example:** ATAN(1.5,2) = 0.927295 (radians)

@COS @COS(x) returns the cosine of angle x. The result lies between −1 and 1, inclusive. Angle x must be expressed in radians.

> **Example:** @COS(45*@PI/180) = 0.707106

@EXP @EXP(x) returns the value of e, approximately 2.718282, raised to the xth power. To incorporate the value e in any calculation, use the function @EXP(1) in that calculation. @EXP is the inverse function of @LN.

Argument x cannot be larger than 709 because the result would be too large for 1-2-3 to store. If x is larger than 230, 1-2-3 can calculate and store the value of @EXP but cannot display it. 1-2-3 cannot display a number greater than 9.9E99.

> **Example:** @EXP(1.25) = 3.490342

@INT @INT(x) returns the integer part of x. It truncates x at the decimal point but does not round it. To round a number, use @ROUND. x can be any value.

> **Example:** @INT(35.45) = 35

@LN @LN(x) computes the natural logarithm (base e) of x. Natural logarithms use the value of e (approximately 2.718282) as a base. @LN is the inverse function of @EXP. To incorporate the value e in any calculation, use the function @EXP(1) in that calculation.

Argument x must be greater than 0.

> **Example:** @LN(2) = 0.693147

@LOG @LOG(x) computes the common logarithm (base 10) of x. @LOG is the base 10 exponent of a number.

Argument x must be greater than 0.

> **Example:** @LOG(100) = 2

@MOD @MOD(x,y) returns the remainder (modulus) of x/y.

Argument x can be any number. Argument y must be a number other than 0. The sign (+ or −) of the result is always the same as the sign of x.

> **Example:** @M"OD(4,3) = 1

@PI @PI returns the number π (approximately 3.1415926). π is the ratio of the circumference of a circle to its diameter.

> **Example:** @PI*4^2 = 50.26548, the area of the circle whose radius is 4

@RAND @RAND generates a random number between 0 and 1. 1-2-3 calculates the same random values, in the same order, during every work session.

Each time 1-2-3 recalculates the worksheet, the value of @RAND changes. To generate random numbers in larger numeric intervals, multiply @RAND by the size of the interval.

Example: @RAND*10 + 1 = any integer between 1 and 10

@ROUND   @ROUND(x,n) rounds number x to n places. 1-2-3 can round on either side of the decimal point; n specifies the power of 10 to which 1-2-3 rounds x.

Argument n must be any integer between –15 and 15, inclusive. Argument x can be any value.

If n is positive, 1-2-3 rounds x to n digits to the right of the decimal point. If n is negative, 1-2-3 rounds x to the positive nth power of 10. For example, if n is –2, 1-2-3 rounds x to the nearest hundred. If n is zero, 1-2-3 rounds x to an integer. If n is not an integer, 1-2-3 uses only its integer part.

Example: @ROUND(134.578,1) = 134.6

@SIN   @SIN(x) returns the sine of angle x.

Angle x must be expressed in radians.

Example: @SIN(.883) = 0.772626

@SQRT   @SQRT(x) returns the positive square root of x.

Argument x must be a positive number.

Example: @SQRT(100) = 10

@TAN   @TAN(x) returns the tangent of angle x.

Angle x must be expressed in radians.

Example: @TAN(.52) = 0.572561

Logical @Functions

1-2-3's logical @functions produce values based on the results of conditional (logical) formulas.

A conditional formula evaluates a condition in the form of an equation. The condition is either true or false. For example, the @ISNUMBER function tests to see if a value in a cell is numeric. If the value is numeric or the cell is blank, @ISNUMBER returns the logical value 1 (true). If the value is not numeric, @ISNUMBER returns the logical value 0 (false).

ERR and NA are special values in 1-2-3, generated either by 1-2-3 or by you when you use the @ERR or @NA function. ERR denotes an error in a formula, and NA denotes that the number needed to complete a formula is not available. Both ERR and NA have a ripple-through effect on formulas, meaning that any formula dependent on a formula containing ERR or NA will also result in ERR or NA. It also means that when you correct the formula containing ERR or provide the unavailable number to the formula containing NA, the results of dependent formulas will become correct.

The @ISERR, @ISNA, @ISNUMBER, and @ISSTRING functions stop this ripple-through effect because they can test for these values before you perform a calculation. The arguments for @ISERR, @ISNA, @ISNUMBER, and @ISSTRING are generally cell addresses or range names. If you use a range name that represents a multiple-cell range, 1-2-3 tests the upper left corner cell.

ERR and NA are both numeric values. A blank cell has the value 0.

@FALSE   @FALSE returns the logical value 0. You can use @FALSE with other @functions to create logical arithmetic formulas that are easy to read.

>   **Example:** @IF(PASSWORD = "music",@TRUE,@FALSE) = 0 when the value in the cell named PASSWORD is not music

@IF   @IF(*condition,x,y*) returns the value *x* if the condition is true or the value *y* if the condition is false.

The condition must be a numeric value or any type of formula that results in a numeric value. It is usually a logical formula. Arguments *x* and *y* can be either numeric or string values.

>   **Example:** @IF(9>8,C3,D3) = the value in C3

@ISAAF   @ISAAF (*name*) returns 1 (true) for an attached add-in @function and 0 (false) for any other entry. *Name* is the name of the add-in @function you want to test.

>   **Example:** @ISAAF("DSUM") = 0 (because @DSUM is a built-in 1-2-3 @function, not an add-in @function)

@ISAPP   @ISAPP(*name*) returns 1 (true) for a currently attached add-in and 0 (false) for any other entry. *Name* is the name of the add-in you want to test.

>   **Example:** @ISAPP("FINANCE") = 1 (if an add-in called FINANCE is currently attached)

@ISERR   @ISERR(*x*) tests to see if *x* contains the value ERR. @ISERR returns 1 if *x* is the value ERR; otherwise, it returns 0. This function stops the ripple-through effect of the value ERR. *x* can be any string, value, location, or condition.

>   **Example:** @ISERR(45/0) = 1

@ISNA   @ISNA(*x*) tests to see if *x* contains the value NA. @ISNA returns 1 if *x* is the value NA; otherwise, it returns 0. This function stops the ripple-through effect of the value NA. *x* can be any string, value, location, or condition.

>   **Example:** @ISNA(B1) = 1 if B1 contains the value NA @ISNA(B1) = 0 if B1 contains any other entry

@ISNUMBER @ISNUMBER(*x*) tests to see if *x* contains a numeric value. @ISNUMBER returns 1 if *x* is a number, NA, ERR, a formula that results in a numeric value, or a blank cell; otherwise, it returns 0. *x* can be any string, value, location, or condition.

> **Example:** @ISNUMBER(745) = 1

@ISSTRING @ISSTRING(*x*) tests to see if *x* contains a string value. @ISSTRING returns 1 if *x* is a string, even if the string contains only a space character or an empty string. If *x* contains any other value or a blank cell, @ISSTRING returns 0. *x* can be any string, value, location, or condition.

> **Example:** @ISSTRING(745) = 0

@TRUE @TRUE returns the logical value 1.

1-2-3 sees the value TRUE as a condition that produces a positive result. For example, the formula @IF(25=5*5, "yes", "no") returns yes because 25=5*5 is a true condition.

When you use the value TRUE in a formula, you can use either @TRUE or the number 1. Using the number 1 may make the meaning of the formula unclear. Using @TRUE prevents any ambiguity.

> **Example:** @IF(PASSWORD = "music",@TRUE,@FALSE) = 1 when
> PASSWORD contains the string music

Special @Functions

Special @functions return information about cells or ranges, find the contents of a cell, or mark places where information is missing or incorrect. These @functions are particularly useful with macros.

The @@ function acts as a pointer by referencing a specific cell whose contents are another address.

The @? function indicates an unknown @function from an add-in program.

The @CELL and @CELLPOINTER functions provide information on a cell's contents, format, and location in a worksheet.

The @CHOOSE function returns a specific numeric or string value from an argument list.

The @COLS, @HLOOKUP, @INDEX, @ROWS, and @VLOOKUP functions locate values in specific cells in a table.

The @ERR and @NA functions mark cells that contain formulas with errors (@ERR) or unavailable values (@NA). They also cause every cell that depends on formulas containing ERR or NA to have those values. This is called a ripple-through effect on the worksheet.

An empty string has a length of 0. An empty string is one that you enter into a cell by typing the label-prefix character ", ^, or '. The cell looks blank, but it has a string value.

@@   @@(*location*) returns the cell or range address specified by *location*.

The location is the address or name of a cell that contains a cell address or name, or a text formula that returns the address or name of a cell. *Location* points to another cell whose contents @@ displays in the cell that contains @@. If *location* is not a valid cell address or range name, or is a multiple-cell range, @@ returns ERR.

Contents of *location*:	Examples:
A cell address written as a label	A33
A range name assigned to a cell	INPUT, where INPUT is the cell name of cell A33

Examples: @@(D4) = 37 when cell D4 contains the label F5 and cell F5 contains the value 37

@@(D4) = Balance when D4 contains the label INPUT, INPUT is the name of cell F6, and cell F6 contains the string Balance

@?   @? is a special @function that 1-2-3 uses to indicate the location of an unknown add-in @function that is referred to by a formula in a worksheet.

1-2-3 works with add-ins that provide their own @functions. If you retrieve a worksheet that contains add-in @functions without first attaching the appropriate add-in, 1-2-3 translates the @function name to @? and interprets the @function as NA.

Note   You cannot enter @? directly in a worksheet.

@CELL   @CELL(*attribute,range*) returns a particular piece of information, called an attribute, about a given cell after you enter a range name or address for the cell and an attribute string from the attribute table (see Table 4.2).

The attribute must be enclosed in quotation marks (" ") and can be in uppercase letters, lowercase letters, or both, for example, "WIDTH", "width", and "Width". You can also enter an attribute by typing a cell address that contains one of the attribute strings. You can enter B2 as the attribute if B2 contains the label WIDTH (or Format, TYPE, contents, and so on).

The range can be a range name or address. If *range* consists of more than one cell (for example, H7..K14), 1-2-3 uses the first cell in the range.

@CELL returns a result for the cell attribute you request about the specified cell. You must press (F9) (CALC) to update cell attributes.

Table 4.2 lists attributes and results.

Example: @CELL("row",JH5..J5) = 5

Attribute	Result
"address"	The absolute cell address (for example, $B$7 or B7)
"row"	The row number (between 1 and 8192)

Table 4.2

Attribute	Result
"col"	The column letter as a number (between 1 and 256)
"contents"	The cell contents
"type"	The type of data in the cell:
	b if the cell is blank (it has no cell entry)
	v if the cell contains a numeric value or formula or a string-valued formula
	l if the cell contains a label
"prefix"	The label prefix:
	' if the cell contains a left-aligned label
	" if the cell contains a right-aligned label
	^ if the cell contains a centered label
	\ if the cell contains a repeating label
	l if the cell contains a nonprinting label
	a blank if the cell is empty or contains a number or any kind of formula
"protect"	The protection status:
	1 if the cell is protected
	0 if the cell is not protected
"filename"	The name of the current file, including the path
"width"	The column width (between 1 and 240 in the current window)
"format"	The numeric format:
	F0 to F15 if fixed; 0 to 15 decimal places
	S0 to S15 if scientific; 0 to 15 decimal places
	C0 to C15 if currency; 0 to 15 decimal places
	G if general
	P0 to P15 if percent; 0 to 15 decimal places
	D1 if DD-MMM-YY
	D2 if DD-MMM
	D3 if MMM-YY
	D4 if MM/DD/YY, DD/MM/YY, DD.MM.YY, YY-MM-DD
	D5 if MM/DD, DD/MM, DD.MM, MM-DD
	D6 if HH:MM:SS AM/PM
	D7 if HH:MM AM/PM
	D8 if HH:MM:SS 24hr, HH.MM.SS 24hr, HH,MM,SS 24hr, or HHhMMmSSs

**Table 4.2
Continued**

Attribute	Result
"format"	The numeric format:
	D9 if HH:MM 24hr, HH.MM 24hr, HH.MM or HHhMMm
	T if text format (cell formula appears in cell)
	H if hidden format
	a blank if the cell contains an empty string

Table 4.2
Continued

If cell B2 contains the label WIDTH, @CELL(B2,G12) = 14 because the column width for cell G12 is 14, and B2 contains the word WIDTH.

@CELLPOINTER @CELLPOINTER(*attribute*) returns information about the current cell and is useful when you are testing cell values in a macro.

This function is similar to the @CELL function. @CELL yields information about a cell whose address or range name you specify. @CELLPOINTER yields information about the current cell, the cell that the cell pointer is currently highlighting. The value of this function changes to reflect the attribute of the cell that the cell pointer was on during the most recent recalculation. Use Table 4.2 to enter a cell attribute.

Examples: @CELLPOINTER("row") = 4 if the cell pointer was in row 4 at the time of the last recalculation

@CELLPOINTER("col") = 26 if the cell pointer was in column Z at the time of the last recalculation

@CHOOSE @CHOOSE(*x,list*) returns the *x*th value or label from *list. Offset x* represents an offset number. An offset number corresponds to the position an item occupies in *list.* The first item has an offset number of 0, the second item has an offset number of 1, and so on. *x* can be 0 or any positive integer that is less than or equal to the number of items in *list* minus 1. *List* can contain one or more values; strings; references to ranges that contain values or strings; or any combination of values, strings, and range references. Use @CHOOSE to enter a list of lookup values without setting a lookup table.

Examples: @CHOOSE(1, "Profit", "Loss", "Bankruptcy") = Loss

@CHOOSE(H5,B1,B2,B3) = the value in cell B2 if H5 contains the value 1.3

@COLS @COLS(*range*) returns the number of columns in *range.* This @function is helpful when used with range names. *range* can be any range name or address.

Examples: @COLS(A3..F7) = 6

@COLS(SCORES) = 6 if the range A3..F7 is named SCORES

@COLS(A3) = 1

@ERR @ERR returns the numeric value ERR.

Use @ERR to force a cell to have the value ERR. All cells containing formulas that depend on this cell's value also assume the value ERR, causing a ripple-through effect on the worksheet.

You cannot substitute the label ERR for the value ERR.

The @functions @COUNT, @ISERR, @ISNA, @ISNUMBER, @ISSTRING, @CELL, and @CELLPOINTER stop the ripple-through effect of ERR values.

> **Example:** @IF(B14>3.2,@ERR,B14) returns ERR if the value in cell B14 is greater than 3.2; otherwise, it returns the value in B14

@HLOOKUP

@HLOOKUP(*x,range,row-offset*) performs a horizontal table lookup. A horizontal table lookup compares the value *x* to each cell in the top, or index, row in the range. When it locates a cell containing a value that matches *x*, it stops moving horizontally across the index row. @HLOOKUP then moves down the column the number of rows specified by *row-offset* to return the answer. If you include formulas in a lookup table, make sure the lookup range includes the row specified by *row-offset*.

@HLOOKUP searches an index row of *range* until it finds a cell containing a numeric value that is larger than the value *x*. It then moves back one cell so that it stops at the cell whose value is the highest number that is less than or equal to the value *x*. For example, if the index row contains the values 10, 20, 30, 40, and 50, and *x* is 33, @HLOOKUP stops at the cell containing 40 and then backs up to the cell containing 30. At this point, @HLOOKUP moves the number of rows specified by the row offset.

> **Example:** @HLOOKUP(2,A1..C5,3) returns the second value in row 3 from the table located in cells A1..C5

@INDEX

@INDEX(*range,column-offset,row-offset*) returns the value of the cell in *range* at the intersection of *column-offset* and *row-offset*.

@INDEX uses *range* as its table range; *column-offset* and *row-offset* specify the number of columns to count over from the first column and how many rows to count down from the top row. The first column is column 0, and the top row is row 0.

Column-offset and *row-offset* represent offset numbers and can be zero or any positive integer that is less than or equal to the number of columns or rows in *range* minus 1.

> **Example:** @INDEX(A3..G7,0,2) returns the value in the first column in row 3 of the range A3..G7

@NA

@NA returns the numeric value NA (not available) when a number is not available to complete a formula. This @function enters NA in the current cell and in all other cells that depend on the formula in the cell.

@NA is useful when you are building a worksheet that will contain data that have not been specified. You can use @NA in cells where the data are to be entered.

Formulas that reference those cells will have the value NA until you supply the correct data. Because NA appears in every cell that depends on the cell containing NA, this @function ripples through the worksheet. You cannot substitute the label NA for the value NA.

The @functions @COUNT, @ISERR, @ISNA, @ISNUMBER, @ISSTRING, @CELL, and @CELLPOINTER stop the ripple-through effect of NA values.

> **Example:** @IF(B14>3.2,@NA,B14) returns NA if the value in cell B14 is greater than 3.2; otherwise, it returns the value in B14

@ROWS @ROWS(*range*) returns the number of rows in *range*. This function is helpful when used with named ranges. *Range* can be any range name or address.

> **Examples:** @ROWS(A3..F7) = 5
>
> @ROWS(SCORES1) = 5 if SCORES1 names the range A3..F7

@VLOOKUP @VLOOKUP(*x,range,column-offset*) performs a vertical table lookup. A vertical table lookup compares the value *x* to each cell in the top, or index, column in *range*. When it locates a cell that contains a value that matches *x*, it stops moving vertically down the index column. @VLOOKUP then moves across that row the number of columns specified by *column-offset* to return the answer. *Column-offset* represents an offset number, which corresponds to the position the column occupies in *range*. *Column-offset* can be zero or any positive integer that is less than or equal to the number of columns in *range* minus 1.

@VLOOKUP searches an index column *range* until it finds a cell containing a numeric value larger than the value *x*. It then moves up one cell so that it stops at the cell whose value is the highest number that is less than or equal to the value *x*. For example, if the index column contains the values 10, 20, 30, 40, and 50, and *x* is 33, @VLOOKUP stops at the cell containing 40 and then moves up to the cell containing 30. At this point, @VLOOKUP moves the number of columns specified by *column-offset*.

> **Example:** @VLOOKUP(3,B2..E5,2) returns the second value in row 3 from the table located in cells B2..E5

String @Functions

String @functions provide information about strings (text) in cells and perform other operations on strings. Strings can be letters, numbers, and special characters, as long as they are label data types.

The string argument can be a literal string, range names, or addresses of cells that contain labels or formulas or @functions that evaluate to a string.

When you enter actual string values as arguments, enclose them in a pair of quotation marks (" "). When you enter string values by cell address or range name, you do not need to use quotation marks. For example, @LEFT("Monthly Expenses",5) returns the word Month. If the string Monthly Expenses was in cell G8, you could also write @LEFT(G8,5).

Many string @functions use offset numbers to locate the characters in a string. Offset numbers always start at position 0. The string Red Shoes contains nine characters. The R is at position 0, the e is at position 1, the d is at position 2, the space is at position 3, and the last s is at position 8. The last position number is always one less than the length of the string.

Use positive integers to indicate an offset number. 1-2-3 interprets an entry with a negative position number as invalid and returns ERR. If you type 4.5 as a position number, 1-2-3 abbreviates it to 4.

The argument start number is an offset number of a character in a string from which you want to begin the calculation.

@Functions can read 240 characters in one string. Therefore, offset numbers can be from 0 to 239 for each string value.

You can create a string that has no letters, numbers, spaces, or special characters by typing a label-prefix character in a cell. This is called an empty string and has a length of 0. An empty string has an LICS code of 0, which differs from a blank cell, which has no LICS code value.

@CHAR @CHAR(x) returns the Lotus International Character Set (LICS) code character that corresponds to the code number x. 1-2-3 stores each character displayed on the screen as one of the numeric character codes in LICS. LICS is an extension of the ASCII character set.

Argument x can be any numeric value between 1 and 255. Values outside the range yield ERR. 1-2-3 abbreviates any fractional numbers to integers.

If your computer does not have a display character for x, @CHAR returns either a character that resembles the desired character or a blank. For characters outside the printable ASCII character set (codes below 32), the LICS code may not correspond to the codes used by your computer. The display driver you include in the 1-2-3 driver set takes care of any required translation.

Examples: @CHAR(52) = 4

@CHAR(65) = A

@CHAR(97) = a

@CLEAN @CLEAN(string) removes the following control characters from string: control characters with ASCII codes below 32, the begin and end attribute characters, as well as the attribute character itself, the merge character (LICS 155) and the character that follows it.

@CODE @CODE(string) returns the LICS code number of the first character in string.

The @CHAR and @CODE functions let you switch between the displayed characters and the LICS character codes that identify them.

Examples: @CODE("4.2") = 52

@CODE("A") = 65

@CODE("Anyone") = 65

@EXACT @EXACT(*string1,string2*) tests whether two strings are exactly the same. If *string1* is exactly the same as *string2*, @EXACT returns 1; otherwise, it returns 0.

This function provides a more precise alternative to the equal operator (=) in a formula because, unlike the equal operator, @EXACT distinguishes between uppercase and lowercase letters and between letters with and without accent marks.

Examples: @EXACT("LONDON", "London") = 0 (false)

+ "LONDON" = "London" = 1 (true) because this formula is not sensitive to uppercase and lowercase letters

@FIND @FIND(*search-string,string,start-number*) finds the position at which the first occurrence of *search-string* begins in *string*.

The @FIND function begins searching *string* at *start-number*. If the search fails, the result is ERR. @FIND is case sensitive.

To extract a substring after locating its starting position with @FIND, use the @MID function.

Examples: @FIND("even", "Seven is not even",0) = 1

@FIND("even", "Seven is not even",2) = 13

@FIND("e", "THE",0) = ERR

@LEFT @LEFT(*string,n*) returns the first *n* characters in *string*. 1-2-3 counts punctuation and spaces as characters.

Example: @LEFT("This is a test",4) = This

@LENGTH @LENGTH(*string*) returns the number of characters found in *string*. 1-2-3 counts punctuation and spaces as characters.

Examples: @LENGTH("computer") = 8

@LENGTH("") = 0

@LENGTH(A5&G12) = the total number of characters found in cells A5 and G12

@LOWER @LOWER(*string*) converts all the uppercase characters in *string* to lowercase.

Example: @LOWER("A FinE THINg") = a fine thing

@MID @MID(*string,start-number,n*) extracts *n* characters from *string* beginning with the character at *start-number*.

The @LEFT and @RIGHT functions are special cases of @MID. They extract a substring from either end of the string value.

If *start-number* is beyond the end of *string,* the result is an empty string, consisting of no characters. If *n* is 0, the result is an empty string. *n* can be any positive number or 0. If *n* is 0, the result of @MID is an empty string.

You can use a large number for *n* if you do not know the length of the string and want to make sure you get all of it. The extra length has no effect on the result.

Examples: @MID("Our finest hour",4,6) = finest

@MID("Our finest hour",25,6) = empty string

@MID("data" & "base",0,4) = data

@N @N(*range*) returns the value in the first cell in *range* as a numeric value. If the cell contains a value, @N returns that value. If the cell contains a label, @N returns the value 0.

Range can be any range name or address.

Examples: @N(!A3) = 0 if cell A3 was empty

@N(B3..B7) = 1981 if cell B3 contained 1981

@PROPER @PROPER(*string*) converts the letters in *string* to proper capitalization, that is, the first letter of each word in uppercase and all others in lowercase.

Examples: @PROPER("A FINE THING") = A Fine Thing

@PROPER("354 - a babcock") = 354 - A Babcock

@REPEAT @REPEAT(*string,n*) duplicates *string* the number of times specified by *n*. *n* can be any positive integer.

@REPEAT differs from a repeating label (a cell entry that begins with a label-prefix backslash) in that the repeating label repeats the label only to fill the current column width. @REPEAT duplicates the string the number of times you specify; it is not limited by the current column width.

Example: @REPEAT("Hello",3) = Hello Hello Hello

@REPLACE @REPLACE(*original-string,start-number,n,new-string*) removes *n* characters from the original string beginning at *start-number* and then inserts *new-string* in the same place. *n* can be any positive integer or 0.

There are several procedures you can perform with @REPLACE:

- By making *n* equal to the number of characters in *original-string,* you can replace the entire original string with *new-string*.

- By specifying a position immediately beyond the end of *original-string* as *start-number,* you can add *new-string* to *original-string.*

- By making *n* equal to 0, you can insert a new string.

- By making *new-string* an empty string, you can delete a string.

Example: @REPLACE("This is the only one",12,4,"first") = This is the first one

@RIGHT @RIGHT(*string,n*) returns the last *n* characters in *string.*

Example: @RIGHT("Allons enfants de la",5) = de la

@S @S(*range*) returns the entry in the first cell in *range* as a label if the cell contains a label; if it contains a value, @S returns an empty string.

Example: @S(A4..A7) = Rent, if A4 contains the label "Rent"

@STRING @STRING(*x,n*) converts a numeric value *x* to a string with *n* decimal places. This @function formats the string as if it were a number, using the fixed numeric format. @STRING also rounds the formatted string value to the number of specified decimal places, just as it would when formatting a number.

To convert a string to its numeric equivalent, use @VALUE; *n* specifies the number of decimal places (0 to 15). *x* can be any value.

Example: @STRING(1234,3) = the string value 1234.000

@TRIM @TRIM(*string*) removes excess space characters from *string.* It removes all spaces that precede the first nonspace character and that follow the last nonspace character. It also replaces all consecutive spaces within the string with single spaces.

Example: @TRIM("too   much   space") = too much space

@UPPER @UPPER(*string*) converts all lowercase letters in *string* to uppercase.

Example: @UPPER("A Fine Thing") = A FINE THING

@VALUE @VALUE(*string*) converts a number entered as a string to its corresponding numeric value. The string may appear as a standard number (456.7), a number in scientific format (4.567E2), or a mixed number (45 $^7/_8$).

1-2-3 ignores numeric values and returns 0 for blank cells and empty strings. Leading and trailing space characters do not affect the result. In some cases, however, a string that contains editing symbols (for instance, a two-character trailing currency sign) yields ERR.

Example: @VALUE("543") = the numeric value 543

Date and Time @Functions

Date and time @functions generate and use serial numbers to represent dates and times. As a result, you can use dates and times in calculations.

Each date between January 1, 1900 and December 31, 2099 has an integer serial number called a date number. The first serial data number is 1, and the last date number is 73050. January 1, 1900 corresponds to 1, and December 31, 2099 corresponds to 73050.

Each moment during the day corresponds to a fractional serial number called a time number. For example, 0.000 is midnight, .5 (or 1/) is noon, and 0.99999 is just before midnight. You can enter a time number as a fraction or as a decimal.

Even though 1-2-3 stores dates and times as serial numbers for calculations, you can format them on the screen to appear as actual dates and times. For example, @DATE(86,10,12) generates the date number 31697. You can format this number to appear on the screen as 12-Oct-86. @TIME(23,59,59) generates the serial time number 0.99999. You can format this number to appear as 23:59:59.

To format dates and times, use the **/R**ange **F**ormat command. 1-2-3 has five possible date formats. The first three formats are permanent, but you can reset the last two formats using the **/W**orksheet **G**lobal **D**efault **O**ther International **D**ate command. The first two of the four time formats are permanent 1-2-3 formats. You can reset the last two formats using the **/W**orksheet **G**lobal **D**efault **O**ther International **T**ime command.

The date and time @functions that generate serial numbers are @DATE, @DATE-VALUE, @NOW, @TIME, and @TIMEVALUE. The data @functions that use serial numbers are @DATE, @MONTH, and @YEAR. The time @functions that use serial numbers are @HOUR, @MINUTE, and @SECOND.

If you enter mixed numbers as date numbers in arguments, 1-2-3 uses their integer part. For example, if you enter 31790.45 as a date number, 1-2-3 sees it as 31790.

@DATE @DATE(*year,month,day*) returns the serial date number of the year, month, and day.

You can extract the year, month, and day from a date number with @YEAR, @MONTH, and @DAY. You can use @MOD to determine the day of the week for a given date. (See page R-137 for a discussion of @MOD.)

The year must be a number between 0 (1900) and 199 (2099), inclusive. The month must be a number between 1 and 12, inclusive. The day must be a number between 1 and 31, inclusive, and it must be a valid date for the given month. For example, you cannot use 31 for April. If the year, month, and day are not valid numbers, 1-2-3 returns the value ERR.

Note Even though there was no February 29, 1900 (it was not a leap year), 1-2-3 assigns a date number to this "day." This does not invalidate any of your date calculations unless you use dates between January 1, 1900 and March 1, 1900.

Example: @DATE(82,9,27) = 30221 (for 27-Sep-82 in D1 format)

@DATEVALUE @DATEVALUE(*string*) returns the serial date number of the string value stating the year, month, and day.

@DATEVALUE is similar to @DATE in that it generates the serial date number for a particular date between January 1, 1900 and December 31, 2099. The difference is that @DATE uses three numeric values as arguments, and @DATEVALUE uses a single string value as its argument. Use @DATEVALUE when you want to convert data entered as labels to date numbers so that you can use the dates in calculations.

The *string* must be in one of the five 1-2-3 date formats and must be enclosed in double quotation marks. 1-2-3's three permanent date formats are D1, DD-MMM-YY; D2, DD-MMM, with the current year automatically included; and D3, MMM-YY, with the date stored as the first of the month.

The two other formats in which you can enter a date are D4 and D5, which have more than one option in each format.

Examples: If you set the D4 format as DD.MM.YY,
@DATEVALUE("23.12.85") = 31404

If you set the D4 format as MM/DD/YY,
@DATEVALUE("12/23/85") = 31404

You need to press (F9) (CALC), to see the results when you change a date format.

Example: @DATEVALUE("23-Aug-86") = 31647

@DAY @DAY(*date-number*) returns the day of the month (1 to 31) of *date-number*.

The date number must be the serial number of the desired date generated by the @DATE, @DATEVALUE, or @NOW function.

Example: @DAY(@DATE(85,3,27)) = 27

@MONTH @MONTH(*date-number*) returns the month (1 to 12) of the year of *date-number*.

The date number must be the serial number of the desired date generated by the @DATE, @DATEVALUE, or @NOW function.

Example: @MONTH(@DATE(85,3,27)) = 3

@YEAR @YEAR(*date-number*) returns the year (0 to 199) of *date-number*.

The date number must be the serial number of the desired date generated by the @DATE, @DATEVALUE, or @NOW function.

Example: @YEAR(@DATEVALUE("14-Feb-2019")) = 119

@NOW @NOW returns the serial number for the current date and time on the computer's clock. This includes both a date number (integer part) and a time number (fractional part). Every time 1-2-3 recalculates, it updates the value of @NOW.

You can format the value of @NOW in one of the date formats or one of the time formats. With a date format, 1-2-3 ignores the fractional part of the number; with a time format, 1-2-3 ignores the integer part of the number. In both cases, 1-2-3 records the date and time.

Examples: @NOW = 30148.5 at noon on January 25, 1985

@MOD(@NOW,7) = a value between 0 and 6, from which you can determine the day of the week

@MOD produces the remainder of the serial number generated by @NOW/7. 1-2-3 sees Sunday as the first day of the week and Saturday as the seventh day. If the result of this @function is 1, the day is Sunday; if the result is 2, the day is Monday; if the result is 0, the day is Saturday.

@HOUR   @HOUR(*time-number*) extracts the hour value from a *time-number* and returns a value between 0 (midnight) and 23 (23:00, or 11:00 PM).

The time number can be any fraction or a fractional serial number generated by @TIME, @TIMEVALUE, or @NOW.

Example: @HOUR(31774.5) = 12 (noon)

@MINUTE   @MINUTE(*time-number*) extracts the minute value from *time-number* and returns a value between 0 and 59.

The time number can be any fraction or a fractional serial number generated by @TIME, @TIMEVALUE, or @NOW.

Example: @MINUTE(0.333) = 59

@SECOND   @SECOND(*time-number*) extracts the second value from *time-number* and returns a value between 0 and 59.

The time number can be any fraction or a fractional serial number generated by @TIME, @TIMEVALUE, or @NOW.

Example: @SECOND(0.333) = 31

@TIME   @TIME(*hour,minutes,seconds*) returns the serial time number of the specified hour, minute, and second. You can extract the hour, minute, and second from a time number with the @HOUR, @MINUTE, and @SECOND functions.

The hour must be any integer between 0 and 23, the minute must be between 0 and 59, and the second must be between 0 and 59. If *hour, minutes,* and *seconds* are not valid numbers, 1-2-3 returns the value ERR.

Example: @TIME(8,19,27) = 0.246840 (or 8:19:27 PM in D6 format)

@TIMEVALUE   @TIMEVALUE(*string*) returns the serial time number for a string stating the hour, minute, and second. Use @TIMEVALUE when you want to convert time entered as labels to time numbers so that they can be used in calculations.

@TIMEVALUE is similar to @TIME in that it generates the serial number fraction that corresponds to a particular time of day. The difference is that @TIME uses three numeric values as arguments, and @TIMEVALUE uses a single string value as its argument.

The string must be in one of the four 1-2-3 time formats and must be enclosed in double quotation marks. 1-2-3's two permanent time formats are D6, HH:MM:SS AM/PM; and D7, HH:MM AM/PM.

The two other formats in which you can enter a time are D8 and D9, which have more than one option in each format.

> **Examples:** If you set the D8 format as HH:MM:SS 24hr,
> @TIMEVALUE("15"12"00") = 0.6333
>
> If you set the D8 format as HH.MM.SS 24hr,
> @TIMEVALUE("15.12.00") = 0.6333

You need to press (F9) (CALC) to see the results when you change a time format.

> **Example:** @TIMEVALUE("3:12:00 PM") = 0.6333 (D6 format)

Financial @Functions

The 1-2-3 financial @functions make calculations that relate to loans, annuities, and cash flows that occur over a term or a period of time.

Interest rates are entered as either percents or decimal fractions. You can type 15.5 percent as 15.5% or as .155. 1-2-3 automatically converts all percentages to decimal values.

You should express the term and the interest rate in the same units of time. To calculate a monthly payment when the interest and term are given in years, divide the annual interest rate by 12 to find the monthly interest rate, and multiply the term by 12 to obtain the number of monthly payment periods.

An annuity is an investment of a series of equal payments. An ordinary annuity is an annuity in which a payment is made at the end of each period. An annuity due is an annuity where each payment is made at the beginning of each period. The financial @functions make calculations by assuming that investments are ordinary annuities.

In the financial examples, monetary results are in cells formatted as Currency, and percentage results are in cells formatted as Percent.

@CTERM   @CTERM(*interest,future-value,present-value*) computes the number of compounding periods it will take an investment (*present-value*) to grow to a *future-value*, earning a fixed *interest* rate per compounding period.

@CTERM uses the following formula to compute the term:

$$\frac{\ln(fv \, / \, pv)}{\ln(1 + int)}$$ where: fv = future value
pv = present value
int = periodic interest rate
$\ln$ = natural logarithm

Example: You have just deposited $10,000 in an account that pays an annual interest rate of 10%, compounded monthly. You want to determine how long it will take to double your investment.

@CTERM(10%/12,20000,10000) returns 83.52, which tells you that it will take 83.52 months, or about seven years, to double your $10,000.

@DDB   @DDB(*cost,salvage,life,period*) computes the depreciation allowance on an asset for a specified period, using the double-declining balance method.

The double-declining balance method accelerates the rate of depreciation so that more depreciation expense occurs (and can be written off) in earlier periods than in later ones. Depreciation stops when the book value of the asset reaches the salvage value. The book value in any period is the total cost minus the total depreciation over all prior periods.

@DDB uses the following formula to compute the double-declining balance depreciation for any period:

$$\frac{(bv * 2)}{n}$$ where: bv = book value in that period
n = life of the asset

1-2-3 adjusts the result of the formula when necessary to ensure that total depreciation taken over the life of the asset equals the asset's cost minus its salvage value.

You give @DDB this information as arguments:

cost	The amount you paid for the asset
salvage	The value of the asset at the end of its life
life	The number of periods it will take to depreciate to the salvage value
period	The period for which you want to find the depreciation allowance

Example: You have just purchased an office machine for $10,000. The useful life of the machine is considered to be eight years, and the salvage value after eight years is $1,200. You want to compute the depreciation expense for the fifth year using the double-declining balance method.

@DDB(10000,1200,8,5) returns $791, which tells you that the depreciation expense for the fifth year will be $791.

@FV   @FV(*payments,interest,term*) determines the future value of an investment. It computes the future value based on a series of equal *payments,* each of a specific amount earning a periodic *interest* rate over the number of payment periods in the *term.*

@FV uses the following formula to compute future value:

$$\frac{pmt\,(1 + int)^n - 1}{int}, \quad \text{where:} \quad \begin{array}{l} pmt = \text{periodic payment} \\ int = \text{periodic interest rate} \\ n = \text{number of periods} \end{array}$$

@FV makes its calculations by assuming that the investment is an ordinary annuity.

> **Example:** You plan to deposit $2,000 each year for the next 20 years into a bank account. The account is paying 10% interest, compounded annually. Interest is paid on the last day of each year. You want to compute the value of your account in 20 years. You make each year's contribution on the last day of the year.
>
> @FV(2000,10%,20) returns $114,550, the value of your account at the end of 20 years.

To compute the future value of an annuity due, use the formula @FV(*payments,interest,term*)*(1 + *interest*).

> **Example:** If you make each year's contribution on the first day of the year, you would compute the amount for an annuity due.
>
> @FV(2000,10%,20)*(1 + 10%) would return $126,005, the value of your account in 20 years, an additional $11,455 over the ordinary annuity.

@IRR   @IRR(*guess,range*) computes the internal rate of return for a series of cash flow values generated by an investment. In general the IRR is the rate that equates the present value of an expected future series of even or uneven cash flows to the initial investment. 1-2-3 assumes that the cash flows are received at regular intervals.

1-2-3 bases its calculations on a series of approximations for the internal rate of return. Because this @function uses approximations, you enter a guess as the first argument. Enter a guess you feel is reasonable for the IRR. Because there may be more than one solution, try another guess if the result does not seem correct. If you get unexpected results with @IRR, you may want to use @NPV to analyze the cash flow.

Guess is a percentage that represents your estimate of the internal rate of return. In general, specify a guess between 0 and 1. If the iteration cannot approximate the result to within 0.0000001 after 20 tries, the result will be the value ERR.

Range is the cell range that contains the cash flow amounts. 1-2-3 considers negative numbers as cash outflows and positive numbers as cash inflows. The first cash flow in *range* must be a negative number.

Example: @IRR(A2,B2..B14) returns 6.11% over a 12-month term if the initial payment is $1000 and the 12 periodic receipts are each $120. Cell A2 contains the guess. In range B2 through B14, B2 contains the value −1000, and B3 through B14 each contain the value 120.

@NPV @NPV(*interest,range*) computes the net present value of a series of future cash flows, discounted at a fixed periodic interest rate. 1-2-3 assumes that the cash flows occur at equal time intervals, that the first cash outflow occurs at the end of the first period, and that subsequent cash outflows occur at the end of subsequent periods.

@NPV uses the following formula to compute net present value:

$$\Sigma \frac{V_i}{(1 + int)^i}$$

where: $V_i...V_n$ = series of cash flows in range
int = interest rate
n = number of cash flows
i = the current iteration
(1 through n)

Example: @NPV(10%,D2..D13) = $340.69 if the assumed interest rate is 10 and D2..D13 contains 12 future cash flows, each of which is $50.

To find the net present value of an investment where you make an initial cash outflow immediately and follow it by a series of future inflows, you must factor the initial outflow separately because it is not affected by the interest.

If INITIAL is your initial outflow, SERIES is a range of future cash flows, and RATE is the periodic interest rate, the overall net present value is calculated by +INITIAL+ @NPV(RATE,SERIES).

Example: +INITIAL+ @NPV(RATE,SERIES) = $904.07 when

INITIAL = ($4,700.00)
RATE   = 14%
SERIES = $1,600.00
            $1,600.00
            $1,600.00
            $1,700.00
            $1,700.00

@PMT @PMT(*principal,interest,term*) computes the amount of the periodic payment on a loan. Most installment loans are computed like ordinary annuities in that payments are made at the end of each payment period.

@PMT uses the following formula to compute the payment:

$$prin^* \frac{int}{1 - (int + 1)^{-n}}$$

where: $prin$ = principal
int = periodic interest rate
n = term

Example: You are considering taking out a $50,000 mortgage for 30 years at an annual interest rate of 12.5%. You want to determine your monthly payment.

@PMT(50000,12.5%/12,30*12) returns your monthly payment, $533.63.

To compute the periodic payment of an annuity due, use the formula @PMT(*principal,interest,term*)/(1 + *interest*).

@PV   @PV(*payments,interest,term*) determines the present value of an investment. It computes the present value based on a series of equal *payments,* each of a specific amount, discounted at a periodic *interest* rate, over the number of periods in the *term.*

@PV uses the following formula to compute the present value:

$$pmt * \frac{1 - (1 + int)^{-n}}{int} \qquad \text{where:} \quad \begin{aligned} prin &= \text{principal} \\ int &= \text{periodic interest rate} \\ n &= \text{term} \end{aligned}$$

Example: You have just won a million dollars. The prize is awarded in 20 annual payments of $50,000 each (a total of $1,000,000 over 20 years). Annual payments are received at the end of each year.

You are given the option of receiving a single lump-sum payment of $400,000 instead of the million-dollar annuity. You want to find out which option is worth more in today's dollars.

If you were to accept the annual payments of $50,000, you assume that you would invest the money at a rate of 12%, compounded annually. @PV(50000,12%,20) returns $373,472, which tells you that the $1,000,000 paid over 20 years is worth $373,472 in present dollars.

Based on your assumptions, the lump-sum payment of $400,000 is worth more than the million-dollar ordinary annuity in present dollars (before taxes).

To compute the present value of an annuity due, use the formula @PV(*payments,interest,term*)*(1 + *interest*).

Example: If the annual payments of $50,000 were made at the beginning (rather than at the end) of each year, you could use the annuity due formula.

@PV(50000,12%,20)*(1 + 12%) returns $418,289. Using the same assumptions, if the annual payments were made at the beginning of each year, the million-dollar annuity would be worth more than the lump-sum payment in present dollars (before taxes).

@RATE   @RATE(*future-value,present-value,term*) returns the periodic interest necessary for a *present-value* to grow to a *future-value* over the number of compounding periods in the *term*. If the investment is compounded monthly, for example, you multiply the value of @RATE by 12 to compute the annual rate.

@RATE uses the following formula to compute the periodic interest rate:

$$(fv / pv)^{1-n} - 1 \quad \text{where:} \quad \begin{aligned} fv &= \text{future value} \\ pv &= \text{present value} \\ n &= \text{term} \end{aligned}$$

Example: You have invested $10,000 in a bond. The bond matures in five years and has a maturity value of $18,000. Interest is compounded monthly. You want to determine the periodic interest rate for this investment.

@RATE(18000,10000,5*12) returns .00984, which tells you that the periodic (monthly) interest rate is 0.984%, just under 1% a month.

To determine the annual rate, multiply the above formula by 12, which yields a result of 11.8%.

@SLN   @SLN(*cost,salvage,life*) computes the straight-line depreciation of an asset for one period.

The straight-line method of depreciation divides the depreciable cost (*cost – salvage*) evenly over the useful life of an asset. The useful life is the number of periods (typically years) over which an asset is depreciated.

@SLN uses the following formula to compute depreciation:

$$\frac{(c - s)}{n} \quad \text{where:} \quad \begin{aligned} c &= \text{cost of the asset} \\ s &= \text{salvage value of the asset} \\ n &= \text{useful life of the asset} \end{aligned}$$

You give @SLN this information as arguments:

cost	The amount you paid for the asset
salvage	The value of the asset at the end of its life
life	The number of years it will take to depreciate to the salvage value

Example: You have purchased an office machine for $10,000. The useful life of this machine is eight years, and the salvage value in any year is $1,200. You want to compute yearly depreciation expense using the straight-line method.

@SLN(10000,1200,8) returns $1100, the annual depreciation allowance.

@SYD   @SYD(*cost,salvage,life,period*) returns the sum-of-the-years'-digits depreciation for a specified period.

The sum-of-the-years'-digits method of depreciation accelerates the rate of depreciation so that more depreciation expense occurs in earlier periods than in later ones. The depreciable cost is the actual cost minus salvage value. The useful life is the number of periods (typically years) over which an asset is depreciated.

@SYD uses the following formula to compute depreciation:

$$\frac{(c - s) * (n - p + 1)}{(n * (n + 1)/2)} \quad \text{where:} \quad \begin{aligned} c &= \text{cost of the asset} \\ s &= \text{salvage value of the asset} \\ n &= \text{useful life of the asset} \\ p &= \text{period for which depreciation} \\ &\quad \text{is being computed} \end{aligned}$$

You give @SYD this information as arguments:

cost	The amount you paid for the asset
salvage	The value of the asset at the end of its life
life	The number of periods it will take to depreciate to the salvage value
period	The period for which you want to find the depreciation allowance

Example: You have just purchased an office machine for $10,000. The useful life of this machine is eight years, and the salvage value after eight years is $1,200. You want to compute the depreciation expense for the fifth year using the sum-of-the-years'-digits method.

@SYD(10000,1200,8,5) returns $978, the depreciation allowance for the fifth year.

@TERM   @TERM(*payments,interest,future-value*) returns the number of *payments* in the term of an ordinary annuity necessary to accumulate a *future-value,* earning a periodic *interest* rate. Each payment is equal to a specific amount.

@TERM uses the following formula to compute the term:

$$\frac{\ln(1 + (fv * int / pmt))}{\ln(1 + int)} \quad \text{where:} \quad \begin{aligned} pmt &= \text{periodic payment} \\ fv &= \text{future value} \\ int &= \text{periodic interest rate} \\ \ln &= \text{natural logarithm} \end{aligned}$$

Example: You deposit $2,000 at the end of each year into a bank account. Your account earns 10% a year, compounded annually. You want to determine how long it will take to accumulate $100,000.

@TERM(2000,10%,100000) returns 19 (when the cell format is fixed, 0), the number of years it will take to accumulate $100,000 in your account.

You want to know how long it will take to pay back a $10,000 loan at 10% annual interest, making payments of $1,175.60 a year. You can calculate the term necessary to pay back a loan by entering the future value as a negative number.

To compute the term of an annuity due, use the formula @TERM(*payments,interest,future-value* / (1 + *interest*)).

Statistical @Functions

1-2-3's statistical @functions perform calculations on lists of values. Each statistical @function has an equivalent database statistical @function.

Every @function in this group except @COUNT accepts only numeric values as single arguments. @COUNT accepts numeric and string values as single arguments.

Numeric arguments can be numbers, cell addresses, cell names, range addresses, and range names. String arguments can be strings enclosed in quotation marks, cell addresses, cell names, range addresses, and range names.

A list contains one or more arguments. Each argument in a list can be a single value or a range. A list can contain both single values and ranges. For example, the argument list in the function @COUNT(B3..B8,C3..C8,D9,J3) is a valid argument list.

A list can include some blank ranges, but not all ranges can be blank. 1-2-3 ignores blank cells in multiple-cell ranges. For example, if you use @AVG to average the values in a range that spans eight cells and there is a blank cell in that range, 1-2-3 divides the sum by 7 to find the correct average. 1-2-3 sees a blank cell used as a single argument in a list as the value 0.

CAUTION   When you use a range to calculate with the statistical @functions, 1-2-3 assigns the value 0 to all labels within that range and includes them in calculations.

All examples are based on the Weekly Sales Report worksheet in Figure 4.1. All monetary results are returned in Currency format. All dates are returned in D1 format.

```
A1:  [W10]                                                          READY

       ┌──────────┬─────────┬───────────┬───────────┬───────────┐  ◄
       │     A    │    B    │     C     │     D     │     E     │  ►
     1 │              WEEKLY SALES REPORT                       │  ▲
     2 │==========================================================  ▼
     3 │DATE        BOOKS SOLD    DAILY SALES    WEEKLY TOTALS   │  ?
     4 │==========================================================
     5 │19-Dec-92      147        $1,180.72     Total Sales: $6,791.74
     6 │20-Dec-92      122        $1,095.56   Avg Sales Amt: $1,131.96
     7 │21-Dec-92      106          $877.68   Highest Amt: $1,610.00
     8 │22-Dec-92       82          $708.48   Lowest  Amt:   $708.48
     9 │23-Dec-92      158        $1,319.30      Days Open:        6
    10 │24-Dec-92      184        $1,610.00  Total Books Sold:   799
    11 │25-Dec-92                           Average Sold Daily: 133.17
    12 │                                         Variance:    1145.47
    13 │                                          Std Dev:      33.84
    14 │
    15 │
    16 │
    17 │
    18 │
    19 │
    20 │30-Sep-91  01:30 PM
```

Figure 4.1

@AVG   @AVG(*list*) computes the average of all values in *list*. @AVG(*list*) is equivalent to the formula @SUM(*list*)/@COUNT(*list*).

> **Example:** @AVG(C5..C11) = $1,131.96, the average sales amount for the week

@COUNT @COUNT(*list*) counts the number of cells in *list*. @COUNT is one of the @functions that stops the ripple-through effect of the values NA and ERR (explained in the section "Special @Functions").

If the list includes only blank ranges, the result is 0. @COUNT(A1..A4) = a value between 0 and 4. If every cell in range A1 through A4 is blank, @COUNT returns 0. If cells A1 through A4 contain one filled cell, it returns 1, and so on.

Each single value in the list adds 1 to the count, even if it is blank; therefore, you should use @COUNT with range arguments. For example, @COUNT(H54) = 1 even if cell H54 is blank.

> **Example:** @COUNT(B5..B11) = 6, the number of days open that week

@MAX   @MAX(*list*) returns the maximum value in *list*.

> **Example:** @MAX(C5..C11) = $1,610.00, the highest daily amount taken in that week

@MIN   @MIN(*list*) returns the minimum value in *list*.

> **Example:** @MIN(C5..C11) = $708.48, the lowest daily amount taken in that week

@STD   @STD(*list*) computes the population standard deviation of the values in *list*. The standard deviation is the square root of the variance.

The standard deviation measures the degree to which individual values in a list vary from the mean (average) of all values in the list. The lower the standard deviation, the less individual values vary from the mean and the more reliable the mean. A standard deviation of 0 indicates that all values in the list are equal.

@STD uses the n method (biased) to compute the standard deviation of population data, which uses the following formula:

$$\sqrt{\frac{\Sigma(V_i - AVG)^2}{n}}$$ where:
n = number of items in *list*
V_i = the ith item in *list*
AVG = average of values in *list*

Example: @STD(B5..B11) = 33.84, the standard deviation for the daily average of books sold that week

If you want to compute the standard deviation of sample data, use the $n - 1$ method (unbiased) by entering the following formula:

@SQRT(@COUNT(*list*)/@COUNT(*list*) − 1)*@STD(*list*)

@SUM   @SUM(*list*) adds the values in *list*.

Example: @SUM(C5..C11) = $6,791.74, the total sales for that week

@SUM(B5..B11) = 799, the total number of books sold that week

@VAR   @VAR(*list*) computes the population variance of the values in *list*. Variance is a measure of the degree to which individual values in a list vary from the mean (average) of all values in the list. The lower the variance, the less individual values vary from the mean and the more reliable the mean. A variance of 0 indicates that all values in the list are equal.

@VAR uses the n method (biased) to compute the variance of population data with the following formula:

$$\frac{\Sigma(V_i - AVG)^2}{n}$$ where:
n = number of items in *list*
V_i = the ith item in *list*
AVG = average of values in *list*

@VAR(SAT__SCORES) computes the variance in SAT scores for the entire freshman class.

If you want to compute the variance for sample data, use the $n - 1$ method (unbiased) by entering the following formula:

@COUNT(*list*) / (@COUNT(*list*) − 1) *@VAR(*list*)

In this example, @COUNT/(COUNT − 1)*@VAR(SAT__SCORES) computes the variances for the whole freshman class when SAT__SCORES includes a random sample of all scores.

Database Statistical @Functions

The database statistical @functions perform the same calculations on a field of a database as the statistical @functions perform on a list. Therefore, to use database statistical @functions, you must set up a database in a worksheet and establish a criteria range. (If you have not yet created a database in 1-2-3, read the section "Data Commands" in Chapter 2.)

Each database statistical @function scans the database, selects the records that match the criteria range, and then performs the calculation on the selected values in the field you specify.

Each database statistical @function has three arguments: *input*, *field*, and *criteria*.

- *Input* is the range. This range must include all the database records and their field names.
- *Field* is the number containing the field. The first column of the input range is field 0, the second column is field 1, the third column is field 2, and so on.
- *Criteria* is the criteria range you set up. The criteria range must contain the same field names as the input range and must include the criteria directly below each field name.

The first row in both the input and criteria ranges must contain the field names of each column. You can set up as many criteria ranges as you want to select values.

@DAVG @DAVG(*input,field,criteria*) averages the values in a *field* of the *input* range that meet the criteria in the *criteria* range.

@DCOUNT @DCOUNT(*input,field,criteria*) counts the nonblank cells in a *field* of the *input* range that meet the criteria in the *criteria* range.

@DMAX @DMAX(*input,field,criteria*) finds the maximum value in a *field* of the *input* range that meets the criteria in the *criteria* range.

@DMIN @DMIN(*input,field,criteria*) finds the minimum value in a *field* of the *input* range that meets the criteria in the *criteria* range.

@DSTD @DSTD(*input,field,criteria*) computes the population standard deviation for values in a *field* of the *input* range that meet the criteria in the *criteria* range.

@DSUM @DSUM(*input,field,criteria*) calculates the sum of the values in a *field* of the *input* range that meet the criteria in the *criteria* range.

@DVAR @DVAR(*input,field,criteria*) computes the population variance for values in a *field* of the *input* range that meet the criteria in the *criteria* range.

Add-In @Functions

Add-in @functions are @functions supplied by add-in programmers. Add-in @functions increase the number of @functions you can use to work with data in 1-2-3. Once you attach an add-in program that has add-in @functions, you can use add-in @functions as you would any built-in 1-2-3 @function.

Follow these steps to use add-in @functions:

1. Start 1-2-3.

2. Use **/A**dd-in **A**ttach to attach the add-in program that provides the @functions.

3. Use **/F**ile **R**etrieve to retrieve the worksheet that contains the add-in @functions.

The add-in @functions remain in memory until you end the 1-2-3 session. You cannot detach add-in @functions to free memory during a session.

Note If you retrieve a worksheet that contains add-in @functions without first attaching the appropriate add-in, each add-in @function is displayed as @? in the control panel and returns the value NA in the worksheet. To correct this, you must attach the add-in and retrieve the worksheet again.

Chapter 5

The PrintGraph Program

The PrintGraph program lets you print graphs from files you create with the /Graph Save command. /Graph Save stores an image of the current graph in a graph file with the extension .PIC. These are the only files PrintGraph can print. During the PrintGraph session, the PrintGraph settings sheet remains on the screen. You select commands from the PrintGraph menu just as you do in 1-2-3.

PrintGraph does not work with all printers. PrintGraph can print graphs only on a graphics printer or plotter. You can use your printer with PrintGraph only if you specify an appropriate driver for it in the driver set that you build during the Install program. Your printer may appear as one of the choices in the Install program. If you have acquired a driver for your printer, you can add it as a single driver.

You cannot start PrintGraph from the 1-2-3 main menu; you must start it from the operating system.

PrintGraph Commands

Before you print the graph, you must choose settings in PrintGraph. Your choice of settings determines layout, proportions, angle, typeface styles, and colors. You also use the settings to configure PrintGraph to your particular graphics printer and to specify the order in which you want to print a series of graphs. Table 5.1 summarizes the PrintGraph commands.

Command	Description
Image-Select	Lets you specify one or more graph files (file extension .PIC) to be printed
Settings	Controls all PrintGraph settings, including the size and proportion of the graph, fonts, colors (if any), and the hardware you want to use

Table 5.1

Command	Description
Go	Starts printing
Align	Tells PrintGraph that the paper is positioned at the top of the page
Page	Advances the paper to the top of the next page
Exit	Ends the PrintGraph session

Table 5.1 Continued

When PrintGraph starts, the PrintGraph settings appear on your screen, and the PrintGraph menu appears on the control panel. You do not need to press slash (/) to make the menu appear. The PrintGraph menu tree is shown below.

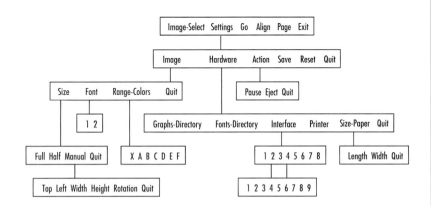

You issue a command by making a selection from the PrintGraph menu. To move the menu pointer to your selection, use ⊖, ⊕, or SPACEBAR to select the option. You can also type the first letter of the option to select it. If you forget what a command or setting does, press F1 (HELP) to display the corresponding Help screen.

The following steps summarize the procedure for printing a graph that you created and saved in 1-2-3:

1. Enter PrintGraph from DOS by typing **PGRAPH** at the operating system prompt.

2. Select **S**ettings from the PrintGraph menu to make any necessary changes.

3. Select **I**mage-Select to indicate the graphs you want to print.

4. Make sure the printer is correctly set up and that the paper is in the right position, then select **A**lign.

5. Select **G**o to begin printing.

If you want to interrupt printing, press CTRL-BREAK.

6. Select **P**age to advance the page when printing is complete.

To print the next graph on the same page, skip this step and select the next graph to print (step 3).

7. When you are done, select **Exit**. When you end PrintGraph, you return to DOS.

Note   You cannot make changes to a graph file when you are in PrintGraph. You must return to 1-2-3 and re-create the graph. (You cannot retrieve a .PIC file in 1-2-3.) After you re-create the graph, you must save it before returning to PrintGraph.

The following sections describe the PrintGraph commands in the order in which they appear in the PrintGraph menu.

Image-Select Command

The Image-Select command lets you specify the graph files that you want to print or preview. When you select **G**o, the selected graphs print in the order in which you choose them.

After selecting Image-Select, an alphabetical menu of graph files in the specified directory is displayed. The menu shows when you created each file and the file's size in bytes. Use ⬆ and ⬇ to highlight a graph file name.

While the list of graph files is on the screen, you can press (F10) (GRAPH) to preview a highlighted graph (if your monitor can display graphs).

A previewed graph in PrintGraph may look clearer than, and be scaled differently from, a graph that 1-2-3 displays. The printed graph prints the correct scaling and the clearer picture. The graph that appears on screen may not reflect the PrintGraph settings you have chosen; PrintGraph always uses the Block1 font for titles, legends, and scale numbers. (See the "Settings Image Font" section in this chapter.)

To select the graph files you want to print, highlight the file name, and then press SPACEBAR. PrintGraph marks a file you select for printing with a # symbol. To unmark a graph file, press SPACEBAR again when the file name is highlighted. To leave the graph file menu, press ⏎.

The graphs you have selected will be printed using the print settings you have specified with the **S**ettings command.

The next time you select **G**o, PrintGraph will print the graph files marked with a # symbol in the order in which you selected them. The names of the graph files you selected appear on the Image-Select screen.

Settings Commands

The PrintGraph settings control the size and proportion of the graph, the fonts and colors, whether PrintGraph saves or resets the current settings, and the hardware you use. Figure 5.1 shows the PrintGraph settings screen with the settings that 1-2-3 supplies. (Your system's default settings may be different.)

```
Copyright 1986, 1991 Lotus Development Corp.  All Rights Reserved.        MENU

Select graphs to print or preview
Image-Select  Settings  Go  Align  Page  Exit
─────────────────────────────────────────────────────────────────────────
    GRAPHS      IMAGE SETTINGS                    HARDWARE SETTINGS
    TO PRINT    Size            Range colors       Graphs directory
                Top        .395  X                   C:\123
                Left       .750  A                 Fonts directory
                Width     6.500  B                   C:\123
                Height    4.691  C                 Interface
                Rotation   .000  D                   Parallel 1
                                 E                 Printer
                Font             F
                1  BLOCK1                          Paper size
                2  BLOCK1                            Width      8.500
                                                     Length    11.000

                                                  ACTION SETTINGS
                                                   Pause  No   Eject  No
```

Figure 5.1

When you change one of the settings, PrintGraph updates the screen display. Use
BACKSPACE to erase characters, and use $\rightarrow$ and $\leftarrow$ to move between existing
characters. Use (ESC) to clear the entry and start again. When you select **G**o,
PrintGraph prints the selected graph images using the current settings. The settings
remain current until you change them or end the PrintGraph session.

Quit appears on several menus. Like (ESC), **Q**uit returns you to the previous menu.

The following sections describe each **S**ettings command. The commands are listed
in the order in which they appear in the Settings menu.

Settings **I**mage

Size Font Range-Colors Quit

Settings **I**mage controls the appearance of a graph.

The **I**mage settings control the way PrintGraph prints the graph: size, font
(typeface), color, angle of rotation, width and height, and top and left margins.

Settings **I**mage **S**ize

Full Half Manual Quit

Settings **I**mage **S**ize determines the size and proportions of the graph on the
paper.

Each setting controls the values (in inches) for margins, height and width, and (in
degrees) rotation. If you use **F**ull or **H**alf, PrintGraph sets the **H**eight and **W**idth
automatically. PrintGraph optimizes these settings for use with 8½-by-11-inch
paper. The height and width settings do not change when you change the
Hardware **S**ize-Paper setting. When you set the values with **S**ettings **S**ize **M**anual,
PrintGraph may display settings slightly different from those you entered.

Differences on the printed graph, however, will not be noticeable. Table 5.2 describes the settings you need to specify.

The **H**eight setting always measures the graph vertically (from top to bottom, as the paper feeds into the printer). The **W**idth setting always measures the graph horizontally (across the page, as it feeds into the printer).

Setting	Meaning
Full	Sets rotation to 90 degrees to print the graph sideways on the page. (The X axis is drawn along the height of the page.) Proportions are close to those you see displayed on the screen. With 8½-by-11-inch paper, this setting prints one graph on a page.
Half	Sets rotation to 0 degrees. (The X axis spans the width of the page.) Proportions are close to those you see displayed on the screen. With 8½-by-11-inch paper, this setting lets you print two graphs on a page. This is the default setting.
Manual	Sets all variables as shown below. Proportions depend on your settings.
Top	Sets the size of the top margin in inches.
Left	Sets the size of the left margin in inches.
Width	Sets the width of the graph (horizontal distance) in inches.
Height	Sets the height of the graph (vertical distance) in inches.
Rotation	Sets the number of degrees the graph is turned counterclockwise. (90 degrees produces a quarter turn to the left.)

Table 5.2

Three of these settings affect the proportions of your graph: width, height, and rotation. If you set these manually and want to retain the standard proportions of the graph, you must consider several things.

When PrintGraph sets a graph's size automatically, it preserves the aspect ratio, or the ratio of the graph's width to its height: approximately 1.385 (X axis) to 1 (Y axis). If you want to maintain these proportions, you must calculate this ratio. For instance, if X = 3.0, then Y = 2.165 (because Y = X/1.385). If Y = 4.5, then X = 6.237 (because X = Y*1.385).

If, however, you change the rotation to anything except 0, you must calculate the aspect ratio again to retain the standard proportions. Height and width are always measured in relation to the page, not in relation to the graph's axes. Thus, if rotation is set to 0 degrees, the height setting refers to the Y axis. If rotation is set to 90 degrees, the height setting refers to the X axis. To maintain the same proportions when setting rotation from 0 to 90 degrees, you must invert the width and height settings.

Rotation settings that turn rectangular graphs along vertical or horizontal axes (0, 90, 180, or 270 degrees) always create right-angled corners. If you select other rotations, you must make another calculation to preserve right-angled corners. Without this calculation, your graphs will be drawn as rhomboids and your pie charts as ellipses.

Pie charts must always retain the standard aspect ratio of 1 (Y axis) to 1.385 (X axis) to preserve their circular shape. The first radial line drawn always runs from the center of the pie toward the title line at the top of the graph. PrintGraph interprets this line as the Y axis when rotating the pie chart.

Settings Image Font

1 2

Settings **I**mage **F**ont determines which font (typeface) PrintGraph uses in printing the graph's text portions.

Follow these steps to establish which typeface PrintGraph uses when printing your graphs:

1. Select **1** or **2** to see the list of available fonts. PrintGraph uses Font 1 for the first line of the graph's title and Font 2 for all other alphanumeric characters in the graph, including the other titles, legends, and scale numbers. If you do not select Font 2, PrintGraph uses Font 1 for the entire graph.

   The available fonts are Block1, Block2, Bold, Forum, Italic1, Italic2, Lotus, Roman1, Roman2, Script1, and Script2.

   The numbers at the end of similar font names indicate how heavy (dark) each font is; for example, Script2 is heavier than Script1. The heavier font produces high-quality graphs only with high-resolution printers and plotters.

Note   Some PrintGraph fonts are designed for plotters, not raster graphics printers such as dot matrix and inkjet printers. In particular, the Italic and Script fonts will probably be unsatisfactory if you use them with a dot matrix printer. The Bold, Forum, and Roman fonts work well on raster printers if you choose a high enough density. The Block fonts provide the best results with a raster printer.

2. Highlight your choice using ⬆ and ⬇. Mark it by pressing SPACEBAR. The # symbol appears to the left of your choice. To remove the # symbol from a selection, highlight the selection and press SPACEBAR again.

3. Press ⏎ to enter your selection and return to the previous menu. Use (ESC) to return from the font listings without making any changes.

Before you print a graph, make sure the fonts directory setting is correct. If you need to change it, select **S**ettings **H**ardware **F**onts-Directory, and specify the correct directory.

CAUTION   If the fonts PrintGraph uses are stored on a removable disk, do not remove the disk from the drive during the PrintGraph session.

Settings Image Range-Colors

X A B C D E F Quit

Settings **I**mage **R**ange-Colors assigns colors to graph ranges.

When you select **R**ange-Colors, PrintGraph displays a menu that lists the graph ranges (**X**, **A** through **F**). Each range is associated with an available color. Depending on the type of printer you are using, this menu may offer several colors or only blank. Use ⇥ and ⇤ to move through the menu and see what colors your system offers.

The color you assign to the X range determines the color of the grid (the box that contains the graphed data and everything, except legends, outside the box). The grid includes scale numbers, titles, and exponents. PrintGraph uses the colors you assign to ranges A through F to draw the graphed data and the legends.

You cannot select **R**ange-Colors until you have specified a printer or plotter.

Pie Charts   When you print a pie chart, two things determine the colors of slices: the values in the B data range when you saved the graph in 1-2-3 (**/G**raph **S**ave) and the colors assigned in PrintGraph (**R**ange-Colors). Each B data range value in 1-2-3 corresponds to a range in PrintGraph, as follows:

B data range values in 1-2-3	Range in PrintGraph
1	X
2	A
3	B
4	C
5	D
6	E
7	F

PrintGraph uses the color you assign to a range in each slice that has the corresponding B-range value. For example, if the B-range slice is 4 (or 104, exploded), PrintGraph prints the slice in the color you assigned to range C using **R**ange-Colors; if the B-range value of a slice is 6, PrintGraph prints it in the color you assigned to range E; and so on.

PrintGraph uses the color you assigned to the X range for labels and titles. It uses the color you assigned to the A range for the pie's border.

Plotter Pens   If you are using a plotter, 1-2-3 prompts you to load the pens in a specific order when you select **G**o. Depending on the plotter, PrintGraph beeps when it is time to change the color of a pen and prompts you to do so. Refer to your plotter's documentation for information on using different pens.

Note   When you print a graph on a remote plotter, the number of pens in the plotter limits the number of colors you can use. In addition, the number of colors you specify when you are using a remote plotter cannot exceed the number of pen stalls in the plotter.

*S*ettings *I*mage *Q*uit	*S*ettings *I*mage *Q*uit returns you to the Settings menu.
*S*ettings *H*ardware	

Graphs-Directory Fonts-Directory Interface Printer Size-Paper Quit

*S*ettings *H*ardware tells PrintGraph how to find and print a graph. These settings tell PrintGraph the type of printer you are using, where your files are located, which interface you require, and what size paper you are using. Unless you change printers or print density, you can usually leave these settings unchanged.

The next sections describe each selection in the Settings Hardware menu.

*S*ettings *H*ardware *G*raphs-Directory	*S*ettings *H*ardware *G*raphs-Directory specifies the directory, including the drive, that PrintGraph searches for graph files (file extension .PIC). You can change this directory. For example, if you plan to use graph files stored on the disk in drive B, enter the specification B:\.
*S*ettings *H*ardware *F*onts-Directory	*S*ettings *H*ardware *F*onts-Directory specifies the directory, including the drive, that PrintGraph searches for font (.FNT) files. These font files should be in your 1-2-3 Release 2.3 program directory. If they are not, type the full path of the directory that contains the font files, then save the settings with *S*ettings *S*ave so that you do not have to specify them again unless you move the font files to another directory.
*S*ettings *H*ardware *I*nterface	

1 2 3 4 5 6 7 8

*S*ettings *H*ardware *I*nterface sets the communication channel between PrintGraph and your printer. Your choice for a setting depends on your computer. Some sample settings follow:

Setting	Meaning
1	Parallel 1 (standard interface for personal computers)
2	Serial 1
3	Parallel 2
4	Serial 2
5	DOS device LPT1
6	DOS device LPT2
7	DOS device LPT3
8	DOS device LPT4

Note   These are sample settings only. PrintGraph needs to know the correct settings for your hardware. If you are unsure about interface types, ports, and baud rates, consult your printer's manual or your dealer. Settings 1 through 4 are for printers physically linked to your system. The rest are for logical devices and are generally used to connect printers over a local area network.

CAUTION   If you use a logical device to print a graph file on a raster printer, you may use substantial disk space on the machine to which the printer is attached. A low-density raster printer used this way requires about 40K of disk space; a high-density printer requires about 500K.

Baud Rates for a Serial Printer

If you specify a serial interface for this setting, you must also tell PrintGraph your printer's baud rate. Baud rate is the speed at which PrintGraph transfers data. You can probably adjust the baud rate your printer uses. If so, select the fastest baud rate that will correctly transmit data without losing it. See your printer's manual for details. Baud rates in order of increasing speed are as follows:

Setting	Baud Rate
1	110
2	150
3	300
4	600
5	1200
6	2400
7	4800
8	9600
9	19200

Before you use a serial port to print 1-2-3 graphs, you must also configure it to the following settings:

Setting	Value
Data bits	8
Stop bits	If 110 baud, 2; otherwise, 1
Parity	None
Handshaking (XON/XOFF)	Enabled

You must change these settings on your printer, not in PrintGraph. See your printer's manual for details.

Settings Hardware Printer   Settings Hardware Printer tells PrintGraph which printer you are using and, in some cases, how densely to print the graph.

When you select Printer, PrintGraph displays a list of graphics printers that you selected with the Install program. Select the type of printer you are currently using. Follow these steps to select the printer from the list PrintGraph displays on your screen:

1. Highlight your choice using ⬆ and ⬇.

2. Mark your selection by pressing SPACEBAR.

3. The # symbol appears to the left of your choice. To remove the # symbol from a selection, highlight the selection and press SPACEBAR again.

4. Press ⏎ to enter your selection and return to the previous menu.

Some printer names on the list are described as low or high density, indicating the relative density, or resolution, of the printing. Denser printing means finer detail in your graphs, but it also means much slower printing. If you are using a dot matrix printer, some fonts will work only if you use high density. (See the "Settings Image Font" section earlier in this chapter for details.)

Settings Hardware Size-Paper

Length Width Quit

Settings Hardware Size-Paper identifies the size of paper you are using with your graphics printer. The default is $8^1/_2$-by-11 inches.

To specify a length of printer paper different from the default length of 11 inches, change the Length setting in PrintGraph. Manually adjust the settings for paper length (sometimes called form length) on your printer. See your printer's manual for information on changing the paper length setting.

If you cannot adjust the paper length setting on your printer manually, leave the PrintGraph default setting of 11 inches.

To adjust the paper's width, change the Width setting in PrintGraph.

Settings Action

Pause Eject Quit

Settings Action controls what PrintGraph does between printing graphs.

Pause controls whether PrintGraph pauses before printing each graph.

Setting	Meaning
Yes	PrintGraph pauses before printing each graph and signals the pause by beeping continuously. Use this setting when you need to change paper or switch settings on a printer between graphs. Press SPACEBAR to continue.
No	PrintGraph does not pause before printing each graph.

Note   When you are printing on a network device, **S**ettings **A**ction **P**ause has no effect on the printer. PrintGraph pauses but does not let you know what is happening at the network device.

Eject controls whether PrintGraph automatically advances the paper to the next page after printing a graph.

Setting	Meaning
Yes	Paper advances to the next page after each graph is printed. Use this setting to print one graph per page. On continuous formfeed paper, the paper advances to the top of a new page before printing resumes. On a plotter, PrintGraph prompts you to insert a new sheet of paper before printing resumes.
No	Paper does not advance after each graph is printed. If PrintGraph determines that the next graph is too long for the current page, the paper advances to the top of the next page. This depends on the Size-Paper ..setting.

Quit returns you to the previous menu.

Settings **S**ave   **S**ettings **S**ave stores PrintGraph settings (except graph images).

Each time you start a session, PrintGraph reads settings from PGRAPH.CNF. You can change these settings any time during the current session. Use **S**ave to copy your changes to PGRAPH.CNF so that they become the new standard for your PrintGraph sessions. 1-2-3 stores the settings, except for the selected graph images, in the file PGRAPH.CNF.

PrintGraph does not remember the settings you change during a session unless you use **S**ettings **S**ave. Each time you start a session or select **R**eset, PrintGraph reads the more recently saved settings.

If you use PrintGraph directly from the disk that contains the PrintGraph program, make sure it is in the disk drive with its write-protect tab removed before you select **S**ave.

Settings **R**eset   **S**ettings **R**eset replaces the current settings with those in PGRAPH.CNF.

Use **R**eset if you have changed, but not saved, the settings during the current session and you want to restore the settings you had when you started the session.

Settings **Q**uit   **S**ettings **Q**uit lets you return to the PrintGraph main menu after changing any setting.

Go Command

Go tells PrintGraph to print the graphs you choose. Before you select **G**o, make sure you have established the right settings and selected all the graphs you want to print. There is no confirmation step. If you want to interrupt printing, press (CTRL)-(BREAK).

If you are using a plotter, PrintGraph prompts you to load the pens in the order of the list PrintGraph displays. When you finish loading the pens, press SPACEBAR.

There may be a brief pause before printing actually begins. PrintGraph uses the settings you selected to format and print the selected graphs on your printer or plotter. As PrintGraph works, the control panel displays messages about PrintGraph's activities. During printing, your printer or plotter may pause for several seconds. When PrintGraph finishes printing, the control panel returns to the PrintGraph main menu.

If you are on a network and PrintGraph returns to the 1-2-3 main menu before printing begins, you can select **P**age to start printing the graph.

Align Command

PrintGraph automatically assumes that the paper is aligned at the top of the print page only at the beginning of a PrintGraph session. If you adjust the paper's position manually after the start of the session so that the top of the page is at the right place to start printing, use **A**lign to tell PrintGraph that the current paper position is at the top of the page.

No paper movement takes place, but PrintGraph now assumes that the paper is correctly positioned at the top of the page in the printer. If you are using a plotter, PrintGraph prompts you to set up the plotter and to press SPACEBAR.

With some printers, you must also set the printer's Top of Page or Home position. See your printer's manual.

Page Command

Page advances the paper one page in your printer or plotter. Use it to separate batches of graphs or whenever you want a blank page.

Exit Command

Select **E**xit to end the PrintGraph session.

CAUTION PrintGraph does not automatically save your current settings. If you want to use them in future sessions, save them before you select this command.

If you select **Y**es, PrintGraph ends, returning you to DOS. If you select **N**o, the PrintGraph session continues.

Chapter 6

*The Translate Utility**

The Translate utility lets you convert 1-2-3 and Symphony worksheet data to other file formats. This allows you to use your 1-2-3 Release 2.3 data with other spreadsheet and database management programs, as well as with previous releases of 1-2-3. Translate also lets you convert database and spreadsheet data from other programs to 1-2-3 and Symphony file formats.

When you translate files, you need to understand the following terms:

- The **source file** is the file you want to translate. It is in the file format of the source product, which is the program used to create the file.

- The **target file** is the new file you create with Translate. It contains source file data that has been translated into the file format of the target product, which is the program you will now use to work with the file.

For example, to translate a 1-2-3 Release 2.3 file named EMPLOYS.WK1 to a dBase III file named EMPLOYS.DBF, 1-2-3 Release 2.3 would be the source product, EMPLOYS.WK1 would be the source file, dBase III would be the target product, and EMPLOYS.DBF would be the target file. Table 6.1 lists all the possible file translations you can perform with the Translate utility.

Table 6.1

Source File	Target Product	Target File
1-2-3 Release 1A	dBase II	.DBF
	dBase III	.DBF
	any product that can read DIF files	.DIF
1-2-3 Release 2	1-2-3 Release 1A	.WKS

*Not included in the Addison-Wesley Lotus 1-2-3, Release 2.3 Education Software Series software.

R-162

Source File	Target Product	Target File
1-2-3 Release 2.01	dBase II	.DBF
1-2-3 Release 2.2	dBase III	.DBF
1-2-3 Release 2.3	any product that can read DIF files	.DIF
	Enable 2.0	.SSF
	Multiplan	.SLK
	SuperCalc4	.CAL
	Symphony 1.0 or 1.01	.WRK
dBase II	1-2-3 Release 1A	.WKS
dBase III	1-2-3 Release 2, 2.01, 2.2, 2.3	.WK1
DIF files	Symphony 1.0 or 1.01	.WRK
Multiplan VisiCalc	Symphony 1.1, 1.2, 2.0, 2.2	.WR1
Enable 2.0 SuperCalc4	1-2-3 Release 2, 2.01, 2.2, 2.3	.WK1
Symphony 1.0	1-2-3 Release 1A	.WKS
Symphony 1.01	dBase II and dBase III	.DBF
	any product that can read DIF files	.DIF
Symphony 1.1	1-2-3 Release 1A	.WKS
Symphony 1.2	dBase II and dBase III	.DBF
Symphony 2.0	any product that can read DIF files	.DIF
Symphony 2.2	Symphony 1.0 or 1.01	.WRK

Table 6.1 Continued

Using Translate

1. Start the Translate utility.

   Make the directory that contains 1-2-3 current. (This is usually the directory named 123R23 that the Install program created.) Then do one of the following:

   From the operating system, type **TRANS,** and then press ⏎.

   From the Access system, select **T**ranslate.

   Starting Translate directly from your computer's operating system prompt gives you more of your computer's memory for work. When you start Translate from the operating system, you return to the operating system when you leave Translate.

   A menu of source products appears on the left side of the screen.

2. Select a source product.

   Highlight the product, and then press ⏎. A list of available target products for the source product you selected appears on the right side of the screen.

3. Select a target product.

   The Translate utility displays Help screens that provide information about the translation you selected, including any restrictions.

4. Press ᴱˢᶜ to leave the Help screens and specify the source file.

   The Translate utility displays a list of files in the current directory that were created with the source product you specified in step 2. To list source files in a different drive or directory, press ᴱˢᶜ, and then use the pointer-movement keys to edit the path. When you are done, press ⏎. The Translate utility displays a list of source files in the directory you specified.

   If a source file's extension is different from the default extension of the source product, you will still be able to translate it.

5. Select the source file you want to translate.

   The Translate utility displays a prompt followed by the default target file name. The Translate utility creates a default target file name by adding the target product extension to the source file name.

6. Press ⏎ to accept the default name the Translate utility suggests, or edit the path or file name or type a new directory or file name and press ⏎.

   The Translate utility displays a progress message that indicates the percentage of data that has been translated. When the translation is complete, the message "Translation successful" appears.

   Note If the Translate utility is unable to translate, it displays an error message with information about the problem. This usually happens when the file you are attempting to translate is not in the correct format or the file has functions that do not translate to the target product directly. For each type of translation, Translate expects the file to be structured in a particular way. For information about the correct format, press ᶠ¹ (HELP).

7. Press ⏎ to translate another file from the same source product, or press ᴱˢᶜ to specify a different source product, or press ᴱˢᶜ twice to display the message "Do you want to leave Translate?" and select **Yes**.

   If you started Translate from the operating system, the operating system prompt appears. If you started Translate from the Access system, the Access menu appears.

Chapter 7

1-2-3 Add-In Utilities

Add-ins are programs, created by Lotus and other software developers, that you can run while you are using 1-2-3 and that provide 1-2-3 with additional capabilities. You never have to leave the worksheet to use an add-in. The program actually becomes part of 1-2-3.

In addition to all the 1-2-3 features available to you through the menus, @functions, and macro commands, 1-2-3 contains five add-in programs, each of which performs a specific task. Table 7.1 lists the five add-in programs.

Add-In	Description
Auditor*	Analyzes formulas in your worksheet files, including dependencies and circular references.
Macro Library Manager	Lets you create and use macro libraries.
Tutor*	Runs an interactive tutorial that shows you many of the features of 1-2-3.
Viewer*	Manages your files by letting you view them without retrieving them.
Wysiwyg*	Transforms 1-2-3 into a spreadsheet publishing tool. Wysiwyg lets you format and print your spreadsheets in ways you wouldn't think possible.

Table 7.1

*Not included in the Addison-Wesley Lotus 1-2-3 Release 2.3 Educational Software Series software. Contact your local sales representative for information about our Wysiwyg package, which is available separately.

Starting the 1-2-3 Add-In Utilities

To use the Add-In commands, select **/A**dd-In from the 1-2-3 main menu, or press (ALT)-(F10) (APP4) if you have not assigned an add-in program to that key.

/**A**dd-In **A**ttach	No-Key **7 8 9 10**

/**A**dd-In **A**ttach loads an add-in into memory. Add-ins remain in memory until you detach them with /**A**dd-In **D**etach, /**A**dd-In **C**lear, /**W**orksheet **G**lobal **D**efault **O**ther **A**dd-In **C**ancel, or until you end the current 1-2-3 session. An attached add-in is not activated until you select /**A**dd-In **I**nvoke or press the key you have assigned to the add-in.

Selecting **No**-Key does not assign the add-in to any specific key. Selecting **7** assigns the add-in to (ALT)-(F7) (APP1). Selecting **8** assigns the add-in to (ALT)-(F8) (APP2). Selecting **9** assigns the add-in to (ALT)-(F9) (APP3). Selecting **10** assigns the add-in to (ALT)-(F10) (APP4).

Note   Once you assign an add-in to a key, that key will no longer appear in the menu during the current 1-2-3 session unless you detach the add-in.

If you do not assign the add-in to a key, you will have to invoke it using /**A**dd-In **I**nvoke.

/**A**dd-In **D**etach   /**A**dd-In **D**etach removes an add-in, freeing the memory it occupied.

/**A**dd-In **I**nvoke   /**A**dd-In **I**nvoke activates an add-in that you have attached with /**A**dd-In **A**ttach. If you assigned the add-in to a key, you can use that key to invoke the add-in.

/**A**dd-In **C**lear   /**A**dd-In **C**lear removes all add-ins, freeing the memory they occupied.

/**Q**uit   /**Q**uit lets you leave 1-2-3.

CAUTION   Before you select /**Q**uit, select /**F**ile **S**ave to save your work. If you do not save changes you have made to the current worksheet before selecting /**Q**uit, 1-2-3 will prompt you to do so.

You must select either **Y**es to leave 1-2-3 or **N**o to cancel the /**Q**uit command and return to READY mode.

The Auditor*

The Auditor analyzes formulas in your worksheet files. You use the Auditor to perform the following tasks:

- Identify all the formulas that depend on a particular cell
- Display cells involved in a circular reference
- Display information about formulas in a file

*Not included in the Addison-Wesley Lotus 1-2-3 Release 2.3 Educational Software Series software.

Before you can use the Auditor, you must load it into memory and invoke it so that 1-2-3 displays the Auditor menu and settings sheet. For information about how to load the Auditor into memory and invoke it, see "Starting the 1-2-3 Add-In Utilities."

The Auditor Settings Sheet

The Auditor settings sheet displays the current audit mode and audit range.

Audit Mode You control the audit mode (how the Auditor identifies cells when you select Precedents, Dependents, Formulas, Recalc-List, or Circs) when you first invoke Auditor, or by selecting Options from the Auditor menu. The Auditor can highlight cells, list them in a range you specify, or move the cell pointer to them one at a time. Table 7.2 lists the available audit report methods.

Report Method	Description
Highlight	Identifies cells in a bright intensity or different color. Use Highlight when you want to examine the relationships among cells visually. Highlight is the default.
List	Identifies cells by listing them in a range you specify.
Trace	Identifies cells by moving the cell pointer to them one at a time.

Table 7.2

Audit Range You specify the audit range you want to use with the Precedents, Dependents, or Formulas command.

Auditor Commands

The Auditor commands identify cells involved in a circular reference and display information about formulas in a file. Table 7.3 summarizes the Auditor commands.

Command	Description
Precedents	Identifies all cells in the audit range referred to by a specified formula.
Dependents	Identifies all formulas in the audit range that depend on a specified cell.
Formulas	Identifies all formulas in the audit range.
Recalc-List	Identifies all formulas in the order that 1-2-3 recalculates them.
Circs	Identifies all cells involved in a circular reference.
Options	Sets or resets options such as the audit range or the way in which the Auditor identifies cells
Quit	Returns 1-2-3 to READY mode.

Table 7.3

Auditor Menu Tree

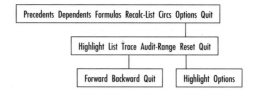

Precedents   Precedents identifies all the cells and ranges that provide data to a formula (so that 1-2-3 can calculate the result of the formula). For example, if cell O7 contains the formula +A3+@SUM(B1..B3), cells A3, B1, B2, and B3 are all precedents of cell O7.

Use **P**recedents to identify the cells that supply data to a formula. The Auditor identifies precedents using the current Auditor option (**H**ighlight, **L**ist, or **T**race).

Dependents   Dependents identifies all the formulas in the audit range that refer to a particular cell. For example, suppose cell E1 contains @SUM(B1..B10), cell E2 contains (B1*2)/A1, and cell E3 contains +B1. Cells E1, E2, and E3 are all dependents of cell B1 because they contain formulas that refer to B1.

Use **D**ependents when you want to see whether a formula refers to a specified cell. The Auditor identifies dependents using the current Auditor option (**H**ighlight, **L**ist, or **T**race).

Formulas   Formulas identifies all the formulas (including linking formulas to cells in other files) in the audit range. The Auditor identifies formulas using the current Auditor option (**H**ighlight, **L**ist, or **T**race).

Recalc-List   Recalc-List identifies formulas in the file in the order of recalculation (**N**atural, **C**olumnwise, or **R**owwise). The Auditor always begins by identifying the formula that 1-2-3 calculates first and ends with the formula that 1-2-3 calculates last.

The Auditor identifies formulas using the current Auditor option (**L**ist or **T**race).

Circs   Circs identifies all the cells in the file that are involved in a circular reference. A circular reference occurs when the recalculation method is **N**atural and a formula either directly or indirectly refers to itself.

For example, if cell M7 contains the formula @AVG(M7..M15), the circular reference is direct. If, on the other hand, cell A1 contains +A2, cell A2 contains +A3, and cell A3 contains +A1, the circular reference is indirect.

Use **C**ircs to identify the cells involved in the circular reference. The Auditor identifies the cells in the circular reference using the current Auditor option (**H**ighlight, **L**ist, or **T**race).

To change the way the Auditor identifies circular references, select **O**ptions **H**ighlight, **O**ptions **L**ist, or **O**ptions **T**race, and then select **Q**uit.

Options   Table 7.4 shows the options that are set or reset by the **O**ptions commands.

Command	Description
Highlight	Identifies cells by displaying them in a bright intensity or different color.
List	Lists information about identified cells in a range you specify.
Trace	Displays identified cells one at a time.
Audit-Range	Specifies the range you want to audit.
Reset	Clears highlights from cells or resets options to the defaults.
Quit	Returns you to the Auditor menu.

Table 7.4

Options **H**ighlight

Options Highlight identifies particular cells (for example, formulas or dependents) by displaying them in a bright intensity or different color. **H**ighlight is the default way of identifying cells.

Use **H**ighlight to quickly examine the relationships among cells.

Options **L**ist

Options List identifies cells by listing information about the contents of the cells in a range you specify.

Use **O**ptions List to examine detailed information about the contents of cells.

Options **T**race

Options **T**race identifies cells one at a time by moving the cell pointer to them. You can go forward or backward through the cells the Auditor identified. When the Auditor cannot find any more cells in a particular direction, it beeps.

Options **A**udit-Range

Options **A**udit-Range specifies the range to audit when you select the **P**recedents, **D**ependents, or **F**ormulas command.

Options **R**eset

Options **R**eset clears highlights from the screen or resets the options to the defaults.

Options **Q**uit

Options **Q**uit returns you to the Auditor menu.

Quit

Quit removes the Auditor menu, but keeps the Auditor in memory. The Auditor remains in memory until you end the 1-2-3 session or until you remove the Auditor from memory.

Use Quit to remove the Auditor menu so you can use 1-2-3 commands to enter or edit worksheet data.

The Macro Library Manager

Creating and Using the Macro Library Manager

The Macro Library Manager add-in lets you create and use macro libraries. A macro library is a range taken from a 1-2-3 worksheet and stored in memory (in an area that is separate from the worksheet) and in a file on disk called a library file (with an .MLB extension). The range can contain a single macro, several macros, a combination of macros and data (including formulas), or just data. Because the Macro Library Manager is an add-in, it does not have to be stored in memory all the time. You can attach it (load it into memory) when you need to use it and detach it (remove it from memory) when you need more memory for completing other tasks.

Using the Macro Library Manager allows you to:

- Use macros, formulas, and ranges of data in a different worksheet from the worksheet in which you created them.

- Leave some data in memory when you clear the worksheet and retrieve a new worksheet file.

- Build sophisticated applications to use with more than one worksheet.

The Macro Library Manager is in a file called MACROMGR.ADN. To start the 1-2-3 Macro Library Manager, see "Starting the 1-2-3 Add-In Utilities."

Table 7.5 summarizes the Macro Library Manager commands.

Command	Description
Load	Lets you copy data from a library file (a file with an .MLB extension) on disk into a library in memory. The library is stored separately from the worksheet.
Save	Lets you move the contents of a worksheet range and its range names into both a macro library in memory and a library file on disk. Range names associated with the cells no longer refer to the worksheet; they now refer to library locations.
Note	Be sure to test your macros in the worksheet before you save them in a library.
Edit	Lets you copy a macro library from memory into the worksheet so that you can make changes to the contents of the library or use it in the worksheet.
CAUTION	The library can be placed in any unprotected area of the worksheet. Make sure that the worksheet location is blank or contains unimportant data because the Macro Library Manager writes over existing data when it copies the library into the worksheet.
Remove	Lets you erase a macro library from memory but leaves a copy of the library intact on disk. (To erase a library file from disk, select /File Erase Other, press (ESC), type *.MLB, and then select the library you want to delete.)

Table 7.5

Command	Description
Name-List	Lets you create a list in the worksheet of the range names contained in a library. The list consists of a column of labels. The list will occupy a single column and as many rows as there are range names in the library.

CAUTION The range name list can be placed in any unprotected area of the worksheet. Make sure that the location is blank or contains unimportant data because the Macro Library Manager writes over existing data when it creates the list.

**Table 7.5
Continued**

Quit	Lets you leave the Macro Library Manager menu but keeps the Macro Library Manager attached. The data in the macro libraries that you have loaded or saved are still available.

Macro Library Manager Tree

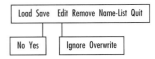

Basic Macro Library Manager Rules

- You must attach the Macro Library Manager before you attempt to save data in a library or load a library file into memory. If you detach the Macro Library Manager during a work session, the macro libraries you have saved or loaded disappear from memory. The library files already on disk are not affected.

- A macro library can contain up to 16,376 cells.

- The Macro Library Manager places a library in memory when you select either the Load or Save command from the Macro Library Manager menu. You can have up to ten libraries in memory simultaneously.

- When you specify the range you want to save in a library, the Macro Library Manager allocates a cell in conventional memory for each cell in the range, even if it is empty. To save memory, try to make your macros as compact as possible and specify ranges with as few empty cells as possible.

- Macro libraries are stored in an area of memory separate from the worksheet. Because a library has no cell coordinates, you cannot refer to data in a library with a cell or range address such as B3..B12. If you want to create a macro in the worksheet that uses data in a macro library, the data in the library must be contained in a named range (such as SALES89), and you must use the range name in the macro.

- /Worksheet Erase and /File Retrieve do not erase macro libraries from memory, so you can erase all data from a worksheet or retrieve a new worksheet without affecting the libraries.

- You use the same techniques to run a macro stored in a library as you would use with a macro in a worksheet.

- You can specify a password when you save data in a macro library. The password can be up to 80 characters long. Passwords protect libraries you created from being edited by others or from being viewed in STEP mode.

- You cannot have two or more libraries in memory with the same name.

- Try to assign unique names to each range you save in the library.

- The Macro Library Manager will not let you save a range in a library if the range includes a reference, or link, to data in another file.

The Tutor (1-2-3-Go!)*

The Tutor add-in utility (also called 1-2-3-Go!) is an online tutorial that teaches you how to use 1-2-3. When you complete 1-2-3-Go!, you will have the basic skills you need to create worksheets, graphs, databases, and macros in 1-2-3.

*Not included in the Addison-Wesley Lotus 1-2-3 Release 2.3 Educational Software Series software.

Starting the Tutor

Unlike the other add-in programs, you can start the Tutor either from the Add-In menu or from the operating system prompt. To start the Tutor from the Add-In menu, follow the steps described in "Starting the 1-2-3 Add-In Utilities." To start the Tutor from the operating system (before you start 1-2-3), complete the following steps:

1. Change to the 1-2-3 program directory (the directory that contains the 1-2-3 files).

2. Type **LEARN123** and then press ⏎.

When you start the Tutor from the operating system, 1-2-3 automatically assigns ⒜ⓛⓣ-Ⓕ⑩ (APP4) as the Tutor key. This key lets you end the Tutor during a lesson and return to the operating system prompt.

Once the Tutor is in memory, it displays the 1-2-3-Go! Table of Contents, from which you can select the tutorial lessons you want to run.

Using the 1-2-3-Go! Table of Contents

The Tutor displays the 1-2-3-Go! Table of Contents each time you start a Tutor session. 1-2-3-Go! covers six topics:

- Read Me First — Provides an overview of 1-2-3-Go! It tells you how to proceed through the lessons and what keys you can use. You should read Read Me First before you go on to the other lessons.

- Building a Worksheet — Teaches you how to identify different parts of a worksheet, enter and edit values and labels, use formulas, link worksheets, format data, and print a worksheet. After you complete this section, you can begin experimenting on your own, or you can complete the remaining three sections in any order.

- Using Graphs — Teaches you how to create different types of graphs; how to specify information for titles, labels, and legends; and how to save graphs for printing.

- Using a Database — Teaches you how to set up a database, sort records in a database, and search for information in a database.

- Working with Macros — Teaches you how to automate your work by creating macros. You will also learn how to document and name macros and how to find and fix errors in macros.

- Wysiwyg-Go! — Teaches you how to use the Wysiwyg add-in.

Each lesson tells you approximately how much time it takes to complete. If you need help while you are using 1-2-3-Go!, you can press (F1) (HELP) for information about the keys you can use.

Ending the Tutor

To end a Tutor session, do one of the following:

- To end a session in the middle of a lesson, press (ALT)-(F10) (APP4), the Tutor key, and then select Quit 1-2-3-Go! from the What's Next? menu. Selecting Quit 1-2-3-Go! returns you to either the worksheet or the operating system, depending on where you started.

- To end a session at the end of a lesson, select Return to 1-2-3-Go! Table of Contents from the What's Next? menu, then select Quit 1-2-3-Go! Selecting Quit 1-2-3-Go! returns you to either the worksheet or the operating system, depending on where you started.

Using Wysiwyg-Go!

Wysiwyg-Go! shows you how to create more professional-looking worksheets with Wysiwyg. To use Wysiwyg-Go! your monitor must be able to display graphics.

Using the Wysiwyg-Go! Menu
The Wysiwyg-Go! menu appears when you start a Wysiwyg-Go! session. Wysiwyg-Go! covers four main topics:

- Formatting a Worksheet — Teaches you how to change fonts; format a line of data in bold and italics, and set off data with lines, outlines, or a drop shadow.

- Including Graphics in a Worksheet — Teaches you how to add a graphic to a worksheet and how to enhance the graph.

- Using Text Ranges — Teaches you how to improve the appearance of text in a worksheet by aligning a label over a range of columns, entering text directly in a worksheet, and reformatting a range of labels you entered in a worksheet.

- Previewing and Printing — Teaches you how to specify a range to print, preview the printed page, print in landscape, and print formatted worksheets.

Ending Wysiwyg-Go!   Select Quit Wysiwyg-Go! from the menu to end a Wysiwyg-Go! session.

The Viewer*

The Viewer manages your files by letting you look at worksheet files before you retrieve or open them, by linking worksheet files while you view their contents, and by looking at the contents of your text files without retrieving them with a different program.

For example, if you want to update your year-end totals but cannot remember which file contains these totals, use the Viewer to scan the contents of all the worksheets in a directory without retrieving any of them. Once you find the file with the year-end totals, you can retrieve it or link to it.

Before you can use the Viewer, you must load it into memory and invoke it so that 1-2-3 displays the Viewer menu and screen. For information about how to load the Viewer into memory and invoke it, see "Starting the 1-2-3 Add-In Utilities."

*Not included in the Addison-Wesley Lotus 1-2-3 Release 2.3 Educational Software Series software.

The Viewer Screen

1-2-3 provides a split-screen display of your data when you invoke the Viewer add-in. The List window on the left displays the list of file names in the current directory. As you scroll through the list of files, you view their contents in the View window on the right.

Moving Around the Viewer   Table 7.6 lists the keys you use to move around the Viewer screen.

Key	Description
↑ or ↓	Moves the highlight up or down one line (List) or one row (View).
→	In the List window, moves the highlight to the View window if the List window contains file names. If the List window contains directory names, it makes the highlighted directory current. In the View window, moves the highlight right one column (in worksheets).
←	In the List window, displays a list of directories or drives. In the View window, moves the highlight left one column or to the List window.

Table 7.6

You can use all pointer-movement keys available in 1-2-3 Release 2.3 in the List window. (For more information on pointer-movement keys, see "Moving Around the Worksheet" in Chapter 1.)

Changing Directories   Use the following procedure to change the directory that the Viewer displays when you select a Viewer command.

1. While in the List window, press ⬅ to move one level up the directory tree. As you hold down ⬅, a list of drive letters appears.

2. To make a directory current, highlight its name and press ➡. Repeat this step until you reach the directory you want.

3. To make the current directory in 1-2-3 the current Viewer directory, press F2 (RESET).

The name of the current Viewer directory always appears below the status line at the top of the screen. When you use the Viewer for the first time, the directory it uses is the current directory in 1-2-3. If you change the current directory in the Viewer, the Viewer remembers the new directory from one Viewer session to another. Even if you change the current directory in 1-2-3 with **/File Dir**, the Viewer continues to use the directory you set in the Viewer.

Viewer Commands

Table 7.7 summarizes the Viewer commands.

Command	Description
Browse	Displays the contents of worksheet and text files as you scroll through the list of files in the current Viewer directory.
Link	Enters one or more linking formulas in the current worksheet after you select one or more source cells in another worksheet file.
Retrieve	Retrieves a worksheet file after you see its contents

Table 7.7

Viewer Menu Tree

Browse Browse displays the contents of a selected file in the current Viewer directory as you scroll through the list of file names in the directory. You can look at worksheet files (1-2-3 and Symphony) and text files.

Use **B**rowse to check the contents of a file quickly without having to retrieve the file. When you look at a worksheet file with the Viewer, you see it just as it appears in READY mode (1-2-3) or SHEET mode (Symphony).

Link   Link displays the contents of a selected file and links one or more selected cells in this file to the target cell in the current worksheet. When the Viewer links cells, it enters in the target cell a linking formula in the following format:

+<<*file reference*>>*cell reference*

file reference is the name of the file you select from the list that the Viewer displays in the List window. (This file is also called the source file.) *cell reference* is the address of the cell in the source file that contains the data you want in the target cell. For example, the Viewer enters in the target cell the formula +<<D:\SALES\QTR1.WK1>>J7 if you select the file QTR1.WK3 in D:\SALES and cell J7.

Use Link to enter a linking formula while you are looking at the contents of the source file, without having to type the linking formula. Also use Link to enter a series of linking formulas, starting at the current cell. For example, suppose you want to enter sales data for six products in the current worksheet, and this sales data is in a file named PRODUCTS.WK1. You can use Link to select PRODUCTS.WK1, then highlight the range that contains the sales data for the six products. The Viewer automatically enters a linking formula in six consecutive cells starting at the target cell.

Retrieve   Retrieve displays the contents of a selected worksheet file as you scroll through the list of files in the current Viewer directory and retrieves the selected file.

Use Retrieve to look at the contents of a file before retrieving it. When you look at a file with the Viewer, you see it just as it appears in READY mode (1-2-3) or SHEET mode (Symphony).

Wysiwyg*

The Wysiwyg add-in transforms 1-2-3 into a spreadsheet publishing tool. You use Wysiwyg commands to add and edit worksheet graphics, format data, print presentation-quality documents, and customize the way 1-2-3 displays worksheets on screen. The name Wysiwyg stands for "What you see is what you get" because what you see on the screen when you use Wysiwyg is nearly identical to what you get when you print the worksheet. Wysiwyg makes printing worksheets and graphs easier and improves the quality of both printed work and your on-screen display.

*Not included in the Addison-Wesley Lotus 1-2-3 Release 2.3 Educational Software Series software. Contact your local sales representative for information about our Wysiwyg package, which is available separately.

Using Wysiwyg

Unlike the other add-ins, Wysiwyg is not a program you use separately from 1-2-3. Instead, you use the Wysiwyg commands directly in your 1-2-3 spreadsheets to enhance their presentation.

You start Wysiwyg the same way you start any of the add-ins. For a description of starting an add-in, see "Starting the 1-2-3 Add-In Utilities." Then, once Wysiwyg is in memory, you can use the Wysiwyg commands at any point during your 1-2-3 session by displaying the Wysiwyg menu and selecting the command you want. To display the Wysiwyg menu, press **:** (colon). The **:** (colon) key displays the Wysiwyg menu, just as the **/** (slash) key displays the 1-2-3 main menu.

Wysiwyg is invoked when the status indicator displays WYSIWYG. For more information on any command, highlight the command with the menu pointer, and then press (F1) (HELP).

Wysiwyg Commands

Table 7.8 summarizes the Wysiwyg commands.

Command	Description
:Worksheet	Set column widths and row heights and inserts and deletes vertical and horizontal (column and row) page breaks.
:Format	Controls the appearance of your worksheets on screen and when printed.
:Graph	Lets you add, edit, and save graphics in a format file associated with a worksheet.
:Print	Creates printed copies of your work that include all formatting done with the Wysiwyg commands.
:Display	Controls how 1-2-3 displays the worksheet on the screen.
:Special	Copies and moves Wysiwyg formats from one range to another, imports formats and graphics from another format file, and exports formats and graphics from the current worksheet to format files on disk.
:Text	Lets you enter and edit text in worksheet ranges as though the words were in paragraphs in a word processor.
:Named-Style	Defines a named style (a collection of Wysiwyg formats taken from a single cell) and applies the named style to a cell or range of cells in the current file.
:Quit	Ends the current Wysiwyg session and returns 1-2-3 to READY mode while Wysiwyg remains attached.

Table 7.8

Display Commands

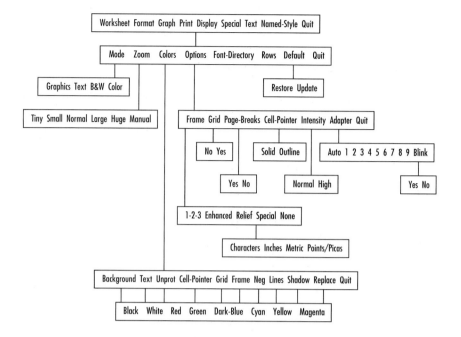

Format Commands

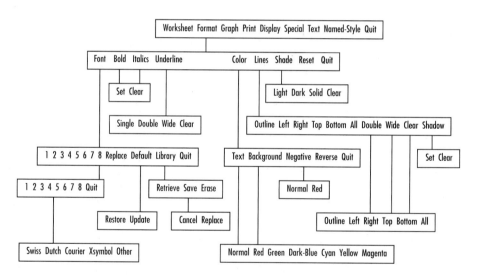

Graph Commands

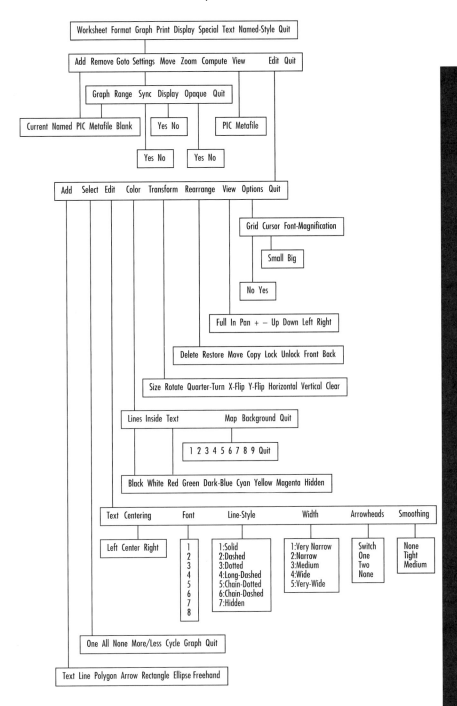

Named-Style Commands

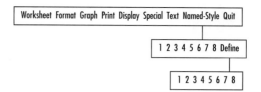

Print Commands

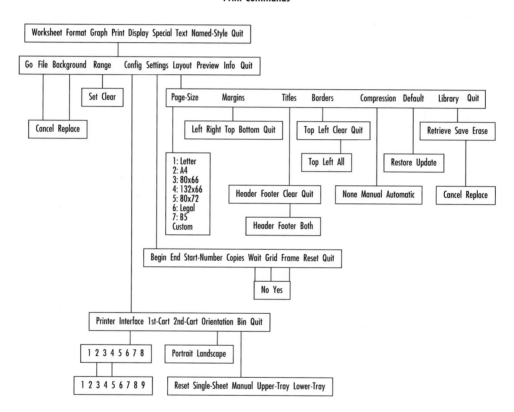

Special Commands

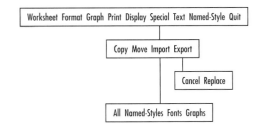

Text Commands

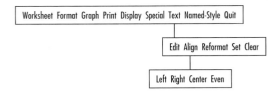

Worksheet Commands

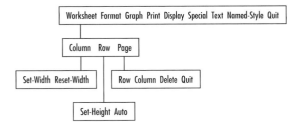

:Worksheet   The **:W**orksheet commands set column widths and row heights and insert and delete vertical and horizontal (column and row) page breaks. Table 7.9 lists the **:W**orksheet commands.

Command	Description
:Worksheet **C**olumn	Lets you set the width of one or more columns or resets one or more columns to the global column width. (A column can be from 1 to 240 characters wide.)
:Worksheet **R**ow	Lets you set the height of one or more rows or automatically sets the height of one or more rows based on the size of the largest font in a given row. (A row can be from 1 to 255 points high.)
:Worksheet **P**age	Lets you insert and delete vertical and horizontal (column and row) page breaks in worksheets. (**:D**isplay **O**ptions **P**age-Breaks **Y**es must be set to see them.)

Table 7.9

:Format The **:F**ormat commands give you control over the appearance of your worksheets on screen and when printed. You can control the format of a single cell or range or of multiple cells and ranges at the same time. **/F**ile **S**ave stores the formats in the format file (.FMT) associated with the current worksheet. Table 7.10 lists the **:F**ormat commands.

Command	Description
:Format **F**ont	Specifies fonts for ranges and the default font for the current worksheet, replaces fonts in the current font set, updates and restores the default font set, and saves font libraries in files on disk. (You can use up to eight fonts in a file.)
:Format **B**old	Adds or removes the boldface attribute from data in a range.
:Format **I**talics	Adds or removes the italics attribute from data in a range.
:Format **U**nderline	Adds or removes single, double, or wide underlines from a range. (Underlines appear under only the data in a cell; they do not appear in blank cells.)
:Format **C**olor	Specifies colors for the background, text, and negative numbers in a range for color monitors and color printers; reverses text colors and background colors. (You can use up to seven colors.)
:Format **L**ines	Adds or removes single, double, or wide horizontal and vertical lines, outlines, and 3-D effects in ranges. (1-2-3 displays lines in the global text color until you change the color globally with **:D**isplay **C**olor **L**ines.)
:Format **S**hade	Adds or removes light, dark, or solid shading from a range. (Solid shading prints in black, even if you have a color printer.)
:Format **R**eset	Resets all formats for the current range to the default formats.
:Format **Q**uit	Returns 1-2-3 to READY mode.

Table 7.10

:Graph The **:G**raph commands let you add, edit, and save graphics in a format file associated with a worksheet. Wysiwyg defines graphics as current or named 1-2-3 graphs or as graphs saved in graph files (.PIC), metafile files (.CGM), or blank placeholders in a worksheet. The **:G**raph commands also let you view graphics in a graphics editing window where you can edit and enhance them. Table 7.11 lists the **:G**raph commands.

Command	Description
:Graph **A**dd	Adds a graphic to a specified range in the worksheet. (Wysiwyg automatically sizes the graphic to fit in the specified range.)
:Graph **R**emove	Clears a graphic range from the worksheet. (1-2-3 data and graphs remain unchanged when the Wysiwyg graphic is removed.)
:Graph **G**oto	Moves the cell pointer to a graphic in the worksheet.
:Graph **S**ettings	Replaces a graphic in the worksheet with another graphic (preserving any graphic enhancement), resizes or moves a graphic in the worksheet, turns the display of graphics on or off, makes the graphics transparent or opaque, and determines whether 1-2-3 updates current and named graphs in the worksheet automatically when data they are based on changes.

Table 7.11

Command	Description
:Graph **M**ove	Moves a graphic to another range in the worksheet. (The row and column dimensions of the original range remain unchanged.)
:Graph **Z**oom	Displays a full-screen view of the selected graphic range in the worksheet. (You must be in graphics mode.) To return from full-screen view of the graphic, press any key.
:Graph **C**ompute	Recalculates and redraws the graphics in the worksheet based on the current worksheet data.
:Graph **V**iew	Lets you view a full-screen display of a graph file (.PIC) or metafile file (.CGM) graphic without adding it to the worksheet. (You must be in graphics mode.)
:Graph **E**dit	Adds and modifies text, objects, and other enhancements, such as arrows, polygons, rectangles, color, text alignment, and freehand drawings. (You must be in graphics mode to use the **:G**raph **E**dit commands.)
:Graph **Q**uit	Returns 1-2-3 to READY mode.

Table 7.11 Continued

:Print   The **:P**rint commands create printed copies of your work that include all formatting done with the Wysiwyg commands. You can print data and graphics on a printer or to an encoded file, or you can print from an encoded file in the background. Table 7.12 lists the **:P**rint commands.

Command	Description
:Print Go	Sends your data to the specified printer and starts printing.
:Print File	Prints your data to an encoded file with the file extension .ENC unless you specify another extension. The files can be printed only on the same type of printer as the printer specified in **:P**rint **C**onfig **P**rinter when the file was created. The file can include 1-2-3 data, graphics, and printer codes for all Wysiwyg options. (You cannot read an encoded file back into 1-2-3.)
:Print Background	Sends a copy of the selected range to an encoded file and then prints the encoded file on a printer while you continue your 1-2-3 session. When the file finishes printing, 1-2-3 deletes the encoded file.
:Print Range	Sets or clears the print range, which is the range of data that Wysiwyg prints.
:Print Config	Specifies the printer, printer interface, font cartridges, orientation of paper, and paper-feed method.
:Print Settings	Specifies which pages to print, page numbering, number of copies to print, whether to print the worksheet frame, whether to print grid lines, and whether to pause for manual paper feed before each page.
:Print Layout	Specifies the page size, margins, headers and footers, border columns and rows, and print compression; updates and restores the default page layout; saves and retrieves page layouts in library files on disk with the file extension .ALS unless you specify another extension.
:Print Preview	Displays, page by page and on screen, how printed pages will look. (To magnify objects on the page, press the + (plus) key; to reduce objects on the page, press the − (minus) key.
:Print Info	Removes or redisplays the Wysiwyg Print Settings dialog box.
:Print Quit	Returns 1-2-3 to READY mode.

Table 7.12

:Display   The **:D**isplay commands control how 1-2-3 displays the worksheet on the screen. Except for **:D**isplay **C**olors and **:D**isplay **M**ode (if you have a color printer), the Display commands do not affect worksheets or graphics you print. Table 7.13 lists the **:D**isplay commands.

Command	Description
:Display mode	Switches the screen display between graphics mode and text mode; displays the worksheet in black and white or in color when in graphics mode.
:Display Zoom	Enlarges the size of displayed cells and their contents up to 400% (decreasing the number of rows and columns displayed on the screen) or reduces the size of displayed cells and their contents down to 16% (increasing the number of rows and columns displayed on the screen).
:Display Colors	Specifies the on-screen colors for the worksheet background and data, cell pointer, grid, worksheet frame, lines, 3-D effect, negative numbers, and data in unprotected ranges when in graphics display mode; modifies the hue (color palette) of the eight colors 1-2-3 uses with Wysiwyg when in graphics mode. (You must select **:Display Mode Color**, not **:Display Mode B&W**.)
:Display Options	Determines whether 1-2-3 displays page breaks and grid lines; determines how 1-2-3 displays the worksheet frame and cell pointer; specifies screen-display brightness and the video adapter to use.
:Display Font-Directory	Specifies the directory in which 1-2-3 looks for display and printer fonts. If you specify a directory that contains no font files and no directory in your DOS path contains fonts, 1-2-3 replaces all display and printer fonts with the system font, Courier, which 1-2-3 uses when Wysiwyg is not attached.
:Display Rows	Specifies the number of worksheet rows to display on screen while 1-2-3 is in graphics mode. (You can select from 16 to 60 worksheet rows.)
:Display Default	Creates a new set of default display settings based on the current settings (**U**pdate) or replaces the current display settings with the default display settings (**R**estore). The default settings are stored in the Wysiwyg configuration file (WYSIWYG.CNF) that 1-2-3 uses automatically when you attach the Wysiwyg add-in.
:Display Quit	Returns 1-2-3 to READY mode.

Table 7.13

:Special   The **:S**pecial commands copy and move Wysiwyg formats from one range to another, import formats and graphics from another format file, and export formats and graphics from the current worksheet to format files on disk. Table 7.14 lists the **:S**pecial commands.

Command	Description
:Special Copy	Copies the Wysiwyg formats of a range to another range. (Data, graphs, and graph enhancements remain unchanged.)
:Special Move	Moves the Wysiwyg formats of a range to another range. (Data, graphs, and graphic enhancements remain unchanged.)

Table 7.14

Command	Description
:Special Import	Reads a Wysiwyg (.FMT) or Allways (.ALL) format file into memory and applies its formats to the current file. Lets you import all format settings, named styles only, fonts only, or graphs only.
:Special Export	Saves the format of the current file in a Wysiwyg (.FMT) or Allways (.ALL) format file on disk.

Table 7.14 Continued

:Text The :Text commands let you enter and edit text in worksheet ranges as though the words were in paragraphs in a word processor. To enter text, or align or justify data previously entered in cells, you specify a text range. The attribute indicator {Text} appears in the control panel when the cell pointer is in a text range. Table 7.15 lists the :Text commands.

Command	Description
:Text Edit	Lets you enter and edit labels in a text range directly in the worksheet instead of in the control panel.
:Text Align	Left-aligns, right-aligns, centers, or even-aligns labels in a text range.
:Text Reformat	Formats a column of long labels so that the labels fit within a text range and look like a paragraph. (To use this command, you must first select :Display Mode Graphics.)
:Text Set	Specifies a text range to use with :Text Align, :Text Edit, or :Text Reformat.
:Text Clear	Removes the alignment settings for a text range and the {Text} formatting description. (Data does not get deleted.)

Table 7.15

:Named-Style The :Named-Style commands define a named style, which is a collection of Wysiwyg formats taken from a single cell, and apply the named style to a cell or range of cells in the current file. Each file can contain up to eight named styles. Table 7.16 lists the :Named-Style commands.

Command	Description
:Named-Style 1:Normal–8:Normal	Assigns one of eight named styles to a range. (If you redefine a named style, any range you formatted with that style is automatically reformatted.)
:Named-Style Define	Creates a named style based on formats in the specified cell. (You can enter a name of up to 6 characters for a named style you define, and you can enter a description of the named style that is up to 37 characters.)

Table 7.16

:Quit The :Quit command lets you end the current Wysiwyg session and return 1-2-3 to READY mode while Wysiwyg remains attached. To invoke Wysiwyg from 1-2-3 READY mode, press : (colon), or move the mouse pointer to the control panel and click the right mouse button to switch menus if necessary.

Appendix A

Printers and Their Compatible Emulations

When you are selecting a printer driver during installation, you may not see the name of your printer on the list the Install program displays. This means that the Lotus 1-2-3 disks do not contain a printer driver for your type of printer.

Because many printers are designed to be compatible with one another, it is possible that your printer is able to emulate another type of printer. Ask your technical resource person or check your printer's manual to see if your printer has this capability. Make any necessary modifications as instructed, and select the printer manufacturer and model that you want to emulate.

The following table shows some printers and what they can emulate. If your printer is listed, select from the list of suggested emulations.

If you have	You can emulate
ALPS ALQ224e or ALPS ALQ324e	Epson LQ series 2500, 1500, 1050, 1000, 850, 800, or 500
ALPS LPX600	HP LaserJet+, IBM Proprinter, or Epson FX-80
Brother M1709	Epson FX series or IBM Proprinter
Citizen America MSP45	Epson FX series or IBM Proprinter
Epson EPL600	HP LaserJet II
Fujitsu RX 7200	HP LaserJet+, Epson FX-85, or IBM Proprinter
Fujitsu RX 7300 or Fujitsu RX 7400	HP LaserJet+ or Epson FX-80
IBM Personal Page Printer 4216	IBM Proprinter XL or PostScript
Mannesmann Tally MT340	Epson FX-185/JX Color, IBM Graphics Printer, or IBM Proprinter

If you have	You can emulate
Panasonic KX P4450 Laser	HP LaserJet or IBM Proprinter
Tandy LP 1000	HP LaserJet+
Texas Instruments OmniLaser 2106	HP LaserJet+
NEC LC 890	HP LaserJet II or PostScript
Okidata ML 321 or other color printers	HP LaserJet II or PostScript

If your printer cannot emulate, find out if it came with a disk containing a printer driver designed for use with 1-2-3 Release 2.3. To add a new driver to the library of available printer drivers, select Add New Drivers from the Advanced Options Screen of the Install Main Menu, and follow the instructions provided. Then select the new driver.

If you cannot use any of these options, select Unlisted from the printer manufacturer list displayed by the Install program, and then select Complete Compatibility from the printer model list. This generic printer driver lets you print text and will work with most printers; however, you may not be able to use every feature of your printer, and you will not be able to print in Wysiwyg or PrintGraph.

Appendix B

New Release 2.3 Software Features

Following is a list of the commands and features that have been added to Lotus 1-2-3 Release 2.2 to create Release 2.3.

File Commands

Command	Task
/File Directory	Edits the default directory for the current 1-2-3 session.
/File View Browse	Scrolls through a list of files and views their contents.
/File View Link	Displays the contents of a worksheet file and links selected cells in this file to the target cell in the current worksheet.
/File View Retrieve	Retrieves a file from disk after it has been viewed.

New Graph Types

Graph type	Description
Area	A line or mixed graph in which a different hatch pattern or color fills the area between each line.
HLCO (stock market)	Tracks a measurable quantity that fluctuates during a specific period.
Horizontal bar	Bar graph with horizontal Y axis.
Horizontal Stacked bar	Bar graph with horizontal Y axis.
Mixed bar and line	Includes both lines and bars.

New Graph Appearance Commands

Command	Task
/Graph Options Scale Y-Scale Display	Displays Y-axis labels on either one or both sides of a graph.
/Graph Type Features Frame	Controls the display of the graph frame, zero lines, and margins
/Graph Type Features 3D-Effect	Displays a 3D bar graph.

Worksheet Commands

Command	Task
/Worksheet Global Default Other Expanded-Memory Enhanced	Stores both cell contents and cell pointers in expanded memory.
/Worksheet Global Default Other Expanded-Memory Standard	Stores cell contents in expanded memory and cell pointers in conventional memory.
/Worksheet Global Default Update	Allows you to save colors specified with Wysiwyg after Wysiwyg is detached.
/Worksheet Global Default Directory	Allows you to enter a split vertical bar as the first character of the default directory name to specify that 1-2-3 should not expand the entry to a full path or convert it to uppercase.
/Worksheet Global Default Status	Tells 1-2-3 to identify the expanded memory setting and the name of the 1-2-3 configuration file.
/Worksheet Global Default Printer	Displays the Default Printer Settings dialog box.

Macro Commands

Command	Task
{APPENDBELOW}	Copies a range of data below a second range.
{APPENDRIGHT}	Copies a range of data to the right of a second range.
{FORM}	Suspends running a macro so that you can enter and edit data in the specified range.
{ABS}	Lets you specify a range when 1-2-3 is in READY mode.
{DEL}	Erases a single cell when 1-2-3 is in READY mode.
{EDIT}	Activates a dialog box after you use {WINDOW}.

Other New Features

- Background printing
- Ability to save printer information to an encoded file
- Mouse support
- Interactive dialog boxes replace settings sheets
- New ways to specify ranges
- Wildcard characters can be used to specify a search string in /Range Search

- Criteria formulas can be entered without using a reference to a cell in the input range
- (DEL) can be used to delete the contents of the current cell when 1-2-3 is in READY mode
- (F4) can be used to specify a range before you select a command
- (F10) (GRAPH) can now be used in many 1-2-3 modes, including displaying the current graph after the **P**rint command has been selected
- 1-2-3 help has enhanced context sensitivity
- New configuration files can be specified when accessing 1-2-3 from the DOS prompt
- New 1-2-3 prompts more closely reflect what selected commands do
- Error messages are displayed in message boxes. You can read a description of the error condition by pressing (F1) (HELP)

New Add-ins*

Add-in	Description
Wysiwig Add-in	Spreadsheet publishing add-in that lets you create presentation-quality 1-2-3 documents and include graphs and graphics in your worksheets.
Auditor Add-in	Identifies and checks formulas in the worksheet.
1-2-3 Go! and Wysiwyg Tutorials	On-line tutorials for teaching 1-2-3 Release 2.3 and for teaching Wysiwyg.
Viewer Add-in	Allows you to view the contents of worksheet, text, and database files on disk or on a network without opening the files.

* These add-ins are not included in the Addison-Wesley 1-2-3 Release 2.3 Educational Software Series software. Contact your local sales representative for information about our Wysiwyg package and tutorial.

Appendix C

Creating a Floppy Disk Version of Lotus 1-2-3, Release 2.3

Once you have installed Lotus 1-2-3 Release 2.3 on a hard disk drive, you can copy selected 1-2-3 files from your hard disk drive to 5¼" or 3½" floppy diskettes to create a floppy disk version of the program.

The 5¼" floppy disk version of Lotus 1-2-3 Release 2.3 will contain two diskettes, a 1-2-3 Program disk, and a PrintGraph disk. This version of 1-2-3 will not allow you to access on-line help.

The 3½" floppy disk version of Lotus 1-2-3 Release 2.3 will contain three diskettes, a 1-2-3 Program disk, a PrintGraph disk, and a Help disk. This version of 1-2-3 has the the same functionality as the Lotus 1-2-3 Release 2.3 Educational Software Series software that you have installed on your hard disk drive.

Before You Begin

1. Install Lotus 1-2-3 Release 2.3 on your hard disk drive, following the directions in Chapter 2, "Installing Lotus 1-2-3 Release 2.3" in Part 1, "Getting Started."

2. If the driver set that you create during the installation process describes a different screen display and printer from the hardware on which you intend to use the floppy disk version of 1-2-3, you must create another driver set that specifies the correct screen display and printer. Follow the instructions on creating more than one driver set in Chapter 2, "Installing Lotus 1-2-3 Release 2.3" in Part 1, "Getting Started." Substitute the name that you give to this driver set for 123.SET in the steps that follow.

3. Format two blank 5¼" diskettes or three blank 3½" diskettes. If necessary, see Chapter 2, "Installing Lotus 1-2-3 Release 2.3" in Part 1, "Getting Started" for instructions on how to format blank diskettes. Label your blank formatted diskettes as follows:

	5 1/4″ version	3.5″ version
Disk 1	1-2-3 Program Disk	1-2-3 Program Disk
Disk 2	PrintGraph Disk	PrintGraph Disk
Disk 3	Not applicable	Help Disk

Creating the 1-2-3 Program Disk

Create the 1-2-3 Program Disk for both the 5 1/4″ or 3 1/2″ versions by copying selected 1-2-3 files from your hard disk drive as follows:

1. Make sure that C:\123R23> is displayed on your computer screen.

2. Insert the blank formatted disk called 1-2-3 Program Disk in the A drive.

Note If you are using a drive other than the A drive, substitute that drive name as appropriate in these instructions.

3. Copy each of the files listed below onto the 1-2-3 Program Disk. To do this,

Type: **Copy <file name> A:**

Press: (↵)

As you copy each file, substitute the names listed below for "file name." For example, if you are copying the file named 123.CMP,

Type: **Copy 123.CMP A:**

File names to copy:

123.CMP	123.EXE	123R23.ICO
123.CNF	123.LLD	123R23.PIF
123.DLD	123.RI	123.SET**
123.DYN		

Note If you have given the driver set you intend to use with your floppy disk version a name other than 123.SET, copy that file onto your floppy disk instead of 123.SET.

4. When you have finished copying each file, check to see that all ten files have been transferred to the 1-2-3 Program Disk. To do this,

Type: **dir A:**

Press: (↵)

DOS will list all the file names contained on the 1-2-3 Program Disk. Compare this list to the list above to make sure that all of the files you need are on the disk. If any of them are missing, copy them to the disk using the instructions in step 3.

Using the 1-2-3 Program Disk

Once you have created your 1-2-3 Program Disk, you can use it to create and print 1-2-3 worksheets, and to create graphs. To run 1-2-3 from your 1-2-3 Program Disk,

1. Make sure that C:\123R23> is displayed on your computer screen.

2. Insert the 1-2-3 Program Disk into drive A and

Type: **A:**

Press: ⏎

The DOS prompt for the A drive, A:\> should appear on your screen.

3. At the DOS prompt for the A drive,

Type: **123**

Press: ⏎

Note   If you have given your driver set a name other than 123.SET, start 1-2-3 by typing **123** followed by a space and the name of the driver set, then press ⏎. It is not necessary to type the extension .SET. For example, to start 123 with a driver set called LASER.SET, type **123 LASER**. If you do not type the name of the driver set, 1-2-3 will use 123.SET to start the program.

The Lotus 1-2-3 logo should appear on your screen briefly, followed by a blank 1-2-3 worksheet.

Using your Data Disk

If you have not already created your 1-2-3 data disk, see Getting Started Chapter 2, "Installing Lotus 1-2-3 Release 2.3" in Part 1, "Getting Started" for instructions on creating a separate floppy disk that contains the data files you will need to work through the tutorials for this text.

Systems with Two Floppy Disk Drives

When you are using the floppy disk version of Lotus 1-2-3 on a system with two floppy disk drives, place your 1-2-3 Program Disk in the A drive, your data disk in the B drive, and start 1-2-3 following the instructions above for using the 1-2-3 Program Disk.

The first time that you start 1-2-3 from the 1-2-3 Program Disk — before you retrieve or save any files — you must change the default directory to the B drive using the instructions for changing the default drive in Getting Started Chapter 3, "Starting and Quitting a 1-2-3 Session" in Part 1, "Getting Started." Substitute the B drive for the A drive as you work through these instructions.

Systems with One Floppy Disk Drive

When you are using the floppy disk version of Lotus 1-2-3 on a system with one floppy disk drive, place your 1-2-3 Program Disk in the A drive, and start 1-2-3 following the instructions above for using the 1-2-3 Program Disk.

The first time that you start 1-2-3 from the 1-2-3 Program Disk — before you retrieve or save any files — you must change the default directory to the A drive using the instructions for changing the default drive in Chapter 3, "Starting and Quitting a 1-2-3 Session" in Part 1, "Getting Started." The 1-2-3 Program Disk must be in place in the A drive throughout this process. Be sure to save your changes to the default directory by selecting **U**pdate.

After you have started 1-2-3 and made any necessary changes to the default directory, you can remove the 1-2-3 Program Disk from the A drive and replace it with your data disk. This is possible because as the computer starts 1-2-3, it loads the program into the computer's short term memory.

Creating the PrintGraph Disk

The PrintGraph Disk will allow you to print the graphs that you create using the 1-2-3 Program Disk. Create the PrintGraph Disk for both the 5¼" or 3½" versions by copying selected 1-2-3 files from your hard disk drive as follows:

1. Make sure that C:\123R23> is displayed on your computer screen.

2. Insert the blank formatted disk labelled PrintGraph Disk in the A drive.

Note   If you are using a drive other than the A drive, substitute that drive name as appropriate in these instructions.

3. Copy each of the files listed below onto the PrintGraph Disk. To do this,

Type: **Copy <file name> A:**

Press: ⏎

As you copy each file, substitute the names listed below for "file name."

File names to copy:

PGRAPH.EXE	BLOCK2.FNT	ITALIC2.FNT	SCRIPT1.FNT
PGRAPH.HLP	BOLD.FNT	LOTUS.FNT	SCRIPT2.FNT
PGRAPH.CNF	FORUM.FNT	ROMAN1.FNT	123.LLD
BLOCK1.FNT	ITALIC1.FNT	ROMAN2.FNT	123.SET**

**Note   As before, if you have given the driver set you intend to use with your floppy disk version a name other than 123.SET, copy that file onto your floppy disk instead of 123.SET.

4. When you have finished copying each file, check to see that all sixteen files have been transferred to the PrintGraph Disk. To do this,

Type: **dir A:**

Press: ⏎

DOS will list all the file names contained on the PrintGraph Disk. Compare this list to the list above to make sure that all of the files you need are on the disk. If any of them are missing, copy them to the disk using the instructions in step 3.

Using the PrintGraph Disk

Once you have created your PrintGraph Disk, you can use it to run the PrintGraph program and print graphs you have created using the 1-2-3 Program Disk. To run the PrintGraph program from your PrintGraph Disk,

1. Make sure that C:\123R23> is displayed on your computer screen.

2. Insert the PrintGraph Disk into drive A and

Type: **A:**

Press: ⌐⏎

The DOS prompt for the A drive, A:\> should appear on your screen.

3. At the DOS prompt for the A drive,

Type: **PGRAPH**

Note If you have given your driver set a name other than 123.SET, start PrintGraph by typing **PGRAPH** followed by a space and the name of the driver set, then press ⌐⏎. It is not necessary to type the extension .SET. For example, to start PrintGraph with a driver set called LASER.SET, type **PGRAPH LASER**. If you do not type the name of the driver set, PrintGraph will use 123.SET to start the program.

The PrintGraph logo screen will appear briefly, followed by the PrintGraph main menu.

Review Chapter 4, "Starting and Quitting PrintGraph" in Part 1, "Getting Started" for information on how to customize your hardware setup. Instructions on printing graphs using PrintGraph appear in appropriate tutorials.

Systems with Two Floppy Disk Drives

When you are using the PrintGraph program on a system with two floppy disk drives, place your PrintGraph Disk in the A drive, your data disk (or disk on which you have stored your graph "picture" files) in the B drive, and start PrintGraph following the instructions above for using the PrintGraph Disk.

The first time that you start PrintGraph from the PrintGraph Disk, before you retrieve any files for printing, you must change the PrintGraph default directory to the B drive using the instructions for changing the PrintGraph default drive in Chapter 4, "Starting and Quitting PrintGraph" in Part 1, "Getting Started." Substitute the B drive for the A drive as you work through these instructions.

Systems with One Floppy Disk Drive

When you are using your floppy disk version of the PrintGraph program on a system with one floppy disk drive, place your PrintGraph Disk in the A drive, and start 1-2-3 following the instructions above for using the PrintGraph Disk.

The first time that you start 1-2-3 from the PrintGraph Disk — before you retrieve or save any files — you must change the PrintGraph default directory to the A drive using the instructions for changing the default drive in Chapter 4, "Starting and Quitting PrintGraph" in Part 1, "Getting Started."

After you have started PrintGraph and made any necessary changes to the default directory, you can remove the PrintGraph Disk from the A drive and replace it with your data disk. This is possible because as the computer starts PrintGraph, it loads the program into the computer's short term memory.

Creating a Help Disk (3½" version only)

The Help Disk will allow you to access on-line help from a 3½" diskette. You cannot create a 5¼" version of the Help Disk because the file containing help will not fit on a low density 5¼" floppy diskette. To create a 3½" Help Disk,

1. Make sure that C:\123R23> is displayed on your computer screen.

2. Insert the blank formatted 3½" disk called Help Disk in the A drive.

Note   If you are using a drive other than the A drive, substitute that drive name as appropriate in these instructions.

3. Copy each the file containing help onto the Help Disk as follows,

Type: **Copy 123.HLP A:**

Using On-line Help (3½" version only)

To access on-line help after you have started 1-2-3 using the 1-2-3 Program Disk, remove the 1-2-3 Program Disk from the A drive, and replace it with the Help Disk. Then,

Press: F1 (HELP).

Note   If you press F1 (HELP) before you put the Help Disk into the A drive, the error message "Cannot find 123.HLP help file" will appear on the screen. Press the ESC key to continue, and be sure to replace the 1-2-3 Program Disk with the Help Disk in the A drive before trying again.

Index

Special characters

,(comma), R-96
&(ampersand), R-16
'(apostrophe), in label prefixes, 19, 23
*(asterisk), as wildcard character, GS-28, R-52
\(backslash)
    in labels, 25–26, 169, R-14, R-50
{}(braces), R-96
^(caret), R-13
    in label prefixes, 23
$(dollar sign), 76, 77
?(question mark), 7, R-81
    as macro command, R-101
    as wildcard character, R-52
"(quote)
    in label prefixes, 23, R-13
    in string arguments, R-96–R-97
}(right brace), R-96
;(semicolon), R-96
'(single quote), R-13
/(slash), 27
~(tilde), R-81

@ABS function, R-121
Absolute cell reference, 75–78
Access system, R-22–R-23
@ACOS function, R-121
/**A**dd-In **A**ttach command, R-166
/**A**dd-In **C**lear command, R-166
/**A**dd-In **D**etach command, R-166
Add-in @functions, R-148–R-149
/**A**dd-In **I**nvoke command, R-166
Add-in utilities, R-165–R-185
    Auditor program, R-166–R-169
    new in Release 2.3, R-190
    Tutor, R-172–R-174
    Viewer, R-174–R-176
    Wysiwyg, R-176–R-185
Addresses. *See* Cell addresses; Range addresses
Advanced macro commands, R-95–R-117
    arguments and, R-96–R-99
    data manipulation, R-99, R-110–R-114
    file manipulation, R-99, R-114–R-117
    flow-of-control, R-99, R-105–R-110
    interactive, R-99, R-101–R-105
    screen control, R-99–R-101
Align command, R-161

Alignment
    of labels, 38, R-31, R-44
    of values, R-12
Ampersand (&), R-16
Anchor cell, 66
Anchoring, 66, R-15
Annuities
    computing payments and, R-141–R-142
    number of payments and, R-144–R-145
Apostrophe ('), in label prefixes, 19, 23
{APPENDBELOW} command, R-110–R-111
{APPENDRIGHT} command, R-110–R-111
Arguments
    condition, R-96
    declaring type of, R-97, R-105–R-106
    in @functions, R-119–R-120
    in macros, R-95–R-98, R-105–R-106
    passing to subroutines, R-98
Arithmetic operators, 40, R-16
Arrow(s), scroll, 7
Arrow keys, 9–11
Ascending sort order, 232–233

Paper
  advancing, R-63, R-160, R-161
  positioning, R-65, R-161
  size of, R-159
Passwords, 152–154, R-52
  in Macro Library Manager,
    R-172
  saving files with, R-55
Path, R-50
Pausing
  of macros, 289, 290–291,
    R-101, R-102
  during printing, R-159–R-160
Period (.) key, in POINT mode,
  R-15
PgDn key, 11–12
PgUp key, 12
@PI function, R-122
.PIC file extension, GS-46, 185,
  R-51, R-157
Pie charts, 164, R-68–R-69
  creating, 205–207
  exploded, 210–211
  printing, R-156
  settings for, R-155
  shading, 207–210
Plotter pens, loading, R-156
@PMT function, R-141–R-142
POINT mode, 66–69
  keys in, 65–69, R-15
Pointer
  cell, 6, 9–15, R-47
  menu, 28
  mouse, 7, 15
Pointer-movement keys, in POINT
  mode, R-15
Pointing, 15, 65–69
Popup dialog boxes, R-8
Precedents command, R-168
Preselection, of ranges, 107
Pressing, R-6
Primary key, 232
/**P**rint **A**lign command, R-65
/**P**rint **C**lear command, R-65
/**P**rint commands, 43–45, 84–85,
  150–151, R-62–R-65
:**P**rint commands, R-180, R-183
/**P**rint **G**o command, R-65
/**P**rint **L**ine command, R-63

/**P**rint **O**ptions commands,
  R-63–R-65
/**P**rint **P**age command, R-63
/**P**rint **R**ange command, R-62
Printer(s)
  communication channel
    between PrintGraph and,
    R-157–R-158
  compatible emulations of,
    R-186–R-187
  default settings for, R-33–R-34
  graphics, GS-23–GS-24
  selecting, GS-45–GS-46, R-159
  serial, baud rates for, R-158
  setup strings for, R-63, R-64
  text, GS-22–GS-23
Printer driver. *See also* Driver sets
  compatible emulations and,
    R-186–R-187
  specifying name for, R-66
PrintGraph program,
  GS-43–GS-47, 185–189,
  215–217, R-150–R-161
  customizing hardware setup for,
    GS-45–GS-47
  exiting from, GS-47, R-161
  menu of, GS-45
  saving graphs for printing with,
    185
  settings in, R-160
  starting, GS-43–GS-45
  using, GS-44–GS-45
Printing
  avoiding gaps in, R-65
  in background, R-59
  commands for, R-25, R-59–R-66
  in compressed mode, 150–152
  density of, R-159
  to encoded file, R-59
  format for, R-64–R-65
  of graphs. *See* PrintGraph
    program
  macros for, 322–324
  pausing during, R-159–R-160
  to printer, R-59
  of ranges, R-60–R-62
  saving graphs for, 185
  settings for, R-65
  specifying driver set name for,
    R-66

starting, R-65
  to text file, R-59
  of worksheets, 43–45, 84–85,
    150–152
  with Wysiwyg, R-180, R-183
.PRN file extension, R-51, R-59
Program files, transferring,
  GS-17–GS-19
Prompt, 14
  DOS, GS-13–GS-14, GS-35
  file name, R-51–R-52
  responding to, R-7
@PROPER function, R-133
Protection, R-32–R-33, R-46–R-47
Punctuation, specifying display
  for, R-35
{PUT} command, R-113
@PV function, R-142

Querying, 235–243
Question mark (?), 7, R-81
  as macro command, R-101
  as wildcard character, R-52
{?} command, R-101
@? function, R-126
Quick installation, GS-10–GS-11
{QUIT} command, 324–325,
  R-109
Quit command, in Auditor, R-169
/**Q**uit command, GS-59, R-166
Quote (")
  in label prefixes, 23, R-13
  in string arguments, R-96–R-97

@RAND function, R-122–R-123
Range(s), 44, R-14–R-15
  adding to graphs, 171–174
  anchored and unanchored, R-15
  commands for, R-26, R-41–R-48
  copying, R-49
  copying contents of,
    R-111–R-112
  criteria, 235, 237
  defining for graphs, 167–168
  erasing contents of, R-44, R-96,
    R-111
  input, 238
  learn, 297